FORENSIC SCIENCE

An Introduction
Second Edition

Richard Saferstein, Ph.D.

Forensic Science Consultant, Mt. Laurel, New Jersey

Prentice Hall

Boston Columbus Indianapolis New York San Francisco Upper Saddle River
Amsterdam Cape Town Dubai London Madrid Milan Munich Paris Montreal Toronto
Delhi Mexico City Sao Paulo Sydney Hong Kong Seoul Singapore Taipei Tokyo

Editorial Director: Vernon Anthony
Executive Editor: Eric Krassow
Editorial Assistant: Lynda Cramer
Director of Marketing: David Gesell
Marketing Manager: Adam Kloza
Senior Marketing Coordinator: Alicia Wozniak
Marketing Assistant: Les Roberts
Senior Managing Editor: JoEllen Gohr
Project Manager: Steve Robb
Audiovisual Project Manager: Janet Portisch
Senior Operations Supervisor: Pat Tonneman
Operations Specialist: Matt Ottenweller

Manager, Visual Research: Beth Brenzel
Manager, Rights and Permissions: Zina Arabia
Photo Researcher: Tim Huddleston
Media Editor: Michelle Churma
Media Project Manager: Karen Bretz
Cover Art: Beth Kun and Linda Punskovsky
Project Management: Emergent Learning, LLC
Editorial and Composition: FeatherSchneider Editorial Services and Abshier House
Printer/Binder: RR Donnelley
Cover Printer: Phoenix-Lehigh Color/Hagerstown

Credits and acknowledgments for materials borrowed from other sources and reproduced, with permission, in this textbook appear on appropriate page within text (or on page 732).

6 7 8 9 10 V063 15 14 13

Prentice Hall
is an imprint of

ISBN 10: 0-13-507433-9
ISBN 13: 978-0-13-507433-6

To my wife Gail, the pillar of my life

Contents

Chapter 1

Introduction 2

Chapter 2

The Crime Scene 42

Chapter 3

Physical Evidence 82

Chapter 4

Properties of Matter and the Analysis of Glass 106

Chapter 5

Drugs 148

Chapter 12

Trace Evidence II: Metals, Paint, and Soil 444

Chapter 13

Forensic Aspects of Fire Investigation 480

Chapter 14

Forensic Investigation of Explosions 508

Chapter 15

Fingerprints 532

Chapter 16

Firearms, Tool Marks, and Other Impressions 572

Preface

The level of sophistication that forensic science has brought to criminal investigations is awesome. But one cannot lose sight of the fact that, once all the drama of a forensic science case is put aside, what remains is an academic subject emphasizing science and technology. It is to this end that this second edition of *Forensic Science: An Introduction* is dedicated.

This book follows the tradition, philosophy, and objectives of my introductory college text, *Criminalistics: An Introduction to Forensic Science*, which is in its tenth edition. In creating this introductory text, every chapter of the college text was examined to improve the clarity of the narrative. This improvement has been accomplished by presenting the science of forensics in a straightforward and student-friendly format. Topics have been rearranged to better integrate scientific methodology with actual forensic application. The reader is offered the option of delving into the more difficult technical aspects of the book by going into the "Inside the Science" features in some chapters, an option that can be bypassed without detracting from a basic comprehension of the subject of forensic science.

Only the most relevant scientific and technological concepts are presented to the reader, so that the subject is not watered down with superfluous discussions that are of no real significance to current forensic science practices. It is the author's belief that, by learning in an interactive environment using the Internet, the reader will be a more motivated and active participant in the learning process. The text is accompanied by a companion web site that provides additional exercises, text information, and MyCrimeKit: WebExtras. The latter serve to expand the coverage of the book through video presentations and MyCrimeKit: Web Extras that enhance the reader's understanding of the subject's more difficult concepts.

One of the constants of forensic science is how frequently its applications become front-page news. Whether the story is sniper shootings or the tragic consequences of the terrorist attacks of 9/11/01, forensic science is at the forefront of the public response. In order to merge theory with practice, a significant number of actual forensic Case Files are included in the text. The intent is for all the case illustrations to capture the interest of the reader and to move forensic science from the domain of the abstract into the real world of criminal investigation.

Within and at the end of each chapter, the student will encounter Quick Reviews and a Chapter Summary that recap all of the major points of the chapter. The end-of-chapter summary is followed by review questions, as well as application and critical thinking exercises designed to have the reader further explore the chapter's content and its significance. In some chapters, virtual crime scene exercises enable the reader to move through various types of crime scenes while identifying and collecting physical evidence.

Acknowledgments

I am most appreciative of the contribution that Lieutenant Andrew (Drew) Donofrio of New Jersey's Bergen County Prosecutor's Office made to *Forensic Science*. I was fortunate to find in Drew a contributor who not only possesses extraordinary skill, knowledge, and hands-on experience with computer forensics, but who was able to combine those attributes with sophisticated communication skills.

Sarah A. Skorupsky-Borg, MSFS, invested an extraordinary amount of time and effort in preparing an accompanying supplement to this text: *Basic Laboratory Exercises for Forensic Science*. Her skills and tenacity in carrying out this task are acknowledged and greatly appreciated.

Many people provided assistance and advice in the preparation of this book. Many faculty members, colleagues, and friends have read and commented on various portions of the text. I would like to acknowledge the contributions of Jeffrey C. Kercheval, Robert Thompson, Roger Ely, Jose R. Almirall, Darlene Brezinski, Gavin Edmonstone, Anita Wonder, Norman Reeves, and Michael Malone.

The following reviewers for the second edition provided insightful and helpful critiques of the manuscript: Kate Allender, Redmond High School; Jill Christman, Canyon Del Oro High School; Charles Fanning, La Habra High School; John Gomola, Sterling Heights High School; Lance Goodlock, Sturgis High School; Dorothy Harris, Quince Orchard High School; Christine Leventhal, Darien High School; Christal Lippencott, Parker High School; Mary Monte, Eastern Technical High School; Kim McNamara, Oak Lawn Community High School; Randy Neider, Reading High School; Stephanie Niedermeyer, Wayne Memorial High School; Baokhanh Paton, Granby Memorial High School; and Jay Phillips, Westside High School.

I also thank the following reviewers of the first edition: Craig Anderson, Galt High School; Margaret Barthel, Ph.D., Freedom High School; Thomas J. Costello, High Point Regional High School; Thomas Donley, The Hotchkiss School; Shelly Duk, Walled Lake Central High School; Mark Feil, Glasgow High School; Myra Frank, Marjory Stoneman Douglas High School; Jim Hurley, Waverly-Shell Rock Community Schools; Lisa Kiann, River Valley High School; Mary Monte, Eastern Technical High School; Mary J. Monte, Woodlawn High School; Kevin Mugridge, Bishop Timon St. Jude High School; Barbara Olsen, Rocky Hill High School; Bruce Parce, Albert Einstein High School; Tod Suttle, Mayfair Middle/High School; Danielle DuChesne Thompson, Mariner High School; and Penny Wolkow, Oakland Mills High School.

The assistance and research efforts of Pamela Cook, Gonul Turhan, and Michelle Tetreault were invaluable and are an integral part of this text. The transformation of *Criminalistics* from a college text into this edition is the result in large part of the editorial skills of John Haley, who reorganized substantial portions of the text and rewrote end-of-chapter questions.

Finally, I am grateful to those law enforcement agencies, government agencies, private individuals, and equipment manufacturers cited in the text for contributing their photographs and illustrations.

About the Author

Richard Saferstein, Ph.D., retired in 1991 after serving twenty-one years as the Chief Forensic Scientist of the New Jersey State Police Laboratory, one of the largest crime laboratories in the United States. He currently acts as a consultant for attorneys and the media in the area of forensic science. During the O. J. Simpson criminal trial, Dr. Saferstein provided extensive commentary on forensic aspects of the case for the *Rivera Live* show, the E! television network, ABC radio, and various radio talk shows. Dr. Saferstein holds degrees from the City College of New York and earned his doctorate degree in chemistry in 1970 from the City University of New York. From 1972 to 1991, he taught an introductory forensic science course in the criminal justice programs at The College of New Jersey and Ocean County College. These teaching experiences played an influential role in Dr. Saferstein's authorship in 1977 of the widely used introductory textbook *Criminalistics: An Introduction to Forensic Science*, currently in its tenth edition. Saferstein's basic philosophy in writing *Criminalistics* is to make forensic science understandable and meaningful to the nonscience reader while giving the reader an appreciation for the scientific principles that underlie the subject.

Dr. Saferstein has authored or co-authored more than forty-four technical papers covering a variety of forensic topics. Dr. Saferstein has authored *Basic Laboratory Exercises for Forensic Science* (Prentice Hall, 2011) and co-authored *Lab Manual for Criminalistics* (Prentice Hall, 2011). He has also edited two editions of the widely used professional reference books *Forensic Science Handbook*, Volume 1 (Prentice Hall, 2002), *Forensic Science Handbook*, Volume 2 (Prentice Hall, 2005), and *Forensic Science Handbook*, Volume 3 (Prentice Hall, 2009). Dr. Saferstein is a member of the American Chemical Society, the American Academy of Forensic Sciences, the Canadian Society of Forensic Scientists, the International Association for Identification, the Mid-Atlantic Association of Forensic Scientists, the Northeastern Association of Forensic Scientists, the Northwestern Association of Forensic Scientists, and the Society of Forensic Toxicologists.

In 2006, Dr. Saferstein received the American Academy of Forensic Sciences Paul L. Kirk award for distinguished service and contributions to the field of criminalistics.

Welcome...

to the exciting second edition of *Forensic Science: An Introduction*. Richard Saferstein has carefully adapted and updated his classic *Criminalistics* text to create a comprehensive program designed specifically for high school students and teachers.

Accessible Text and Motivational 4-Color Presentation

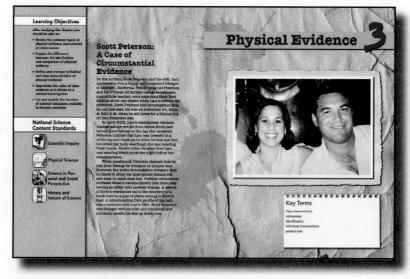

The new layout and design make learning forensic science even more motivating and exciting.

Students live in a visual world, and the functional use of full color conveys forensic science to today's students. Over 150 full-color photos and illustrations motivate students to read.

Chapter Openers

Each chapter opens with a real-life case study and stunning visual that captures students' interest and brings content to life.

Learning Objectives help students focus on the key takeaways for that chapter.

National Science Education Standards align with the chapter content and highlight the multidisciplinary nature of forensic science.

Dimensional Illustrations

The full-color art program helps students better understand key forensics concepts.

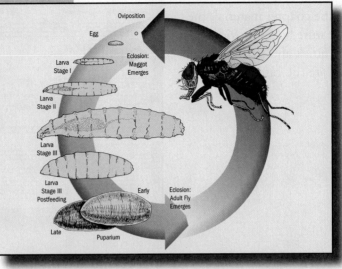

Open and Accessible Design

New design elements bring the course content to life and provide visual cues to guide student reading.

Key Terms

Forensic-specific vocabulary is highlighted in the text and defined in the margins.

Engaging Case Files

Linked to the chapter material, the Case File feature boxes provide students with quick and pertinent facts about real forensic cases.

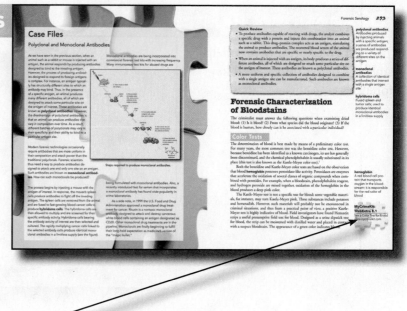

WebExtras

Interactive activities and in-depth information are just a click away. Hand-picked by the author, WebExtras drive students online to explore a wide range of forensic topics in greater depth.

Quick Labs

Quick Lab: Crime-Scene Sketch

Materials:

Graph paper   Notepad   Rulers
Tape measure/meter stick   Mock crime scene

Procedure:

You have been introduced to the appropriate steps to process a crime scene. An important part of this process is surveying the scene, taking diligent notes, and creating a sketch of the scene. With a partner or small group, create a sketch of the scene presented to you and keep notes of what evidence you find. In your sketch, provide an accurate depiction of the entire scene with dimension measurements as well as location measurements for all pieces of physical evidence.

Follow-Up Questions:

1. Why is it important to take diligent notes when processing the crime scene?
2. What is the chain of custody?
3. Why do we sketch the crime scene as well as take photographs of it?

Quick Lab: Anthropometric Activity

Materials:

Meter sticks   Rulers/tape measures   Student worksheets

Procedure:

First, read the section on anthropometry from the chapter. Next, pair up with two other students and pick up your materials. Each person should measure both of the other people in the group and record the results on the Anthropometric Measurements worksheet. Afterward, discuss the follow-up questions below.

Follow-Up Questions:

1. Did any of your measurements match those of your partners? Were there any measurements for which several members of your group showed identical results? What might that suggest about the usefulness of that measurement for identification?
2. Compare all the measurements recorded for a single individual. Did every person who measured that individual obtain the same results? What factors may contribute to any differences in the results?
3. Do you believe that anthropometry would be a good way to identify people who are trying to hide their identity? Explain your answer.

Inquiry is at the heart of science, and it's no exception here. In-text Quick Labs are hands-on activities that allow students to apply and experience key forensic concepts.

Application and Critical Thinking

Each chapter contains many activities designed to encourage application of critical thinking skills as they pertain to everyday life.

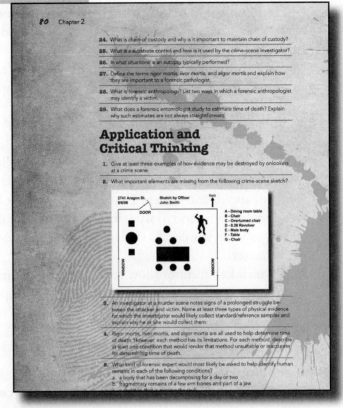

80 Chapter 2

24. What is chain of custody and why is it important to maintain chain of custody?

25. What is a substrate control and how is it used by the crime-scene investigator?

26. In what situations is an autopsy typically performed?

27. Define the terms *rigor mortis, livor mortis,* and *algor mortis* and explain how they are important to a forensic pathologist.

28. What is forensic anthropology? List two ways in which a forensic anthropologist may identify a victim.

29. What does a forensic entomologist study to estimate time of death? Explain why such estimates are not always straightforward.

Application and Critical Thinking

1. Give at least three examples of how evidence may be destroyed by onlookers at a crime scene.

2. What important elements are missing from the following crime-scene sketch?

3. An investigator at a murder scene notes signs of a prolonged struggle between the attacker and victim. Name at least three types of physical evidence for which the investigator would likely collect standard/reference samples and explain why he or she would collect them.

4. Rigor mortis, livor mortis, and algor mortis are all used to help determine time of death. However, each method has its limitations. For each method, describe at least one condition that would render that method unsuitable or inaccurate for determining time of death.

5. What kind of forensic expert would most likely be asked to help identify human remains in each of the following conditions?
a. a body that has been decomposing for a day or two
b. fragmentary remains of a few arm bones and part of a jaw

Chapter Review and Assessment

Each chapter provides a point-by-point summary of key concepts, with explanations that reinforce the materials covered.

Chapter Review

- Physical evidence includes any and all objects that can establish that a crime has been committed or can link the crime and its victim or its perpetrator.

- Forensic science begins at the crime scene, where investigators must recognize and properly preserve evidence for laboratory examination.

- The first officer to arrive must secure the crime scene.

- Investigators record the crime scene by using photographs, sketches, and notes and make a preliminary examination of the scene as the perpetrator left it.

- The search pattern selected at a crime scene depends on the size and locale of the scene and the number of collectors participating in the search.

- Many items of evidence may be detected only through examination at the crime laboratory. For this reason, it is important to collect possible carriers of trace evidence, such as clothing, vacuum sweepings, and fingernail scrapings, in addition to more discernible items.

- Each item of physical evidence collected at a crime scene must be placed in a separate appropriate container to prevent damage through contact or cross-contamination.

- Investigators must maintain the chain of custody, a record for denoting the location of the evidence.

- Proper standard/reference samples, such as hairs, blood, and fibers, must be collected at the crime scene and from appropriate subjects for comparison purposes in the laboratory.

- An autopsy is normally performed if a death is suspicious or unexplained.

- Rigor mortis occurs after death and results in the stiffening of body parts in the position they are in when death occurs. Livor mortis occurs after death and results in the settling of blood in areas of the body closest to the ground. Algor mortis refers to postmortem changes that cause a body to continually cool to ambient or room temperature.

- Forensic anthropology is concerned primarily with the identification and examination of human skeletal remains.

- A forensic entomologist studies the development of insect larvae in a body to estimate time of death.

New to This Edition

- Updated content on crime data and forensics technology throughout.
- New sections on anthropology, entomology, and odontology.
- Expanded coverage of blood spatter.
- Updated end-of-chapter questions to fit the needs and level of today's high school student, including new Application and Critical Thinking questions.
- New, briefer end-of-chapter summaries.
- Additional illustrations throughout.
- New and improved art program.
- New integration of Web-based media–MyCrime Kit and Virtual Labs.
- National Science Education Standards correlated to each chapter.
- New, enhanced, and current Case Files feature that links the content to real-world crime cases.
- New Inside the Science feature focuses the student on the science behind the topic.
- New Quick Review checks student learning and retention before getting too far ahead in each chapter.
- New Quick Lab features allow teachers to assign quick and easy lab exercises in the classroom with little prep time and easy-to-find supplies.

Student and Teacher Supplements

New and improved lab manual:
Basic Laboratory Exercises for Forensic Science (for purchase, ISBN: 013510534X)

The *Basic Laboratory Exercises* workbook brings the real world of forensic science into the classroom with hands-on activities from fingerprinting to bloodstain analysis, and from forensic entomology to forensic anthropology.

New to this edition:
Teacher's Wraparound Edition (ISBN: 0135089301)

The Teacher's Wraparound Edition features:

- Teacher's notes.
- Classroom management and planning tips.
- Lesson plans for customized instruction.
- Point-of-use teaching tips.
- Additional class and lab activities.

Companion Web Site (www.MyCrimeKit.com)

- Upon purchase students and teachers are given access to MyCrimeKit™. This site provides a broad range of materials, including book-specific learning objectives, chapter summaries, flashcards and practice tests, as well as video clips and activities to aid student learning and comprehension. Also included in MyCrimeKit are Research Navigator and weblinks that give students access to powerful and reliable research material. High school teachers can obtain teacher and student preview or adoption access for MyCrimeKit™ by either of the following means: Register online at **www.PearsonSchool.com/Access_ Request** (using Option 2) or ask your Pearson sales representative for an Access Code Card (Adoption Card 0-13-034391-9; Preview Card 0-13-111589-8).
- Also available are Virtual Forensic Science Labs. These multimedia lab animations allow students to walk through various lab exercises right from their computer.

Teacher Resource DVD (ISBN: 0135110475)

This one-stop teacher resource includes:

- NEW! Teacher Prep Forensic Lab Videos–unique videos prepared by high school instructors to walk teachers through preparing and executing forensic science labs.
- Instructor's Guide with high school-focused lesson plans.
- New PowerPoint Lecture Presentations for each chapter.
- TestGen software with an expanded Test Bank that includes hundreds of questions in a variety of formats.
- Answers keys for all questions and activities in the Student Edition.

Instructor's Manual (ISBN: 0135105315)

This collection of resources includes teaching tips, answers to *Basic Laboratory Exercises for Forensic Science*, detailed lesson plans, and much more.

Learning Objectives

After studying this chapter you should be able to:

- Define forensic science and list the major disciplines it encompasses

- Recognize the major contributors to the development of forensic science

- Account for the rapid growth of forensic laboratories in the past 40 years

- Describe the services of a typical comprehensive crime laboratory in the criminal justice system

- Compare and contrast the *Frye* and *Daubert* decisions relating to the admissibility of scientific evidence in the courtroom

- Explain the role and responsibilities of the expert witness

- List the specialized forensic services, aside from the crime laboratory, that are generally available to law enforcement personnel

- Learn where to search for information about forensic science on the Internet

National Science Content Standards

Scientific Inquiry

Physical Science

Life Science

Ted Bundy, Serial Killer

The name Ted Bundy is synonymous with the term serial killer. This handsome, gregarious, and worldly onetime law student is believed to be responsible for 40 murders between 1964 and 1978. His reign of terror stretched from the Pacific Northwest down to California and into Utah, Idaho, and Colorado, finally ending in Florida. His victims were typically young women, usually murdered with a blunt instrument or by strangulation, and sexually assaulted before and after death.

First convicted in Utah in 1976 on a charge of kidnapping, Bundy managed to escape after his extradition to Colorado on a murder charge. Ultimately, Bundy found his way to the Tallahassee area of Florida. There he unleashed mayhem, killing two women at a Florida State University sorority house and then murdering a 12-year-old girl three weeks later. Fortunately, future victims were spared when Bundy was arrested while driving a stolen vehicle. As police investigated the sorority murders, they noted that one victim, who had been beaten over the head with a log, raped, and strangled, also had bite marks on her left buttock and breast.

Supremely confident that he could beat the sorority murder charges, the arrogant Bundy insisted on acting as his own attorney. His unfounded optimism was shattered in the courtroom when a forensic odontologist matched the bite mark on the victim's buttock to Bundy's front teeth. Bundy was ultimately executed in 1989.

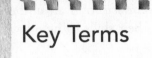

Key Terms

expert witness

Locard's exchange principle

scientific method

Definition and Scope of Forensic Science

Forensic science in its broadest definition is the application of science to law. As our society has grown more complex, it has become more dependent on rules of law to regulate the activities of its members. Forensic science applies the knowledge and technology of science to the definition and enforcement of such laws.

Each year, as government finds it increasingly necessary to regulate the activities that most intimately influence our daily lives, science merges more closely with civil and criminal law. Consider, for example, the laws and agencies that regulate the quality of our food, the nature and potency of drugs, the extent of automobile emissions, the kind of fuel oil we burn, the purity of our drinking water, and the pesticides we use on our crops and plants. It would be difficult to conceive of any food and drug regulation or environmental protection act that could be effectively monitored and enforced without the assistance of scientific technology and the skill of the scientific community.

Laws are continually being broadened and revised to counter the alarming increase in crime rates. In response to public concern, law enforcement agencies have expanded their patrol and investigative functions, hoping to stem the rising tide of crime. At the same time they are looking more to the scientific community for advice and technical support for their efforts. Can the technology that put astronauts on the moon, split the atom, and eradicated most dreaded diseases be enlisted in this critical battle? Unfortunately, science cannot offer final and authoritative solutions to problems that stem from a maze of social and psychological factors. However, as the contents of this book will attest, science occupies an important and unique role in the criminal justice system—a role that relates to the scientist's ability to supply accurate and objective information that reflects the events that have occurred at a crime. A good deal of work remains to be done if the full potential of science as applied to criminal investigations is to be realized.

Considering the vast array of civil and criminal laws that regulate society, forensic science, in its broadest sense, has become so comprehensive a subject as to make a meaningful introductory textbook treatment of its role and techniques most difficult, if not overwhelming. For this reason, we must find practical limits that narrow the scope of the subject. Fortunately, common usage provides us with such a limited definition: **Forensic science is the application of science to the criminal and civil laws that are enforced by police agencies in a criminal justice system.** *Forensic science* is an umbrella term encompassing a myriad of professions that use their skills to help law enforcement officials conduct their investigations.

The diversity of professions practicing forensic science is illustrated by the 11 sections of the American Academy of Forensic Science, the largest forensic science organization in the world:

1. **Criminalistics**

2. **Digital and Multimedia Sciences**

3. **Engineering Science**

4. General

5. Jurisprudence

6. Odontology

7. Pathology/Biology

8. Physical Anthropology

9. Psychiatry/Behavioral Sciences

10. Questioned Documents

11. Toxicology

Even within the limited definition just presented, we will restrict our discussion in this book to only the areas of chemistry, biology, physics, geology, and computer technology, which are useful for determining the evidential value of crime-scene and related evidence, omitting any references to medicine and law. Forensic pathology, psychology, anthropology, and odontology encompass important and relevant areas of knowledge and practice in law enforcement, each being an integral part of the total forensic science service that is provided to any up-to-date criminal justice system. However, except for brief discussions, these subjects go beyond the intended range of this book, and the reader is referred elsewhere for discussions of their applications and techniques.[1] Instead, we will attempt to focus on the services of what has popularly become known as the crime laboratory, where the principles and techniques of the physical and natural sciences are practiced and applied to the analysis of crime-scene evidence.

For many, the term criminalistics seems more descriptive than forensic science for describing the services of a crime laboratory. The two terms will be used interchangeably in this text. Regardless of title—criminalist or forensic scientist—the trend of events has made the scientist in the crime laboratory an active participant in the criminal justice system.

Prime time television shows like *CSI: Crime Scene Investigation* have greatly increased the public's awareness of the use of science in criminal and civil investigations (see Figure 1-1). However, by simplifying scientific procedures to fit into the available airtime, these shows have created unrealistic expectations of forensic science skills within both the public and the legal community. In these shows, members of the CSI team collect evidence at the crime scene, process all evidence, question witnesses, interrogate suspects, carry out search warrants, and testify in court. In the real world, these tasks are almost always delegated to different people in different parts of the criminal justice system. Procedures that could take days, weeks, months, or years in reality appear on these shows to take mere minutes. This false image is especially relevant to the public's high interest in and expectations for DNA evidence.

The dramatization of forensic science on television has led the public to believe that every crime scene will yield forensic evidence and produces unrealistic expectations that a prosecutor's case should always be bolstered and supported by forensic evidence. This phenomenon is known as the "CSI effect." Some jurists have come to believe that this phenomenon ultimately detracts from the search for truth and justice in the courtroom.

FIGURE 1–1
Scene from *CSI*, a forensic science television show.
Courtesy Picture Desk, Inc./Kobal Collection

History and Development of Forensic Science

Forensic science owes its origins first to the individuals who developed the principles and techniques needed to identify or compare physical evidence and second to those who recognized the need to merge these principles into a coherent discipline that could be practically applied to a criminal justice system.

The roots of forensic science reach back many centuries, and history records a number of instances in which individuals used close observation of evidence and applied basic scientific principles to solve crimes. Not until relatively recently, however, did forensic science take on the more careful and systematic approach that characterizes the modern discipline.

Early Developments

One of the earliest records of applying forensics to solve criminal cases comes from third-century China. A manuscript titled *Yi Yu Ji* (*A Collection of Criminal Cases*) reports how a coroner solved a case in which a woman was suspected of murdering her husband and burning the body, then claiming that he died in an accidental fire. Noticing that the husband's corpse had no ashes in its mouth, the coroner performed an experiment to test the woman's story. He burned two pigs—one alive and one dead—and then checked for ashes inside the mouth of each. He found ashes in the mouth of the pig that was alive before it was burned, but none in the mouth of the pig that was dead beforehand. The coroner thus concluded that the husband, too, was dead before his body was burned. Confronted with this evidence, the woman admitted her guilt. The Chinese were also among the first to recognize the potential of fingerprints as a means of identification.

Although cases such as that of the Chinese coroner are noteworthy, this kind of scientific approach to criminal investigation was for many years the exception rather than the rule. Limited knowledge of anatomy and pathology hampered the development of forensic science until the late 17th and early 18th centuries. For example, the first recorded notes about fingerprint characteristics were prepared in 1686 by Marcello Malpighi, a professor of anatomy at the University of Bologna in Italy. Malpighi, however, did not acknowledge the value of fingerprints as a method of identification. The first scientific paper about the nature of fingerprints did not appear until more than a century later, but that work also did not recognize their potential as a form of identification.

Initial Scientific Advances

As physicians gained a greater understanding of the workings of the body, the first scientific treatises on forensic science began to appear, such as the 1798 work *A Treatise on Forensic Medicine and Public Health* by the French physician François-Emanuel Fodéré. Breakthroughs in chemistry at this time also helped forensic science take significant strides forward. In 1775, the Swedish chemist Carl Wilhelm Scheele devised the first successful test for detecting the poison arsenic in corpses. By 1806, the German chemist Valentin Ross had discovered a more precise method for detecting small amounts of arsenic in the walls of a victim's stomach. The most significant early figure in this area was Mathieu Orfila, a Spaniard who is considered the father of forensic toxicology. In 1814, Orfila published the first scientific treatise on the detection of poisons and their effects on animals. This treatise established forensic toxicology as a legitimate scientific endeavor.

The mid-1800s saw a spate of advances in several scientific disciplines that furthered the field of forensic science. In 1828, William Nichol invented the polarizing microscope. Eleven years later, Henri-Louis Bayard formulated the first procedures for microscopic detection of sperm. Other developments during this time included the first microcrystalline test for hemoglobin (1853) and the first presumptive test for blood (1863). Such tests soon found practical applications in criminal trials. Toxicological evidence at trial was first used in 1839, when a Scottish chemist named James

FIGURE 1-2 Mathieu Orfila.
Courtesy The Granger Collection, New York

Marsh testified on the detection of arsenic in a victim's body. During the 1850s and 1860s, the new science of photography was also used in forensics, recording images of prisoners and crime scenes.

Late 19th-Century Progress

By the late 19th century, public officials were beginning to apply knowledge from virtually all scientific disciplines to the study of crime. Anthropology and morphology (the study of the structure of living organisms) were applied to the first system of personal identification, devised by the French scientist Alphonse Bertillon in 1879. Bertillon's system, which he dubbed anthropometry, was a systematic procedure that involved taking a series of body measurements as a means of distinguishing one individual from another. For nearly two decades, this system was considered the most accurate method of personal identification, before being replaced by fingerprinting in the early 1900s. Bertillon's early efforts earned him the distinction of being known as the father of criminal identification.

Bertillon's anthropometry, however, would soon be supplanted by the more reliable method of identification by fingerprinting. Two years before the publication of Bertillon's system, the U.S. microscopist Thomas Taylor suggested that fingerprints could be used as a means of identification, but his ideas were not immediately followed up. Three years later, the Scottish physician Henry Faulds made a similar assertion in a paper published in the journal *Nature*. However, the Englishman Francis Henry Galton undertook the first definitive study of fingerprints and developed a methodology of classifying them for filing. In 1892, Galton published a book titled *Finger Prints*, which contained the first statistical proof supporting the uniqueness of his method of personal identification. His work went on to describe the basic principles that form the present system of identification by fingerprints.

The first treatise describing the application of scientific disciplines to the field of criminal investigation was written by Hans Gross in 1893. Gross, a public prosecutor and judge in Graz, Austria, spent many years studying and developing principles of criminal investigation. In his classic book, *Handbuch für Untersuchungsrichter als System der Kriminalistik* (later published in English under the title *Criminal Investigation*), he detailed the assistance that investigators could expect from the fields of microscopy, chemistry, physics, mineralogy, zoology, botany, anthropometry, and fingerprinting. He later introduced the forensic journal *Archiv für Kriminal Anthropologie und Kriminalistik*, which still reports improved methods of scientific crime detection.

Ironically, the best-known figure in 19th-century forensics was not a real person, but a fictional character, the legendary detective Sherlock Holmes. Many people today believe that Holmes's creator, Sir Arthur Conan Doyle, had a considerable influence on popularizing scientific crime-detection methods. In adventures with his partner and biographer, Dr. John Watson, Holmes first applied the newly developing principles of serology (the study of blood and bodily fluids), fingerprinting, firearms identification, and questioned-document examination long before their value was recognized and accepted by real-life criminal investigators. Holmes's feats excited the imagination of an emerging generation of forensic scientists and criminal investigators. Even in the first Sherlock Holmes novel, *A Study in Scarlet*, published in 1887, we find examples of Doyle's uncanny ability to describe scientific methods of detection years before they were actually discovered and implemented. For instance, here in the following quote, Holmes probes and recognizes the potential usefulness of forensic serology to criminal investigation.

FIGURE 1–3 Bertillon's system of bodily measurements as used for the identification of an individual.
Courtesy Sirchie Finger Print Laboratories, Inc., Youngsville, N.C., www.sirchie.com

"I've found it. I've found it," he shouted to my companion, running towards us with a test tube in his hand. "I have found a reagent which is precipitated by hemoglobin and by nothing else. . . . Why, man, it is the most practical medico-legal discovery for years. Don't you see that it gives us an infallible test for blood stains? . . . The old guaiacum test was very clumsy and uncertain. So is the microscopic examination for blood corpuscles. The latter is valueless if the stains are a few hours old. Now, this appears to act as well whether the blood is old or new. Had this test been invented, there are hundreds of men now walking the earth who would long ago have paid the penalty of their crimes. . . . Criminal cases are continually hinging upon that one point. A man is suspected of a crime months perhaps after it has been committed. His linen or clothes are examined and brownish stains discovered upon them. Are they blood stains, or rust stains, or fruit stains, or what are they? That is a question which has puzzled many an expert, and why? Because there was no reliable test. Now we have the Sherlock Holmes test, and there will no longer be any difficulty."

FIGURE 1–4 Sir Arthur Conan Doyle's legendary detective Sherlock Holmes applied many of the principles of modern forensic science long before they were adopted widely by police. *© Paul C. Chauncey/ CORBIS. All rights reserved.*

20th-Century Breakthroughs

The pace of technological change quickened considerably in the 20th century, and with it the rate of advancement in the field of forensic science. In 1901, Dr. Karl Landsteiner discovered that blood can be grouped into different categories, now recognized as the blood types A, B, AB, and O. The possibility that blood grouping could be useful in identifying an individual intrigued Dr. Leone Lattes, a professor at the Institute of Forensic Medicine at the University of Turin in Italy. In 1915, Lattes devised a relatively simple procedure for determining the blood group of a dried bloodstain, a technique that he immediately applied to criminal investigations.

At around the same time, Albert S. Osborn was conducting pioneering work in document examination. In 1910, Osborn wrote the first significant text in this field, *Questioned Documents*. This book is still considered a primary reference for document examiners. Osborn's development of the fundamental principles of document examination was responsible for the acceptance of documents as scientific evidence by the courts.

One of the most important contributors to the field in the early 20th century was the Frenchman Edmond Locard. Although Hans Gross was a pioneer advocate of the use of the scientific method in criminal investigation, Locard first demonstrated how the principles enunciated by Gross could be incorporated within a workable crime laboratory. Locard's formal education was in both medicine and law. In 1910, he persuaded the Lyons police department to give him two attic rooms and two assistants to start a police laboratory. During Locard's first years of work, the only available instruments were a microscope and a rudimentary spectrometer. However, his enthusiasm quickly overcame the technical and monetary deficiencies he encountered. From these modest beginnings, Locard's research and accomplishments became known throughout the world by forensic scientists and criminal investigators. Eventually he became the founder and director of the Institute of Criminalistics at the University of Lyons; this quickly developed into a leading international center for study and research in forensic science.

Locard asserted that when two objects come into contact with each other, a cross-transfer of materials occurs (**Locard's exchange principle**). He strongly believed that every criminal can be connected to a crime by dust particles carried from the crime scene. This concept was reinforced by a series of successful and well-publicized investigations. In one case, presented with counterfeit coins and the names of three suspects, Locard urged the police to bring the suspects' clothing to his laboratory. On careful examination, he located small metallic particles in all the garments. Chemical analysis revealed that the particles and coins were composed of exactly the same metallic elements. Confronted with this evidence, the suspects were arrested and soon confessed to the crime. After World War I, Locard's successes served as an impetus for the formation of police laboratories in Vienna, Berlin, Sweden, Finland, and Holland.

The microscope came into widespread use in forensic science during the 20th century, and its applications grew dramatically. Perhaps the leading figure in the field of microscopy was Dr. Walter C. McCrone. During his lifetime, McCrone became the world's preeminent microscopist. Through his books, journal publications, and research institute, he was a tireless advocate for applying microscopy

Locard's exchange principle
When two objects come into contact with one another, there is exchange of materials between them

to analytical problems, particularly forensic science cases. McCrone's exceptional communication skills made him a much-sought-after instructor, and he educated thousands of forensic scientists throughout the world in the application of microscopic techniques. Dr. McCrone used microscopy, often in conjunction with other analytical methodologies, to examine evidence in thousands of criminal and civil cases throughout a long and illustrious career.

Another trailblazer in forensic applications of microscopy was U.S. Army Colonel Calvin Goddard, who refined the techniques of firearms examination by using the comparison microscope. Goddard's work allowed investigators to determine whether a particular gun has fired a bullet by comparing the bullet with one that has been test-fired from the suspect's weapon. His expertise established the comparison microscope as the indispensable tool of the modern firearms examiner.

Modern Scientific Advances

Since the mid-20th century, a revolution in computer technology has made possible a quantum leap forward in human knowledge. The resulting explosion of scientific advances has dramatically impacted the field of forensic science by introducing a wide array of sophisticated techniques for analyzing evidence related to a crime. Procedures such as chromatography, spectrophotometry, and electrophoresis (all discussed in later chapters) allow the modern forensic scientist to determine with astounding accuracy the identity of a suspect substance, and to connect even tiny fragments of evidence to a particular person and place.

The most significant modern advance in forensic science undoubtedly has been the discovery and refinement of DNA typing in the late 20th and early 21st centuries. Sir Alec Jeffreys developed the first DNA profiling test in 1984, and two years later he applied it for the first time to solve a crime by identifying Colin Pitchfork as the murderer of two young English girls. The same case also marked the first time DNA profiling established the innocence of a criminal suspect. Made possible by scientific breakthroughs in the 1950s and 1960s, DNA typing offers law enforcement officials a powerful tool for establishing the precise identity of a suspect, even when only a small amount of physical evidence is available. Combined with the modern analytical tools mentioned earlier, DNA typing has revolutionized the practice of forensic science.

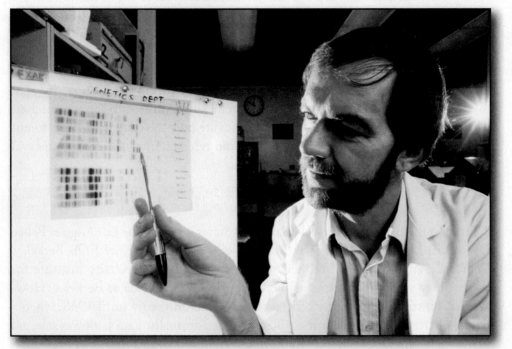

FIGURE 1–6
Sir Alec Jeffreys.
Courtesy Homer Sykes, Alamy Images Royalty Free

Another significant recent development in forensics is the establishment of computerized databases on physical evidence such as fingerprints, markings on bullets and shell casings, and DNA. These databases have proven to be invaluable, enabling law enforcement officials to compare evidence found at crime scenes to records of thousands of pieces of similar information. This has significantly reduced the time required to analyze evidence and increased the accuracy of the work done by police and forensic investigators.

Although this brief narrative is by no means a complete summary of historical advances in forensics, it provides an idea of the progress made in the field by dedicated scientists and law enforcement personnel. Even Sherlock Holmes probably couldn't have imagined the lengths to which science today is applied in the service of criminal investigation.

Quick Review

- Forensic science is the application of science to criminal and civil laws that are enforced by police agencies in a criminal justice system.

- The first system of personal identification was called anthropometry. It distinguished one individual from another based on a series of body measurements.

- Forensic science owes its origins to individuals such as Bertillon, Galton, Lattes, Goddard, Osborn, and Locard, who developed the principles and techniques needed to identify or compare physical evidence.

- Locard's exchange principle states that when two objects come into contact with each other, there is exchange of materials between them. This cross-transfer of materials can connect a criminal suspect to his or her victim.

Crime Laboratories

The steady advance of forensic science technologies during the 20th century led to the establishment of the first facilities specifically dedicated to forensic analysis of criminal evidence. These crime laboratories are now the centers for both forensic investigation of ongoing criminal cases and research into new techniques and procedures to aid investigators in the future.

History of Crime Labs in the United States

The oldest forensic laboratory in the United States is that of the Los Angeles Police Department, created in 1923 by August Vollmer, a police chief from Berkeley, California. In the 1930s, Vollmer headed the first U.S. university institute for criminology and criminalistics at the University of California at Berkeley. However, this institute lacked any official status in the university until 1948, when a school of criminology was formed. The famous criminalist Paul Kirk was selected to head its criminalistics department. Many graduates of this school have gone on to develop forensic laboratories in other parts of the state and country.

In 1932, the Federal Bureau of Investigation (FBI), under the directorship of J. Edgar Hoover, organized a national laboratory that offered forensic services to all law enforcement agencies in the country. During its formative stages, Hoover consulted extensively with business executives, manufacturers, and scientists whose knowledge and experience guided the new facility through its infancy. The FBI Laboratory is now the world's largest forensic laboratory, performing more than one million examinations every year. Its accomplishments have earned it worldwide recognition, and its structure and organization have served as a model for forensic laboratories formed at the state and local levels in the United States as well as in other countries. Furthermore, the opening of the FBI's Forensic Science Research and Training Center in 1981 gave the United States, for the first time, a facility dedicated to conducting research to develop new and reliable scientific methods that can be applied to forensic science. This facility is also used to train crime laboratory personnel in the latest forensic science techniques and methods.

(a)

(b)

FIGURE 1–7
(a) Exterior and (b) interior views of the FBI crime laboratory in Quantico, Virginia. *Courtesy AP Wide World Photos*

Despite the existence of the FBI Laboratory, the United States has no national system of forensic laboratories. Instead, many local law enforcement jurisdictions—city, county, and state—around the country each operate their own independent crime labs. California, for example, has numerous federal, state, county, and city crime laboratories, many of which operate independently. However, in 1972 the California Department of Justice created a network of integrated state-operated crime laboratories consisting of regional and satellite facilities. An informal exchange of information and expertise occurs within California's criminalist community through a regional professional society, the California Association of Criminalists. This organization was the forerunner of a number of regional organizations that have developed throughout the United States to foster cooperation among the nation's growing community of criminalists.

Organization of a Crime Laboratory

The development of crime laboratories in the United States has been characterized by rapid growth accompanied by a lack of national and regional planning and coordination. Approximately four hundred public crime laboratories operate at various levels of government—federal, state, county, and municipal. The size and diversity of crime laboratories make it impossible to select any one model that best describes a typical crime laboratory. Although most of these facilities function as part of a police department, others operate under the direction of the prosecutor's or district attorney's office; some work with the laboratories of the medical examiner or coroner. Far fewer are affiliated with universities or exist as independent agencies in government. Laboratory staff sizes range from one person to more than a hundred, and their services may be diverse or specialized, depending on the responsibilities of the agency that houses the laboratory.

The Growth of Crime Laboratories Crime laboratories have mostly been organized by agencies that either foresaw their potential application to criminal investigation or were pressed by the increasing demands of casework. Several reasons explain the unparalleled growth of crime laboratories during the past 35 years. Supreme Court decisions in the 1960s were responsible for greater police emphasis on securing scientifically evaluated evidence. The requirement to advise criminal suspects of their constitutional rights and their right of immediate access to counsel has all but eliminated confessions as a routine investigative tool. Successful prosecution of criminal cases requires a thorough and professional police investigation, frequently incorporating the skills of forensic science experts. Modern technology has provided forensic scientists with many new skills and techniques to meet the challenges accompanying their increased participation in the criminal justice system.

Coinciding with changing judicial requirements has been the staggering increase in crime rates in the United States over the past 40 years. This factor alone would probably have accounted for the increased use of crime laboratory services by police agencies, but only a small percentage of police investigations generate evidence requiring scientific examination. There is, however, one important exception to this observation: drug-related arrests. All illicit-drug seizures must be sent to a forensic laboratory for confirmatory chemical analysis before the case can be adjudicated. Since the mid-1960s, drug abuse has accelerated to nearly uncontrollable levels and has resulted in crime laboratories being inundated with drug specimens. Current estimates indicate that nearly half of all requests for examination of forensic evidence deal with abused drugs.

A more recent impetus leading to the growth and maturation of crime laboratories has been the advent of DNA profiling. Since the early 1990s, this technology has progressed to the point at which traces of blood, semen stains, hair, and saliva residues left behind on stamps, cups, bite marks, and so on have made possible the individualization or near-individualization of biological evidence. To meet the demands of DNA technology, crime labs have expanded staff and in many cases modernized their physical plants. The labor-intensive demands and sophisticated requirements of the technology have affected the structure of the forensic laboratory as has no other technology in the past 50 years. Likewise, DNA profiling has become the dominant factor in explaining how the general public perceives the workings and capabilities of the modern crime laboratory.

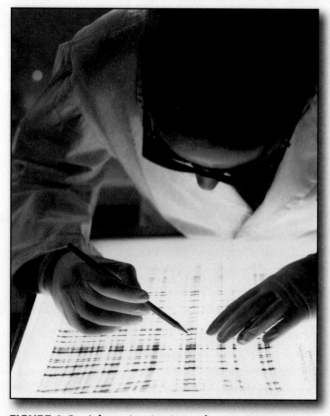

FIGURE 1–8 A forensic scientist performing DNA analysis.
Courtesy Mauro Fermariello, Photo Researchers, Inc.

In coming years thousands of forensic scientists will be added to the rolls of both public and private forensic laboratories to process crime-scene evidence for DNA and to acquire DNA profiles, as mandated by state laws, from the hundreds of thousands of individuals convicted of crimes. This endeavor has already added many new scientists to the field and will eventually more than double the number of scientists employed by forensic laboratories in the United States.

A major problem facing the forensic DNA community is the substantial backlog of unanalyzed DNA samples from crime scenes. The number of unanalyzed casework DNA samples reported by state and national agencies is more than 57,000. The estimated number of untested convicted offender samples is more than 500,000. In an attempt to eliminate the backlog of convicted offender or arrestee samples to be analyzed and entered into the Combined DNA Index System (CODIS), the federal government has initiated funding for in-house analysis of samples at the crime laboratory or outsourcing samples to private laboratories for analysis.

Beginning in 2008, California began collecting DNA samples from all people arrested on suspicion of a felony, not waiting until a person is convicted. The state's database, with approximately one million DNA profiles, is already the third largest in the world, behind those maintained by the United Kingdom and the FBI. The federal government plans to begin doing the same.

Crime Laboratories in the United States Historically, a federal system of government, combined with a desire to retain local control, has produced a variety of independent laboratories in the United States, precluding the creation of a national system. Crime laboratories to a large extent mirror the fragmented law enforcement structure that exists on the national, state, and local levels. The federal government has no single law enforcement or investigative agency with unlimited jurisdiction.

Four major federal crime laboratories have been created to help investigate and enforce criminal laws that extend beyond the jurisdictional boundaries of state and local forces. The FBI (Department of Justice) maintains the largest crime laboratory in the world. An ultramodern facility housing the FBI's forensic science services is located in Quantico, Virginia. Its expertise and technology support its broad investigative powers. The Drug Enforcement Administration laboratories (Department of Justice) analyze drugs seized in violation of federal laws regulating the production, sale, and transportation of drugs. The laboratories of the Bureau of Alcohol, Tobacco, Firearms and Explosives (Department of Justice) analyze alcoholic beverages and documents relating to alcohol and firearm excise tax law enforcement and examine weapons, explosive devices, and related evidence to enforce the Gun Control Act of 1968 and the Organized Crime Control Act of 1970. The U.S. Postal Inspection Service maintains laboratories concerned with criminal investigations relating to the postal service. Each of these federal facilities offers its expertise to any local agency that requests assistance in relevant investigative matters.

Most state governments maintain a crime laboratory to service state and local law enforcement agencies that do not have ready access to a laboratory. Some states, such as Alabama, California, Illinois, Michigan, New Jersey, Texas, Washington, Oregon, Virginia, and Florida, have developed a comprehensive statewide system of regional or satellite laboratories. These operate under the direction of a central facility and provide forensic services to most areas of the state. The concept of a regional laboratory operating as part of a statewide system has increased the accessibility of many local law enforcement agencies to a crime laboratory, while minimizing duplication of services and ensuring maximum interlaboratory cooperation through the sharing of expertise and equipment.

Local laboratories provide services to county and municipal agencies. Generally, these facilities operate independently of the state crime laboratory and are financed directly by local government. However, as costs have risen, some counties have combined resources and created multicounty laboratories to service their jurisdictions. Many of the larger cities in the United States maintain their own crime laboratories, usually under the direction of the local police department. Frequently, high population and high crime rates combine to make a municipal facility, such as that of New York City, the largest crime laboratory in the state.

Crime Laboratories Abroad Like the United States, most countries in the world have created and now maintain forensic facilities. In contrast to the American system of independent local laboratories, Great Britain has developed a national system of regional laboratories under the direction of the government's Home Office. England and Wales are serviced by six regional laboratories, including the Metropolitan Police Laboratory (established in 1935), which services London. In the early 1990s, the British Home Office reorganized the country's forensic laboratories into the Forensic Science Service and instituted a system in which police agencies are charged a fee for services rendered by the laboratory. The fees are based on "products," or a set of examinations that are packaged together and designed to be suitable for particular types of physical evidence. The fee-for-service concept has encouraged the creation of a number of private laboratories that provide services to both police and criminal defense attorneys. One such organization, LGC in the United Kingdom, employs more than one thousand forensic scientists.

In Canada, forensic services are provided by three government-funded institutes: (1) six Royal Canadian Mounted Police regional laboratories, (2) the Centre of Forensic Sciences in Toronto, and (3) the Institute of Legal Medicine and Police Science in Montreal. Altogether, more than a hundred countries throughout the world have at least one laboratory facility offering forensic science services.

Services of the Crime Laboratory

Bearing in mind the independent development of crime laboratories in the United States, the wide variation in total services offered in different communities is not surprising. There are many reasons for this, including (1) variations in local laws, (2) the different capabilities and functions of the organization to which a laboratory is attached, and (3) budgetary and staffing limitations.

In recent years, many local crime laboratories have been created solely to process drug specimens. Often these facilities were staffed with few personnel and operated under limited budgets. Although many have expanded their forensic services, some still primarily perform drug analyses. However, even among crime laboratories providing services beyond drug identification, the diversity and quality of services rendered varies significantly. For the purposes of this text, I have arbitrarily designated the following units as those that should constitute a "full-service" crime laboratory.

Basic Services Provided by Full-Service Crime Laboratories

Physical science unit. The physical science unit applies principles and techniques of chemistry, physics, and geology to the identification and comparison of crime-scene evidence. It is staffed by criminalists who have the expertise to use chemical tests and modern analytical instrumentation to examine items as diverse as drugs, glass, paint, explosives, and soil. In a laboratory that has a staff large enough to permit specialization, the responsibilities of this unit may be further subdivided into drug identification, soil and mineral analysis, and examination of a variety of trace physical evidence.

Biology unit. The biology unit is staffed with biologists and biochemists who identify and perform DNA profiling on dried bloodstains and other body fluids, compare hairs and fibers, and identify and compare botanical materials such as wood and plants.

Firearms unit. The firearms unit examines firearms, discharged bullets, cartridge cases, shotgun shells, and ammunition of all types. Garments and other objects are also examined to detect firearms discharge residues and to approximate the distance from a target at which a weapon was fired. The basic principles of firearms examination are also applied here to the comparison of marks made by tools.

FIGURE 1–9
A forensic analyst examining a firearm. *Courtesy Mediacolors, Alamy Images*

Document examination unit. The document examination unit studies the handwriting and typewriting on questioned documents to ascertain authenticity and/or source. Related responsibilities include analyzing paper and ink and examining indented writings (the term usually applied to the partially visible depressions appearing on a sheet of paper underneath the one on which the visible writing appears), obliterations, erasures, and burned or charred documents.

Photography unit. A complete photographic laboratory examines and records physical evidence. Its procedures may require the use of highly specialized photographic techniques, such as digital imaging, infrared, ultraviolet, and X-ray photography, to make invisible information visible to the naked eye. This unit also prepares photographic exhibits for courtroom presentation.

Optional Services Provided by Full-Service Crime Laboratories

Toxicology unit. The toxicology group examines body fluids and organs to determine the presence or absence of drugs and poisons. Frequently, such functions are shared with or may be the sole responsibility of a separate laboratory facility placed under the direction of the medical examiner's or coroner's office.

In most jurisdictions, field instruments such as the Intoxilyzer are used to determine the alcoholic consumption of individuals. Often the toxicology section also trains operators and maintains and services these instruments.

Latent fingerprint unit. The latent fingerprint unit processes and examines evidence for latent fingerprints when they are submitted in conjunction with other laboratory examinations.

Polygraph unit. The polygraph, or lie detector, has come to be recognized as an essential tool of the criminal investigator rather than the forensic scientist. However, during the formative years of polygraph technology, many police agencies incorporated this unit into the laboratory's administrative structure, where it sometimes remains today. In any case, its functions are handled by people trained in the techniques of criminal investigation and interrogation.

Voiceprint analysis unit. In cases involving telephoned threats or tape-recorded messages, investigators may require the skills of the voiceprint analysis unit to tie the voice to a particular suspect. To this end, a good deal of casework has been performed with the sound spectrograph, an instrument that transforms speech into a visual graphic display called a voiceprint. The validity of this technique as a means of personal identification rests on the premise that the sound patterns produced in speech are unique to the individual and that the voiceprint displays this uniqueness.

Crime-scene investigation unit. The concept of incorporating crime-scene evidence collection into the total forensic science service is slowly gaining recognition in the United States. This unit dispatches specially trained personnel (civilian and/or police) to the crime scene to collect and preserve physical evidence that will later be processed at the crime laboratory.

Whatever the organizational structure of a forensic science laboratory may be, specialization must not impede the overall coordination of services demanded by today's criminal investigator. Laboratory administrators need to keep open the lines of communication between analysts (civilian and uniform), crime-scene investigators, and police personnel. Inevitably, forensic investigations require the skills of many individuals. One notoriously high-profile investigation illustrates this process—the search for the source of the anthrax letters mailed shortly after September 11, 2001. Figure 1–10 shows one of the letters and illustrates the multitude of skills required in the investigation—skills possessed by forensic chemists and biologists, fingerprint examiners, and forensic document examiners.

Other Forensic Science Services Even though this textbook is devoted to describing the services normally provided by a crime laboratory, the field of forensic science is by no means limited to the areas covered in this book. A number of specialized forensic science services outside the crime laboratory are routinely available to law enforcement personnel. These services are important aids to a criminal investigation and require the involvement of individuals who have highly specialized skills.

Three specialized forensic services—forensic pathology, forensic anthropology, and forensic entomology—are frequently employed at a murder scene and will be discussed at greater length when we examine crime-scene procedures in Chapter 2. Other services, such as those discussed next, are used in a wide variety of criminal investigations.

**MyCrimeKit:
WebExtra 1.1**
Take a Tour of a Forensic Laboratory
www.mycrimekit.com

Fingerprints may be detectable on paper using a variety of chemical developing techniques (Chapter 15).

Paper examination may identify a manufacturer. General appearance, watermarks, fiber analysis, and chemical analysis of pigments, additives, and fillers may reveal a paper's origin (Chapter 17).

DNA may be recovered from saliva residues on the back of a stamp (Chapter 9). However, in this case, the stamp is printed onto the envelope.

Ink analysis may reveal a pen's manufacturer (Chapter 17).

Trace evidence, such as hairs and fibers, may be present within the contents of the envelope. (Chapter 11)

Photocopier toner may reveal its manufacturer through chemical and physical properties (Chapter 17).

Indented writing may be deposited on paper left underneath a sheet of paper being written upon. Electrostatic imaging is used to visualize indented impressions on paper (Chapter 17).

Handwriting examination reveals that block lettering is consistent with a single writer who wrote three other anthrax letters (Chapter 17).

DNA may be recovered from saliva used to seal an envelope (Chapter 9).

Cellophane tape was used to seal four envelopes containing the anthrax letters. The fitting together of the serrated ends of the tape strips confirmed that they were torn in succession from the same roll of tape (Chapter 3).

FIGURE 1–10
An envelope containing anthrax spores along with an anonymous letter was sent to the office of Senator Tom Daschle shortly after the terrorist attacks of September 11, 2001. A variety of forensic skills were used to examine the envelope and letter. Also, bar codes placed on the front and back of the envelope by mail-sorting machines contain address information and information about where the envelope was first processed.
Courtesy Getty Images, Inc.—Liaison

Forensic psychiatry. Forensic psychiatry is a specialized area that examines the relationship between human behavior and legal proceedings. Forensic psychiatrists are retained for both civil and criminal litigations. In civil cases, they typically perform tasks such as determining whether an individual is competent to make decisions about preparing a will, settling property, or refusing medical treatment. In criminal cases, forensic psychologists evaluate behavioral disorders and determine whether defendants are competent to stand trial. Forensic psychiatrists also examine behavior patterns of criminals as an aid in developing a suspect's behavioral profile.

Forensic odontology. Practitioners of forensic odontology help identify victims based on dental evidence when the body is left in an unrecognizable state. Teeth are composed of enamel, the hardest substance in the body. Because of enamel's resilience, the teeth outlast tissues and organs as decomposition begins. The characteristics of teeth, their alignment, and the overall structure of the mouth provide individual evidence for identifying a specific person. With the use of dental records such as X-rays and dental casts or even a photograph of the person's smile, a set of dental remains can be compared to a suspected victim. Another application of forensic odontology to criminal investigations is bite mark analysis. Bite marks are sometimes left on the victim in assault cases. A forensic odontologist can compare the marks left on a victim and the tooth structure of the suspect.

Forensic engineering. Forensic engineers are concerned with failure analysis, accident reconstruction, and causes and origins of fires or explosions. Forensic engineers answer questions such as these: How did an accident or structural failure occur? Were the parties involved responsible? If so, how were they responsible? Accident scenes are examined, photographs are reviewed, and any mechanical objects involved are inspected.

**MyCrimeKit:
WebExtra 1.2**
Explore Forensic Dentistry
www.mycrimekit.com

FIGURE 1–11   (a) Bite mark on victim's body. (b) Comparison to suspect's teeth. *Courtesy David Sweet, DMD, Ph.D., DABFO BOLD Forensic Laboratory, Vancouver, B.C., Canada*

(a)   (b)

Forensic computer and digital analysis. Forensic computer science is a new and fast-growing field that involves identifying, collecting, preserving, and examining information derived from computers and other digital devices, such as cell phones. Law enforcement aspects of this work normally involve recovering deleted or overwritten data from a computer's hard drive and tracking hacking activities within a compromised system. This field of forensic computer analysis will be addressed in detail in Chapter 18.

Quick Review

- The development of crime laboratories in the United States has been characterized by rapid growth accompanied by a lack of national and regional planning and coordination.

- Four major reasons for the increase in the number of crime laboratories in the United States since the 1960s are as follows: (1) the fact that the requirement to advise criminal suspects of their constitutional rights and their right of immediate access to counsel has all but eliminated confessions as a routine investigative tool; (2) the staggering increase in crime rates in the United States; (3) the fact that all illicit-drug seizures must be sent to a forensic laboratory for confirmatory chemical analysis before the case can be adjudicated in court; and (4) the advent of DNA profiling.

- The technical support provided by crime laboratories can be assigned to five basic services: the physical science unit, the biology unit, the firearms unit, the document examination unit, and the photography unit.

- Some crime laboratories offer optional services such as toxicology, fingerprint analysis, polygraph administration, voiceprint analysis, and crime-scene investigation.

- Special forensic science services available to the law enforcement community include forensic pathology, forensic anthropology, forensic entomology, forensic psychiatry, forensic odontology, forensic engineering, and forensic computer and digital analysis.

The Functions of the Forensic Scientist

Although a forensic scientist relies primarily on scientific knowledge and skill, only half of the job is performed in the laboratory. The other half takes place in the courtroom, where the ultimate significance of the evidence is determined. The forensic scientist must not only analyze physical evidence but also persuade a jury to accept the conclusions derived from that analysis.

Analyzing Physical Evidence

First and foremost, the forensic scientist must be skilled in applying the principles and techniques of the physical and natural sciences to analyze the many types of physical evidence that may be recovered during a criminal investigation. Of the three major avenues available to police investigators for assistance in solving a crime—confessions, eyewitness accounts by victims or witnesses, and evaluation of physical evidence retrieved from the crime scene—only physical evidence is free of inherent error or bias.

Criminal cases are replete with examples of individuals who were incorrectly charged with and convicted of committing a crime because of faulty memories or lapses in judgment. For example, investigators may be led astray during their preliminary evaluation of the events and circumstances surrounding the commission of a crime. These errors may be compounded by misleading eyewitness statements and inappropriate confessions. These same concerns don't apply to physical evidence.

What about physical evidence allows investigators to sort out facts as they are and not what one wishes they were? The hallmark of physical evidence is that it must undergo scientific inquiry. Science derives its integrity from adherence to strict guidelines that ensure careful and systematic collection, organization, and analysis of information—a process known as the **scientific method**. The underlying principles of the scientific method provide a safety net to ensure that the outcome of an investigation is not tainted by human emotion or compromised by distorting, belittling, or ignoring contrary evidence.

scientific method
A process that uses strict guidelines to ensure careful and systematic collection, organization, and analysis of information

The scientific method begins by formulating a question worthy of investigation, such as who committed a particular crime. The investigator next formulates a hypothesis, a reasonable explanation proposed to answer the question. What follows is the basic foundation of scientific inquiry—the testing of the hypothesis through experimentation. The testing process must be thorough and recognized by other scientists as valid. Scientists and investigators must accept the experimental findings even when they wish they were different. Finally, when the hypothesis is validated by experimentation, it becomes suitable as scientific evidence, appropriate for use in a criminal investigation and ultimately available for admission in a court of law.

Determining Admissibility of Evidence In rejecting the scientific validity of the lie detector (polygraph), the District of Columbia Circuit Court in 1923 set forth what has since become a standard guideline for determining the judicial admissibility of scientific examinations. In *Frye v. United States*,[2] the court ruled that in order to be admitted as evidence at trial, the questioned procedure, technique, or principles must be "generally accepted" by a meaningful segment of the relevant scientific community. In practice, this approach requires the proponent of a scientific test to present to the court a collection of experts who can testify that the scientific issue before the court is generally accepted by the relevant members of the scientific community. Furthermore, in determining whether a novel technique meets criteria associated with "general acceptance," courts have frequently taken note of books and papers written on the subject, as well as prior judicial decisions relating to the reliability and general acceptance of the technique. In recent years, many observers have questioned whether this approach is sufficiently flexible to deal with new scientific issues that may not have gained widespread support within the scientific community.

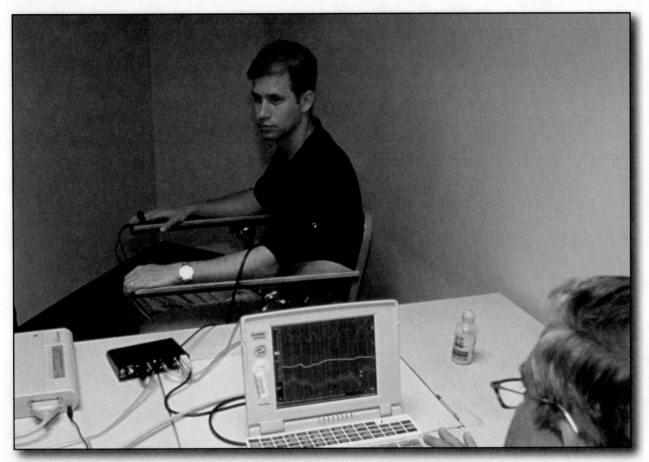

FIGURE 1–12 An individual undergoing a polygraph test. *Courtesy Stock Connection Blue/Alamy*

The Federal Rules of Evidence offer an alternative to the *Frye* standard, one that some courts believe espouses a more flexible standard for admitting scientific evidence. Part of the Federal Rules of Evidence governs the admissibility of all evidence, including expert testimony, in federal courts, and many states have adopted codes similar to those of the Federal Rules. Specifically, Rule 702 of the Federal Rules of Evidence sets a different standard from "general acceptance" for admissibility of expert testimony. Under this standard, a witness "qualified as an expert by knowledge, skill, experience, training, or education" may offer expert testimony on a scientific or technical matter if "(1) the testimony is based upon sufficient facts or data, (2) the testimony is the product of reliable principles and methods, and (3) the witness has applied the principles and methods reliably to the facts of the case."

In a landmark ruling in the 1993 case of *Daubert v. Merrell Dow Pharmaceuticals, Inc.,*[3] the U.S. Supreme Court asserted that "general acceptance," or the *Frye* standard, is not an absolute prerequisite to the admissibility of scientific evidence under the Federal Rules of Evidence. According to the Court, the Rules of Evidence—especially Rule 702—assign to the trial judge the task of ensuring that an expert's testimony rests on a reliable foundation and is relevant to the case.

Although this ruling applies only to federal courts, many state courts are expected to use this decision as a guideline in setting standards for the admissibility of scientific evidence.

Judging Scientific Evidence In *Daubert*, the Court advocates that trial judges assume the ultimate responsibility for acting as a "gatekeeper" in judging the admissibility and reliability of scientific evidence presented in their courts. The Court offered some guidelines as to how a judge can gauge the veracity of scientific evidence, emphasizing that the inquiry should be flexible. Suggested areas of inquiry include the following:

1. **Whether the scientific technique or theory can be (and has been) tested**

2. **Whether the technique or theory has been subject to peer review and publication**

3. **The technique's potential rate of error**

4. **Existence and maintenance of standards controlling the technique's operation**

5. **Whether the scientific theory or method has attracted widespread acceptance within a relevant scientific community**

FIGURE 1–13
Sketch of a US Supreme Court hearing.
Courtesy Art Lien

Some legal experts have expressed concern that abandoning *Frye's* general-acceptance test will result in the introduction of absurd and irrational pseudoscientific claims in the courtroom. The Supreme Court rejected these concerns, pointing out the inherent strengths of the American judicial process in identifying unreliable evidence:

In this regard the respondent seems to us to be overly pessimistic about the capabilities of the jury and of the adversary system generally. Vigorous cross-examination, presentation of contrary evidence, and careful instruction on the burden of proof are the traditional and appropriate means of attacking shaky but admissible evidence.

In a 1999 decision, *Kumho Tire Co., Ltd. v. Carmichael,*[4] the Court unanimously ruled that the "gatekeeping" role of the trial judge applied not only to scientific testimony, but to all expert testimony:

We conclude that Daubert's general holding—setting forth the trial judge's general "gatekeeping" obligation—applies not only to testimony based on "scientific" knowledge, but also to testimony based on "technical" and "other specialized" knowledge. . . . We also conclude that a trial court may consider one or more of the more specific factors that Daubert mentioned when doing so will help determine that testimony's reliability. But, as the Court stated in Daubert, the test of reliability is "flexible," and Daubert's list of specific factors neither necessarily nor exclusively applies to all experts in every case.

The case of *Coppolino v. State*[5] (examined more closely in the following case study) exemplifies the flexibility and wide discretion that the *Daubert* ruling, 25 years later, apparently gave to trial judges in matters of scientific inquiry. The issue at question was whether the results of a new procedure that have not been widely accepted in the scientific community are necessarily inadmissible as evidence. The court rejected this argument, recognizing that researchers must devise new scientific tests to solve the special problems that continually arise in the forensic laboratory.

The *Coppolino* ruling acknowledged that even well-established scientific procedures were once new and unproven and noted the court's duty to protect the public when weighing the admissibility of a new test. In the words of the concurring opinion, "Society need not tolerate homicide until there develops a body of medical literature about some particular lethal agent." The court emphasized, however, that although these tests may be new and unique, they are admissible only if they are based on scientifically valid principles and techniques.

Providing Expert Testimony

Because the results of their work may ultimately be a factor in determining a person's guilt or innocence, forensic scientists may be required to testify about their methods and conclusions at a trial or hearing. Trial courts have broad discretion in accepting an individual as an **expert witness** on any particular subject. Generally, if a witness can establish to the satisfaction of a trial judge that he or she possesses a particular skill or has knowledge in a trade or profession that will aid the court in determining the truth of the matter at issue, that individual will be accepted as an expert witness. Depending on the subject area in question, the court will usually consider knowledge acquired through experience, training, education, or a combination as sufficient grounds for qualification as an expert witness.

In court, an expert witness may be asked questions intended to demonstrate his or her ability and competence pertaining to the matter at hand. Competency

expert witness
An individual whom the court determines to possess knowledge relevant to the trial that is not expected of the average layperson

Case Files

Dr. Coppolino's Deadly House Calls

A frantic late-night telephone call brought a local physician to the Florida home of Drs. Carl and Carmela Coppolino. The physician arrived to find Carmela beyond help. Carmela Coppolino's body, unexamined by anyone, was buried in her family's plot in her home state of New Jersey.

A little more than a month later, Carl married a moneyed socialite, Mary Gibson. News of Carl's marriage infuriated Marjorie Farber, a former New Jersey neighbor of Dr. Coppolino who had been a having an affair with the good doctor. Soon Marjorie had an interesting story to recount to investigators. Her husband's death two years before, although ruled to be from natural causes, had actually been murder! Carl, an anesthesiologist, had given Marjorie a syringe containing some medication and told her to inject her husband, William, while he was sleeping. Ultimately, Marjorie claimed, she was unable to inject the full dose and called Carl, who finished the job by suffocating William with a pillow.

Marjorie Farber's astonishing story was supported in part by Carl's recent increase in his wife's life insurance. Carmela's $65,000 policy, along with his new wife's fortune, would keep Dr. Coppolino in high society for the rest of his life. Based on this information, authorities in New Jersey and Florida now obtained exhumation orders for both William Farber and Carmela Coppolino. After examination of both bodies, Dr. Coppolino was charged with the murders of William and Carmela.

Officials decided to try Dr. Coppolino first in New Jersey for the murder of William Farber. The Farber autopsy did not reveal any evidence of poisoning, but seemed to show strong evidence of strangulation. The absence of toxicological findings left the jury to deliberate the conflicting medical expert testimony versus the sensational story told by a scorned and embittered woman. In the end, Dr. Coppolino was acquitted.

The Florida trial presented another chance to bring Carl Coppolino to justice. Recalling Dr. Coppolino's career as an anesthesiologist, it was theorized that Coppolino had exploited his access to the many potent drugs used during surgery to commit these murders, specifically an injectable paralytic agent called succinylcholine chloride.

After having Carmela's body exhumed, it was found that Carmela had been injected in her left buttock shortly before her death. Ultimately, a completely novel procedure for detecting succinylcholine chloride was devised. Elevated levels of succinic acid were found in Carmela's brain, which proved that she had received a large dose of the paralytic drug shortly before her death. This evidence, along with the finding of the same drug residues in the injection site on her buttock, was presented in the Florida murder trial of Carl Coppolino, who was convicted of second-degree murder.

may be established by having the witness cite educational degrees, participation in special courses, membership in professional societies, and any professional articles or books published. Also important is the number of years of occupational experience the witness has in areas related to the matter before the court.

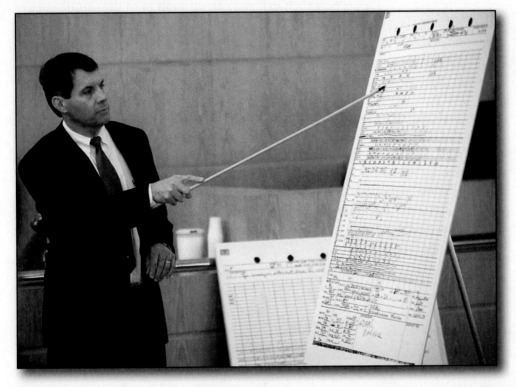

FIGURE 1–14
An expert witness testifying in court. *Courtesy Jeff Siner, Corbis/Sygma*

Unfortunately, few schools confer degrees in forensic science. Most chemists, biologists, geologists, and physicists prepare themselves for careers in forensic science by combining training under an experienced examiner with independent study. Of course, formal education in the physical sciences provides a firm foundation for learning and understanding the principles and techniques of forensic science. Nevertheless, for the most part, courts must rely on training and years of experience as a measurement of the knowledge and ability of the expert.

Before the judge rules on the witness's qualifications, the opposing attorney may cross-examine the witness and point out weaknesses in background and knowledge. Most courts are reluctant to disqualify an individual as an expert even when presented with someone whose background is only remotely associated with the issue at hand. The question of what credentials are suitable for qualification as an expert is ambiguous and highly subjective and one that the courts wisely try to avoid.

The weight that a judge or jury assigns to "expert" testimony in subsequent deliberations is, however, quite another matter. Undoubtedly, education and experience have considerable bearing on the value assigned to the expert's opinions. Just as important may be his or her demeanor and ability to explain scientific data and conclusions clearly, concisely, and logically to a judge and jury composed of nonscientists. The problem of sorting out the strengths and weaknesses of expert testimony falls to prosecution and defense counsel.

MyCrimeKit:
WebExtra 1.3
Watch a Forensic Witness
Testify—I
www.mycrimekit.com

MyCrimeKit:
WebExtra 1.4
Watch a Forensic Witness
Testify—II
www.mycrimekit.com

The ordinary or lay witness must testify on events or observations that arise from personal knowledge. This testimony must be factual and, with few exceptions, cannot contain the personal opinions of the witness. On the other hand, the expert witness is called on to evaluate evidence when the court lacks the expertise to do so. This expert then expresses an opinion as to the significance of the findings. The views expressed are accepted only as representing the expert's opinion and may later be accepted or ignored in jury deliberations.

The expert cannot render any view with absolute certainty. At best, he or she may only be able to offer an opinion based on a reasonable scientific certainty derived from training and experience. Obviously, the expert is expected to defend vigorously the techniques and conclusions of the analysis, but at the same time must not be reluctant to discuss impartially any findings that could minimize the significance of the analysis. The forensic scientist should not be an advocate of one party's cause, but only an advocate of truth. An adversary system of justice must give the prosecutor and defense ample opportunity to offer expert opinions and to argue the merits of such testimony. Ultimately, the duty of the judge or jury is to weigh the pros and cons of all the information presented in deciding guilt or innocence.

Furnishing Training in the Proper Recognition, Collection, and Preservation of Physical Evidence

The competence of a laboratory staff and the sophistication of its analytical equipment have little or no value if relevant evidence cannot be properly recognized, collected, and preserved at the site of a crime. For this reason, the forensic staff must have responsibilities that will influence the conduct of the crime-scene investigation.

The most direct and effective response to this problem has been to dispatch specially trained evidence-collection technicians to the crime scene. A growing number of crime laboratories and the police agencies they service keep trained "evidence technicians" on 24-hour call to help criminal investigators retrieve evidence. These technicians are trained by the laboratory staff to recognize and gather pertinent physical evidence at the crime scene. They are assigned to the laboratory full-time for continued exposure to forensic techniques and procedures. They have at their disposal all the proper tools and supplies for proper collection and packaging of evidence for future scientific examination.

Unfortunately, many police forces still have not adopted this approach. Often a patrol officer or detective collects the evidence. The individual's effectiveness in this role depends on the extent of his or her training and working relationship with the laboratory. For maximum use of the skills of the crime laboratory, training of the crime-scene investigator must go beyond superficial classroom lectures to involve extensive personal contact with the forensic scientist. Each must become aware of the other's problems, techniques, and limitations.

The training of police officers in evidence collection and their familiarization with the capabilities of a crime laboratory should not be restricted to a select group of personnel on the force. Every officer engaged in fieldwork, whether it be traffic, patrol, investigation, or juvenile control, often must process evidence for laboratory examination. Obviously, it would be difficult and time consuming to give everyone the in-depth training and attention that a qualified criminal investigator requires. However, familiarity with crime laboratory services and capabilities can be gained through periodic lectures, laboratory tours, and dissemination of manuals prepared by the laboratory staff that outline the proper methods for collecting and submitting physical evidence to the laboratory.

A brief outline describing the proper collection and packaging of common types of physical evidence is found in the <u>Appendix</u>. The procedures and information summarized in this appendix are discussed in greater detail in forthcoming chapters.

FIGURE 1–15 Representative evidence-collection guides prepared by various police agencies.

Quick Review

- A forensic scientist must be skilled in applying the principles and techniques of the physical and natural sciences to analyzing evidence that may be recovered during a criminal investigation.

- The cases *Frye v. United States* and *Daubert v. Merrell Dow Pharmaceuticals, Inc.* set guidelines for determining the admissibility of scientific evidence into the courtroom.

- An expert witness evaluates evidence based on specialized training and experience.

- Forensic scientists participate in training law enforcement personnel in the proper recognition, collection, and preservation of physical evidence.

Exploring Forensic Science on the Internet

There are no limits to the amount or type of information that can be found on the Internet. The fields of law enforcement and forensic science have not been left behind by advancing computer technology. Extensive information about forensic science is available on the Internet. The types of Web pages range from simple explanations of the various fields of forensics to intricate details of crime-scene reconstruction. People can also find information on which colleges offer degree programs in forensics or pages posted by law enforcement agencies that detail their activities, as well as possible employment opportunities.

General Forensics Sites

Reddy's Forensic Home Page (www.forensicpage.com) is a valuable starting point. This site is a collection of forensic Web pages listed under categories such as new links in forensics; general forensic information sources; associations, colleges, and societies; literature and journals; forensic laboratories; general Web pages; forensic-related mailing lists and newsgroups; universities; conferences; and various forensic fields of expertise.

Another Web site offering a multitude of information related to forensic science is Zeno's Forensic Site (www.forensic.to/forensic.html). Here users can find links to forensic education and expert consultation, as well as a wealth of information concerning specific fields of forensic science.

A comprehensive and useful Web site for those interested in law enforcement is Officer.com (www.officer.com). This comprehensive collection of criminal justice resources is organized into easy-to-read subdirectories that relate to topics such as law enforcement agencies, police association and organization sites, criminal justice organizations, law research pages, and police mailing-list directories.

An Introduction to Forensic Firearm Identification This Web site contains an extensive collection of information relating to the identification of firearms. An individual can explore in detail how to examine bullets, cartridge cases, and clothing for gunshot residues and suspect shooters' hands for primer residues. Information on the latest technology involving the automated firearms search system IBIS can also be found on this site.

Carpenter's Forensic Science Resources This site provides a bibliography with hypertext references pertaining to various aspects of criminal investigations involving forensic evidence. For example, the user can find references about DNA, fingerprints, hairs, fibers, and questioned documents as they relate to crime scenes and assist investigations. This Web site is an excellent place to start a research project in forensic science.

Crime Scene Investigator Network For those who are interested in learning the process of crime-scene investigation, this site provides detailed guidelines and information regarding crime-scene response and the collection and preservation of evidence. For example, information concerning the packaging and analysis of bloodstains, seminal fluids, hairs, fibers, paint, glass, firearms, documents,

MyCrimeKit: WebExtra 1.5

An Introduction to Forensic Firearm Indentification
www.mycrimekit.com

MyCrimeKit: WebExtra 1.6

Carpenter's Forensic Science Resources
www.mycrimekit.com

MyCrimeKit: WebExtra 1.7

Crime Scene Investigator Network
www.mycrimekit.com

and fingerprints can be found through this Web site. It explains the importance of inspecting the crime scene and the impact forensic evidence has on the investigation.

Crimes and Clues Users interested in learning about the forensic aspects of fingerprinting will find this a useful and informative Web site. The site covers the history of fingerprints, as well as subjects pertaining to the development of latent fingerprints. The user will also find links to other Web sites covering a variety of subjects pertaining to crime-scene investigation, documentation of the crime scene, and expert testimony.

Interactive Investigator—Détective Interactif At this outstanding site, visitors can obtain general information and an introduction to the main aspects of forensic science from a database on the subject. They can also explore actual evidence gathered from notorious crime scenes. Users will be able to employ deductive skills and forensic knowledge while playing an interactive game in which they must help Detective Wilson and Detective Marlow solve a gruesome murder.

The Chemical Detective This site offers descriptions of relevant forensic science disciplines. Topics such as fingerprints, fire and arson, and DNA analysis are described in informative layperson's terms. Case histories describe the application of forensic evidence to criminal investigations. Emphasis is placed on securing and documenting the crime scene. The site directs the reader to other important forensic links.

Questioned-Document Examination This basic, informative Web page answers frequently asked questions concerning document examination, explains the application of typical document examinations, and details the basic facts and theory of handwriting and signatures. There are also links to noted document examination cases that present the user with real-life applications of forensic document examination.

MyCrimeKit: WebExtra 1.8
Crimes and Clues
www.mycrimekit.com

MyCrimeKit: WebExtra 1.9
Interactive Investigator
www.mycrimekit.com

MyCrimeKit: WebExtra 1.10
The Chemical Detective
www.mycrimekit.com

MyCrimeKit: WebExtra 1.11
Questioned-Document Examination
www.mycrimekit.com

Chapter Review

- Forensic science is the application of science to criminal and civil laws that are enforced by police agencies in a criminal justice system.

- The first system of personal identification was called anthropometry. It distinguished one individual from another based on a series of body measurements.

- Forensic science owes its origins to individuals such as Bertillon, Galton, Lattes, Goddard, Osborn, and Locard, who developed the principles and techniques needed to identify or compare physical evidence.

- Locard's exchange principle states that when two objects come into contact with each other, there is exchange of materials between them. This cross-transfer of materials can connect a criminal suspect to his or her victim.

- The development of crime laboratories in the United States has been characterized by rapid growth accompanied by a lack of national and regional planning and coordination.

- Four major reasons for the increase in the number of crime laboratories in the United States since the 1960s are as follows: (1) the fact that the requirement to advise criminal suspects of their constitutional rights and their right of immediate access to counsel has all but eliminated confessions as a routine investigative tool; (2) the staggering increase in crime rates in the United States; (3) the fact that all illicit-drug seizures must be sent to a forensic laboratory for confirmatory chemical analysis before the case can be adjudicated in court; and (4) the advent of DNA profiling.

- The technical support provided by crime laboratories can be assigned to five basic services: the physical science unit, the biology unit, the firearms unit, the document examination unit, and the photography unit.

- Some crime laboratories offer optional services such as toxicology, fingerprint analysis, polygraph administration, voiceprint analysis, and crime-scene investigation.

- Special forensic science services available to the law enforcement community include forensic pathology, forensic anthropology, forensic entomology, forensic psychiatry, forensic odontology, forensic engineering, and forensic computer and digital analysis.

- A forensic scientist must be skilled in applying the principles and techniques of the physical and natural sciences to analyzing evidence that may be recovered during a criminal investigation.

- The cases *Frye v. United States* and *Daubert v. Merrell Dow Pharmaceuticals, Inc.* set guidelines for determining the admissibility of scientific evidence into the courtroom.

- An expert witness evaluates evidence based on specialized training and experience.

- Forensic scientists participate in training law enforcement personnel in the proper recognition, collection, and preservation of physical evidence.

Review Questions

1. All the following are basic services provided by "full-service crime laboratories" except:
   a. biology unit.
   b. firearms unit.
   c. document examination unit.
   d. toxicology unit.

2. The standard guideline for determining the judicial admissibility of scientific examination stemmed from which court ruling?
   a. *Mincey v. Arizona*
   b. *Kumho Tire Co., Ltd. v. Carmichael*
   c. *Frye v. United States*
   d. *Coppolino v. State*

3. The scientist who maintained that when a criminal came in contact with an object or person a cross-transfer of evidence would occur was
   a. Hans Gross.
   b. Walter McCrone.
   c. Edmond Locard.
   d. Albert Osborn.

4. Which individual contributed knowledge to the forensic characterization of blood?
   a. Albert Osborn
   b. Calvin Goddard
   c. Alec Jeffries
   d. Thomas Taylor

5. The basic functions of a forensic scientist include:
   a. furnishing training on the proper collection of physical evidence.
   b. analysis of physical evidence.
   c. providing expert testimony.
   d. all of the above.

6. True or False: The first forensic laboratory in the United States was created in 1923.

7. True or False: The United States is one of only a handful of countries in the world that have created and now maintain forensic facilities.

8. True or False: In 1993 the U.S. Supreme Court decided that the *Frye v. United States* precedent is an absolute prerequisite to the admissibility of scientific evidence.

9. True or False: Only individuals who have accredited professional credentials from recognized university or medical programs are allowed to testify in court as an expert witness.

10. True or False: Strict guidelines that ensure careful and systematic collection, organization, and analysis of information is a process known as the scientific method.

11. Define forensic science.

12. What was the name of the first system of personal identification? What criteria did it use to distinguish individuals?

13. What was Francis Henry Galton's major contribution to forensic science? How did this advancement improve forensic science?

14. Who is known as "the father of forensic toxicology" and why?

15. Name two major contributions to forensic science made by Hans Gross. Why are they considered important to forensic science?

16. With what area of forensic investigation are Karl Landsteiner and Louis Lattes associated?

17. Who was the first person to apply the principles of forensic science to a working crime laboratory? What crime was he investigating?

18. What is Locard's exchange principle?

19. With what instrument did Dr. Walter C. McCrone make significant contributions to forensic science?

20. List four major reasons for the increase in the number of crime laboratories in the United States since the 1960s.

21. List four government agencies that offer forensic services at the federal level.

22. The current system of crime laboratories in the United States can best be described as
    a. centralized.
    b. regional.
    c. decentralized.
    d. national.

23. List three advantages of having regional crime laboratories operate as part of a statewide system. Are there any disadvantages to this setup?

24. How does the organization of Great Britain's forensic laboratories differ from that of the United States? Is this advantageous?

25. Which unit examines body fluids and organs for drugs and poisons?

26. Which unit examines and compares tool marks?

27. What part of the body do forensic odontologists use to identify a victim? Why is this body part particularly useful as a source of identification?

28. Describe the criteria for admissibility of scientific evidence as laid out in *Frye v. United States*.

29. In its decision in *Daubert v. Merrell Dow Pharmaceuticals, Inc.*, whom did the U.S. Supreme Court charge with ensuring that an expert's testimony rests on a reliable foundation and is relevant to the case?

30. What is an expert witness?

31. What is the main difference between the testimony given by an expert witness and that given by a lay witness?

Chapter 1

Application and Critical Thinking

1. Most crime labs in the United States are funded and operated by the government and provide services free to police and prosecutors. Great Britain, however, uses a quasi-governmental agency that charges fees for its services and keeps any profits it makes. Suggest potential strengths and weaknesses of each system.

2. Police investigating an apparent suicide collect the following items at the scene: a note purportedly written by the victim, a revolver bearing very faint fingerprints, and traces of skin and blood under the victim's fingernails. What units of the crime laboratory will examine each piece of evidence?

3. List at least three advantages of having an evidence-collection unit process a crime scene instead of a patrol officer or detective.

4. What legal issue was raised on appeal by the defense in Carl Coppolino's Florida murder trial? What court ruling is most relevant to the decision to reject the appeal? Explain your answer.

5.   A Timeline of Forensic Science

The following images depict different types of evidence or techniques for analyzing evidence. Place the images in order pertaining to the time in history (least recent to most recent) at which that evidence or technique was first introduced. Do this using the letter assigned to each image.

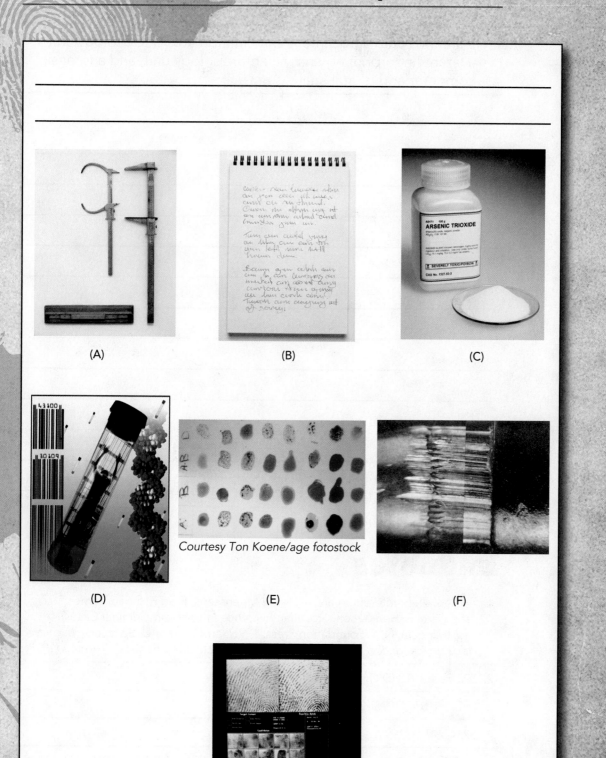

Courtesy Ton Koene/age fotostock

6. Evidence Processing at the Crime Laboratory

You are the evidence technician at the front desk of the state crime lab. You receive the following items of evidence to check in on a very busy day. You must indicate which unit each piece of evidence must be sent to for analysis. Your crime lab has a criminalistics (physical science) unit, a drug unit, a biology unit, a firearms unit, a document examination unit, a toxicology unit, a latent fingerprinting unit, an anthropology unit, and a forensic computer and digital analysis unit.

a.

b.

c.

d.

e.

f.

g.

h.

i.

j.

k.

l.

m.

Endnotes

1. Two excellent references are André A. Moenssens, Fred E. Inbau, James Starrs, and Carol E. Henderson, *Scientific Evidence in Civil and Criminal Cases, 4th ed.* (Mineola, N.Y.: Foundation Press, 1995); and Werner U. Spitz, ed., *Medico-legal Investigation of Death, 3rd ed.* (Springfield, Ill.: Charles C. Thomas, 1993).

2. 293 Fed. 1013 (D.C. Cir. 1923).

3. 509 U.S. 579 (1993).

4. 526 U.S 137 (1999).

5. 223 So. 2d 68 (Fla. App. 1968), app. dismissed, 234 So. 2d (Fla. 1969), cert. denied, 399 U.S. 927 (1970).

(A)

(B)

(C)

(D)

(E)

(F)

(G)

(H)

(I)

(J)

(K)

(L)

(M)

JonBenet Ramsey: Who Did It?

Patsy and John Ramsey were in the upper crust of Boulder, Colorado, society. In the span of five short years, John had built his computer company into a billion-dollar corporation. In addition to financial success, the Ramseys also had a beautiful 6-year-old daughter, JonBenet.

Just after five A.M. on December 26, 1996, Patsy Ramsey awoke and walked downstairs to her kitchen. At the foot of the staircase, she found a two-and-a-half-page note saying that JonBenet had been kidnapped. The note contained a ransom demand of $118,000. When the police arrived to investigate, it was quite apparent to all that JonBenet was missing.

In retrospect, some serious mistakes were made in securing the crime scene—the Ramsey household. Initially, the police conducted a cursory search of the house, but failed to find JonBenet. The house was not sealed off; in fact, four friends along with the Ramsey pastor were let into the home and allowed to move about at will. John was permitted to leave the premises unattended for one and a half hours. One hour after his return, John and two of his friends searched the house again. This time John went down into the basement, where he discovered JonBenet's body. He removed a white blanket from JonBenet and carried her upstairs, placing the body on the living room floor.

The murder of JonBenet Ramsey remains as baffling a mystery today as it was on its first day. Ample physical evidence supports the theory that the crime was committed by an outsider, as well as the competing theory that JonBenet was murdered by someone who resided in the Ramsey household. Perhaps better care at securing and processing the crime scene could have resolved some of the crime's outstanding questions.

The Crime Scene

Key Terms

algor mortis

autopsy

buccal swab

chain of custody

finished sketch

livor mortis

physical evidence

rigor mortis

rough sketch

standard/reference sample

substrate control

Physical Evidence and the Crime Scene

physical evidence
Any object that can establish that a crime has or has not been committed or can link a crime and its victim or its perpetrator

As automobiles run on gasoline, crime laboratories "run" on **physical evidence**. Physical evidence encompasses any and all objects that can establish that a crime has or has not been committed or can link a crime and its victim or its perpetrator. But if physical evidence is to be used effectively to aid the investigator, its presence first must be recognized at the crime scene. If all the natural and commercial objects within a reasonable distance of a crime were gathered so that the scientist could uncover significant clues from them, the deluge of material would quickly immobilize the laboratory facility. Physical evidence achieves its optimum value in criminal investigations only when its collection is performed with a selectivity governed by the collector's thorough knowledge of the crime laboratory's techniques, capabilities, and limitations.

Forthcoming chapters discuss methods and techniques available to forensic scientists to evaluate physical evidence. Although current technology has given the crime laboratory capabilities far exceeding those of past decades, these advances are no excuse for complacency on the part of criminal investigators. Crime laboratories do not solve crimes; only a thorough and competent investigation conducted by professional police officers will enhance the chances for a successful criminal investigation. Forensic science is, and will continue to be, an important element of the total investigative process, but it is only one aspect of an endeavor that must be a team effort. The investigator who believes the crime laboratory to be a solution for carelessness or ineptness is in for a rude awakening.

Forensic science begins at the crime scene. If the investigator cannot recognize physical evidence or cannot properly preserve it for laboratory examination, no amount of sophisticated laboratory instrumentation or technical expertise can salvage the situation. The know-how for conducting a proper crime-scene search for physical evidence is within the grasp of any police department, regardless of its size. With proper training, police agencies can ensure competent performance at crime scenes. In many jurisdictions, police agencies have delegated this task to a specialized team of technicians. However, the techniques of crime-scene investigation are easy to master and certainly lie within the bounds of comprehension of the average police officer.

Not all crime scenes require retrieval of physical evidence, and limited resources and personnel have forced many police agencies to restrict their efforts in this area to crimes of a more serious nature. Once the commitment is made to process a crime site for physical evidence, however, certain fundamental practices must be followed.

Preserving and Recording the Crime Scene

In order to be useful to investigators, evidence at a crime scene must be preserved and recorded in its original condition as much as possible. Failure to protect a crime scene properly or record its details accurately may result in the destruction or altering of evidence, or hinder the search for the perpetrator by misleading investigators about the facts of the incident.

Secure and Isolate the Crime Scene

The first officer arriving on the scene of a crime must preserve and protect the area as much as possible. Of course, first priority should be given to obtaining medical assistance for individuals in need of it and to arresting the perpetrator. However, as soon as possible, extensive efforts must be made to exclude all unauthorized personnel from the scene. As additional officers arrive, measures are immediately initiated to isolate the area. (See Figure 2–1.) Ropes or barricades along with strategic positioning of guards will prevent unauthorized access to the area.

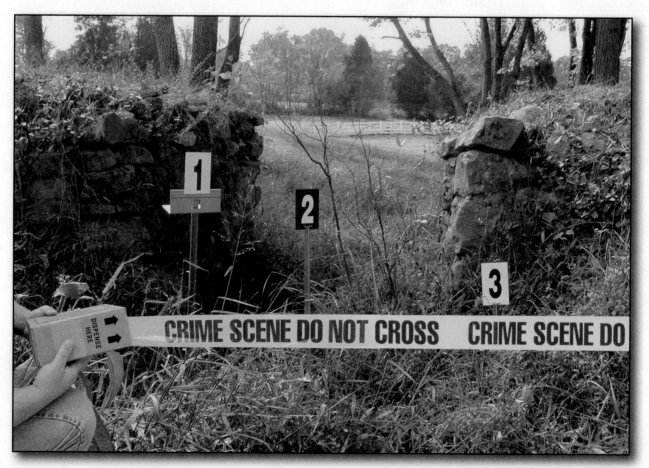

FIGURE 2–1   The first investigators to arrive must secure the crime scene and establish the crime-scene perimeter. *Courtesy Sirchie Finger Print Laboratories, Inc., Youngsville, N.C., www.sirchie.com*

Sometimes the exclusion of unauthorized personnel proves more difficult than expected. Violent crimes are especially susceptible to attention from higher-level police officials and members of the press, as well as by emotionally charged neighbors and curiosity seekers. Every individual who enters the scene has the potential to destroy physical evidence, even if by unintentional carelessness. To exercise proper control over the crime scene, the officer protecting it must have the authority to exclude everyone, including fellow police officers not directly involved in processing the site or in conducting the investigation. Seasoned criminal investigators are always prepared to relate horror stories about crime scenes where physical evidence was rendered totally valueless by hordes of people who trampled through the site. Securing and isolating the crime scene are critical steps in an investigation, the accomplishment of which is the mark of a trained and professional crime-scene investigative team.

Once the scene has been secured, a lead investigator starts evaluating the area. First, he or she determines the boundaries of the scene and then establishes the perpetrator's path of entry and exit. Logic dictates that obvious items of crime-scene evidence will first come to the attention of the crime-scene investigator. These items must be documented and photographed. The investigator then proceeds with an initial walk-through of the scene to gain an overview of the situation and develop a strategy for systematically examining and documenting the entire crime scene.

Record the Scene

Investigators have only a limited amount of time to work a crime site in its untouched state. The opportunity to permanently record the scene in its original state must not be lost. Such records not only will prove useful during the subsequent investigation, but also are required for presentation at a trial in order to document the condition of the crime site and to delineate the location of physical evidence. Photography, sketches, and notes are the three methods for crime-scene recording (see Figure 2–2). Ideally all three should be employed; however, personnel and monetary limitations often prohibit the use of photography at every crime site. Under these circumstances, departmental guidelines will establish priorities for deploying photographic resources. However, there is no reason not to make sketches and notes at the crime scene.

Photography The most important prerequisite for photographing a crime scene is for it to be unaltered. Unless injured people are involved, objects must not be moved until they have been photographed from all necessary angles. If objects are removed, positions changed, or items added, the photographs may not be admissible as evidence at a trial, and their intended value will be lost. If evidence has been removed or moved before photography, the fact should be noted in the report, but the evidence should not be reintroduced into the scene in order to take photographs.

Each crime scene should be photographed as completely as possible. This means that the crime scene should include the area in which the crime actually took place and all adjacent areas where important acts occurred immediately before or after the commission of the crime. Overview photographs of the entire

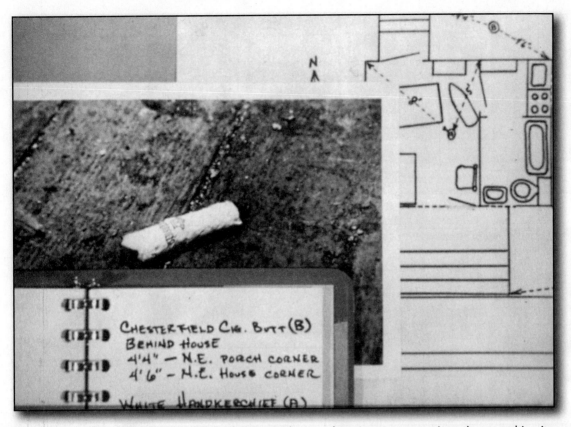

FIGURE 2–2 The finding of an evidential cigarette butt at the crime scene requires photographing it, making a sketch showing its relation to the crime scene, and recording the find in field notes. *Courtesy Police Science Services, Niles, Ill.*

scene and surrounding area, including points of exit and entry, must be taken from various angles. If the crime took place indoors, the entire room should be photographed to show each wall area. Rooms adjacent to the actual crime site must be similarly photographed. If the crime scene includes a body, photographs must be taken to show the body's position and location relative to the entire scene. Close-up photos depicting injuries and weapons lying near the body are also necessary. After the body is removed from the scene, the surface beneath the body should be photographed.

As items of physical evidence are discovered, they are photographed to show their position and location relative to the entire scene. After these overviews are taken, close-ups should be taken to record the details of the object itself. When the size of an item is significant, a ruler or other measuring scale may be inserted near the object and included in the photograph as a point of reference.

The digital revolution promises to bring enhanced photographic capabilities to the crime scene. For example, individual images of the crime scene captured with a digital camera can be stitched together electronically to reveal a near three-dimensional panoramic view of the crime scene (see Figure 2–3). With the aid of a computer, any area of the scene captured digitally can be enhanced and examined in fine detail.

The use of videotape or digital video at crime scenes is becoming increasingly popular because the cost of this equipment is decreasing. The same principles used in crime-scene photographs apply to videotaping or digital video. As with

MyCrimeKit: WebExtra 2.1
Making a Photographic Record of the Crime Scene
www.mycrimekit.com

FIGURE 2–3 Individual images (top) are shown before being electronically stitched together into a single panoramic image (bottom). Individual photographs should be taken with about a 30 percent overlap. *Courtesy Imaging Forensics, Fountain Valley, Calif., www.imagingforensics.com*

conventional photography, videotaping or digital video should include the entire scene and the immediate surrounding area. Long shots as well as close-ups should be taken in a slow and systematic manner. Furthermore, it is desirable to have one crime-scene investigator narrate the events and scenes being recorded while another does the actual shooting.

Although videotaping or digital video can capture the sounds and scenes of the crime site with relative ease, the technique cannot at this time be used in place of still photography. The still photograph remains unsurpassed in the definition of detail it provides to the human eye.

Sketches Once photographs have been taken, the crime-scene investigator sketches the scene. The investigator may have neither the skill nor the time to make a polished sketch of the scene. However, this is not required during the early phase of the investigation. What is necessary is a **rough sketch** containing an accurate depiction of the dimensions of the scene and showing the location of all objects having a bearing on the case.

A rough sketch is illustrated in Figure 2–4. It shows all recovered items of physical evidence, as well as other important features of the crime scene. Objects are located in the sketch by distance measurements from two fixed points, such as the walls of a room. Distances shown on the sketch must be accurate and not

rough sketch

A sketch, drawn at the crime scene, that contains an accurate depiction of the dimensions of the scene and shows the location of all objects having a bearing on the case the result of a guess or estimate. For this reason, all measurements are made with a tape measure. The simplest way to designate an item in a sketch is to assign it a number or letter. A legend or list placed below the sketch then correlates the letter to the item's description. The sketch should also show a compass heading designating north.

FIGURE 2–4
Rough-sketch diagram of a crime scene. *Courtesy Sirchie Finger Print Laboratories, Inc., Youngsville, N.C., www.sirchie.com*

finished sketch
A precise rendering of the crime scene, usually drawn to scale

Unlike the rough sketch, the **finished sketch** in Figure 2–5 is constructed with care and concern for aesthetic appearance. When the finished sketch is completed, it must reflect information contained within the rough sketch in order to be admissible evidence in a courtroom. Computer-aided drafting (CAD) has become the standard method for reconstructing crime scenes from rough sketches. The software, ranging from simple, low-cost programs to complex, expensive ones, contains predrawn intersections, roadways, buildings, and rooms onto which information can be entered (see Figure 2–6). A generous symbol library provides a variety of images that can be used to add intricate details such as blood spatters to a crime-scene sketch. Equipped with a zoom function, computerized sketching can focus on a specific area for a more detailed picture. The CAD programs allow the user to select scale size so that the final product can be produced in a size suitable for courtroom presentation.

FIGURE 2–5
Finished sketch of a crime scene. *Courtesy Sirchie Finger Print Laboratories, Inc., Youngsville, N.C., www. sirchie.com*

FIGURE 2–6
Construction of a crime-scene diagram with the aid of a computer-aided drafting program.
Courtesy Sirchie Finger Print Laboratories, Inc., Youngsville, N.C., www. sirchie.com

Notes Note taking must be a constant activity throughout the processing of the crime scene. These notes must include a detailed written description of the scene with the location of items of physical evidence recovered. They must also identify the time an item of physical evidence was discovered, by whom, how and by whom it was packaged and marked, and the disposition of the item after it was collected. The note taker must keep in mind that this written record may be the only source of information for refreshing one's memory months, perhaps years, after a crime has been processed. The notes must be sufficiently detailed to anticipate this need. Tape-recording notes at a scene can be advantageous—detailed notes can be taped much faster than they can be written. Another method of recording notes is to narrate a video recording of the crime scene. This has the advantage of combining note taking with photography. However, at some point the tape must be transcribed into a written document.

Quick Review

- Physical evidence includes any and all objects that can establish that a crime has been committed or can link the crime and its victim or its perpetrator.

- Forensic science begins at the crime scene, where investigators must recognize and properly preserve evidence for laboratory examination.

- The first officer to arrive must secure the crime scene.

- Investigators record the crime scene by using photographs, sketches, and notes and make a preliminary examination of the scene as the perpetrator left it.

Dealing with Physical Evidence

After the lead detective has conducted a preliminary walk-through, a more thorough search for physical evidence begins. Once found, physical evidence must be collected and stored in a way that preserves its integrity for forensic comparison and analysis. As a result, law enforcement officials have developed specific procedures for finding, collecting, and transporting physical evidence that preserve its evidentiary value.

Conduct a Systematic Search for Evidence

The search for physical evidence at a crime scene must be thorough and systematic. For a factual, unbiased reconstruction of the crime, the investigator, relying on his or her training and experience, must not overlook any pertinent evidence. Even when suspects are immediately seized and the motives and circumstances of the crime are readily apparent, a thorough search for physical evidence must be conducted at once. Failure in this, even though it may seem unnecessary, can lead to accusations of negligence or charges that the investigative agency knowingly "covered up" evidence that would be detrimental to its case.

The investigator in charge assigns the personnel responsible for searching a crime scene. Except in major crimes, or when the evidence is complex, a forensic scientist is usually not needed at the crime scene; his or her role appropriately begins when evidence is submitted to the crime laboratory. As has already been observed, some police agencies have trained field evidence technicians to search for physical evidence at the crime scene. They have the equipment and skill to photograph the scene and examine it for the presence of fingerprints, footprints, tool marks, or any other type of evidence that may be relevant to the crime.

Considerations in Searching the Crime Scene How one conducts a crime-scene search will depend on the locale and size of the area, as well as on the actions of the suspect(s) and victim(s) at the scene. When possible, one person should supervise and coordinate the collection of evidence. Without proper control, the search may be conducted in an atmosphere of confusion with needless duplication of effort. Evidence collectors may subdivide the scene into segments and search each segment individually, or the search may start at some outer point and gradually move toward the center of the scene in a circular fashion (see Figure 2–7). The areas searched must include all probable points of entry and exit used by the criminals.

What to search for will be determined by the particular circumstances of the crime. Obviously, the skill of crime-scene investigators at recognizing evidence and searching relevant locations is paramount to successful processing of the crime scene. Although training will impart general knowledge for conducting a proper crime-scene investigation, ultimately the investigator must rely on the experience gained from numerous investigations to formulate a successful strategy for recovering relevant physical evidence at crime scenes. For example, in

Spiral search method

Grid method

start

end

Strip or line search

Quadrant or zone search

FIGURE 2–7
Several typical examples of crime-scene search patterns. The pattern selected normally depends on the size and locale of the scene and the number of collectors participating in the search.

a homicide case, the search will center on the weapon and any type of evidence left as a result of contact between the victim and the assailant. The cross-transfer of evidence, such as hairs, fibers, and blood, between individuals involved in the crime is particularly useful for linking suspects to the crime scene and for corroborating events that transpired during the commission of the crime. During the investigation of a burglary, efforts will be made to locate tool marks at the point of entry. In most crimes, a thorough and systematic search for latent fingerprints is required.

Vehicle searches must be carefully planned and systematically carried out. The nature of the case determines how detailed the search must be. In hit-and-run cases, the outside and undercarriage of the car must be examined with care. Particular attention is paid to looking for any evidence resulting from a cross-transfer of evidence between the car and the victim—including blood, tissue, hair, fibers, and fabric impressions. Traces of paint or broken glass may be located on the victim. In cases of homicide, burglary, kidnapping, and so on, all areas of the vehicle, inside and outside, are searched with equal care for physical evidence.

Collect Physical Evidence

Physical evidence can be anything from massive objects to microscopic traces. Often, many items of evidence are obvious in their presence, but others may be detected only through examination in the crime laboratory. For example, minute traces of blood may be discovered on garments only after a thorough search in the laboratory; the presence of hairs and fibers may be revealed in vacuum sweepings or on garments only after close laboratory scrutiny. For this reason, it is important to collect possible carriers of trace evidence in addition to more discernible items. Hence, it may be necessary to take custody of all clothing worn by the participants in a crime. Each clothing item should be handled carefully and wrapped separately to avoid loss of trace materials.

Critical areas of the crime scene should be vacuumed and the sweepings submitted to the laboratory for analysis. The sweepings from different areas must be collected and packaged separately. A portable vacuum cleaner equipped with a special filter attachment is suitable for this purpose (see Figure 2–8). Additionally, fingernail scrapings from individuals who were in contact with other individuals may contain minute fragments of evidence capable of linking the assailant and victim. The undersurface of each nail is best scraped with a dull object such as a toothpick to avoid cutting the skin. These scrapings will be subjected to microscopic examination in the laboratory.

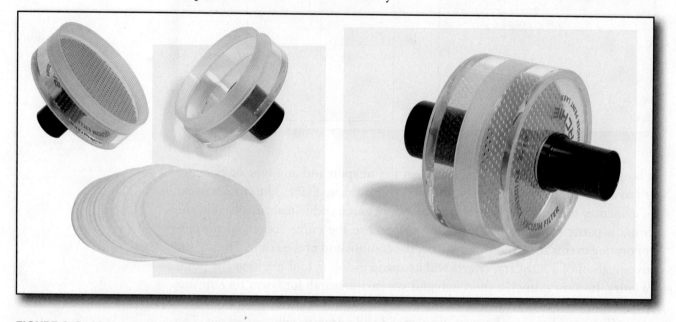

FIGURE 2–8 Vacuum sweeper attachment, constructed of clear plastic in two pieces that are joined by a threaded joint. A metal screen is mounted in one half to support a filter paper to collect debris. The unit attaches to the hose of the vacuum sweeper. After a designated area of the crime scene is vacuumed, the filter paper is removed and retained for laboratory examination. *Courtesy Sirchie Finger Print Laboratories, Inc., Youngsville, N.C., www.sirchie.com*

The search for physical evidence must extend beyond the crime scene to the autopsy room of a deceased victim. Here, the medical examiner or coroner carefully examines the victim to establish a cause and manner of death. Tissues and organs are retained for pathological and toxicological examination. At the same time, arrangements must be made between the examiner and investigator to secure a variety of items that may be obtainable from the body for laboratory examination. The following are to be collected and sent to the forensic laboratory:

1. **Victim's clothing**
2. **Fingernail scrapings**
3. **Head and pubic hairs**
4. **Blood (for DNA typing)**

5. Vaginal, anal, and oral swabs (in sex-related crimes)

6. Recovered bullets from the body

7. Hand swabs from shooting victims (for gunshot residue analysis)

Once the body is buried, efforts at obtaining these items may prove difficult or futile. Furthermore, a lengthy delay in obtaining many of these items will diminish or destroy their forensic value.

Many police departments have recently purchased and equipped "mobile crime laboratories" (see Figure 2–9) for their evidence technicians. However, the term mobile crime laboratory is a misnomer. These vehicles carry the necessary supplies to protect the crime scene; photograph, collect, and package physical evidence; and develop latent prints. They are not designed to carry out the functions of a chemical laboratory. Crime-scene search vehicle would be a more appropriate but perhaps less dramatic name for such a vehicle.

FIGURE 2–9 Inside view of a mobile crime-scene van: (a) driver's side and (b) passenger's side. *Courtesy Sirchie Finger Print Laboratories, Inc., Youngsville, N.C., www.sirchie.com*

Procedures for Collecting and Packaging Physical Evidence Physical evidence must be handled and processed in a way that prevents any change from taking place between the time it is removed from the crime scene and the time it is received by the crime laboratory. Changes can arise through contamination, breakage, evaporation, accidental scratching or bending, or improper or careless packaging.

The integrity of evidence is best maintained when the item is kept in its original condition as found at the crime site. Whenever possible, evidence should be submitted to the laboratory intact. Blood, hairs, fibers, soil particles, and other types of trace evidence should not normally be removed from garments, weapons, or other articles that bear them. Instead, the entire object should be sent to the laboratory for processing.

Of course, if evidence is adhering to an object in a precarious manner, good judgment dictates removing and packaging the item. If evidence is found adhering to a large structure, such as a door, wall, or floor, common sense must be used; remove the specimen with a forceps or other appropriate tool. In the case of a bloodstain, one may either scrape the stain off the surface, transfer the stain to a moistened swab, or cut out the area of the object bearing the stain.

Each different item or similar items collected at different locations must be placed in separate containers. Packaging evidence separately prevents damage through contact and prevents cross-contamination.

Tools for Evidence Collection The well-prepared evidence collector arrives at a crime scene with a large assortment of packaging materials and tools, ready to encounter any type of situation. Forceps and similar tools may be used to pick up small items. Unbreakable plastic pill bottles with pressure lids are excellent containers for hairs, glass, fibers, and various other kinds of small or trace evidence. Alternatively, manila envelopes, screw-cap glass vials, or cardboard pillboxes are adequate containers for most trace evidence encountered at crime sites. Ordinary mailing envelopes should not be used as evidence containers because powders and fine particles will leak out of their corners.

Small amounts of trace evidence can also be conveniently packaged in a carefully folded paper, using what is known as a "druggist fold." This consists of folding one end of the paper over one-third, then folding the other end (one-third)

FIGURE 2–10
A druggist fold is used to package paint transfer evidence. *Courtesy Sirchie Finger Print Laboratories, Inc., Youngsville, N.C., www.sirchie.com*

over that, and repeating the process from the other two sides. After the paper is folded in this manner, the outside two edges are tucked into each other to produce a closed container that keeps the specimen from falling out (see Figure 2–10).

Although manila envelopes, pillboxes, or sealable plastic bags (see Figure 2–11) are good universal containers for most trace evidence, two frequent finds at crime scenes warrant special attention. If bloodstained materials are stored in airtight containers, the accumulation of moisture may encourage the growth of mold, which can destroy the evidential value of blood. In these instances, wrapping paper, manila envelopes, or paper bags are recommended packaging materials (see Figure 2–12). All items of clothing must be air-dried and placed individually in separate paper bags to ensure constant circulation of air through them. This will prevent the formation of mold and mildew. On the other hand, charred debris recovered from the scene of a suspicious fire must be sealed in an airtight container to prevent the evaporation of volatile petroleum residues. New paint cans or tightly sealed jars are recommended in such situations (see Figure 2–13).

A detailed description of the proper collection and packaging of various types of physical evidence will be discussed in forthcoming chapters; additionally, most of this information is summarized in the evidence guide found in the Appendix.

FIGURE 2–11 (a) Manila evidence envelope, (b) metal pillboxes, (c) sealable plastic evidence bag. *Courtesy Sirchie Finger Print Laboratories, Inc., Youngsville, N.C., www.sirchie.com*

FIGURE 2–12
Paper bags are recommended evidence containers for objects suspected of containing blood and semen stains. Each object should be packaged in a separate bag. *Courtesy Sirchie Finger Print Laboratories, Inc., Youngsville, N.C., www.sirchie.com*

FIGURE 2–13
Air-tight metal cans used to package arson evidence. *Courtesy Sirchie Finger Print Laboratories, Inc., Youngsville, N.C., www.sirchie.com*

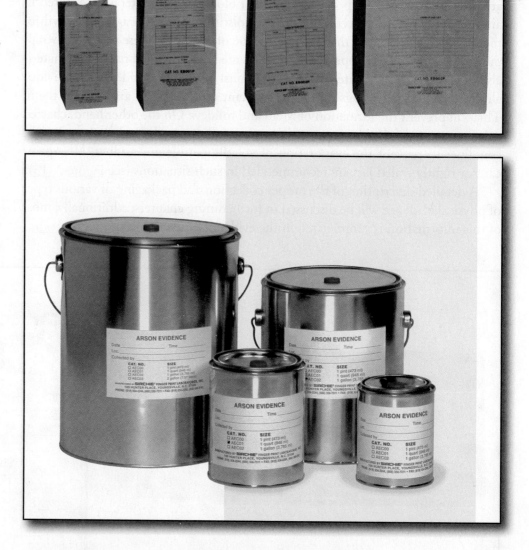

chain of custody
A list of all people who came into possession of an item of evidence

Maintain the Chain of Custody

Continuity of possession, or the **chain of custody**, must be established whenever evidence is presented in court as an exhibit. This means that every person who handled or examined the evidence must be accounted for. Failure to substantiate the evidence's chain of custody may lead to serious questions regarding the authenticity and integrity of the evidence and the examinations of it. Adhering to standard procedures in recording the location of evidence, marking it for identification, and properly completing evidence submission forms for laboratory analysis is the best guarantee that the evidence will withstand inquiries of what happened to it from the time of its finding to its presentation in court.

All items of physical evidence should be carefully packaged and marked upon their retrieval at crime sites. This should be done with the utmost care to avoid destroying their evidential value or restricting the number and kind of examinations to which the criminalist may subject them. If possible, the evidence itself should be marked for identification. Normally, the collector's initials and the date of collection are inscribed directly on the article. However, if the evidence collector is unsure of the necessity of marking the item itself, or of where to mark it, it is best to omit this step. Where appropriate, the evidence is to be tagged for identification.

Once an evidence container is selected for the evidence, whether a box, bag, vial, or can, it also must be marked for identification. A minimum record would show the collector's initials, location of the evidence, and date of collection. If the evidence is turned over to another individual for care or delivery to the laboratory, this transfer must be recorded in notes and other appropriate forms. In fact, every individual who possesses the evidence must maintain a written record of its acquisition and disposition. Frequently, all of the individuals involved in the collection and transportation of the evidence may be requested to testify in court. Thus, to avoid confusion and to retain complete control of the evidence at all times, the chain of custody should be kept to a minimum.

Obtain Standard/Reference Samples

The examination of evidence, whether soil, blood, glass, hair, fibers, and so on, often requires comparison with a known **standard/reference sample**. Although most investigators have little difficulty recognizing and collecting relevant crime-scene evidence, few seem aware of the necessity and importance of providing the crime lab with a thorough sampling of standard/reference materials. Such materials may be obtained from the victim, a suspect, or other known sources. For instance, investigation of a hit-and-run incident may require the removal of standard/reference paint from a suspect vehicle. This will permit its comparison to paint recovered at the scene.

The presence of standard/reference samples greatly facilitates the work of the forensic scientist. For example, hair found at a crime scene will be of optimum value only when compared to standard/reference hairs removed from the suspect and victim. Likewise, bloodstained evidence must be accompanied by a whole-blood or **buccal swab** standard/reference sample obtained from all relevant crime-scene participants. The quality and quantity of standard/reference specimens often determine the evidential value of crime-scene evidence, and these standard/reference specimens must be treated with equal care.

Some types of evidence must also be accompanied by the collection of **substrate controls**. These are materials close to areas where physical evidence has been deposited. For example, substrate controls are normally collected at arson scenes. If an investigator suspects that a particular surface has been exposed to gasoline or some other accelerant, the investigator should also collect a piece of the same surface material that is believed not to have been exposed to the accelerant. At the laboratory, the substrate control is tested to ensure that the surface on which the accelerant was deposited does not interfere with testing procedures. Another common example of a substrate control is a material on which a bloodstain has been deposited. Unstained areas close to the stain may be sampled to determine whether this material can interfere with the interpretation of laboratory results. Thorough collection and proper packaging of standard/reference specimens and substrate controls are the mark of a skilled investigator.

standard/reference sample
Physical evidence whose origin is known, such as blood or hair from a suspect, that can be compared to crime-scene evidence

buccal swab
A swab of the inner portion of the cheek, performed to collect cells for use in determining the DNA profile of an individual

substrate control
Uncontaminated surface material close to an area where physical evidence has been deposited; used to ensure that the surface on which a sample has been deposited does not interfere with laboratory tests

Submit Evidence to the Laboratory

Evidence is usually submitted to the laboratory either by personal delivery or by mail shipment. The method of transmittal is determined by the distance the submitting agency must travel to the laboratory and the urgency of the case. If the evidence is delivered personally, the deliverer should be familiar with the case, to facilitate any discussions between laboratory personnel and the deliverer concerning specific aspects of the case.

If desired, most evidence can be conveniently shipped by mail. However, postal regulations restrict the shipment of certain chemicals and live ammunition and prohibit the mailing of explosives. In such situations, the laboratory must be consulted to determine the disposition of these substances. Care must also be exercised in the packaging of evidence in order to prevent breakage or other accidental destruction while it is in transit to the laboratory.

Most laboratories require that an evidence submission form accompany all evidence submitted (see Figure 2–14). This form must be properly completed. Its information will enable the laboratory analyst to make an intelligent and complete examination of the evidence. Particular attention should be paid to providing the laboratory with a brief description of the case history. This information

FIGURE 2–14
An example of a properly completed evidence submission form. *Courtesy New Jersey State Police*

will allow the examiner to analyze the specimens in a logical sequence and make the proper comparisons, and it will also facilitate the search for trace quantities of evidence.

The particular kind of examination requested for each type of evidence should be delineated. However, the analyst will not be bound to adhere strictly to the specific tests requested by the investigator. During the examination new evidence may be uncovered, and as a result the complexity of the case may change. Furthermore, the analyst may find the initial requests incomplete or not totally relevant to the case. Finally, a list of items submitted for examination must be included on the evidence submission form. Each item is to be packaged separately and assigned a number or letter, which should be listed in an orderly and logical sequence on the form.

Quick Review

- The search pattern selected at a crime scene depends on the size and locale of the scene and the number of collectors participating in the search.

- Many items of evidence may be detected only through examination at the crime laboratory. For this reason, it is important to collect possible carriers of trace evidence, such as clothing, vacuum sweepings, and fingernail scrapings, in addition to more discernible items.

- Each item of physical evidence collected at a crime scene must be placed in a separate appropriate container to prevent damage through contact or cross-contamination.

- Investigators must maintain the chain of custody, a record for denoting the location of the evidence.

- Proper standard/reference samples, such as hairs, blood, and fibers, must be collected at the crime scene and from appropriate subjects for comparison purposes in the laboratory.

The Murder Scene: Death and Autopsies

Unfortunately, the most important piece of evidence at many crime scenes is the dead body of a victim. When foul play is suspected, a victim's corpse is subjected to the same kind of intense physical analysis as any other piece of evidence. This task falls primarily to a forensic pathologist, often aided by the skills of specialists including forensic anthropologists and forensic entomologists. In its broadest sense, forensic pathology involves the study of medicine as it relates to the application of the law, particularly criminal law. In practice, this most often involves the investigation of sudden, unnatural, unexplained, or violent deaths.

Role of the Forensic Pathologist

Typically, forensic pathologists, in their role as medical examiners or coroners, must answer several basic questions: Who is the victim? What injuries are present? When did the injuries occur? Why and how were the injuries produced? The primary role of the medical examiner is to determine the cause of death. If a cause cannot be found through observation, an **autopsy** is normally performed to establish the cause of death. The manner in which death occurred is classified into five categories: natural, homicide, suicide, accident, or undetermined, based on the circumstances surrounding the incident.

Frequently, medical examiners must perform autopsies if a death is deemed suspicious or unexplained. The cause of death may not always be what it seems at first glance. For example, a decedent with a gunshot wound and a gun in his hand may appear to have committed suicide. However, an autopsy may reveal that the victim actually died of suffocation and the gunshot wound occurred after death to cover up the circumstances surrounding the commission of a crime.

autopsy
The medical dissection and examination of a body in order to determine the cause of death

FIGURE 2–15 Medical examiners work on a dissected corpse laid on an examination table in a morgue.
Courtesy Alamy Images

MyCrimeKit:
WebExtra 2.2
See How an Autopsy Is Performed
www.mycrimekit.com

Estimating Time of Death

After a human body expires, it goes through several stages of decomposition. A medical examiner can often estimate the time of death by evaluating the stage of decomposition in which the victim was found. Immediately following death, the muscles relax and then become rigid. This condition, **rigor mortis**, manifests itself within the first 24 hours and disappears within 36 hours.

Another condition occurring in the early stages of decomposition is **livor mortis**. When the human heart stops pumping, the blood begins to settle in the parts of the body closest to the ground. The skin appears dark blue or purple in these areas. The onset of this condition begins immediately and continues for up to 12 hours after death. The skin does not appear discolored in areas where the body is restricted by either clothing or an object pressing against the body. This information can be useful in determining whether the victim's position was changed after death.

Other physical and chemical changes within the body also help approximate the time of death. **Algor mortis** is the process by which the body temperature continually cools after death until it reaches the ambient or room temperature. The rate of heat loss is influenced by factors such as the location and size of the body, the victim's clothing, and weather conditions. Because of such factors, this method can only estimate the approximate time period since death. As a general rule, beginning about an hour after death, the body loses heat at a rate of approximately 1–1½°F per hour until the body reaches the environmental temperature.

Another approach helpful for estimating the time of death is to determine potassium levels in the ocular fluid (fluid within the eye, also known as the vitreous humor). After death, cells within the inner surface of the eyeball release potassium into the ocular fluid. By analyzing the amount of potassium present at various intervals after death, the forensic pathologist can determine the rate at which potassium is released into the vitreous humor and use it to approximate the time of death. During the autopsy, other factors may indicate the time period in which death occurred. For example, the amount of food in the stomach can help estimate when a person's last meal was eaten. This information can be valuable when investigating a death.

Role of the Forensic Anthrolpologist

Forensic anthropology is concerned primarily with the identification and examination of human skeletal remains. Skeletal bones are remarkably durable and undergo an extremely slow breakdown process that lasts decades or centuries. Because of their resistance to rapid decomposition, skeletal remains can provide a multitude of individual characteristics. An examination of bones may reveal their sex, approximate age, race, height, and physical injury.

Recovering and Processing Remains Thorough documentation is required throughout the processes of recovery and examination of human remains. The sites where human remains are found must be treated as a crime scene (see Figure 2–16). These sites are usually located by civilians who then contact law enforcement personnel. The scene should be secured as soon as possible to prevent any further alteration of the scene. The scene should then be searched to locate all bones if they are scattered or other aspects of evidence such as footwear impressions or discarded items. Some tools can be useful in the search for evidence at a "tomb" site, including aerial photography, metal detectors, ground-penetrating radar, infrared photography, apparatuses that detect the gases produced by biological decomposition, and so-called cadaver dogs that detect the odors caused by biological decomposition. All items that are found must be tagged,

rigor mortis
A medical condition that occurs after death and results in the stiffening of muscle mass; the rigidity of the body begins within 24 hours of death and disappears within 36 hours of death

livor mortis
A medical condition that occurs after death and results in the settling of blood in areas of the body closest to the ground

algor mortis
A process that occurs after death in which the body temperature continually cools until it reaches the ambient or room temperature

photographed, sketched, and documented in notes. Once all bones and other evidence are found, a scene sketch should be made to show the exact location of each item (preferably using Global Positioning System [GPS] coordinates) and the spatial relationship of all evidence. Once the skeletal remains have been recovered, they can be examined to deduce information about the identity of the decedent.

FIGURE 2–16
Crime-scene site showing a pelvis partly buried in sand and a femur lying across a pistol. *Courtesy Paul Sledzik/National Transportation Safety Board.*

Determining Victim Characteristics The gender of the decedent can be determined by the size and shape of various skeletal features, especially those in the pelvis and skull or cranium. Female pelvic bones tend to show a wider, more circular opening than that of a male pelvis because of a woman's child-bearing capabilities. The female sacrum (flat bone above the tailbone) is wider and shorter (see Figure 2–17[a]); the length and width of the male sacrum are roughly equal (see Figure 2–17[b]). The angle formed at the bottom of the pelvis (subpubic angle) is approximately a right angle (90 degrees) in females and acute (less than 90 degrees) in males. In general, male craniums are larger in overall size than those of females. A male cranium tends to have a more pronounced brow bone and mastoid process (a bony protrusion behind the jaw) than a female cranium (see Figure 2–18). See Table 2–1 for a summary of the differing features of female and male skeletons from head to toe. These are typical cases; not all skeletons may display the given characteristics to indicate the gender of the decedent.

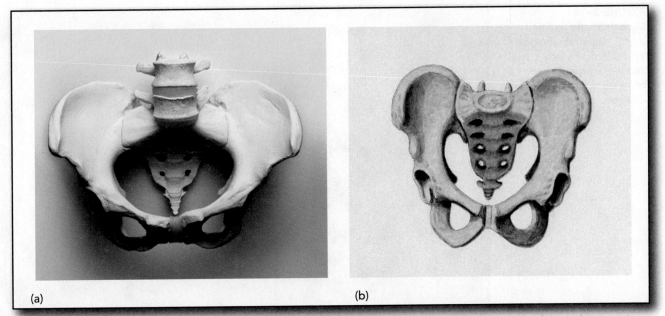

(a)   (b)

FIGURE 2–17   (a) Frontal shot of female pelvis and hips. This view shows the wide, circular nature of the pelvic opening and the short, wide nature of the sacrum. (b) Human male pelvis. This view shows the narrow pelvic opening and long, narrow sacrum. *Courtesy of Dorling Kindersley Media Library*

Table 2–1
Summary of Skeletal Features by Gender

	Female	Male
Cranium (skull)	Medium to large in size	Large in size
Forehead	High in height, vaulted, rounded	Low in height, sloped backward
Brow bone	Diminished	Pronounced
Mastoid process	Diminished or absent	Pronounced
Mandible (jaw) Angle	Obtuse (>90 degrees)	Approximately right (90 degrees)
Pelvis opening	Wide, circular	Narrow, noncircular
Sacrum	Short, wide, turned outward	Approximately equal width/length, turned inward
Subpubic angle	Approximately right (90 degrees)	Acute (<90 degrees)
Femur	Narrow, angled inward from pelvis	Thick, relatively straight from pelvis
Overall skeleton	Slender	Robust

FIGURE 2–18
Male (left) and female (right) human skulls showing male skull's larger size and more pronounced brow bone. *Courtesy Corbis*

The method for determining the age of a decedent varies depending on the victim's growth stage. For infants and toddlers, age can be estimated by the length of the long bones (femur and humerus) when compared to a known growth curve. Different sections of the skull also fuse together at different stages during early development, and the appearance of fused or divided sections can be used to estimate the age of bones still in early developmental stages (see Figure 2–19). In infant skeletons, formation of teeth can be used in age determination. This is based on the fact that permanent teeth start to form at birth. If the skeletal remains belong to a child, the age of the decedent may be determined by observing the fusion or lack of fusion of epiphyseal regions of bones such as

FIGURE 2–19
A lateral view of a fetal skull showing the separated bones of the skull before they have had a chance to fuse. *Courtesy Ralph T. Hutchings*

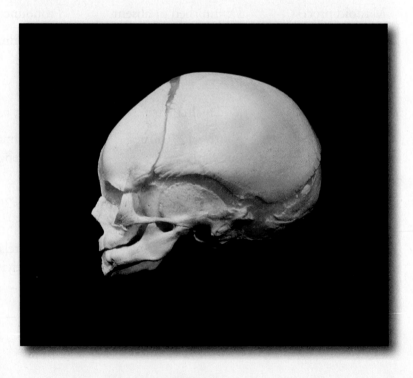

those of the mandible (lower jaw), fingers, wrist, long bones, and clavicle (see Figure 2–20). The average age at which each of these regions fuses is known and can be compared against the state of the remains to provide a range of possible ages for the decedent. A child's cranium may also be identified by the smaller size and the presence of developing teeth (see Figure 2–21). After age 21, age is estimated by the level of change experienced by the surfaces of the bones, especially in areas of common wear such as the pubic symphysis. The pubic symphyseal face shown in Figure 2–22 is a raised platform that slowly changes over the years from a rough, rugged surface to a smooth, well-defined area. See Table 2–2 for a summary of the skeletal closures by age. It is important to note that these are average ages for closures; not all skeletons display closures at the given ages.

FIGURE 2–20
Colored X-rays of healthy human hands at 3 years (left) and at 20 years. Bones are red with flesh blue. The child's hand has areas of cartilage in the joints between the finger bones (epiphyseal areas), where bone growth and fusion will occur. In the adult hand, all the bones are present and the joints have closed. *Courtesy Photo Researchers Inc.*

FIGURE 2–21
The skull of a young child, with part of the jaw cut away to show the developing teeth. *Courtesy Ralph T. Hutchings*

FIGURE 2–22
The symphysis pubis shown magnified beneath human pelvic bones. *Courtesy Pearson Education Custom Publishing*

Table 2–2
Summary of Skeletal Closures by Age

Age (months)	Closure
6–9	Mandible (jaw) fused
4–6	Humerus head bones fused
7–8	Pelvis frontal bones fused
4–16	Femur shaft sections built
9–13	Elbow bones fused
10	Finger bones fused
16–18	Femur head bones fused to shaft bones
18	Wrist bones fused
18–21	Humerus head bones fused to shaft bones
18–24	Sternum fused to clavicle
20–25	Pelvic bones fully formed
21–22	Clavicle fused
21–30	Labodial suture (rear of cranium) fused
24–30	Sacrum bones fused
30–32	Sagittal suture (center of cranium) fused
48–50	Coronal suture (front of cranium) fused

Although the categorization of "race" has come under scrutiny and is hard to define, forensic anthropologists use broad classes to characterize the likely (but not definite) ancestry of skeletal remains. The possible racial ancestry of the decedent can be assessed by the appearance of various cranial features on the skeletal remains. For example, eye orbits tend to be circular in Mongoloid skeletons (Asian descent), oval in Caucasoid skeletons (European descent), and square in Negroid skeletons (African descent). The frontal plane of the cranium may also vary. The frontal plane of Mongoloid craniums may be flat or projected outward, that of Caucasoid craniums is flat, and that of Negroid craniums is projected outward. The nasal cavity tends to be small and rounded in Mongoloids, long and narrow in Caucasoids, and wide in Negroids. Skeletal remains of Asian ancestry, including those of Native American descent, also tend to have "scooped-out" or shovel-shaped incisor teeth. See Table 2–3 for a summary of the differing features of skeletons that can indicate ancestry. These are typical cases; not all skeletons may display the given characteristics to indicate the ancestry of the decedent.

Table 2–3

Summary of Skeletal Characteristics Indicating Racial Ancestry

	Eye Orbitals	Nasal Cavity	Incisors	Cranium Frontal Plane
Caucasoid	Oval	Long, narrow	Smooth	Flat
Mongoloid	Circular	Small, rounded	Shoveled interior	Flat or projected outward
Negroid	Square	Wide	Smooth	Projected outward

The height of the victim when alive can be estimated by measuring the long bones of the skeleton, especially in the lower limbs. Even partial bones can yield useful results. However, meaningful stature calculations from known equations must be based on the determined sex and race of the remains. See Table 2–4 for example equations used to calculate the height of the decedent from skeletal remains. These equations should yield estimations within 5 cm of actual height.

Table 2–4

Equations for Height Calculation from Skeletal Remains

	Caucasoid	Negroid	Unknown Ancestry
Female	Height (cm) = femur length (cm) × 2.47 + 54.10	Height (cm) = femur length (cm) × 2.28 + 59.76	Height (cm) = femur length (cm) × 3.01 + 32.52
	Height (cm) = humerus length (cm) × 3.36 + 57.97	Height (cm) = humerus length (cm) × 3.08 + 64.67	Height (cm) = humerus length (cm) × 4.62 + 19.00
Male	Height (cm) = femur length (cm) × 2.32 + 65.53	Height (cm) = femur length (cm) × 2.10 + 72.22	Height (cm) = femur length (cm) × 2.71 + 45.86
	Height (cm) = humerus length (cm) × 2.89 + 78.10	Height (cm) = humerus length (cm) × 2.88 + 75.48	Height (cm) = humerus length (cm) × 4.62 + 19.00

Case Files

Identifying a Serial Killer's Victims

The worst serial killer in America calmly admitted his guilt as he led investigators to a crawl space under his house. There, John Wayne Gacy had buried 28 young men, after brutally raping and murdering them in cold blood. Because no identification was found with the bodies, the police were forced to examine missing-person reports for leads. However, these boys and men were so alike in age, race, and stature that police were unable to make individual identifications for most of the victims. Clyde Snow, the world-renowned foren-sic anthropologist from Oklahoma, was asked to help the investigators make these difficult identifications.

Snow began by making a 35-point examination of each skull for comparison to known individuals. By examining each skeleton, he made sure each bone was correctly attributed to an individual. This was crucial to later efforts because some of the victims had been buried on top of older graves, mingling their remains. Once Snow was sure all the bones were sorted prop-erly, he began his in-depth study. Long bones such as the femur (thigh bone) were used to estimate each individual's height. This helped narrow the search when attempting to match the victims with the descriptions of missing people.

After narrowing the possibilities to missing people fitting the general description, investigators consulted potential victims' hospital and dental records. Evi-dence of injury, illness, surgery, or other unique skeletal defects were used to make identifications. Snow also pointed out features that gave clues to the victim's be-havior and medical history. For example, he discovered that one of Gacy's victims had an old fracture of his left arm, and that his left scapula (shoulder blade) and arm bore the telltale signs of a left-handed individual. These details were matched to a missing-person re-port, and another young victim was identified.

For the most difficult cases, Snow called in the help of forensic sculptor and facial reconstructionist Betty Pat Gatliff. She used clay and depth markers to put the flesh back on the faces of these forgotten boys in the hopes that someone would recognize them after their photographs were released to the media. Her efforts were successful, but investigators found some families unwilling to accept the idea that their loved ones were among Gacy's victims. Even with Gatliff's help, nine of Gacy's victims remain unidentified.

Other Contributions of Forensic Anthropology A forensic anthropologist may also create facial reconstructions to help identify skeletal remains. Facial reconstruction uses the victim's actual cranium and takes into account the estimated age, ancestry, and gender (see Figure 2–23). With the help of this technique, a composite of the victim can be drawn and advertised in an attempt to identify the victim.

FIGURE 2–23
Trooper Sarah Foster, a Michigan State Police forensic artist, works on a three-dimensional facial reconstruction from an unidentified human skull at Richmond post in Richmond, MI. *Courtesy AP World Wide Photos*

Forensic anthropologists are also helpful in identifying victims of a mass disaster such as a plane crash. When such a tragedy occurs, forensic anthropologists can help identify victims through the collection of bone fragments. Definite identification of remains can be made only by analyzing the decedent's DNA profile, fingerprints, or medical records. Recovered remains may still contain some soft tissue material, which may yield a DNA profile for identification purposes. Sometimes the tissue of the hand is still present, though dried out. It may be possible to rehydrate the tissue to recover fingerprints. However, usually the identification of the remains will depend on medical records, especially dental records of the individual.

Role of the Forensic Entomologist

The study of insects and their relation to a criminal investigation is known as forensic entomology. Such a practice is commonly used to estimate the time of death when the circumstances surrounding the crime are unknown. This determination can be carried out by studying the stage of development of maggots or insect sequence of arrival.

Determining Time of Death After decomposition begins, necrophilious insects, or insects that feed on dead tissue, are the first to infest the body, usually within 24 hours. The most common and important of these is the blowfly recognized by its green or blue color. Blowfly eggs are laid in human remains and ultimately hatch into maggots, or fly larvae, which consume human organs and tissues (see Figure 2–24). Typically, a single blowfly can lay up to 2,000 eggs during its lifetime. The resulting larvae gather and feed as a "maggot mass" on the decomposing remains. Forensic entomologists can approximate how long a body has been left exposed by examining the stage of development of the fly larvae. This kind of determination is best for a timeline of hours to approximately one month, because the blowfly goes through the stages of its life cycle at known time intervals and sequence. By determining the most developed stage of fly found on the body, entomologists can approximate the postmortem interval (PMI), or the time that has elapsed since death (see Figure 2–25). Newly emerged flies are of important forensic interest, as they indicate that an entire blowfly cycle has been completed on the decomposing body. Likewise, empty pupal cases indicate that a fly has completed its entire life cycle on the body. Flies known as cheese skippers are primarily found on human corpses in the later stages of decomposition long after the blowflies have left the corpse.

FIGURE 2–24
A scanning electron micrograph of two-hour-old blowfly maggots. *Courtesy Dr. Jeremy Burgess/Photo Researchers, Inc.*

These determinations are not always straightforward, however. The time required for stage development is affected by environmental influences such as geographical location, climate, weather conditions, and the presence of drugs. For example, cold temperatures hinder the development of fly eggs into adult flies. The forensic entomologist must consider these conditions when estimating the PMI.

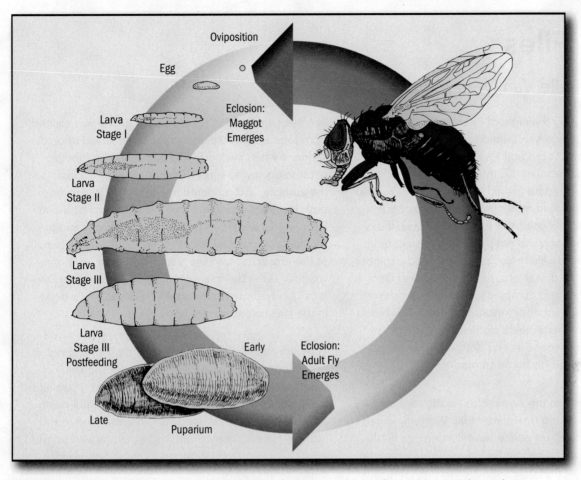

FIGURE 2–25 Typical blowfly life cycle from egg deposition to adult fly emergence. This cycle is representative of any one of nearly 90 species of blowflies in North America. *Courtesy E. P. Catts, Ph.D., deceased, and Neal H. Haskell, Ph.D., forensic entomology consultant, www.forensic-entolmology.com*

Information about the arrival of other species of insects may also help determine the PMI. The sequence of arrival of these groups depends mostly on the body's natural decomposition process. Predator insects generally arrive and prey on the necrophilious insects. Several kinds of beetles will be found, either feeding directly on the corpse's tissues or as predators feeding on blowfly eggs and maggots present on the corpse. Next, omnivore insects arrive at the body. These insects feed on the body, on other insects, and on surrounding vegetation. Ants and wasps are an example of omnivore insects. Last comes the arrival of indigenous insects, such as spiders, whose presence on or near the body is coincidental as they move about their environment.

Case Files

The Danielle Van Dam Murder Case

Sometime during the night of February 1, 2002, 7-year-old Danielle Van Dam disappeared from her bedroom in the Sabre Springs suburb of San Diego, California. On February 27, three and a half weeks later, searchers found her naked body in a trash-covered lot about 25 miles from her home. Because of the high degree of decomposition of the girl's remains, the medical examiner could not pinpoint the exact time of the girl's death. Her neighbor, 50-year-old engineer David Westerfield, was accused of kidnapping Danielle, killing her, and dumping her body in the desert. During the subsequent investigation, Danielle's blood was found on Westerfield's clothes, her fingerprints and blood were found in his RV, and child pornography was found on his home computer.

The actual time of the 7-year-old's death became a central issue during the murder trial. Westerfield had been under constant police surveillance since February 4. Any suggestion that Danielle was placed at the dump site after that date would have eliminated him as a suspect. Conflicting expert testimony was elicited from forensic entomologists who were called upon to estimate when the body was dumped. The forensic entomologist who went to the dump site, witnessed the autopsy, and collected and analyzed insects from both locations estimated that Danielle died between February 16 and 18. A forensic entomologist and a forensic anthropologist both called to testify on behalf of the prosecution noted that the very hot, very dry weather at the dump site might have mummified Danielle's body almost immediately, thus causing a delay in the flies colonizing the body.

The jurors convicted Westerfield of the kidnapping and murder of Danielle Van Dam, and a San Diego judge sentenced David Westerfield to death. Danielle Van Dam's parents filed and settled a wrongful death suit against Westerfield requiring his automotive and homeowners' insurance carriers to pay the Van Dams an undisclosed amount, reported to be between $400,000 and $1 million.

The known sequence of arrival of different insect groups can help determine the PMI. This method is usually used when months have elapsed between the time when the decedent died and when the body was found. In order to make an accurate estimate, the forensic entomologist must compare the species found on the body to experimental data from that geographical area. The entomologist then looks first for what earlier groups are missing. This sets a minimum PMI. For example, if experiments in that area have shown that all necrophilious insects leave the body after about 3 months and no necrophilious insects are found on the body, it can be deduced that the decedent has been deceased for at least 3 months. If a particular entomologist is very familiar with the insect patterns of an area, he or she may be able to further define the PMI range by looking for what groups have not yet arrived. This method may also be useful to determine season of death. However, it is important to remember that the diversity of insects found on a body is also affected by the body's location, weather and temperature conditions, habitat characteristics, indigenous species, and characteristics of the body.

Other Contributions of Forensic Entomology Entomological evidence can also provide other pertinent information. In general, insects first colonize the body's natural moist orifices. However, if open wounds are present, they prefer to colonize there first. Because decomposition processes may conceal wounds, colonization away from natural orifices may help locate wounds on the body. If maggots are found extensively on the hands and forearms, for example, this suggests the presence of defensive wounds on the victim. Insects that have fed on the body may also have accumulated any drugs present in the flesh, and these insects can yield the identity of these drugs.

If resources allow, all insect evidence should be carefully collected by a forensic entomology expert. When this is not possible, collection should be carried out by an investigator with experience in death investigation. The entire body and the area where insect evidence was found must be photographed and documented before collection. Specimen samples should be taken from each area on the body where they are found and labeled to show where they were collected from.

Quick Review

- An autopsy is normally performed if a death is suspicious or unexplained.

- Rigor mortis occurs after death and results in the stiffening of body parts in the position they are in when death occurs. Livor mortis occurs after death and results in the settling of blood in areas of the body closest to the ground. Algor mortis refers to postmortem changes that cause a body to continually cool to ambient or room temperature.

- Forensic anthropology is concerned primarily with the identification and examination of human skeletal remains.

- A forensic entomologist studies the development of insect larvae in a body to estimate time of death.

Chapter Review

- Physical evidence includes any and all objects that can establish that a crime has been committed or can link the crime and its victim or its perpetrator.

- Forensic science begins at the crime scene, where investigators must recognize and properly preserve evidence for laboratory examination.

- The first officer to arrive must secure the crime scene.

- Investigators record the crime scene by using photographs, sketches, and notes and make a preliminary examination of the scene as the perpetrator left it.

- The search pattern selected at a crime scene depends on the size and locale of the scene and the number of collectors participating in the search.

- Many items of evidence may be detected only through examination at the crime laboratory. For this reason, it is important to collect possible carriers of trace evidence, such as clothing, vacuum sweepings, and fingernail scrapings, in addition to more discernible items.

- Each item of physical evidence collected at a crime scene must be placed in a separate appropriate container to prevent damage through contact or cross-contamination.

- Investigators must maintain the chain of custody, a record for denoting the location of the evidence.

- Proper standard/reference samples, such as hairs, blood, and fibers, must be collected at the crime scene and from appropriate subjects for comparison purposes in the laboratory.

- An autopsy is normally performed if a death is suspicious or unexplained.

- Rigor mortis occurs after death and results in the stiffening of body parts in the position they are in when death occurs. Livor mortis occurs after death and results in the settling of blood in areas of the body closest to the ground. Algor mortis refers to postmortem changes that cause a body to continually cool to ambient or room temperature.

- Forensic anthropology is concerned primarily with the identification and examination of human skeletal remains.

- A forensic entomologist studies the development of insect larvae in a body to estimate time of death.

Quick Lab: Crime-Scene Sketch

Materials:

Graph paper   Notepad   Rulers
Tape measure/meter stick   Mock crime scene

Procedure:

You have been introduced to the appropriate steps to process a crime scene. An important part of this process is surveying the scene, taking diligent notes, and creating a sketch of the scene. With a partner or small group, create a sketch of the scene presented to you and keep notes of what evidence you find. In your sketch, provide an accurate depiction of the entire scene with dimension measurements as well as location measurements for all pieces of physical evidence.

Follow-Up Questions:

1. Why is it important to take diligent notes when processing the crime scene?

2. What is the chain of custody?

3. Why do we sketch the crime scene as well as take photographs of it?

Quick Lab: Anthropometric Activity

Materials:

Meter sticks   Rulers/tape measures   Student worksheets

Procedure:

First, read the section on anthropometry from the chapter. Next, pair up with two other students and pick up your materials. Each person should measure both of the other people in the group and record the results on the Anthropometric Measurements worksheet. Afterward, discuss the follow-up questions below.

Follow-Up Questions:

1. Did any of your measurements match those of your partners? Were there any measurements for which several members of your group showed identical results? What might that suggest about the usefulness of that measurement for identification?

2. Compare all the measurements recorded for a single individual. Did every person who measured that individual obtain the same results? What factors may contribute to any differences in the results?

3. Do you believe that anthropometry would be a good way to identify people who are trying to hide their identity? Explain your answer.

Quick Lab Worksheet: Anthropometric Measurements

Directions: Please record each measurement in centimeters for each member of your group.

1. Height: cm

2. Sitting height: cm

3. Length of outstretched arm from one index fingertip to the other: cm

3. Length of outstretched arm from shoulder to the index fingertip: cm

4. Length of lower arm from elbow to wrist: cm

5. Length of right ear: cm

2. Length of head from front to back: cm

Review Questions

1. All of the following are items to be collected from a deceased's body and sent to the forensic laboratory except:
   a. ocular fluid.
   b. head and pubic hairs.
   c. fingernail scrapings.
   d. blood.

2. Which of the following is not an allowance made to justify a warrantless search?
   a. the need to prevent the eventual loss of evidence over time
   b. the existence of emergency circumstances
   c. a search made by consent of the parties involved
   d. a search made incident to a lawful arrest

3. The most important prerequisite for photographing a crime scene is
   a. to place items in indirect light so that nuances can be picked up in the photograph.
   b. to place rulers or other items in the photographs to show scale.
   c. that the crime scene is in an unaltered condition.
   d. that the photographer start with close-ups of any important object and back up to get the full scale.

4. Uncontaminated surface material close to an area where physical evidence has been deposited is
   a. a standard sample.
   b. a reference sample.
   c. a substrate control.
   d. ground material.

5. Physical and chemical changes that occur following death include all of the following except:
   a. livor mortis
   b. biogor mortis
   c. algor mortis
   d. rigor mortis

6. True or False: In order for physical evidence to be used effectively for aiding an investigator, it must first be photographed and tagged as evidence and turned over to the officer in charge of the crime scene.

7. True or False: Before taking photographs of the crime scene, the investigator first draws a rough sketch, containing an accurate depiction of the dimensions of the scene and showing the location of all objects.

8. True or False: If bloodstained materials are stored in airtight containers, such as pill bottles or vials, the accumulation of moisture may encourage the growth of mold, which can destroy the evidential value of blood.

9. True or False: The examination of evidence requires comparison with a substrate control to ensure the evidentiary value of the crime-scene evidence.

10. True or False: Charred debris recovered from the scene of a suspicious fire may be sealed in a plastic evidence container.

11. What is physical evidence? Give three examples of physical evidence that may be found at a crime scene.

12. What is the first step in processing a crime scene?

13. Why is it important to exclude onlookers from a crime scene?

14. Name three methods for recording a crime scene and list one unique advantage of each.

15. What is the most important prerequisite for video recording a crime scene?

16. Name and describe the two kinds of sketches prepared for a crime scene.

17. What information must be included in written notes made at the crime scene?

18. List at least four pieces of evidence from a murder scene that must be collected and sent to the forensic laboratory. Why must these items be collected at the crime scene instead of later?

19. What is the best way to maintain the integrity of physical evidence?

20. Describe the best way for an investigator to handle trace evidence found on articles collected at the crime scene. Name two exceptions to this general rule.

21. Describe a druggist's fold and explain why it is a better way to store trace evidence than an ordinary mailing envelope.

22. Why should all items of evidence be placed in separate containers?

23. Name one type of evidence that should be stored in an airtight container and one type that should not be stored in such a container. Explain why each type of evidence should be stored (or not stored) in this way.

24. What is chain of custody and why is it important to maintain chain of custody?

25. What is a substrate control and how is it used by the crime-scene investigator?

26. In what situations is an autopsy typically performed?

27. Define the terms *rigor mortis*, *livor mortis*, and *algor mortis* and explain how they are important to a forensic pathologist.

28. What is forensic anthropology? List two ways in which a forensic anthropologist may identify a victim.

29. What does a forensic entomologist study to estimate time of death? Explain why such estimates are not always straightforward.

Application and Critical Thinking

1. Give at least three examples of how evidence may be destroyed by onlookers at a crime scene.

2. What important elements are missing from the following crime-scene sketch?

3. An investigator at a murder scene notes signs of a prolonged struggle between the attacker and victim. Name at least three types of physical evidence for which the investigator would likely collect standard/reference samples and explain why he or she would collect them.

4. Rigor mortis, livor mortis, and algor mortis are all used to help determine time of death. However, each method has its limitations. For each method, describe at least one condition that would render that method unsuitable or inaccurate for determining time of death.

5. What kind of forensic expert would most likely be asked to help identify human remains in each of the following conditions?
   a. a body that has been decomposing for a day or two
   b. fragmentary remains of a few arm bones and part of a jaw
   c. a skeleton that is missing the skull

6. Creating a Forensic Anthropology Victim Profile

A nearly complete human skeleton has been found. The skeleton has the features shown in the accompanying table and images. Approximate the gender, ancestry, age range, and height of the individual based on this information.

CRANIUM	Size	Medium
	Forehead	Rounded, projected outward
	Mastoid process	Absent
	Jaw	Angle = 110 degrees
	Teeth	All permanent
	Sagittal suture	Not fused
	Coronal suture	Not fused
	Eye orbits	Squared
	Nasal cavity	Large, wide
	Incisors	Smooth
PELVIS	Opening	See Figure PH-02-2
	Sacrum	See Figure PH-02-2
	Subpubic angle	90-100 degrees
LONG BONES	Femur	Fully fused, 44.1 cm long
	Clavicle	Fully fused

FIGURE PH-02-2
Frontal shot of pelvis and hips. *Courtesy Dorling Kindersley Media Library*

Gender _____   Ancestry _____

Age Range _____   Height _____

7. Sequence of Insect Arrival in Forensic Entomology

The following images depict the sequence of events at the site of a decomposing body. Place the arrival events in order of occurrence from earliest to latest.

(A) _____

(B) _____

(C) _____

Courtesy Corbis/Superstock

(D) _____

(E) _____

(F) _____

Courtesy Ian Thraves/Alamy

Learning Objectives

After studying this chapter you should be able to:

- Review the common types of physical evidence encountered at crime scenes

- Explain the difference between the idenfication and comparison of physical evidence

- Define and contrast individual and class characteristics of physical evidence

- Appreciate the value of class evidence as it relates to a criminal investigation

- List and explain the function of national databases available to forensic scientists

National Science Content Standards

 Scientific Inquiry

 Physical Science

 Science in Personal and Social Perspective

 History and Nature of Science

Scott Peterson: A Case of Circumstantial Evidence

On the surface, Scott Peterson and his wife, Laci, appeared to live a happy and contented lifestyle in Modesto, California. The 30-year-old Peterson and his 27-year-old former college sweetheart, a substitute teacher, were expecting their first child in about one month when Laci suddenly disappeared. Scott Peterson told investigators that he had last seen his wife on December 24, 2002, at 9:30 A.M. when he left home for a fishing trip off San Francisco Bay.

In April 2003, Laci's decomposed remains washed ashore not far from where Scott said he had gone fishing on the day she vanished. Peterson claimed that Laci was dressed in a white top and black pants when he last saw her, but when her body was found she was wearing khaki pants. Scott's sister recalled that Laci was wearing khaki pants the night before her disappearance.

When questioned, Peterson claimed that he had gone fishing for sturgeon or striped bass. However, the police investigation revealed that he failed to bring the appropriate fishing rod and lines to catch such fish. Further revelations surfaced when it became known that Scott was having an affair with another woman. A search of Scott's warehouse led to the recovery of a black hair on a pair of pliers resting in Scott's boat. A mitochondrial DNA profile of the hair was consistent with Laci's DNA. Scott Peterson was charged with murder and convicted and currently awaits his fate on death row.

Physical Evidence 3

It would be impossible to list all the objects that could conceivably be important to a crime; every crime scene obviously has to be treated on an individual basis, having its own peculiar history, circumstances, and problems. It is practical, however, to list items whose scientific examination is likely to yield significant results in ascertaining the nature and circumstances of a crime. The investigator who is thoroughly familiar with the recognition, collection, and analysis of these items, as well as with laboratory procedures and capabilities, can make logical decisions when the uncommon and unexpected are encountered at the crime scene. Just as important, a qualified evidence collector cannot rely on collection procedures memorized from a pamphlet but must be able to make innovative, on-the-spot decisions at the crime scene.

Common Types of Physical Evidence

Blood, semen, and saliva All suspected blood, semen, or saliva—liquid or dried, animal or human—present in a form that suggests a relation to the offense or the people involved in a crime. This category includes blood or semen dried onto fabrics or other objects, as well as cigarette butts that may contain saliva residues. These substances are subjected to serological and biochemical analysis to determine their identity and possible origin.

Documents Any handwriting and typewriting submitted so that authenticity or source can be determined. Related items include paper, ink, indented writings, obliterations, and burned or charred documents.

Drugs Any substance seized in violation of laws regulating the sale, manufacture, distribution, and use of drugs.

Explosives Any device containing an explosive charge, as well as all objects removed from the scene of an explosion that are suspected to contain the residues of an explosive.

Fibers Any natural or synthetic fiber whose transfer may be useful in establishing a relationship between objects and/or people.

Fingerprints All prints of this nature, hidden (latent) and visible.

Firearms and ammunition Any firearm, as well as discharged or intact ammunition, suspected of being involved in a criminal offense.

Glass Any glass particle or fragment that may have been transferred to a person or object involved in a crime. Windowpanes containing holes made by a bullet or other projectile are included in this category.

Hair Any animal or human hair present that could link a person with a crime.

Impressions Tire markings, shoe prints, depressions in soft soils, and all other forms of tracks. Glove and other fabric impressions, as well as bite marks in skin or foodstuffs, are also included.

Organs and physiological fluids Body organs and fluids are submitted for analysis to detect the possible existence of drugs and poisons. This category includes blood to be analyzed for the presence of alcohol and other drugs.

Paint Any paint, liquid or dried, that may have been transferred from the surface of one object to another during the commission of a crime. A common example is the transfer of paint from one vehicle to another during an automobile collision.

Petroleum products Any petroleum product removed from a suspect or recovered from a crime scene. The most common examples are gasoline residues removed from the scene of an arson, or grease and oil stains whose presence may suggest involvement in a crime.

Plastic bags A disposable polyethylene bag such as a garbage bag may be evidential in a homicide or drug case. Examinations are conducted to associate a bag with a similar bag in the possession of a suspect.

Plastic, rubber, and other polymers Remnants of these manufactured materials recovered at crime scenes may be linked to objects recovered in the possession of a criminal suspect.

Powder residues Any item suspected of containing powder residues resulting from the discharge of a firearm (see Figure 3–1).

FIGURE 3–1 The gun is fired at a set distance from the target, and the gunpowder left on the target is compared to powder stains found on a victim's clothing. The density and shape of the powder stains vary with the distance the gun was fired. *Courtesy Arresting Images*

Serial numbers This category includes all stolen property submitted to the laboratory for the restoration of erased identification numbers.

Soil and minerals All items containing soil or minerals that could link a person or object to a particular location. Common examples are soil embedded in shoes and insulation found on garments.

Tool marks This category includes any object suspected of containing the impression of another object that served as a tool in a crime. For example, a screwdriver or crowbar could produce tool marks by being impressed into or scraped along a surface of a wall.

Vehicle lights Examination of vehicle headlights and taillights is normally conducted to determine whether a light was on or off at the time of impact.

Wood and other vegetative matter Any fragments of wood, sawdust, shavings, or vegetative matter discovered on clothing, shoes, or tools that could link a person or object to a crime location.

Quick Review

- Biological crime-scene evidence includes blood, saliva, semen, DNA, hair, organs, and physiological fluids.

- Impression crime-scene evidence includes tire markings, shoe prints, depressions in soft soils, all other forms of tracks, glove and other fabric impressions, tool marks, and bite marks.

- Manufactured items considered common items of crime-scene evidence include firearms, ammunition, fibers, paint, glass, petroleum products, plastic bags, rubber, polymers, and vehicle headlights.

The Examination of Physical Evidence

Physical evidence is usually examined by a forensic scientist for identification or comparison.

Identification

identification
The process of determining a substance's physical or chemical identity

Identification has as its purpose the determination of the physical or chemical identity of a substance with as near absolute certainty as existing analytical techniques will permit. For example, the crime laboratory is frequently asked to identify the chemical composition of preparations that may contain illicit drugs such as heroin, cocaine, or barbiturates. It may be asked to identify gasoline in residues recovered from the debris of a fire, or it may have to identify the nature of explosive residues—for example, dynamite or TNT. Also, the identification of blood, semen, hair, or wood would, as a matter of routine, include a determination of species origin. For example, did a bloodstain originate from a human as opposed to a dog or cat? Each of these requests requires the analysis and ultimate identification of a specific physical or chemical substance to the exclusion of all other possible substances.

The process of identification first requires the adoption of testing procedures that give characteristic results for specific standard materials. Once these test results have been established, they may be permanently recorded and used repeatedly to prove the identity of suspect materials. For example, to ascertain that a particular suspect powder is heroin, the test results on the powder must be identical to those that have been previously obtained from a known heroin sample.

Second, identification requires that the number and type of tests needed to identify a substance be sufficient to exclude all other substances. This means that the examiner must devise a specific analytical scheme that will eliminate all but one substance from consideration. Hence, if the examiner concludes that a white powder contains heroin, the test results must have been comprehensive enough to have excluded all other drugs—or, for that matter, all other substances—from consideration.

Simple rules cannot be devised for defining what constitutes a thorough and foolproof analytical scheme. Each type of evidence obviously requires different tests, and each test has a different degree of specificity. Thus, one substance could conceivably be identified by one test, whereas another may require the combination of five or six different tests to arrive at an identification. In a science in which the practitioner has little or no control over the quality and quantity of the specimens received, a standard series of tests cannot encompass all possible problems and pitfalls. So the forensic scientist must determine at what point the analysis can be concluded and the criteria for positive identification satisfied; for this, he or she must rely on knowledge gained through education and experience. Ultimately, the conclusion will have to be substantiated beyond any reasonable doubt in a court of law.

Comparison

A **comparison** analysis subjects a suspect specimen and a standard/reference specimen to the same tests and examinations in order to determine whether they have a common origin. For example, the forensic scientist may place a suspect at a particular location by noting the similarities of a hair found at the crime scene to hairs removed from a suspect's head (Figure 3–2). Or a paint chip found on a hit-and-run victim's garment may be compared with paint removed from a vehicle suspected of being involved in the incident.

comparison
The process of ascertaining whether two or more objects have a common origin

FIGURE 3–2
Side-by-side comparison hairs. *Courtesy Chris Palenik, Microtrace, Elgin, IL., www.microtracescientific. com*

The forensic comparison is actually a two-step procedure. First, combinations of select properties are chosen from the suspect and the standard/reference specimen for comparison. The question of which and how many properties are selected obviously depends on the type of materials being examined. (This subject will receive a good deal of discussion in forthcoming chapters.) The overriding consideration must be the ultimate evidential value of the conclusion.

This brings us to the second objective. Once the examination has been completed, the forensic scientist must draw a conclusion about the origins of the specimens. Do they or do they not come from the same source? Certainly if one or more of the properties selected for comparison do not agree, the analyst will conclude that the specimens are not the same and hence could not have originated from the same source. Suppose, on the other hand, that all the properties do compare and the specimens, as far as the examiner can determine, are indistinguishable. Does it logically follow that they come from the same source? Not necessarily so.

To comprehend the evidential value of a comparison, one must appreciate the role that probability has in ascertaining the origins of two or more specimens. Simply defined, probability is the frequency of occurrence of an event. If a coin is flipped 100 times, in theory we can expect heads to come up 50 times. Hence, the probability of the event (heads) occurring is 50 in 100. In other words, probability defines the odds that a certain event will occur.

individual characteristics
Properties of evidence that can be attributed to a common source with an extremely high degree of certainty

Individual Characteristics Evidence that can be associated with a common source with an extremely high degree of probability is said to possess **individual characteristics**. Examples of such associations are the matching ridge characteristics of two fingerprints, the comparison of random striations (markings) on bullets or tool marks, the comparison of irregular and random wear patterns in tire or footwear impressions, the comparison of handwriting characteristics, the fitting together of the irregular edges of broken objects in the manner of a jigsaw puzzle (see Figure 3–3), or matching sequentially made plastic bags by striation marks running across the bags (see Figure 3–4).

In all of these cases, it is not possible to state with mathematical exactness the probability that the specimens are of common origin; it can only be concluded that this probability is so high as to defy mathematical calculations or human comprehension. Furthermore, the conclusion of common origin must be substantiated by the practical experience of the examiner. For example, the French scientist Victor Balthazard has mathematically determined that the probability of two individuals having the same fingerprints is one in 1×10^{60}, or 1 followed by 60 zeros. This probability is so small as to exclude the possibility of any two individuals having the same fingerprints. This contention is also supported by the experience of fingerprint examiners who, after classifying millions of prints over the past hundred years, have never found any two to be exactly alike.

class characteristics
Properties of evidence that can be associated only with a group and never with a single source

Class Characteristics One disappointment awaiting the investigator unfamiliar with the limitations of forensic science is the frequent inability of the laboratory to relate physical evidence to a common origin with a high degree of certainty. Evidence is said to possess **class characteristics** when it can be associated only with a group and never with a single source. Here again, probability is a determining factor. For example, if we compare two single-layer automobile paint chips

FIGURE 3–3 The body of a woman was found with evidence of beating about the head and a stablike wound in the neck. Her husband was charged with the murder. The pathologist found a knife blade tip in the wound in the neck. The knife blade tip was compared with the broken blade of a penknife found in the trousers pocket of the accused. Note that in addition to the fit of the indentations on the edges, the scratch marks running across the blade tip correspond in detail to those on the broken blade. *Courtesy Centre of Forensic Sciences, Toronto*

FIGURE 3–4 The bound body of a young woman was recovered from a river. Her head was covered with a black polyethylene trash bag (shown on the right). Among the items recovered from one of several suspects was a black polyethylene trash bag (shown on the left). A side-by-side comparison of the two bags' extrusion marks and pigment bands showed them to be consecutively manufactured. This information allowed investigators to focus their attention on one suspect, who ultimately was convicted of the homicide.

of a similar color, their chance of originating from the same car is not nearly as great as when we compare two paint chips with seven similar layers of paint, not all of which were part of the car's original color. The former will have class characteristics and could be associated at best only with one car model (which may number in the thousands), whereas the latter may be judged to have individual characteristics and to have a high probability of originating from one specific car.

Blood offers another good example of evidence that can have class characteristics. For example, suppose that two blood specimens are compared and both are found to be of human origin, type A. The frequency of occurrence in the population of type A blood is 26 percent—hardly offering a basis for establishing the

product rule
A formula for determining how frequently a certain combination of characteristics occurs in a population; the product rule states that one must first determine the probability of each characteristic occurring separately, then multiply together the frequencies of all independently occurring characteristics; the result is the overall frequency of occurrence for that particular combination of characteristics

common origin of the stains. However, if other blood factors are also determined and are found to compare, the probability that the two blood specimens originated from a common source increases. Thus, if one uses a series of blood factors that occur independently of each other, then one can apply the **product rule** to calculate the overall frequency of occurrence of the blood in a population. In this case, the product rule states that multiplying together the frequency of each factor present in a blood sample will determine how common blood containing that combination of factors is in the general population.

For example, in the O. J. Simpson murder case, a bloodstain located at the crime scene was found to contain a number of factors that compared to O. J.'s blood:

Blood Factors	Frequency
A	26%
EsD	85%
PGM 2+2–	2%

The product of all the frequencies shown in the table determines the probability that any one individual possesses such a combination of blood factors. In this instance, applying the product rule, $0.26 \times 0.85 \times 0.02$ equals 0.0044. Thus, only 0.44 percent, or less than 1 in 200 people, would be expected to have this particular combination of blood factors. These bloodstain factors did not match either of the two victims, Nicole Brown Simpson or Ronald Goldman, thus eliminating them as possible sources of the blood. Although the forensic scientist has still not individualized the bloodstains to one person (in this case, O. J. Simpson), data have been provided that will permit investigators and the courts to better assess the evidential value of the crime-scene stain.

As we will learn in Chapter 9, the product rule is used to determine the frequency of occurrence of DNA profiles typically determined from blood and other biological materials. Importantly, modern DNA technology provides enough factors to allow an analyst to individualize blood, semen, and other biological materials to a single person.

Quick Review
- Two methods used by forensic scientists when examining physical evidence are identification and comparison.

- Identification is the process of determining a substance's chemical or physical identity to the exclusion of all other substances; for example, drugs, explosives, petroleum products, blood, semen, and hair species.

- A comparison analysis determines whether a suspect specimen and a standard/reference specimen have a common origin.

- Evidence that can be associated with a common source with an extremely high degree of probability is said to possess individual characteristics.

- Evidence associated with only a group is said to have class characteristics.

- The overall frequency of occurrence of an event can be obtained by multiplying the frequencies of all independently occurring instances related to that event. This is known as the product rule.

The Significance of Physical Evidence

One of the current weaknesses of forensic science is the inability of the examiner to assign exact or even approximate probability values to the comparison of most class physical evidence. For example, what is the probability that a nylon fiber originated from a particular sweater, or that a hair came from a particular person's head, or that a paint chip came from a car suspected to have been involved in a hit-and-run accident? Few statistical data are available from which to derive this information, and in a society that is increasingly dependent on mass-produced products, the gathering of such data is becoming an increasingly elusive goal.

One of the primary endeavors of forensic scientists must be to create and update statistical databases for evaluating the significance of class physical evidence. Of course, when such information—for example, the population frequency of blood factors—is available, it is used; but for the most part, the forensic scientist must rely on personal experience when interpreting the significance of class physical evidence.

People who are unfamiliar with the realities of modern criminalistics are often disappointed to learn that most items of physical evidence retrieved at crime scenes cannot be linked definitively to a single person or object. Although investigators always try to uncover physical evidence with individual characteristics—such as fingerprints, tool marks, and bullets—the chances of finding class physical evidence are far greater. To deny or belittle the value of such evidence is to reject the potential role that criminalistics can play in a criminal investigation.

FIGURE 3–5 A computer-generated image of DNA superimposed on a fingerprint representing two of the most frequently found individualized items of evidence at crime scenes. *Courtesy Photo Researchers, Inc.*

In practice, criminal cases are fashioned for the courtroom around a collection of diverse elements, each pointing to the guilt or involvement of a party in a criminal act. Often, most of the evidence gathered is subjective, prone to human error and bias. The believability of eyewitness accounts, confessions, and informant testimony can all be disputed, maligned, and subjected to severe attack and skepticism in the courtroom. Under these circumstances, errors in human judgment are often magnified to detract from the credibility of the witness.

Assessing the Value of Physical Evidence

The value of class physical evidence lies in its ability to corroborate events with data in a manner that is, as nearly as possible, free of human error and bias. It is the thread that binds together other investigative findings that are more dependent on human judgments and, therefore, more prone to human failings. The fact that scientists have not yet learned to individualize many kinds of physical evidence means that criminal investigators should not abdicate or falter in their pursuit of all investigative leads. However, the ability of scientists to achieve a high degree of success in evaluating class physical evidence means that criminal investigators can pursue their work with a much greater chance of success.

Admittedly, defining the significance of an item of class evidence in exact mathematical terms is usually a difficult if not impossible goal. Although class evidence is by its nature not unique, meaningful items of physical evidence, such as those listed at the beginning of this chapter, are extremely diverse in our environment. Select, for example, a colored fiber from an article of clothing and try to locate the exact same color on the clothing of random individuals you meet, or select a car color and try to match it to other automobiles you see on local streets. Furthermore, keep in mind that a forensic comparison goes beyond a mere color comparison and involves examining and comparing a variety of chemical and/or physical properties (Figure 3–6). The chances are low of encountering two indistinguishable items of physical evidence at a crime scene that actually originated from different sources. Obviously, given these circumstances, only objects that exhibit significant diversity are appropriate for classification as physical evidence.

FIGURE 3-6 Side-by-side comparison of fibers. *Courtesy Chris Palenik, Microtrace, Elgin, IL., www.microtracescientific.com*

In the same way, when one is dealing with more than one type of class evidence, their collective presence may lead to an extremely high certainty that they originated from the same source. As the number of different objects linking an individual to a crime increases, the probability of involvement increases dramatically. A classic example of this situation can be found in the evidence presented at the trial of Wayne Williams. Wayne Williams was charged with the murders of two individuals in the Atlanta, Georgia, metropolitan area; he was also linked to the murders of ten other boys and young men. An essential element of the state's case involved the association of Williams with the victims through a variety of fiber evidence. Twenty-eight different types of fibers linked Williams to the murder victims, evidence that the forensic examiner characterized as "overwhelming."

Cautions and Limitations in Dealing with Physical Evidence

In further evaluating the contribution of physical evidence, one cannot overlook one important reality in the courtroom: the weight or significance accorded physical evidence is a determination left entirely to the trier of fact, usually a jury of laypeople. Given the high esteem in which scientists are generally held by society and the infallible image created for forensic science by books and television, scientifically evaluated evidence often takes on an aura of special reliability and trustworthiness in the courtroom. Often physical evidence, whether individual or class, is accorded great weight during jury deliberations and becomes a primary factor in reinforcing or overcoming lingering doubts about guilt or innocence. In fact, a number of jurists have already cautioned against giving carte blanche approval to admitting scientific testimony without first considering its relevance to the case. Given the potential weight of scientific evidence, failure to take proper safeguards may unfairly prejudice a case against the accused.

Physical evidence may also exclude or exonerate a person from suspicion. For instance, if type A blood is linked to the suspect, all individuals who have types B, AB, and O blood can be eliminated from consideration. Because it is not possible to assess at the crime scene what value, if any, the scientist will find in the evidence collected, or what significance such findings will ultimately have to a jury, thorough collection and scientific evaluation of physical evidence must become a routine part of all criminal investigations.

Just when an item of physical evidence crosses the line that distinguishes class from individual is a difficult question to answer and is often the source of heated debate and honest disagreement among forensic scientists. How many striations are necessary to individualize a mark to a single tool and no other? How many color layers individualize a paint chip to a single car? How many ridge characteristics individualize a fingerprint, and how many handwriting characteristics tie a person to a signature? These questions defy simple answers. The task of the forensic scientist is to find as many characteristics as possible to compare one substance with another. The significance attached to the findings is decided by the quality and composition of the evidence, the case history, and the examiner's experience. Ultimately, the conclusion can range from mere speculation to near certainty.

There are practical limits to the properties and characteristics the forensic scientist can select for comparison. Carried to the extreme, no two things in this world are alike in every detail. Modern analytical techniques have become so sophisticated and sensitive that the criminalist must define the limits of natural variation among materials when interpreting the data gathered from a comparative analysis. For example, we will learn in the next chapter that two properties, density and refractive index, are best suited for comparing two pieces of glass. But the latest techniques that have been developed to measure these properties are so sensitive that they can even distinguish glass originating from a single pane of glass. Certainly this goes beyond the desires of a criminalist trying to determine only whether two glass particles originated from the same window. Similarly, if the surface of a paint chip is magnified 1,600 times with a powerful scanning electron microscope, it is apparent that the fine details that are revealed could not be duplicated in any other paint chip. Under these circumstances, no two paint chips, even those coming from the same surface, could ever compare in the true sense of the word. Therefore, practicality dictates that such examinations be conducted at a less revealing, but more meaningful, magnification (see Figure 3–7).

(a) (b)

FIGURE 3-7   (a) Two-layer paint chip magnified 244 times with a scanning electron microscope. (b) The same paint chip viewed at a magnification of 1,600 times. *Courtesy Jeff Albright*

Distinguishing evidential variations from natural variations is not always an easy task. Learning how to use the microscope and all the other modern instruments in a crime laboratory properly is one thing; gaining the proficiency needed to interpret the observations and data is another. As new crime laboratories are created and others expand to meet the requirements of the law enforcement community, many individuals are starting new careers in forensic science. They must be cautioned that merely reading relevant textbooks and journals is no substitute for experience in this most practical of sciences.

Quick Review

- The value of class physical evidence lies in its ability to corroborate events with data in a manner that is, as nearly as possible, free of human error and bias.

- As the number of different objects linking an individual to a crime scene increases, so does the likelihood of that individual's involvement with the crime.

- A person may be exonerated or excluded from suspicion if physical evidence collected at a crime scene is found to be different from standard/reference samples collected from that subject.

Forensic Databases

In a criminal investigation, the ultimate contribution a criminalist can make is to link a suspect to a crime through comparative analysis. This comparison defines the unique role of the criminalist in a criminal investigation. Of course, a one-on-one comparison requires a suspect. Little or nothing of evidential value can be accomplished if crime-scene investigators acquire fingerprints, hairs, fibers, paint, blood, and semen without the ability to link these items to a suspect. In this respect, computer technology has dramatically altered the role of the crime laboratory in the investigative process.

No longer is the crime laboratory a passive bystander waiting for investigators to uncover clues about who may have committed a crime. Today, the crime laboratory is on the forefront of the investigation seeking to identify perpetrators. This dramatic enhancement of the role of forensic science in criminal investigation has come about through the creation of computerized databases that not only link all 50 states, but tie together police agencies throughout the world.

Fingerprint Databases

The premier model of all forensic database systems is the *Integrated Automated Fingerprint Identification System* (IAFIS), a national fingerprint and criminal history system maintained by the FBI and launched in 1999. IAFIS contains fingerprints and corresponding criminal history information for nearly 50 million subjects (or 500 million fingerprint images), which are submitted voluntarily to the FBI by state, local, and federal law enforcement agencies.

A crime-scene fingerprint or latent fingerprint is a dramatic find for the criminal investigator. Once the quality of the print has been deemed suitable for the IAFIS search, the latent-print examiner creates a digital image of the print with either a digital camera or a scanner. Next, the examiner, with the aid of a coder, marks points on the print to guide the computerized search (see Figure 3–8). The print is then electronically submitted to IAFIS, and within minutes the search is completed against all fingerprint images in IAFIS; the examiner may receive a list of potential candidates and their corresponding fingerprints for comparison and verification (see Figure 3–9).

FIGURE 3-8 A forensic scientist using the AFIS database. *Courtesy Arresting Images*

FIGURE 3-9
The computerized search of a fingerprint database first requires that selected ridge characteristics be designated by a coder. The positions of these ridge characteristics serve as a basis for comparing the print against fingerprints. *Courtesy Sirchie Finger Print Laboratories, Inc., Youngsville, N.C., www. sirchie.com*

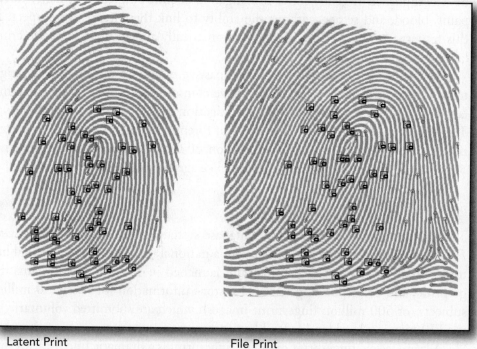

Latent Print   File Print

Many countries throughout the world have created national automated fingerprint identification systems that are comparable to the FBI's model. For example, a computerized fingerprint database containing nearly nine million ten-print records connects the Home Office and 43 police forces throughout England and Wales.

Case Files

Gerald Wallace

In 1975, police found Gerald Wallace's body on his living room couch. He had been savagely beaten, his hands bound with an electric cord. Detectives searched his ransacked house, cataloging every piece of evidence they could find. None of it led to the murderer. They had no witnesses. Sixteen years after the fact, a lone fingerprint, lifted from a cigarette pack found in Wallace's house and kept for 16 years in the police files, was entered into the Pennsylvania State Police AFIS database. Within minutes, it hit a match. That print, police say, gave investigators the identity of a man who had been at the house the night of the murder. Police talked to him. He led them to other witnesses, who led them to the man police ultimately charged with the murder of Gerald Wallace.

DNA Databases

In 1998, the FBI's *Combined DNA Index System* (CODIS) became fully operational. CODIS enables federal, state, and local crime laboratories to electronically exchange and compare DNA profiles, thereby linking crimes to each other and to convicted offenders (see Figure 3–10). All 50 states have enacted legislation to establish a data bank containing DNA profiles of individuals convicted of felony sexual offenses (and other crimes, depending on each state's statute).

FIGURE 3-10 A forensic scientist using the CODIS database. *Courtesy Arresting Images*

Case Files

The Center City Rapist

Fort Collins, Colorado, and Philadelphia, Pennsylvania, are separated by nearly 1,800 miles, but in 2001 they were tragically linked though DNA. Troy Graves left the Philadelphia area in 1999, joined the Air Force, and settled down with his wife in Colorado. A frenzied string of eight sexual assaults around the Colorado University campus set off a manhunt that ultimately resulted in the arrest of Graves. However, his DNA profile inextricably identified him as Philadelphia's notorious "Center City rapist." This assailant attacked four women in 1997 and brutally murdered Shannon Schieber, a Wharton School graduate student, in 1998. His last known attack in Philadelphia was the rape of an 18-year-old student in August 1999, shortly before he left the city. In 2002 Graves was returned to Philadelphia, where he was sentenced to life in prison without parole.

CODIS creates investigative leads from two sources: the *forensic index* and the *offender index*. The forensic index currently contains about 110,000 profiles from unsolved crime-scene evidence. Based on a match, police in multiple jurisdictions can identify serial crimes, allowing coordination of investigations and sharing of leads developed independently. The offender index contains the profiles of nearly seven million convicted or arrested individuals. The FBI has joined 15 states that collect DNA samples from those awaiting trial and detained immigrants. This information will be entered into an *arrestee index* database. Unfortunately, hundreds of thousands of samples are backlogged, still awaiting DNA analysis and entry into CODIS. Law enforcement agencies search this index against DNA profiles recovered from biological evidence found at unsolved crime scenes. This approach has been tremendously successful in identifying perpetrators because most crimes involving biological evidence are committed by repeat offenders.

Several countries throughout the world have initiated national DNA data banks. The United Kingdom's National DNA Database, established in 1995, was the world's first national database. Currently it holds about four million profiles, and DNA can be taken for entry into the database from anyone arrested for an offense likely to involve a prison term. In a typical month, matches are found linking suspects to 26 murders; 57 rapes and other sexual offenses; and three thousand motor vehicle, property and drug crimes.

Other Databases

The *National Integrated Ballistics Information Network* (NIBIN), maintained by the Bureau of Alcohol, Tobacco, Firearms, and Explosives, allows firearms analysts to acquire, digitize, and compare markings made by a firearm on bullets and cartridge casings recovered from crime scenes. The NIBIN program currently has 236 sites that are electronically joined to 16 multistate regions.

The heart of NIBIN is the *Integrated Ballistic Identification System* (IBIS), comprising a microscope and a computer unit that can capture an image of a bullet or cartridge casing. The images are then forwarded to a regional server,

Case Files

Aztec Gold Metallic Hit and Run

A 53-year-old man was walking his dog in the early morning hours. He was struck and killed by an unknown vehicle and later found lying in the roadway. No witnesses were present, and the police had no leads regarding the suspect vehicle. A gold metallic painted plastic fragment recovered from the scene and the victim's clothing were submitted to the Virginia Department of Forensic Science for analysis.

The victim's clothing was scraped, and several minute gold metallic paint particles were recovered. Most of these particles contained only topcoats, whereas one minute particle contained two primer layers and a limited amount of colorcoat. The color of the primer surface layer was similar to that typically associated with some Fords. Subsequent spectral searches in the Paint Data Query (PDQ) database indicated that the paint most likely originated from a 1990 or newer Ford.

The most discriminating aspect of this paint was the unusual-looking gold metallic topcoat color. A search of automotive repaint books yielded only one color that closely matched the paint recovered in the case. The color, Aztec Gold Metallic, was determined to have been used only on 1997 Ford Mustangs.

The results of the examination were relayed via telephone to the investigating detective. The investigating detective quickly determined that only 11,000 1997 Ford Mustangs were produced in Aztec Gold Metallic. Only two of these vehicles were registered, and had been previously stopped, in the jurisdiction of the offense. Ninety minutes after the make, model, and year information was relayed to the investigator, he called back to say he had located a suspect vehicle. Molding from the vehicle and known paint samples were submitted for comparison. Subsequent laboratory comparisons showed that the painted plastic piece recovered from the scene could be physically fitted together with the molding, and paint recovered from the victim's clothing was consistent with paint samples taken from the suspect vehicle.

Source: Brenda Christy, Virginia Department of Forensic Science

where they are stored and correlated against other images in the regional database. IBIS does not positively match bullets or casings fired from the same weapon; this must be done by a firearms examiner. IBIS does, however, facilitate the work of the firearms examiner by producing a short list of candidates for the examiner to manually compare. Nearly 900,000 pieces of crime-scene evidence have been entered in NIBIN and more than 10,000 "hits" have been recorded, many of them yielding investigative information not obtainable by other means.

The *International Forensic Automotive Paint Data Query* (PDQ) database contains chemical and color information pertaining to original automotive paints. This database, developed and maintained by the Forensic Laboratory Services of the Royal Canadian Mounted Police (RCMP), contains information about make, model, year, and assembly plant on more than 13,000 vehicles, with a library of more than 50,000 layers of paint. Contributors to the PDQ include the RCMP and forensic laboratories in Ontario and Quebec, as well as 40 U.S. forensic laboratories and police agencies in 21 other countries. Accredited users of PDQ are required to submit 60 new automotive paint samples per year for addition to the database. The PDQ database has found its greatest utility in the investigation of hit-and-runs by providing police with possible make, model, and year information to aid in the search for the unknown vehicle.

Case Files

NIBIN Links Handgun to Suspects

After a series of armed robberies in which suspects fired shots, the sheriff's office of Broward County, Florida, entered the cartridge casings from the crime scenes into NIBIN. Through NIBIN, four of the armed robberies were linked to the same .40-caliber handgun. A short time later, sheriff's deputies noticed suspicious activity around a local business. When they attempted to interview the suspects, the suspects fled in a vehicle. During the chase, the suspects attempted to dispose of a handgun; deputies recovered the gun after making the arrests. The gun was test-fired and the resulting evidence entered into NIBIN, which indicated a possible link between this handgun and the four previous armed robberies. Firearms examiners confirmed the link by examining the original evidence. The suspects were arrested and charged with four prior armed robbery offenses.

The previously described databases are maintained and controlled by government agencies. There is one exception: a commercially available computer retrieval system for comparing and identifying crime-scene shoe prints known as SICAR (shoeprint image capture and retrieval).[1] SICAR's pattern-coding system enables an analyst to create a simple description of a shoe print by assigning codes to individual pattern features (see Figure 3–11). Shoe print images can be entered into SICAR by either a scanner or a digital camera. This product has a comprehensive shoe sole database (Solemate) that includes more than 17,000 footwear entries, representing more than seven hundred shoe brands, providing investigators with a means for linking a crime-scene footwear impression to a particular shoe manufacturer.

FIGURE 3-11
The crime-scene footwear print on the right is being searched against eight thousand sole patterns to determine its make and model.
Courtesy Foster & Freeman Limited, Worcestershire, U.K., www.fosterfreeman.co.uk

Quick Review

- The creation of computerized databases for fingerprints, criminal histories, DNA profiles, markings on bullets and cartridges, automotive paints, and shoe prints has dramatically enhanced the role of forensic science in criminal investigation.

- IAFIS is the Integrated Automated Fingerprint Identification System, a national fingerprint and criminal history database maintained by the FBI. IAFIS allows criminal investigators to compare fingerprints at a crime scene to an index of 500 million known prints. CODIS is the FBI's Combined DNA Index System. It enables federal, state, and local crime laboratories to electronically exchange and compare DNA profiles, linking crimes to each other and to convicted offenders.

Chapter Review

- Biological crime-scene evidence includes blood, saliva, semen, DNA, hair, organs, and physiological fluids.

- Impression crime-scene evidence includes tire markings, shoe prints, depressions in soft soils, all other forms of tracks, glove and other fabric impressions, tool marks, and bite marks.

- Manufactured items considered common items of crime-scene evidence include firearms, ammunition, fibers, paint, glass, petroleum products, plastic bags, rubber, polymers, and vehicle headlights.

- Two methods used by forensic scientists when examining physical evidence are identification and comparison.

- Identification is the process of determining a substance's chemical or physical identity to the exclusion of all other substances; for example, drugs, explosives, petroleum products, blood, semen, and hair species.

- A comparison analysis determines whether a suspect specimen and a standard/reference specimen have a common origin.

- Evidence that can be associated with a common source with an extremely high degree of probability is said to possess individual characteristics.

- Evidence associated with only a group is said to have class characteristics.

- The overall frequency of occurrence of an event can be obtained by multiplying the frequencies of all independently occurring instances related to that event. This is known as the product rule.

- The value of class physical evidence lies in its ability to corroborate events with data in a manner that is, as nearly as possible, free of human error and bias.

- As the number of different objects linking an individual to a crime scene increases, so does the likelihood of that individual's involvement with the crime.

- A person may be exonerated or excluded from suspicion if physical evidence collected at a crime scene is found to be different from standard/reference samples collected from that subject.

- The creation of computerized databases for fingerprints, criminal histories, DNA profiles, markings on bullets and cartridges, automotive paints, and shoe prints has dramatically enhanced the role of forensic science in criminal investigation.

- IAFIS is the Integrated Automated Fingerprint Identification System, a national fingerprint and criminal history database maintained by the FBI. IAFIS allows criminal investigators to compare fingerprints at a crime scene to an index of 500 million known prints. CODIS is the FBI's Combined DNA Index System. It enables federal, state, and local crime laboratories to electronically exchange and compare DNA profiles, linking crimes to each other and to convicted offenders.

Properties of Matter and the Analysis of Glass

4

Key Terms

amorphous solid
atom
Becke line
birefringence
Celsius scale
chemical property
compound
concentric fracture
crystalline solid
density
dispersion
electromagnetic spectrum
element

Fahrenheit scale
frequency
gas
intensive property
laminated glass
laser
liquid
mass
matter
periodic table
phase
photon
physical property

physical state
radial fracture
refraction
refractive index
solid
sublimation
tempered glass
visible light
wavelength
weight
X-ray

Properties of Matter

The forensic scientist must constantly determine the properties that impart distinguishing characteristics to matter, giving it a unique identity. The continuing search for distinctive properties ends only when the scientist has completely individualized a substance to one correct source. Properties are the identifying characteristics of substances. In this and succeeding chapters, we will examine properties that are most useful for characterizing soil, glass, and other physical evidence. However, before we begin, we can simplify our understanding of the nature of properties by classifying them into two broad categories: physical and chemical.

Physical properties describe a substance without reference to any other substance. For example, weight, volume, color, boiling point, and melting point are typical physical properties that can be measured for a particular substance without altering the material's composition through a chemical reaction; they are associated only with the physical existence of that substance. A **chemical property** describes the behavior of a substance when it reacts or combines with another substance. For example, when wood burns, it chemically combines with oxygen in the air to form new substances; this transformation describes a chemical property of wood. In the crime laboratory, a routine procedure for determining the presence of heroin in a suspect specimen is to react it with a chemical reagent known as the Marquis reagent, which turns purple in the presence of heroin. This color transformation becomes a chemical property of heroin and provides a convenient test for its identification (see Figure 4–1).

physical property
A property that describes the behavior of a substance without reference to any other substance

chemical property
A property that describes the behavior of a substance when it combines with another substance

FIGURE 4–1 The color change associated with a drug color test represents an example of a chemical property that can be used to identify the drug of interest. *Courtesy Drug Enforcement Administration*

Which physical and chemical properties the forensic scientist ultimately chooses to observe and measure depends on the type of material that is being examined. Logic requires, however, that if the property can be assigned a numerical value, it must relate to a standard system of measurement accepted throughout the scientific community. That standard system is called the metric system.

Inside the Science

The Metric System

Although scientists, including forensic scientists, throughout the world have been using the metric system of measurement for more than a century, the United States still uses the cumbersome "English system" to express length in inches, feet, or yards; weight in ounces or pounds; and volume in pints or quarts. The inherent difficulty of this system is that no simple numerical relationship exists between the various units of measurement. For example, to convert inches to feet one must know that 1 foot is equal to 12 inches; the conversion of ounces to pounds requires the knowledge that 16 ounces is equivalent to 1 pound.

In 1791, the French Academy of Science devised the simple system of measurement known as the metric system. This system uses a simple decimal relationship so that a unit of length, volume, or mass can be converted into a subunit by simply multiplying or dividing by a multiple of 10—for example, 10, 100, or 1,000. Even though the United States has not yet adopted the metric system, its system of currency is decimal and, hence, is analogous to the metric system. The basic unit of currency is the dollar. A dollar is divided into 10 equal units called dimes, and each dime is further divided into 10 equal units of cents.

The metric system has basic units of measurement for length, mass, and volume: the meter, gram, and liter, respectively. These three basic units can be converted into subunits that are decimal multiples of the basic unit by simply attaching a prefix to the unit name. The following are common prefixes and their equivalent decimal value:

Prefix	Equivalent Value
deci-	1/10 or 0.1
centi-	1/100 or 0.01
milli-	1/1,000 or 0.001
micro-	1/1,000,000 or 0.000001
nano-	1/1,000,000,000 or 0.000000001
kilo-	1,000
mega-	1,000,000

Hence, 1/10 or 0.1 gram (g) is the same as a decigram (dg), 1/100 or 0.01 meter is equal to a centimeter (cm), and 1/1000 liter (0.001) is a milliliter (mL). A metric conversion is carried out simply by moving the decimal point to the right or left and inserting the proper prefix to show the direction and number of places that the decimal point has been moved. For example, if the weight of a powder is 0.0165 gram, it may be more convenient to multiply this value by 100 and express it as 1.65 centigrams or by 1,000 to show it as its equivalent value of 16.5 milligrams. Similarly, an object that weighs 264,450 grams may be expressed as 264.45 kilograms simply by dividing it by 1,000. It is important to remember that in any of these conversions, the value of the measurement has not changed; 0.0165 gram is still equivalent to 1.65 centigrams, just as one dollar is still equal to 100 cents. We have simply adjusted the position of the decimal and shown the extent of the adjustment with a prefix.

One interesting aspect of the metric system is that volume can be defined in terms of length. A liter by definition is the volume of a cube with sides of length 10 centimeters. One liter is therefore equivalent to a volume of (10 cm)^3, or 1,000 cubic centimeters (cc). Thus, 1/1,000 liter or 1 milliliter (mL) is equal to 1 cubic centimeter (cc) (see Figure 1). Scientists commonly use the subunits mL and cc interchangeably to express volume.

FIGURE 1   Volume equivalencies in the metric system.

FIGURE 2   Comparison of the metric and English systems of length measurement; 2.54 centimeters = 1 inch.

At times, it may be necessary to convert units from the metric system into the English system, or vice versa (see Figure 2). To accomplish this, we must consult references that list English units and their metric equivalents. Some of the more useful equivalents follow:

1 inch = 2.54 centimeters
1 meter = 39.37 inches
1 pound = 453.6 grams
1 liter = 1.06 quarts
1 kilogram = 2.2 pounds

The general mathematical procedures for converting from one system to another can be illustrated by converting 12 inches into centimeters. To change inches into centimeters, we need to know that there are 2.54 centimeters per inch. Hence, if we multiply 12 inches by 2.54 centimeters per inch (12 in. × 2.54 cm/in.), the unit of inches will cancel out, leaving the product 30.48 cm. Similarly, converting grams to pounds, 227 grams is equivalent to 227 g × 1 lb/453.6 g or 0.5 lb.

The Nature of Matter

Before examining physical and chemical properties that are important to the forensic scientist, it is important to understand the basic nature of matter, which comprises all substances. **Matter** is anything that has mass and occupies space.

Elements and Compounds

As we examine the world that surrounds us and consider the countless variety of materials that we encounter, we must consider one of humankind's most remarkable accomplishments, the discovery of the concept of the atom, to explain the composition of all matter. This search had its earliest contribution from the ancient Greek philosophers, who suggested air, water, fire, and earth as matter's fundamental building blocks. It culminated with the development of the atomic theory and the discovery of matter's simplest identity, the element.

Table 4–1
List of Elements with Their Symbols and Atomic Masses

Element	Symbol	Atomic Mass[a] (amu)
Actinium	Ac	(227)
Aluminum	Al	26.9815
Americium	Am	(243)
Antimony	Sb	121.75
Argon	Ar	39.948
Arsenic	As	74.9216
Astatine	At	(210)
Barium	Ba	137.34
Berkelium	Bk	(247)
Beryllium	Be	9.01218
Bismuth	Bi	208.9806
Bohrium	Bh	(262)
Boron	B	10.81
Bromine	Br	79.904
Cadmium	Cd	112.40
Calcium	Ca	40.08
Californium	Cf	(251)
Carbon	C	12.011
Cerium	Ce	140.12
Cesium	Cs	132.9055
Chlorine	Cl	35.453
Chromium	Cr	51.996
Cobalt	Co	58.9332
Copernicium	Cp	(285)
Copper	Cu	63.546
Curium	Cm	(247)
Darmstadtium	Ds	(271)
Dubnium	Db	(260)

Table 4–1 *(continued)*
List of Elements with Their Symbols and Atomic Masses

Element	Symbol	Atomic Mass[a] (amu)
Dysprosium	Dy	162.50
Einsteinium	Es	(254)
Erbium	Er	167.26
Europium	Eu	151.96
Fermium	Fm	(253)
Fluorine	F	18.9984
Francium	Fr	(223)
Gadolinium	Gd	157.25
Gallium	Ga	69.72
Germanium	Ge	72.59
Gold	Au	196.9665
Hafnium	Hf	178.49
Hassium	Hs	(265)
Helium	He	4.00260
Holmium	Ho	164.9303
Hydrogen	H	1.0080
Indium	In	114.82
Iodine	I	126.9045
Iridium	Ir	192.22
Iron	Fe	55.847
Krypton	Kr	83.80
Lanthanum	La	138.9055
Lawrencium	Lr	(257)
Lead	Pb	207.2
Lithium	Li	6.941
Lutetium	Lu	174.97
Magnesium	Mg	24.305
Manganese	Mn	54.9380
Meitnerium	Mt	(266)
Mendelevium	Md	(256)
Mercury	Hg	200.59
Molybdenum	Mo	95.94
Neodymium	Nd	144.24
Neon	Ne	20.179
Neptunium	Np	237.0482
Nickel	Ni	58.71
Niobium	Nb	92.9064
Nitrogen	N	14.0067
Nobelium	No	(254)
Osmium	Os	190.2
Oxygen	O	15.9994
Palladium	Pd	106.4
Phosphorus	P	30.9738
Platinum	Pt	195.09
Plutonium	Pu	(244)

Polonium	Po	(209)
Potassium	K	39.102
Praseodymium	Pr	140.9077
Promethium	Pm	(145)
Protactinium	Pa	231.0359
Radium	Ra	226.0254
Radon	Rn	(222)
Rhenium	Re	186.2
Rhodium	Rh	102.9055
Roentgenium	Rg	(272)
Rubidium	Rb	85.4678
Ruthenium	Ru	101.07
Rutherfordium	Rf	(257)
Samarium	Sm	105.4
Scandium	Sc	44.9559
Seaborgium	Sg	(263)
Selenium	Se	78.96
Silicon	Si	28.086
Silver	Ag	107.868
Sodium	Na	22.9898
Strontium	Sr	87.62
Sulfur	S	32.06
Tantalum	Ta	180.9479
Technetium	Tc	98.9062
Thallium	Tl	204.37
Terbium	Tb	158.9254
Tellurium	Te	127.60
Thorium	Th	232.0381
Thulium	Tm	168.9342
Tin	Sn	118.69
Titanium	Ti	47.90
Tungsten	W	183.85
Ununhexium	Uuh	(292)
Ununoctium	Uuo	(294)
Ununpentium	Uup	(288)
Ununquadium	Uuq	(289)
Ununseptium	Uus	(unknown)
Ununtrium	Uut	(284)
Uranium	U	238.029
Vanadium	V	50.9414
Xenon	Xe	131.3
Ytterbium	Yb	173.04
Yttrium	Y	88.9059
Zinc	Zn	65.57
Zirconium	Zr	91.22

[a]Based on the assigned relative atomic mass of C = exactly 12; parentheses denote the mass number of the isotope with the longest half-life.

element
A fundamental particle of matter that cannot be broken down into simpler substances by chemical means

periodic table
A chart of all the known elements arranged in a systematic fashion

An **element** is a fundamental particle of matter that cannot be broken down into simpler substances by chemical means. Elements provide the building blocks from which all matter is composed. At present, 118 elements have been identified (see Table 4–1); of these, 89 occur naturally on the earth, and the remainder have been created in the laboratory.

Figure 4–2 shows the **periodic table**, a chart of all the known elements arranged in a systematic fashion. This table is most useful to chemists because it arranges elements with similar chemical properties in the same vertical or horizontal rows. Vertical rows of elements in the table are called groups or families; horizontal rows are called series. Elements in the same group have similar properties (for example, atomic mass or density) and exhibit a clear trend in properties as one moves down the group. As a result, groups are considered the most important way of classifying the elements. In some parts of the table, however, similarities in properties of the elements in the same row makes the series a more useful method for classification.

FIGURE 4–2
The Periodic table.

For convenience, chemists have chosen letter symbols to represent the elements. Many of these symbols come from the first letter of the element's English name—for example, carbon (C), hydrogen (H), and oxygen (O). Others are two-letter abbreviations of the English name—calcium (Ca) and zinc (Zn). Some symbols are derived from the first letters of Latin or Greek names. Thus, the symbol for silver, Ag, comes from the Latin name argentum; copper, Cu, from the Latin cuprum; and helium, He, from the Greek name helios.

atom
The smallest unit of an element that can exist and still retain its identity as that element

compound
A pure substance composed of two or more elements

The smallest particle of an element that can exist and still retain its identity as that element is the **atom**. When we write the symbol C we mean one atom of carbon; the chemical symbol for carbon dioxide, CO_2, signifies one atom of carbon combined with two atoms of oxygen. When two or more elements are combined, as with carbon dioxide, a new substance is created, different in its physical and chemical properties from its elemental components. This new material is called a **compound**. Compounds contain at least two elements. Considering that there are 89 natural elements, it is easy to imagine the large number of possible elemental combinations that may form compounds. Not surprisingly, more than 16 million known compounds have already been identified.

Just as the atom is the basic unit of an element, the molecule is the smallest unit of a compound. Thus, a molecule of carbon dioxide is represented by the symbol CO_2, and a molecule of table salt is symbolized by NaCl, representing the combination of one atom of the element sodium (Na) with one atom of the element chlorine (Cl).

States of Matter

As we look around us and view the materials that make up the earth, it becomes an awesome task even to attempt to estimate the number of different kinds of matter. A much more logical approach is to classify matter according to the physical form it takes. These forms are called **physical states**. There are three such states: solid, liquid, and gas (vapor).

In the **solid** state, molecules of matter are held closely together by strong attractive forces. This tightly packed molecular arrangement makes solid matter rigid and gives it a definite shape and volume. In a **liquid**, the attractive forces between molecules are weaker. The molecules are in contact with one another, but are not held as rigidly in place. Like a solid, a liquid also occupies a specific volume, but its fluidity causes it to take the shape of the container in which it resides. The attractive forces between molecules in a **gas** are much weaker still, allowing them to move freely. Thus, gaseous matter has neither a definite shape nor volume, and it will completely fill any container into which it is placed.

Changes of State Substances can change from one state to another. For example, as water is heated, it is converted from a liquid form into a vapor. At a high enough temperature (100°C), water boils and rapidly changes into steam. Similarly, at 0°C, water solidifies or freezes into ice. Under certain conditions, some solids can be converted directly into a gaseous state. For instance, a piece of dry ice (solid carbon dioxide) left standing at room temperature quickly forms carbon dioxide vapor and disappears. This change of state from a solid to a gas is called **sublimation**.

In each of these examples, no new chemical species are formed; matter simply changes from one physical state to another. Water, whether in the form of liquid, ice, or steam, remains chemically H_2O. Simply, what has been altered are the attractive forces between the water molecules. In a solid, these forces are very strong, and the molecules are held closely together in a rigid state. In a liquid, the attractive forces are not as strong, and the molecules have more mobility. Finally, in the vapor state, appreciable attractive forces no longer exist between the molecules; thus, they may move in any direction at will.

Phases Chemists are forever combining different substances, no matter whether they are in the solid, liquid, or gaseous states, hoping to create new and useful products. Not all attempts at mixing matter are productive. For instance, oil spills demonstrate that oil and water do not mix. Whenever substances can be distinguished by a visible boundary, different **phases** are said to exist.

Oil floating on water is an example of a two-phase system. The oil and water each constitute a separate liquid phase, clearly distinct from each other. Similarly, when sugar is first added to water, it will not dissolve, and two distinctly different

physical state
The physical form taken by matter: solid, liquid, or gas

solid
A state of matter in which molecules are held closely together by strong attractive forces

liquid
A state of matter in which the attractive forces are strong enough to allow molecules to be in contact with one another but too weak to hold them rigidly in place

gas (vapor)
A state of matter in which the attractive forces between molecules are weak enough to permit them to move with complete freedom

sublimation
A change of state from a solid directly into a gas

phase
A uniform substance separated from other substances by definite visible boundaries

phases exist: the solid sugar and the liquid water. However, after stirring, all the sugar dissolves, leaving just one liquid phase. As we shall see, forensic scientists use the existence of different phases to identify and classify evidence found at a crime scene.

Quick Review

- Physical properties such as weight, volume, color, boiling point, and melting point describe a substance without reference to any other substance. A chemical property describes the behavior of a substance when it reacts or combines with another substance.

- Matter is anything that has mass and occupies space. An element is a fundamental particle of matter that cannot be broken down into simpler substances by chemical means.

- The smallest particle of an element that can exist and still retain its identity as that element is the atom.

- A compound is a pure substance composed of two or more elements. The smallest unit of a compound is a molecule.

- The three states of matter are solid, liquid, and gas.

- Sublimation is a change of state from a solid to a gas.

- A phase is a uniform body of matter distinguished from other matter by definite visible boundaries.

Theory of Light

As with matter, knowledge of the nature and behavior of light is fundamental to understanding physical properties important to the examination of forensic evidence. Two simple models explain light's behavior. The first model describes light as a continuous wave; the second depicts it as a stream of discrete energy particles. Together, these two very different descriptions explain all of the observed properties of light, but by itself, no one model can explain all the facets of the behavior of light.

Light as a Wave

wavelength
The distance between crests of adjacent waves

frequency
The number of waves that pass a given point per unit of time

The wave concept depicts light as having an up-and-down motion of a continuous wave, as shown in Figure 4–3. Such a wave can be characterized by two distinct properties: wavelength and frequency. The distance between two consecutive crests (high points) or troughs (low points) of a wave is called the **wavelength**; it is designated by the Greek letter lambda (λ) and is typically measured in nanometers (nm), or millionths of a meter. The number of crests (or troughs) passing any one given point in a unit of time is defined as the **frequency** of the wave. Frequency is normally designated by the letter f and is expressed in cycles per second (cps). Frequency and wavelength are inversely proportional to one another, as shown by the relationship expressed in Equation (4–1):

$$F = c / \lambda$$

EQUATION 4-1

In the equation, *c* represents the speed of light.

Many of us have held a glass prism up toward the sunlight and watched it transform light into the colors of the rainbow. The process of separating light into its component colors is called **dispersion**. Visible light usually travels at a constant velocity of nearly 300 million meters per second. However, on passing through the glass of a prism, each color component of light is slowed to a speed slightly different from those of the others, causing each component to bend at a different angle as it emerges from the prism (see Figure 4–4). This bending of light waves because of a change in velocity is called **refraction**.

dispersion
The separation of light into its component wavelengths

refraction
The bending of a light wave caused by a change in its velocity

FIGURE 4–3
The frequency of the lower wave is twice that of the upper wave.

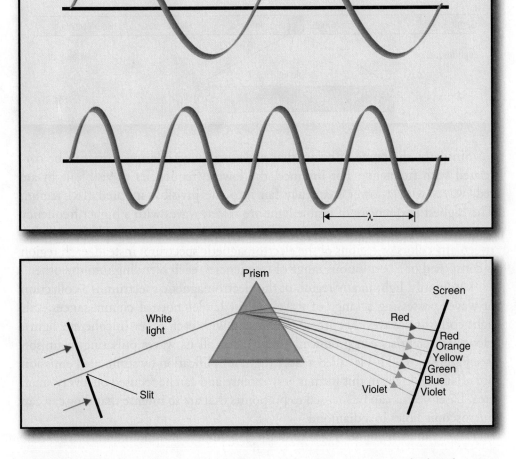

FIGURE 4–4
Representation of the dispersion of light by a glass prism.

The observation that a substance has a color is consistent with this description of white light. For example, when light passes through a red glass, the glass absorbs all the component colors of light except red, which passes through or is transmitted by the glass. Likewise, one can determine the color of an opaque

visible light
Colored light ranging
from red to violet in
the electromagnetic
spectrum

**electromagnetic
spectrum**
The entire range of
radiation from the most
energetic cosmic rays
to the least energetic
radio waves

FIGURE 4–5
The electromagnetic
spectrum.

object by observing its ability to absorb some of the component colors of light while reflecting others back to the eye. Color is thus a visual indication that objects absorb certain portions of **visible light** and transmit or reflect others. Scientists have long recognized this phenomenon and have learned to characterize different chemical substances by the type and quantity of light they absorb. This has important applications for the identification and classification of forensic evidence.

The Electromagnetic Spectrum Visible light is only a small part of a large family of radiation waves known as the **electromagnetic spectrum** (see Figure 4–5). All electromagnetic waves travel at the speed of light (*c*) and are distinguishable from one another only by their different wavelengths or frequencies. Hence, the only property that distinguishes **X-rays** from radio waves is the different frequencies the two types of waves possess.

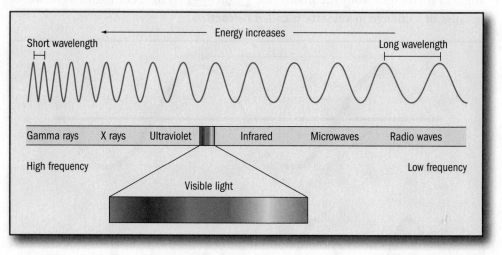

X-ray
The high-energy,
short-wavelength form
of electromagnetic
radiation

Similarly, the range of colors that make up the visible spectrum can be correlated with frequency. For instance, the lowest frequencies of visible light are red; waves with a lower frequency fall into the invisible infrared (IR) region. The highest frequencies of visible light are violet; waves with a higher frequency extend into the invisible ultraviolet (UV) region. No definite boundaries exist between any colors or regions of the electromagnetic spectrum; instead, each region is composed of a continuous range of frequencies, each blending into the other.

Ordinarily, light in any region of the electromagnetic spectrum is a collection of waves possessing a range of wavelengths. Under normal circumstances, this light comprises waves that are all out of step with each other (incoherent light). However, scientists can produce light that has all its waves pulsating in unison (see Figure 4–6). This is called a **laser** (light amplification by stimulated emission of radiation). Light in this form is very intense and can be focused on a very small area. Laser beams can be focused to pinpoints that are so intense that they can zap microscopic holes in a diamond.

laser
An acronym for light
amplification by
stimulated emission of
radiation; light that has
all its waves pulsating
in unison

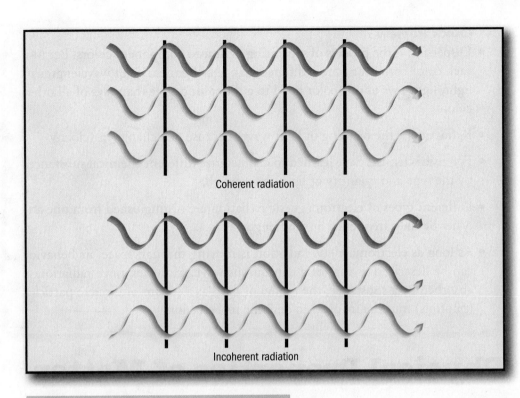

FIGURE 4–6
Coherent and incoherent radiation.

Coherent radiation

Incoherent radiation

Light as a Particle

As long as electromagnetic radiation is moving through space, its behavior can be described as that of a continuous wave. However, once radiation is absorbed by a substance, the model of light as a stream of discrete particles must be invoked to describe its behavior. Here, light is depicted as consisting of energy particles that are known as **photons**. Each photon has a definite amount of energy associated with its behavior. This energy is related to the frequency of light, as shown by Equation (4–2):

$$E = hf$$

where E specifies the energy of the photon, f is the frequency of radiation, and h is a universal constant called Planck's constant. As shown by Equation (4–2), the energy of a photon is directly proportional to its frequency. Therefore, the photons of ultraviolet light will be more energetic than the photons of visible or infrared light, and exposure to the more energetic photons of X-rays presents more danger to human health than exposure to the photons of radio waves.

Just as a substance can absorb visible light to produce color, many of the invisible radiations of the electromagnetic spectrum are likewise absorbed. This absorption phenomenon is the basis for spectrophotometry, an analytical technique that measures the quantity of radiation that a particular material absorbs as a function of wavelength or frequency. We will examine spectrophotometry in more detail when we discuss the forensic analysis of drugs in Chapter 5.

photon
A discrete particle of electromagnetic radiation

EQUATION 4-2

Physical Properties of Matter

Temperature

Determining the physical properties of any material often requires measuring its temperature. For instance, the temperatures at which a substance melts or boils are readily determinable characteristics that will help identify it. Temperature is a measure of heat intensity, or the amount of heat in a substance. Temperature is usually measured by placing a thermometer in contact with a substance. The familiar mercury-in-glass thermometer functions because mercury expands more than glass when heated and contracts more than glass when cooled. Thus, the length of the mercury column in the glass tube measures the surrounding environment's temperature.

The construction of a temperature scale requires two reference points and a choice of units. The reference points most conveniently chosen are the freezing point and boiling point of water. The two most common temperature scales used are the **Fahrenheit** and **Celsius** (formerly called centigrade) **scales** (see Figure 4–7).

The Fahrenheit scale is based on the assignment of a value of 32°F to the freezing point of water and a value of 212°F to its boiling point. The difference between the two points is evenly divided into 180 units. Thus, a degree Fahrenheit is 1/180 of the temperature change between the freezing point and boiling point of water. The Celsius scale is derived by assigning the freezing point of water a value of 0°C and its boiling point a value of 100°C. A degree Celsius is thus 1/100 of the temperature change between the two reference points. Scientists in most countries use the Celsius scale to measure temperature.

Farenheit scale
The temperature scale that defines the melting point of ice as 32° and the boiling point of water as 212°, with 180 equal divisions or degrees between

Celsius scale
The temperature scale that defines the melting point of ice as 0° and the boiling point of water as 100°, with 100 equal divisions or degrees between

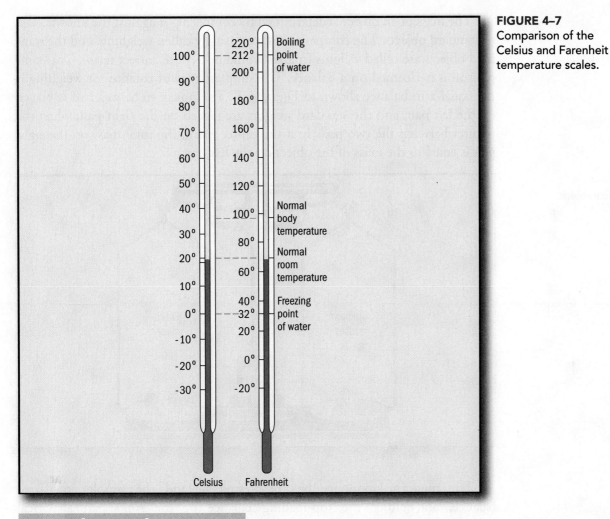

FIGURE 4–7
Comparison of the Celsius and Farenheit temperature scales.

Weight and Mass

The force with which gravity attracts a body is called **weight**. If your weight is 180 pounds, this means that the earth's gravity is pulling you down with a force of 180 pounds; on the moon, where the force of gravity is one-sixth that of the earth, your weight would be 30 pounds.

Mass differs from weight because it refers to the amount of matter an object contains and is independent of its location on the earth or any other place in the universe. The mathematical relationship between weight (w) and mass (m) is shown in Equation (4–3), where g is the acceleration imparted to a body by the force of gravity.

$$w = mg$$

The weight of a body is seen to be directly proportional to its mass; hence, a large mass weighs more than a small mass.

In the metric system, the mass of an object is always specified, rather than its weight. The basic unit of mass is the gram. An object that has a mass of 40 grams on the earth will have a mass of 40 grams anywhere else in the universe. Normally, however, the terms mass and weight are used interchangeably, and we often speak of the weight of an object when we really mean its mass.

weight
The force with which gravity attracts a body

mass
A constant property that refers to the amount of matter an object contains

EQUATION 4-3

The mass of an object is determined by comparing it against the known mass of standard objects. The comparison is confusingly called weighing, and the standard objects are called weights (masses would be a more correct term). The comparison is performed on a balance. The simplest type of balance for weighing is the equal-arm balance shown in <u>Figure 4–8</u>. The object to be weighed is placed on the left pan, and the standard weights are placed on the right pan; when the pointer between the two pans is at the center mark, the total mass on the right pan is equal to the mass of the object on the left pan.

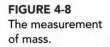

FIGURE 4-8
The measurement of mass.

The modern laboratory has progressed beyond the simple equal-arm balance, and either the top-loading balance or the single-pan analytical balance (see <u>Figure 4–9</u>) is now likely to be used. The choice depends on the accuracy required and the amount of material being weighed. Each works on the same counterbalancing principle as the simple equal-arm balance, but the second pan, the one on which the standard weights are placed, is hidden from view within the balance's housing. Once the object whose weight is to be determined is placed on the visible pan, the operator selects the proper standard weights (also contained with the housing) by manually turning a set of knobs located on the front side of the balance. At the point of balance, the weights selected are automatically recorded on digital and optical readout scales. Other versions of single-pan balances rely on an electromagnetic field to generate a current to balance the force pressing down on the pan from the sample being weighed. When the scale is properly calibrated, the amount of current needed to keep the pan balanced is used to determine the weight of the sample. The strength of the current is converted to a digitized signal for a readout. The top-loading balance can accurately weigh an object to the nearest 1 milligram or 0.001 gram; the analytical balance is even more accurate, weighing to the nearest tenth of a milligram or 0.0001 gram.

FIGURE 4-9
(a) Top-loading balance. *Courtesy Scientech, Inc., Boulder, CO, www.scientech-inc.com,* (b) Single-pan analytical balance. *Courtesy Sirchie Finger Print Laboratories, Inc., Youngsville, N.C., www.sirchie.com*

(a)

(b)

Density

An important physical property of matter with respect to the analysis of certain kinds of physical evidence is **density**. Density is defined as mass per unit volume (see Equation (4–4)).

$$\text{Density} = \frac{\text{mass}}{\text{volume}}$$

Density is an **intensive property** of matter—that is, it remains the same regardless of the size of an object; thus, it is a characteristic property of a substance and can be used in identification. Solids tend to be more dense than liquids, and liquids more dense than gases. The densities of some common substances are shown in Table 4–2.

A simple procedure for determining the density of a solid is illustrated in Figure 4–10. First, the solid is weighed on a balance against known standard gram weights to determine its mass. The solid's volume is then determined from the volume of water it displaces. This is easily measured by filling a cylinder with a known volume of water (V_1), adding the object, and measuring the new water level (V_2). The difference ($V_2 - V_1$) in milliliters is equal to the volume of the solid. Density can now be calculated from Equation 4–4 in grams per milliliter.

density
A physical property of matter that is equivalent to the mass per unit volume of a substance

EQUATION 4-4

intensive property
A property that is not dependent on the size of an object

FIGURE 4-10
A simple procedure for determining the density of a solid is to first weigh it and then measure its volume by noting the volume of water it displaces.

Mass = 20 g

$$\text{Density} = \frac{\text{Mass}}{\text{Volume }(v_2 - v_1)}$$

$$\text{Density} = \frac{75g}{(50ml - 40ml)}$$

$$\text{Density} = \frac{75g}{10ml} = 7.5g/ml$$

Volume

Table 4–2
Densities of Select Materials (at 20°C Unless Otherwise Stated)

Substance	Density (g/mL)
Solids	
Silver	10.5
Lead	11.5
Iron	7.8
Aluminum	2.7
Window glass	2.47–2.54
Ice (0°C)	0.92
Liquids	
Mercury	13.6
Benzene	0.88
Ethyl alcohol	0.79
Gasoline	0.69
Water at 4°C	1.00
Water at 20°C	0.998
Gases	
Air (0°C)	0.0013
Chlorine (0°C)	0.0032
Oxygen (0°C)	0.0014
Carbon dioxide (0°C)	0.0020

The volumes of gases and liquids vary considerably with temperature; hence, when determining density, it is important to control and record the temperature at which the measurements are made. For example, 1 gram of water occupies a volume of 1 milliliter at 4°C and thus has a density of 1.0 g/mL. However, as the temperature of water increases, its volume expands. Therefore, at 20°C (room temperature), 1 gram of water occupies a volume of 1.002 mL and has a density of 0.998 g/mL.

The observation that a solid object either sinks, floats, or remains suspended when immersed in a liquid can be accounted for by the property of density. For instance, if the density of a solid is greater than that of the liquid in which it is immersed, the object sinks; if the solid's density is less than that of the liquid, it floats; and when the solid and liquid have equal densities, the solid remains suspended in the liquid medium. As we will see shortly, these observations provide a convenient technique for comparing the densities of solid objects.

Refractive Index

As we noted earlier, the bending of a light wave because of a change in velocity is called refraction. The phenomenon of refraction is apparent when we view an object that is immersed in a transparent medium such as water; because we are accustomed to thinking that light travels in a straight line, we often forget to account for refraction. For instance, suppose a ball is observed at the bottom of a swimming pool; the light rays reflected from the ball travel through the water and into the air to reach the eye. As the rays leave the water and enter the air, their velocity suddenly increases, causing them to be refracted. However, because of our assumption that light travels in a straight line, our eyes deceive us and make us think we see an object lying at a higher point than is actually the case. This phenomenon is illustrated in Figure 4–11.

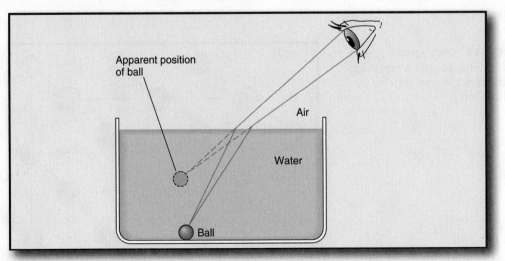

Apparent position of ball

Air

Water

Ball

FIGURE 4-11
Light is refracted when it travels obliquely from one medium to another.

The ratio of the velocity of light in a vacuum to its speed in any medium determines the **refractive index** of that medium and is expressed as follows:

$$\text{Refractive Index} = \frac{\text{velocity of light in vacuum}}{\text{velocity of light in medium}}$$

refractive index
The ratio of the speed of light in a vacuum to its speed in a given medium

EQUATION 4-5

For example, at 25°C the refractive index of water is 1.333. This means that light travels 1.333 times as fast in a vacuum as it does in water at this temperature.

Like density, the refractive index is an intensive physical property of matter and characterizes a substance. However, any procedure used to determine a substance's refractive index must be performed under carefully controlled temperature and lighting conditions, because the refractive index of a substance varies with its temperature and the wavelength of light passing through it. Nearly all tabulated refractive indices are determined at a standard wavelength, usually 589.3 nanometers; this is the predominant wavelength emitted by sodium light and is commonly known as the sodium D light.

When a transparent solid is immersed in a liquid with a similar refractive index, light is not refracted as it passes from the liquid into the solid. For this reason, the eye cannot distinguish the liquid–solid boundary, and the solid seems to disappear from view. This observation, as we will see, offers the forensic scientist a rather simple method for comparing the refractive indices of transparent solids.

Normally, we expect a solid or a liquid to exhibit only one refractive index value for each wavelength of light; however, many crystalline solids have two refractive indices whose values depend in part on the direction from which the light enters the crystal with respect to the crystal axis. **Crystalline solids** have definite geometric forms because of the orderly arrangement of the fundamental particle of a solid, the atom.

In any type of crystal, the relative locations and distances between its atoms repeat throughout the solid. Figure 4–12 shows the crystalline structure of sodium chloride, or ordinary table salt. Sodium chloride is an example of a cubic crystal in which each sodium atom is surrounded by six chlorine atoms and each chlorine atom by six sodium atoms, except at the crystal surface. Not all solids are crystalline; some, such as glass, have their atoms arranged randomly throughout the solid; these materials are known as **amorphous solids**.

crystalline solid
A solid in which the constituent atoms have a regular arrangement

amorphous solid
A solid in which the constituent atoms or molecules are arranged in random or disordered positions

FIGURE 4–12 Diagram of a sodium chloride crystal. Sodium is represented by the dark spheres, chlorine by the light spheres.

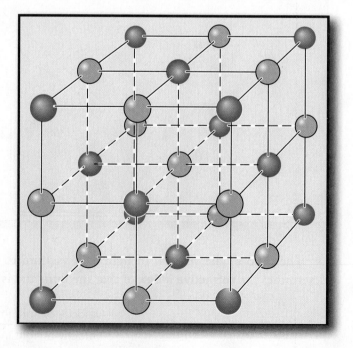

Most crystals, excluding those that have cubic configurations, refract a beam of light into two different light-ray components. This phenomenon, known as double refraction, can be observed by studying the behavior of the crystal calcite. When the calcite is laid on a printed page, the observer sees not one but two images of each word covered. The two light rays that create the double image are refracted at different angles, and each has a different refractive index value. The indices of refraction for calcite are 1.486 and 1.658, and subtracting the two values yields a difference of 0.172; this difference is known as **birefringence**. Thus, the optical properties of crystals provide points of identification that help characterize them.

Now that we have investigated various chemical and physical properties of objects, we are ready to apply some of these properties to the characterization of glass, an item of evidence frequently retrieved at crime scenes and often sent to the crime laboratory for examination.

birefringence
A difference in the two indices of refraction exhibited by most crystalline materials

Quick Review

- Temperature is a measure of heat intensity, or the amount of heat in a substance.

- In science, the most commonly used temperature scale is the Celsius scale, which is derived by assigning the freezing point of water a value of 0°C and its boiling point a value of 100°C.

- Weight is the force with which gravity attracts a body. Mass is a constant property of matter that reflects the amount of material present.

- The formula for calculating the density of an object is mass per unit volume.

- The ratio of the velocity of light in a vacuum to its speed in any medium determines the refractive index of that medium.

- Crystalline solids have definite geometric forms because of the orderly arrangement of their atoms.

- Crystalline solids refract a beam of light in two different light-ray components, resulting in double refraction. Birefringence is the numerical difference between these two refractive indices.

Forensic Analysis of Glass

Glass that is broken and shattered into fragments and minute particles during the commission of a crime can be used to place a suspect at the crime scene. For example, chips of broken glass from a window may lodge in a suspect's shoes or garments during a burglary; particles of headlight glass found at the scene of a hit-and-run accident may confirm the identity of a suspect vehicle. All of these possibilities require the comparison of glass fragments found on the suspect, whether a person or vehicle, with the shattered glass remaining at the crime scene.

Composition of Glass

Glass is a hard, brittle, amorphous substance composed of sand (silicon oxides) mixed with various metal oxides. When sand is mixed with other metal oxides, melted at high temperatures, and then cooled to a rigid condition without crystallization, the product is glass. Soda (sodium carbonate) is normally added to the sand to lower its melting point and make it easier to work with. Another necessary ingredient is lime (calcium oxide), which is added to prevent the "soda-lime" glass from dissolving in water. The forensic scientist is often asked to analyze soda-lime glass, which is used for manufacturing most window and bottle glass. Usually the molten glass is cooled on top of a bath of molten tin. This manufacturing process produces flat glass typically used for windows. This type of glass is called float glass.

The common metal oxides found in soda-lime glass are sodium, calcium, magnesium, and aluminum. In addition, a wide variety of special glasses can be made by substituting in whole or in part other metal oxides for the silica, sodium, and calcium oxides. For example, automobile headlights and heat-resistant glass, such as Pyrex, are manufactured by adding boron oxide to the oxide mix. These glasses are therefore known as borosilicates.

Another type of glass that the reader may be familiar with is **tempered glass**. This glass is made stronger than ordinary window glass by introducing stress through rapid heating and cooling of the glass surfaces. When tempered glass breaks, it does not shatter but rather fragments or "dices" into small squares with little splintering (see Figure 4–13). Because of this safety feature, tempered glass is used in the side and rear windows of automobiles sold in the United States. The windshields of all cars manufactured in the United States are constructed from **laminated glass**. This glass derives its strength by sandwiching one layer of plastic between two pieces of ordinary window glass.

tempered glass
Glass to which strength is added by introducing stress through rapid heating and cooling of the glass surfaces

laminated glass
Two sheets of ordinary glass bonded together with a plastic film

FIGURE 4-13 When tempered glass breaks, it usually holds together without splintering. *Courtesy Robert Ilewellyn, Alamy Images*

Comparing Glass Fragments

For the forensic scientist, comparing glass consists of finding and measuring the properties that will associate one glass fragment with another while minimizing or eliminating the possible existence of other sources. Considering the prevalence of glass in our society, it is easy to appreciate the magnitude of this analytical problem. Obviously, glass possesses its greatest evidential value when it can be individualized to one source. Such a determination, however, can be made only when the suspect and crime-scene fragments are assembled and physically fitted together. Comparisons of this type require piecing together irregular edges of broken glass as well as matching all irregularities and striations on the broken surfaces (see Figure 4–14). The possibility that two pieces of glass originating from different sources will fit together exactly is so unlikely as to exclude all other sources from practical consideration.

FIGURE 4-14   Match of broken glass. Note the physical fit of the edges. *Courtesy Sirchie Finger Print Laboratories, Inc., Youngsville, N.C., www.sirchie.com*

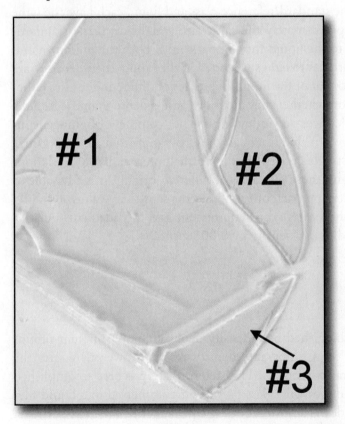

Unfortunately, most glass evidence is either too fragmentary or too minute to permit a comparison of this type. In such instances, the search for individual properties has proven fruitless. For example, the general chemical composition of various window glasses within the capability of current analytical methods has so far been found to be relatively uniform among various manufacturers and thus offers no basis for individualization. However, as more sensitive analytical techniques are developed, trace elements present in glass may prove to be distinctive and measurable characteristics.

The physical properties of density and refractive indexes are used most successfully for characterizing glass particles. However, these properties are class characteristics, which cannot provide the sole criteria for individualizing glass to a common source. They do, however, give the analyst sufficient data to evaluate the significance of a glass comparison, and the absence of comparable density and refractive index values will certainly exclude glass fragments that originate from different sources.

Measuring and Comparing Density

Recall that a solid particle will either float, sink, or remain suspended in a liquid, depending on its density relative to the liquid medium. This knowledge gives the criminalist a rather precise and rapid method for comparing densities of glass.

In a method known as flotation, a standard/reference glass particle is immersed in a liquid; a mixture of bromoform and bromobenzene may be used. The composition of the liquid is carefully adjusted by adding small amounts of bromoform or bromobenzene until the glass chip remains suspended in the liquid medium. At this point, the standard/reference glass and liquid each have the same density. Glass chips of approximately the same size and shape as the standard/reference are now added to the liquid for comparison. If both the unknown and the standard/reference particles remain suspended in the liquid, their densities are equal to each other and to that of the liquid.[1] Particles of different densities either sink or float, depending on whether they are more or less dense than the liquid.

The density of a single sheet of window glass is not completely homogeneous throughout. It has a range of values that can differ by as much as 0.0003 g/mL. Therefore, in order to distinguish between the normal internal density variations of a single sheet of glass and those of glasses of different origins, it is advisable to let the comparative density approach but not exceed a sensitivity value of 0.0003 g/mL. The flotation method meets this requirement and can adequately distinguish glass particles that differ in density by 0.001 g/mL.

Determining and Comparing Refractive Index

Once glass has been distinguished by a density determination, different origins are immediately concluded. Comparable density results, however, require the added comparison of refractive indices. This determination is best accomplished by the immersion method. For this, glass particles are immersed in a liquid medium whose refractive index is adjusted until it equals that of the glass particles. At this point, known as the match point, the observer notes the disappearance of the **Becke line**, indicating minimum contrast between the glass and liquid medium. The Becke line is a bright halo observed near the border of a particle that is immersed in a liquid of a different refractive index. This halo disappears when the medium and fragment have similar refractive indices.

The refractive index of an immersion fluid is best adjusted by changing the temperature of the liquid. Temperature control is, of course, critical to the success of the procedure. One approach is to heat the liquid in a special apparatus known as a hot stage (see Figure 4–15). The glass is immersed in a boiling liquid, usually a silicone oil, and heated at the rate of 0.2°C per minute until the match point

Becke line
A bright halo observed near the border of a particle immersed in a liquid of a different refractive index

FIGURE 4-15 Hot-stage microscope. *Courtesy Chris Palenik, Microtrace, Elgin, IL, www.microtracescientific. com*

is reached. The examiner then observes the disappearance of the Becke line on minute glass particles that are illuminated with sodium D light or at other wavelengths of light. If all the glass fragments examined have similar match points, it can be concluded that they have comparable refractive indices (see Figure 4–16). Furthermore, the examiner can determine the refractive index value of the immersion fluid as it changes with temperature. With this information, the exact numerical value of the glass refractive index can be calculated at the match point temperature.[2]

As with density, glass fragments removed from a single sheet of plate glass may not have a uniform refractive index value; instead, their values may vary by as much as 0.0002. Hence, for comparison purposes, the difference in refractive index between a standard/reference and questioned glass must exceed this value. This allows the examiner to differentiate between the normal internal variations present in a sheet of glass and those present in glasses that originated from completely different sources.

FIGURE 4-16 Determining the refractive index of glass. (a) Glass particles are immersed in a liquid of a much higher refractive index at a temperature of 77°C. (b) At 87°C the liquid still has a higher refractive index than the glass. (c) The refractive index of the liquid is closest to that of the glass at 97°C, as shown by the disappearance of the glass and the Becke lines. (d) At the higher temperature of 117°C, the liquid has a much lower index than the glass, and the glass is plainly visible. *Courtesy Walter C. McCrone*

Classification of Glass Samples

A significant difference in either density or refractive index proves that the glasses examined do not have a common origin. But what if two pieces of glass exhibit comparable densities and comparable refractive indices? How certain can one be that they did, indeed, come from the same source? After all, there are untold millions of windows and other glass objects in this world.

To provide a reasonable answer to this question, the FBI Laboratory has collected density and refractive index values from glass submitted to it for examination. What has emerged is a data bank correlating these values to their frequency of occurrence in the glass population of the United States. This collection is available to all forensic laboratories in the United States. This means that once a criminalist has completed a comparison of glass fragments, he or she can correlate their density and refractive index values to their frequency of occurrence and assess the probability that the fragments came from the same source.

Figure 4–17 shows the distribution of refractive index values (measured with sodium D light) for approximately two thousand glasses analyzed by the FBI. The wide distribution of values clearly demonstrates that the refractive index is

Inside the Science

GRIM 3

An automated approach for measuring the refractive index of glass fragments by temperature control using the immersion method with a hot stage is with the instrument known as GRIM 3 (glass refractive index measurement)* (see Figure 1). The GRIM 3 is a personal computer/video system designed to automate the measurements of the match temperature and refractive index for glass fragments. This instrument uses a video camera to view the glass fragments as they are being heated. As the immersion oil is heated or cooled, the contrast of the video image is measured continually until a minimum, the match point, is detected (see Figure 2). The match point temperature is then converted to a refractive index using stored calibration data.

*Note: There is a 5-degree error factor with this formula. This means that calculations are good to plus or minus 5 degrees of the actual value of the angle of impact. The measurements for length and width should be made with a ruler, micrometer, or photographic loupe.

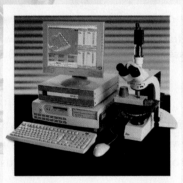

FIGURE 1 An automated system for glass fragment identification. *Courtesy Foster & Freeman, Worcestershire, U.K., www. fosterfreeman.co.uk*

FIGURE 2 GRIM 3 identifies the refraction match point by monitoring a video image of glass fragment immersed in an oil. As the immersion oil is heated or cooled, the contrast of the image is measured continuously until a minimum, the match point, is detected. *Courtesy Foster & Freeman, Worcestershire, U.K., www.fosterfreeman.co.uk*

a highly distinctive property of glass and is thus useful for defining its frequency of occurrence and hence its evidential value. For example, a glass fragment with a refractive index value of 1.5290 is found in approximately only 1 out of 2,000 specimens, while glass with a value of 1.5180 occurs approximately in 22 glasses out of 2,000.

FIGURE 4-17 Frequency of occurence of refractive index values (measured with sodium D light) for approximately two thousand flat glass specimens received by the FBI Laboratory. *Courtesy FBI Laboratory, Washington, D.C.*

The distinction between tempered and nontempered glass particles can be made by slowly heating and then cooling the glass (a process known as annealing). The change in the refractive index value for tempered glass upon annealing is significantly greater when compared to nontempered glass and thus serves as a point of distinction.[3]

Glass Fractures

radial fracture
A crack in a glass that extends outward like the spoke of a wheel from the point at which the glass was struck

concentric fracture
A crack in a glass that forms a rough circle around the point of impact

Glass bends in response to any force that is exerted on any one of its surfaces; when the limit of its elasticity is reached, the glass fractures. Frequently, fractured window glass reveals information about the force and direction of an impact; such knowledge may be useful for reconstructing events at a crime-scene investigation.

The penetration of ordinary window glass by a projectile, whether a bullet or a stone, produces a familiar fracture pattern in which cracks both radiate outward and encircle the hole, as shown in Figure 4–18. The radiating lines are appropriately known as **radial fractures**, and the circular lines are termed **concentric fractures**.

FIGURE 4-18 Radial and concentric fracture lines in a sheet of glass. *Courtesy Sirchie Finger Print Laboratories, Inc., Youngsville, N.C., www. sirchie.com*

Often it is difficult to determine just from the size and shape of a hole in glass whether it was made by a bullet or by some other projectile. For instance, a small stone thrown at a comparatively high speed against a pane of glass often produces a hole very similar to that produced by a bullet. On the other hand, a large stone can completely shatter a pane of glass in a manner closely resembling the result of a close-range shot. However, in the latter instance, the presence of gunpowder deposits on the shattered glass fragments points to damage caused by a firearm.

When it penetrates glass, a high-velocity projectile such as a bullet often leaves a round, crater-shaped hole surrounded by a nearly symmetrical pattern of radial and concentric cracks. The hole is inevitably wider on the exit side (see Figure 4–19), and hence examining it is an important step in determining the direction of impact. However, as the velocity of the penetrating projectile decreases, the irregularity of the shape of the hole and of its surrounding cracks increases, so that at some point the hole shape will not help determine the direction of impact. At this point, examining the radial and concentric fracture lines may help determine the direction of impact.

FIGURE 4-19 Crater-shaped hole made by a projectile passing through glass. The upper surface is the exit side of the projectile. *Courtesy Getty Images, Inc.-Photodisc/Royalty Free*

When a force pushes on one side of a pane of glass, the elasticity of the glass permits it to bend in the direction of the force applied. Once the elastic limit is exceeded, the glass begins to crack. As shown in Figure 4–20, the first fractures form on the surface opposite that of the penetrating force and develop into radial lines. The continued motion of the force places tension on the front surface of the glass, resulting in the formation of concentric cracks. An examination of the edges of the radial and concentric cracks frequently reveals stress markings (Wallner lines) whose shape can be related to the side on which the window first cracked.

FIGURE 4-20 Production of radial and concentric fractures in glass. (a) Radial cracks are formed first, beginning on the side of the glass opposite to the destructive force. (b) Concentric cracks occur afterward, starting on the same side as the force.

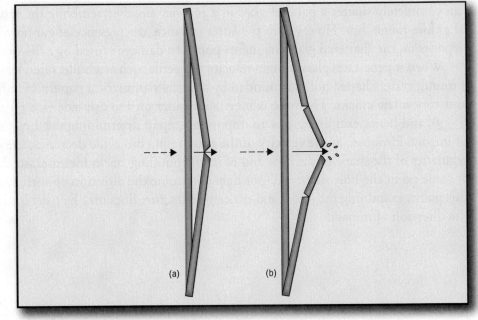

(a)   (b)

Stress marks, shown in Figure 4–21, are shaped like arches that are perpendicular to one glass surface and curved nearly parallel to the opposite surface. The importance of stress marks stems from the observation that the perpendicular edge always faces the surface on which the crack originated. Thus, in examining the stress marks on the edge of a radial crack near the point of impact, the perpendicular end is always found opposite the side from which the force of impact was applied. For a concentric fracture, the perpendicular end always faces the surface on which the force originated. A convenient way for remembering these observations is the 3R rule—Radial cracks form a Right angle on the Reverse side of the force. These facts enable the examiner to determine the side on which a window was broken. Unfortunately, the absence of radial or concentric fracture lines prevents these observations from being applied to broken tempered glass.

FIGURE 4-21 Stress marks on the edge of a radial glass fracture. Arrow indicates direction of force.

When there have been successive penetrations of glass, it is frequently possible to determine the sequence of impact by observing the existing fracture lines and their points of termination. A fracture always terminates at an existing line of fracture. In Figure 4–22, the fracture on the left preceded that on the right; we know this because the latter's radial fracture lines terminate at the cracks of the former.

FIGURE 4-22
Two bullet holes in a piece of glass. The left hole preceded the right hole.

FIGURE 4-23 The presence of black tungsten oxide on the upper filament indicates that the filament was on when it was exposed to air. The lower filament was off, but its surface was coated with a yellow/white tungsten oxide, which was vaporized from the upper ("on") filament and condensed onto the lower filament.

Collection and Preservation of Glass Evidence

The gathering of glass evidence at the crime scene and from the suspect must be thorough if the examiner is to have any chance to individualize the fragments to a common source. If even the remotest possibility exists that fragments may be pieced together, every effort must be made to collect all the glass found. For example, evidence collection at hit-and-run scenes must include all the broken parts of the headlight and reflector lenses. This evidence may ultimately prove invaluable in placing a suspect vehicle at the accident scene by matching the fragments with glass remaining in the headlight or reflector shell of the suspect vehicle. In addition, examining the headlight's filaments may reveal whether an automobile's headlights were on or off before the impact (see Figure 4–23).

When an individual fit is improbable, the evidence collector must submit all glass evidence found in the possession of the suspect along with a sample of broken glass remaining at the crime scene. This standard/reference glass should always be taken from any remaining glass in the window or door frames, as close as possible to the point of breakage. About one square inch of sample is usually adequate for this purpose. The glass fragments should be packaged in solid containers to avoid further breakage. If the suspect's shoes and/or clothing are to be examined for the presence of glass fragments, they should be individually wrapped in paper and transmitted to the laboratory. The field investigator should avoid removing such evidence from garments unless absolutely necessary for its preservation.

When a determination of the direction of impact is desired, all broken glass must be recovered and submitted for analysis. Wherever possible, the exterior and interior surfaces of the glass must be indicated. When this is not immediately apparent, the presence of dirt, paint, grease, or putty may indicate the exterior surface of the glass.

Quick Review

- To compare glass fragments, a forensic scientist evaluates two important physical properties: density and refractive index.

- The immersion method is used to determine a glass fragment's refractive index. It involves immersing a glass particle in a liquid medium whose refractive index is adjusted by varying its temperature. At the refractive index match point the contrast between the glass and liquid is at a minimum.

- The flotation method is used to determine a glass fragment's density. It involves immersing a glass particle in a liquid whose density is carefully adjusted by adding small amounts of an appropriate liquid until the glass chip remains suspended in the liquid medium.

- By analyzing the radial and concentric fracture patterns in glass, the forensic scientist can determine the direction of impact by applying the 3R rule: Radial cracks form a Right angle on the Reverse side of the force.

Chapter Review

- Physical properties such as weight, volume, color, boiling point, and melting point describe a substance without reference to any other substance. A chemical property describes the behavior of a substance when it reacts or combines with another substance.

- Matter is anything that has mass and occupies space. An element is a fundamental particle of matter that cannot be broken down into simpler substances by chemical means.

- The smallest particle of an element that can exist and still retain its identity as that element is the atom.

- A compound is a pure substance composed of two or more elements. The smallest unit of a compound is a molecule.

- The three states of matter are solid, liquid, and gas.

- Sublimation is a change of state from a solid to a gas.

- A phase is a uniform body of matter distinguished from other matter by definite visible boundaries.

- Dispersion is the process of separating light into component colors. Because each color corresponds to a different range of frequencies or wavelengths of light, light rays of one color bend to a different degree than rays of all other colors.

- Refraction is the bending of light waves because of a change in velocity.

- Forensic scientists have learned to characterize different chemical substances by the type and quantity of light they absorb.

- Different types of electromagnetic radiation are distinguished from one another by their frequency or wavelength.

- As long as electromagnetic radiation is moving through space, its behavior can be described as that of a continuous wave. However, once radiation is absorbed by a substance, the model of light as a stream of discrete particles (photons) must be invoked to describe its behavior.

- Temperature is a measure of heat intensity, or the amount of heat in a substance.

- In science, the most commonly used temperature scale is the Celsius scale, which is derived by assigning the freezing point of water a value of 0°C and its boiling point a value of 100°C.

- Weight is the force with which gravity attracts a body. Mass is a constant property of matter that reflects the amount of material present.

- The formula for calculating the density of an object is mass per unit volume.

- The ratio of the velocity of light in a vacuum to its speed in any medium determines the refractive index of that medium.

- Crystalline solids have definite geometric forms because of the orderly arrangement of their atoms.

- Crystalline solids refract a beam of light in two different light-ray components, resulting in double refraction. Birefringence is the numerical difference between these two refractive indices.

- To compare glass fragments, a forensic scientist evaluates two important physical properties: density and refractive index.

- The immersion method is used to determine a glass fragment's refractive index. It involves immersing a glass particle in a liquid medium whose refractive index is adjusted by varying its temperature. At the refractive index match point the contrast between the glass and liquid is at a minimum.

- The flotation method is used to determine a glass fragment's density. It involves immersing a glass particle in a liquid whose density is carefully adjusted by adding small amounts of an appropriate liquid until the glass chip remains suspended in the liquid medium.

- By analyzing the radial and concentric fracture patterns in glass, the forensic scientist can determine the direction of impact by applying the 3R rule: Radial cracks form a Right angle on the Reverse side of the force.

Quick Lab: Glass and Density
Materials:

Meter sticks
Rulers/tape measures
Student worksheets

Procedure:

Density can be used to determine what type of glass evidence we are dealing with. Not all glass objects are made of the same type of glass, so it is important to determine what type of glass we have as evidence. Make sure when handling glass to use the forceps and not your fingers; be careful! First measure and record the mass of the piece of glass in grams using the scale. Fill the beaker with enough water that the glass will be covered when placed in it and record the amount in milliliters. Then place the piece of glass in the water and again record the new measurement from the beaker. Now subtract the first (just water) measurement from the second (water and glass) measurement; this is the volume of the glass. Determine the density of the glass by dividing the mass by the volume. Complete this for all the glass types.

Follow-Up Questions:

1. What are some different objects that would be found as glass evidence?

2. Before your teacher reveals what density each type of glass was, try to guess which type of glass would be denser. Which type would be less dense? Why?

3. What is an intensive property?

Review Questions

1. Which of the following is not a physical state of matter?
   a. solid
   b. plasma
   c. liquid
   d. vapor

2. If the density of a solid is greater than the liquid medium in which it is immersed, the object will
   a. sink.
   b. float.
   c. be suspended in the medium.
   d. lose density.

3. A bright halo that is observed near the border of a particle immersed in a liquid of a different refractive index is known as
   a. birefringence.
   b. the Becke line.
   c. a type line.
   d. the refraction point.

4. Wavelength is
   a. the distance between crests of adjacent waves.
   b. the speed of a wave.
   c. the distance from the crest of a wave to the trough.
   d. the number of waves that pass a given point in a second.

5. Refractive index measures the speed of light in a vacuum to its speed in
   a. air.
   b. water.
   c. glass.
   d. any given substance.

6. True or False: Visible light is only a small part of a large family of radiation that lies outside the range of the electromagnetic spectrum.

7. True or False: The physical properties of density and refractive index are used most successfully for characterizing glass particles.

8. True or False: A significant difference in either density or refractive index proves that the glasses examined have a common origin.

9. True or False: A high-velocity projectile, such as a bullet, will often leave a round, crater-shaped hole that is surrounded by a nearly symmetrical pattern of radial and concentric cracks.

10. True or False: The "3R rule" states that "radial cracks form a right angle on the reverse side of the force."

11. What is the difference between a physical property and a chemical property?

12. Define *matter* and *element*. How are matter and elements related?

13. What is the smallest particle of an element that can exist and still retain its identity?

14. What is a compound? Name three common compounds and give the chemical symbol for each.

15. What is the smallest unit of a compound?

16. Name the three states of matter. What chemical property of a substance determines its state?

17. What is sublimation?

18. What is a phase? Give an example of a two-phase system.

19. Define *dispersion* and explain how it is related to wavelength and frequency.

20. What is refraction?

21. Explain how color is related to the behavior of light. How do forensic scientists use this knowledge in their work?

22. What property distinguishes different types of electromagnetic radiation from one another?

23. Define *temperature* and name the two most common temperature scales.

24. What is weight? How does weight differ from mass?

25. How is the mass of an object determined? List three devices used for comparing the masses of different objects.

26. What is the formula for calculating the density of an object?

27. What is an intensive property? Name three intensive properties of matter.

28. What is the main ingredient in ordinary glass?

29. What kind of glass is used commonly in bottles and windows? How did this type of glass acquire its name?

30. What are tempered glass and laminated glass? On what part of an automobile is each type typically used?

31. What is the only way to individualize glass fragments found at a crime scene to a single source?

32. What physical properties are used most often to characterize glass particles? What is the main drawback of using these properties to characterize glass?

33. Define *flotation* and describe how it works.

34. Describe how a forensic scientist determines the refractive indices of suspect glass fragments.

35. How might a forensic scientist tell which of two fractures on a piece of glass was created earlier?

Application and Critical Thinking

1. Use metric conversions to answer the following questions:
 a. Who is taller—someone who measures 6 feet, 3 inches, or someone who measures 1.9 meters?
 b. Which is heavier—a package that weighs 210 pounds or one that weighs 90 kilograms?
 c. Which holds more water—a 2-gallon bottle or an 8-liter bottle?

2. The following table shows the force of gravity on other planets relative to the force of gravity on the earth. For example, the force of gravity on the moon is only 0.166 (about one-sixth) that of the earth.

Table 1
The Force of Gravity on Other Planets

Planet	Gravity Relative to Earth
Mercury	0.378
Venus	0.907
Moon	0.166
Earth	1.000
Mars	0.377
Jupiter	2.533
Saturn	1.064
Uranus	0.889
Neptune	1.125
Pluto	0.067

Using this information, along with your knowledge of the difference between mass and weight, answer the following questions:
 a. Which weighs more—a 100-pound Great Dane on Pluto or a 25-pound terrier on Mars?
 b. Which weighs more—a quarter-pound hamburger on Jupiter or a 12-ounce steak on Venus?
 c. Which has a greater mass—a 300-pound football player on Saturn or an 800-pound gorilla on Mercury?
 d. If a car has a mass of 4,500 pounds on the earth, how much will it weigh on Neptune?

3. An accident investigator arrives at the scene of a hit-and-run collision. The driver who remained at the scene reports that the windshield or a side window of the car that struck him shattered on impact. The investigator searches the accident site and collects a large number of fragments of tempered glass. This is the only type of glass recovered from the scene. How can the glass evidence help the investigator locate the vehicle that fled the scene?

4. Indicate the order in which the bullet holes were made in the glass depicted in the figure below. Explain the reason for your answer.

5. The right side of figure below depicts stress marks on the edge of a glass fracture caused by the application of force. If this is a radial fracture, from which side of the glass (left or right) was the force applied? From which side was force applied if it is a concentric fracture? Explain the reason for your answers.

Visual Lab: Forensic Glass Analysis
To perform a virtual glass analysis, go to www.pearsoncustom.com/us/vlm

Endnotes

1. As an added step, the analyst can determine the exact numerical density value of the particles of glass by transferring the liquid to a density meter, which will electrically measure and calculate the liquid's density. See A. P. Beveridge and C. Semen, "Glass Density Measurement Using a Calculating Digital Density Meter," *Canadian Society of Forensic Science Journal 12* (1979): 113.

2. A. R. Cassista and P. M. L. Sandercock, "Precision of Glass Refractive Index Measurements: Temperature Variation and Double Variation Methods, and the Value of Dispersion," *Canadian Society of Forensic Science Journal 27* (1994): 203.

3. G. Edmondstone, "The Identification of Heat Strengthened Glass in Windshields," *Canadian Society of Forensic Science Journal* 30 (1997): 181.

Pablo Escobar, Drug Lord

In 1989, *Forbes* magazine listed Pablo Escobar as the seventh richest man in the world. Escobar began his climb to wealth as a teenage car thief in the streets of Medellin, Colombia, and eventually moved into the cocaine-smuggling business. At the peak of his power in the mid-1980s, he was shipping as much as 11 tons of cocaine per flight in jetliners to the United States. Law enforcement officials estimate that the Medellin cartel controlled 80 percent of the world's cocaine market and was taking in about $25 billion annually.

Escobar ruthlessly ruled by the gun: murdering, assassinating, and kidnapping. He was responsible for killing three presidential candidates in Colombia as well as the storming of the Colombian Supreme Court, which resulted in the murder of half the justices. All the while, Escobar curried favor with the Colombian general public by cultivating a Robin Hood image and distributing money to the poor.

In 1991, hoping to avoid extradition to the United States, Escobar turned himself in to the Colombian government and agreed to be sent to prison. However, the prison compound could easily be mistaken for a country club. There he continued his high-flying lifestyle, trafficking by telephone and even murdering a few associates. When the Colombian government attempted to move Escobar to another jail, he escaped, again fearing extradition to the United States.

Pressured by the U.S. government, Colombia organized a task force dedicated to apprehending Escobar. The manhunt for Escobar ended on December 2, 1993, when he was cornered on the roof of one of his hideouts. A shootout ensued and Escobar was fatally wounded by a bullet behind his ear.

Key Terms

anabolic steroids
analgesic
chromatography
confirmation
depressant
hallucinogen
infrared
ion
microcrystalline test

monochromator
narcotic
physical dependence
psychological dependence
screening test
spectrophotometry
stimulant
ultraviolet

A *drug* can be defined as a natural or synthetic substance that is used to produce physiological or psychological effects in humans or other higher-order animals. However, this colorless clinical definition does not really tell us what drugs are; in their modern context, drugs mean something different to each person. To some, drugs are a necessity for sustaining and prolonging life; to others, drugs provide an escape from the pressures of life; to still others, they are a means of ending it.

Considering the wide application and acceptance of drugs in our society, it was perhaps inevitable that a segment of our population would abuse them. During the 1960s, successive waves of hallucinogens, amphetamines, and barbiturates found their way out of laboratories, pharmacies, and medicine chests and into the streets. During this decade, marijuana became the most widely used illicit drug in the United States, and alcohol consumption continued to rise—today 90 million Americans drink alcohol regularly, and 10 million of these are hopelessly addicted or have severe problems in coping with their drinking habits. In the 1970s, heroin addiction emerged as a national problem, and today the United States is in the midst of an epidemic of cocaine abuse.

FIGURE 5–1
Drug bust.
Courtesy Syracuse Newspapers/The Image Works

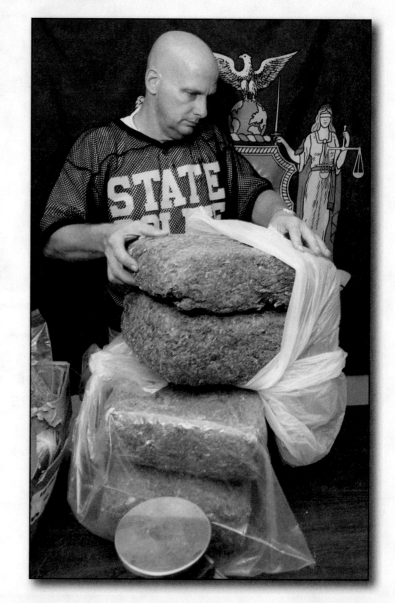

Drug abuse has grown from a problem generally associated with members of the lower end of the socioeconomic ladder to one that cuts across all social and ethnic classes of society. Today, approximately 23 million people in the United States use illicit drugs, including about a half million heroin addicts and nearly six million users of cocaine. In the United States, more than 75 percent of the evidence evaluated in crime laboratories is drug related. The deluge of drug specimens has forced the expansion of existing crime laboratories and the creation of new ones. For many concerned forensic scientists, the crime laboratory's preoccupation with drug evidence represents a serious distraction from time that could be devoted to evaluating evidence related to homicides and other types of serious crimes. However, the increasing caseloads associated with drug evidence have justified the expansion of forensic laboratory services. This expansion has increased the overall analytical capabilities of crime laboratories.

Drug Dependence

In assessing the potential danger of drugs, society has become particularly conscious of their effects on human behavior. In fact, the first drugs to be regulated by law in the early years of the twentieth century were those deemed to have "habit-forming" properties. The early laws were aimed primarily at controlling opium and its derivatives, cocaine, and later marijuana. The ability of a drug to induce dependence after repeated use is submerged in a complex array of physiological and social factors.

Dependence on drugs exists in numerous patterns and in all degrees of intensity, depending on the nature of the drug, the route of administration, the dose, the frequency of administration, and the individual's rate of metabolism. Furthermore, nondrug factors play an equally crucial role in determining the behavioral patterns associated with drug use. The personal characteristics of the user, his or her expectations about the drug experience, society's attitudes and possible responses, and the setting in which the drug is used are all major determinants of drug dependence.

The question of how to define and measure a drug's influence on the individual and its danger to society is difficult to assess. The nature and significance of drug dependence must be considered from two overlapping points of view: the interaction of the drug with the individual, and the drug's impact on society. It will be useful to approach the problem from two distinctly different aspects of human behavior—**psychological dependence** and **physical dependence**.

Psychological Dependence

The common denominator that characterizes all types of repeated drug use is the creation of a psychological dependence for continued use of the drug. It is important to discard the unrealistic image that all drug users are hopeless "addicts" who are social dropouts. Most users present quite a normal appearance and remain both socially and economically integrated in the life of the community.

The reasons why some people abstain from drugs while others become moderately or heavily involved are difficult if not impossible to delineate. Psychological needs arise from numerous personal and social factors that inevitably stem

psychological dependence
The conditioned use of a drug caused by underlying emotional needs

physical dependence
Physiological need for a drug brought about by its regular use and characterized by withdrawal sickness when administration of the drug abruptly stops

from the individual's desire to create a sense of well-being and to escape from reality. In some cases, the individual may seek relief from personal problems or stressful situations, or may be trying to sustain a physical and emotional state that permits an improved level of performance. Whatever the reasons, the underlying psychological needs and the desire to fulfill them create a conditioned pattern of drug abuse (see Figure 5–2).

FIGURE 5–2
Young people drinking.
*Courtesy Daytona Beach
News-Journal/Jim Tiller/
AP Wide World Photos*

The intensity of the psychological dependence associated with a drug's use is difficult to define and largely depends on the nature of the drug used. For drugs such as alcohol, heroin, amphetamines, barbiturates, and cocaine, continued use will likely result in a high degree of involvement. Other drugs, such as marijuana and codeine, appear to have a considerably lower potential for the development of psychological dependence. However, this does not imply that repeated abuse of drugs deemed to have a low potential for psychological dependence is safe or will always produce low psychological dependence. We have no precise way to measure or predict the impact of drug abuse on the individual. Even if a system could be devised for controlling the many possible variables affecting a user's response, the unpredictability of the human personality would still have to be considered.

Our general knowledge of alcohol consumption should warn us of the fallacy of generalizing when attempting to describe the danger of drug abuse. Obviously, not all alcohol drinkers are psychologically addicted to the drug; most are "social" drinkers who drink in reasonable amounts and on an irregular basis. Many people have progressed beyond this stage and consider alcohol a necessary crutch for dealing with life's stresses and anxieties. However, alcohol abusers exhibit a wide range of behavioral patterns, and to a large extent the determination of the degree of psychological dependence must be made individually. Likewise, it would be wrong to generalize that all users of marijuana can at worst develop a low degree of dependence on the drug. A wide range of factors also influence marijuana's effect, and heavy users of the drug expose themselves to the danger of developing a high degree of psychological dependence.

Physical Dependence

Although emotional well-being is the primary motive leading to repeated and intensive use of a drug, certain drugs, taken in sufficient dose and frequency, can produce physiological changes that encourage their continued use. Once the user abstains from such a drug, severe physical illness follows. The desire to avoid this withdrawal sickness, or abstinence syndrome, ultimately causes physical dependence, or addiction. Hence, for the addict who is accustomed to receiving large doses of heroin, the thought of abstaining and encountering body chills, vomiting, stomach cramps, convulsions, insomnia, pain, and hallucinations is a powerful inducement for continued drug use.

Interestingly, some of the more widely abused drugs have little or no potential for creating physical dependence. Drugs such as marijuana, LSD, and cocaine create strong anxieties when their repeated use is discontinued; however, no medical evidence attributes these discomforts to physiological reactions that accompany withdrawal sickness. On the other hand, use of alcohol, heroin, and barbiturates can result in development of physical dependence.

Physical dependence develops only when the drug user adheres to a regular schedule of drug intake; that is, the interval between doses must be short enough so that the effects of the drug never wear off completely. For example, the interval between injections of heroin for the drug addict probably does not exceed six to eight hours. Beyond this time the addict begins to experience the uncomfortable symptoms of withdrawal. Many heroin users avoid taking the drug regularly for fear of becoming physically addicted to its use. Similarly, the risk of developing physical dependence on alcohol becomes greatest when the consumption is characterized by a continuing pattern of daily use in large quantities.

Table 5–1 categorizes some of the more commonly abused drugs according to their effect on the body and summarizes their tendency to produce psychological dependence and to induce physical dependence with repeated use.

Societal Aspects of Drug Use

The social impact of drug dependence is directly related to the extent to which the user has become preoccupied with the drug. Here, the most important element is the extent to which drug use has become interwoven in the fabric of the user's life. The more frequently the drug satisfies the person's need, the greater the likelihood that he or she will become preoccupied with its use, with a consequent neglect of individual and social responsibilities. Personal health, economic relationships, and family obligations may all suffer as the drug-seeking behavior increases in frequency and intensity and dominates the individual's life. Extreme drug dependence may lead to behavior that has serious implications for the public's safety, health, and welfare.

Table 5–1
**The Potential of Some Commonly Abused Drugs
to Produce Dependence with Regular Use**

Drug	Psychological Dependence	Physical Dependence
Narcotics		
Morphine	High	Yes
Heroin	High	Yes
Methadone	High	Yes
Codeine	Low	Yes
Depressants		
Barbiturates (short-acting)	High	Yes
Barbiturates (long-acting)	Low	Yes
Alcohol	High	Yes
Methaqualone (Quaalude)	High	Yes
Meprobamate (Miltown, Equanil)	Moderate	Yes
Diazepam (Valium)	Moderate	Yes
Chlordiazepoxide (Librium)	Moderate	Yes
Stimulants		
Amphetamines	High	Unknown
Cocaine	High	No
Caffeine	Low	No
Nicotine	High	Yes
Hallucinogens		
Marijuana	Low	No
LSD	Low	No
Phencyclidine (PCP)	High	No

Drug dependence in its broadest sense involves much of the world's population. As a result, a complex array of individual, social, cultural, legal, and medical factors ultimately influence society's decision to prohibit or impose strict controls on a drug's distribution and use. Invariably, society must weigh the beneficial aspects of the drug against the ultimate harm its abuse will do to the individual and to society as a whole. Obviously, many forms of drug dependence do not carry sufficient adverse social consequences to warrant their prohibition, as illustrated by the widespread use of such drug-containing substances as tobacco and coffee. Although the heavy and prolonged use of these drugs may eventually damage body organs and injure an individual's health, there is no evidence that they result in antisocial behavior, even with prolonged or excessive use. Hence, society is willing to accept the widespread use of these substances.

We are certainly all aware of the disastrous failure in the United States to prohibit the use of alcohol during the 1920s and the current debate on whether marijuana should be legalized. Each of these issues emphasizes the delicate balance between individual desires and needs and society's concern with the consequences of drug abuse; moreover, this balance is continuously subject to change and re-evaluation.

> **Quick Review**
> - A drug is a natural or synthetic substance that is used to produce physiological or psychological effects in humans or other animals.
>
> - Nondrug factors that play a part in drug dependence include the personal characteristics of the user, his or her expectations about the drug experience, society's attitudes and possible responses, and the setting in which the drug is used.
>
> - Physical dependence is defined as the physiological need for a drug that has been brought about by its regular use. Psychological dependence is the conditioned use of a drug caused by underlying emotional needs.

Types of Drugs

Narcotic Drugs

The term **narcotic** is derived from the Greek word *narkotikos*, meaning numbness or deadening. Although pharmacologists classify narcotic drugs as substances that relieve pain and produce sleep, the term narcotic has become popularly associated with any drug that is socially unacceptable. As a consequence of this incorrect usage, many drugs are improperly called narcotics.

This confusion has produced legal definitions that differ from the pharmacological actions of many drugs. For example, until the early 1970s, most drug laws in the United States incorrectly designated marijuana as a narcotic. Even today, federal law classifies cocaine as a narcotic drug, although pharmacologically, cocaine is actually a powerful central nervous system stimulant, possessing properties opposite those normally associated with the depressant effects of a narcotic.

Opiates Medical professionals apply the term opiate to most of the drugs properly classified as narcotics. Opiates behave pharmacologically like morphine, a painkiller derived from opium—a gummy, milky juice exuded through a cut made in the unripe pod of the Asian poppy (Papaver somniferium). Although morphine is readily extracted from opium, the most commonly used opium-based drug is heroin, which is produced by reacting morphine with acetic anhydride or acetyl chloride (see Figure 5–3). Heroin's high solubility in water makes its street preparation for intravenous administration rather simple, because only by injection are heroin's effects felt almost instantaneously and with maximum sensitivity. The solution is drawn into a syringe or eyedropper for injection under the skin (see Figure 5–4).

narcotic
A drug that induces sleep and depresses vital body functions such as blood pressure, pulse rate, and breathing rate

FIGURE 5–3
The opium poppy and its derivatives. Shown are the poppy plant, crude and smoking opium, codeine, heroin, and morphine.
Courtesy Pearson Education/PH College

FIGURE 5–4
Heroin paraphernalia.
Courtesy Drug Enforcement Administration, Washington, D.C.

analgesic
A substance that lessens or eliminates pain

Heroin and other narcotic drugs are **analgesics**—that is, they relieve pain by depressing the central nervous system. Besides being a powerful analgesic, heroin produces a "high" that is accompanied by drowsiness and a deep sense of well-being. The effect is short, generally lasting only three to four hours. Regular use of heroin—or any other narcotic drug—invariably leads to physical dependence, with all of its dire consequences.

Codeine is also present in opium, but it is usually prepared synthetically from morphine. It is commonly used as a cough suppressant in prescription cough syrup. Codeine, only one-sixth as strong as morphine, is not an attractive street drug for addicts.

Inside the Science

What's in That Bag?

The content of a typical heroin bag is an excellent example of the uncertainty attached to buying illicit drugs. For many years into the 1960s and early 1970s, the average bag contained 15 to 20 percent heroin. Currently, the average purity of heroin obtained in the illicit U.S. market is approximately 35 percent. The addict rarely knows or cares what comprises the other 65 percent or so of the material. Traditionally, quinine has been the most common diluent of heroin. Like heroin, it has a bitter taste and was probably originally used to obscure the actual potency of a heroin preparation from those who wished to taste-test the material before buying it. Other diluents commonly added to heroin are starch, lactose, procaine (Novocain), and mannitol.

Synthetic Opiates A number of narcotic drugs are not naturally derived from opium. However, because they have similar physiological effects on the body as the opium narcotics, they are also commonly referred to as opiates.

Methadone is perhaps the best known synthetic opiate. In the 1960s, scientists discovered that a person who received periodic doses of methadone would not get high if he or she then took heroin or morphine. Although methadone is pharmacologically related to heroin, its administration appears to eliminate the addict's desire for heroin, with minimal side effects. These discoveries led to the establishment of controversial methadone maintenance programs in which heroin addicts receive methadone to reduce or prevent future heroin use. Physicians increasingly prescribe methadone for pain relief. Unfortunately the wide availability of methadone for legitimate medical purposes has recently led to greater quantities of the drug being diverted into the illicit market.

In 1995, the U.S. Food and Drug Administration (FDA) approved for use the pain-killing drug OxyContin. The active ingredient in OxyContin is oxycodone, a synthetic closely related to morphine and heroin in its chemical structure. OxyContin is an analgesic narcotic that has effects similar to those of heroin. It is prescribed to a million patients for treatment of chronic pain, with doctors writing close to seven million OxyContin prescriptions each year. The drug is compounded with a time-release formulation that the manufacturer initially believed would reduce the risk of abuse and addiction. This has not turned out to be the case. It is estimated that close to a quarter of a million individuals abuse the drug.

Because it is a legal drug that is diverted from legitimate sources, OxyContin is obtained differently from illegal drugs. Pharmacy robberies, forged prescriptions, and theft of the drug from patients with a legitimate prescription are ways in which abusers access OxyContin. Some abusers visit numerous doctors and receive prescriptions even though their medical condition may not warrant it.

Hallucinogens

Hallucinogens are drugs that can cause marked alterations in normal thought processes, perceptions, and moods. Perhaps the most popular and controversial member of this class of drugs is marijuana.

hallucinogen
A substance that induces changes in normal thought processes, perceptions, and moods

Marijuana Marijuana easily qualifies as the most widely used illicit drug in the United States today. For instance, more than 43 million Americans have tried marijuana, according to the latest surveys, and almost half that number may be regular users. Marijuana is a preparation derived from the plant Cannabis. Most botanists believe there is only one species of the plant, Cannabis sativa L. The marijuana preparation normally consists of crushed leaves mixed in varying proportions with the plant's flower, stem, and seed. The plant secretes a sticky resin known as hashish. The resinous material can also be extracted from the plant by soaking in a solvent such as alcohol. On the illicit-drug market, hashish usually appears in the form of compressed vegetation containing a high percentage of resin. A potent form of marijuana is known as sinsemilla. This is made from the unfertilized flowering tops of the female Cannabis plants, attained by removing all male plants from the growing field at the first sign of their appearance. It follows that the production of sinsemilla requires a great deal of attention and care, and the plant is therefore cultivated on small plots.

The Cannabis plant contains a chemical known as tetrahydrocannabinol, or THC, which produces the psychoactive effects experienced by users. The THC content of Cannabis varies in different parts of the plant. The greatest concentration is usually found in the resin. Declining concentrations are typically found in the flowers and leaves, respectively. Little THC is found in the stem, roots, or seeds of the plant. The potency and resulting effect of the drug fluctuate, depending on the relative proportion of these plant parts in the marijuana mixture consumed by the user. The most common method of administration is by smoking either the dried flowers and leaves, or various preparations of hashish (see Figure 5–5). Marijuana is also occasionally taken orally, typically baked in sweets such as brownies or cookies.

Any study of marijuana's effect on humans must consider the potency of the marijuana preparation. An interesting insight into the relationship between dosage level and marijuana's pharmacological effect was presented in the first report of the National Commission on Marijuana and Drug Abuse:

> At low, usual "social" doses. the user may experience an increased sense of well-being; initial restlessness and hilarity followed by a dreamy, carefree state of relaxation; alteration of sensory perceptions including expansion of space and time; a more vivid sense of touch, sight, smell, taste, and sound; a feeling of hunger, especially a craving for sweets; and subtle changes in thought formation and expression. To an unknowing observer, an indi-

vidual in this state of consciousness would not appear noticeably different from his normal state.

At higher, moderate doses these same reactions are intensified but the changes in the individual would still be scarcely noticeable to an observer. At very high doses, psychotomimetic phenomena may be experienced. These include distortion of body image, loss of personal identity, sensory and mental illusions, fantasies, and hallucinations.[1]

FIGURE 5-5
Several rolled marijuana cigarettes lie on a pile of crushed dried marijuana leaves next to a tobacco cigarette. *Courtesy Drug Enforcement Administration, Washington, D.C.*

In addition to its widespread illegal use, accumulating evidence suggests that marijuana has potential medical uses. Two promising areas of research are marijuana's reduction of excessive eye pressure in glaucoma and the lessening of nausea caused by powerful anticancer drugs. Marijuana may also be useful as a muscle relaxant.

No current evidence suggests that experimental or intermittent use causes physical or psychological harm. Marijuana does not cause physical dependence. However, the risk of harm lies instead in heavy, long-term use, particularly of the more potent preparations. Heavy users can develop a strong psychological dependence on the drug. Some effects of marijuana use include increased heart rate, dry mouth, reddened eyes, impaired motor skills and concentration, and, frequently, hunger and an increased desire for sweets.

Other Hallucinogens A substantial number of other substances with widely varying chemical compositions are also used recreationally because of their hallucinogenic properties. These include both naturally occurring substances such as mescaline and psilocybin and synthetically created drugs including lysergic acid diethylamide (LSD) and phencyclidine (PCP).

Inside the Science

Marijuana and Hashish

Marijuana is a weed that grows wild under most climatic conditions. The plant grows to a height of 5 to 15 feet and is characterized by an odd number of leaflets on each leaf. Normally, each leaf contains five to nine leaflets, all with serrated or saw-tooth edges (see Figure 1).

The potency of marijuana depends on its form. Marijuana in the form of loose vegetation has an average THC content of about 3–4.5 percent. The more potent sinsemilla form averages about 6–12 percent in THC content.

Hashish preparations average about 2–8 percent THC. On the illicit-drug market, hashish usually appears in the form of compressed vegetation containing a high percentage of resin (see Figure 2). A particularly potent form of hashish is known as *liquid hashish* or *hashish oil*. Hashish in this form is normally a viscous substance, dark green with a tarry consistency.

FIGURE 1 The marijuana leaf. *Courtesy Drug Enforcement Administration, Washington, D.C.*

Liquid hashish is produced by efficiently extracting the THC-rich resin from the marijuana plant with an appropriate solvent, such as alcohol. Liquid hashish typically varies between 8–22 percent in THC content. Because of its extraordinary potency, one drop of the material can produce a "high."

FIGURE 2 Blocks of hashish leaves and flowering tops of the marijuana plant. *Courtesy James King-Holmes, Photo Researchers, Inc.*

Case Files

A Brief History of Marijuana

Marijuana and its related products have been in use legally and illegally for almost three thousand years. The first reference to medical use of marijuana is in a pharmacy book written about 2737 B.C. by the Chinese emperor Shen Nung, who recommended it for "female weakness, gout, rheumatism, malaria, beriberi, constipation, and absent-mindedness." In China, at that time, and even today, the marijuana or hemp plant was also a major source of fiber for rope production. Marijuana's mood-altering powers probably did not receive wide attention until about 1000 B.C., when it became an integral part of Hindu culture in India. After A.D. 500, marijuana began creeping westward, and references to it began to appear in Persian and Arabian literature.

The plant was probably brought to Europe by Napoleon's soldiers when they returned from Egypt in the early 19th century. In Europe, the drug excited the interest of many physicians who foresaw its application for treating a wide range of ailments. At this time, it also found some use as a painkiller and mild sedative. In later years, these applications were either forgotten or ignored.

Marijuana was first introduced into the United States around 1920. The weed was smuggled by Mexican laborers across the border into Texas. American soldiers also brought the plant in from the ports of Havana, Tampico, and Veracruz. Although its use was confined to a small segment of the population, its popularity quickly spread from the border and Gulf states into most major U.S. cities. By 1937, the federal government and 46 states had laws prohibiting the use or possession of marijuana. Under most of these laws, marijuana was subject to the same rigorous penalties applicable to morphine, heroin, and cocaine and was often erroneously designated a narcotic.

LSD is synthesized from lysergic acid, a substance derived from ergot, which is a type of fungus that attacks certain grasses and grains. The drug appears in a variety of forms—as a pill, added to a cube of sugar, or absorbed onto a small piece of paper—and is taken orally. Its hallucinogenic effects were first described by the Swiss chemist Albert Hofmann after he accidentally ingested some of the material in his laboratory in 1943. LSD produces marked changes in mood, leading to laughing or crying at the slightest provocation. Feelings of anxiety and tension almost always accompany LSD use. LSD is very potent; as little as 25 micrograms is enough to start vivid visual hallucinations that can last for about 12 hours. Although physical dependence does not develop with continued use, the individual user may be prone to flashbacks and psychotic reactions even after use is discontinued.

Abuse of the hallucinogen phencyclidine, commonly called PCP, has recently grown to alarming proportions. Because this drug can be synthesized by simple chemical processes, it is manufactured surreptitiously for the illicit market in so-called clandestine laboratories (see Figure 5–6). These laboratories range from large, sophisticated operations to small labs located in a garage or bathroom. Small-time operators normally have little or no training in chemistry and employ "cookbook" methods to synthesize the drug. Some of the more knowledgeable and experienced operators have been able to achieve clandestine production levels that approach a commercial level of operation.

FIGURE 5–6
Scene from a clandestine drug laboratory. *Courtesy Drug Enforcement Administration, Washington, D.C.*

Phencyclidine is often mixed with other drugs, such as LSD or amphetamines, and is sold as a powder ("angel dust"), capsule, or tablet, or as a liquid sprayed on plant leaves. The drug is smoked, ingested, or sniffed. Following oral intake of moderate doses (1–6 milligrams), the user first experiences feelings of strength and invulnerability, along with a dreamy sense of detachment. However, the user soon becomes unresponsive, confused, and agitated. Depression, irritability, feelings of isolation, audio and visual hallucinations, and sometimes paranoia accompany PCP use. Severe depression, tendencies toward violence, and suicide accompany long-term daily use of the drug. In some cases, the PCP user experiences sudden schizophrenic behavior days after the drug has been taken.

Depressants

depressant
A substance that slows down, or depresses, the functions of the central nervous system

Depressants are drugs that slow down, or depress, the central nervous system. Several types of drugs fall under this category, including the most widely used drug in the United States—alcohol.

Alcohol (Ethyl Alcohol) Many people overlook the fact that alcohol is a drug; its major behavioral effects derive from its depressant action on the central nervous system. In the United States, the alcohol industry annually produces more than one billion gallons of spirits, wine, and beer for which 90 million consumers pay nearly $40 billion. Unquestionably, these and other statistics support the fact that alcohol is the most widely used and abused drug.

The behavioral patterns of alcohol intoxication vary and depend in part on such factors as social setting, amount consumed, and the personal expectation of the individual with regard to alcohol. When alcohol enters the body's bloodstream, it quickly travels to the brain, where it suppresses the brain's control of thought processes and muscle coordination.

Low doses of alcohol tend to inhibit the mental processes of judgment, memory, and concentration. The drinker's personality becomes expansive, and he or

FIGURE 5–7
Rows of alcohol bottles behind a bar. *Courtesy Jeremy Liebman/Stone/ Getty Images*

she exudes confidence. When taken in moderate doses, alcohol reduces coordination substantially, inhibits orderly thought processes and speech patterns, and slows reaction times. Under these conditions, the ability to walk or drive becomes noticeably impaired. In the next chapter, we examine in greater detail the relationship between alcohol blood levels and driving ability. Higher doses of alcohol may cause the user to become highly irritable and emotional; displays of anger and crying are not uncommon. Extremely high doses may cause an individual to lapse into unconsciousness or even a comatose state that may precede a fatal depression of circulatory and respiratory functions.

Barbiturates Barbiturates are derivatives of barbituric acid, a substance first synthesized by a German chemist, Adolf von Bayer, more than a hundred years ago. They are commonly referred to as "downers" because they relax the user, create a feeling of well-being, and produce sleep. Like alcohol, barbiturates suppress the vital functions of the central nervous system. Twenty-five barbiturate derivatives are currently used in medical practice in the United States; however, five—amobarbital, secobarbital, phenobarbital, pentobarbital, and butabarbital—tend to be used for most medical applications.

Normally, barbiturate users take these drugs orally. The average sedative dose is about 10–70 milligrams. When taken in this fashion, the drug enters the blood through the walls of the small intestine. Some barbiturates, such as phenobarbital, are classified as long-acting barbiturates. They are absorbed into the bloodstream more slowly than others and therefore produce less pronounced effects than faster-acting barbiturates. The slow action of phenobarbital accounts for its low incidence of abuse. Apparently, barbiturate abusers prefer the faster-acting varieties—secobarbital, pentobarbital, and amobarbital.

Since the early 1970s, a nonbarbiturate depressant, methaqualone (Quaalude), has appeared on the illicit-drug scene. Methaqualone is a powerful sedative and muscle relaxant that possesses many of the depressant properties of barbiturates.

When taken in prescribed amounts, barbiturates are relatively safe, but in instances of extensive and prolonged use, physical dependence can develop.

Antipsychotics and Antianxiety Drugs Although antipsychotics and antianxiety drugs can be considered depressants, they differ from barbiturates in the extent of their actions on the central nervous system. Generally, these drugs produce a relaxing tranquility without impairing high-thinking faculties or inducing sleep. Antipsychotics such as reserpine and chlorpromazine have been used to reduce the anxieties and tensions of mental patients. Antianxiety drugs are commonly prescribed to deal with the everyday tensions of many healthy people. These drugs include meprobamate (Miltown), chlordiazepoxide (Librium), and diazepam (Valium).

In the past 35 years, the use of these drugs—particularly antianxiety drugs—has grown dramatically. Medical evidence shows that these drugs produce psychological and physical dependence with repeated and high levels of usage. For this reason, the widespread prescribing of antianxiety drugs to overcome the pressures and tensions of life has worried many who fear the creation of a legalized drug culture.

"Huffing" Since the early 1960s, "huffing," the practice of sniffing materials containing volatile solvents (airplane glue or model cement, for example), has grown in popularity. Another dimension has recently been added to the problem with the increasing number of incidents involving the sniffing of aerosol gas propellants, such as freon. All materials abused by huffing contain volatile or gaseous substances that are primarily central nervous system depressants. Although toluene (a solvent used in airplane glue) seems to be the most popular solvent to sniff, others can produce comparable physiological effects. These chemicals include naphtha, methyl ethyl ketone (antifreeze), gasoline, and trichloroethylene (dry-cleaning solvent).

The usual immediate effects of huffing are a feeling of exhilaration and euphoria combined with slurred speech, impaired judgment, and double vision. Finally, the user may experience drowsiness and stupor, with these depressant effects slowly wearing off as the user returns to a normal state. Most experts believe that users become physiologically dependent on the effects achieved by huffing. However, little evidence suggests that solvent inhalation is addictive. But huffers expose themselves to the dangers of liver, heart, and brain damage from the chemicals they have inhaled. Even worse, sniffing of some solvents, particularly halogenated hydrocarbons such as freon and related gases, is accompanied by a significant risk of death.

Stimulants

The term **stimulant** refers to a range of drugs that stimulate, or speed up, the central nervous system.

Amphetamines Amphetamines are a group of synthetic stimulants that share a similar chemical structure and are commonly referred to in the terminology of the drug culture as "uppers" or "speed." They are typically taken either orally or via intravenous injection and provide a feeling of well-being and increased alert-

stimulant
A substance that speeds up, or stimulates, the central nervous system

ness that is followed by a decrease in fatigue and a loss of appetite. However, these apparent benefits of the drug are accompanied by restlessness and instability or apprehension, and once the stimulant effect wears off, depression may set in.

In the United States, the most serious form of amphetamine abuse stems from intravenous injection of amphetamine or its chemical derivative, methamphetamine (see Figure 5–8). The desire for a more intense amphetamine experience is the primary motive for this route of administration. The initial sensation of a "flash" or "rush," followed by an intense feeling of pleasure, constitutes the principal appeal of the intravenous route for the user. During a "speed binge," the individual may inject 500–1,000 milligrams of amphetamines every two to three hours. Users have reported experiencing a euphoria that produces hyperactivity, with a feeling of clarity of vision as well as hallucinations. As the effect of the amphetamines wears off, the individual lapses into a period of exhaustion and may sleep continuously for one or two days. Following this, the user often experiences a prolonged period of severe depression, lasting from days to weeks.

FIGURE 5–8
Granular amphetamine beside a razor blade. *Courtesy Cordelia Molloy, Photo Researchers, Inc.*

A smokable form of methamphetamine known as "ice" is reportedly in heavy demand in some areas of the United States. Ice is prepared by slowly evaporating a methamphetamine solution to produce large, crystal-clear "rocks." Like crack cocaine (discussed next), ice is smoked and produces effects similar to those of crack cocaine, but the effects last longer. Once the effects of ice wear off, users often become depressed and may sleep for days. Chronic users exhibit violent destructive behavior and acute psychosis similar to paranoid schizophrenia. Repeated use of amphetamines leads to a strong psychological dependence, which encourages their continued administration.

Cocaine Between 1884 and 1887, pioneering psychologist Sigmund Freud created something of a sensation in European medical circles by describing his experiments with a new drug. He reported a substance of seemingly limitless potential as a source of "exhilaration and lasting euphoria" that permitted "intensive mental or physical work [to be] performed without fatigue. . . . It is as though the need for food and sleep was completely banished."

The object of Freud's enthusiasm was cocaine, a drug stimulant extracted from the leaves of *Erythroxylon coca*, a plant grown in tropical Asia and the Andes mountains of South America (see Figure 5–9). At one time, cocaine had wide medical application as a local painkiller or anesthetic. However, this function has now been largely replaced by other drugs, primarily procaine and lidocaine. Cocaine is also a powerful stimulant to the central nervous system, and its effects resemble those caused by the amphetamines—namely, increased alertness and vigor, accompanied by the suppression of hunger, fatigue, and boredom. Most commonly, cocaine is sniffed or "snorted" and is absorbed into the body through the mucous membranes of the nose.

FIGURE 5–9
Coca leaves and illicit
forms of cocaine.
*Courtesy Drug Enforce-
ment Administration,
Washington, D.C.*

coca leaves and cocaine

One form of cocaine that has gained widespread popularity in the drug culture is known as *crack*. The process used to make crack is simple. Ordinary cocaine is mixed with baking soda and water into a solution that is then heated in a pot. This material is then dried and broken into tiny chunks that dealers sell as crack rocks. Crack is freebase cocaine and is sufficiently volatile to be smoked, usually in glass pipes. Crack, like cocaine that is snorted, produces a feeling of euphoria by stimulating a pleasure center in the base of the brain, in an area connected to nerves that are responsible for emotions.

Cocaine stimulates this pleasure center to a far greater degree than it would ever normally be stimulated. The result is euphoria—a feeling of increased energy, of being mentally more alert, of feeling really good. The faster the cocaine level rises in the brain, the greater the euphoria, and the surest way to obtain a fast rise in the brain's cocaine level is to smoke crack. Inhaling the cocaine vapor gets a large wallop of the drug to the brain in less than 15 seconds—about as fast as injecting it and much faster than snorting it. The dark side of crack, however, is that the euphoria fades quickly as cocaine levels drop, leaving the user feeling depressed, anxious, pleasureless. The desire to return to a euphoric feeling is so intense that crack users quickly develop a habit for the drug that is almost impossible to overcome. Only a small percentage of crack abusers will ever be cured of this drug habit.

In the United States, cocaine abuse is on the rise. Many people are apparently using cocaine to improve their ability to work and to keep going when tired. Although there is no evidence of physical dependency accompanying cocaine's repeated use, abstention from cocaine after prolonged use brings on severe bouts of mental depression, which produce a strong compulsion to resume using the drug. In fact, laboratory experiments with animals have demonstrated that of all the commonly abused drugs, cocaine produces the strongest psychological compulsions for continued use.

The United States spends millions of dollars annually in attempting to control cultivation of the coca leaf in various South American countries and to prevent cocaine trafficking into the United States. Three-quarters of the cocaine smuggled into the United States is refined in clandestine laboratories in Colombia. The profits are astronomical. Peruvian farmers may be paid $200 for enough coca leaves to make one pound of cocaine. The refined cocaine is worth $1,000 when it leaves Colombia and sells at retail in the United States for up to $20,000.

Club Drugs

The term *club drugs* refers to synthetic drugs that are often used at nightclubs, bars, and raves (all-night dance parties). Substances that are used as club drugs include, but are not limited to, MDMA (Ecstasy, see Figure 5–10), GHB (gamma hydroxybutyrate), Rohypnol "Roofies" (flunitrazyrate), ketamine, and methamphetamine. These drugs have become popular at the dance scene as a way to stimulate the rave experience. A high incidence of use has been found among teens and young adults.

GHB and Rohypnol are central nervous system depressants that are often connected with drug-facilitated sexual assault, rape, and robbery. Effects accompanying the use of GHB include dizziness, sedation, headache, and nausea. Recreational users have reported euphoria, relaxation, disinhibition, and increased libido (sex drive). Rohypnol causes muscle relaxation, loss of consciousness, and an inability to remember what happened during the hours after ingesting the

FIGURE 5–10
Ecstasy, a popular
club drug. *Courtesy
Rusty Kennedy, AP Wide
World Photos*

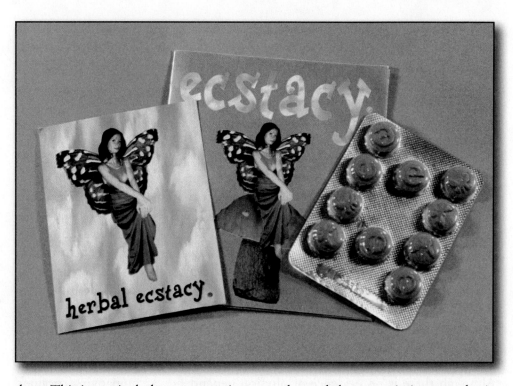

FIGURE 5–10
Ecstasy, a popular club drug. *Courtesy Rusty Kennedy, AP Wide World Photos*

drug. This is particularly a concern in a sexual assault because victims are physically unable to resist the attack. Unsuspecting victims become drowsy or dizzy. Effects are even stronger when the drug is combined with alcohol because the user experiences memory loss, blackouts, and disinhibition. Drugs such as Rohypnol and GHB are odorless, colorless, and tasteless, and thus remain undetected when slipped into a drink.

Methylenedioxymethamphetamine, also known as MDMA or Ecstasy, is a synthetic, mind-altering drug that exhibits many hallucinogenic and amphetamine-like effects. Ecstasy was originally patented as an appetite suppressant and was later discovered to induce feelings of happiness and relaxation. Recreational drug users find that Ecstasy enhances self-awareness and decreases inhibitions. However, seizures, muscle breakdown, stroke, kidney failure, and cardiovascular system failure often accompany chronic abuse of Ecstasy. In addition, chronic use of Ecstasy leads to serious damage to the areas of the brain responsible for thought and memory. Ecstasy increases heart rate and blood pressure; produces muscle tension, teeth grinding, and nausea; and causes psychological difficulties such as confusion, severe anxiety, and paranoia. The drug can cause significant increases in body temperature from the combination of the drug's stimulant effect with the often hot, crowded atmosphere of a rave club.

Ketamine is primarily used in veterinary medicine as an animal anesthetic. When used by humans, the drug can cause euphoria and feelings of unreality accompanied by visual hallucinations. Ketamine can also cause impaired motor function, high blood pressure, amnesia, and mild respiratory depression.

Anabolic Steroids

Anabolic steroids are synthetic compounds that are chemically related to the male sex hormone testosterone. Testosterone has two different effects on the body. It promotes the development of secondary male characteristics (androgenic effects), and it accelerates muscle growth (anabolic effects). Efforts to promote muscle growth and to minimize the hormone's androgenic effects have led to the synthesis of numerous anabolic steroids. However, a steroid free of the accompanying harmful side effects of an androgen drug has not yet been developed.

Incidence of steroid abuse first received widespread public attention when both amateur and professional athletes were discovered using these substances to enhance their performance. Interestingly, current research on male athletes given anabolic steroids has generally found little or, at best, marginal evidence of enhanced strength or performance. Although the full extent of anabolic steroid abuse by the general public is not fully known, the U.S. government is sufficiently concerned to regulate the availability of these drugs to the general population and to severely punish individuals for illegal possession and distribution of anabolic steroids. In 1991, anabolic steroids were classified as controlled dangerous substances, and the Drug Enforcement Administration was given enforcement power to prevent their illegal use and distribution (see Figure 5–11).

anabolic steroids
Synthetic compounds, chemically related to the male sex hormone testosterone, that are used to promote muscle growth

FIGURE 5–11
Anabolic steroids: a vial of testosterone and a syringe. Testosterone, the male sex hormone, is sometimes abused by athletes for its protein-building (anabolic) effect. *Courtesy Photo Researchers Inc.*

Anabolic steroids are usually taken by individuals who are unfamiliar with the harmful medical side effects. Liver cancer and other liver malfunctions have been linked to steroid use. These drugs also cause masculinizing effects in females, infertility, and diminished sex drive in males. For teenagers, anabolic steroids result in premature halting of bone growth. Anabolic steroids can also cause unpredictable effects on mood and personality, leading to unprovoked acts of anger and destructive behavior. Depression is also a frequent side effect of anabolic steroid abuse.

Quick Review

- Narcotic drugs are analgesics, meaning they relieve pain by depressing the central nervous system.

- The most common source for narcotic drugs is opium. Morphine is extracted from opium and used to synthesize heroin.

- Opiates are not derived from opium or morphine, but they have the same physiological effects on the body. Examples of opiates include methadone and OxyContin (oxycodone).

- Hallucinogens cause marked changes in normal thought processes, perceptions, and moods. Marijuana is the most well-known drug in this class. Other hallucinogens include LSD, mescaline, PCP, psilocybin, and MDMA (Ecstasy).

- Depressants decrease the activity of the central nervous system, calm irritability and excitability, and produce sleep. Depressants include alcohol (ethanol), barbiturates, tranquilizers, and various substances that can be sniffed, such as airplane glue or model cement.

- Stimulants increase the activity of the central nervous system and are taken to increase alertness and activity. Stimulants include amphetamines, sometimes known as "uppers" or "speed," and cocaine, which in its freebase form is known as *crack*.

- Club drugs are synthetic drugs that are used at nightclubs, bars, and raves (all-night dance parties). Some club drugs act as stimulants; others have depressant effects.

- Anabolic steroids are synthetic compounds that are chemically related to the male sex hormone testosterone. Anabolic steroids are often abused by individuals who are interested in accelerating muscle growth.

Drug-Control Laws

The provisions of drug laws are of particular interest to the criminalist, because they may impose specific analytical requirements on drug analysis. For example, the severity of a penalty associated with the manufacture, distribution, possession, and use of a drug may depend on the weight of the drug or its concentration in a mixture. In such cases, the chemist's report must contain all information that is needed to properly charge a suspect under the provisions of the existing law.

The provisions of any drug-control law are an outgrowth of national and local law enforcement requirements and customs, as well as the result of moral and political philosophies. These factors have produced a wide spectrum of national and local drug-control laws. Although their detailed discussion is beyond the intended scope of this book, a brief description of the U.S. federal law known as the Controlled Substances Act will illustrate a legal drug classification system that has been created to prevent and control drug abuse. Many states have modeled their own drug-control laws after this act, an important step in establishing uniform drug-control laws throughout the United States.

Controlled Substances Act

The federal law establishes five schedules of classification for controlled dangerous substances on the basis of a drug's potential for abuse, potential for physical and psychological dependence, and medical value. This classification system is extremely flexible in that the U.S. attorney general has the authority to add, delete, or reschedule a drug as more information becomes available.

Schedule I. Schedule I drugs have a high potential for abuse, have no currently accepted medical use in the United States, and/or lack accepted safety for use in treatment under medical supervision. Drugs controlled under this schedule include heroin, marijuana, methaqualone, and LSD.

Schedule II. Schedule II drugs have a high potential for abuse, a currently accepted medical use or a medical use with severe restrictions, and a potential for severe psychological or physical dependence. Schedule II drugs include opium and its derivatives not listed in schedule I, cocaine, methadone, phencyclidine (PCP), most amphetamine preparations, and most barbiturate preparations containing amobarbital, secobarbital, and pentobarbital. Dronabinol, the synthetic equivalent of the active ingredient in marijuana, has been placed in schedule II in recognition of its growing medical uses in treating glaucoma and chemotherapy patients.

Schedule III. Schedule III drugs have less potential for abuse than those in schedules I and II, a currently accepted medical use in the United States, and a potential for low or moderate physical dependence or high psychological dependence. Schedule III controls, among other substances, all barbiturate preparations (except phenobarbital) not covered under schedule II and certain codeine preparations. Anabolic steroids were added to this schedule in 1991.

Schedule IV. Schedule IV drugs have a low potential for abuse relative to schedule III drugs and have a current medical use in the United States; their abuse may lead to limited dependence relative to schedule III drugs. Drugs controlled in this schedule include propoxyphene (Darvon), phenobarbital, and tranquilizers such as meprobamate (Miltown), diazepam (Valium), and chlordiazepoxide (Librium).

Schedule V. Schedule V drugs must show low abuse potential, have medical use in the United States, and have less potential for producing dependence than schedule IV drugs. Schedule V controls certain opiate drug mixtures that contain nonnarcotic medicinal ingredients.

Controlled dangerous substances listed in schedules I and II are subject to manufacturing quotas set by the attorney general. For example, eight billion doses of amphetamines were manufactured in the United States in 1971. In 1972, production quotas were established reducing amphetamine production approximately 80 percent below 1971 levels.

Table 5–2
Control Mechanisms of the Controlled Substances Act

Schedule	Registration	Record Keeping	Manufacturing Quotas	Distribution Restrictions	Dispensing Limits	Import–Export		Security	Manufacturer/Distributor Enforcement Administration	Criminal Penalties for Individual Trafficking (First Offense)
						Narcotic	Nonnarcotic			
I	Required	Separate	Yes	Order forms	Research use only	Permit	Permit	Vault/safe	Yes	0–20 years/$1 million
II	Required	Separate	Yes	Order forms	Rx: written; no Refills	Permit	Permit	Vault/safe	Yes	0–20 years/$1 million
III	Required	Readily retrievable	No, but some drugs limited by schedule II quotas	Records required	Rx: written or oral; with medical authorization refills up to 5 times in 6 months	Permit	Declaration	Secure storage area	Yes, narcotic No, nonnarcotic	0–5 years/$250,000
IV	Required	Readily retrievable	No, but some drugs limited by schedule II quotas	Records required	Rx: written or oral; with medical authorization refills up to 5 times in 6 months	Permit	Declaration	Secure storage area	Manufacturer only, narcotic No, nonnarcotic	0–3 years/$250,000
V	Required	Readily retrievable	No, but some drugs limited by schedule II quotas	Records required	Over-the-counter (Rx drugs limited to MD's order) refills up to 5 times	Permit to import; declaration to export	Declaration	Secure storage area	Manufacturer only, narcotic No, nonnarcotic	0–1 year/$100,000

Source: Drug Enforcement Administration, Washington, D.C.

Criminal Penalties under the Act

The criminal penalties for unauthorized manufacture, sale, or possession of controlled dangerous substances are related to the schedules as well. The most severe penalties are associated with drugs listed in schedules I and II. For example, for drugs included in schedules I and II, a first offense is punishable by up to 20 years in prison and/or a fine of up to $1 million for an individual or up to $5 million for other than individuals. Table 5–2 summarizes the control mechanisms and penalties for each schedule of the Controlled Substances Act.

The Controlled Substances Act stipulates that an offense involving a controlled substance *analog*, a chemical substance substantially similar in chemical structure to a controlled substance, triggers penalties as if it were a controlled substance listed in schedule I. This section is designed to combat the proliferation of so-called *designer drugs*—substances that are chemically related to some controlled drugs and are pharmacologically very potent. These substances are manufactured by skilled individuals in clandestine laboratories, with the knowledge that their products will not be covered by the schedules of the Controlled Substances Act. For instance, fentanyl is a powerful narcotic that is commercially marketed for medical use and is also listed as a controlled dangerous substance. This drug is about one hundred times as potent as morphine. A number of substances chemically related to fentanyl have been synthesized by underground chemists and sold on the street. The first such substance encountered was sold under the street name China White. These drugs have been responsible for more than a hundred overdose deaths in California and nearly 20 deaths in western Pennsylvania. As designer drugs, such as China White, are identified and linked to drug abuse, they are placed in appropriate schedules.

The Controlled Substances Act also reflects an effort to decrease the prevalence of clandestine drug laboratories designed to manufacture controlled substances. The act regulates the manufacture and distribution of *precursors*, the chemical compounds used by clandestine drug laboratories to synthesize abused drugs. Targeted precursor chemicals are listed in the definition section of the Controlled Substances Act. Severe penalties are provided for a person who possesses a listed precursor chemical with the intent to manufacture a controlled substance or who possesses or distributes a listed chemical knowing, or having reasonable cause to believe, that the listed chemical will be used to manufacture a controlled substance. In addition, precursors to PCP, amphetamines, and methamphetamines are enumerated specifically in schedule II, making them subject to regulation in the same manner as other schedule II substances.

Quick Review
- Federal law establishes five schedules of classification for controlled dangerous substances on the basis of a drug's potential for abuse, potential for physical and psychological dependence, and medical value.

Forensic Drug Analysis

One only has to look into the evidence vaults of crime laboratories to appreciate the assortment of drug specimens that confront the criminalist. The presence of a huge array of powders, tablets, capsules, vegetable matter, liquids, pipes, cigarettes, cookers, and syringes is testimony to the vitality and sophistication of the illicit-drug market. If outward appearance is not evidence enough of the difficult analytical chore facing the forensic chemist, consider the complexity of the drug preparations themselves. Usually these contain active drug ingredients of unknown origin and identity, as well as additives—for example, sugar, starch, and quinine—that dilute their potency and stretch their value on the illicit-drug market. Do not forget that illicit-drug dealers are not hampered by government regulations that ensure the quality and consistency of a product.

When a forensic chemist picks up a drug specimen for analysis, he or she should be prepared for all contingencies. The analysis must leave no room for error, because its results will have a direct bearing on the process of determining the guilt or innocence of a defendant. There is no middle ground in drug identification—either the specimen is a specific drug or it is not—and once a positive conclusion is drawn, the chemist must be prepared to support and defend the validity of the results in a court of law.

Screening and Confirmation

The challenge or difficulty of forensic drug identification comes in selecting analytical procedures that will ensure specific identification of a drug. Presented with a substance of unknown origin and composition, the forensic chemist must develop a plan of action that will ultimately yield the drug's identity. This plan, or scheme of analysis, is divided into two phases.

First, faced with the prospect that the unknown substance may be any one of a thousand or more commonly encountered drugs, the analyst must use **screening tests** to reduce these possibilities to a small and manageable number. This objective is often accomplished by subjecting the material to a series of color tests that produce characteristic colors for the more commonly encountered illicit drugs. Even if these tests produce negative results, their value lies in having excluded certain drugs from further consideration.

Once the number of possibilities has been reduced substantially, the second phase of the analysis is devoted to pinpointing and confirming the drug's identity. In an era in which crime laboratories receive voluminous quantities of drug evidence, it is impractical to subject a drug to all the chemical and instrumental tests available. Indeed, it is more realistic to view these techniques as a large analytical arsenal. The chemist, aided by training and experience, must choose tests that will most conveniently identify a particular drug.

Forensic chemists often use a specific test to identify a drug substance to the exclusion of all other known chemical substances. A single test that identifies a substance is known as a **confirmation**. The analytical scheme sometimes consists of a series of nonspecific or presumptive tests. Each test in itself is insufficient to prove the drug's identity; however, the proper analytical scheme encompasses a combination of test results that characterize one and only one chemical

screening test
A preliminary test used to reduce the number of possible identities of an unknown substance

confirmation
A single test that specifically identifies a substance

substance—the drug under investigation. Furthermore, experimental evidence must confirm that the probability of any other substance responding in an identical manner to the scheme selected is so small as to be beyond any reasonable scientific certainty.

Another consideration in selecting an analytical technique is the need for either a *qualitative* or a *quantitative* determination. The former relates just to the identity of the material, whereas the latter refers to the percentage combination of the components of a mixture. Hence, a qualitative identification of a powder may reveal the presence of heroin and quinine, whereas a quantitative analysis may conclude the presence of 10 percent heroin and 90 percent quinine.

Obviously, a qualitative identification must precede any attempt at quantitation, for little value is served by attempting to quantitate a material without first determining its identity. Essentially, a qualitative analysis of a material requires the determination of numerous properties using a variety of analytical techniques. On the other hand, a quantitative measurement is usually accomplished by precise measurement of a single property of the material.

Forensic chemists normally rely on several tests for a routine drug-identification scheme: color tests, microcrystalline tests, chromatography, spectrophotometry, and mass spectrometry.

Color Tests

Many drugs yield characteristic colors when brought into contact with specific chemical reagents. Not only do these tests provide a useful indicator of a drug's presence, but they are also used by investigators in the field to examine materials suspected of containing a drug (see Figure 5–12).[2] However, color tests are useful for screening purposes only and are never taken as conclusive identification of unknown drugs.

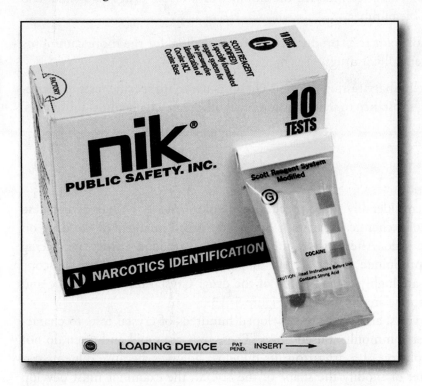

FIGURE 5–12
A field color test kit for cocaine. The suspect drug is placed in the plastic pouch. Tubes containing chemicals are broken open, and the color of the chemical reaction is observed. *Courtesy Tri-Tech, Inc., Southport, N.C., www.tritechusa.com*

Five primary color test reagents are as follows:

1. **Marquis.** The reagent turns purple in the presence of heroin and morphine and most opium derivatives. Marquis also becomes orange-brown when mixed with amphetamines and methamphetamines.

2. **Dillie-Koppanyi.** This is a valuable screening test for barbiturates, in whose presence the reagent turns violet-blue in color.

3. **Duquenois-Levine.** This is a valuable color test for marijuana, performed by adding a series of chemical solutions, to the suspect vegetation. A positive result is shown by a purple color when chloroform is added.

4. **Van Urk.** The reagent turns blue-purple in the presence of LSD. However, owing to the extremely small quantities of LSD in illicit preparations, this test is difficult to conduct under field conditions.

5. **Scott Test.** This is a color test for cocaine. A powder containing cocaine turns a cobalt thiocyanate solution blue. Upon addition of hydrochloric acid, the blue color is transformed to a clear pink color. Upon addition of chloroform, if cocaine is present, the blue color reappears in the chloroform layer.

Quick Review
- Analysts use screening tests to determine the identity of drugs present in a sample. These tests reduce the number of possible drugs to a small and manageable number.

- A series of color tests produce characteristic colors for the more commonly encountered illicit drugs.

- After preliminary testing, forensic chemists use more specific tests to identify a drug substance to the exclusion of all other known chemical substances.

Microcrystalline Tests

microcrystalline test
A test that identifies a specific substance based on the color and shape of crystals formed when the substance is mixed with specific reagents

A technique considerably more specific than color tests is the **microcrystalline test**. A drop of a chemical reagent is added to a small quantity of the drug on a microscopic slide. After a short time, a chemical reaction ensues, producing a crystalline precipitate. The size and shape of the crystals, under microscope examination, are highly characteristic of the drug. Crystal tests for cocaine and methamphetamine are illustrated in Figure 5–13.

Over the years, analysts have developed hundreds of crystal tests to characterize the most commonly abused drugs. These tests are rapid and often do not require the isolation of a drug from its diluents; however, because diluents can sometimes alter or modify the shape of the crystal, the examiner must develop experience in interpreting the results of the test.

(a)

(b)

FIGURE 5–13 (a) A photograph of a cocaine crystal formed in platinum chloride (400x). (b) A photomicrograph of a methamphetamine crystal formed in gold chloride (400x). *Courtesy David P. Blackburn, San Bermardino County Sheriff's Department, San Bernardino, Calif.*

Most color and crystal tests are largely empirical—that is, scientists do not fully understand why they produce the results that they do. From the forensic chemist's point of view, this is not important. When the tests are properly chosen and used in proper combination, their results constitute an analytical scheme that is characteristic for one and only one drug.

Chromatography

Chromatography is a means of separating and tentatively identifying the components of a mixture. It is particularly useful for analyzing drug specimens, which may be diluted with practically any material in order to increase the quantity of the product available to prospective customers. The task of identifying an illicit-drug preparation would be arduous without the aid of chromatographic methods to first separate the mixture into its components.

Theory of Chromatography The theory of chromatography is based on the fact that chemical substances tend to partially escape into the surrounding environment when dissolved in a liquid or when absorbed on a solid surface. For example, if a beaker of water is covered with a bell jar, as shown in Figure 5–14, gas molecules (represented by green balls) escape from the water into the surrounding enclosed air. The molecules that remain are said to be in the liquid phase; the molecules that have escaped into the air are said to be in the gas phase.

As the gas molecules escape into the surrounding air, they accumulate above the water; random motion carries some of them back into the water. Eventually, a point is reached at which the number of molecules leaving the water equals the number returning. At this time, the liquid and gas phases are in equilibrium. If the temperature of the water is increased, the equilibrium state readjusts itself to a point at which more gas molecules move into the gas phase.

This behavior was first observed in 1803 by British chemist William Henry. His explanation of this phenomenon, known appropriately as Henry's law, may be stated as follows: **When a volatile chemical compound is dissolved in a**

chromatography
Any of several analytical techniques for separating organic mixtures into their components by attraction to a stationary phase while being propelled by a moving phase

FIGURE 5–14
Evaporation of a liquid.

liquid and is brought to equilibrium with air, there is a fixed ratio between the concentration of the volatile compound in air and its concentration in the liquid, and this ratio remains constant for a given temperature.

The distribution of a gas between the liquid and gas phases is determined by the solubility of the gas; that is, how easily the gas dissolves in the liquid. The higher its solubility, the greater the tendency of the gas molecules to remain in the liquid phase. If two different gases are simultaneously dissolved in the same liquid, each reaches a state of equilibrium with the surrounding air independently of the other. For example, as shown in Figure 5–15, gas A (green molecules) and gas B (blue molecules) are both dissolved in water. At equilibrium, gas A has a greater number of molecules dissolved in the water than does gas B. This is so because gas A is more soluble in water than gas B.

FIGURE 5–15
At equilibrium, there are more gas A molecules (green molecules) than gas B molecules (blue molecules) in the liquid phase.

Thin-Layer Chromatography Thin-layer chromatography (TLC) uses a solid stationary phase and a moving liquid phase to separate the constituents of a mixture. Thin-layer chromatography is a powerful tool for solving many of the analytical problems presented to the forensic scientist. The method is both rapid and

Inside the Science

The Chromatographic Process

In Figures 5–14 and 5–15, both phases—liquid and gas—were kept stationary; that is, they were not moving. During a chromatographic process, however, this is not the case. Instead, one phase is always made to move continuously in one direction over a stationary or fixed phase. For example, in Figure 5–15, chromatography will occur only when the air is forced to move continuously in one direction over the water. Because gas B (blue molecules) has a greater percentage of its molecules in the moving phase than does gas A (green molecules), the molecules of gas B will travel over the liquid at a faster pace than those of gas A. Eventually, when the moving phase has advanced a reasonable distance, the molecules of gas B will become entirely separated from those of gas A, and the chromatographic process will be complete. This process is illustrated in Figure 1.

FIGURE 1   In this illustration of chromatography, the blue molecules have a greater affinity for the upper phase and hence will be pushed along at a faster rate by the moving air. Eventually, the two sets of molecules will separate from each other, completing the chromatographic process.

Inside the Science (CONTINUED)

Simply, we can think of chromatography as being analogous to a race between chemical compounds. At the starting line, all the participating substances are mixed together; however, as the race progresses, materials that prefer the moving phase slowly pull ahead of those substances that prefer to remain in the stationary phase. Finally, at the end of the race, all the participants are separated, each crossing the finish line at different times.

The different types of chromatographic systems are as varied as the number of stationary and moving-phase combinations that can be devised. However, two chromatographic processes—gas chromatography and thin-layer chromatography—are most applicable for solving many analytical problems in the crime laboratory.

sensitive; moreover, less than 100 micrograms of suspect material are required for the analysis. In addition, the equipment necessary for TLC work has minimal cost and space requirements. Importantly, numerous samples can be analyzed simultaneously on one thin-layer plate. This technique is principally used to detect and identify components in complex mixtures.

Theory of Thin-Layer Chromatography. In TLC, the components of a suspect mixture are separated as they travel up a glass plate, eventually appearing as a series of dark or colored spots on the plate. This action is then compared to a standard sample separation of a specific drug, such as heroin. If both the standard and the suspect substance travel the same distance up the plate, they can tentatively be identified as being produced by the same substance.

Figure 5–16 shows a sample suspected of containing heroin and quinine that has been chromatographed alongside known heroin and quinine standards. The distance the unknown material migrated up the suspect plate is compared to the distances that heroin and quinine migrated up a standard sample plate. If the distances are the same, a tentative identification can be made. However, such an identification cannot be considered definitive, because numerous other substances can migrate the same distance up the plate when chromatographed under similar conditions. Thus, thin-layer chromatography alone cannot provide an absolute identification; it must be used in conjunction with other testing procedures to prove absolute identity.

TLC in Practice. A thin-layer plate is prepared by coating a glass plate or plastic backing with a thin film of a granular material, usually silica gel or aluminum oxide. This granular material serves as the solid stationary phase and is usually held in place on the plate with a binding agent such as plaster of Paris. If the sample to be analyzed is a solid, it must first be dissolved in a suitable solvent and a few microliters of the solution spotted with a capillary tube onto the granular surface near the

FIGURE 5–16
Chromatograms of known heroin (1) and quinine (2) standards alongside suspect sample (3).

lower edge of the plate. A liquid sample may be applied directly to the plate in the same manner. The plate is then placed upright into a closed chamber that contains a selected liquid, with care that the liquid does not touch the sample spot.

The liquid slowly rises up the plate by capillary action. This rising liquid is the moving phase in thin-layer chromatography. As the liquid moves past the sample spot, the components of the sample become distributed between the stationary solid phase and the moving liquid phase. The components with the greatest affinity for the moving phase travel up the plate faster than those that have greater affinity for the stationary phase. When the liquid front has moved a sufficient distance (usually 10 cm), the development is complete, and the plate is removed from the chamber and dried (see Figure 5–17). An example of the chromatographic separation of ink is shown in Figure 5–18.

Because most compounds are colorless, no separation will be noticed after development unless the materials are visualized. To accomplish this, the plates are placed under ultraviolet light, revealing fluorescent materials (those that emit visible light when exposed to light of a shorter wavelength) as bright spots on a dark background. When a fluorescent dye has been incorporated into the solid phase, nonfluorescent substances appear as dark spots against a fluorescent background when exposed to the ultraviolet light.

In a second method of visualization, the plate is sprayed with a chemical reagent that reacts with the separated substances and causes them to form colored spots. Figure 5–19 shows the chromatogram of a marijuana extract that has been separated into its components by TLC and visualized by having been sprayed with a chemical reagent.

FIGURE 5–17
(a) In thin-layer chromatography, a liquid sample is spotted onto the granular surface of a gel-coated plate. (b) The plate is placed into a closed chamber that contains a liquid. As the liquid rises up the plate, the components of the sample distribute themselves between the coating and the moving liquid. The mixture is separated, with substances with a greater affinity for the moving liquid traveling up the plate at a faster speed.

Very thin coating of silica gel or aluminum oxide

Sample spot

(a)

Rising solvent; original spot has separated into several spots

(b)

(a) (b) (c)

FIGURE 5–18 (a) The liquid phase begins to move up the stationary phase. (b) Liquid moves past the ink spot carrying the ink components up the stationary phase. (c) The moving liquid has separated the ink into its several components. *Courtesy Richard Megna/Fundamental Photographs, NYC, Photos a and b*

The distance a spot has traveled up a thin-layer plate can be assigned a numerical value known as the R_f value. This value is defined as the distance traveled by the component divided by the distance traveled by the moving liquid phase. For example, in Figure 5–16 the moving phase traveled 10 centimeters up the plate before the plate was removed from the tank. After visualization, the heroin spot moved 8 centimeters, for an R_f value of 0.8; the quinine migrated 4 centimeters, for an R_f value of 0.4.

FIGURE 5–19
Thin-layer chromatogram of a marijuana extract.
Courtesy Sirchie Finger Print Laboratories, Inc., Youngsville, N.C., www.sirchie.com

Gas Chromatography (GC) Gas chromatography (GC) separates mixtures based on their distribution between a stationary liquid phase and a moving gas phase. In gas chromatography, the moving phase is called the *carrier gas*, which flows through a column constructed of stainless steel or glass. The stationary phase is a thin film of liquid within the column.

Two types of columns are used: the *packed column* and the *capillary column*. With the packed column, the stationary phase is a thin film of liquid fixed onto small granular particles packed into the column. This column, usually constructed of stainless steel or glass, is 2 to 6 meters long and about 3 millimeters in diameter. Capillary columns are composed of glass and are much longer than packed columns—15 to 60 meters long. These types of columns are very narrow, ranging from 0.25 to 0.75 millimeter in diameter. Capillary columns can be made narrower than packed columns because their stationary liquid phase is actually coated as a very thin film directly onto the column's inner wall.

As the carrier gas flows through the packed or capillary column, it carries with it the components of a mixture that have been injected into the column.

Components with a greater affinity for the moving gas phase travel through the column more quickly than those with a greater affinity for the stationary liquid phase. Eventually, after the mixture has traversed the length of the column, it emerges separated into its components.

The time required for a component to emerge from the column from the time of its injection into the column is known as the *retention time*, which is a useful identifying characteristic of a material. Figure 5–20(a) shows the chromatogram of two barbiturates; each barbiturate has tentatively been identified by comparing its retention time to those of known barbiturates, shown in Figure 5–20(b). However, because other substances may have comparable retention times under similar chromatographic conditions, gas chromatography cannot be considered an absolute means of identification. Conclusions derived from this technique must be confirmed by other testing procedures.

MyCrimeKit:
WebExtra 5.1

Watch Animated Depictions of Thin-Layer Chromatography and Gas Chromatography www.mycrimekit.com

FIGURE 5–20
(a) An unknown mixture of barbiturates is identified by comparing its retention times to (b), a known mixture of barbiturates. *Courtesy Varian Inc., Palo Alto, Calif.*

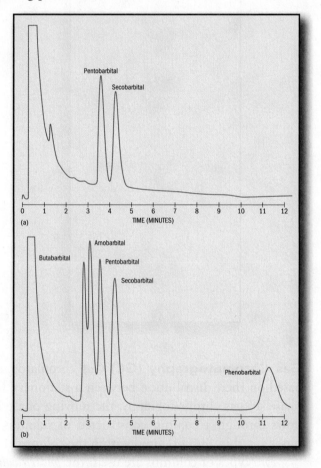

MyCrimeKit:
WebExtra 5.2

Watch the Gas Chromatograph at Work www.mycrimekit.com

Gas chromatography is widely used because of its ability to resolve a highly complex mixture into its components, usually within minutes. It has an added advantage in that it is extremely sensitive and can yield quantitative results. Gas chromatography has sufficient sensitivity to detect and quantitate materials at the nanogram (0.000000001 gram or 1×10^9 gram) level.[3]

Inside the Science

The Gas Chromatograph

A simplified scheme of the gas chromatograph is shown in <u>Figure 5–21</u>. The operation of the instrument can be summed up briefly as follows: The carrier gas is fed into the column at a constant rate. The carrier gas is chemically inert and is generally nitrogen or helium. The sample under investigation is injected as a liquid into a heated injection port with a syringe, where it is immediately vaporized and swept into the column by the carrier gas. The column itself is heated in an oven in order to keep the sample in a vapor state as it travels through the column. In the column, the components of the sample travel in the direction of the carrier gas flow at speeds that are determined by their distribution between the stationary and moving phases. If the analyst has selected the proper liquid phase and has made the column long enough, the components of the sample will be completely separated as they emerge from the column.

1. Sample
2. Injector
3. Carrier gas
4. Column
5. Detector
6. Power supply
7. Recorder
8. Chromatogram

FIGURE 5–21 Basic gas chromatography. Gas chromatography permits rapid separation of complex mixtures into individual compounds and allows identification and quantitative determination of each compound. As shown, a sample is introduced by a syringe (1) into a heated injection chamber (2). A constant stream of nitrogen gas (3) flows through the injector, carrying the sample into the column (4), which contains a thin film of liquid. The sample is separated in the column, and the carrier gas and separated components emerge from the column and enter the detector (5). Signals developed by the detector activate the recorder (7), which makes a permanent record of the separation by tracing a series of peaks on the chromatograph (8). The time of elution identifies the component present, and the peak area identifies the concentration.
Courtesy Varian Inc., Palo Alto, Calif.

Inside the Science (CONTINUED)

As each component emerges from the column, it enters a detector. One type of detector uses a flame to ionize the emerging chemical substance, thus generating an electrical signal. The signal is recorded on a strip-chart recorder as a function of time. This written record of the separation is called a chromatogram. A gas chromatogram is a plot of the recorder response (vertical axis) versus time (horizontal axis). A typical chromatogram shows a series of peaks, each peak corresponding to one component of the mixture.

Spectrophotometry

The technique of chromatography is particularly suited for analyzing illicit drugs, because it can separate a drug from other substances that may be present in the drug preparation. However, chromatography has the drawback of not being able to specifically identify the material under investigation. For this reason, other analytical tools are frequently used to identify drugs. These include the technique of **spectrophotometry**, which can identify a substance by exposing it to a specific type of electromagnetic radiation.

spectrophotometry
An analytical method for identifying a substance by its selective absorption of different wavelengths of light

Theory of Spectrophotometry We have already observed in the description of color that an object does not absorb all the visible light it is exposed to; instead, it selectively absorbs some frequencies and reflects or transmits others. Similarly, the absorption of other types of electromagnetic radiation by chemical substances is also selective. Selective absorption of a substance is measured by an instrument called a *spectrophotometer*, which produces a graph or *absorption spectrum* that depicts the absorption of light as a function of wavelength or frequency. The absorption of ultraviolet (UV), visible, and infrared (IR) radiation is particularly applicable for obtaining qualitative data pertaining to the identification of drugs.

Absorption at a single wavelength or frequency of light is not 100 percent complete—some radiation is transmitted or reflected by the material. Just how much radiation a substance absorbs is defined by a fundamental relationship known as Beer's law, shown in Equation (5–1):

EQUATION 5-1

$$A = kc$$

Here, A symbolizes the absorption or the quantity of light taken up at a single frequency, c is the concentration of the absorbing material, and k is a proportionality constant. This relationship shows that the quantity of light absorbed at any frequency is directly proportional to the concentration of the absorbing species; the more material you have, the more radiation it will absorb. By defining the relationship between absorbance and concentration, Beer's law permits spectrophotometry to be used as a technique for quantification.

Ultraviolet and Visible Spectrophotometry Ultraviolet (UV) and visible spectrophotometry measure the absorbance of UV and visible light as a function of wavelength or frequency. For example, the UV absorption spectrum of heroin shows a maximum absorption band at a wavelength of 278 nanometers (see Figure 5–22). This shows that the simplicity of a UV spectrum facilitates its use as a tool for determining a material's probable identity. For instance, a white powder may have a UV spectrum comparable to heroin and therefore may be tentatively identified as such. (Fortunately, sugar and starch, common diluents of heroin, do not absorb UV light.)

This technique, however, does not provide a definitive result; other drugs or materials may have a UV absorption spectrum similar to that of heroin. Nevertheless, UV spectrophotometry is often useful in establishing the probable identity of a drug. For example, if an unknown substance yields a UV spectrum that resembles that of amphetamine (see Figure 5–23), thousands of substances are immediately eliminated from consideration, and the analyst can begin to identify the material from a relatively small number of possibilities. A comprehensive collection of UV drug spectra provides an index that can rapidly be searched in order to tentatively identify a drug or, failing that, at least to exclude certain drugs from consideration.

Infrared Spectrophotometry In contrast to the simplicity of a UV spectrum, absorption in the **infrared** region provides a far more complex pattern. Figure 5–24 depicts the IR spectra of heroin and secobarbital. Here, the absorption bands are so numerous that each spectrum can provide enough characteristics to identify a substance specifically. Different materials always have distinctively

ultraviolet
Invisible long frequencies of light beyond violet in the visible spectrum

FIGURE 5–22
Ultraviolet spectrum of heroin.

infrared
Invisible short frequencies of light before red in the visible spectrum

FIGURE 5–23
Ultraviolet spectrum
of amphetamine.

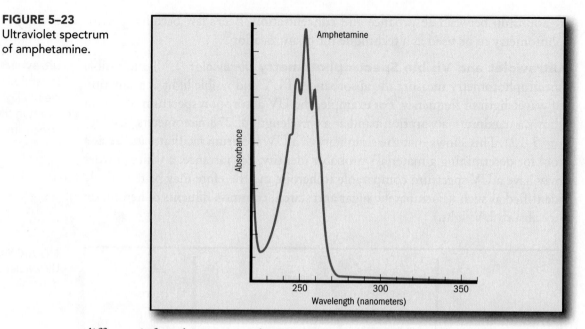

different infrared spectra; each IR spectrum is therefore equivalent to a "finger-print" of that substance and no other. This technique is one of the few tests available to the forensic scientist that can be considered specific in itself for identification. The IR spectra of thousands of organic compounds have been collected, indexed, and cataloged as invaluable references for identifying organic substances. The selective absorption of light by drugs in the UV and IR regions of the electromagnetic spectrum provides a valuable technique for characterizing drugs.

FIGURE 5-24
(a) Infrared spectrum
    of heroin.
(b) Infrared spectrum
    of secobarbital.

**MyCrimeKit:
WebExtra 5.3**

See How a Spectropho-
tometer Works
www.mycrimekit.com

Inside the Science

The Spectrophotometer

Prism disperses radiation into component wavelengths

Radiation source   Monochromator   Sample cell   Detector   Recorder

Prism   Slit

The spectrophotometer measures and records the absorption spectrum of a chemical. The basic components of a simple spectrophotometer are the same regardless of whether it is designed to measure the absorption of UV, visible, or IR radiation. These components are illustrated diagrammatically in the figure above. They include (1) a radiation source, (2) a monochromator or frequency selector, (3) a sample holder, (4) a detector to convert electromagnetic radiation into an electrical signal, and (5) a recorder to produce a record of the signal.

The choice of source varies with the type of radiation desired. For visible radiation, an ordinary tungsten bulb provides a convenient source of radiation. In the UV region, a hydrogen or deuterium discharge lamp is normally used, and a heated molded rod containing a mixture of rare-earth oxides is a good source of IR light.

Slit allows only selected wavelengths or frequencies of radiation to pass through

Radiation source   Monochromator   Sample cell   Detector   Recorder

Prism   Slit

The function of the **monochromator** is to select a single wavelength or frequency of light from the source—monochromatic light. Some inexpensive spectrophotometers pass the light through colored glass filters to remove all radiation from the beam except for a desired range of wavelengths.

Inside the Science (CONTINUED)

More precise spectrophotometers may use a prism or diffraction grating to disperse radiation into its component wavelengths or frequencies. A diffraction grating is made by scratching thousands of parallel lines on a transparent surface such as glass. As light passes through the narrow spacings between the lines, it spreads out and produces a spectrum similar to that formed by a prism. The desired wavelength is obtained when the dispersed radiation is focused onto a narrow slit that permits only selected wavelengths to pass through.

Radiation passes through sample, which absorbs certain frequencies

Radiation source   Monochromator   Prism   Slit   Sample cell   Detector   Recorder

Most laboratory infrared spectrophotometers use Fourier transform analysis to measure the wavelengths of light at which a material absorbs in the infrared spectrum. This approach does not use any dispersive elements that select single wavelengths or frequencies of light emitted from a source; instead, the heart of a Fourier transform infrared (FT-IR) spectrometer is the Michelson interferometer. The interferometer uses a beam-splitting prism and two mirrors, one movable and one stationary, to direct light toward a sample. As the wavelengths pass through the sample and reach a detector, they are all measured simultaneously. A mathematical operation, the Fourier transform method, is used to decode the measured signals and record the wavelength data. These Fourier calculations are rapidly carried out by a computer. In a matter of seconds, a computer-operated FT-IR instrument can produce an infrared absorption pattern compatible to one generated by a prism instrument.

Radiation source   Monochromator   Prism   Slit   Sample cell   Detector measures absorption of radiation by the sample and converts the radiation into an electrical signal   Recorder

Inside the Science (CONTINUED)

Sample preparation varies with the type of radiation being studied. Absorption spectra in the UV and visible regions are usually obtained from samples that have been dissolved in an appropriate solvent. Because the cells holding the solution must be transparent to the light being measured, glass cells are used in the visible region and quartz cells in the ultraviolet region. Practically all substances absorb in some region of the IR spectrum, so sampling techniques must be modified to measure absorption in this spectral region; special cells made out of sodium chloride or potassium bromide are commonly used because they do not absorb light over a wide range of the IR portion of the electromagnetic spectrum.

Recorder translates electrical signal into recording of the absorption spectrum

Radiation source   Monochromator   Sample cell   Detector   Recorder

Prism   Slit

The absorption spectrum of a chemical substance allows spectrophotometry to be used for identification.

The detector measures the quantity of radiation that passes through the sample by converting it to an electrical signal. UV and visible spectrophotometers use photoelectric tube detectors. A signal is generated when the photons strike the tube surface to produce a current that is directly proportional to the intensity of the light transmitted through the sample. When this signal is compared to the intensity of light that is transmitted to the detector in the absence of an absorbing material, the absorbance of a substance can be determined at each wavelength or frequency of light selected. The signal from the detection system is then fed into a recorder, which plots absorbance as a function of wavelength or frequency. Modern spectrophotometers are designed to trace an entire absorption spectrum automatically.

Mass Spectrometry

monochromator
A device for isolating individual wavelengths or frequencies of light

A previous section discussed the operation of the gas chromatograph. This instrument is one of the most important tools in a crime laboratory. Its ability to separate the components of a complex mixture is unsurpassed. However, gas chromatography has one important drawback—its inability to produce specific identification. A forensic chemist cannot unequivocally state the identification of a substance based solely on a retention time as determined by the gas chromatograph. Fortunately, coupling the gas chromatograph to a mass spectrometer has largely overcome this problem.

A mixture's components are first separated on the gas chromatograph. A direct connection between the gas chromatograph column and the mass spectrometer then allows each component to flow into the spectrometer as it emerges from the gas chromatograph. In the mass spectrometer, the material enters a high-vacuum chamber where a beam of high-energy electrons is aimed at the sample molecules. The electrons collide with the molecules, causing them to lose electrons and to acquire a positive charge. These positively charged molecules, or **ions**, are unstable or are formed with excess energy and almost instantaneously decompose into numerous smaller fragments. The fragments then pass through an electric or magnetic field, where they are separated according to their masses. The unique feature of mass spectrometry is that under carefully controlled conditions, no two substances produce the same fragmentation pattern. In essence, one can think of this pattern as a "fingerprint" of the substance being examined (see Figure 5–25).

ion
An atom or molecule bearing a positive or negative charge

FIGURE 5–25
How GC/MS works. Left to right, the sample is separated into its components by the gas chromatograph, and then the components are ionized and identified by characteristic fragmentation patterns of the spectra produced by the mass spectrometer. *Courtesy Agilent Technologies, Inc., Palo Alto, Calif.*

The technique thus provides a specific means for identifying a chemical structure. It is also sensitive to minute concentrations. Mass spectrometry is most widely used to identify drugs; however, further research is expected to yield significant applications to identifying other types of physical evidence. Figure 5–26 illustrates the mass spectra of heroin and cocaine; here, each line represents a fragment of a different mass (actually the ratio of mass to charge), and the line height reflects the relative abundance of each fragment. Note how different the fragmentation patterns of heroin and cocaine are. Each mass spectrum is unique to each drug and therefore provides a specific test for identifying that substance.

The combination of the gas chromatograph and mass spectrometer (GC/MS) is further enhanced when a computer is added to the system. The integrated gas chromatograph/mass spectrometer/computer system provides the ultimate in speed, accuracy, and sensitivity. With the ability to record and store in its memory several hundred mass spectra, such a system can detect and identify substances present in only one-millionth-of-a-gram quantities. Furthermore, the computer can be programmed to compare an unknown spectrum against a comprehensive library of mass spectra stored in its memory. The advent of personal computers and microcircuitry has made it possible to design mass spectrometer systems that can fit on a small table. Such a unit is pictured in Figure 5–27. With data obtained from a GC/MS determination, a forensic analyst can, with one instrument, separate the components of a complex drug mixture and then unequivocally identify each substance present in the mixture. (see Figure 5–28).

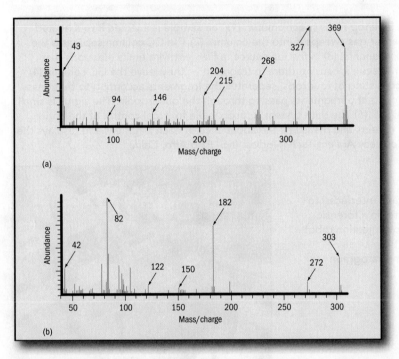

FIGURE 5–26
(a) Mass spectrum of heroin.
(b) Mass spectrum of cocaine.

The Identification of Marijuana

Enforcement of laws prohibiting the sale and use of marijuana accounts for a high percentage of drug arrests in the United States. Any trial or hearing involving a seizure of marijuana requires identification of the material before the issue of guilt or innocence can be decided.

Unlike most other drugs received by the crime laboratory, marijuana (Cannabis sativa L.) possesses botanical features that impart identifiable characteristics. Because most marijuana specimens consist of small leaf fragments, their identification must be partially based on botanical features observed under the microscope by a trained expert. This approach is further augmented with a chemical test that will independently confirm the findings of the botanical examination.

The identification of marijuana by microscopic methods depends largely on observing short hairs shaped like "bear claws" on the upper side of the leaf (see the SEM photo in Figure 7–14). These hairs are known as cystolithic hairs. Further

MyCrimeKit:
WebExtra 5.4
Watch an Animation of a Mass Spectrometer
www.mycrimekit.com

1. Injection port 3. Ion source 4. Quadrupole 6. Data system 2. GC column 5. Detector

FIGURE 5–27 A tabletop mass spectrometer. (1) The sample is injected into a heated inlet port, and a carrier gas sweeps it into the column. (2) The GC column separates the mixture into its components. (3) In the ion source, a filament wire emits electrons that strike the sample molecules, causing them to fragment as they leave the GC column. (4) The quadrupole, consisting of four rods, separates the fragments according to their mass. (5) The detector counts the fragments passing through the quadrupole. The signal is small and must be amplified. (6) The data system is responsible for total control of the entire GC/MS system. It detects and measures the abundance of each fragment and displays the mass spectrum. *Courtesy Agilent Technologies, Inc., Palo Alto, Calif.*

FIGURE 5–28
A gas chromatograph interfaced to a mass spectrometer in a forensic laboratory. A sample injection robot transfers samples from small vials to the gas chromatograph

verification of the identity of marijuana is confirmed by the presence of longer, nonglandular hairs on the opposite side of the leaf.

The Duquenois-Levine color test, described earlier in this chapter, is a highly but not totally specific test for marijuana. However, when used in combination with a botanical examination, the results constitute a specific identification of marijuana. In addition, the analyst may be unable to obtain a microscopic identification of the marijuana leaf, as in the case of hashish or hashish oil. Here, the color test has to be supplemented by another examination, preferably thin-layer chromatography. This method involves separating chemical constituents found in the suspect resin on a thin-layer plate. The separated components are compared on the same plate to those obtained from a known marijuana extract, as shown in Figure 5–19. In this manner, a positive TLC comparison, used in conjunction with the Duquenois-Levine color test, constitutes a specific identification for marijuana.

Quick Review

- Chromatography is a means of separating and tentatively identifying the components of a mixture.

- TLC uses a solid stationary phase, usually coated onto a glass plate, and a mobile liquid phase to separate the components of the mixture.

- Gas chromatography (GC) separates mixtures on the basis of their distribution between a stationary liquid phase and a mobile gas phase.

- Spectrophotometry is the study of the absorption of light by chemical substances.

- Most forensic laboratories use ultraviolet (UV) and infrared (IR) spectrophotometers to characterize chemical compounds.

- IR spectrophotometry provides a far more complex pattern than UV spectrophotometry. Because different materials have distinctively different infrared spectra, each IR spectrum is equivalent to a "fingerprint" of that substance.

- Mass spectrometry characterizes organic molecules by observing their fragmentation pattern after their collision with a beam of high-energy electrons.

- Infrared spectrophotometry and mass spectrophotometry typically are used to specifically identify a drug substance.

Collection and Preservation of Drug Evidence

Preparation of drug evidence for submission to the crime laboratory is normally relatively simple, accomplished with minimal precautions in the field. The field investigator must ensure that the evidence is properly packaged and labeled for delivery to the laboratory. Considering the countless forms and varieties of drug evidence seized, it is not practical to prescribe any single packaging procedure for fulfilling these requirements. Generally, common sense is the best guide in such situations, keeping in mind that the package must prevent loss and/or cross-contamination of the contents. Often, the original container in which the drug was seized will suffice to meet these requirements. Specimens suspected of containing volatile solvents, such as those involved in glue-sniffing cases, must be packaged in an airtight container to prevent evaporation of the solvent. All packages must be marked with sufficient information to ensure identification by the officer in future legal proceedings and to establish the chain of custody.

To aid the drug analyst, the investigator should supply any background information that may relate to a drug's identity. Analysis time can be markedly reduced when the chemist has this information. For the same reason, the results of drug-screening tests used in the field must also be transmitted to the laboratory. However, although these tests may indicate the presence of a drug and may help the officer establish probable cause to search and arrest a suspect, they do not offer conclusive evidence of a drug's identity.

Chapter Review

- A drug is a natural or synthetic substance that is used to produce physiological or psychological effects in humans or other animals.

- Nondrug factors that play a part in drug dependence include the personal characteristics of the user, his or her expectations about the drug experience, society's attitudes and possible responses, and the setting in which the drug is used.

- Physical dependence is defined as the physiological need for a drug that has been brought about by its regular use. Psychological dependence is the conditioned use of a drug caused by underlying emotional needs.

- Narcotic drugs are analgesics, meaning they relieve pain by depressing the central nervous system.

- The most common source for narcotic drugs is opium. Morphine is extracted from opium and used to synthesize heroin.

- Opiates are not derived from opium or morphine, but they have the same physiological effects on the body. Examples of opiates include methadone and OxyContin (oxycodone).

- Hallucinogens cause marked changes in normal thought processes, perceptions, and moods. Marijuana is the most well-known drug in this class. Other hallucinogens include LSD, mescaline, PCP, psilocybin, and MDMA (Ecstasy).

- Depressants decrease the activity of the central nervous system, calm irritability and excitability, and produce sleep. Depressants include alcohol (ethanol), barbiturates, tranquilizers, and various substances that can be sniffed, such as airplane glue or model cement.

- Stimulants increase the activity of the central nervous system and are taken to increase alertness and activity. Stimulants include amphetamines, sometimes known as "uppers" or "speed," and cocaine, which in its freebase form is known as crack.

- Club drugs are synthetic drugs that are used at nightclubs, bars, and raves (all-night dance parties). Some club drugs act as stimulants; others have depressant effects.

- Anabolic steroids are synthetic compounds that are chemically related to the male sex hormone testosterone. Anabolic steroids are often abused by individuals who are interested in accelerating muscle growth.

- Federal law establishes five schedules of classification for controlled dangerous substances on the basis of a drug's potential for abuse, potential for physical and psychological dependence, and medical value.

- Analysts use screening tests to determine the identity of drugs present in a sample. These tests reduce the number of possible drugs to a small and manageable number.

- A series of color tests produce characteristic colors for the more commonly encountered illicit drugs.

- After preliminary testing, forensic chemists use more specific tests to identify a drug substance to the exclusion of all other known chemical substances.

- Chromatography is a means of separating and tentatively identifying the components of a mixture.

- TLC uses a solid stationary phase, usually coated onto a glass plate, and a mobile liquid phase to separate the components of the mixture.

- Gas chromatography (GC) separates mixtures on the basis of their distribution between a stationary liquid phase and a mobile gas phase.

- Spectrophotometry is the study of the absorption of light by chemical substances.

- Most forensic laboratories use ultraviolet (UV) and infrared (IR) spectrophotometers to characterize chemical compounds.

- IR spectrophotometry provides a far more complex pattern than UV spectrophotometry. Because different materials have distinctively different infrared spectra, each IR spectrum is equivalent to a "fingerprint" of that substance.

- Mass spectrometry characterizes organic molecules by observing their fragmentation pattern after their collision with a beam of high-energy electrons.

- Infrared spectrophotometry and mass spectrophotometry typically are used to specifically identify a drug substance.

Quick Lab: Chromatography

Materials:

Roll of chromatography paper
5 different types of markers/pens
Thin piece of wire about 5 inches long
Beaker
Water

Procedure:

Chromatography is a process that can be used to identify different substances that make up a mixture. In forensics this process can be used on many types of evidence. In this activity you will perform paper chromatography to identify the components of different types of ink. Cut a piece of chromatography paper that is about 5 inches long. Select one of the markers/pens and place a dot at one end of the paper, leaving a small gap between the dot and end of paper. At the other end, push the wire through the paper so that the paper is hanging off of the wire with the dot end down. Fill the bottom of the beaker with water. Place the wire across the top of the beaker with the paper hanging in the beaker so that the dot end of the paper is in the water, but the dot is just above the water. Allow 5 minutes for the separation to occur. When the ink has stopped separating, take the paper out of the beaker and let it dry. Repeat the process for all the markers/pens. Your teacher could give you an unknown ink to test and compare to the samples you have just tested.

Follow-Up Questions:

1. Did all of the inks separate during the process? If not, why do you think certain inks did not separate?

2. Besides ink, what other types of evidence could chromatography be used with?

3. Did you find a match to the unknown ink? Was it exactly the same as one of the other inks? If not, what was different?

Quick Lab: Drug Screening Test

Materials:

Ward's Natural Science Crime Scene Drug Bust Kit

Procedure:

Often drugs are part of an investigation in forensics. Suspects may need to be tested to see if they have been using or may be on some type of drug. To do this, a screening test is completed. Follow the directions of the kit to see how some screening tests are completed.

Follow-up questions can be found in the kit handout section.

Quick Lab:
What Is the White Powder?

Materials:

Table salt
Baking soda
Cornstarch
Sugar
Flour
Water
Vinegar
Iodine
Bunsen burner/candle
Aluminum foil
Tongs
Slides
Toothpicks

Procedure:

Unknown substances may be found at crime scenes. When this happens, it is important to be able to identify what substance is actually present. In this activity you will test five white powders to look for differences among them in order to identify an unknown sample. First, mix each powder individually with water. Do this by placing a small amount of the powder on a slide and adding a drop of water to it; mix with a toothpick. Record what you observe. Do this for each powder. Repeat this process twice more, once using vinegar and once using iodine instead of water. Do not get iodine on anything but the slide; it stains! Next create a foil tray that will hold a small sample of powder. Carefully light the candle or the Bunsen burner; be sure to have eye protection on for this part of the activity. Place a small amount of the powder on the tray and use the tongs to hold it over the candle for a minute. Record your observations. Repeat this for each powder. When you are finished, your teacher may choose to give you an unknown powder sample for you to test and determine which powder it is.

Follow-Up Questions:

1. Of the different tests performed, which one would be the best to use to identify an unknown powder?

2. In this activity you tested pure samples. Would this be the case if you were investigating a crime in the real world? Explain your answer.

3. Were you able to identify the unknown sample provided by your teacher?

Review Questions

1. In chromatography, the distribution of a gas between the liquid and gas phases is determined by
   a. the solubility of the gas in the liquid.
   b. the volume of the gas in the container.
   c. the density of the gas relative to the liquid.
   d. the mass of the gas relative to the liquid.

2. Spectrophotometry uses which light source?
   a. visible
   b. UV
   c. Infrared
   d. all of the above

3. The higher the solubility of a gas in a liquid, the greater the tendency of the gas molecules to
   a. move from a liquid phase to a gaseous or vapor phase.
   b. remain in the liquid phase.
   c. move from a liquid phase to a solid state.
   d. disperse.

4. All of the following are chromatographic processes found to be applicable for solving analytical problems encountered in the crime laboratory except:
   a. thin-layer chromatography
   b. gas chromatography
   c. GC/MS
   d. solid-state chromatography

5. Which of the following tests can be considered specific in itself for identification purposes?
   a. mass spectrometry
   b. gas spectrometry
   c. gas chromatography
   d. electromagnetic radiation

6. True or False: Although cocaine is legally classified as a narcotic, pharmacologically it is actually a powerful central nervous system stimulant.

7. True or False: The quantity of a substance separated by gas chromatography can be determined by its R_f value.

8. True or False: The gas chromatography/mass spectrometry (GC/MS) combination produces a fragmentation pattern that serves as a virtual "fingerprint" of a chemical substance because, with few exceptions, no two substances fragment in the same fashion.

9. True or False: Chromatography is a means of separating and tentatively identifying the components of a mixture.

10. True or False: Infrared spectrophotometry allows for the identification of different materials because different organic substances always produce distinctive infrared spectra.

11. What is a drug? How has drug use affected the growth of crime laboratories in the United States?

12. Name three nondrug factors that play a part in drug dependence.

13. Define physical dependence and psychological dependence.

14. What is the pharmacological definition of a narcotic?

15. What is the source of most narcotic analgesics? Name two popular drugs prepared from this substance.

16. Name two synthetic opiates and describe the purpose for which each typically is used.

17. What is a hallucinogen? Name three commonly used hallucinogens.

18. What is the most widely used illicit drug in the United States? What is the active ingredient in this drug?

19. Arrange the following parts or products of the Cannabis plant in order of THC content, from highest to lowest concentration of THC: flowers, leaves, resin, seeds, stem.

20. List three potential medical uses of marijuana.

21. What is angel dust and what are the negative consequences of long-term use?

22. What is the most widely abused drug in the United States?

23. In what class of drugs do alcohol and barbiturates belong? What is the main physiological effect of such drugs?

24. What is a stimulant? Name two widely used stimulants.

25. Name two potent forms of methamphetamine. How is each of these drugs typically taken into the body?

26. What popular stimulant is derived from a plant that grows in the Andes mountains of South America?

27. What is crack, and how is it produced?

28. Name club drugs belonging to three different classes of drugs and indicate the class to which each belongs.

29. What are anabolic steroids, and why were they developed?

30. What is the difference between a screening test and a confirmation test?

31. Name two types of empirical tests used to identify drugs. Why are these tests referred to as empirical?

32. What is the difference between a qualitative evaluation and a quantitative evaluation?

33. Why is chromatography particularly well suited to the needs of a drug analyst?

34. Name three distinct advantages of gas chromatography in the identification of drugs.

35. What is the main drawback of gas chromatography in the identification of drugs?

36. What phenomenon forms the basis of spectrophotometry?

37. What is the main advantage of infrared spectrophotometry over ultraviolet or visible-light spectrophotometry?

38. With what analytical device is a gas chromatograph often connected to analyze drug mixtures, and why?

Application and Critical Thinking

1. An individual who has been using a drug for an extended period of time suddenly finds himself unable to secure more of the drug. He acts nervous and irritable and is hyperactive. He seems almost desperate to find more of the drug, but experiences no sickness, pain, or other outward physical discomfort. Based on his behavior, what drugs might he possibly have been using? Explain your answer.

2. Following are descriptions of behavior that are characteristic among users of certain classes of drugs. For each description, indicate the class of drug (narcotics, stimulants, and so on) for which the behavior is most characteristic. For each description, also name at least one drug that produces the described effects.
   a. slurred speech, slow reaction time, impaired judgment, reduced coordination
   b. intense emotional responses, anxiety, altered sensory perceptions
   c. alertness, feelings of strength and confidence, rapid speech and movement, decreased appetite
   d. drowsiness, intense feeling of well-being, relief from pain

3. Following are descriptions of four hypothetical drugs. According to the Controlled Substances Act, under which drug schedule would each substance be classified?
   a. This drug has a high potential for psychological dependence, it currently has accepted medical uses in the United States, and the distributor is not required to report to the U.S. Drug Enforcement Administration.
   b. This drug has medical use in the United States, is not limited by manufacturing quotas, and may be exported without a permit.
   c. This drug must be stored in a vault or safe, requires separate record keeping, and may be distributed with a prescription.
   d. This drug may not be imported or exported without a permit, is subject to manufacturing quotas, and currently has no medical use in the United States.

4. A police officer stops a motorist who is driving erratically and notices a bag of white powder on the front seat of the car that he suspects contains heroin. The officer brings the bag to you, a forensic scientist in the local crime lab. Name one screening test that you might perform to determine the presence of heroin. Assuming the powder tests positive for heroin, what should you do next?

5. The figure below shows a chromatogram of a known mixture of barbiturates. Based on this figure, answer the following questions:
   a. What barbiturate detected by the chromatogram had the longest retention time?
   b. Which barbiturate had the shortest retention time?
   c. What is the approximate retention time of amobarbital?

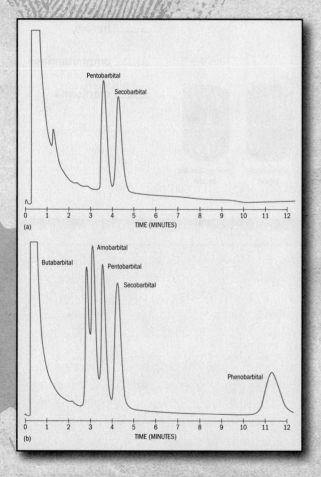

6. When investigating a potential warehouse for storing illegal drugs, the police collected a variety of drugs. The drugs were tested with presumptive color tests to determine their possible identity. The test tubes shown in the figure display the positive color tests. Match the drug on the right with the color test on the left and name the test.

A	B	C	D	E
purple liquid	pink layer above blue chloroform layer	purple liquid above green vegetation	violet-blue liquid	orange-brown liquid

_____ cocaine

_____ barbituates

_____ heroin

_____ amphetamines

_____ marijuana

Virtual Lab: Thin-Layer Chromatography

To perform a virtual thin-layer chromatography lab, go to www.pearsoncus-tom.com/us/vlm

Virtual Lab: Drug Identification

To perform a virtual drug identification, go to www.pearsoncustom.com/us/vlm

Endnotes

1. *Marijuana—A Signal of Misunderstanding* (Washington, D.C.: U.S. Government Printing Office, 1972), p. 56.

2. Field-test color kits for drugs can be purchased from various commercial manufacturers.

3. Powers of 10 are quite useful and simple for handling large or small numbers. The exponent expresses the number of places the decimal point must be moved. If it is positive, the decimal point is moved to the right; if it is negative, the decimal point is moved to the left. Thus, to express 1×10^{-9} as a number, the decimal point is simply moved nine places to the left of 1.

Learning Objectives

After studying this chapter you should be able to:

- Explain how alcohol is absorbed into the bloodstream, transported throughout the body, and eliminated by oxidation and excretion

- Understand the process by which alcohol is excreted in the breath via the lungs

- Understand the concepts of infrared and fuel cell breath-testing devices for alcohol testing

- Describe commonly employed field sobriety tests to assess alcohol impairment

- List and contrast laboratory procedures for measuring the concentration of alcohol in the blood

- Relate the precautions to be taken to properly preserve blood in order to analyze its alcohol content

- Understand the significance of implied-consent laws and the *Schmerber* v. *California* case to traffic enforcement

- Describe techniques that forensic toxicologists use to isolate and identify drugs and poisons

- Appreciate the significance of finding a drug in human tissues and organs to assessing impairment

National Science Content Standards

  Scientific Inquiry

 Science and Technology

 Physical Science

 Science in Personal and Social Perspective

 Life Science

 History and Nature of Science

Harold Shipman, Dr. Death

Kathleen Grundy's sudden death in 1998 was shocking news to her daughter, Angela Woodruff. Mrs. Grundy, an 81-year-old widow, was believed to be in good health when her physician, Dr. Harold Shipman, visited her a few hours before her demise. Some hours later, when friends came to her home to check on her whereabouts, they found Mrs. Grundy lying on a sofa fully dressed and dead.

Dr. Shipman pronounced her dead and informed her daughter that an autopsy was not necessary. A few days later, Mrs. Woodruff was surprised to learn that a will had surfaced leaving all of Mrs. Grundy's money to Dr. Shipman. The will was immediately recognized as a forgery and led to the exhumation of Mrs. Grundy's body. A toxicological analysis of the remains revealed a lethal quantity of morphine.

In retrospect, there was good reason to suspect that Dr. Shipman was capable of foul play. In the 1970s, he was asked to leave a medical practice because of a drug abuse problem and charges that he obtained drugs by forgery and deception. However, Dr. Shipman was quickly back to practicing medicine. By 1998, local undertakers became suspicious at the number of his patients who were dying. What is more, they all seemed to be elderly women who were found sitting in a chair or lying fully clothed on a bed. As police investigated, the horror of Dr. Shipman's deeds became apparent. One clinical audit estimated that Dr. Shipman killed at least 236 of his patients over a 24-year period. Most of the deaths were attributed to fatal doses of heroin or morphine. Toxicological analysis on seven exhumed bodies clearly showed significant quantities of morphine. Convicted of murder, Dr. Shipman hanged himself in his jail cell in 2004.

Forensic Toxicology

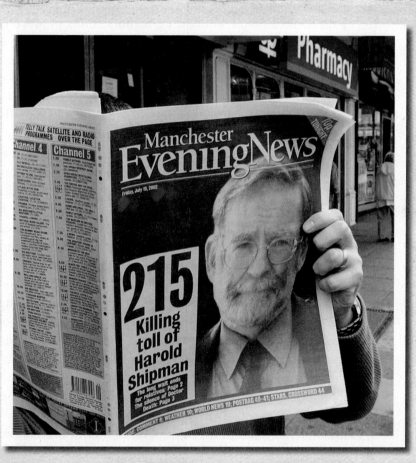

Key Terms

absorption	excretion
acid	fuel cell detector
alveoli	metabolism
anticoagulant	oxidation
artery	pH scale
base	preservative
capillary	toxicologist
catalyst	vein

The Role of Forensic Toxicology

It is no secret that in spite of the concerted efforts of law enforcement agencies to prevent distribution and sale of illicit drugs, thousands die every year from intentional or unintentional administration of drugs, and many more innocent lives are lost as a result of the erratic and frequently uncontrollable behavior of individuals under the influence of drugs. But one should not automatically attribute these occurrences to the wide proliferation of illicit-drug markets. For example, in the United States alone, drug manufacturers produce enough sedatives and antidepressants each year to provide every man, woman, and child with about 40 pills. All of the statistical and medical evidence shows ethyl alcohol, a legal over-the-counter drug, to be the most heavily abused drug in Western countries.

toxicologist
An individual whose job is to detect and identify drugs and poisons in body fluids, tissues, and organs

Because the uncontrolled use of drugs has become a worldwide problem affecting all segments of society, the role of the **toxicologist** has taken on new and added significance. Toxicologists detect and identify drugs and poisons in body fluids, tissues, and organs. Their services are required not only in such legal institutions as crime laboratories and medical examiners' offices; they also reach into hospital laboratories—where identifying a drug overdose may represent the difference between life and death—and into various health facilities that monitor the intake of drugs and other toxic substances. Primary examples include performing blood tests on children exposed to leaded paints and analyzing the urine of addicts enrolled in methadone maintenance programs.

The role of the forensic toxicologist is limited to matters that pertain to violations of criminal law. However, responsibility for performing toxicological services in a criminal justice system varies considerably throughout the United States. In systems with a crime laboratory independent of the medical examiner, this responsibility may reside with one or the other or may be shared by both. Some systems, however, take advantage of the expertise of government health department laboratories and assign this role to them. Nevertheless, whatever facility handles this work, its caseload will reflect the prevailing popularity of the drugs that are abused in the community. In most cases, this means that the forensic toxicologist handles numerous requests to determine the presence of alcohol in the body.

Forty percent of all traffic deaths in the United States, nearly 17,500 fatalities per year, are alcohol related, along with more than 2 million injuries each year requiring hospital treatment. This highway death toll, as well as the untold damage to life, limb, and property, shows the dangerous consequences of alcohol abuse (see Figure 6–1). Because of the prevalence of alcohol in the toxicologist's work, we will begin by taking a closer look at how the body processes and responds to alcohol.

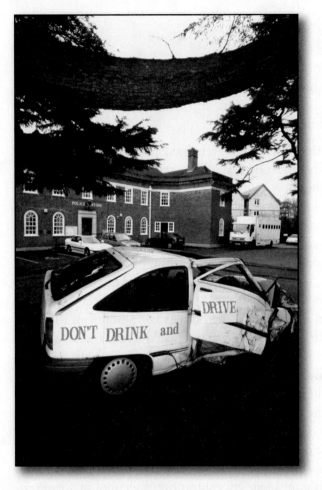

FIGURE 6–1
Alcohol consumption
increases the risk of traffic
accidents and fatalities.
A crashed car is on display
as part of a Don't Drink
and Drive campaign.
Courtesy Peter Arnold, Inc.

Quick Review

- Forensic toxicologists detect and identify drugs and poisons in body fluids, tissues, and organs in matters that pertain to violations of criminal laws.

- Ethyl alcohol is the most heavily abused drug in Western countries.

Toxicology of Alcohol

The subject of the analysis of alcohol immediately confronts us with the primary objective of forensic toxicology—detecting and isolating drugs in the body to determine their influence on human behavior. Knowing how the body metabolizes alcohol provides the key to understanding its effects on human behavior. In the case of alcohol, however, the problem is further complicated by practical considerations. The predominant role of the automobile in our society has mandated the imposition of laws to protect the public from the drinking driver. This has meant that toxicologists have had to devise rapid and specific procedures for measuring the degree of alcohol intoxication. The methods used must be suitably designed to test hundreds of thousands of motorists annually without causing them undue physical harm or unreasonable inconvenience, while at the same time providing a reliable diagnosis that can be supported and defended within the framework of the legal system.

The Metabolism of Alcohol

All chemicals that enter the body are eventually broken down by chemicals in the body and transformed into other chemicals that are easier to eliminate. This process of transformation, called **metabolism**, consists of three basic steps: absorption, distribution, and elimination.

Absorption and Distribution Alcohol, or ethyl alcohol, is a colorless liquid normally diluted with water and consumed as a beverage. Alcohol appears in the blood within minutes after it has been consumed and slowly increases in concentration while it is being absorbed from the stomach and the small intestine into the bloodstream. During the **absorption** phase, alcohol slowly enters the body's bloodstream and is carried to all parts of the body. When the absorption period is completed, the alcohol becomes distributed uniformly throughout the watery portions of the body—that is, throughout about two-thirds of the body volume. Fat, bones, and hair are low in water content and therefore contain little alcohol, whereas alcohol concentration in the rest of the body is fairly uniform. After absorption is completed, a maximum alcohol level is reached in the blood, and the postabsorption period begins. Then, the alcohol concentration slowly decreases until a zero level is again reached.

Many factors determine the rate at which alcohol is absorbed into the bloodstream, including the total time taken to consume the drink, the alcohol content of the beverage, the amount consumed, and the quantity and type of food present in the stomach at the time of drinking. With so many variables, it is difficult to predict just how long the absorption process will require. For example, beer is absorbed more slowly than an equivalent concentration of alcohol in water, apparently because of the carbohydrates present in beer. Also, alcohol consumed on an empty stomach is absorbed faster than an equivalent amount of alcohol taken when there is food in the stomach. The longer the total time required for complete absorption to occur, the lower the peak alcohol concentration in the blood (see Figure 6–2). Depending on a combination of factors, maximum blood-alcohol concentration may not be reached until two or three hours have elapsed from the time of consumption. However, under normal social drinking conditions, it takes anywhere from 30 to 90 minutes from the time of the final drink until the absorption process is completed.

Elimination As the alcohol is circulated by the bloodstream, the body begins to eliminate it. Alcohol is eliminated through two mechanisms—**oxidation** and **excretion**. Nearly all of the alcohol (95–98 percent) consumed is eventually oxidized to carbon dioxide and water. Oxidation takes place almost entirely in the liver. Here, in the presence of the enzyme alcohol dehydrogenase, the alcohol is converted into acetaldehyde and then to acetic acid. The acetic acid is subsequently oxidized in practically all parts of the body to carbon dioxide and water.

The remaining alcohol is excreted unchanged in the breath, urine, and perspiration. Most significantly, the amount of alcohol exhaled in the breath is in direct proportion to the concentration of alcohol in the blood. This observation has had a tremendous impact on the technology and procedures used for blood-alcohol testing. The development of instruments to reliably measure breath for its alcohol

---

metabolism
The transformation of a chemical in the body to other chemicals to facilitate its elimination from the body

absorption
Passage of alcohol across the wall of the stomach and small intestine into the bloodstream

oxidation
The combination of oxygen with other substances to produce new products

excretion
Elimination of alcohol from the body in an unchanged state; alcohol is normally excreted in breath and urine

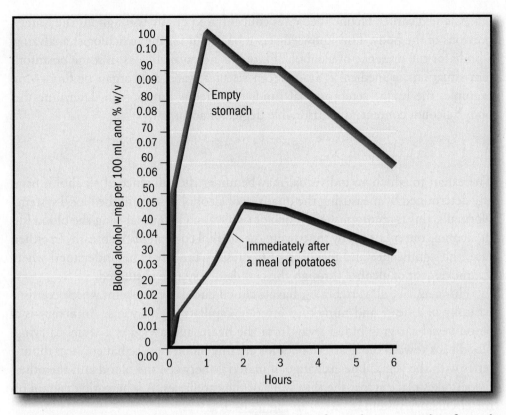

FIGURE 6–2
Blood-alcohol concentrations after ingestion of 2 ounces of pure alcohol mixed in 8 ounces of water (equivalent to about 5 ounces of 80-proof vodka). *Courtesy U.S. Department of Transportation, Washington, D.C.*

content has made possible the testing of millions of people in a rapid, safe, and convenient manner.

The fate of alcohol in the body is therefore relatively simple—namely, absorption into the bloodstream, distribution throughout the body's water, and finally, elimination by oxidation and excretion. The elimination or "burn-off" rate of alcohol varies in different individuals; 0.015 percent w/v (weight per volume) per hour seems to be an average value once the absorption process is complete.[1] However, this figure is an average that varies by as much as 30 percent among individuals.

Blood-Alcohol Concentration Logically, the most obvious measure of intoxication would be the amount of liquor a person has consumed. Unfortunately, most arrests are made after the fact, when such information is not available to legal authorities; furthermore, even if these data could be collected, numerous related factors, such as body weight and the rate of alcohol's absorption into the body, are so variable that it would be impossible to prescribe uniform standards that would yield reliable alcohol intoxication levels for all individuals.

Theoretically, for a true determination of the quantity of alcohol impairing an individual's normal body functions, it would be best to remove a portion of brain tissue and analyze it for alcohol content. For obvious reasons, this cannot be done on living subjects. Consequently, toxicologists concentrate on the blood, which provides the medium for circulating alcohol throughout the body, carrying it to all tissues, including the brain. Fortunately, experimental evidence supports this approach and shows blood-alcohol concentration to be directly proportional to the concentration of alcohol in the brain. From the medicolegal point of view, blood-alcohol levels have become the accepted standard for relating alcohol intake to its effect on the body.

As noted earlier, alcohol becomes concentrated evenly throughout the watery portions of the body. This knowledge can be useful for the toxicologist analyzing a body for the presence of alcohol. If blood is not available, as in some postmortem situations, a medical examiner can select a water-rich organ or fluid—for example, the brain, cerebrospinal fluid, or vitreous humor—to determine the body's alcohol content to a reasonable degree of accuracy.

Alcohol in the Circulatory System

The extent to which an individual may be under the influence of alcohol is usually determined by measuring the quantity of alcohol present in the blood system. Normally, this is accomplished in one of two ways: (1) by analyzing the blood for its alcohol content or (2) by measuring the alcohol content of the breath. In either case, the significance and meaning of the results can better be understood when the movement of alcohol through the circulatory system is studied.

Humans, like all vertebrates, have a closed circulatory system, which consists basically of a heart and numerous arteries, capillaries, and veins. An **artery** is a blood vessel carrying blood away from the heart, and a **vein** is a vessel carrying blood back toward the heart. **Capillaries** are tiny blood vessels that connect the arteries with the veins. The exchange of materials between the blood and the other tissues takes place across the thin walls of the capillaries. A schematic diagram of the circulatory system is shown in Figure 6–3.

artery
A blood vessel that carries blood away from the heart

vein
A blood vessel that carries blood toward the heart

capillary
A tiny blood vessel that receives blood from arteries and carries it to veins, and across whose walls exchange of materials between the blood and the tissues takes place

FIGURE 6–3
Simplified diagram of the human circulatory system. Dark vessels contain oxygenated blood; light vessels contain deoxygenated blood.

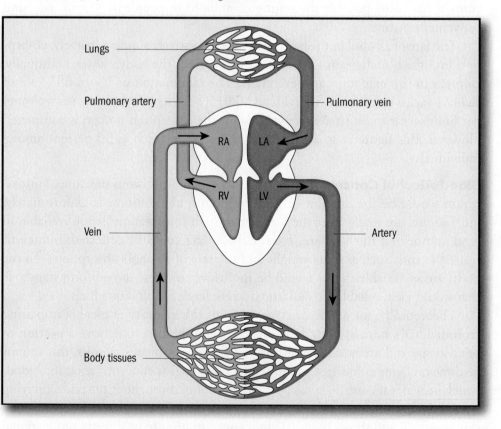

Ingestion and Distribution Let us now trace the movement of alcohol through the human circulatory system. After alcohol is ingested, it moves down the esophagus into the stomach. About 20 percent of the alcohol is absorbed through the stomach walls into the portal vein of the blood system. The remaining alcohol passes into the blood through the walls of the small intestine. Once in the blood, the alcohol is carried to the liver, where enzymes begin to break it down.

As the blood (still carrying the alcohol) leaves the liver, it moves up to the heart. The blood enters the upper right chamber of the heart, called the right atrium (or auricle), and is forced into the lower right chamber of the heart, known as the right ventricle. Having returned to the heart from its circulation through the tissues, the blood at this time contains very little oxygen and much carbon dioxide. Consequently, the blood must be pumped up to the lungs, through the pulmonary artery, to be replenished with oxygen.

Aeration In the lungs, the respiratory system bridges with the circulatory system so that oxygen can enter the blood and carbon dioxide can leave it. As shown in Figure 6–4, the pulmonary artery branches into capillaries lying close to tiny pear-shaped sacs called **alveoli**. The lungs contain about 250 million alveoli, all located at the ends of the bronchial tubes. The bronchial tubes connect to the windpipe (trachea), which leads up to the mouth and nose (see Figure 6–5). At the surface of the alveolar sacs, blood flowing through the capillaries comes in contact with fresh oxygenated air in the sacs.

alveoli
Small sacs in the lungs through whose walls air and other gases are exchanged between the breath and the blood

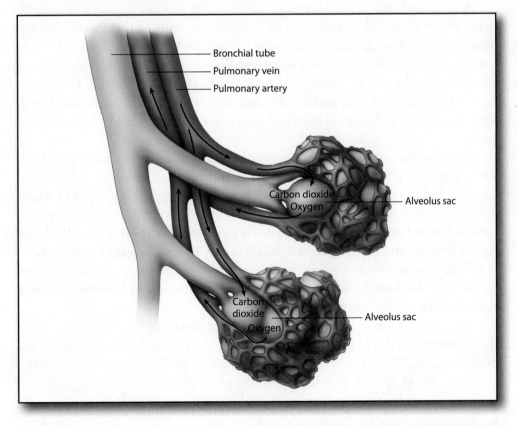

Bronchial tube
Pulmonary vein
Pulmonary artery

Carbon dioxide
Oxygen
Alveolus sac

Carbon dioxide
Oxygen
Alveolus sac

FIGURE 6–4
Gas exchange in the lungs. Blood flows from the pulmonary artery into vessels that lie close to the walls of the alveoli sacs. Here the blood gives up its carbon dioxide and absorbs oxygen. The oxygenated blood leaves the lungs via the pulmonary vein and returns to the heart.

FIGURE 6–5
The respiratory system. The trachea connects the nose and mouth to the bronchial tubes. The bronchial tubes divide into numerous branches that terminate in the alveoli sacs in the lungs.

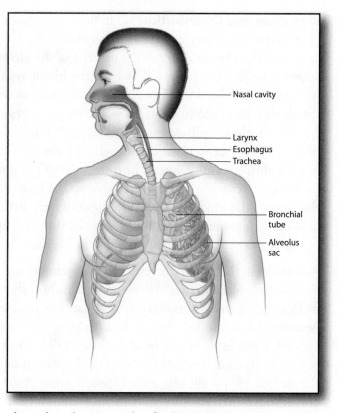

Nasal cavity

Larynx
Esophagus
Trachea

Bronchial tube

Alveolus sac

A rapid exchange now takes place between the fresh air in the sacs and the spent air in the blood. Oxygen passes through the walls of the alveoli into the blood while carbon dioxide is discharged from the blood into the air. If, during this exchange, alcohol or any other volatile substance is in the blood, it too will pass into the alveoli. During breathing, the carbon dioxide and alcohol are expelled through the nose and mouth, and the alveoli sacs are replenished with fresh oxygenated air breathed into the lungs, allowing the process to begin all over again.

The distribution of alcohol between the blood and alveolar air is similar to the example of a gas dissolved in an enclosed beaker of water, as described in Chapter 5. Here again, one can use Henry's law (see pages 177-178) to explain how the alcohol will divide itself between the air and blood. Henry's Law may now be restated as follows: **When a volatile chemical (alcohol) is dissolved in a liquid (blood) and is brought to equilibrium with air (alveolar breath), there is a fixed ratio between the concentration of the volatile compound (alcohol) in air (alveolar breath) and its concentration in the liquid (blood), and this ratio is constant for a given temperature.**

The temperature at which the breath leaves the mouth is normally 34°C. At this temperature, the ratio of alcohol in the blood to alcohol in alveolar air is approximately 2,100 to 1. In other words, 1 milliliter of blood contains nearly the same amount of alcohol as 2,100 milliliters of alveolar breath. Henry's law thus becomes a basis for relating breath to blood-alcohol concentration.

Recirculation and Absorption Now let's return to the circulating blood. After emerging from the lungs, the oxygenated blood is rushed back to the upper left chamber of the heart (left atrium) by the pulmonary vein. When the left atrium contracts, it forces the blood through a valve into the left ventricle, which is the lower left chamber of the heart. The left ventricle then pumps the freshly oxygenated blood into the arteries, which carry the blood to all parts of the body. Each of these arteries, in turn, branches into smaller arteries, which eventually connect with the numerous tiny capillaries embedded in the tissues. Here the alcohol moves out of the blood and into the tissues. The blood then runs from the capillaries into tiny veins that fuse to form larger veins. These veins eventually lead back to the heart to complete the circuit.

During absorption, the concentration of alcohol in the arterial blood is considerably higher than the concentration of alcohol in the venous blood. One typical study revealed a subject's arterial blood-alcohol level to be 41 percent higher than the venous level 30 minutes after the last drink.[2] This difference is thought to exist because of the rapid diffusion of alcohol into the body tissues from venous blood during the early phases of absorption. Because the administration of a blood test requires drawing venous blood from the arm, this test is clearly to the advantage of a subject who may still be in the absorption stage. However, once absorption is complete, the alcohol becomes equally distributed throughout the blood system.

Quick Review

- Alcohol appears in the blood within minutes after it has been taken by mouth. It slowly increases in concentration while it is being absorbed from the stomach and the small intestine into the bloodstream.

- When all of the alcohol has been absorbed, a maximum alcohol level is reached in the blood, and the postabsorption period begins. During postabsorption, the alcohol concentration slowly decreases until a zero level is reached.

- Elimination of alcohol throughout the body is accomplished through oxidation and excretion. Oxidation takes place almost entirely in the liver, while alcohol is excreted unchanged in the breath, urine, and perspiration.

- Breath testing devices operate on the principle that the ratio between the concentration of alcohol in alveolar breath and its concentration in blood is fixed.

Testing for Intoxication

From a practical point of view, the idea of drawing blood from a vein to test motorists suspected of being under the influence of alcohol simply does not provide a convenient method for monitoring drivers. The need to transport the suspect to a location where a medically qualified person can draw blood would be costly and time consuming, considering the hundreds of tests that the average police department must conduct every year. The methods used must be designed to test hundreds of thousands of motorists annually without causing them undue physical harm or unreasonable inconvenience, while providing a reliable diagnosis that can be supported and defended within the framework of the legal system. This means that toxicologists have had to devise rapid and specific procedures for measuring a driver's degree of alcohol intoxication that can be easily administered in the field.

Breath Testing for Alcohol

The most widespread method for rapidly determining alcohol intoxication is breath testing. A breath tester is simply a device for collecting and measuring the alcohol content of alveolar breath. As we saw earlier, alcohol is expelled unchanged in the breath of a person who has been drinking. A breath-test measures the alcohol concentration in the pulmonary artery by measuring its concentration in alveolar breath. Thus, breath analysis provides an easily obtainable specimen along with a rapid and accurate result.

Breath-test results obtained during the absorption phase may be higher than results obtained from a simultaneous analysis of venous blood. However, the former are more reflective of the concentration of alcohol reaching the brain and, therefore, more accurately reflect the effects of alcohol on the subject. Again, once absorption is complete, the difference between a blood test and a breath test should be minimal.

Breath-Test Instruments The first widely used instrument for measuring the alcohol content of alveolar breath was the Breathalyzer, developed in 1954 by R. F. Borkenstein, who was a captain in the Indiana State Police. Although the Breathalyzer has undergone several modifications since its development, the basic theory and design of the instrument have not changed. The "Inside the Science" feature on the Breathalyzer explains the working of the device in greater detail.

Starting in the 1970s, the Breathalyzer was phased out and replaced by other instruments for measuring the alcoholic content of alveolar breath. Like the Breathalyzer, they assume that the ratio of alcohol in the blood to alcohol in alveolar breath is 2,100 to 1 at a mouth temperature of 34°C. Unlike the Breathalyzer, modern breath testers are free of chemicals. These devices include infrared light absorption devices and **fuel cell detectors**.

fuel cell detector
A detector in which a chemical reaction involving alcohol produces electricity

A fuel cell like the one in "Inside the Science" converts a fuel and an oxidant into an electrical current. In evidential breath testing devices that use this concept, breath alcohol is the fuel and atmospheric oxygen is the oxidant. Alcohol is converted in the fuel cell into acetic acid, generating a current that is proportional to the quantity of alcohol present in the breath.

Infrared and fuel-cell-based breath testers are microprocessor controlled so that all an operator has to do is press a start button and the instrument automatically moves through a sequence of steps that produce a printout of the subject's test results. These instruments also perform self-diagnostic tests to ascertain whether the instrument is in proper operating condition.

Considerations in Breath Testing An important feature of breath-testing instruments is that they can be connected to an external alcohol standard or simulator in the form of either a liquid or a gas. The liquid simulator comprises a known concentration of alcohol in water. It is heated to a controlled temperature, and the vapor formed above the liquid is pumped into the instrument. Dry-gas standards typically consist of a known concentration of alcohol mixed with an inert gas and compressed in cylinders. The external standard is automatically sampled by the breath-testing instrument before and/or after the subject's breath sample is taken and recorded. Thus, the operator can check the accuracy of the instrument against the known alcohol standard.

Inside the Science

The Breathalyzer

The Breathalyzer is a device for collecting and measuring the alcohol content of alveolar breath (see Figure 1). The subject blows into a mouthpiece that leads into a metal cylinder. The last portion of breath (alveolar breath) is trapped in the cylinder. The amount of breath collected in this manner is 52.5 milliliters, or 1/40 of 2,100 milliliters.* We have already seen that the amount of alcohol in 2,100 milliliters of alveolar breath approximates that in 1 milliliter of blood. Hence, in essence, the Breathalyzer is designed to measure the alcohol concentration present in 1/40 of a milliliter of blood.

FIGURE 1
Schematic diagram of a Breathalyzer. *Courtesy Draeger Safety, Inc., Breathalyzer Division, Durango, Colo.*

*Actually, the collection cylinder is designed to hold 56.5 milliliters of breath. This is because, having left the mouth at 34°C, the breath will expand when heated to 50°C in the cylinder. Furthermore, added breath is needed to compensate for the air that remains in the delivery tube leading to the test ampoule.

The quantity of alcohol in the trapped breath is measured by passing the breath into a glass ampoule containing potassium dichromate, sulfuric acid, and water. Any alcohol in the breath immediately dissolves in the dichromate solution and is oxidized to acetic acid. In the oxidation process, potassium dichromate is also destroyed. The extent of this destruction is measured by the Breathalyzer and is related to the quantity of alcohol passed into the ampoule.

Inside the Science (CONTINUED)

Basically, the Breathalyzer is a spectrophotometer (see Chapter 5) designed to measure the absorption of light passing through the potassium dichromate solution at a single wavelength. To better understand its operation, let's examine what is happening in the ampoule when alcohol is converted to acetic acid. Whenever a chemical reaction occurs between two or more substances, chemists use a chemical equation as a shorthand method to describe the changes taking place. The equation serves two purposes: it identifies the participants, and it describes the quantitative aspects of the reaction.

The following equation depicts the chemical reaction taking place in the ampoule:

$$2K_2Cr_2O_7 \quad + \quad 3C_2H_5OH \quad + \quad 8H_2SO_4 \quad \rightarrow$$

potassium   ethyl   sulfuric   yields
dichromate   alcohol   acid

$$2Cr_2(SO_4)_3 \quad + \quad 2K_2SO_4 \quad + \quad 3CH_3COOH \quad + \quad 11H_2O$$

chromium   potassium   acetic   water
sulfate   sulfate   acid

From this chemical equation, we can see that there is always a fixed relationship between the number of potassium dichromate molecules reacting with the alcohol. Two molecules of potassium dichromate always combine with three molecules of ethyl alcohol. Hence, determining the amount of potassium dichromate consumed is an indirect way to determine the quantity of alcohol originally present. Silver nitrate is also present in the Breathalyzer ampoule; however, this substance acts only as a catalyst to speed up the rate of reaction between potassium dichromate and ethyl alcohol. As a **catalyst**, silver nitrate undergoes no net change itself during the reaction.

catalyst
A substance that accelerates
the rate of a chemical reaction
but is not itself permanently
changed by the reaction

Inside the Science

Infrared Light Absorption

In principle, infrared instruments operate no differently from the spectro-photometers described in Chapter 5. An evidential testing instrument that incorporates the principle of infrared light absorption is shown in Figure 1. Any alcohol present in the subject's breath flows into the instrument's breath chamber. As shown in Figure 2, a beam of infrared light is aimed through the chamber. A filter is used to select a wavelength of infrared light that alcohol will absorb. As the infrared light passes through the chamber, it interacts with the alcohol, which causes the light to decrease in intensity. The decrease in light intensity is measured by a photoelectric

FIGURE 1 (a) An infrared breath testing instrument—the Data Master DMT. (b) A subject blowing into the DMT breath tester. *Courtesy National Patent Analytical Systems, Inc., Mansfield, Ohio, www.npas.com*

detector that gives a signal proportional to the concentration of alcohol present in the breath sample. This information is processed by an electronic microprocessor, and the percent blood-alcohol concentration is displayed on a digital readout. Also, the blood-alcohol level is printed on a card to produce a permanent record of the test result. Most infrared breath testers aim a second infrared beam into the same chamber to check for acetone or other chemical interferences on the breath. If the instrument detects differences in the relative response of the two infrared beams that does not conform to ethyl alcohol, the operator is immediately informed of the presence of an "interferant."

Inside the Science (CONTINUED)

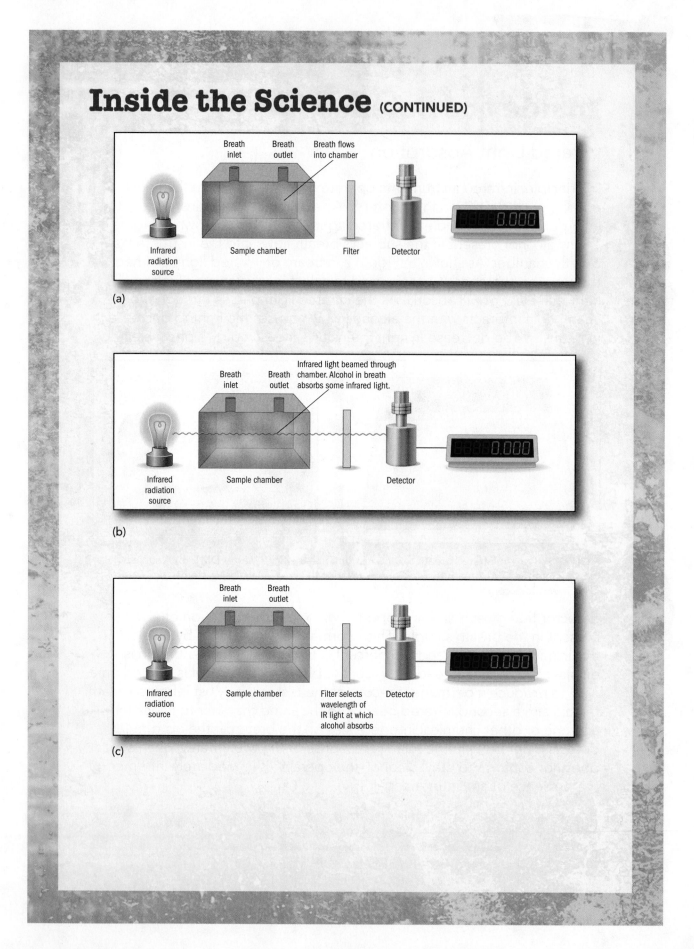

(a)

(b)

(c)

Inside the Science (CONTINUED)

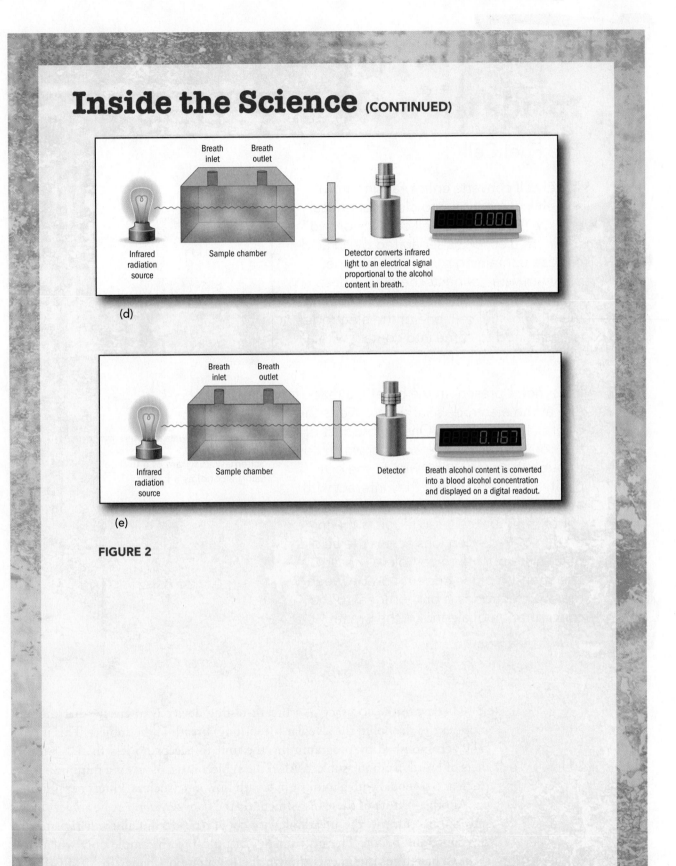

(d)

(e)

FIGURE 2

Inside the Science

The Fuel Cell

A fuel cell converts energy arising from a chemical reaction into electrochemical energy. A typical fuel cell consists of two platinum electrodes separated by an acid- or base-containing porous membrane. A platinum wire connects the electrodes and allows a current to flow between them. In the alcohol fuel cell, one of the electrodes is positioned to come into contact with a subject's breath sample.

If alcohol is present in the breath, a reaction at the electrode's surface converts the alcohol to acetic acid. One by-product of this conversion is free electrons, which flow through the connecting wire to the opposite electrode, where they interact with atmospheric oxygen to form water (see the figure). The fuel cell also requires the migration of hydrogen ions across the acidic porous membrane to complete the circuit. The strength of the current flow between the two electrodes is proportional to the concentration of alcohol in the breath.

Schematic diagram of a fuel cell using alcohol as a fuel.

The key to the accuracy of a breath-testing device is to ensure that the unit captures the alcohol in the alveolar (deep-lung) breath of the subject. This is typically accomplished by programming the unit to accept no less than 1.1 to 1.5 liters of breath from the subject. Also, the subject must blow for a minimum time (such as 6 seconds) with a minimum breath flow rate (such as 3 liters per minute).

Another feature of these instruments is the *slope detector*. As the subject blows into the instrument, the breath-alcohol concentration initially will rise steadily as a function of time. The instrument accepts a breath sample only when consecutive breath measurements show little or no rate of change in breath-alcohol concentration. This approach ensures that the breath sample being measured is alveolar or deep-lung breath and thus most closely relates to the true blood-alcohol concentration of the subject being tested.

A breath-test operator must take other steps to ensure that the breath-test result truly reflects the actual blood-alcohol concentration of the subject. A major consideration is to avoid measuring "mouth alcohol" resulting from regurgitation, belching, or recent intake of an alcoholic beverage. Also, the recent gargling of an alcohol-containing mouthwash can lead to the presence of mouth alcohol. As a result, the alcohol concentration detected in the exhaled breath is higher than the concentration in the alveolar breath. To avoid this possibility, the operator must not allow the subject to take any foreign material into his or her mouth for at least 15 to 20 minutes before the breath test. Likewise, the subject should be observed not to have belched or regurgitated during this period. Mouth alcohol has been shown to dissipate after 15 to 20 minutes from its inception.

Independent measurement of duplicate breath samples taken within a few minutes of each other is another extremely important check of the integrity of the breath test. Acceptable agreement between the two tests taken minutes apart significantly reduces the possibility of errors arising from the operator, mouth alcohol, instrument component failures, and spurious electric signals.

Field Sobriety Testing

A police officer who suspects that an individual is under the influence of alcohol usually conducts a series of preliminary tests before ordering the suspect to submit to an evidential breath or blood test. These preliminary, or field sobriety, tests are normally performed to ascertain the degree of the suspect's physical impairment and whether an evidential test is justified.

Field sobriety tests usually consist of a series of psychophysical tests and a preliminary breath test (if such devices are authorized and available for use). A portable handheld, roadside breath tester is shown in Figure 6–6. This device, about the size of a pack of cigarettes, weighs 5 ounces and uses a fuel cell to measure the alcohol content of a breath sample. The fuel cell absorbs the alcohol from the breath sample, oxidizes it, and produces an electrical current proportional to the breath-alcohol content. This instrument can typically perform for three to five years before the fuel cell needs to be replaced. Breath-test results obtained with devices such as those shown in Figure 6–6 must be considered preliminary and nonevidential. They should only establish probable cause for requiring an individual to submit to a more thorough breath or blood test.

FIGURE 6–6   (a) The Alco-Sensor FST. (b) A subject blowing into the roadside tester device. *Courtesy Intoximeters, Inc., St. Louis, Mo., www.intox.com*

Horizontal-gaze nystagmus, walk and turn, and the one-leg stand constitute a series of reliable and effective psychophysical tests. Horizontal-gaze nystagmus is an involuntary jerking of the eye as it moves to the side. A person experiencing nystagmus is usually unaware that the jerking is happening and is unable to stop or control it. The subject being tested is asked to follow a penlight or some other object with his or her eye as far to the side as the eye can go. The more intoxicated the person is, the less the eye has to move toward the side before jerking or nystagmus begins. Usually, when a person's blood-alcohol concentration is in the range of 0.10 percent, the jerking begins before the eyeball has moved 45 degrees to the side (see Figure 6–7). Higher blood-alcohol concentration causes jerking at smaller angles. Also, if the suspect has taken a drug that also causes nystagmus (such as phencyclidine, barbiturates, and other depressants), the nystagmus onset angle may occur much earlier than would be expected from alcohol alone.

FIGURE 6–7
When a person's blood-alcohol level is in the range of 0.10 percent, jerking of the eye during the horizontal-gaze nystagmus test begins before the eyeball has moved 45 degrees to the side.

Eye looking straight ahead

45°

Walk and turn and the one-leg stand are divided-attention tasks, testing the subject's ability to comprehend and execute two or more simple instructions at one time. The ability to understand and simultaneously carry out more than two instructions is significantly affected by increasing blood-alcohol levels. Walk and turn requires the suspect to maintain balance while standing heel-to-toe and at the same time listening to and comprehending the test instructions. During the walking stage, the suspect must walk a straight line, touching heel-to-toe for nine steps, then turn around on the line and repeat the process. The one-leg stand requires the suspect to maintain balance while standing with heels together listening to the instructions. During the balancing stage, the suspect must stand on one foot while holding the other foot several inches off the ground for 30 seconds; simultaneously, the suspect must count out loud during the 30-second time period.

Quick Review

- Modern breath testers are free of chemicals. They include infrared light absorption devices and fuel cell detectors.

- The key to the accuracy of a breath testing device is to ensure that the unit captures the alcohol in the alveolar (deep-lung) breath of the subject.

- Many breath testers collect a set volume of breath and expose it to infrared light. The instrument measures alcohol concentration in breath by measuring the degree of the interaction of the light with alcohol in the collected breath sample.

- Law enforcement officers use field sobriety tests to estimate a motorist's degree of physical impairment by alcohol and to determine whether an evidential test for alcohol is justified.

- The horizontal-gaze nystagmus test, walk and turn, and the one-leg stand are all considered reliable and effective psychophysical tests for alcohol impairment.

The Analysis of Blood for Alcohol

Gas chromatography offers the toxicologist the most widely used approach for determining alcohol levels in blood. Under proper gas chromatographic conditions, alcohol can be separated from other volatiles in the blood. By comparing the resultant alcohol peak area to ones obtained with known blood-alcohol standards, the investigator can calculate the alcohol level with a high degree of accuracy (see Figure 6–8).

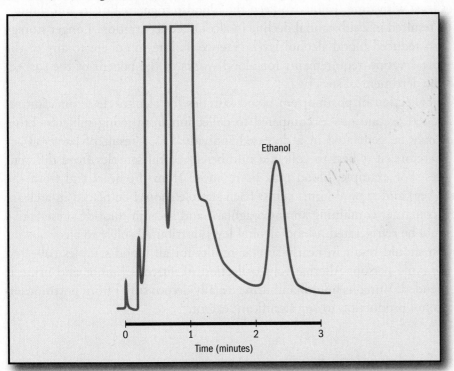

FIGURE 6–8
Gas chromatogram showing ethyl alcohol (ethanol) in whole blood. *Courtesy Vaian Inc., Palo Alto, Calif.*

Another procedure for alcohol analysis involves the oxidation of alcohol to acetaldehyde. This reaction is carried out in the presence of the enzyme alcohol dehydrogenase and the coenzyme nicotin-amide-adenine dinucleotide (NAD). As the oxidation proceeds, NAD is converted into another chemical species, NADH. The extent of this conversion is measured by a spectrophotometer and is related to alcohol concentration. This approach to blood-alcohol testing is normally associated with instruments used in a clinical or hospital setting. On the other hand, forensic laboratories normally use gas chromatography for determining blood-alcohol content.

Collection and Preservation of Blood

Blood must always be drawn under medically accepted conditions by a qualified individual. It is important to apply a nonalcoholic disinfectant before the suspect's skin is penetrated with a sterile needle or lancet. It is important to negate any argument that an alcoholic disinfectant may have inadvertently contributed to a falsely high blood-alcohol result. Nonalcoholic disinfectants such as aqueous benzalkonium chloride (Zepiran), aqueous mercuric chloride, or povidone-iodine (Betadine) are recommended for this purpose.

Once blood is removed from an individual, it is best preserved sealed in an airtight container after adding an anticoagulant and a preservative. The blood should be stored in a refrigerator until delivery to the toxicology laboratory. The addition of an **anticoagulant**, such as EDTA or potassium oxalate, prevents clotting; a **preservative**, such as sodium fluoride, inhibits the growth of microorganisms capable of destroying alcohol.

anticoagulant
A substance that prevents coagulation or clotting of blood

preservative
A substance that stops the growth of microorganisms in blood

One study performed to determine the stability of alcohol in blood removed from living individuals found that the most significant factors affecting alcohol's stability in blood are storage temperature, the presence of a preservative, and the time of storage.[3] Not a single blood specimen examined showed an increase in alcohol level with time. Failure to keep the blood refrigerated or to add sodium fluoride resulted in a substantial decline in alcohol concentration. Longer storage times also reduced blood-alcohol levels. Hence, failure to adhere to any of the proper preservation requirements for blood works to the benefit of the suspect and to the detriment of society.

The collection of postmortem blood samples for alcohol determination requires added precautions as compared to collection from living subjects. Ethyl alcohol may be generated in a deceased individual as a result of bacterial action. Therefore, it is best to collect a number of blood samples from different body sites. For example, blood may be removed from the heart and from the femoral (leg) and cubital (arm) veins. Each sample should be placed in a clean, airtight container containing an anticoagulant and sodium fluoride preservative and should be refrigerated. Blood-alcohol levels attributed solely to alcohol consumption should result in nearly similar results for all blood samples collected from the same person. Alternatively, collection of vitreous humor and urine is recommended. Vitreous humor and urine usually do not suffer from postmortem ethyl alcohol production to any significant extent.

Quick Review

- Gas chromatography is the most widely used approach for determining blood-alcohol levels in forensic laboratories.

- An anticoagulant should be added to a blood sample to prevent clotting; a preservative should be added to inhibit the growth of microorganisms capable of destroying alcohol.

Alcohol and the Law

Constitutionally, every state in the United States must establish and administer statutes regulating the operation of motor vehicles. Although such an arrangement might encourage diverse laws defining permissible blood-alcohol levels, this has not been the case. Since the 1930s, both the American Medical Association and the National Safety Council have exerted considerable influence in persuading the states to establish uniform and reasonable blood-alcohol standards.

Blood-Alcohol Laws

The American Medical Association and the National Safety Council initially recommended that a person with a blood-alcohol concentration in excess of 0.15 percent w/v was to be considered under the influence of alcohol.[4] However, continued experimental studies showed a clear correlation between drinking and driving impairment at blood-alcohol levels much below 0.15 percent w/v. These findings eventually led to a lowering of the blood-concentration standard for intoxication from 0.15 percent w/v to its current 0.08 percent w/v.

In 1992, the U.S. Department of Transportation (DOT) recommended that states adopt 0.08 percent blood-alcohol concentration as the legal measure of drunk driving. This recommendation was enacted into federal law in 2000. All 50 states have now established *per se* laws, meaning that any individual meeting or exceeding a defined blood-alcohol level (usually 0.08 percent) shall be deemed intoxicated. No other proof of alcohol impairment is necessary. The 0.08 percent level applies only to noncommercial drivers, as the federal government has set the maximum allowable blood-alcohol concentration for commercial truck and bus drivers at 0.04 percent.

Several Western countries have also set 0.08 percent w/v as the blood-alcohol level above which it is an offense to drive a motor vehicle, including Canada, Italy, Switzerland, and the United Kingdom. Finland, France, Germany, Ireland, Japan, the Netherlands, and Norway have a 0.05 percent limit. Australian states have adopted a 0.05 percent blood-alcohol concentration level. Sweden has lowered its blood-alcohol concentration limit to 0.02 percent.

As shown in Figure 6–9, a person is about four times as likely to become involved in an automobile accident at the 0.08 percent level as a sober individual. At the 0.15 percent level, the chances are 25 times as much for involvement in an automobile accident as compared to a sober driver. The reader can estimate the relationship of blood-alcohol levels to body weight and the quantity of 80-proof liquor consumed by referring to Figure 6–10.

MyCrimeKit: WebExtra 6.1
Your Blood-Alcohol Level
www.mycrimekit.com

FIGURE 6–9
Diagram of increased driving risk in relation to blood-alcohol concentration. *Courtesy U.S. Department of Transportation, Washington, D.C.*

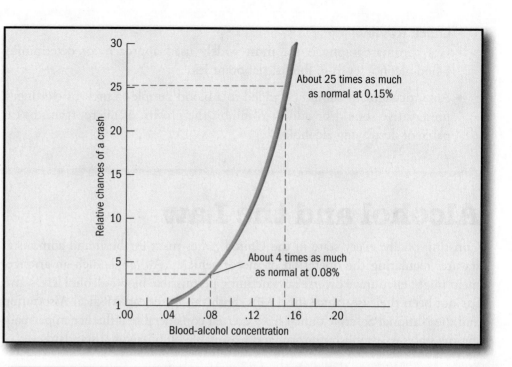

FIGURE 6–10
To use this diagram, lay a straightedge across the suspect's weight and the number of ounces he or she has consumed on an empty or full stomach. The point where the edge hits the right-hand column is one's maximum blood-alcohol level. The rate of elimination of alcohol from the bloodstream is approximately 0.015 percent per hour. Therefore, to calculate one's actual blood-alcohol level, subtract 0.015 from the number in the right-hand column for each hour from the start of drinking.

Constitutional Issues

The Fifth Amendment to the U.S. Constitution guarantees all citizens protection against *self-incrimination*—that is, against being forced to make an admission that would prove one's own guilt in a legal matter. Because consenting to a breath test for alcohol may be considered a form of self-incrimination, the National Highway Traffic Safety Administration (NHTSA) recommended an *implied consent* law to prevent a person from refusing to take a test on those constitutional grounds. This law states that the operator of a motor vehicle on a public highway must either consent to a test for alcohol intoxication, if requested, or lose his or her license for some designated period—usually six months to one year.

The leading case relating to the constitutionality of collecting a blood specimen for alcohol testing, as well as for obtaining other types of physical evidence from a suspect without consent, is *Schmerber v. California.*[5] While being treated at a Los Angeles hospital for injuries sustained in an automobile collision, Schmerber was arrested for driving under the influence of alcohol. Despite Schmerber's objections, a physician took a blood sample from him at the direction of the police. Schmerber was convicted of driving while intoxicated, and he subsequently appealed the decision. The case eventually reached the U.S. Supreme Court, where Schmerber argued that his privilege against self-incrimination had been violated by the introduction of the results of the blood test at his trial. The Court ruled against him, reasoning that the Fifth Amendment prohibits only compelling a suspect to give *testimonial* evidence that may prove to be self-incriminating; being compelled to furnish *physical evidence*, such as fingerprints, photographs, measurements, and blood samples, the Court ruled, was not protected by the Fifth Amendment.

The Court also addressed the question of whether the police violated Schmerber's Fourth Amendment protection against unreasonable search and seizure by taking a blood specimen from him without a search warrant. The Court upheld the constitutionality of the blood removal, reasoning in this case that the police were confronted with an emergency situation. By the time police officials would have obtained a warrant, Schmerber's blood-alcohol levels would have declined significantly as a result of natural body elimination processes. In effect, the evidence would have been destroyed. The Court also emphasized that the blood specimen was taken in a medically accepted manner and without unreasonable force. This opinion in no way condones warrantless taking of blood for alcohol or drug testing under all circumstances. The reasonableness of actions a police officer may take to compel an individual to yield evidence can be judged only on a case-by-case basis.

Quick Review

- The current legal measure of drunk driving in the United States is a blood-alcohol concentration of 0.08 percent, or 0.08 grams of alcohol per 100 milliliters of blood.

- An implied-consent law states that the operator of a motor vehicle on a public highway must either consent to a test for alcohol intoxication, if requested, or lose his or her license for some designated period—usually six months to one year.

The Role of the Toxicologist

Once the forensic toxicologist ventures beyond the analysis of alcohol, he or she encounters an encyclopedic maze of drugs and poisons. Even a cursory discussion of the problems and handicaps imposed on toxicologists is enough to develop a sense of appreciation for their accomplishments and ingenuity.

Challenges Facing the Toxicologist

The toxicologist is presented with body fluids and/or organs and asked to examine them for drugs and poisons. If he or she is fortunate, which is not often, some clue as to the type of toxic substance present may develop from the victim's symptoms, a postmortem pathological examination, an examination of the victim's personal effects, or the nearby presence of empty drug containers or household chemicals. Without such supportive information, the toxicologist must use general screening procedures with the hope of narrowing thousands of possibilities to one.

If this task does not seem monumental, consider that the toxicologist is not dealing with drugs at the concentration levels found in powders and pills. By the time a drug specimen reaches the toxicology laboratory, it has been dissipated and distributed throughout the body. The drug analyst may have gram or milligram quantities of material to work with, but the toxicologist must be satisfied with nanogram or at best microgram amounts, acquired only after careful extraction from body fluids and organs.

FIGURE 6–11
Scientist analyzing blood samples.
Courtesy Risto Bozovic, AP Wide World Photos

Furthermore, the body is an active chemistry laboratory, and no one can appreciate this observation more than a toxicologist. Few substances enter and completely leave the body in the same chemical state. The drug that is injected is not always the substance extracted from the body tissues. Therefore, a thorough understanding of how the body alters or metabolizes the chemical structure of a drug is essential in detecting its presence.

It would, for example, be futile and frustrating to search exhaustively for heroin in the human body. This drug is almost immediately metabolized to morphine on entering the bloodstream. Even with this information, the search may still prove impossible unless the examiner also knows that only a small percentage of morphine is excreted unchanged in urine. For the most part, morphine becomes chemically bonded to body carbohydrates before elimination in urine. Thus, successful detection of morphine requires that its extraction be planned in accordance with a knowledge of its chemical fate in the body.

Another example of how one needs to know how a drug metabolizes itself in the body is exemplified by the investigation of the death of Anna Nicole Smith. In her case, the sedative chloral hydrate was a major contributor to her death and its presence was detected by its active metabolite, trichloroethanol (see the Case File on page 233).

Last, when and if the toxicologist has surmounted all of these obstacles and has finally detected, identified, and quantitated a drug or poison, he or she must assess the substance's toxicity. Fortunately, there is published information relating to the toxic levels of most drugs. However, even when such data are available, their interpretation must assume that the victim's physiological behavior agrees with that of subjects of previous studies. Such an assumption may not be entirely valid without knowing the subject's case history. No experienced toxicologist would be surprised to find an individual tolerating a toxic level of a drug that would have killed most other people.

Case Files

Celebrity Toxicology
Michael Jackson: The Demise of a Superstar

A call to 911 had the desperate tone of urgency. The voice of a young man implored an ambulance to hurry to the home of pop star Michael Jackson. The unconscious performer was in cardiac arrest and was not responding to CPR. The 50-year old Jackson was pronounced dead upon arrival at a regional medical center. When the initial autopsy results revealed no signs of foul play, rumors immediately began to swirl around a drug-related death. News media coverage showed investigators carrying bags full of medical supplies out of the Jackson residence. Hence, it came as no surprise that the forensic toxicology report accompanying Jackson's autopsy showed that the entertainer had died of a drug overdose.

Apparently, Jackson had become accustomed to receiving sedatives to help him sleep. On the morning of his death, his physician gave Mr. Jackson a tab of valium. At 2 a.m., he administered the sedative loraze-pam, and at 3 a.m. the physician administered another sedative, midazolam. Those drugs were administered again at 5 a.m. and 7:30 a.m., but Mr. Jackson still was unable to sleep. Finally, at about 10:40 a.m., Jackson's doctor gave him 25 milligrams of propofol, at which point Mr. Jackson went to sleep. Propofol's is a power-ful sedative whose principal use is the maintenance of surgical anesthesia. All of the drugs administered to Jackson were sedatives that act in concert to depress the activities of the central nervous system. Hence, it comes as no surprise that this drug cocktail resulted in cardiac arrest and death.

Courtesy AP Wide World Photos

Case Files

Accidental Overdose: The Tragedy of Anna Nicole Smith

Rumors exploded in the media when former model, Playboy playmate, reality television star, and favorite tabloid subject Anna Nicole Smith was found unconscious in her hotel room at the Seminole Hard Rock Hotel & Casino in Hollywood, Florida. She was taken to Memorial Legal Hospital, where she was declared dead at age 39. Analysis of Smith's blood postmortem revealed an array of prescribed medications. Most pronounced was a toxic level of a metabolite of the sedative chloral hydrate. A part of the contents of the toxicology report from Smith's autopsy are shown here.

FINAL PATHOLOGICAL DIAGNOSES:

I. ACUTE COMBINED DRUG INTOXICATION

    A. Toxic/legal drug:

       Chloral Hydrate (Noctec)

1.	Trichloroethanol (TCE)	75 mg/L (active metabolite)
2.	Trichloroacetic acid (TCA) (inactive metabolite)	85 mg/L

    B. Therapeutic drugs:

1.	Diphenhydramine (Benadryl)	0.11 mg/L
2.	Clonazepam (Klonopin)	0.04 mg/L
3.	Diazepam (Valium)	0.21 mg/L
4.	Nordiazepam (metabolite)	0.38 mg/L
5.	Temazepam (metabolite)	0.09 mg/L
6.	Oxazepam	0.09 mg/L
7.	Lorazepam	0.022 mg/L

    C. Other non-contributory drugs present (atropine, topiramate, ciprofloxacin, acetaminophen)

Although many of the drugs present were detected at levels consistent with typical doses of the prescribed medications, it was their presence in combination with chloral hydrate that exacerbated the toxic level of chloral hydrate. The lethal combination of these prescription drugs caused failure of both her circulatory and respiratory systems and resulted in her death. The investigators determined that the overdose of chloral hydrate and other drugs was accidental and not a suicide. This was due to the nonexcessive levels of most of the prescription medications and the discovery of a significant amount of chloral hydrate still remaining in its original container; had she intended to kill herself she would have likely downed it all. Anna Nicole Smith was a victim of accidental overmedication.

Courtesy Landov Media

Case Files

Death by Tylenol

In 1982, two firefighters from a Chicago suburb were casually discussing four bizarre deaths that had recently taken place in a neighboring area. As they discussed the circumstances of the deaths, they realized that each of the victims had taken Tylenol. Their suspicions were immediately reported to police investigators. Tragically, before the general public could be alerted, three more victims died after taking poison-laced Tylenol capsules. Seven individuals, all in the Chicago area, were the first victims to die from what has become known as product tampering.

A forensic chemical analysis of Tylenol capsules recovered from the victims' residences showed that the capsules were filled with potassium cyanide in a quantity ten thousand times what was needed to kill an average person. It was quickly determined that the cyanide was not introduced into the bottles at the factory. Instead, the perpetrator methodically emptied each of 20 to 30 capsules and then refilled them with potassium cyanide. The tampered capsules were rebottled, carefully repackaged, and placed on the shelves of six different stores. The case of the Tylenol murders remains unsolved, and the $100,000 reward offered by Tylenol's manufacturer remains unclaimed.

Collection and Preservation of Toxicological Evidence

The toxicologist's capabilities depend directly on input from the attending physician, medical examiner, and police investigator. It is a tribute to forensic toxicologists, who must often labor under conditions that do not afford such cooperation, that they can achieve the high level of proficiency that they do.

Generally, with a deceased person, the medical examiner decides what biological specimens must be shipped to the toxicology laboratory for analysis. However, a living person suspected of being under the influence of a drug presents a completely different problem, and few options are available. When possible, both blood and urine are taken from any suspected drug user. The entire urine void (sample) is collected and submitted for toxicological analysis. Preferably, two consecutive voids should be collected in separate specimen containers.

When a licensed physician or registered nurse is available, a sample of blood should also be collected. The amount of blood taken depends on the type of examination to be conducted. Comprehensive toxicological tests for drugs and poisons can conveniently be carried out on a minimum of 10 milliliters of blood. A determination solely for the presence of alcohol will require much less—approximately 5 milliliters of blood. However, many therapeutic drugs, such as tranquilizers and barbiturates, taken in combination with a small, nonintoxicating amount of alcohol, produce behavioral patterns resembling alcohol intoxication. For this reason, the toxicologist must be given enough blood to perform a comprehensive analysis for drugs in cases of low alcohol concentrations.

Techniques Used in Toxicology

For the toxicologist, the upsurge in drug use and abuse has meant that the overwhelming majority of fatal and nonfatal toxic agents are drugs. Not surprisingly, a relatively small number of drugs—namely, those discussed in <u>Chapter 5</u>—comprise nearly all the toxic agents encountered. Of these, alcohol, marijuana, and cocaine account for 90 percent or more of the drugs encountered in a typical toxicology laboratory.

Like the drug analyst, the toxicologist must devise an analytical scheme to detect, isolate, and identify a toxic substance. The first chore is to remove and isolate drugs and other toxic agents from the biological materials submitted as evidence. Because drugs constitute a large portion of the toxic materials found, a good deal of effort must be devoted to their extraction and detection. Many different procedures are used, and a useful description of them would be too detailed for this text. We can best understand the underlying principle of drug extraction by observing that many drugs fall into the categories of acids and bases.

Acids and Bases Although several definitions exist for these two classes, a simple one states that an **acid** is a compound capable of donating a hydrogen ion (or a hydrogen atom minus its electron) to another compound with reasonable ease. Conversely, a **base** is a molecule capable of accepting a hydrogen ion shed by an acid. The idea of acidity and basicity can be expressed in terms of a simple numerical value that relates to the concentration of the hydrogen ion (H+) in a liquid medium such as water. Chemists use the **pH scale** to do this. This scale runs from 0 to 14:

$$pH =$$
$$0\ 1\ 2\ 3\ 4\ 5\ 6\ 7\ 8\ 9\ 10\ 11\ 12\ 13\ 14$$

Increasing acidity   Neutral   Increasing basicity

Normally, water is neither acid nor basic—in other words, it is neutral, with a pH of 7. However, when an acidic substance—for example, sulfuric acid or hydrochloric acid—is added to the water, it adds excess hydrogen ions, and the pH value becomes less than 7. The lower the number, the more acidic the water. Similarly, when a basic substance—for example, sodium hydroxide or ammonium hydroxide—is added to water, it removes hydrogen ions, thus making water basic. The more basic the water, the higher its pH value.

By controlling the pH of a water solution into which blood, urine, or tissues are dissolved, the toxicologist can control the type of drug that is recovered. For example, acid drugs are easily extracted from an acidified water solution (pH less than 7) with organic solvents such as chloroform. Similarly, basic drugs are readily removed from a basic water solution (pH greater than 7) with organic solvents. This simple approach gives the toxicologist a general technique for extracting and categorizing drugs. Some of the more commonly encountered drugs may be classified as follows:

Acid Drugs: Barbiturates, Acetylsalicylic acid (aspirin)
Basic Drugs: Phencyclidine, Methadone, Amphetamines, Cocaine

acid
A compound capable of donating a hydrogen ion (H+) to another compound

base
A compound capable of accepting a hydrogen ion (H+)

pH scale
A scale used to express the basicity or acidity of a substance. A pH of 7 is neutral; lower values are acidic and higher values basic

Screening and Confirmation Once the specimen has been extracted and divided into acidic and basic fractions, the toxicologist can identify the drugs present. The strategy for identifying abused drugs entails a two-step approach: screening and confirmation (see Figure 6–12). A screening test normally gives quick insight into the likelihood that a specimen contains a drug substance. This test allows a toxicologist to examine a large number of specimens within a short period of time for a wide range of drugs. Any positive results from a screening test are tentative at best and must be verified with a confirmation test.

FIGURE 6–12 Biological fluids and tissues are extracted for acidic and basic drugs by controlling the pH of a water solution in which they are dissolved. Once this is accomplished, the toxicologist analyzes for drugs by using screening and confirmation test procedures.

Screening Tests. The three most widely used screening tests are thin-layer chromatography (TLC), gas chromatography (GC), and immunoassay. The techniques of GC and TLC are described in Chapter 5. The third technique, immunoassay, has proven to be a useful screening tool in toxicology laboratories. Its principles are very different from any of the analytical techniques we have discussed so far. Basically, immunoassay is based on specific drug antibody reactions. We will learn about this concept in Chapter 8. The primary advantage of immunoassay is its ability to detect small concentrations of drugs in body fluids and organs. In fact, this technique provides the best approach for detecting the low drug levels normally associated with smoking marijuana.

Confirmation Tests. A positive screening test may be due to a substance's close chemical structure to an abused drug. For this reason, the toxicologist must follow up any positive screening test with a confirmation test. Because of the potential impact of the results of a drug finding on an individual, only the most conclusive confirmation procedures should be used.

Gas chromatography/mass spectrometry is generally accepted as the confirmation test of choice. As we learned in Chapter 5, the combination of gas chromatography and mass spectrometry provides a one-step confirmation test of unequaled sensitivity and specificity. Figure 6–13 illustrates the process. After being introduced to the gas chromatograph, the sample is separated into its components. When the separated sample component leaves the column of the gas chromatograph, it enters the mass spectrometer, where it is bombarded with high-energy electrons. This bombardment causes the sample to break up into fragments, producing a fragmentation pattern or mass spectrum for each sample. For most compounds, the mass spectrum represents a unique "fingerprint" pattern that can be used for identification.

FIGURE 6–13 The combination of the gas chromatograph and the mass spectrometer enables forensic toxicologists to separate the components of a drug mixture and provides specific identification of a drug substance.

There is tremendous interest in drug-testing programs conducted not only in criminal matters but for industry and government as well. Urine testing for drugs is becoming common for job applicants and employees in the workplace. Likewise, the U.S. military has an extensive drug urine-testing program for its members. Many urine-testing programs rely on private laboratories to perform the required analyses. In any case, when the test results form the basis for taking action against an individual, both a screening and confirmation test must be incorporated into the testing protocol to ensure the integrity of the laboratory's conclusions.

Detecting Drugs in Hair When a forensic toxicological examination on a living person is required, practicality limits available specimens to blood and urine. Most drugs remain in the bloodstream for about 24 hours; in urine, they normally are present up to 72 hours. However, it may be necessary to go further back in time to ascertain whether a subject has been abusing a drug. If so, the only viable alternative to blood and urine is head hair.

Hair is nourished by blood flowing through capillaries located close to the hair root. Drugs present in blood diffuse through the capillary walls into the base of the hair and become permanently entrapped in the hair's hardening protein structure. As the hair continues to grow, the drug's location on the hair shaft becomes a historical marker for delineating drug intake. Given that the average human head hair grows at the rate of 1 centimeter per month, analyzing segments of hair for drug content may define the timeline for drug use, dating it back over a period of weeks, months, or even years, depending on the hair's length.

However, caution is required in interpreting the timeline. The chronology of drug intake may be distorted by drugs penetrating the hair's surface as a result of environmental exposure, or drugs may enter the hair's surface through sweat. Nevertheless, drug hair analysis is the only viable approach for measuring long-term abuse of a drug.

Detecting Nondrug Poisons Although forensic toxicologists devote most of their efforts to detecting drugs, they also test for a wide variety of other toxic substances. Some of these are rare elements, not widely or commercially available. Others are so common that virtually everyone is exposed to nontoxic amounts of them every day.

Heavy Metals. One group of poisons once commonly encountered in criminal cases of murder are known as heavy metals. They include arsenic, bismuth, antimony, mercury, and thallium. These days, however, the forensic toxicologist only occasionally encounters heavy metals because severe environmental protection regulations restrict their availability to the general public. Nevertheless, as the following case study makes clear, their use is by no means only a historical curiosity.

To screen for many of these metals, the investigator may dissolve the suspect body fluid or tissue in a hydrochloric acid solution and insert a copper strip into the solution. This process is known as the Reinsch test. The appearance of a silvery or dark coating on the copper indicates the presence of a heavy metal. Such a finding must be confirmed by analytical techniques suitable for inorganic analysis—namely, emission spectroscopy, or X-ray diffraction. These procedures are discussed in more detail in Chapters 11 and 13.

Carbon Monoxide. Unlike heavy metals, carbon monoxide still represents one of the most common poisons encountered in a forensic laboratory. When carbon monoxide enters the human body, it is primarily absorbed by the red blood cells, where it combines with hemoglobin to form carboxyhemoglobin. An average red blood cell contains about 280 million molecules of hemoglobin. Oxygen normally combines with hemoglobin, which transports the oxygen throughout the body. However, if a high percentage of the hemoglobin combines with carbon monoxide, not enough is left to carry sufficient oxygen to the tissues, and death by asphyxiation quickly follows.

There are two basic methods for measuring the concentration of carbon monoxide in the blood. Spectrophotometric methods examine the visible spectrum of blood to determine the amount of carboxyhemoglobin relative to oxyhemoglobin or total hemoglobin; also, a volume of blood can be treated with a reagent to liberate the carbon monoxide, which is then measured by gas chromatography.

The amount of carbon monoxide in blood is generally expressed as percent saturation. This represents the extent to which the available hemoglobin has been converted to carboxyhemoglobin. The transition from normal or occupational levels of carbon monoxide to toxic levels is not sharply defined. It depends, among other things, on the age, health, and general fitness of each individual. In a healthy middle-aged individual, a carbon monoxide blood saturation greater than 50–60 percent is considered fatal. However, in combination with alcohol or other depressants, fatal levels may be significantly lower. For instance, a carbon monoxide saturation of 35–40 percent may prove fatal in the presence of a blood-alcohol concentration of 0.20 percent w/v. Interestingly, chain smokers may have a constant carbon monoxide level of 8–10 percent from the carbon monoxide in cigarette smoke.

Inhaling automobile fumes is a relatively common way to commit suicide (see Figure 6–14). A garden or vacuum cleaner hose is often used to connect the tail-

Case Files

Joann Curley: Caught by a Hair

A vibrant young woman named Joann Curley rushed to the Wilkes-Barre (Pennsylvania) General Hospital—her husband, Bobby, was having an attack and required immediate medical attention. Bobby was experiencing a burning sensation in his feet, numbness in his hands, a flushed face, and intense sweating. After being discharged, Bobby experienced another bout of debilitating pain and numbness. He was admitted to another hospital. There doctors observed extreme alopecia, or hair loss.

Test results of Bobby's urine showed high levels of the heavy metal thallium in his body. Thallium, a rare and highly toxic metal that was used decades ago in substances such as rat poison and to treat ringworm and gout, was found in sufficient quantities to cause Bobby's sickness. The use of thallium was banned in the United States in 1984. Now, at least, Bobby could be treated. However, before Bobby's doctors could treat him for thallium poisoning, he experienced cardiac arrest and slipped into a coma. Joann Curley made the difficult decision to remove her husband of 13 months from life support equipment. He died shortly thereafter.

Investigators also learned that Bobby had changed his life insurance to list his wife, Joann, as the beneficiary of his $300,000 policy. Based on this information, police consulted a forensic toxicologist in an effort to glean as much from the physical evidence in Bobby Curley's body as possible. The toxicologist conducted segmental analysis of Bobby's hair, an analytical method based on the predictable rate of hair growth on the human scalp: an average of 1 centimeter per month. Bobby had approximately 5 inches (12.5 centimeters) of hair, which represents almost 12 months of hair growth. Each section tested represented a specific period of time in the final year of Bobby's life.

The hair analysis confirmed that Bobby Curley was poisoned with thallium. The first few doses were small, which probably barely made him sick at the time. Gradually, over a year or more, Bobby was receiving more doses of thallium until he finally succumbed to a massive dose three or four days before his death. After careful scrutiny of the timeline, investigators concluded that only Joann Curley had access to Bobby during each of these intervals. She also had motive, in the amount of $300,000.

Presented with the timeline and the solid toxicological evidence against her, Joann Curley pleaded guilty to murder. As part of her plea agreement, she provided a 40-page written confession of how she haphazardly dosed Bobby with some rat poison she found in her basement. She admitted that she murdered him for the money she would receive from Bobby's life insurance policy.

---

pipe with the vehicle's interior, or the engine is allowed to run in a closed garage. A level of carbon monoxide sufficient to cause death accumulates in five to ten minutes in a closed single-car garage.

The level of carbon monoxide in the blood of a victim found dead at the scene of a fire is significant in ascertaining whether foul play has occurred. High levels of carbon monoxide in the blood prove that the victim breathed the combustion products of the fire and was alive when the fire began. Many attempts at covering up a murder by setting fire to a victim's house or car have been uncovered in this manner.

FIGURE 6–14
Inhaling carbon monoxide fumes from an automobile is a common way to commit suicide.
Courtesy Dorling Kindersley Media Library

The Significance of Toxicological Findings

Once a drug is found and identified, the toxicologist assesses its influence on the behavior of the individual. Interpreting the results of a toxicology finding is one of the toxicologist's more difficult chores. Recall that many countries have designated a specific blood-alcohol level at which an individual is deemed under the influence of alcohol. These levels were established as a result of numerous studies conducted over several years to measure the effects of alcohol levels on driving performance. However, no such legal guidelines are available to the toxicologist who must judge how a drug other than alcohol affects an individual's performance or physical state.

For many drugs, blood concentration levels are readily determined and can be used to estimate the pharmacological effects of the drug on the individual. Often, when dealing with a living person, the toxicologist has the added benefit of knowing what a police officer may have observed about an individual's behavior and motor skills. For a deceased person, drug levels in various body organs and tissues provide additional information about the individual's state at the time of death. However, before drawing conclusions about drug-induced behavior, the analyst must consider other factors, including the age, physical condition, and tolerance of the drug user.

With prolonged use of a drug, an individual may become less responsive to a drug's effects and tolerate blood-drug concentrations that would kill a casual drug user. Therefore, knowledge of an individual's history of drug use is important in evaluating drug concentrations. Another consideration is additive or synergistic effects of the interaction of two or more drugs, which may produce a highly intoxicated or comatose state even though none of the drugs alone is present at high or toxic levels. The combination of alcohol with barbiturates or narcotics is a common example of a potentially lethal drug combination.

The concentration of a drug present in urine is a poor indicator of how extensively an individual's behavior or state is influenced by the drug. Urine is formed outside the body's circulatory system, and consequently drug levels can build up in it over a relatively long period of time. Some drugs are found in the urine one to three days after they have been taken and long after their effects on the user have disappeared. Nevertheless, the value of this information should not be discounted. Urine drug levels, like blood levels, are best used by law enforcement authorities and the courts to corroborate other investigative and medical findings regarding an individual's condition. Hence, for an individual arrested for suspicion of being under the influence of a drug, a toxicologist's determinations supplement the observations of the arresting officer, including the results of a drug influence evaluation (discussed next).

For a deceased person, the medical examiner or coroner must establish a cause of death. However, before a conclusive determination is made, the examining physician depends on the forensic toxicologist to demonstrate the presence or absence of a drug or poison in the tissues or body fluids of the deceased. Only through the combined efforts of the toxicologist and the medical examiner (or coroner) can society be assured that death investigations achieve high professional and legal standards.

The Drug Recognition Expert

Whereas recognizing alcohol-impaired performance is an expertise generally accorded to police officers by the courts, recognizing drug-induced intoxication is much more difficult and generally not part of police training. During the 1970s, the Los Angeles Police Department developed and tested a series of clinical and psychophysical examinations that a trained police officer could use to identify and differentiate between types of drug impairment. This program has evolved into a national program to train police as drug recognition experts. Normally, a three- to five-month training program is required to certify an officer as a drug recognition expert (DRE).

The DRE program incorporates standardized methods for examining suspects to determine whether they have taken one or more drugs. The process is systematic and standard; to ensure that each subject has been tested in a routine fashion, each DRE must complete a standard Drug Influence Evaluation form (see

FIGURE 6–15
DREs must complete the Drug Influence Evaluation form to ensure that each subject has been tested in a routine fashion.

Figure 6–15). The entire drug evaluation takes approximately 30 to 40 minutes. The components of the 12-step process are summarized in Table 6–1.

Table 6–1

Components of the Drug Recognition Process

1. **The Breath-Alcohol Test.**
   By obtaining an accurate and immediate measurement of the suspect's blood-alcohol concentration, the drug recognition expert (DRE) can determine whether alcohol may be contributing to the suspect's observable impairment and whether the concentration of alcohol is sufficient to be the sole cause of that impairment.

2. **Interview with the Arresting Officer.**
   Spending a few minutes with the arresting officer often enables the DRE to determine the most promising areas of investigation.

3. **The Preliminary Examination.**
   This structured series of questions, specific observations, and simple tests provides the first opportunity to examine the suspect closely. It is designed to determine whether the suspect is suffering from an injury or from another condition unrelated to drug consumption. It also affords an opportunity to begin assessing the suspect's appearance and behavior for signs of possible drug influence.

4. **The Eye Examination.**
   Certain categories of drugs induce nystagmus, an involuntary, spasmodic motion of the eyeball. Nystagmus is an indicator of drug-induced impairment. The inability of the eyes to converge toward the bridge of the nose also indicates the possible presence of certain types of drugs.

5. **Divided-Attention Psychophysical Tests.**
   These tests check balance and physical orientation and include the walk and turn, the one-leg stand, the Romberg balance, and the finger-to-nose.

6. **Vital Signs Examinations.**
   Precise measurements of blood pressure, pulse rate, and body temperature are taken. Certain drugs elevate these signs; others depress them.

7. **Dark Room Examinations.**
   The size of the suspect's pupils in room light, near-total darkness, indirect light, and direct light is checked. Some drugs cause the pupils to either dilate or constrict.

8. **Examination for Muscle Rigidity.**
   Certain categories of drugs cause the muscles to become hypertense and quite rigid. Others may cause the muscles to relax and become flaccid.

9. **Examination for Injection Sites.**
   Users of certain categories of drugs routinely or occasionally inject their drugs. Evidence of needle use may be found on veins along the neck, arms, and hands.

10. **Suspect's Statements and Other Observations.**
    The next step is to attempt to interview the suspect concerning the drug or drugs he or she has ingested. Of course, the interview must be conducted in full compliance of the suspect's constitutional rights.

11. **Opinions of the Evaluator.**
    Using the information obtained in the previous ten steps, the DRE can make an informed decision about whether the suspect is impaired by drugs and, if so, what category or combination of categories is the probable cause of the impairment.

12. **The Toxicological Examination.**
    The DRE should obtain a blood or urine sample from the suspect for laboratory analysis in order to secure scientific, admissible evidence to substantiate his or her conclusions.

The DRE evaluation process can suggest the presence of the following seven broad categories of drugs:

1. **Central nervous system depressants**
2. **Central nervous system stimulants**
3. **Hallucinogens**
4. **Dissociative anesthetics (includes phencyclidine and its analogs)**
5. **Inhalants**
6. **Narcotic analgesics**
7. **Cannabis**

The DRE program is not designed to be a substitute for toxicological testing. The toxicologist can often determine that a suspect has a particular drug in his or her body. But the toxicologist often cannot infer with reasonable certainty that the suspect was impaired at a specific time. On the other hand, the DRE can supply credible evidence that the suspect was impaired at a specific time and that the nature of the impairment was consistent with a particular family of drugs. But the DRE program usually cannot determine which specific drug was ingested. Proving drug intoxication requires a coordinated effort and the production of competent data from both the DRE and the forensic toxicologist.

Quick Review

- The forensic toxicologist must devise an analytical scheme to detect, isolate, and identify toxic drug substances extracted from biological fluids, tissues, and organs.

- A screening test gives quick insight into the likelihood that a specimen contains a drug substance. Positive results arising from a screening test are tentative at best and must be verified with a confirmation test.

- The most widely used screening tests are thin-layer chromatography, gas chromatography, and immunoassay. Gas chromatography/mass spectrometry is generally accepted as the confirmation test of choice.

- Once a drug is extracted and identified, a toxicologist may be required to judge the drug's effect on an individual's natural performance or physical state.

Chapter Review

- Forensic toxicologists detect and identify drugs and poisons in body fluids, tissues, and organs in matters that pertain to violations of criminal laws.

- Ethyl alcohol is the most heavily abused drug in Western countries.

- Alcohol appears in the blood within minutes after it has been taken by mouth. It slowly increases in concentration while it is being absorbed from the stomach and the small intestine into the bloodstream.

- When all of the alcohol has been absorbed, a maximum alcohol level is reached in the blood, and the postabsorption period begins. During postabsorption, the alcohol concentration slowly decreases until a zero level is reached.

- Elimination of alcohol throughout the body is accomplished through oxidation and excretion. Oxidation takes place almost entirely in the liver, while alcohol is excreted unchanged in the breath, urine, and perspiration.

- Breath-testing devices operate on the principle that the ratio between the concentration of alcohol in alveolar breath and its concentration in blood is fixed.

- Modern breath testers are free of chemicals. They include infrared light absorption devices and fuel cell detectors.

- The key to the accuracy of a breath-testing device is to ensure that the unit captures the alcohol in the alveolar (deep-lung) breath of the subject.

- Many breath testers collect a set volume of breath and expose it to infrared light. The instrument measures alcohol concentration in breath by measuring the degree of the interaction of the light with alcohol in the collected breath sample.

- Law enforcement officers use field sobriety tests to estimate a motorist's degree of physical impairment by alcohol and to determine whether an evidential test for alcohol is justified.

- The horizontal-gaze nystagmus test, walk and turn, and the one-leg stand are all considered reliable and effective psychophysical tests for alcohol impairment.

- Gas chromatography is the most widely used approach for determining blood-alcohol levels in forensic laboratories.

- An anticoagulant should be added to a blood sample to prevent clotting; a preservative should be added to inhibit the growth of microorganisms capable of destroying alcohol.

- The current legal measure of drunk driving in the United States is a blood-alcohol concentration of 0.08 percent, or 0.08 grams of alcohol per 100 milliliters of blood.

- An implied-consent law states that the operator of a motor vehicle on a public highway must either consent to a test for alcohol intoxication, if requested, or lose his or her license for some designated period—usually six months to one year.

- The forensic toxicologist must devise an analytical scheme to detect, isolate, and identify toxic drug substances extracted from biological fluids, tissues, and organs.

- A screening test gives quick insight into the likelihood that a specimen contains a drug substance. Positive results arising from a screening test are tentative at best and must be verified with a confirmation test.

- The most widely used screening tests are thin-layer chromatography, gas chromatography, and immunoassay. Gas chromatography/mass spectrometry is generally accepted as the confirmation test of choice.

- Once a drug is extracted and identified, a toxicologist may be required to judge the drug's effect on an individual's natural performance or physical state.

Quick Lab: pH Test

Materials:

pH paper with color indicator chart

Liquid samples of acid and base substances (examples: tap water, bottled water, soda, ice tea, baking soda in water, salt water, lime juice, cleaning solution, liquid soap)

Procedure:

pH can help toxicologists determine what type of toxin may be present in a sample. This activity will allow you to identify the pH of some common substances. Before you begin, write a guess of what you think the pH of each sample will be. Now, take a piece of pH paper and dip into the first sample for a few seconds. Compare the pH paper to the color indicator chart and determine what the pH is of the sample. Record your observations. Repeat this for each sample.

Follow-Up Questions:

1. How many samples did you guess correctly before testing them? Which ones were they?

2. Create a pH chart. Use the labels *Acid, Base,* and *Neutral.* Also label where each item you tested would be on your chart.

3. A toxicologist would test samples of what to determine the pH of the toxin in a body?

Review Questions

1. About 95–98 percent of alcohol is oxidized to what two substances?
   a. carbon dioxide and dehydrogenase
   b. water and acetic acid
   c. acetaldehyde and acetic acid
   d. water and carbon dioxide

2. Carbon monoxide combines with what component of blood?
   a. carboxyhemoglobin
   b. hemoglobin
   c. oxyhemoglobin
   d. white blood cells

3. With a blood-alcohol level at 0.15 percent, the chance for involvement in an automobile accident is
   a. 10 times as great
   b. 25 times as great
   c. 50 times as great
   d. 75 times as great

4. Which of the following drugs would not have a pH of increasing basicity?
   a. phencyclidine
   b. amphetamines
   c. cocaine
   d. barbiturates

5. What percentage of alcohol is absorbed through the stomach walls into the portal vein of the blood system?
   a. 20 percent
   b. 70 percent
   c. 1 percent
   d. 10 percent

6. True or False: The role of the forensic toxicologist is limited to matters that pertain to violations of the law.

7. True or False: A breath test, used to measure alcohol, reflects the alcohol concentration in the pulmonary vein.

8. True or False: After a screening test has been used to determine the identity of an abused drug, the confirmation test of choice is thin-layer chromatography.

9. True or False: The concentration of a drug present in urine is an excellent indicator of how extensively an individual's behavior or state is influenced by the drug.

10. True or False: The technique used most widely by forensic toxicologists for detecting alcohol in blood is the gas chromatograph.

11. What is a toxicologist? Name three settings in which a toxicologist often works.

12. What is the most widely abused drug in Western countries?

13. Define *metabolism*.

14. List and describe the three stages of alcohol's fate in the human body.

15. Name at least three factors that influence the rate at which alcohol is absorbed into the bloodstream.

16. Alcohol that is not oxidized is expelled unchanged in what bodily excretions?

17. The amount of alcohol exhaled in the breath is in direct proportion to what?

18. For a longer total time required for complete absorption, will the peak blood-alcohol concentration be higher or lower?

19. List and describe the functions of the three types of blood vessels in the circulatory system.

20. Through the walls of which organ is most alcohol absorbed into the bloodstream? In what other organ does the remainder of absorption occur?

21. What are alveoli and what role do they play in circulation?

22. What scientific observation forms the theoretical basis for breath testing?

23. Briefly describe how a fuel cell detector measures blood-alcohol concentration.

24. What is mouth alcohol and how does it affect the accuracy of a breath test? Name three potential sources of mouth alcohol.

25. What is a field sobriety test? What two general types of test are included in a field sobriety test?

26. What type of disinfectant must be applied to a subject's skin before drawing blood? Why must such a disinfectant be applied?

27. What type of container best ensures the preservation of blood samples?

28. What two substances should be added to a blood sample after collection and why?

29. How do each of the following factors affect alcohol's stability in blood: storage temperature, the presence of a preservative, and the time of storage?

30. When collecting postmortem blood samples for alcohol determination, why is it best to collect a number of blood samples from different body sites?

31. What blood-alcohol concentration is the current legal measure of drunk driving in the United States, as established by the National Highway Traffic Safety Administration?

32. What is a *per se* law?

33. What is an implied-consent law? Why were such laws implemented?

34. Describe two challenges toxicologists face in detecting drugs and determining their toxicity.

35. What three drugs account for 90 percent or more of the drugs encountered in a typical toxicology laboratory?

36. What is the first task of a forensic toxicologist when establishing an analytical scheme to detect and identify drugs?

37. What are acids and bases? How are they used to extract and categorize drugs?

38. What are the three screening tests most widely used by forensic toxicologists? What is the confirmation test of choice?

39. Which of the following is not classified as a heavy metal?
   a. lead
   b. arsenic
   c. mercury
   d. thallium

40. Explain how inhaling carbon monoxide can cause death.

41. Why is the concentration of a drug present in urine a poor indicator of how extensively an individual's behavior or state is influenced by the drug?

Application and Critical Thinking

1. Answer the following questions about driving risk associated with drinking and blood-alcohol concentration:
   a. Randy is just barely legally intoxicated. How much more likely is he to have an accident compared with someone who is sober?
   b. Marissa, who has been drinking, is 15 times as likely to have an accident as her sober friend, Christine. What is Marissa's approximate blood-alcohol concentration?
   c. After several drinks, Charles is ten times as likely to have an accident as a sober person. Is he more or less intoxicated than James, whose blood-alcohol level is 0.10?
   d. Under the original blood-alcohol standards recommended by the NHTSA, a person considered just barely legally intoxicated was how much more likely to have an accident than a sober individual?

2. Following is a description of four individuals who have been drinking. Rank them from highest to lowest blood-alcohol concentration:
   a. John, who weighs 200 pounds and has consumed eight 8-ounce drinks on a full stomach
   b. Frank, who weighs 170 pounds and has consumed four 8-ounce drinks on an empty stomach
   c. Gary, who weighs 240 pounds and has consumed six 8-ounce drinks on an empty stomach
   d. Stephen, who weighs 180 pounds and has consumed six 8-ounce drinks on a full stomach

3. Following is a description of four individuals who have been drinking. In which (if any) of the following countries would each be considered legally drunk: the United States, Australia, and Sweden?
   a. Bill, who weighs 150 pounds and has consumed three 8-ounce drinks on an empty stomach
   b. Sally, who weighs 110 pounds and has consumed three 8-ounce drinks on a full stomach
   c. Rich, who weighs 200 pounds and has consumed six 8-ounce drinks on an empty stomach
   d. Carrie, who weighs 140 pounds and has consumed four 8-ounce drinks on a full stomach

4. You are a forensic scientist who has been asked to test two blood samples. You know that one sample is suspected of containing barbiturates and the other contains no drugs; however, you cannot tell the two samples apart. Describe how you would use the concept of pH to determine which sample contains barbiturates. Explain your reasoning.

5. You are investigating an arson scene and you find a corpse in the rubble, but you suspect that the victim did not die as a result of the fire. Instead, you suspect that the victim was murdered earlier, and that the blaze was started to cover up the murder. How would you go about determining whether the victim died before the fire?

6. Three individuals are stopped at a DUI checkpoint at ten p.m. Before performing the on-site breath test, the checkpoint officer asks each of them about their activities before they were stopped in order to estimate the expected blood-alcohol reading estimation (and to gauge their honesty). Use the testimony of each person that follows and the diagram in Figure 6–9 to estimate the expected BAC (blood-alcohol concentration). Indicate whether this is above or below the legal limit for operating a vehicle.
   a. Larry Questring had a large meal at an Italian restaurant with his wife. He ingested 8 ounces of 80-proof Frangelico between seven p.m. and nine p.m. Larry weighs approximately 180 pounds.
      Estimated BAC at ten p.m.:
   b. Paul Raunetz is driving home from a bar. He drove there after finishing his workday without stopping to eat. At the bar, he had four shots of tequila (1 ounce each, 80 proof) and five shots of whiskey (1 oz each, 80 proof) between six p.m. and nine p.m. Paul weighs approximately 130 pounds.
      Estimated BAC at ten p.m..
   c. Thomas Wold is returning home after an NFL game that started at six p.m. and ended at nine p.m. While watching the game, he ingested two hot dogs, a hot pretzel, peanuts, cheese fries, two diet sodas, ice cream, and six gin-and-tonics. Each gin-and-tonic contained 2 ounces of 80-proof gin. Thomas weighs approximately 240 pounds.
      Estimated BAC at ten p.m.:

Endnotes

1. In the United States, laws that define blood-alcohol levels almost exclusively use the unit *percent weight per volume*—% w/v. Hence, 0.015 percent w/v is equivalent to 0.015 grams of alcohol per 100 milliliters of blood, or 15 milligrams of alcohol per 100 milliliters.

2. R. B. Forney et al., "Alcohol Distribution in the Vascular System: Concentrations of Orally Administered Alcohol in Blood from Various Points in the Vascular System and in Rebreathed Air during Absorption," *Quarterly Journal of Studies on Alcohol* 25 (1964): 205.

3. G. A. Brown et al., "The Stability of Ethanol in Stored Blood," *Analytica Chemica Acta* 66 (1973): 271.

4. 0.15 percent w/v is equivalent to 0.15 grams of alcohol per 100 milliliters of blood, or 150 milligrams per 100 milliliters.

5. 384 U.S. 757 (1966).

The Lindbergh Baby Case

On the evening of March 1, 1932, a kidnapper crept up his homemade ladder and stole the baby of Charles and Anne Lindbergh directly from the second-floor nursery of their house in Hopewell, New Jersey. The only evidence of his coming was a ransom note, the ladder, a chisel, and the tragic absence of the infant. A couple of months later, although the $50,000 ransom had been paid, the baby turned up dead in the woods a mile away. There was no additional sign of the killer. Fortunately, when finally studied by wood technologist Arthur Koehler, the abandoned ladder yielded some important investigative clues.

By studying the types of wood used and the cutter marks on the wood, Koehler ascertained where the materials might have come from and what specific equipment was used to create them. Koehler traced the wood from a South Carolina mill to a lumberyard in the Bronx, New York. Unfortunately the trail went cold, as the lumberyard did not keep sales records of purchases. The break in the case came in 1934, when Bruno Richard Hauptmann paid for gasoline with a bill that matched a serial number on the ransom money. Koehler showed that microscopic markings on the wood were made by a tool in Hauptmann's possession. Ultimately, handwriting analysis of the ransom note clearly showed it to be written by Hauptmann.

The Microscope

Key Terms

binocular

condenser

depth of focus

eyepiece lens

field of view

microspectrophotometer

monocular

objective lens

parfocal

polarized light

polarizer

real image

transmitted illumination

vertical or reflected illumination

virtual image

A microscope is an optical instrument that uses a lens or a combination of lenses to magnify and resolve the fine details of an object. The earliest methods for examining physical evidence in crime laboratories relied almost solely on the microscope to study the structure and composition of matter. Even the advent of modern analytical instrumentation and techniques has done little to diminish the usefulness of the microscope for forensic analysis. If anything, the development of the powerful scanning electron microscope promises to add a new dimension to forensic science heretofore unattainable within the limits of the ordinary light microscope.

Basics of the Microscope

The earliest and simplest microscope was the single lens commonly referred to as a magnifying glass. The handheld magnifying glass makes things appear larger than they are because of the way light rays are refracted, or bent, in passing from the air into the glass and back into the air. The magnified image is observed by looking through the lens, as shown in Figure 7–1. Such an image is known as a **virtual image**; it can be seen only by looking through a lens and cannot be viewed directly. This is distinguished from a **real image**, which can be seen directly, like the image that is projected onto a motion picture screen.

virtual image
An image that cannot be seen directly, but can be seen only by a viewer looking through a lens

real image
An image that can be seen directly with the naked eye

FIGURE 7–1
The passage of light through a lens, showing how magnification is obtained.

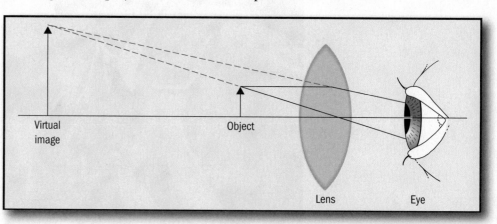

The ordinary magnifying glass can achieve a magnification of about 5 to 10 times. Higher magnifying power is obtainable only with a compound microscope, constructed of two lenses mounted at each end of a hollow tube. The object to be magnified is placed under the lower lens, called the **objective lens**, and the magnified image is viewed through the upper lens, known as the **eyepiece lens**. As shown in Figure 7–2, the objective lens forms a real, inverted, magnified image of the object. The eyepiece, acting just like a simple magnifying glass, further magnifies this image into a virtual image, which is seen by the eye. The combined magnifying power of both lenses can produce an image magnified up to 1,500 times.

objective lens
The lower lens of a compound microscope; it is positioned directly over the specimen

eyepiece lens
The upper lens of a compound microscope, into which the viewer looks

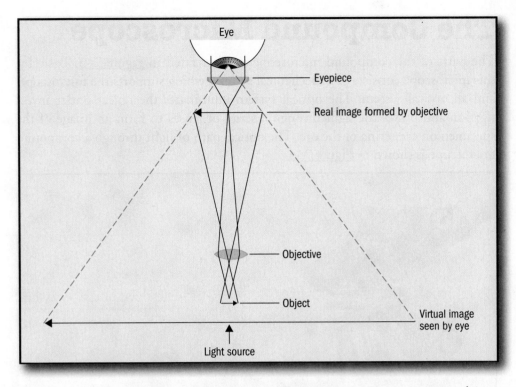

FIGURE 7–2
The principle of the compound microscope. The passage of light through two lenses forms the virtual image of the object seen by the eye.

The optical principles of the compound microscope are incorporated into the basic design of different types of light microscopes. The microscopes most applicable for examining forensic specimens are as follows:

- the compound microscope
- the comparison microscope
- the stereoscopic microscope
- the polarizing microscope
- the microspectrophotometer

After describing these five microscopes, we will talk about a completely different approach to microscopy, the scanning electron microscope (SEM). This instrument focuses a beam of electrons, instead of visible light, onto the specimen to produce a magnified image. The principle and design of this microscope permit magnifying powers as high as 100,000 times.

Quick Review
- A microscope is an optical instrument that uses a lens or a combination of lenses to magnify and resolve the fine details of an object.
- Two types of images are virtual images and real images. A real image can be seen directly with the naked eye; a virtual image can be seen only by a viewer looking through a lens.
- The eyepiece lens is the upper lens through which the viewer looks. The objective lens is the lower lens that is positioned directly over the specimen.

The Compound Microscope

The parts of the compound microscope are illustrated in <u>Figure 7–3</u>. Basically, this microscope consists of a mechanical system, which supports the microscope, and an optical system. The optical system illuminates the object under investigation and passes the light through a series of lenses to form an image of the specimen on the retina of the eye. The optical path of light through a compound microscope is shown in <u>Figure 7–4</u>.

FIGURE 7–3
Parts of the coumpound microscope: (1) base, (2) arm, (3) stage, (4) body tube, (5) coarse adjustment, (6) fine adjustment, (7) illuminator, (8) condenser, (9) objective lens, and (10) eyepiece lens. *Courtesy Leica Microsystems, Buffalo, N.Y., www. leica-microsystems.com*

Construction of the Compound Microscope

The mechanical system of the compound microscope is composed of six parts:

Base The support on which the instrument rests.

Arm A C-shaped upright structure, hinged to the base, that supports the microscope and acts as a handle for carrying.

Stage The horizontal plate on which the specimens are placed for study. The specimens are normally mounted on glass slides that are held firmly in place on the stage by spring clips.

DIALUX

FIGURE 7–4
Optics of the compound microscope. *Courtesy Leica Microsystems, Buffalo, N.Y., www.leica-microsystems.com*

Body Tube A cylindrical hollow tube on which the objective and eyepiece lenses are mounted at opposite ends. This tube is merely a corridor through which light passes from one lens to another.

Coarse Adjustment This knob focuses the microscope lenses on the specimen by raising and lowering the body tube.

Fine Adjustment The movements effected by this knob are similar to those of the coarse adjustment but are of a much smaller magnitude.

The optical system is made up of four parts:

Illuminator Most modern microscopes use artificial light supplied by a lightbulb to illuminate the specimen being examined. If the specimen is transparent, the light is directed up toward and through the specimen stage from an illuminator built into the base of the microscope. This is known as **transmitted illumination**. When the object is opaque—that is, not transparent—the light source must be placed above the specimen so that it can reflect off the specimen's surface and into the lens system of the microscope. This type of illumination is known as **vertical or reflected illumination**.

Condenser The **condenser** is a lens system under the microscope stage that collects light rays from the base illuminator and focuses them on the specimen. The simplest condenser is known as the Abbé condenser. It consists of two lenses held together in a metal mount. The condenser also includes an iris diaphragm that can be opened or closed to control the amount of light passing into the condenser.

transmitted illumination
Light that passes up from the condenser and through the specimen; it is used to examine transparent specimens

vertical or reflected illumination
Illumination of a specimen from above; it is used to examine opaque specimens

condenser
The lens system under the microscope stage that collects light rays from the base illuminator and focuses them onto the specimen

parfocal
Describes a microscope such that when an image is focused with one objective in position, the other objective can be rotated into place and the field will remain in focus

monocular
Describes a microscope with one eyepiece

binocular
Describes a microscope with two eyepieces

Objective Lens This is the lens positioned closest to the specimen. To facilitate changing from one objective lens to another, several objectives are mounted on a revolving nosepiece or turret located above the specimen. Most microscopes are **parfocal**, meaning that when the microscope is focused with one objective in position, the other objective can be rotated into place by revolving the nosepiece while the specimen remains very nearly in correct focus.

Eyepiece or Ocular Lens This is the lens closest to the eye. A microscope with only one eyepiece is **monocular**; one constructed with two eyepieces (one for each eye) is **binocular**.

Magnification and Resolution

Each microscope lens is inscribed with a number signifying its magnifying power. The image viewed by the microscopist will have a total magnification equal to the product of the magnifying power of the objective and eyepiece lenses. For example, an eyepiece lens with a magnification of 10 times (10×) used in combination with an objective lens of 10× has a total magnification power of 100×. Most forensic work requires a 10× eyepiece in combination with either a 4×, 10×, 20×, or 45× objective (see Figure 7–5). The respective magnifications will be 40×, 100×, 200×, and 450×.

In addition, each objective lens is inscribed with its numerical aperture (N.A.). The ability of an objective lens to resolve details into separate images instead of one blurred image is directly proportional to the numerical aperture value of the objective lens. For example, an objective lens of N.A. 1.30 can separate details at half the distance of a lens with an N.A. of 0.65. The maximum useful magnification of a compound microscope is approximately 1,000 times the N.A. of the objective being used. This magnification is sufficient to permit the eye to see all the detail that can be resolved. Any effort to increase the total magnification beyond this figure will yield no additional detail and is referred to as *empty magnification*.

FIGURE 7–5
A microscope's revolving nosepiece shows the objective lenses available to view the specimen and their corresponding magnifications. *Courtesy Getty Images - Stockbyte*

Although a new student of the microscope may be tempted to immediately choose the highest magnifying power available to view a specimen, the experienced microscopist weighs a number of important factors before choosing a magnifying power. A first consideration must be the size of the specimen area, or the **field of view**, that the examiner wishes to study. As magnifying power increases, the field of view decreases. Thus, it is best to first select a low magnification in which a good general overall view of the specimen is seen, and to switch later to a higher power in which a smaller portion of the specimen can be viewed in more detail.

The **depth of focus** is also a function of magnifying power. After a focus has been achieved on a specimen, the depth of focus defines the thickness of that specimen. Areas above and below this region will be blurred and can be viewed only when the focus is readjusted. Depth of focus decreases as magnifying power increases.

field of view
The area of the specimen that can be seen after it is magnified

depth of focus
The thickness of a specimen that is entirely in focus under a microscope

Quick Review

- Transparent illumination is light directed up toward and through a specimen from an illuminator built into the base of the microscope. It is used to view transparent specimens. Vertical or reflected illumination is light from a source above the specimen that reflects off the specimen's surface and into the lens system of the microscope. It is used to view opaque specimens.

- A condenser is a lens system under the microscope stage that collects light rays from the base illuminator and focuses them on the specimen.

- A monocular microscope has one eyepiece; a binocular microscope has two eyepieces.

- One determines the total magnification of a compound microscope by multiplying the magnifying power of the eyepiece lens by the magnifying power of the objective lens.

- When you increase a compound microscope's magnification, its field of view and depth of focus decrease.

The Comparison Microscope

Forensic microscopy often requires a side-by-side comparison of specimens. This kind of examination can best be performed with a comparison microscope, such as the one pictured in Figure 7–6.

Basically, the comparison microscope is two compound microscopes combined into one unit. The unique feature of its design is that it uses a bridge incorporating a series of mirrors and lenses to join two independent objective lenses into a single binocular unit. A viewer looking through the eyepiece lenses of the comparison microscope observes a circular field, equally divided into two parts by a fine line. The specimen mounted under the left-hand objective appears in the left half of the field, and the specimen under the right-hand objective appears in the right half of the field. It is important to closely match the optical characteristics of the objective lenses to ensure that both specimens are seen at equal

MyCrimeKit:
WebExtra 7.1

Explore the Concept of Magnification with a Compound Microscope
www.mycrimekit.com

MyCrimeKit:
WebExtra 7.2

Scan a Sample under the Compound Microscope
www.mycrimekit.com

MyCrimeKit:
WebExtra 7.3

Observe the Concept of Depth of Focus
www.mycrimekit.com

FIGURE 7–6
The comparison micro-
scope—two independent
objective lenses joined together by an optical bridge.
*Courtesy Mikael Karisson/
Arresting Images*

**MyCrimeKit:
WebExtra 7.4**
Practice Matching Bullets
with the Aid of a 3D
Interactive Illustration
www.mycrimekit.com

magnification and with minimal but identical lens distortions. Comparison microscopes designed to compare opaque objects, such as bullets and cartridges, are
equipped with vertical or reflected illumination. Comparison microscopes used
to compare hairs or fibers use transmitted illumination.

Figure 7–7 shows the striation markings on two bullets that have been placed
under the objective lenses of a comparison microscope. Modern firearms examination began with the introduction of the comparison microscope, with its ability to give the firearms examiner a side-by-side magnified view of bullets. Bullets
that are fired through the same rifle barrel display comparable rifling markings on
their surfaces. Matching the majority of striations present on each bullet justifies
a conclusion that both bullets traveled through the same barrel.

Quick Review

- The comparison microscope consists of two independent objective lenses
joined by an optical bridge to a common eyepiece lens. A viewer looking
through the eyepiece lens observes the objects under investigation side-by-
side in a circular field that is equally divided into two parts.

- Modern firearms examination began with the introduction of the comparison microscope, which gives the examiner a side-by-side magnified view
of bullets.

FIGURE 7–7
Photomicrograph taken through a comparison microscope. On the right are the stiation markings on the test-fired bullet, fired through the suspect weapon. On the left are the markings of the crime-scene bullet. *Courtesy Orlando/Getty Images Inc.—Hutton Archive*

The Stereoscopic Microscope

The details that characterize the structures of many types of physical evidence do not always require examination under very high magnifications. For such specimens, the stereoscopic microscope has proven quite adequate, providing magnifying powers from 10× to 125×. This microscope has the advantage of presenting a distinctive three-dimensional image of an object. Also, whereas the image formed by the compound microscope is inverted and reversed (upside-down and backward), the stereoscopic microscope is more convenient because prisms in its light path create a right-side-up image.

The stereoscopic microscope, shown in Figure 7–8, is actually two monocular compound microscopes properly spaced and aligned to present a three-dimensional image of a specimen to the viewer, who looks through both eyepiece lenses. The light path of a stereoscopic microscope is shown in Figure 7–9.

The stereoscopic microscope is undoubtedly the most frequently used and versatile microscope found in the crime laboratory. Its wide field of view and great depth of focus make it an ideal instrument for locating trace evidence in debris, garments, weapons, and tools. Furthermore, its potentially large working distance (the distance between the objective lens and the specimen) makes it ideal for microscopic examination of big, bulky items. When fitted with vertical illumination, the stereoscopic microscope becomes the primary tool for characterizing physical evidence as diverse as paint, soil, gunpowder residues, and marijuana.

MyCrimeKit: WebExtra 7.5
Explore the Stereoscopic Microscope
www.mycrimekit.com

FIGURE 7–8
A stereoscopic microscope.
*Courtesy Mikael Karisson/
Arresting Images*

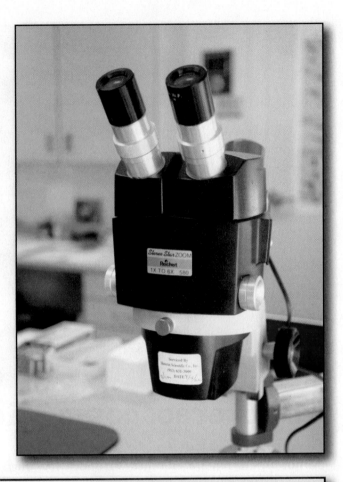

FIGURE 7-9
Schematic diagram of a
stereoscopic microscope.
This microscope is actually
two separate monocular
microscopes, each with its
own set of lenses except
for the lowest objective
lens, which is common to
both microscopes.

Quick Review

- The stereoscopic microscope consists of two monocular compound microscopes properly spaced and aligned to present a three-dimensional image of a specimen to the viewer, who looks through both eyepiece lenses.

- The large working distance of the stereoscopic microscope makes it ideal for microscopic examination of big, bulky items.

The Polarizing Microscope

Recall from Chapter 4 that light's wavelike motion in space can be invoked to explain many facets of its behavior. The waves that compose a beam of light can be pictured as vibrating in all directions perpendicular to the direction in which the light is traveling. However, when a beam of light passes through certain types of specially fabricated crystalline substances, it emerges vibrating in only one plane. Light that is confined to a single plane of vibration is said to be plane-polarized. The device that creates **polarized light** in this manner is called a **polarizer**. A common example of this phenomenon is the passage of sunlight through polarized sunglasses. By transmitting light vibrating in the vertical plane only, these sunglasses eliminate or reduce light glare. Most glare consists of partially polarized light that has been reflected off horizontal surfaces and thus is vibrating in a horizontal plane.

Because polarized light appears no different to the eye from ordinary light, special means must be devised for detecting it. This is accomplished simply by placing a second polarizing crystal, called an analyzer, in the path of the polarized beam. As shown in Figure 7–10, if the polarizer and analyzer are aligned parallel to each other, the polarized light passes through and is seen by the eye. If, on the other hand, the polarizer and analyzer are set perpendicular to one another, or are "crossed," no light penetrates, and the result is total darkness or extinction.

polarized light
Light confined to a single plane of vibration

polarizer
A device that permits the passage of light waves vibrating in only one plane

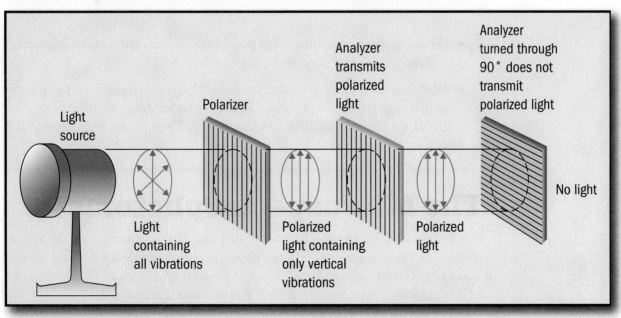

FIGURE 7-10 Polarization of light.

In this manner, a compound or stereoscopic microscope can be outfitted with a polarizer and analyzer to allow the viewer to detect polarized light. Such a microscope is known as a polarizing microscope. Essentially, the polarizer is placed between the light source and the sample stage to polarize the light before it passes through the specimen. The polarized light penetrating the specimen must then pass through an analyzer before it reaches the eyepiece and finally the eye. Normally the polarizer and analyzer are "crossed" so that when no specimen is in place, the field appears dark. However, introducing a specimen that polarizes light reorients the polarized light, allowing it to pass through the analyzer. This result produces vivid colors and intensity contrasts that make the specimen readily distinguishable.

The most obvious and important applications of this microscope relate to studying materials that polarize light. For example, as we learned in Chapter 4, many crystalline substances are birefringent; that is, they split a beam of light into two light-ray components of different refractive index values. What makes this observation particularly relevant to our discussion of the polarizing microscope is that the light beams are polarized at right angles to each other. Thus, polarizing microscopy has found wide application for the examination of birefringent minerals present in soil.

By using the immersion method and selecting the proper immersion liquids, a refractive index corresponding to each plane of polarized light can be determined. Thus, when a mineral is viewed under polarized light in a liquid that matches one of its refractive indices, the Becke line will no longer be visible. This information, plus observations on crystal color, form, and so on, makes it possible for the microscopist to identify the mineral. Similarly, criminalists use the fact that many synthetic fibers are birefringent to characterize them with a polarizing microscope.

MyCrimeKit: WebExtra 7.6

Explore the Polarizing Microscope—I
www.mycrimekit.com

MyCrimeKit: WebExtra 7.7

Explore the Polarizing Microscope—II
www.mycrimekit.com

Quick Review

- Light that is confined to a single plane of vibration is said to be plane-polarized.

- The polarizing microscope made possible the examination of the interaction of plane-polarized light with matter.

- Polarizing microscopy is used to study birefringent materials, that is, materials that have a double refraction. Refractive index data provide information that helps identify minerals present in a soil sample or the identity of a synthetic fiber.

The Microspectrophotometer

Few instruments in a crime laboratory can match the versatility of the microscope. The microscope's magnifying power is indispensable for finding minute traces of physical evidence. Many items of physical evidence can be characterized by a microscopic examination of their morphological features. Likewise, the microscope can be used to study how light interacts with the material under investigation, or it can be used to observe the effects that other chemical substances have on such evidence. Each of these features allows an examiner to better characterize and identify physical evidence. Recently, linking the microscope to a computerized spectrophotometer has added a new dimension to its capability. This combination has given rise to a new instrument called the **microspectrophotometer**. In many respects, this is an ideal marriage from the forensic scientist's viewpoint.

In Chapter 5, we saw how a chemist can use selective absorption of light by materials to characterize them. In particular, light in the ultraviolet, visible, and infrared regions of the electromagnetic spectrum is most helpful for this purpose. Unfortunately, in the past, forensic chemists were unable to take full advantage of the capabilities of spectrophotometry for examining trace evidence, because most spectrophotometers are not well suited for examining the very small particles frequently encountered as evidence.

With the development of the microspectrophotometer, a forensic analyst can view a particle under a microscope while a beam of light is directed at the particle to obtain its absorption spectrum. Depending on the type of light employed, an examiner can acquire either a visible or an IR spectral pattern of the substance being viewed under the microscope. The obvious advantage of this approach is to provide added information to characterize trace quantities of evidence. A microspectrophotometer designed to measure the uptake of visible light by materials is shown in Figure 7–11.

microspectro-photometer
An instrument that links a microscope to a spectrophotometer

FIGURE 7–11
A visible-light microspec-trophotometer.
*Courtesy CRAIC Technologies Inc., Altadena, Calif.
www.microspectra.com*

Visual comparison of color is usually one of the first steps in examining paint, fiber, and ink evidence. Such comparisons are easily obtained using a comparison microscope. A forensic scientist can use the microspectrophotometer to compare the color of materials visually while plotting an absorption spectrum for each item under examination. This displays the exact wavelengths at which each item absorbs in the visible-light spectrum. Occasionally colors that appear similar by visual examination show significant differences in their absorption spectra. An example of this approach is shown in Figure 7–12, in which the microspectrophotometer is used to distinguish counterfeit and authentic currency by comparing the spectral patterns of inked lines on the paper.

FIGURE 7-12 Two $50 bills are shown at top; one is genuine and the other is counterfeit. Below each bill is a microphotograph of an inked line present on each bill. Each line was examined under a visible-light microspectrophotometer. As shown, the visible absorption spectrum of each line is readily differentiated, thus allowing the examiner to distinguish a counterfeit bill from genuine currency. *Courtesy Peter W. Pfefferli, forensic scientist, Lausanne, Switzerland*

Another emerging technique in forensic science is the use of the infrared microspectrophotometer to examine fibers and paints. The "fingerprint" IR spectrum (see page 187) is unique for each chemical substance. Therefore, obtaining such a spectrum from either a fiber or a paint chip allows the analyst to better identify and compare the type of chemicals from which these materials are manufactured. With a microspectrophotometer, a forensic analyst can view a substance through the microscope and at the same time have the instrument plot the infrared absorption spectrum for that material.

Quick Review
- The microspectrophotometer is a spectrophotometer coupled with a light microscope. The device allows an examiner studying a specimen under the microscope to obtain the visible-light or IR spectrum of the material.

The Scanning Electron Microscope (SEM)

All the microscopes described thus far use light coming off the specimen to produce a magnified image. The scanning electron microscope (SEM) is, however, a special case in the family of microscopes (see Figure 7–13). The image is formed by aiming a beam of electrons onto the specimen and studying electron emissions on a closed TV circuit.

FIGURE 7–13
A scanning electron microscope. *Courtesy Jeol USA Inc., Peabody, Mass., www.jeolusa.com*

In the SEM, a hot tungsten filament emits a beam of electrons, which is focused by electromagnets onto the surface of the specimen. This primary electron beam causes the elements that make up the upper layers of the specimen to emit electrons known as secondary electrons. About 20–30 percent of the primary electrons rebound off the surface of the specimen. These electrons are known as *backscattered electrons*. The emitted electrons (both secondary and backscattered) are collected, and the amplified signal is displayed on a cathode-ray or TV tube. By scanning the primary electron beam across the specimen's surface in synchronization with the cathode-ray tube, the SEM converts the emitted electrons into an image of the specimen for display on the cathode-ray tube.

The major attractions of the SEM image are its high magnification, high resolution, and great depth of focus. In its usual mode, the SEM has a magnification that ranges from 10× to 100,000×. Its depth of focus is some 300 times better than optical systems at similar magnifications, and the resultant picture is almost stereoscopic in appearance. Its great depth of field and magnification are exemplified by the magnification of cystolithic hair on the marijuana leaf, as shown in Figure 7–14. An SEM image of a vehicle's headlight filaments may reveal whether the headlights were on or off at the time of a collision (see Figures 7–15 and 7–16).

FIGURE 7–14
The cystolithic hairs of the marijuana leaf, as viewed with a screening electron microscope (800x).
Courtesy Jeff Albright

Another facet of scanning electron microscopy has been the use of X-ray production to determine the elemental composition of a specimen. X-rays are generated when the electron beam of the scanning electron microscope strikes a target. When the SEM is coupled to an X-ray analyzer, the emitted X-rays can be sorted according to their energy values and used to build a picture of the elemental distribution in the specimen. Because each element emits X-rays of characteristic energy values, the X-ray analyzer can identify the elements present in a specimen. Furthermore, the element's concentration can be determined by measuring the intensity of the X-ray emission.

FIGURE 7–15
The melted ends of a hot filament break indicate that the headlights were on when an accident occurred. *Courtesy Jeol USA Inc., Peabody, Mass., www.jeolusa.com*

FIGURE 7–16
The sharp ends of a cold filament break indicate that the headlights were off when an accident occurred. *Courtesy Jeol USA, Inc., Peabody, Mass., www.jeolusa.com*

One application of scanning electron microscopy has been to determine whether a suspect has recently fired a gun. In this case, an attempt is made to remove any gunshot particles that remain on a shooter's hands by lifting them off with a piece of adhesive tape. The tape is then examined under the SEM for the presence of particles that may have originated from the bullet primer. These particles can be characterized by their size, shape, and elemental composition. As shown in Figure 7–17, when the sample of gunshot residue is exposed to a beam of electrons from the scanning electron microscope, X-rays are emitted. These X-rays are passed into a detector, where they are converted into electrical signals. These signals are sorted and displayed according to the energies of the emitted X-rays. Through the use of this technique, the elements lead, antimony, and barium, frequently found in most primers, can be rapidly detected and identified.

FIGURE 7–17 A schematic diagram of a scanning electron microscope displaying the image of a gunshot residue particle. Simultaneously, an X-ray analyzer detects and displays X-ray emissions from the elements lead (Pb), antimony (Sb), and barium (Ba) present in the particle.

MyCrimeKit:
WebExtra 7.8

Explore the Scanning
Electron Microscope
www.mycrimekit.com

Forensic Palynology:
Pollen and Spores as Evidence

Of the many plant species on earth, more than half a million produce pollen or spores. The pollen or spores produced by each species has a unique type of ornamentation and morphology. This means that pollen or spores can be identified and used to provide links between a crime scene and a person or object if examined by a trained analyst. This technique is called forensic palynology and includes the collection and examination of pollen and spores connected with crime scenes, illegal activities, or terrorism. Microscopy is the principal tool used in the field of forensic palynology.

Characteristics of Spores and Pollen In nature, pollen grains are the single-celled male gametophytes (reproductive cells) of seed-bearing plants. The pollen grain wall (*exine*) is durable because it protects and carries "the sperms" needed for plant reproduction. Spores consist of both the male and female gametes of plants such as algae, fungi, mosses, and ferns. Pollen-producing plants are either *anemophilous* (their pollen is dispersed by wind) or *entomophilous* (their pollen is carried and dispersed by insects or small animals). Fairly precise geographical locations can often be identified by the presence of different mixtures of airborne pollens produced by anemophilous plants. For example, it may be possible to identify a geographical origin by a profile of the pollen samples retrieved from a suspect's clothing simply by the type and percentages of airborne pollen grains. Entomophilous plants usually produce a small amount of pollen that is very sticky in nature. Therefore, this type of pollen is very rarely deposited on clothing or other objects except by direct contact with the plant. This information is useful when reconstructing the events of a crime because it indicates that the clothing, a vehicle, or other objects may have come into direct contact with plant types found at a crime scene.

Analysis of Spores and Pollen Both spores and pollen are microscopic in size and are produced by the adult plants and dispersed by the millions, and both can be analyzed using similar methods that use a variety of microscopic techniques. Using a compound light microscope with magnification capabilities up to 1,000×, analysts usually can identify pollen and spores as coming from a specific plant family or genus, and at times even a unique species. However, often the pollen or spores of related species may appear so similar that identification of the species is possible only with careful analysis using an SEM (see Figure 7–18).

FIGURE 7–18
Scanning electron micrograph of ragweed pollen magnified 950 times.
Courtesy Medical-on-Line/ Alamy

Unique shapes, aperture type, and surface ornamentation are typically used to identify spore samples. Useful features for characterizing pollen grains include shape, apertures, and wall and surface sculpturing. Shapes of pollen grains include spheres, triangles, ellipses, hexagons, pentagons, and many other geometric variations. *Apertures* are the openings on pollen grains from which the pollen tube grows and carries the sperms to the egg to complete fertilization. *Sculpturing* of the pollen refers to the pattern of the pollen grain surface.

To avoid destruction or contamination, early collection of forensic pollen samples for analysis is important and should be completed as soon as possible at a crime scene by a trained palynologist. This kind of expert's first task is to calculate the estimated production and dispersal patterns of spores and pollen (called the

Case Files

Clues from the Cornfield

A case exemplifying the application of forensic palynology to a criminal investigation occurred when a victim was kidnapped, robbed, and then murdered in the eastern part of the American Midwest. The victim's car was stolen, but later abandoned when it got stuck in mud near a busy highway. The next night a drifter was arrested in a nearby town for breaking into a closed store. While in jail awaiting trial, the drifter told a fellow inmate about his car being stuck in the mud and that he would not be in jail but for that mishap. The other prisoner, hoping to work a deal for a lighter sentence, told this story to the sheriff.

During the investigation of the crime scene, one of the law enforcement agents noticed that there was a large field of mature corn (maize, Zea mays) growing between the dirt road, where the stolen car had been abandoned in the mud, and the nearby highway leading to the next town. The investigator wondered if traces of torn maize leaves on the suspect's clothing might link him to the crime scene. Fortunately, the drifter's shirt and pants had been removed and stored in sterile paper bags when he was arrested. As with all prisoners in that region, he had been given a pair of orange overalls to wear while in jail.

The shirt and pants were sent to a botanist who was asked to search for traces of maize leaves on the clothing. The botanist was also a palynologist, and thus also collected samples and searched for traces of pollen. The pollen samples provided the best results. The samples collected from the suspect's shirt revealed that the neck and shoulder region of the shirt had high concentrations of fresh maize pollen. The forensic sample collected from the pants also contained maize pollen, but in a lower percentage. The forensic pollen data indicated that the drifter had recently walked through a maize field, similar to the one between the abandoned car and the highway. As he walked through the field, he had brushed against blooming male tassels on the corn plants that were about head high. This accounted for the high amount of maize pollen found on the shoulder and neck area of the shirt. Lesser amounts of maize pollen also fell on his pants as he walked through the field. While the suspect awaited trial, additional evidence and several fingerprints from the victim's farm also linked him to the murder.

Source: V. M. Bryant and G. D. Jones, "Forensic Palynology: Current Status of a Rarely Used Technique in the United States of America," *Forensic Science International*, vol. 163 (2006), pp.183–197.

pollen rain) for the crime scene or area of interest, and then using that information to produce a kind of "pollen fingerprint" of that location.

The information gained from the analysis of pollen and spore evidence has many possible uses. It can link a suspect or object to the crime scene or the victim, prove or disprove a suspect's alibi, include or exclude suspects, track the previous whereabouts of some item or suspect, or indicate the geographical origin of some item. In the past, pollen and spore evidence has also helped locate human remains and concealed burial sites, established the season or time of death of a victim, located the source areas of illegal drugs and fake pharmaceuticals, imprisoned terrorists, and proven the perpetration of illegal poaching or the adulteration of commercial foods.

Quick Review

- The scanning electron microscope (SEM) bombards a specimen with a beam of electrons instead of light to produce a highly magnified image. This produces X-ray emissions that can be used to characterize elements present in the material.

- Forensic palynology involves the collection and examination of pollen and spores connected with crime scenes, illegal activities, or terrorism. The scanning electron microscope is the principal tool used in the field of forensic palynology.

Chapter Review

- A microscope is an optical instrument that uses a lens or a combination of lenses to magnify and resolve the fine details of an object.

- Two types of images are virtual images and real images. A real image can be seen directly with the naked eye; a virtual image can be seen only by a viewer looking through a lens.

- The eyepiece lens is the upper lens through which the viewer looks. The objective lens is the lower lens that is positioned directly over the specimen.

- Transparent illumination is light directed up toward and through a specimen from an illuminator built into the base of the microscope. It is used to view transparent specimens. Vertical or reflected illumination is light from a source above the specimen that reflects off the specimen's surface and into the lens system of the microscope. It is used to view opaque specimens.

- A condenser is a lens system under the microscope stage that collects light rays from the base illuminator and focuses them on the specimen.

- A monocular microscope has one eyepiece; a binocular microscope has two eyepieces.

- One determines the total magnification of a compound microscope by multiplying the magnifying power of the eyepiece lens by the magnifying power of the objective lens.

- When you increase a compound microscope's magnification, its field of view and depth of focus decrease.

- The comparison microscope consists of two independent objective lenses joined by an optical bridge to a common eyepiece lens. A viewer looking through the eyepiece lens observes the objects under investigation side-by-side in a circular field that is equally divided into two parts.

- Modern firearms examination began with the introduction of the comparison microscope, which gives the examiner a side-by-side magnified view of bullets.

- The stereoscopic microscope consists of two monocular compound microscopes properly spaced and aligned to present a three-dimensional image of a specimen to the viewer, who looks through both eyepiece lenses.

- The large working distance of the stereoscopic microscope makes it ideal for microscopic examination of big, bulky items.

- Light that is confined to a single plane of vibration is said to be plane-polarized.

- The polarizing microscope made possible the examination of the interaction of plane-polarized light with matter.

- Polarizing microscopy is used to study birefringent materials, that is, materials that have a double refraction. Refractive index data provide information that helps identify minerals present in a soil sample or the identity of a synthetic fiber.

- The microspectrophotometer is a spectrophotometer coupled with a light microscope. The device allows an examiner studying a specimen under the microscope to obtain the visible-light or IR spectrum of the material.

- The scanning electron microscope (SEM) bombards a specimen with a beam of electrons instead of light to produce a highly magnified image. This produces X-ray emissions that can be used to characterize elements present in the material.

- Forensic palynology involves the collection and examination of pollen and spores connected with crime scenes, illegal activities, or terrorism. The scanning electron microscope is the principal tool used in the field of forensic palynology.

Quick Lab: Focusing the Microscope

Materials:

Compound light microscope
Prepared slides

Procedure:

The microscope is one of the most important tools in the laboratory. The first step in using the microscope is being able to focus on what you want to see. Take a prepared slide and place it on the stage, securing it in place with the stage clips. Always start with the low-power objective lens in place. Use the coarse adjustment knob (the larger knob) to bring the object into view. To bring the object into focus, always focus upward to avoid crushing the slide with the lens. Once you can see the object, use the fine adjustment knob (the smaller knob) to focus the item. If the slide needs to be adjusted, many microscopes have stage adjustment knobs that will move the stage or slide. If your microscope does not, you will have to manually move the slide. Once you have the object focused in the center of your view, try to view the object under high power. To do this, move the high-power lens into place above the slide. Use the fine adjustment knob to focus the object; you should not have to use the coarse adjustment knob (doing so may break the slide).

Follow-Up Questions:

1. To determine total magnification, multiply the objective lens power by the eyepiece lens power. What was the total magnification of your microscope when you were viewing the object under low power? What about under high power?

2. Besides magnification, what did you observe about the real image (what your naked eye saw on the slide) compared to the virtual image (what you saw looking through the scope)?

3. Did you observe anything when you moved the slide on the stage while looking through the scope?

Quick Lab: Creating Wet-Mount Slides

Materials:

Compound light microscope
Slide with cover slip
Water with dropper
Sample object (examples: hair, soil, thread, paper)

Procedure:

To view some objects, it is better to create a wet-mount slide. This helps create a clearer view than a regular slide would allow. To create a wet-mount slide, place the sample you want to view on the slide. Now, place a drop of water on the sample. Take the cover slip and slowly cover the sample so that there are no air bubbles in the water; these would block your view of the sample. The slide is now ready to be viewed on the scope. Remember the steps to focus your slide.

Follow-Up Questions:

1. After looking at the sample as a wet-mount slide, create a regular slide with the same type of sample. Do you see a difference between the two types of slides and the images they produce?

2. Other than the sample you viewed, can you think of any other types of evidence that could be viewed using a wet-mount slide?

Review Questions

1. Which of the following is not a part of the mechanical system of a compound microscope?
   a. coarse adjustment
   b. objective lens
   c. body tube
   d. stage

2. Which microscope is the most frequently used and versatile microscope found in the crime laboratory?
   a. the comparison microscope
   b. the stereoscopic microscope
   c. the compound microscope
   d. the polarizing microscope

3. The major attractions of the scanning electron microscope (SEM) include all of the following except:
   a. its high magnification
   b. its ability to polarize light
   c. its high resolution
   d. its great depth of focus

4. Which microscope can be used to determine whether a suspect has recently fired a gun?
   a. a scanning electron microscope
   b. a polarizing microscope
   c. a compound microscope
   d. a comparison microscope

5. The "fingerprint" IR spectrum can be seen using a
   a. scanning electron microscope.
   b. microspectrophotometer.
   c. polarizing microscope.
   d. stereoscopic microscope.

6. True or False: The mechanical system of a microscope is composed of six parts.

7. True or False: The magnification of a microscope with a 10× eyepiece and a 10× objective will be 1,000×.

8. True or False: The polarizing microscope is best used for forensic microscopy requiring a side-by-side comparison.

9. True or False: The stereoscopic microscope is the most frequently used and versatile microscope found in the crime laboratory.

10. True or False: With the development of the scanning electron microscope, a forensic analyst can now view a particle under a microscope while, at the same time, a beam of light is directed at the particle in order to obtain its absorption spectrum.

11. Name two types of images and explain the difference between them.

12. List and define the two types of lenses in an ordinary microscope.

13. Name two types of illumination and explain the difference between them. What types of specimens are viewed under each type of illumination?

14. What is a condenser? Name and describe the simplest type of condenser.

15. Define parfocal.

16. What is the difference between a monocular and a binocular microscope?

17. How does one determine the total magnification of a compound microscope?

18. What does numerical aperture describe?

19. What is the maximum useful magnification for a compound microscope? Why?

20. What happens to a compound microscope's field of view when you increase its magnification? How does this affect the way a microscopist views specimens under a compound microscope?

21. What is a comparison microscope? How is the image viewed through a comparison microscope different from one viewed through an ordinary or compound microscope?

22. When using a comparison microscope, why is it important to closely match the optical characteristics of the objective lenses?

23. What is the most frequently used and versatile microscope found in the crime laboratory? List three reasons why this type of microscope is so widely used.

24. What is plane-polarized light?

25. Name two types of physical evidence that are often characterized using a polarizing microscope.

26. What is a microspectrophotometer? What advantage does it enjoy over the spectrophotometer for analyzing physical evidence?

27. Briefly explain how a scanning electron microscope (SEM) produces an image.

28. What device can be coupled to an SEM to produce a picture of the elemental distribution of a specimen? Briefly describe how this combination of devices can be used to determine whether a suspect has recently fired a gun.

Application and Critical Thinking

1. A compound microscope has eyepiece lenses of 10×, 15×, and 20× magnification and objective lenses with 4×, 10×, 25×, 50×, and 100× magnifications. Determine the total magnification power of every possible combination of lenses. Which combinations of lenses would a forensic scientist be unlikely to use and why?

2. What type of microscope would a forensic scientist most likely use in each of the following situations? Explain your answers.
   a. examining two bullets to see if they were fired by the same gun
   b. determining the chemical composition of paint chips
   c. identifying birefringent minerals present in soil
   d. examining a large specimen, such as a tool or piece of clothing
   e. examining extremely tiny specimens that require very high magnification

Learning Objectives

After studying this chapter you should be able to:

- List the A-B-O antigens and antibodies found in the blood for each of the four blood types: A, B, AB, and O

- Understand and describe how whole blood is typed

- List and describe forensic tests used to characterize a stain as blood

- Understand the concept of antigen–antibody interactions and how they are applied to species identification and drug identification

- Contrast chromosomes and genes

- Learn how the Punnett square is used to determine the genotypes and phenotypes of offspring

- List the laboratory tests necessary to characterize seminal stains

- Explain how suspect blood and semen stains are properly preserved for laboratory examination

- Describe the proper collection of physical evidence in a rape investigation

National Science Content Standards

 Scientific Inquiry

 Life Science

 Science and Technology

 History and Nature Of Science

The Green River Killer

This case takes its name from the Green River, which flows through Washington state and empties into Puget Sound in Seattle. Within a six-month span in 1982, the bodies of five females were discovered in or near the river. Most of the victims were known prostitutes who were strangled and apparently raped. As police focused their attention on an area known as Sea-Tac Strip, a haven for prostitutes, girls mysteriously disappeared with increasing frequency. By the end of 1986, the body count in the Seattle region rose to 40; all were believed to have been murdered by the Green River Killer.

As the investigation pressed on into 1987, the police renewed their interest in one suspect, Gary Ridgway, a local truck painter. Ridgway had been known to frequent the Sea-Tac Strip. Interestingly, in 1984 Ridgway had passed a lie detector test regarding the Green River killings. Now with a search warrant in hand, police searched Ridgway's residence and also obtained hair and saliva samples from him. Again, insufficient evidence caused Ridgway to be released from custody.

With the exception of one killing in 1998, the murder spree stopped in 1990, and the case remained dormant for nearly ten years. However, the advent of DNA testing brought renewed vigor to the investigation. In 2001, semen samples collected from three early victims of the Green River Killer were compared to saliva that had been collected from Ridgway in 1987. The DNA profiles matched, and the police had their man. An added forensic link to Ridgway was made by the location of minute amounts of spray paint on the clothing of six victims that compared to paints collected from Ridgway's workplace. Ridgway ultimately avoided the death penalty by confessing to the murders of 48 women.

Forensic Serology

Key Terms

acid phosphatase
agglutination
allele
antibody
antigen
antiserum
aspermia
chromosome
deoxyribonucleic acid
   (DNA)
egg

enzyme
erythrocyte
gene
genotype
hemoglobin
heterozygous
homozygous
hybridoma cells
locus
luminol
monoclonal antibodies

oligospermia
phenotype
plasma
polyclonal antibodies
precipitin
serology
serum
sperm
X chromosome
Y chromosome
zygote

In 1901, Karl Landsteiner announced one of the most significant discoveries of the 20th century—the typing of blood—a finding that 29 years later earned him a Nobel Prize (see Figure 8–1). For years physicians had attempted to transfuse blood from one individual to another. Their efforts often ended in failure because the transfused blood tended to coagulate, or clot, in the body of the recipient, causing instantaneous death. Landsteiner was the first to recognize that all human blood was not the same; instead, he found that blood is distinguishable by its group or type.

FIGURE 8–1 Portrait of Karl Landsteiner (1868-1943), Austrian-US pathologist and Nobel Laureate. *Photo Researchers Inc.*

Out of Landsteiner's work came the classification system that we call the A-B-O system. Now physicians had the key for properly matching the blood of a donor to that of a recipient. One blood type cannot be mixed with a different blood type without disastrous consequences. This discovery, of course, had important implications for blood transfusion and the millions of lives it has since saved.

Meanwhile, Landsteiner's findings opened a new field of research in the biological sciences. Others began to pursue the identification of additional characteristics that could further differentiate blood. By 1937, the Rh factor in blood had been demonstrated and, shortly thereafter, numerous blood factors or groups were discovered. More than 100 different blood factors have been identified. However, the ones in the A-B-O system are still the most important for properly matching a donor and recipient for a transfusion.

Until the early 1990s, forensic scientists focused on blood factors, such as A-B-O, as offering the best means for linking blood to an individual. What made these factors so attractive was that in theory no two individuals, except for identical twins, could be expected to have the same combination of blood factors. In other words, blood factors are controlled genetically and have the potential of being a highly distinctive feature for personal identification. What makes this observation so relevant is the great frequency of bloodstains at crime scenes, especially crimes of the most serious nature— homicides, assaults, and rapes. Consider, for example, a transfer of blood between the victim and assailant during a struggle; that is, the victim's blood is transferred to the suspect's garment or vice versa. If the criminalist could individualize human blood by identifying all of its known factors, the result would be strong evidence for linking the suspect to the crime scene.

The advent of DNA technology has dramatically altered the approach of forensic scientists toward individualization of bloodstains and other biological evidence. The search for genetically controlled blood factors in bloodstains has been abandoned in favor of characterizing biological evidence by select regions of our **deoxyribonucleic acid (DNA)**, which carries the body's genetic information. As a result, the individualization of dried blood and other biological evidence has

deoxyribonucleic acid (DNA)

The molecules that carry the body's genetic information

become a reality and has significantly altered the role that crime laboratories play in criminal investigations. In fact, as we will learn in the next chapter, the high sensitivity of DNA analysis has even altered the types of materials collected from crime scenes in the search for DNA.

The next chapter is devoted to discussing recent breakthroughs in associating blood and semen stains with a single individual through characterization of DNA. This chapter focuses on underlying biological concepts that forensic scientists historically relied on as they sought to characterize and individualize biological evidence before the dawning of the age of DNA.

The Nature of Blood

The word *blood* refers to a complex mixture of cells, enzymes, proteins, and inorganic substances. The fluid portion of blood is called **plasma**; it is composed principally of water and accounts for 55 percent of blood content. Suspended in the plasma are solid materials consisting chiefly of several types of cells—red blood cells (**erythrocytes**), white blood cells (leukocytes), and platelets. The solid portion of blood accounts for 45 percent of its content. Blood clots when a protein in the plasma known as fibrin traps and enmeshes the red blood cells. If the clotted material were removed, a pale yellowish liquid known as **serum** would be left.

Obviously, considering the complexity of blood, any discussion of its function and chemistry would have to be extensive, extending beyond the scope of this text. It is certainly far more relevant at this point to concentrate our discussion on the blood components that are directly pertinent to the forensic aspects of blood identification—the red blood cells and the blood serum.

plasma
The fluid portion of unclotted blood

erythrocyte
A red blood cell

serum
The liquid that separates from the blood when a clot is formed

Antigens and Antibodies

Red blood cells transport oxygen from the lungs to the body tissues and remove carbon dioxide from tissues by transporting it back to the lungs, where it is exhaled. However, for reasons unrelated to the red blood cell's transporting mission, on the surface of each cell are millions of characteristic chemical structures called **antigens**. Antigens impart specific characteristics to the red blood cells. Blood antigens are grouped into systems depending on their relationship to one another. More than 15 blood antigen systems have been identified to date; of these, the A-B-O and Rh systems are the most important.

If an individual is type A, this simply indicates that each red blood cell has A antigens on its surface; similarly, all type B individuals have B antigens, and the red blood cells of type AB individuals contain both A and B antigens. Type O individuals have neither A nor B antigens on their cells. Hence, the presence or absence of A and B antigens on the red blood cells determines a person's blood type in the A-B-O system.

Another important blood antigen has been designated as the *Rh factor*, or D antigen. People with the D antigen are said to be *Rh positive*; those without this antigen are *Rh negative*. In routine blood banking, the presence or absence of the three antigens—A, B, and D—must be determined in testing compatibility of the donor and recipient.

antigen
A substance, usually a protein, that stimulates the body to produce antibodies against it

antibody
A protein in the blood serum that destroys or inactivates a specific antigen

antiserum
Blood serum that contains specific antibodies

agglutination
The clumping together of red blood cells by the action of an antibody

FIGURE 8–2
Agglutination.

Serum is important because it contains proteins known as **antibodies**. The fundamental principle of blood typing is that for every antigen, there exists a specific antibody. Each antibody symbol contains the prefix *anti-*, followed by the name of the antigen for which it is specific. Hence, anti-A is specific only for A antigen, anti-B for B antigen, and anti-D for D antigen. The serum-containing antibody is referred to as the **antiserum**, meaning a serum that reacts against something (antigens).

An antibody reacts only with its specific antigen and no other. Thus, if serum containing anti-B is added to red blood cells carrying the B antigen, the two will combine, causing the antibody to attach itself to the cell. Antibodies are normally *bivalent*—that is, they have two reactive sites. This means that each antibody can simultaneously be attached to antigens located on two different red blood cells. This creates a vast network of cross-linked cells usually seen as clumping or **agglutination** (see Figure 8–2).

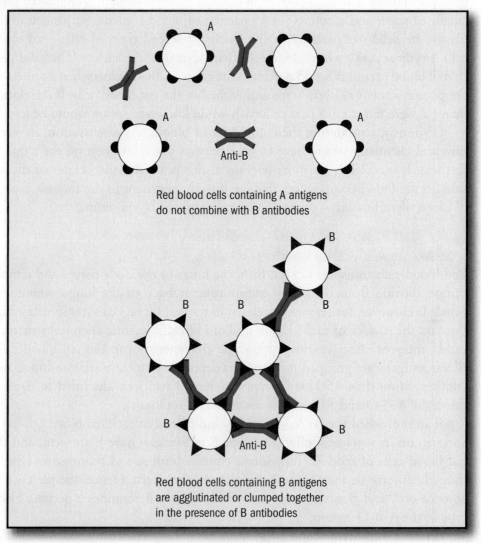

Red blood cells containing A antigens do not combine with B antibodies

Red blood cells containing B antigens are agglutinated or clumped together in the presence of B antibodies

Let's look a little more closely at this phenomenon. In normal blood, shown in Figure 8–3(a), antigens on red blood cells and antibodies coexist without destroying each other because the antibodies present are not specific toward any of the antigens. However, suppose a foreign serum added to the blood introduces a new antibody. This results in a specific antigen–antibody reaction that immediately causes the red blood cells to link together, or agglutinate, as shown in <u>Figure 8–3(b)</u>.

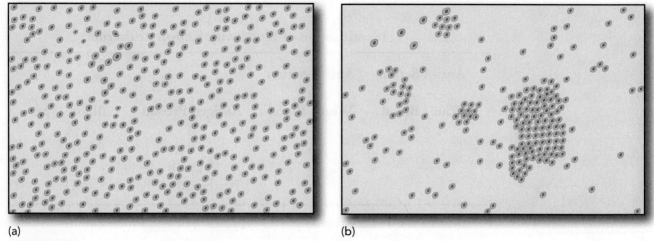

(a)   (b)

FIGURE 8–3
(a) Microscopic view of normal and red blood cells (500×). (b) Microscopic view of agglutinated red blood cells (500×).

Evidently, nature has taken this situation into account, because when we examine the serum of type A blood, we find anti-B and no anti-A. Similarly, type B blood contains only anti-A, type O blood has both anti-A and anti-B, and type AB blood contains neither anti-A nor anti-B. The antigen and antibody components of normal blood are summarized in the following table:

Blood Type	Antigens on Red Blood Cells	Antibodies in Serum
A	A	Anti-B
B	B	Anti-A
AB	AB	Neither anti-A nor anti-B
O	Neither A nor B	Both anti-A and anti-B

The reasons for the fatal consequences of mixing incompatible blood during a transfusion should now be quite obvious. For example, the transfusion of type A blood into a type B patient will cause the natural anti-A in the blood of the type B patient to react promptly with the incoming A antigens, resulting in agglutination. In addition, the incoming anti-B of the donor will react with the B antigens of the patient.

Blood Typing

The term **serology** describes a broad scope of laboratory tests that use specific antigen and serum antibody reactions. The most widespread application of serology is the typing of whole blood for its A-B-O identity. In determining the A-B-O blood type, only two antiserums are needed—anti-A and anti-B. For routine blood typing, both of these antiserums are commercially available.

<u>Table 8–1</u> summarizes how the identity of each of the four blood groups is established when the blood is tested with anti-A and anti-B serum. Type A blood is agglutinated by anti-A serum; type B blood is agglutinated by anti-B

serology
The study of antigen–antibody reactions

serum; type AB blood is agglutinated by both anti-A and anti-B; and type O blood is not agglutinated by either the anti-A or anti-B serum (see Figure 8–4).

Table 8–1
Identification of Blood with Known Antiserum

Anti-A Serum + Whole Blood	Anti-B Serum + Whole Blood	Antigen Present	Blood Type
+	–	A	A
–	+	B	B
+	+	A and B	AB
–	–	Neither A nor B	O

Note: + shows agglutination; – shows absence of agglutination.

FIGURE 8-4
A blood type test for types A, B, AB, and O. Antisera from right to left are A+B, B, and A. *Courtesy Tek Image/Photo Researchers, Inc.*

The identification of natural antibodies present in blood offers another way to determine blood type. Testing blood for the presence of anti-A and anti-B requires using red blood cells that have known antigens. Again, these cells are commercially available. Hence, when A cells are added to a blood specimen, agglutination occurs only in the presence of anti-A. Similarly, B cells agglutinate only in the presence of anti-B. All four A-B-O types can be identified in this manner by testing blood with known A and B cells, as summarized in Table 8–2.

Table 8–2
Identification of Blood with Known Cells

A Cells + Blood	B Cells + Blood	Antibody Present	Blood Type
+	–	Anti-A	B
–	+	Anti-B	A
+	+	Both anti-A and anti-B	O
–	–	Neither anti-A nor anti-B	AB

Note: + shows agglutination; – shows absence of agglutination.

The population distribution of blood types varies with location and race throughout the world. In the United States, a typical distribution is as follows:

O	**A**	**B**	**AB**
43%	42%	12%	3%

Quick Review

- Serology involves a broad scope of laboratory tests that use specific antigen and serum antibody reactions.

- An antibody reacts or agglutinates only with its specific antigen. The concept of specific antigen–antibody reactions has been applied to techniques for detecting abused drugs in blood and urine.

- Every red blood cell contains either an A antigen, a B antigen, or no antigen (this is called type O). The type of antigen on one's red blood cells determines one's A-B-O blood type. People with type A blood have A antigens on their red blood cells, those with type B blood have B antigens, and those with type O blood have no antigens on their red blood cells.

Immunoassay Techniques

The concept of a specific antigen–antibody reaction is finding application in other areas unrelated to blood typing. Most significantly, this approach has been extended to the detection of drugs in blood and urine. Antibodies that react with drugs do not exist naturally; however, they can be produced in animals such as rabbits by first combining the drug with a protein and injecting this combination into the animal. This drug–protein complex acts as an antigen stimulating the animal to produce antibodies (see Figure 8–5). The recovered blood serum of the animal now contains antibodies that are specific or nearly specific to the drug.

FIGURE 8–5 Stimulating production of drug antibodies.

Currently, thousands of individuals regularly submit to urinalysis tests for the presence of abused drugs. These individuals include military personnel, transportation industry employees, police and corrections personnel, and subjects requiring pre-employment drug screening. Immunoassay testing for drugs has proven quite suitable for handling the large volume of specimens that must be rapidly analyzed for drug content on a daily basis. Testing laboratories have access to many commercially prepared sera arising from animals being injected with any one of a variety of drugs. A particular serum that has been added to a urine specimen is designed to interact with either opiates, cannabinoids, cocaine, amphetamines, phencyclidine, barbiturates, methadone, or other drugs. A word of caution: immunoassay is only presumptive in nature, and its result must be confirmed by additional testing.

Radioimmunoassay

Although EMIT is currently a popular immunoassay technique in forensic laboratories, other immunoassay procedures are commercially available. For example, radioimmunoassay (RIA) uses drugs labeled with radioactive tags. Whether using an enzyme tag as in EMIT or a radioactive tag as in RIA, the analyst must be cautious because immunoassay techniques are not totally specific for any drug. Substances with a chemical structure similar to the drug in question may cross-react with the antibody to give a false-positive reaction. A word of caution: immunoassay is only presumptive in nature and always must be confirmed by another reliable analytical procedure.

Case Files

Enzyme-Multiplied Immunoassay Technique (EMIT)

Several immunological assay techniques are commercially available for detecting drugs through an antigen–antibody reaction. One such technique, the *enzyme-multiplied immunoassay technique (EMIT)*, has gained widespread popularity among toxicologists because of its speed and high sensitivity for detecting drugs in urine.

competes with the labeled methadone to bind with the methadone antibodies. The quantity of chemically labeled methadone left uncombined is then measured, and this value is related to the concentration of methadone originally present in the urine.

In the EMIT assay, a drug that may be present in a urine specimen will compete with added labeled drug for a limited number of antibody binding sites. The labeled drugs are indicated by an asterisk. Once the competition for antibody sites is completed, the number of remaining unbound labeled drug is proportional to the drug's concentration in urine.

A typical EMIT analysis begins by adding to a subject's urine antibodies that bind to a particular type or class of drug being looked for. This is followed by adding to the urine a chemically labeled version of the drug. As shown in the figure, a competition will ensue between the labeled and unlabeled drug (if it's present in the subject's urine) to bind with the antibody. If this competition does occur in a person's urine, it signifies that that the urine screen test was positive for the drug being tested. For example, to check someone's urine for methadone, the analyst would add methadone antibodies and chemically labeled methadone to the urine. Any methadone present in the urine immediately

One of the most frequent uses of EMIT in forensic laboratories has been for screening the urine of suspected marijuana users. The primary pharmacologically active agent in marijuana is tetrahydrocannabinol, or THC. To facilitate the elimination of THC, the body converts it to a series of substances called *metabolites* that are more readily excreted. The major THC metabolite found in urine is a substance called *THC-9-carboxylic acid*. Antibodies against this metabolite are prepared for EMIT testing. Normally the urine of marijuana users contains a small quantity of THC-9-carboxylic acid (less than one-millionth of a gram); however, this level is readily detected by EMIT.

The greatest problem with detecting marijuana in urine is interpretation of the test results. Although marijuana use results in the detection of THC metabolites, it is difficult to determine when the individual actually used marijuana. In individuals who use marijuana frequently, detection is possible within two to five days after the last use of the drug. However, some individuals may yield positive results up to thirty days after the last use of marijuana.

Case Files

Polyclonal and Monoclonal Antibodies

As we have seen in the previous section, when an animal such as a rabbit or mouse is injected with an antigen, the animal responds by producing antibodies designed to bind to the invading antigen. However, the process of producing antibodies designed to respond to foreign antigens is complex. For instance, an antigen typically has structurally different sites to which an antibody may bind. Thus, in the presence of a specific antigen, an animal produces many different antibodies, all of which are designed to attack some particular site on the antigen of interest. These antibodies are known as **polyclonal antibodies**. However, the disadvantage of polyclonal antibodies is that an animal can produce antibodies that vary in composition over time. As a result, different batches of polyclonals may vary in their specificity and their ability to bind to a particular antigen site.

Modern forensic technologies occasionally require antibodies that are more uniform in their composition and attack power than the traditional polyclonals. Forensic scientists thus need a way to produce antibodies designed to attack one and only one site on an antigen. Such antibodies are known as **monoclonal antibodies**. How can such monoclonals be produced?

The process begins by injecting a mouse with the antigen of interest. In response, the mouse's spleen cells produce antibodies to fight off the invading antigen. The spleen cells are removed from the animal and are fused to fast-growing blood cancer cells to produce **hybridoma cells**. The hybridoma cells are then allowed to multiply and are screened for their specific antibody activity. Hybridoma cells bearing the antibody activity of interest are then selected and cultured. The rapidly multiplying cancer cells linked to the selected antibody cells produce identical monoclonal antibodies in a limitless supply (see the figure).

Monoclonal antibodies are being incorporated into commercial forensic test kits with increasing frequency. Many immunoassay test kits for abused drugs are

1. Inject mouse or rabbit with antigen.

2. Remove spleen and isolate spleen cells, which produce antibodies to the antigen of interest.

3. Fuse spleen cells with malignant cells, which grow well in culture.

4. Grow hybrid cells and isolate ones that produce the antibody of interest.

5. Culture the hybrid cells to create a virtually limitless supply of antibodies.

Antigen

Antibodies

Spleen cells

Malignant blood cells

Spleen cell

Hybridoma cells

Monoclonal antibodies

Steps required to produce monoclonal antibodies.

being formulated with monoclonal antibodies. Also, a recently introduced test for semen that incorporates a monoclonal antibody has found wide popularity in crime laboratories.

As a side note, in 1999 the U.S. Food and Drug Administration approved a monoclonal drug treatment for cancer. Rituxin is a nontoxic monoclonal antibody designed to attack and destroy cancerous white blood cells containing an antigen designated as CD20. Other monoclonal drug treatments are in the pipeline. Monoclonals are finally beginning to fulfill their long-held expectation as medicine's version of the "magic bullet."

Quick Review

- To produce antibodies capable of reacting with drugs, the analyst combines a specific drug with a protein and injects this combination into an animal such as a rabbit. This drug–protein complex acts as an antigen, stimulating the animal to produce antibodies. The recovered blood serum of the animal now contains antibodies that are specific or nearly specific to the drug.

- When an animal is injected with an antigen, its body produces a series of different antibodies, all of which are designed to attack some particular site on the antigen of interest. These antibodies are known as polyclonal antibodies.

- A more uniform and specific collection of antibodies designed to combine with a single antigen site can be manufactured. Such antibodies are known as monoclonal antibodies.

polyclonal antibodies
Antibodies produced by injecting animals with a specific antigen; a series of antibodies are produced responding to a variety of different sites on the antigen

monoclonal antibodies
A collection of identical antibodies that interact with a single antigen site

hybridoma cells
Fused spleen and tumor cells; used to produce identical monoclonal antibodies in a limitless supply

Forensic Characterization of Bloodstains

The criminalist must answer the following questions when examining dried blood: (1) Is it blood? (2) From what species did the blood originate? (3) If the blood is human, how closely can it be associated with a particular individual?

Color Tests

The determination of blood is best made by means of a preliminary color test. For many years, the most common test was the benzidine color test. However, because benzidine has been identified as a known carcinogen, its use has generally been discontinued, and the chemical phenolphthalein is usually substituted in its place (this test is also known as the Kastle-Meyer color test).[1]

Both the benzidine and Kastle-Meyer color tests are based on the observation that blood **hemoglobin** possesses peroxidase-like activity. Peroxidases are enzymes that accelerate the oxidation of several classes of organic compounds when combined with peroxides. For example, when a bloodstain, phenolphthalein reagent, and hydrogen peroxide are mixed together, oxidation of the hemoglobin in the blood produces a deep pink color.

The Kastle-Meyer test is not a specific test for blood; some vegetable materials, for instance, may turn Kastle-Meyer pink. These substances include potatoes and horseradish. However, such materials will probably not be encountered in criminal situations, and thus from a practical point of view, a positive Kastle-Meyer test is highly indicative of blood. Field investigators have found Hemastix strips a useful presumptive field test for blood. Designed as a urine dipstick test for blood, the strip can be moistened with distilled water and placed in contact with a suspect bloodstain. The appearance of a green color indicates blood.

hemoglobin
A red blood cell protein that transports oxygen in the bloodstream; it is responsible for the red color of blood

MyCrimeKit: WebExtra 8.1

See a Color Test for Blood
www.mycrimekit.com

Luminol and Bluestar

Another important presumptive identification test for blood is the **luminol** test.[2] Unlike the benzidine and Kastle-Meyer tests, the reaction of luminol with blood produces light rather than color. By spraying luminol reagent onto a suspect item, investigators can quickly screen large areas for bloodstains. The sprayed objects must be located in a darkened area while being viewed for the emission of light (luminescence); any bloodstains produce a faint blue glow (see Figure 8–6).

FIGURE 8–6
Blood reacting to Luminol and displaying luminescence.

luminol
The most sensitive chemical test that is capable of presumptively detecting bloodstains diluted to as little as 1 in 100,000; its reaction with blood emits light and thus requires the result to be observed in a darkened area

A relatively new product, Bluestar, is now available to be used in place of luminol (http://www.bluestar-forensic.com). Bluestar is easy to mix in the field. Its reaction with blood can be observed readily without having to create complete darkness. The luminol and Bluestar tests are extremely sensitive—capable of detecting bloodstains diluted to as little as 1 in 100,000. For this reason, spraying large areas such as carpets, walls, flooring, or the interior of a vehicle may reveal blood traces or patterns that would have gone unnoticed under normal lighting conditions (see Figure 8–7). It is important to note that luminol and Bluestar do not interfere with any subsequent DNA testing.[3]

Microcrystalline Tests

The identification of blood can be made more specific if microcrystalline tests are performed on the material. Several tests are available; the two most popular ones are the Takayama and Teichmann tests. Both depend on the addition of specific chemicals to the blood to form characteristic crystals containing hemoglobin derivatives. Crystal tests are far less sensitive than color tests for blood identification and are more susceptible to interference from contaminants that may be present in the stain.

(a)

FIGURE 8–7
(a) A section of a linoleum floor photographed under normal light. This floor was located in the residence of a missing person. (b) Same section of the floor shown in (a) after spraying with luminol. A circular pattern was revealed. Investigators concluded that the circular blood pattern was left by the bottom of a bucket carried about during the cleaning up of the blood. A small clump of sponge, blood, and hair was found near where this photograph was taken. *Courtesy North Carolina State Bureau of Investigation*

(b)

Precipitin Test

Once the stain has been characterized as blood, the serologist determines whether the blood is of human or animal origin. The standard test is the **precipitin** test. Precipitin tests are based on the fact that when animals (usually rabbits) are injected with human blood, antibodies form that react with the invading human blood to neutralize its presence. The investigator can recover these antibodies by bleeding the animal and isolating the blood serum, which contains antibodies that specifically react with human antigens. For this reason, the serum is known

precipitin
An antibody that reacts with its corresponding antigen to form a precipitate

as human antiserum. In the same manner, by injecting rabbits with the blood of other known animals, virtually any kind of animal antiserum can be produced. Antiserums are commercially available for humans and for a variety of commonly encountered animals—for example, dogs, cats, and deer.

Several techniques have been devised for performing precipitin tests on bloodstains. The classic method is to layer an extract of the bloodstain on top of the human antiserum in a capillary tube. Human blood, or for that matter, any protein of human origin in the extract, reacts specifically with antibodies present in the antiserum, as indicated by the formation of a cloudy ring or band at the interface of the two liquids (see Figure 8–8).

FIGURE 8-8
The precipitin test.

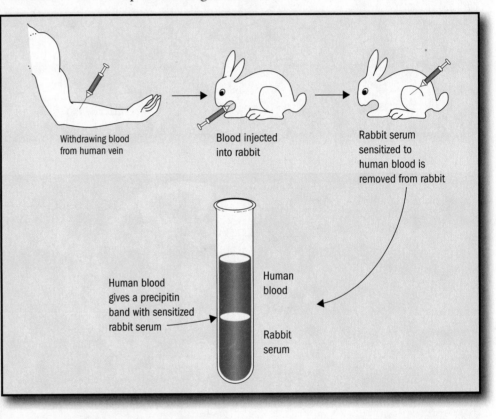

Withdrawing blood
from human vein

Blood injected
into rabbit

Rabbit serum
sensitized to
human blood is
removed from rabbit

Human blood
gives a precipitin
band with sensitized
rabbit serum

Human
blood

Rabbit
serum

Gel Diffusion

Another method, called *gel diffusion*, takes advantage of the fact that antibodies and antigens diffuse or move toward one another on a plate coated with a gel medium made from a natural polymer called agar. The extracted bloodstain and the human antiserum are placed in separate holes opposite each other on the gel. If the blood is human, a line of precipitation forms where the antigens and antibodies meet (see Figure 8–9).

Similarly, the antigens and antibodies can be induced to move toward one another under the influence of an electrical field. In the *electrophoretic method* (examined in detail in Chapter 9), an electrical potential is applied to the gel medium; a specific antigen–antibody reaction is denoted by a line of precipitation formed between the hole containing the blood extract and the hole containing the human antiserum (see Figure 8–10).

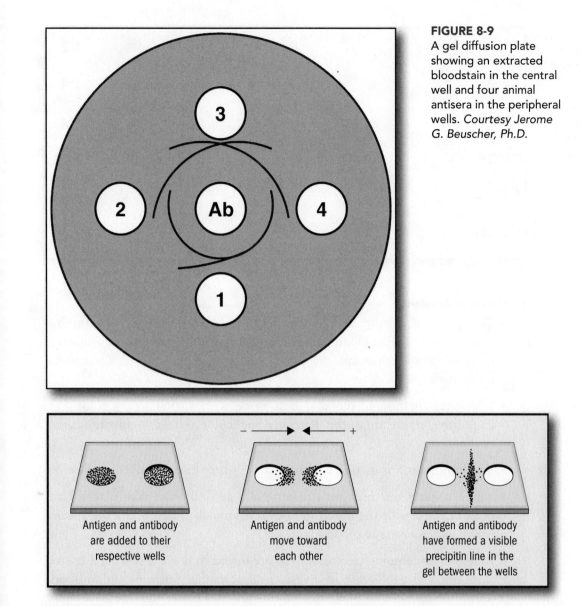

FIGURE 8-9
A gel diffusion plate showing an extracted bloodstain in the central well and four animal antisera in the peripheral wells. *Courtesy Jerome G. Beuscher, Ph.D.*

Antigen and antibody are added to their respective wells

Antigen and antibody move toward each other

Antigen and antibody have formed a visible precipitin line in the gel between the wells

FIGURE 8–10 Antigens and antibodies moving towards one another under the influence of an electrical potential.

The precipitin test is very sensitive and requires only a small amount of blood for testing. Human bloodstains dried for 10 to 15 years and longer may still give a positive precipitin reaction. Even extracts of tissue from mummies four to five thousand years old have given positive reactions with this test. Furthermore, human bloodstains diluted by washing in water and left with only a faint color may still yield a positive precipitin reaction (see Figure 8–11).

Once it has been determined that the bloodstain is human, an effort must be made to associate or disassociate the stain with a particular individual. Until the mid-1990s, routine characterization of bloodstains included the determination of A-B-O types; however, the widespread use of DNA profiling or typing has relegated this subject to one of historical interest only.

Quick Review

- The criminalist must answer the following questions when examining dried blood: (1) Is it blood? (2) From what species did the blood originate? (3) If the blood is human, how closely can it be associated with a particular individual?

- The determination of blood is best made with a preliminary color test. A positive result from the Kastle-Meyer color test is highly indicative of blood.

- The luminol test is used to find trace amounts of blood at crime scenes.

- The precipitin test uses antisera normally derived from rabbits that have been injected with the blood of a known animal to determine the species origin of a questioned bloodstain.

- Materials undergoing electrophoresis are forced to move across a gel-coated plate under the influence of an electrical potential. Antigens and antibodies can be induced to move toward one another under the influence of an electrical field.

Principles of Heredity

All of the antigens and polymorphic enzymes and proteins that have been described in previous sections are genetically controlled traits. That is, they are inherited from parents and become a permanent feature of a person's biological makeup from the moment he or she is conceived. Determining the identity of these traits, then, not only provides us with a picture of how one individual compares to or differs from another, but also gives us an insight into the basic biological substances that determine our overall makeup as human beings and the mechanism by which those substances are transmitted from one generation to the next.

Genes and Chromosomes

Hereditary material is transmitted via microscopic units called **genes**. The gene is the basic unit of heredity. Each gene by itself or in concert with other genes controls the development of a specific characteristic in the new individual; the genes determine the nature and growth of virtually every body structure.

The genes are positioned on **chromosomes**, threadlike bodies that appear in the nucleus of every body cell (see Figure 8–12). Almost all human cells contain 46 chromosomes, mated in 23 pairs (see Figure 8–13). The only exceptions are the human reproductive cells, the **egg** and **sperm**, which contain 23 unmated chromosomes. During fertilization, a sperm and egg combine so that each contributes 23 chromosomes to form the new cell (**zygote**). Hence, the new individual begins life properly with 23 mated chromosome pairs. Because the genes are positioned on the chromosomes, the new individual inherits genetic material from each parent.

gene
The basic unit of heredity, consisting of a DNA segment located on a chromosome

chromosome
A threadlike structure in the cell nucleus, along which the genes are located

egg
The female reproductive cell

sperm
The male reproductive cell

zygote
The cell arising from the union of an egg and a sperm cell

FIGURE 8-12
Computer-enhanced photomicrograph image of human chromosomes. *Courtesy Alfred Pasieka, Science Photo Library/Photo Researchers, Inc.*

**MyCrimeKit:
WebExtra 8.2**
Learn about the Structure of Our Genes
www.mycrimekit.com

Actually, two dissimilar chromosomes are involved in the determination of sex. The egg cell always contains a long chromosome known as the **X chromosome**; the sperm cell may contain either a long X chromosome or a short **Y chromosome**. When an X-carrying sperm fertilizes an egg, the new cell is XX and develops into a female. A Y-carrying sperm produces an XY fertilized egg and develops into a male. Because the sperm cell determines the nature of the chromosome pair, we can say that the father biologically determines the sex of the child.

X chromosome
The female sex chromosome

Y chromosome
The male sex chromosome

FIGURE 8–13
Fluorescent light micrograph of the 46 chromosomes from a normal human female. *Courtesy Photo Researchers Inc.*

locus
The physical location of a gene on a chromosome

allele
Any of several alternative forms of a gene located at the same point on a particular pair of chromosomes

homozygous
Having two identical allelic genes on two corresponding positions of a pair of chromosomes

heterozygous
Having two different allelic genes on two corresponding positions of a pair of chromosomes

Alleles Just as chromosomes come together in pairs, so do the genes they bear. The position a gene occupies on a chromosome is its **locus**. Genes that govern a given characteristic are similarly positioned on the chromosomes inherited from the mother and father. Thus, a gene for eye color on the mother's chromosome will be aligned with a gene for eye color on the corresponding chromosome inherited from the father. Alternative forms of genes that influence a given characteristic and are aligned with one another on a chromosome pair are known as **alleles**.

Inheritance of blood type offers a simple example of allele genes in humans. An individual's blood type is determined by three genes, designated A, B, and O. A gene pair made up of two similar alleles—for example, AA and BB—is said to be **homozygous**. For example, if the chromosome inherited from the father carries the A gene and the chromosome inherited from the mother carries the same gene, the offspring will have an AA combination. Thus, when an individual inherits two similar genes from his or her parents, there is no problem in determining the blood type of that person. An individual with an AA combination will always be type A, a BB will be type B, and an OO will be type O.

A gene pair made up of two different alleles—AO, for example—is said to be **heterozygous**. For example, if the chromosome from one parent carries the A gene and the chromosome from the other parent carries the O gene, the genetic makeup of the offspring will be AO. When two different genes are inherited, one gene will be dominant—that is, the characteristic coded for by that gene is expressed. The other gene will be recessive—that is, its characteristics remain hidden. In the case of blood types, A and B genes are dominant and the O gene is recessive. Thus, with an AO combination, A is always dominant over O, and the individual is typed as A. Similarly, a BO combination is typed as B. In the case of AB, the genes are *codominant*, and the individual's blood type will be AB. The recessive characteristics of O appear only when both recessive genes are present in combination OO, which is typed simply as O.

Genotypes and Phenotypes A pair of allele genes together constitutes the **genotype** of the individual. However, no known laboratory test can determine an individual's A-B-O genotype. For example, a person's outward characteristic, or **phenotype**, may be type A, but this does not tell us whether the genotype is AA or AO. The genotype can be determined only by studying the family history of the individual. If the genotypes of both parents are known, that of their possible offspring can be forecast.

An easy way to determine an individual's genotype is to construct a Punnett square. To do this, write along a horizontal line the two genes of the male parent, and in the vertical column write the two kinds of female genes present, as shown. In our example, we assume the male parent is type O and therefore has to be an OO genotype; the female parent is type AB and can be only an AB genotype:

genotype
The particular combination of genes present in the cells of an individual

phenotype
The physical manifestation of a genetic trait such as shape, color, or blood type

Next, write in each box the corresponding gene contributed from the female and then from the male. The squares will contain all the possible genotype combinations that the parents can produce in their offspring:

	O	O
A	AO	AO
B	BO	BO

In this case, 50 percent of the offspring are likely to be AO and the other 50 percent BO. These are the only genotypes possible from this combination. Because O is recessive, 50 percent of the offspring will probably be type A and 50 percent type B. From this example, we can see that no blood group gene can appear in a child unless it is present in at least one of the parents.

Paternity Testing

Although the genotyping of blood factors has useful applications for studying the transmission of blood characteristics from one generation to the next, it has no direct relevance to criminal investigations. It does, however, have important implications in disputed-paternity cases, which are normally encountered in civil, not criminal, courts.

Many cases of disputed paternity can be resolved by comparing the blood group genotypes of the suspected parents and offspring. For instance, suppose the male in the preceding Punnett square example is suspected of fathering a child by the female. If the child has type AB blood, the suspected father will be cleared because a type O father and a type AB mother cannot have a type AB child. On the other hand, if the child has type A or type B, the most that can be said is that the suspect may be the father. This does not mean that he is the father, just that he is not excluded based on blood typing. Obviously, many other males also have type O blood. Of course, the more blood group systems that are tested, the better

MyCrimeKit: WebExtra 8.3
Learn about the Chromosomes Present in Our Cells
www.mycrimekit.com

MyCrimeKit: WebExtra 8.4
See How Genes Position Themselves on a Chromosome Pair
www.mycrimekit.com

MyCrimeKit: WebExtra 8.5
See How Genes Define Our Genetic Makeup
www.mycrimekit.com

the chances of excluding an innocent male from involvement. Conversely, if no discrepancies are found between the offspring and the suspect father, the more certain one can be that the suspect is indeed the father.

In fact, routine paternity testing involves characterizing blood factors other than A-B-O. For example, the HLA (human leukocyte antigen) test relies on identifying a complex system of antigens on white blood cells. If this test cannot exclude a suspect as the father of a child, the chances are better than 90 percent that he is the father. Paternity-testing laboratories have implemented DNA test procedures that can raise the odds of establishing paternity beyond 99 percent.

Quick Review

- The gene is the basic unit of heredity. A chromosome is a threadlike structure in the cell nucleus, along which the genes are located.

- Most human cells contain 46 chromosomes, arranged in 23 mated pairs. The only exceptions are the human reproductive cells, the egg and sperm, which contain 23 unmated chromosomes.

- During fertilization, a sperm and egg combine so that each contributes 23 chromosomes to form the new cell, or zygote, that develops into the offspring.

- An allele is any of several alternative forms of genes that influence a given characteristic and that are aligned with one another on a chromosome pair.

- A heterozygous gene pair is made up of two different alleles; a homozygous gene pair is made up of two similar alleles.

- When two different genes are inherited, the characteristic coded for by a dominant gene is expressed. The characteristic coded for by a recessive gene remains hidden.

- A genotype is the particular combination of genes present in the cells of an individual. A phenotype is the physical manifestation of a genetic trait.

Forensic Characterization of Semen

Many cases received in a forensic laboratory involve sexual offenses, making it necessary to examine exhibits for the presence of seminal stains. The normal male releases 2.5 to 6 milliliters of seminal fluid during an ejaculation. Each milliliter contains 100 million or more spermatozoa, the male reproductive cells. The forensic examination of articles for seminal stains can actually be considered a two-step process. First, before any tests can be conducted, the stain must be located (see Figure 8–14). Considering the number and soiled condition of outer garments, undergarments, and possible bedclothing submitted for examination, this may prove to be an arduous task. Once located, the stain must be subjected to tests that will prove its identity. This will most likely include testing for the DNA profile of the individual from whom it originated.

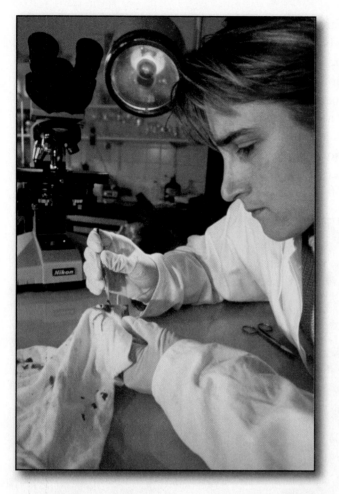

FIGURE 8-14
A forensic analyst examines a garment for blood and semen deposits. *Courtesy Photo Researchers Inc.*

Testing for Seminal Stains

Often seminal stains are visible on a fabric because they exhibit a stiff, crusty appearance. However, reliance on such appearance for locating the stain is unreliable and is useful only when the stain is in an obvious area. If the fabric has been washed or contains only minute quantities of semen, visual examination offers little chance of detecting the stain. The best way to locate and at the same time characterize a seminal stain is to perform the *acid phosphatase color test*.

Acid Phosphatase Test Acid phosphatase is an **enzyme** that is secreted by the prostate gland into seminal fluid. Its concentrations in seminal fluid are up to 400 times those found in any other body fluid. Its presence can easily be detected when it comes in contact with an acidic solution of sodium alpha naphthylphosphate and Fast Blue B dye. Also, 4-methyl umbelliferyl phosphate (MUP) fluoresces (emits light) under UV light when it comes in contact with acid phosphatase.

The utility of the acid phosphatase test is apparent when it becomes necessary to search many garments or large fabric areas for seminal stains. Simply moistening a filter paper with water and rubbing it lightly over the suspect area transfers any acid phosphatase present to the filter paper. Placing a drop or two of the sodium alpha naphthylphosphate and Fast Blue B solution on the paper produces a purple color that indicates the acid phosphatase enzyme. In this manner, any fabric or surface can be systematically searched for seminal stains.

acid phosphatase
An enzyme found in high concentration in semen

enzyme
A protein that acts as a catalyst for certain specific reactions

If it is necessary to search extremely large areas—for example, a bedsheet or carpet—the article can be tested in sections, narrowing the location of the stain with each successive test. Alternatively, the garment can be pressed against a suitably sized piece of moistened filter paper. The paper is then sprayed with MUP solution. Semen stains appear as strongly fluorescent areas under UV light. A negative reaction can be interpreted as absence of semen. Although some vegetable and fruit juices (such as cauliflower and watermelon), fungi, contraceptive creams, and vaginal secretions give a positive response to the acid phosphatase test, none of these substances normally reacts with the speed of seminal fluid. A reaction time of less than 30 seconds is considered a strong indication of semen.

FIGURE 8–15
Photomicrograph of human spermatozoa (300x). *Courtesy John Walsh/Photo Researchers, Inc.*

Microscopic Examination of Semen Semen can be unequivocally identified by the presence of spermatozoa. When spermatozoa are located through a microscope examination, the stain is definitely identified as having been derived from semen. *Spermatozoa* are slender, elongated structures 50–70 microns long, each with a head and a thin flagellate tail (see Figure 8–15). The criminalist can normally locate them by immersing the stained material in a small volume of water. Rapidly stirring the liquid transfers a small percentage of the spermatozoa present into the water. A drop of the water is dried onto a microscope slide, then stained and examined under a compound microscope at a magnification of approximately 400×.[4]

Considering the extremely large number of spermatozoa found in seminal fluid (the normal male releases 250–600 million spermatozoa during ejaculation), the chance of locating one should be very good; however, this is not always true. One reason is that spermatozoa bind tightly to cloth materials.[5] Also, spermatozoa are extremely brittle when dry and easily disintegrate if the stain is washed or when the stain is rubbed against another object, as happens frequently in the handling and packaging of this type of evidence. Furthermore, sexual crimes may involve males who have an abnormally low sperm count, a condition known as **oligospermia**, or who have no spermatozoa at all in their seminal fluid (**aspermia**). Significantly, aspermatic individuals are increasing in numbers because of the growing popularity of vasectomies.

oligospermia
An abnormally low sperm count

aspermia
The absence of sperm; sterility in males

Prostate-Specific Antigen (PSA) Analysts often examine stains or swabs that they suspect contain semen (because of the presence of acid phosphatase), but that yield no detectable spermatozoa. How, then, can one reliably prove the presence of semen? The solution to this problem came with the discovery in the 1970s of a protein called *p30* or *prostate-specific antigen (PSA)*. At first, this protein was thought to be prostate specific and hence a unique identifier of semen. However, additional research has shown that low levels of *p30* may be detectable in other human tissues. A more reasonable approach to the unequivocal identification of semen is to use a positive *p30* test in combination with an acid phosphatase color test having a reaction time less than 30 seconds.

When p30 is isolated and injected into a rabbit, it stimulates the production of polyclonal antibodies (anti-p30). The serum collected from these immunized rabbits can then be used to test suspected semen stains. As shown in Figure 8-16, the stain extract is placed in one well of an electrophoretic plate and the anti-p30 in an opposite well. When an electric potential is applied, the antigens and antibodies move toward each other. The formation of a visible line midway between the two wells shows the presence of p30 in the stain and indicates that the stain was seminal.

A more elegant approach to identifying PSA (p30) is shown in Figure 8–17. First, a monoclonal PSA antibody is attached to a dye and placed on a porous membrane. Next, an extract from a sample suspected of containing PSA is placed on the membrane. If PSA is present in the extract, it combines with the monoclonal PSA antibody to form a PSA antigen–monoclonal PSA antibody complex.

FIGURE 8–16
PSA testing by electrophoresis.

FIGURE 8–17
An antibody-antigen-antibody sandwich or complex is seen as a colored band. This signifies the presence of PSA in the extract of a stain. and positively identifies human semen.

This complex migrates along the membrane, where it interacts with a polyclonal PSA antibody embedded in the membrane. The antibody–antigen–antibody "sandwich" that forms is apparent by the presence of a colored line (see Figure 8–17). This monoclonal antibody technique is about 100 times as sensitive as the electrophoretic method for detecting PSA.[6]

Once the material is proven to be semen, the next task is to associate the semen as closely as possible with an individual. As we will learn in Chapter 9, forensic scientists can link seminal material to one individual with DNA technology. Just as important is the knowledge that this technology can exonerate many of those wrongfully accused of sexual assault.

Quick Review

- The best way to locate and characterize a seminal stain is to perform the acid phosphatase color test.

- The presence of spermatozoa proves that a sample stain contains semen. The presence of the protein called prostate specific antigen (PSA), also known as p30, indicates that a stain contains semen.

- Forensic scientists can link seminal material to an individual by DNA typing.

Collection of Rape Evidence

Seminal constituents on a rape victim are important evidence that sexual intercourse has taken place, but their absence does not necessarily mean that a rape did not occur. Physical injuries such as bruises and bleeding tend to confirm that a violent assault occurred. Furthermore, the forceful physical contact between victim and assailant may result in a transfer of physical evidence—blood, semen, hairs, and fibers. The presence of such evidence helps forge a vital link in the chain of circumstances surrounding a sexual crime.

To protect this kind of evidence, all the outer garments and undergarments from the people involved should be carefully removed and packaged separately in paper (not plastic) bags. Place a clean bedsheet on the floor and lay a clean paper sheet over it. The victim must remove her shoes before standing on the paper. Have the person disrobe while standing on the paper in order to collect any loose foreign material falling from the clothing. Collect each piece of clothing as it is removed and place in separate paper bags to avoid cross-contamination. Carefully fold the paper sheet so that all foreign materials are contained inside. If appropriate, bedding or the object on which the assault took place should be submitted to the laboratory for processing.

Items suspected of containing seminal stains must be handled carefully. Folding an article through the stain may cause it to flake off, as will rubbing the stained area against the surface of the packaging material. If, under unusual circumstances, it is not possible to transport the stained article to the laboratory, the stained area should be cut out and submitted with an unstained piece as a substrate control.

In the laboratory, analysts try to link seminal material to a donor(s) using DNA typing. Because an individual may transfer his or her DNA types to a stain through perspiration, investigators must handle stained articles with care, minimizing direct personal contact. The evidence collector must wear disposable latex gloves when such evidence must be touched.

The rape victim must undergo a medical examination as soon as possible after the assault. At this time, the appropriate items of physical evidence are collected by trained personnel. Evidence collectors should have an evidence-collection kit from the local crime laboratory (see Figure 8–18).

FIGURE 8–18A
Victim rape collection kit showing the kit envelope, kit instructions, medical history and assault information forms, and foreign materials collection bag. *Courtesy Tri-Tech, Inc., Southport, N.C., www.tritechusa.com*

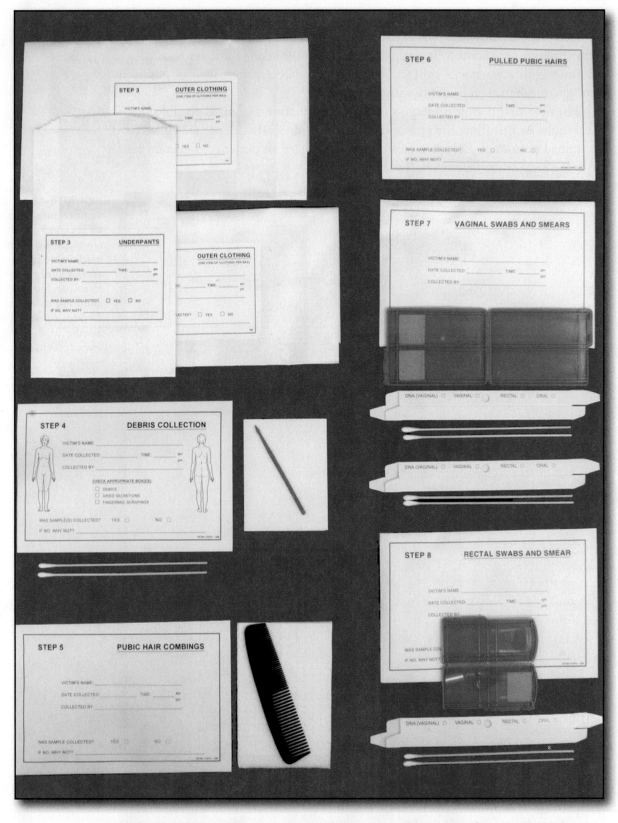

FIGURE 8–18B Victim rape collection kit showing collection bags for outer clothing, underpants, debris, pubic hair combings, pubic hair standard/reference samples, vaginal swabs, and rectal swabs. *Courtesy Tri-Tech, Inc., Southport, N.C., www.tritechusa.com*

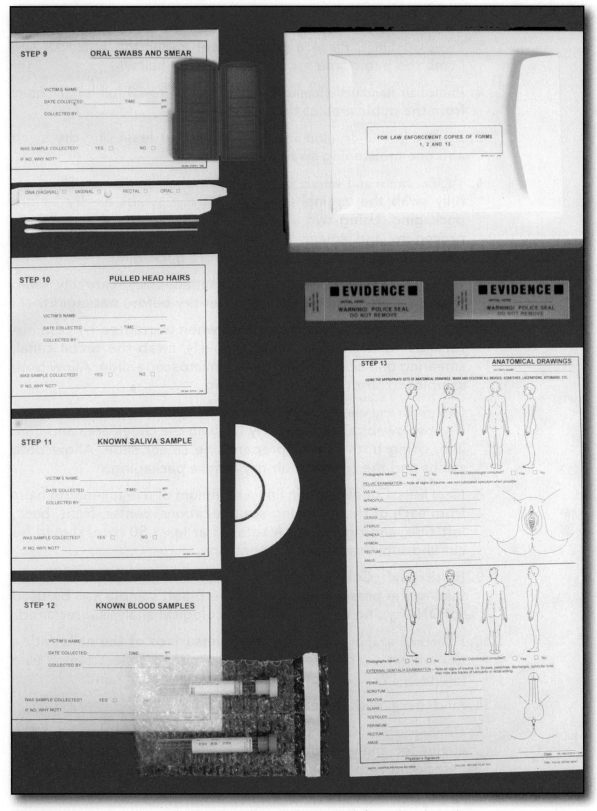

FIGURE 8–18C Victim rape collection kit showing collection bags for oral swabs and smear, pulled head hair standard/reference, known saliva sample, known blood samples, and anatomical drawings. *Courtesy Tri-Tech, Inc., Southport, N.C., www.tritechusa.com*

The following items of physical evidence are to be collected:

1. **Pubic combings.** Place a paper towel under the buttocks and comb the pubic area for loose or foreign hairs.

2. **Pubic hair standard/reference samples.** Cut 15 to 20 full-length hairs from the pubic area at the skin line.

3. **External genital dry-skin areas.** Swab with at least one dry swab and one moistening swab.

4. **Vaginal swabs and smear.** Using two swabs simultaneously, carefully swab the vaginal area and let the swabs air-dry before packaging. Using two additional swabs, repeat the swabbing procedure and smear the swabs onto separate microscope slides, allowing them to air-dry before packaging.

5. **Cervix swabs.** Using two swabs simultaneously, carefully swab the cervix area and let the swabs air-dry before packaging.

6. **Rectal swabs and smear.** To be taken when warranted by case history. Using two swabs simultaneously, swab the rectal canal, smearing one of the swabs onto a microscope slide. Allow both samples to air-dry before packaging.

7. **Oral swabs and smear.** To be taken if oral–genital contact occurred. Use two swabs simultaneously to swab the cheek area and gum line. Using both swabs, prepare one smear slide. Allow both swabs and the smear to air-dry before packaging.

8. **Head hairs.** Cut at the skin line a minimum of five full-length hairs from each of the following scalp locations: center, front, back, left side, and right side. A total of at least 50 hairs should be cut and submitted to the laboratory.

9. **Blood sample.** Collect at least 20 milliliters in a vacuum tube containing the preservative EDTA. The blood sample can be used for DNA typing as well as for toxicological analysis if required.

10. **Fingernail scrapings.** Scrape the undersurface of the nails with a dull object over a piece of clean paper to collect debris (see Figure 8–19). Use separate paper, one for each hand.

11. **All clothing.** Package as described earlier.

12. **Urine specimen.** Collect 30 milliliters or more of urine from the victim for analysis for Rohypnol, GHB, and other substances associated with drug-facilitated sexual assaults (Figure 8-20).

FIGURE 8–19
Victims of violent crimes, such as rape, sometimes have fragments of the perpetrator's skin under their fingernails. This makes it important for the evidence collector to obtain fingernail scrapings from the victim. *Courtesy Arresting Images*

Often during the investigation of a sexual assault, the victim reports that a perpetrator engaged in biting, sucking, or licking of areas of the victim's body. As we will learn <u>in the next chapter</u>, the tremendous sensitivity associated with DNA technology offers investigators the opportunity to identify a perpetuator's DNA types from saliva residues collected off the skin. The most efficient way to recover saliva residues from the skin is to first swab the suspect area with a rotating motion using a cotton swab moistened with distilled water. A second, dry swab is then rotated over the skin to recover the moist remains on the skin's surface from the wet swab. The swabs are air-dried and packaged together as a single sample.[7] If a suspect is apprehended, the following items are routinely collected:

FIGURE 8–20
Box and blister packs of Rohypnol tranquilizer pills. This has gained notoriety as a "date rape" drug. Analysts may test for its presence in a victim's blood or urine. *Courtesy Photo Researchers Inc.*

Case Files

DNA Transfer

A common mode of DNA Transfer occurs when skin cells from the walls of the victim's vagina are transferred onto the suspect during intercourse. Subsequent penile contact with the inner surface of the suspect's underwear often leads to the recovery of the female victim's DNA from the underwear's inner surface. The power of DNA is illustrated in a case in which the female victim of a rape had consensual sexual intercourse with a male partner before being assaulted by a different male. DNA extracted from the inside front area of the suspect's underwear revealed a female DNA profile matching that of the victim. The added bonus in this case was finding male DNA on the same underwear that matched that of the consensual partner.

Source: Gary G. Verret, "Sexual Assault Cases with No Primary Transfer of Biological Material from Suspect to Victim: Evidence of Secondary and Tertiary Transfer of Biological Material from Victim to Suspect's Undergarments," *Proceedings of the Canadian Society of Forensic Science*, Toronto, Ontario, November 2001.

MyCrimeKit: WebExtra 8.6

Step into the Role of the First Responding Officer at a Sexual Assault Scene
www.mycrimekit.com

1. **All clothing and any other items believed to have been worn at the time of assault.**

2. **Pubic hair combings.**

3. **Pulled head and pubic hair standard/reference samples.**

4. **A penile swab taken within 24 hours of the assault, when appropriate to the case history.**

5. **A blood sample or buccal swab for DNA-typing purposes.**

MyCrimeKit: WebExtra 8.7

Assume the Duties of an Evidence-Collection Technician at a Sexual Assault Scene
www.mycrimekit.com

The advent of DNA profiling has forced investigators to rethink what items are evidential in a sexual assault. As we will learn in Chapter 9, DNA levels in the range of one-billionth of a gram are now routinely characterized in crime laboratories. In the past, scant attention was paid to the underwear recovered from a male who was suspected of being involved in a sexual assault; seminal constituents on a man's underwear had little or no investigative value. Today, the sensitivity of DNA analysis has created new areas of investigation. It is possible to link a victim and an assailant by analyzing biological material recovered from the interior front surface of a male suspect's underwear. This is especially important when investigations have failed to yield the presence of suspect's DNA on exhibits recovered from the victim.

The persistence of seminal constituents in the vagina may help determine the time of an alleged sexual attack. Although spermatozoa in the vaginal cavity provide evidence of intercourse, important information regarding the time of sexual activity can be obtained from the knowledge that motile (living) sperm generally survive for four to six hours in the vaginal cavity of a living female. However, a successful search for motile sperm requires a microscopic examination of a vaginal smear immediately after it is taken from the victim. A more extensive examination of vaginal collections is later made at a forensic laboratory. Nonmotile sperm may be found in a living female for up to three days after intercourse and occasionally up to six days later. However, intact sperm (sperm with tails) are not normally found 16 hours after intercourse but have been found as late as 72 hours after intercourse. The likelihood of finding seminal acid phosphatase in the vaginal cavity markedly decreases with time following intercourse, with little chance of identifying this substance 48 hours after intercourse.[8] Hence, with the possibility of prolonged persistence of both spermatozoa and acid phosphatase in the vaginal cavity after intercourse, investigators should determine when and if voluntary sexual activity last occurred before the sexual assault. This information will help in evaluating the significance of finding these seminal constituents in a female victim. Blood or buccal swabs for DNA analysis should be taken from any consensual partner who had sex with the victim within 72 hours of the assault.

Another significant indicator of recent sexual activity is p30. This semen marker normally is not detected in the vaginal cavity beyond 24 hours following intercourse.[9]

Quick Review
- A rape victim must undergo a medical examination as soon as possible after the assault. At that time clothing, hairs, and vaginal and rectal swabs can be collected for subsequent laboratory examination.

Chapter Review

- Serology involves a broad scope of laboratory tests that use specific antigen and serum antibody reactions.

- An antibody reacts or agglutinates only with its specific antigen. The concept of specific antigen–antibody reactions has been applied to techniques for detecting abused drugs in blood and urine.

- Every red blood cell contains either an A antigen, a B antigen, or no antigen (this is called type O). The type of antigen on one's red blood cells determines one's A-B-O blood type. People with type A blood have A antigens on their red blood cells, those with type B blood have B antigens, and those with type O blood have no antigens on their red blood cells.

- To produce antibodies capable of reacting with drugs, the analyst combines a specific drug with a protein and injects this combination into an animal such as a rabbit. This drug–protein complex acts as an antigen, stimulating the animal to produce antibodies. The recovered blood serum of the animal now contains antibodies that are specific or nearly specific to the drug.

- When an animal is injected with an antigen, its body produces a series of different antibodies, all of which are designed to attack some particular site on the antigen of interest. These antibodies are known as polyclonal antibodies.

- A more uniform and specific collection of antibodies designed to combine with a single antigen site can be manufactured. Such antibodies are known as monoclonal antibodies.

- The criminalist must answer the following questions when examining dried blood: (1) Is it blood? (2) From what species did the blood originate? (3) If the blood is human, how closely can it be associated with a particular individual?

- The determination of blood is best made with a preliminary color test. A positive result from the Kastle-Meyer color test is highly indicative of blood.

- The luminol test is used to find trace amounts of blood at crime scenes.

- The precipitin test uses antisera normally derived from rabbits that have been injected with the blood of a known animal to determine the species origin of a questioned bloodstain.

- Materials undergoing electrophoresis are forced to move across a gel-coated plate under the influence of an electrical potential. Antigens and antibodies can be induced to move toward one another under the influence of an electrical field.

- The gene is the basic unit of heredity. A chromosome is a threadlike structure in the cell nucleus, along which the genes are located.

- Most human cells contain 46 chromosomes, arranged in 23 mated pairs. The only exceptions are the human reproductive cells, the egg and sperm, which contain 23 unmated chromosomes.

- During fertilization, a sperm and egg combine so that each contributes 23 chromosomes to form the new cell, or zygote, that develops into the off-spring.

- An allele is any of several alternative forms of genes that influence a given characteristic and that are aligned with one another on a chromosome pair.

- A heterozygous gene pair is made up of two different alleles; a homozygous gene pair is made up of two similar alleles.

- When two different genes are inherited, the characteristic coded for by a dominant gene is expressed. The characteristic coded for by a recessive gene remains hidden.

- A genotype is the particular combination of genes present in the cells of an individual. A phenotype is the physical manifestation of a genetic trait.

- The best way to locate and characterize a seminal stain is to perform the acid phosphatase color test.

- The presence of spermatozoa, proves that a sample stain contains semen. The presence of the protein called prostate specific antigen (PSA), also known as p30, indicates that a stain contains semen.

- Forensic scientists can link seminal material to an individual by DNA typing.

- A rape victim must undergo a medical examination as soon as possible after the assault. At that time clothing, hairs, and vaginal and rectal swabs can be collected for subsequent laboratory examination.

Quick Lab: Blood Typing

Materials:

Ward's Simulated Blood Typing "Whodunit" Lab

Procedure:

In this lab you will test different blood samples from a crime scene. Follow the directions included with the lab instructions.

Follow-Up Questions:

Complete the handout included with the lab.

Quick Lab: Luminol Test

Materials:

Luminol (powder needs to be mixed with water)
Spray bottle
Simulated blood
Piece of wood or flooring
UV light source

Procedure:

Apply some blood to the wood/flooring. Than try to completely clean it, as if you were trying to cover up a crime. If the teacher does not have the luminol mixed for you, follow instructions on how to mix it. Using the spray bottle, apply some luminol to the wood/flooring that you cleaned. Keep the room dark for this step. You may shine the UV light on the area where you sprayed the luminol; this may help if you do not see a reaction right away.

Follow-Up Questions:

1. Did you observe any reaction when the room was dark? When you shined the UV light on the wood/flooring? If so, what did you observe?

2. How does luminol detect bloodstains?

3. What is luminescence?

Review Questions

1. Type AB blood contains
   a. anti-A antibodies and B antigens.
   b. anti-A antigens and anti-B antibodies.
   c. both A and B antigens.
   d. both anti-A and anti-B antibodies.

2. All nucleated human cells contain
   a. 64 chromosomes.
   b. 46 chromosomes.
   c. 32 chromosomes.
   d. 23 chromosomes.

3. Which of the following questions must the criminalist be prepared to answer when examining dried blood?
   a. Is it blood?
   b. From what species did the blood originate?
   c. How closely can human blood be associated with a single individual?
   d. all of the above

4. The determination of whether a substance is blood is best made by means of a preliminary color test such as the Kastle-Meyer color test, which uses the chemical
   a. benzidine.
   b. p30.
   c. phenolphthalein.
   d. precipitin.

5. In which phenotype pairings can the genotypes of the individuals be directly known?
   a. type AB and type O
   b. type A and type B
   c. type B and type O
   d. type A and type AB

6. True or False: The advent of DNA technology has dramatically altered the approach forensic scientists have taken toward the individualization of blood-stains and other biological evidence.

7. True or False: The fundamental principle of blood typing is that for every anti-gen, there exists a specific antibody.

8. True or False: The standard test used to determine whether a blood stain is of human or animal origin is the precipitin test.

9. True or False: Today it is possible for forensic scientists to successfully link seminal material to one individual with DNA technology.

10. True or False: The presence or absence of four antigens determines an indi-vidual's blood type in the A-B-O system.

11. What technique supplanted blood typing for associating bloodstain evidence with a particular individual?

12. What is plasma? What percentage of blood content does plasma account for?

13. Which of the following types of cells are not contained in plasma?
a. phagocytes
b. leukocytes
c. erythrocytes
d. platelets

14. What are antigens and antibodies? What part of the blood contains antibodies?

15. Describe how antibodies and antigens determine one's A-B-O blood type.

16. What is the fourth important antigen other than A, B, and O?

17. What happens when serum containing B antibodies is added to red blood cells carrying the B antigen? Will the same thing happen if serum containing B antibodies is added to red blood cells carrying the A antigen? Explain your answer.

18. Briefly describe how antibodies capable of reacting with drugs are produced in animals.

19. What is the greatest problem associated with detecting marijuana in urine?

20. What is the difference between monoclonal and polyclonal antibodies?

21. Name the most common color test for blood and briefly describe how it identifies bloodstains.

22. Briefly describe how luminol is used to detect bloodstains.

23. What is the standard test used to determine whether blood is of human or animal origin? Briefly state the principle underlying the test.

24. Which technique takes advantage of the fact that antibodies and antigens move toward one another on a plate coated with medium made from a natural polymer called agar?

25. In what technique can antigens and antibodies be induced to move toward one another under the influence of an electrical field?

26. Define gene and chromosome.

27. How many chromosomes do most human cells contain, and how are chromosomes arranged in the cell? What cells are the exception to this rule? How are these cells different from all other cells?

28. Describe how genetic material is transferred from parents to offspring.

29. What is an allele?

30. What is the difference between a heterozygous gene pair and a homozygous gene pair?

31. What is the difference between a dominant and a recessive gene?

32. Define genotype and phenotype. What is the only way to determine an individual's genotype?

33. The best way to locate and characterize a seminal stain is to perform what test? In what situation is this test particularly useful?

34. Define oligospermia and aspermia.

35. The presence of what protein indicates that a sample stain contains semen? What two techniques are used to detect this protein?

36. Besides swabbing for semen constituents, what other bodily fluids should be collected from a rape victim during a medical examination?

37. What items should be collected from the suspected perpetrator of a sexual assault?

Application and Critical Thinking

1. Complete the following Punnett squares and answer the questions that follow.

Subject: Greg   Subject: Dale   Subject: Maura

   a. Among this group of people, which blood type(s) is most likely to be expressed? Which blood type is least likely to be expressed? Explain your answers.

   b. What blood type is Greg most likely to have? Explain your answer.

   c. Which person is least likely to have type B blood? Explain your answer.

   d. In which, if any, of these people may a recessive gene express itself? Explain your answer.

2. Suppose that Greg and Maura have a child. Construct all of the possible Punnett squares for that child and answer the following questions:

   a. What blood type(s) is the child most likely to have?

   b. What genotype(s) is the child most likely to have?

   c. If Maura and Greg have the same genotype, what blood type is the child most likely to have? What are the chances that the child will have type O blood? Explain your answers.

3. Police investigating the scene of a sexual assault recover a large blanket that they believe may contain useful physical evidence. They take it to the laboratory of forensic serologist Scott Alden, asking him to test it for the presence of semen. Noticing faint pink stains on the blanket, Scott asks the investigating detective if he is aware of anything that might recently have been spilled on the blanket. The detective reports that an overturned bowl of grapes and watermelon was found at the scene, as well as a broken glass that had contained wine. After the detective departs, Scott chooses and administers what he considers the best test for analyzing the piece of evidence in his possession. Three minutes after completion of the test, the blanket shows a positive reaction. What test did Scott choose and what was his conclusion? Explain your answer.

4. Criminalist Cathy Richards is collecting evidence from the victim of a sexual assault. She places a sheet on the floor, asks the victim to disrobe, and places the clothing in a paper bag. After collecting pubic combings and pubic hair samples, she takes two vaginal swabs, which she allows to air-dry before packaging. Finally, Cathy collects blood, urine, and scalp hair samples from the victim. What mistakes, if any, did she make in collecting this evidence?

5. Police have been called to the scene of a hit-and-run accident on a busy rural highway. This is a major highway, but the surrounding area is not densely populated. There is a lot of wildlife in the area, including deer, raccoons, and skunks. The victim has been transferred to a local hospital, and police have interviewed several witnesses. All witnesses recall the same make and model of car, a silver compact. Police recover possible bloodstains from the bumper of three vehicles (Vehicles A, B, and C). The Kastle-Meyer presumptive color test for blood was positive for all stains.

When questioned about the blood, suspects A, B, and C all claim the blood originated from wildlife they accidentally hit. Your job as the forensic scientist assigned to the case is to first determine whether the blood samples are animal or human blood. Also, determine whether the blood on any of the suspected vehicles matches the victim's blood type of AB, Rh negative.
a. Use the results of each test to determine whether the blood on each suspect's bumper is of human origin.

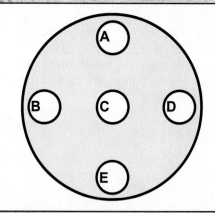

A = human antiserum, B = racoon antiserum, D = deer antiserum, E = skunk antiserum

Blood sample extract from Vehicle A is placed in the center (C):

Vehicle A Blood Origin

Blood sample extract from Vehicle B is placed in the center (C):

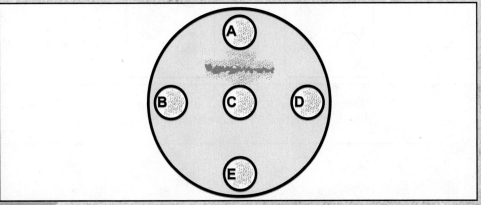

Vehicle B Blood Origin

Blood sample extract from Vehicle C is placed in the center (C):

Vehicle C Blood Origin

b. Using the following blood-typing results, indicate the apparent blood type recovered from Vehicles B and C. Determine whether the blood from the car of each suspect is consistent with the victim's blood type of AB negative.

| Blood type | Blood type |
| Consistent with victim? | Consistent with victim? |

_____

**Visual Lab:
Conduct an Analysis
of a Bloodstain**

To perform a virtual analysis of a blood-stain, go to www.pearsoncustom.com/us/vlm

Endnotes

1. S. Tobe et al., "Evaluation of Six Presumptive Tests for Blood, Their Specificity, Sensitivity, and Effect on High Molecular-Weight DNA," *Journal of Forensic Sciences* 52 (2007): 102.

2. The luminol reagent is prepared by mixing 0.1 gram 3-amino-phthalhydrazide and 5.0 grams sodium carbonate in 100 milliliters distilled water. Before use, 0.7 gram sodium perborate is added to the solution.

3. A. M. Gross et al., "The Effect of Luminol on Presumptive Tests and DNA Analysis Using the Polymerase Chain Reaction," *Journal of Forensic Sciences* 44 (1999): 837.

4. J. P. Allery et al., "Cytological Detection of Spermatozoa: Comparison of Three Staining Methods," *Journal of Forensic Sciences* 46 (2001): 349.

5. In one study, only a maximum of 4 sperm cells out of 1,000 could be extracted from a cotton patch and observed under the microscope. Edwin Jones (Ventura County Sheriff's Department, Ventura, Calif.), personal communication.

6. J. Kearsey, H. Louie, and H. Poon, "Validation Study of the Onestep ABAcard® PSA Test Kit for RCMP Casework," *Canadian Society of Forensic Science Journal* 34 (2001): 63.

7. D. Sweet et al., "An Improved Method to Recover Saliva from Human Skin: The Double Swab Technique," *Journal of Forensic Sciences* 42 (1997): 320.

8. Anne Davies and Elizabeth Wilson, "The Persistence of Seminal Constituents in the Human Vagina," *Forensic Science* 3 (1974): 45.

9. Kearsey, Louie, and Poon, "Validation Study of the Onestep ABAcard® PSA Test Kit."

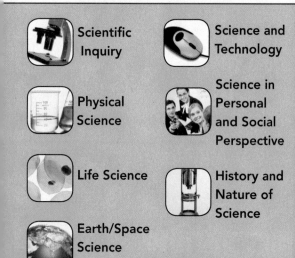
O. J. Simpson— A Mountain of Evidence

On June 12, 1994, police arrived at the home of Nicole Simpson only to view a horrific scene. The bodies of O. J. Simpson's estranged wife and her friend Ron Goldman were found on the path leading to the front door of Nicole's home. Both bodies were covered in blood and had received deep knife wounds. Nicole's head was nearly severed from her body. This was not a well-planned murder. A trail of blood led away from the murder scene. Blood was found in O. J. Simpson's Bronco. Blood drops were on O. J.'s driveway and in the foyer of his home. A blood-soaked sock was located in O. J. Simpson's bedroom, and a bloodstained glove rested outside his residence.

As DNA was extracted and profiled from each bloodstained article, a picture emerged that seemed to irrefutably link Simpson to the murders. A trail of DNA leaving the crime scene was consistent with O. J.'s profile, as was the DNA found entering Simpson's home. Simpson's DNA profile was found in the Bronco along with that of both victims. The glove contained the DNA profiles of Nicole and Ron, and the sock had Nicole's DNA profile. At trial, the defense team valiantly fought back. Miscues in evidence collection were craftily exploited. The defense strategy was to paint a picture of not only an incompetent investigation, but one that was tinged with dishonest police planting evidence. The strategy worked. O. J. Simpson was acquitted of murder.

DNA:
The Indispensable
Forensic Science Tool

Key Terms

amelogenin gene
amino acids
buccal cells
chromosome
complementary base pairing
deoxyribonucleic acid (DNA)
electrophoresis
epithelial cells
human genome
hybridization

low copy number
mitochondria
multiplexing
nucleotide
picogram
polymer
polymerase chain reaction (PCR)
primer
proteins

replication
restriction enzymes
restriction fragment length polymorphisms (RFLPs)
sequencing
short tandem repeat (STR)
substrate control
tandem repeat
touch DNA
Y-STRs

Understanding DNA

deoxyribonucleic acid (DNA)
The molecules carrying the body's genetic information; DNA is double stranded in the shape of a double helix

The discovery of **deoxyribonucleic acid (DNA)**, the deciphering of its structure, and the decoding of its genetic information were turning points in our understanding of the underlying concepts of inheritance. Now, with incredible speed, as molecular biologists unravel the basic structure of genes, we can create new products through genetic engineering and develop diagnostic tools and treatments for genetic disorders.

For a number of years, these developments were of seemingly peripheral interest to forensic scientists. All that changed when, in 1985, what started out as a more or less routine investigation into the structure of a human gene led to the discovery that portions of the DNA structure of certain genes are as unique to each individual as fingerprints. Alec Jeffreys and his colleagues at Leicester University, England, who were responsible for these revelations, named the process for isolating and reading these DNA markers *DNA fingerprinting*. As researchers uncovered new approaches and variations to the original Jeffreys technique, the terms *DNA profiling* and *DNA typing* came to be applied to describe this relatively new technology.

This discovery caught the imagination of the forensic science community, because forensic scientists have long searched for ways to definitively link biological evidence such as blood, semen, hair, and tissue to a single individual. Although conventional testing procedures had gone a long way toward narrowing the source of biological materials, individualization remained an elusive goal. DNA typing has allowed forensic scientists to accomplish this goal. Although the technique is still relatively new, DNA typing has become routine in public crime laboratories. It also has been made available to interested parties through the services of a number of skilled private laboratories. In the United States, courts have overwhelmingly admitted DNA evidence and accepted the reliability of its scientific underpinnings.

What Is DNA?

chromosomes
A threadlike structure in the cell nucleus composed of DNA, along which the genes are located

Inside each of 60 trillion cells in the human body are strands of genetic material called **chromosomes**. Arranged along the chromosomes, like beads on a thread, are nearly 25,000 genes. The gene is the fundamental unit of heredity. It instructs body cells to make proteins that determine everything including hair color and susceptibility to diseases. Each gene is composed of DNA designed to carry out a single body function.

Although DNA was first discovered in 1868, scientists were slow to understand and appreciate its fundamental role in inheritance. Painstakingly, researchers developed evidence that DNA was probably the substance by which genetic instructions are passed from one generation to the next. However, the first major breakthrough in comprehending how DNA works did not occur until the early 1950s, when two researchers, James Watson and Francis Crick, deduced the structure of DNA (see Figure 9–1). It turns out that DNA is an extraordinary molecule skillfully designed to control the genetic traits of all living cells, plant and animal.

polymer
A substance composed of a large number of atoms; these atoms are usually arranged in repeating units, or monomers

The Structure of DNA Before examining the implications of Watson and Crick's discovery, let's see how DNA is constructed. DNA is a **polymer**. A polymer is a

FIGURE 9–1
The discoverers of the structure of DNA. James Watson at left and Francis Crick, seen with their model of part of a DNA molecule. *Courtesy Photo Researchers Inc.*

very large molecule made by linking a series of repeating units, or monomers. In this case, the units are known as **nucleotides**.

Nucleotides. A nucleotide is composed of a sugar molecule, a phosphorus atom surrounded by four oxygen atoms, and a nitrogen-containing molecule called a base. Figure 9–2 shows how nucleotides can be strung together to form a DNA strand. In this figure, S designates the sugar component, which is joined with a phosphate group to form the backbone of the DNA strand. Projecting from the backbone are the bases.

nucleotide
A repeating unit of DNA consisting of one of four bases—adenine, guanine, cytosine, or thymine—attached to a phosphate–sugar group

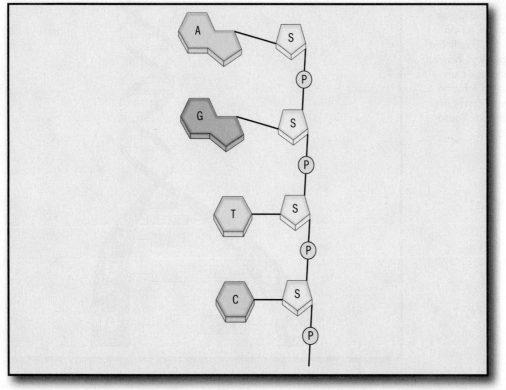

FIGURE 9–2
How nucleotides can be linked to form a DNA strand. S designates the sugar component, which is joined with phosphate groups (P) to form the backbone of DNA. Projecting from the backbone are four bases: A, adenine; G, guanine; T, thymine; and C, cytosine.

The key to understanding how DNA works is to appreciate the fact that only four types of bases are associated with DNA: adenine, cytosine, guanine, and thymine. To simplify our discussion of DNA, we will designate each of these bases by the first letter of their names. Hence, A will stand for adenine, C for cytosine, G for guanine, and T for thymine.

Again, notice in <u>Figure 9–2</u> how the bases project from the backbone of DNA. Also, although this figure shows a DNA strand of four bases, keep in mind that in theory there is no limit to the length of the DNA strand; a DNA strand can be composed of a long chain with millions of bases. This information was well known to Watson and Crick by the time they set about to detail the structure of DNA. Their efforts led them to discover that the DNA molecule is composed of two DNA strands coiled into a double helix. This can be thought of as resembling two wires twisted around each other.

As Watson and Crick manipulated scale models of DNA strands, they realized that the only way the bases on each strand could be properly aligned with each other in a double-helix configuration was to place base A opposite T and G opposite C. Watson and Crick had solved the puzzle of the double helix and presented the world with a simple but elegant picture of DNA (see <u>Figure 9–3</u>).

complementary base pairing
The specific pairing of base A with T and base C with G in double-stranded DNA

Complementary Base Pairing. The only arrangement possible in the double-helix configuration is the pairing of bases A to T and G to C, a concept that has become known as **complementary base pairing**. Although A–T and G–C pairs are always required, there are no restrictions on how the bases are sequenced on a DNA strand. Thus, one can observe the sequences T–A–T–T or G–T–A–A or G–T–C–A. When these sequences are joined with their complements in a double-helix configuration, they pair as follows:

FIGURE 9–3
A representation of a DNA double helix. Notice how bases G and C pair with each other, as do bases A and T. This is the only arrangement in which two DNA strands can align with each other in a double-helix configuration. *Courtesy of Photo Researchers, Inc.*

Any base can follow another on a DNA strand, which means that the possible number of different sequence combinations is staggering. Consider that the average human chromosome has DNA containing 100 million base pairs. All of the human chromosomes taken together contain about 3 billion base pairs. From these numbers, we can begin to appreciate the diversity of DNA and hence the diversity of living organisms. DNA is like a book of instructions. The alphabet used to create the book is simple enough: A, T, G, and C. The order in which these letters are arranged defines the role and function of a DNA molecule.

DNA at Work The inheritable traits that are controlled by DNA arise out of its ability to direct the production of complex molecules called **proteins**. Proteins are made by linking a combination of **amino acids**. Although thousands of proteins exist, they can all be derived from a combination of up to 20 known amino acids. The sequence of amino acids in a protein chain determines the shape and function of the protein.

Let's look at one example: The protein hemoglobin is found in our red blood cells. It carries oxygen to our body cells and removes carbon dioxide from these cells. One of the four amino acid chains of "normal" hemoglobin is shown in Figure 9–4(a). Studies of individuals who have sickle-cell anemia show that this inheritable disorder arises from the presence of "abnormal" hemoglobin in their red blood cells. An amino acid chain for "abnormal" hemoglobin is shown in Figure 9–4(b). Note that the sole difference between "normal" and "abnormal," or sickle-cell hemoglobin, arises from the substitution of one amino acid for another in the protein chain (see Figure 9–5).

**MyCrimeKit:
WebExtra 9.1**
What Is DNA?
www.mycrimekit.com

proteins
Polymers of amino acids that play basic roles in the structure and function of living things

amino acids
The building blocks of proteins

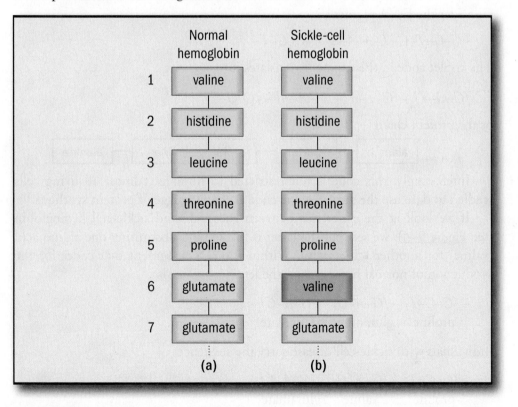

FIGURE 9–4   (a) A string of amino acids composes one of the protein chains of hemoglobin. (b) Substitution of just one amino acid for another in the protein chain results in sickle-cell hemoglobin.

FIGURE 9–5
Sickle cell anemia is an inherited anomaly in which the red blood cells contain an abnormal form of hemoglobin. Decreased oxygen supply causes normal red blood cells to change their form into sickles. *Courtesy Photo Researchers, Inc.*

The genetic information that determines the amino acid sequence for every protein manufactured in the human body is stored in DNA in a genetic code that relies on the sequence of bases along the DNA strand. The alphabet of DNA is simple—*A, T, G,* and *C*—but the key to deciphering the genetic code is to know that each amino acid is coded by a sequence of three bases. Thus, the amino acid alanine is coded by the combination *C–G–T*; the amino acid aspartate is coded by the combination *C–T–A*; and the amino acid phenylalanine is coded by the combination *A–A–A*. With this code in hand, we can now see how the amino acid sequence in a protein chain is determined by the structure of DNA. Consider the DNA segment

–C–G–T–C–T–A–A–A–A–C–G–T–

The triplet code in this segment translates into

[C–G–T] – [C–T–A] – [A–A–A] – [C–G–T]

or the protein chain

Interestingly, this code is not restricted to humans. Almost all living cells studied to date use the same genetic code as the language of protein synthesis.[1]

If we look at the difference between "normal" and sickle-cell hemoglobin (see Figure 9–4), we see that the latter is formed by substituting one amino acid (valine) for another (glutamate). Within the DNA segment that codes for the production of normal hemoglobin, the letter sequence is

– [C–C–T] – [G–A–G] – [G–A–G] –
proline   glutamate   glutamate

Individuals with sickle-cell disease carry the sequence

– [C–C–T] – [G–T–G] – [G–A–G] –
proline   valine   glutamate

Thus, we see that a single base or letter change (T has been substituted for A in valine) is the underlying cause of sickle-cell anemia, demonstrating the delicate chemical balance between health and disease in the human body.

As scientists unravel the base sequences of DNA, they obtain a greater appreciation for the roles of proteins in the chemistry of life. Already the genes responsible for hemophilia, Duchenne muscular dystrophy, and Huntington's disease have been located. Once scientists have isolated a disease-causing gene, they can determine the protein that the gene has directed the cell to manufacture. By studying these proteins—or the absence of them—scientists will be able to devise a treatment for genetic disorders.

A 13-year project to determine the order of bases on all 23 pairs of human chromosomes (also called the **human genome**) is now complete. Knowing the location on a specific chromosome at which DNA codes for production of a particular protein is useful for diagnosing and treating genetic diseases. This information is also crucial for understanding the underlying causes of cancer. Also, comparing the human genome with that of other organisms will help us understand the role and implications of evolution.

human genome
The order of bases on all 23 pairs of human chromosomes

Quick Review

- The gene is the fundamental unit of heredity. Each gene is composed of DNA specifically designed to control the genetic traits of our cells.

- DNA is constructed as a very large molecule made by linking a series of repeating units called nucleotides.

- Four types of bases are associated with the DNA structure: adenine (*A*), guanine (*G*), cytosine (*C*), and thymine (*T*).

- The bases on each strand of DNA are aligned in a double-helix configuration so that adenine pairs with thymine and guanine pairs with cytosine. This concept is known as complementary base pairing.

- The order in which the base pairs are arranged defines the role and function of a DNA molecule.

Replication of DNA

Once the double-helix structure of DNA was discovered, how DNA duplicated itself before cell division became apparent. The concept of base pairing in DNA suggests the analogy of positive and negative photographic film. Each strand of DNA in the double helix has the same information; one can make a positive print from a negative or a negative from a positive.

The Process of Replication

DNA **replication**—the synthesis of new DNA from existing DNA—begins with the unwinding of the DNA strands in the double helix. Each strand is then exposed to a collection of free nucleotides. Letter by letter, the double helix is re-created as the nucleotides are assembled in the proper order, as dictated by the principle of base pairing (*A* with *T* and *G* with *C*). The result is the emergence of two identical copies of DNA where before there was only one (see Figure 9–6). A cell can now pass on its genetic identity when it divides.

replication
The synthesis of new DNA from existing DNA

Many enzymes and proteins are involved in unwinding the DNA strands, keeping the two DNA strands apart, and assembling the new DNA strands. For example, DNA polymerases are enzymes that assemble a new DNA strand in the proper base sequence determined by the original or parent DNA strand. DNA polymerases also "proofread" the growing DNA double helices for mismatched base pairs, which are replaced with correct bases.

FIGURE 9–6
Replication of DNA. The strands of the original DNA molecule are separated, and two new strands are assembled.

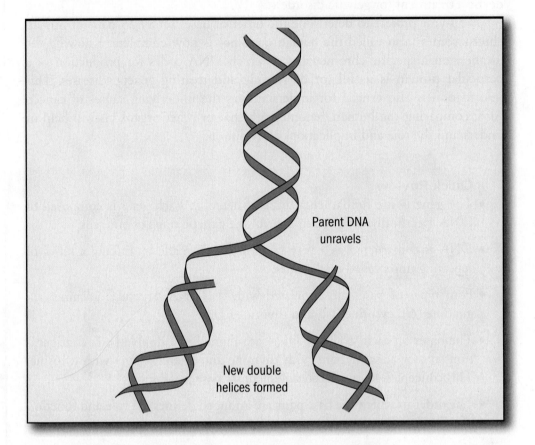

Parent DNA
unravels

New double
helices formed

Polymerase Chain Reaction

Until recently, the phenomenon of DNA replication appeared to be only of academic interest to forensic scientists interested in DNA for identification. However, this changed when researchers perfected the technology of using DNA polymerases to copy a DNA strand located outside a living cell. This relatively new laboratory technique is known as **polymerase chain reaction (PCR)**.

In PCR, small quantities of DNA or broken pieces of DNA found in crime-scene evidence can be copied with the aid of a DNA polymerase. The copying process can be accomplished in an automated fashion using a DNA Thermal Cycler (see Figure 9–7). Each cycle of the PCR technique results in a doubling of the DNA. Within a few hours, 30 cycles can multiply DNA a billionfold. Once DNA copies are in hand, they can be analyzed by any of the methods of modern molecular biology. The ability to multiply small bits of DNA opens new and exciting avenues for forensic scientists to explore. It means that sample size is no longer a limitation in characterizing DNA recovered from crime-scene evidence.

polymerase chain reaction (PCR)
A technique for replicating or copying a portion of a DNA strand outside a living cell

FIGURE 9–7
The DNA Thermal Cycler, an instrument that automates the rapid and precise temperature changes required to copy a DNA strand. Within a matter of hours, DNA can be multiplied a billionfold. *Courtesy Applied Biosystems, Foster City, Calif.*

Quick Review

- DNA replication begins with the unwinding of the DNA strands in the double helix. The double helix is re-created as the nucleotides are assembled in the proper order (A with T and G with C). Two identical copies of DNA emerge from the process.

- PCR (polymerase chain reaction) is a technique for replicating or copying a portion of a DNA strand outside a living cell.

- Recombinant DNA is a process by which the DNA of an organism is altered by inserting into it fragments of DNA from another organism (see Inside the Science on the following pages).

Inside the Science

Recombinant DNA

The relationship between the base letters on a DNA strand and the type of protein specified for manufacture by the sequence of these letters is called the genetic code. Once a particular DNA site has been identified as controlling the production of a certain protein, molecular biologists can take advantage of the natural chemical-producing abilities of the DNA site. This undertaking has given rise to the technology known as recombinant DNA.

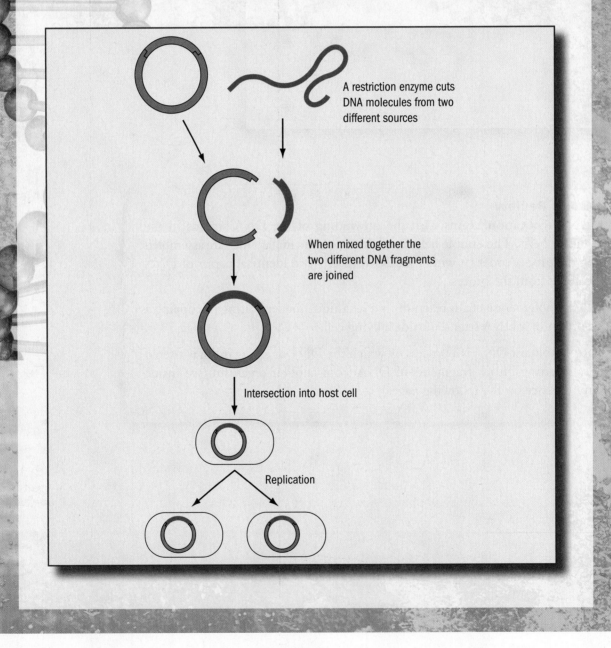

A restriction enzyme cuts DNA molecules from two different sources

When mixed together the two different DNA fragments are joined

Intersection into host cell

Replication

Inside the Science (CONTINUED)

Recombinant DNA relies on the ability of certain chemicals, known as restriction enzymes, to cut DNA into fragments that can later be incorporated into another DNA strand. Restriction enzymes can be thought of as highly specialized scissors that cut a DNA molecule when they recognize a specific sequence of bases. At present, more than 150 restriction enzymes are commercially available. Thus, molecular biologists have a great deal of flexibility in choosing the portion of a DNA strand they wish to cut out.

Once a portion of the DNA strand has been cut out with the aid of a restriction enzyme, the next step in the recombinant DNA process is to insert the isolated DNA segment into a foreign DNA strand (normally, bacterium DNA is selected). Many types of bacteria contain DNA shaped in a circle. A restriction enzyme is used to cut open the circular DNA; then the foreign DNA is spliced in to re-form the circle (see figure). The newly fashioned DNA is reintroduced into the bacterial cells. As the bacteria multiply rapidly in their usual fashion, copies of altered DNA are passed on to all descendants.

The commercial implications of recombinant DNA technology are enormous. For example, the gene that produces human growth hormone has been introduced into goldfish and carp, and the gene that produces growth hormone in rainbow trout has been introduced into carp. In each case, the gene-altered fish have grown significantly faster and larger than their natural relatives. If altered bacteria are infused with the DNA segment that makes human insulin, for example, the bacteria make human insulin. Because bacteria multiply so rapidly, it is not long before significant amounts of insulin can be recovered and used to treat diabetes. In this manner, other naturally occurring substances can be produced in commercial quantities for the treatment of human ailments. Likewise, plant genetic engineering holds promise for increasing global food production.

DNA Typing with Tandem Repeats

Geneticists have discovered that portions of the DNA molecule contain sequences of letters that are repeated numerous times. In fact, more than 30 percent of the human genome is composed of repeating segments of DNA. These repeating sequences, or **tandem repeats**, seem to act as filler or spacers between the coding regions of DNA. Although these repeating segments do not seem to affect our outward appearance or control any other basic genetic function, they are nevertheless part of our genetic makeup, inherited from our parents in the manner illustrated by the Punnett square (page 301). The origin and significance of these tandem repeats is a mystery, but to forensic scientists they offer a means of distinguishing one individual from another through DNA typing.

Restriction Fragment Length Polymorphisms

Forensic scientists first began applying DNA technology to human identity in 1985. From the beginning, attention has focused on the tandem repeats of the genome. These repeats can be visualized as a string of connected boxes with each box having the same core sequence of DNA bases (see Figure 9–8). All humans have the same type of repeats, but there is tremendous variation in the number of repeats that each of us has.

G-C-T G-G-T G-C-T G-G-C C-T-C
Fifteen-base core

Until the mid-1990s, the forensic community aimed its efforts at characterizing repeat segments known as **restriction fragment length polymorphisms (RFLPs)**. These repeats are cut out of the DNA double helix by a **restriction enzyme** that acts like a pair of scissors. The forensic science community selected a number of different RFLPs for performing DNA typing. Typically a core sequence is 15 to 35 bases long and repeats itself up to a thousand times.

Let's examine some DNA strands with regions of repeating base sequences to see how this process works. Figure 9–9 illustrates a portion of a pair of chromosomes. Note that each chromosome is composed of two DNA strands wrapped in a double-helix configuration. Each chromosome has a region that contains repeating bases. For the sake of simplicity in illustrating the RFLP method, we assume that the core repeat is only three bases long with a sequence of *T–A–G*.

Note an important distinction between the two chromosomes: the chromosome on the left has three repeating sequences of *T–A–G*, whereas the one on the right has two repeating sequences of *T–A–G*. As with any genetic trait, these repeating sequences were inherited from the parents. In this example, one parent

---

tandem repeat
Region of a chromosome that contains multiple copies of a core DNA sequence arranged in a repeating fashion

FIGURE 9–8
A DNA segment consisting of a series of repeating DNA units. In this illustration, the fifteen-base core can repeat itself hundreds of times. The entire DNA segment is typically hundreds to thousands of bases long.

restriction fragment length polymorphisms (RFLPs)
Different fragment lengths of base pairs that result from cutting a DNA molecule with restriction enzymes

restriction enzyme
Chemical that acts as scissors to cut DNA molecules at specific locations

FIGURE 9–9
Intertwined strands of DNA representing segments of two chromosomes. Note that the chromosome segment on the left contains three repeating sequences of *T-A-G*, while the chromosome segment on the right has two repeating sequences of *T-A-G*.

contributed the chromosome containing the three repeating sequences, and the other parent passed on the chromosome containing the two repeating sequences.

The key to understanding DNA typing lies in the knowledge that within the world's population, numerous possibilities exist for the number of times a particular sequence of base letters can repeat itself on a DNA strand. The possibilities become even greater when one deals with two chromosomes, each containing different lengths of repeating sequences. During RFLP typing, restriction enzymes cut up chromosomes into hundreds of fragments, some containing repeating sequences from the DNA molecule. In our example, shown in Figure 9–9, the chromosome pair, when cut, will yield two different fragment lengths of *T–A–G*.

Electrophoresis The length differences associated with DNA strands or RFLPs allow forensic scientists to distinguish one person from another. In actuality, these strands are relatively long, often consisting of thousands of bases. Once the DNA molecules have been cut up by the restriction enzyme, the resulting fragments must be sorted out. This is accomplished by separating the fragments by **electrophoresis**.

During the electrophoretic process, DNA from various sources, cut up by restriction enzymes, is placed on a plate coated with a gel medium. When the gel is subjected to an electric potential, the DNA fragments migrate across the plate. Because smaller DNA fragments move faster along the plate than do larger fragments, the process separates the fragments according to size.

electrophoresis
A technique for separating molecules through their migration on a support medium under the influence of an electrical potential

Hybridization Once the electrophoresis process is completed, the double-stranded fragments of DNA are chemically treated so that the strands separate from each other. The fragments are then transferred to a nylon membrane in much the same way as one would transfer an ink line onto a blotter. This transfer process is called *Southern blotting*, named after its developer, Edward Southern. To visualize the separated RFLPs, the nylon sheet is treated with radioactively labeled probes containing a base sequence complementary to the RFLPs being identified (a process called **hybridization**).

hybridization
The process of joining two complementary strands of DNA to form a double-stranded molecule

DNA Typing with RFLP In our example, we aim to identify RFLPs composed of a repeating string of letters spelling *T–A–G*. Hence, the appropriate probes would have the complementary letter sequence *A–T–C*, as shown in the following diagram, so that the probes can specifically bind to the desired RFLP. (Note: The asterisk designates a radioactive label.)

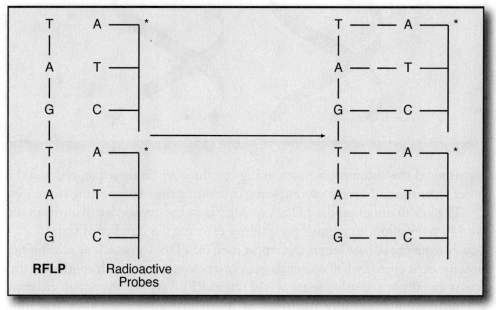

Next, the nylon sheet is placed against X-ray film and exposed for several days. The radioactive decay products strike the film. When the film is processed, bands appear where the radioactive probes stuck to the fragments on the nylon sheet. The length of each fragment is determined by running known DNA fragment lengths alongside the test specimens and comparing the distances they migrated across the plate. The entire DNA-typing process is depicted in Figure 9–10.

A typical DNA fragment pattern shows two bands (one RFLP from each chromosome). When comparing the DNA fragment patterns of two or more specimens, one merely looks for a match between the band sets. For example, in Figure 9–11, DNA extracted from a crime-scene stain matches the DNA recovered from one of three suspects. Although only a limited number of people in a population would have the same DNA fragment pattern as the suspect, this test in itself cannot be used to individualize the stain to the suspect. However,

FIGURE 9–10
The DNA RFLP
typing process.

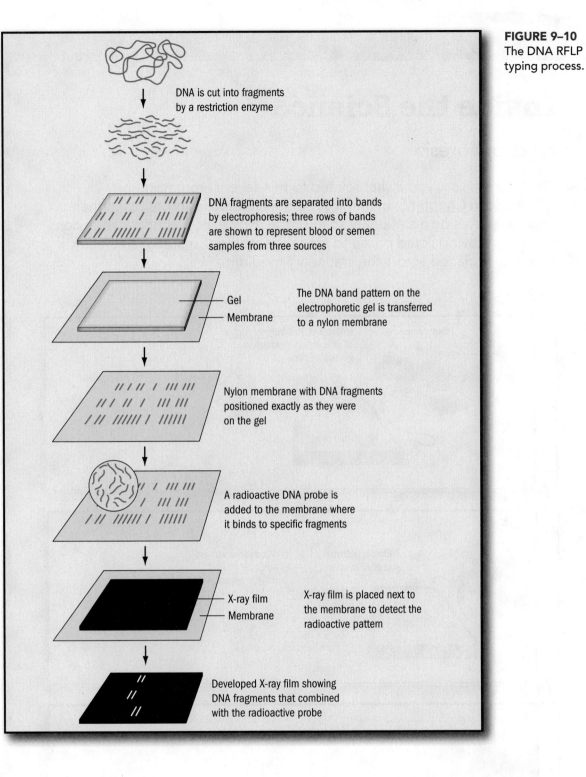

DNA is cut into fragments
by a restriction enzyme

DNA fragments are separated into bands
by electrophoresis; three rows of bands
are shown to represent blood or semen
samples from three sources

Gel
Membrane

The DNA band pattern on the
electrophoretic gel is transferred
to a nylon membrane

Nylon membrane with DNA fragments
positioned exactly as they were
on the gel

A radioactive DNA probe is
added to the membrane where
it binds to specific fragments

X-ray film
Membrane

X-ray film is placed next to
the membrane to detect the
radioactive pattern

Developed X-ray film showing
DNA fragments that combined
with the radioactive probe

Inside the Science

Electrophoresis

Electrophoresis is somewhat related to thin-layer chromatography (discussed in Chapter 5) in that it separates materials according to their migration rates on a stationary solid phase. However, electrophoresis does not use a moving liquid phase to move the material; instead, an electrical potential is placed across the stationary medium.

FIGURE 1

(a) Power source — Mixtures of DNA fragments of different sizes placed on gel-coated plate — Gel-coated plate

(b) Power source — Electric potential applied to plate — Substances with an electrical charge migrate across plate

(c) Power source — Separated proteins allow analyst to characterize DNA in dried blood — Longer fragments move more slowly — Shorter fragments move more quickly — Completed gel

Inside the Science (CONTINUED)

The nature of the medium can vary; most forensic applications call for a starch or agar gel coated onto a glass plate. Under these conditions, only substances that possess an electrical charge migrate across the stationary phase (see Figure 1). Because many substances in blood carry an electrical charge, they can be separated and identified by electrophoresis. The technique is particularly useful for separating and identifying complex biochemical mixtures. In forensic science, electrophoresis is most useful for characterizing proteins and DNA in dried blood (see Figure 2).

FIGURE 2   DNA fragments separated by gel electrophoresis are visualized under a UV light. *Courtesy Simon Fraser/Photo Researchers, Inc.*

Forensic serologists have developed several electrophoretic procedures for characterizing DNA in dried blood. Mixtures of DNA fragments can be separated by gel electrophoresis by taking advantage of the fact that the rate of movement of DNA across a gel-coated plate depends on the molecule's size. Smaller DNA fragments move faster along the plate than larger DNA fragments. After completing the electrophoresis run, the separated DNA is stained with a suitable developing agent for visual observation.

by using additional DNA probes, each of which recognizes different repeating DNA segments (other than *T–A–G*), a high degree of discrimination or even near individualization can be achieved. For example, if each probe selected yielded a DNA type having a frequency of occurrence of one in a hundred in a population, then four different probes would have a combined frequency of one in 100 million (1/100 × 1/100 × 1/100 × 1/100).

FIGURE 9–11
A DNA profile pattern of a suspect and its match to crime-scene DNA. From left to right, lane 1 is a DNA standard marker; lane 2 is the crime-scene DNA; and lanes 3 to 5 are control samples from suspects 1, 2, and 3, respectively. Crime-scene DNA matches suspect 2. *Courtesy Edvotek, The Biotechnology Education Company, www.edvotek.com*

RFLP DNA typing has the distinction of being the first scientifically accepted protocol in the United States used for forensic characterization of DNA. However, its utility has been short lived. New technology incorporating polymerase chain reaction (PCR) has supplanted RFLP. In its short history, perhaps RFLP's most startling impact related to the impeachment trial of President Bill Clinton. The whole complexion of the investigation regarding the relationship of the president with a White House intern, Monica Lewinsky, changed when it was revealed that Ms. Lewinsky possessed a dress that she claimed was stained with the president's semen. The FBI Laboratory was asked to compare the DNA extracted from the dress stain with that of the president. A seven-probe RFLP match was obtained between the president's DNA and the stain. The combined frequency of occurrence for the seven DNA types found was nearly one in eight trillion, an undeniable link. The dress and a copy of the FBI DNA report are shown in <u>Figure 9–12</u>.

FIGURE 9–12
The dress and the FBI
Report of Examination
for a semen stain located
on the dress.

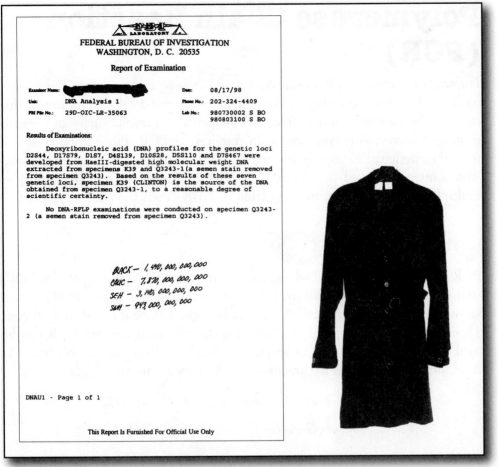

FEDERAL BUREAU OF INVESTIGATION
WASHINGTON, D. C. 20535

Report of Examination

Examiner Name: ███████████ Date: 08/17/98

Unit: DNA Analysis 1 Phone No.: 202-324-4409

FBI File No.: 29D-OIC-LR-35063 Lab No.: 980730002 S BO
980803100 S BO

Results of Examinations:

Deoxyribonucleic acid (DNA) profiles for the genetic loci
D2S44, D17S79, D1S7, D4S139, D10S28, D5S110 and D7S467 were
developed from HaeIII-digested high molecular weight DNA
extracted from specimens K39 and Q3243-1 (a semen stain removed
from specimen Q3243). Based on the results of these seven
genetic loci, specimen K39 (CLINTON) is the source of the DNA
obtained from specimen Q3243-1, to a reasonable degree of
scientific certainty.

No DNA-RFLP examinations were conducted on specimen Q3243-
2 (a semen stain removed from specimen Q3243).

BLACK — 1,440,000,000,000
CAUC — 7,870,000,000,000
SEH — 3,140,000,000,000
SWH — 943,000,000,000

DNAU1 - Page 1 of 1

This Report Is Furnished For Official Use Only

Quick Review

- Portions of the DNA molecule contain sequences of bases that are repeated numerous times. These tandem repeats offer a means of distinguishing one individual from another through DNA typing.

- Length differences associated with relatively long repeating DNA strands—called restriction fragment length polymorphisms (RFLPs)—formed the basis for one of the first DNA-typing procedures.

- In the laboratory, DNA molecules are cut up by a restriction enzyme, and the resulting fragments are sorted out by electrophoresis.

- Materials undergoing electrophoresis are forced to move across a gel-coated plate under the influence of an electrical potential. Substances such as DNA can be separated and characterized using electrophoresis.

- A typical DNA fragment pattern shows two bands (one RFLP from each chromosome).

Polymerase Chain Reaction (PCR)

For nearly a decade, RFLP was the dominant DNA-typing procedure in the United States. However, its utility quickly ended by the mid-1990s. What caused this change? The answer is quite simple: the emergence of a revolutionary and elegant technique known as polymerase chain reaction, or PCR. Put simply, PCR is a technique designed to copy or multiply DNA strands. For the forensic scientist, who is often presented with minute quantities of materials, the opportunity to multiply the quantity of sample available for analysis was too good to pass up.

The PCR Process

PCR is the outgrowth of knowledge gained from an understanding of how DNA strands naturally replicate within a cell. The most important feature of PCR is the knowledge that an enzyme called DNA polymerase can be directed to synthesize a specific region of DNA. In a relatively straightforward manner, PCR can be used to repeatedly duplicate or amplify a strand of DNA millions of times. As an example, let's consider a segment of DNA that we want to duplicate by PCR:

$$-G-T-C-T-C-A-G-C-T-T-\textbf{\textit{C-C-A-G}}-$$

$$-\textbf{\textit{C-A-G-A}}-G-T-C-G-A-A-G-G-T-C-$$

To perform PCR on this DNA segment, short sequences of DNA on each side of the region of interest must be identified. In the example shown here, the short sequences are designated by boldface letters in the DNA segment. These short DNA segments must be available in a pure form known as a **primer** if the PCR technique is going to work.

The first step in PCR is to heat the DNA strands to about 94°C. At this temperature, the double-stranded DNA molecules separate completely:

$$-G-T-C-T-C-A-G-C-T-T-C-C-A-G-$$

$$-C-A-G-A-G-T-C-G-A-A-G-G-T-C-$$

The second step is to add the primers to the separated strands and allow the primers to combine, or hybridize, with the strands by lowering the test-tube temperature to about 60°C.

$$-G-T-C-T-C-A-G-C-T-T-C-C-A-G-$$
$$C-A-G-A$$
$$C-C-A-G$$
$$-C-A-G-A-G-T-C-G-A-A-G-G-T-C-$$

primer
A short strand of DNA used to target a region of DNA for replication by PCR

The third step is to add the DNA polymerase and a mixture of free nucleotides (A, C, G, T) to the separated strands (see Figure 9–13). When the test tube is heated to 72°C, the polymerase enzyme directs the rebuilding of a double-stranded DNA molecule, extending the primers by adding the appropriate bases, one at a time, resulting in the production of two complete pairs of double-stranded DNA segments:

$$–G–T–C–T–C–A–G–C–T–T–C–C–A–G–$$
$$C–A–G–A–G–T–C–G–A–A–G–G–T–C–$$

$$–G–T–C–T–C–A–G–C–T–T–C–C–A–G$$
$$–C–A–G–A–G–T–C–G–A–A–G–G–T–C–$$

This completes the first cycle of the PCR technique, which results in a doubling of the number of DNA strands from one to two. The cycle of heating, cooling, and strand rebuilding is then repeated, resulting in a further doubling of the DNA strands. On completion of the second cycle, four double-stranded DNA molecules have been created from the original double-stranded DNA sample. Typically, 28 to 32 cycles are carried out to yield more than one billion copies of the original DNA molecule. Each cycle takes less than two minutes.

FIGURE 9-13
Vial of DNA Polymerase used in PCR for replication of DNA. *Courtesy Beth Plowes - Proteapix*

MyCrimeKit: WebExtra 9.3
View a Polymerase Chain Reaction
www.mycrimekit.com

Advantages of PCR

Why couldn't the PCR technology be applied to RFLP DNA typing? Simply put, the RFLP strands are too long, often containing thousands of bases. PCR is best used with DNA strands that are no longer than a couple of hundred bases. The obvious solution to this problem is to characterize DNA strands that are much shorter than RFLPs.

Another advantage in moving to shorter DNA strands is that they would be expected to be more stable and less subject to degradation brought about by adverse environmental conditions. The long RFLP strands tend to break apart under adverse conditions not uncommon at crime scenes.

From the forensic scientist's viewpoint, PCR offers a third distinct advantage in that it can amplify minute quantities of DNA, thus overcoming the limited-sample-size problem often associated with crime-scene evidence. With PCR, less than one-billionth of a gram of DNA is required for analysis. Consequently, PCR can characterize DNA extracted from small quantities of blood, semen, and saliva. The extraordinary sensitivity of PCR allows forensic analysts to characterize small quantities of DNA that could never be detected by RFLP. For instance, PCR has been applied to the identification of saliva residues found on envelopes, stamps, soda cans, and cigarette butts.

Quick Review

- Polymerase chain reaction (PCR) can amplify minute quantities of DNA. The technique evolved from an understanding of how DNA strands naturally replicate within a cell.

- PCR technology cannot be applied to RFLP DNA typing because RFLP strands are too long, often numbering in the thousands of bases. PCR is best used with DNA strands that are no longer than a couple of hundred bases.

- Long RFLP strands tend to break apart under the adverse conditions at many crime scenes. The shorter DNA strands used in PCR are more stable and less subject to degradation caused by adverse environmental conditions.

Short Tandem Repeats (STRs)

short tandem repeat (STR)
A region of a DNA molecule that contains short segments of three to seven repeating base pairs

The latest method of DNA typing, **short tandem repeat (STR)** analysis, has emerged as the most successful and widely used DNA-profiling procedure. STRs are locations (loci) on the chromosome that contain short sequence elements that repeat themselves within the DNA molecule. They serve as helpful markers for identification because they are found in great abundance throughout the human genome.

STRs normally consist of repeating sequences of three to seven bases; the entire strand of an STR is also very short, less than 450 bases long. These strands are significantly shorter than those encountered in the RFLP procedure. This means that STRs are much less susceptible to degradation and are often recovered from bodies or stains that have been subject to extreme decomposition. Also, because of their shortness, STRs are an ideal candidate for multiplication by PCR, thus overcoming the limited-sample-size problem often associated with crime-scene evidence. Only one-billionth of a gram or less of DNA is required—1/50 to 1/100 the amount normally required for RFLP analysis.

To understand the utility of STRs in forensic science, let's look at one commonly used STR known as TH01. This DNA segment contains the repeating sequence *A–A–T–G*. Seven TH01 variants have been identified in the human genome. These variants contain 5 to 11 repeats of *A–A–T–G*. Figure 9–14 illustrates two such TH01 variants, one containing 6 repeats and the other containing 8 repeats of *A–A–T–G*.

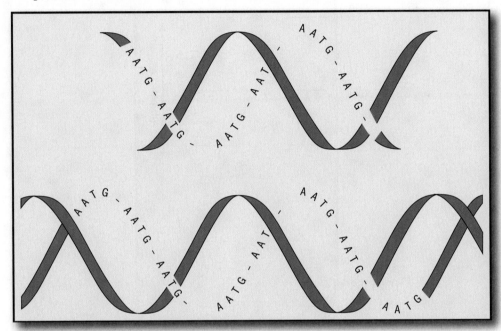

FIGURE 9–14 Variants of the short tandem repeat TH01. The upper DNA strand contains six repeats of the sequence *A-A-T-G*; the lower DNA strand contains eight repeats of the sequence *A-A-T-G*. This DNA type is known as TH01 6, 8.

During a forensic examination, TH01 is extracted from biological materials and amplified by PCR as described earlier. The ability to copy an STR means that extremely small amounts of the molecule can be detected and analyzed. Once the STRs have been copied or amplified, they are separated by electrophoresis. By examining the distance the STR has migrated on the electrophoretic plate, one can determine the number of *A–A–T–G* repeats in the STR. Every person has two STR types for TH01, one inherited from each parent. Thus, for example, one may find in a semen stain TH01 with six repeats and eight repeats. This combination of TH01 is found in approximately 3.5 percent of the population.

Multiplexing

What makes STRs so attractive to forensic scientists is that hundreds of different types of STRs are found in human genes. The more STRs one can characterize, the smaller the percentage of the population from which these STRs can emanate. This gives rise to the concept of **multiplexing**. Using PCR technology, one can simultaneously extract and amplify a combination of different STRs.

One STR system on the commercial market is the STR Blue Kit.[2] This kit provides the necessary materials for amplifying and detecting three STRs (a process

multiplexing
A technique that simultaneously detects more than one DNA marker in a single analysis

called *triplexing*)—D3S1358, vWA, and FGA. The design of the system ensures that the size of the STRs does not overlap, thereby allowing each marker to be viewed clearly on an electrophoretic gel, as shown in Figure 9–15. In the United States, the forensic science community has standardized on 13 STRs for entry into a national database known as the Combined DNA Index System (CODIS).

FIGURE 9-15
Triplex system containing three loci: FGA, vWA, and D3S1358, indicating a match between the questioned and the standard/reference stains.

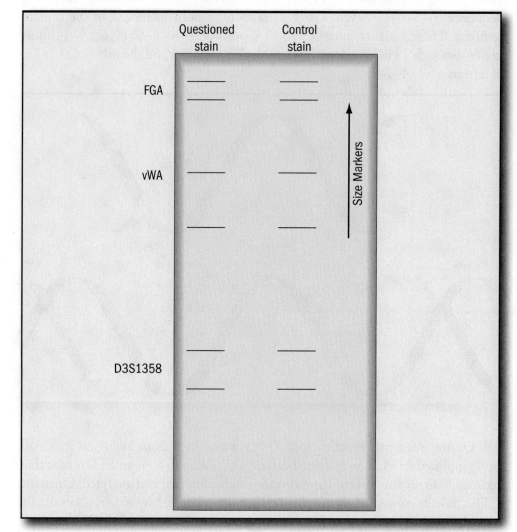

When an STR is selected for analysis, not only must the identity and number of core repeats be defined, but the sequence of bases flanking the repeats must also be known. This knowledge allows commercial manufacturers of STR-typing kits to prepare the correct primers to delineate the STR segment to be amplified by PCR. Figure 9–16 illustrates how appropriate primers are used to define the region of DNA to be amplified. Also, a mix of different primers aimed at different STRs will be used to simultaneously amplify a multitude of STRs (multiplexing). In fact, one STR kit on the commercial market can simultaneously make copies of 15 different STRs (see Figure 9–17).

**MyCrimeKit:
WebExtra 9.4**
See the 13 CODIS STRs and Their Chromosomal Positions
www.mycrimekit.com

FIGURE 9–16
Appropriate primers flanking the repeat units of a DNA segment must be selected and put in place to initiate the PCR process.

FIGURE 9–17
STR profile for 15 loci. *Courtesy H. Edward Grotjan, Ph.D.*

DNA Typing with STRs

The 13 CODIS STRs are listed in Table 9–1 along with their probabilities of identity. The probability of identity is a measure of the likelihood that two individuals selected at random will have an identical STR type. The smaller the value of this probability, the more discriminating the STR. A high degree of discrimination and even individualization can be attained by analyzing a combination of STRs (multiplexing). Because STRs occur independently of each other, the probability of biological evidence having a particular combination of STR types is determined by the product of their frequency of occurrence in a population. This combination is referred to as the *product rule*. Hence, the greater the number of STRs characterized, the smaller the frequency of occurrence of the analyzed sample in the general population.

The combination of the first three STRs shown in Table 9–1 typically produces a frequency of occurrence of about 1 in 5,000. A combination of the first six STRs typically yields a frequency of occurrence in the range of 1 in two million for the Caucasian population, and if the top nine STRs are determined in combination, this frequency declines to about 1 in one billion. The combination of all 13 STRs shown in Table 9–1 typically produces frequencies of occurrence that measure in the range of 1 in 575 trillion for Caucasian Americans and 1 in 900 trillion for African Americans. Importantly, several commercially available kits allow forensic scientists to profile STRs in the kinds of combinations cited here.

Table 9–1
The Thirteen CODIS STRs and Their Probability of Identities

STR	African American	U.S. Caucasian
D3S1358	0.094	0.075
vWA	0.063	0.062
FGA	0.033	0.036
TH01	0.109	0.081
TPOX	0.090	0.195
CSF1PO	0.081	0.112
D5S818	0.112	0.158
D13S317	0.136	0.085
D7S820	0.080	0.065
D8S1179	0.082	0.067
D21S11	0.034	0.039
D18S51	0.029	0.028
D16S539	0.070	0.089

Source: The Future of Forensic DNA Testing: Predictions of the Research and Development Working Group. Washington, D.C.: National Institute of Justice, Department of Justice, 2000, p. 41.

Capillary Electrophorensics

MyCrimeKit: WebExtra 9.5

Calculate the Frequency of Occurrence of a DNA Profile
www.mycrimekit.com

The separation of STRs can typically be carried out on a flat gel-coated electrophoretic plate, as described earlier. However, the need to reduce analysis time and to automate sampling and data collection has led to the emergence of *capillary electrophoresis* as the preferred technology for characterization of STRs. Capillary electrophoresis is carried out in a thin glass column rather than on the surface of a coated-glass plate.

As illustrated in Figure 9–18, each end of the column is immersed in a reservoir of buffer liquid that also holds electrodes (coated with platinum) to supply high-voltage energy. The column is coated with a gel polymer, and the DNA-containing sample solution is injected into one end of the column with a syringe. The STR fragments then move through the column under the influence of an electrical potential at a speed that is related to the length of the STR fragments. The other end of the column is connected to a detector that tracks the separated STRs as they emerge from the column. As the DNA peaks pass through the detector, they are recorded on a display known as an electropherogram.

FIGURE 9–18
Capillary electrophoresis technology has evolved from the traditional flat gel electrophoresis approach. The separation of DNA segments is carried out on the interior wall of a glass capillary tube coated with a gel polymer and kept at a constant voltage. The size of the DNA fragments determines the speed at which they move through the column. This figure illustrates the separation of three sets of STRs (triplexing).

amelogenin gene
A genetic locus useful for determining sex

Sex Identification Using STR

Manufacturers of commercial STR kits typically used by crime laboratories provide one additional piece of useful information along with STR types: the sex of the DNA contributor. The focus of attention here is the **amelogenin gene** located on both the X and Y chromosomes. This gene, which is actually the gene for tooth pulp, has an interesting characteristic in that it is shorter by six bases in the X chromosome than in the Y chromosome. Hence, when the amelogenin gene is amplified by PCR and separated by electrophoresis, males, who have an X and a Y chromosome, show two bands; females, who have two X chromosomes, have just one band. Typically, these results are obtained in conjunction with STR types.

Another tool in the arsenal of the DNA analyst is the ability to type STRs located on the Y chromosome. The Y chromosome is male specific and is always paired with the X chromosome. More than 20 different **Y-STR** markers have been identified, and a commercial kit allows for the characterization of 17 Y chromosome STRs. When can it be advantageous to seek out Y-STR types? Generally, Y-STRs are useful for analyzing blood, saliva, or a vaginal swab that is a mix originating from more than one male. For example, Y-STRs prove useful when multiple males are involved in a sexual assault.

Keep in mind that STR types derived from the Y chromosome originate only from this single male chromosome. A female subject, or one with an XX chromosome pattern, does not contribute any DNA information. Also, unlike a conventional STR analysis that is derived from two chromosomes and typically shows two bands or peaks, a Y-STR has only one band or peak for each STR type.

For example, the traditional STR DNA pattern may prove to be overly complex in the case of a vaginal swab containing the semen of two males. Each STR type would be expected to show four bands, two from each male. Also complicating the appearance of the DNA profile may be the presence of DNA from skin cells emanating from the walls of the vagina. In this circumstance, homing in on the Y chromosome greatly simplifies the appearance and interpretation of the DNA profile. Thus, when presented with a DNA mixture of two males and one female, each STR type would be expected to show six bands. However, the same mixture subjected to Y-STR analysis would show only two bands (one band for each male) for each Y-STR type.

Y-STRs
Short tandem repeats located on the human Y chromosome

MyCrimeKit: WebExtra 9.6
Understand the Operational Principles of Capillary Electrophoresis
www.mycrimekit.com

MyCrimeKit: WebExtra 9.7
See the Electropherogram Record from One Individual's DNA
www.mycrimekit.com

MyCrimeKit: WebExtra 9.8
View an Animation Depicting Y-STRs
www.mycrimekit.com

Significance of DNA Typing

STR DNA typing has become an essential and basic investigative tool in the law enforcement community. The technology has progressed at a rapid rate and in only a few years has surmounted numerous legal challenges to become vital evidence for resolving violent crimes and sex offenses. DNA evidence is impartial, implicating the guilty and exonerating the innocent.

Significantly, about 25 percent of the DNA examinations conducted by the FBI Laboratory since 1989 have excluded suspects identified by police as the source of DNA evidence collected from the crime scene. In a number of well-publicized cases, DNA evidence has exonerated individuals who have been wrongly convicted and imprisoned. The importance of DNA analyses in criminal investigations has also placed added burdens on crime laboratories to improve their quality-assurance procedures and to ensure the correctness of their results. In several well-publicized instances, the accuracy of DNA tests conducted by government-funded laboratories has been called into question.

Quick Review

- STRs are locations on the chromosome that contain short sequences that repeat themselves within the DNA molecule. They serve as useful markers for identification because they are found in great abundance throughout the human genome.

- The entire strand of an STR is very short, less than 450 bases long. This makes STRs much less susceptible to degradation, and they are often recovered from bodies or stains that have been subjected to extreme decomposition.

- The more STRs one can characterize, the smaller the percentage of the population from which a particular combination of STRs can emanate. This gives rise to the concept of multiplexing, in which the forensic scientist can simultaneously extract and amplify a combination of different STRs.

- With STR, as little as 125 picograms of DNA is required for analysis—1/100 the amount normally required for RFLP analysis.

Mitochondrial DNA

Typically, when one describes DNA in the context of a criminal investigation, the subject is assumed to be the DNA in the nucleus of a cell. Actually, a human cell contains two types of DNA—nuclear and mitochondrial. The first constitutes the 23 pairs of chromosomes in the nuclei of our cells. Each parent contributes to the genetic makeup of these chromosomes. Mitochondrial DNA (mtDNA), on the other hand, is found outside the nucleus of the cell and is inherited solely from the mother.

Mitochondria are cell structures found in all human cells (see Figure 9–19). They are the power plants of the body, providing about 90 percent of the energy that the body needs to function. A single mitochondrion contains several loops of DNA, all of which are involved in energy generation. Further, because each cell in our bodies contains hundreds to thousands of mitochondria, there are hundreds to thousands of mtDNA copies in a human cell. This compares to just one set of nuclear DNA located in that same cell.

mitochondria
Small structures outside the nucleus that supply energy to the cell

Forensic scientists rely on mtDNA to identify a subject when nuclear DNA is significantly degraded, such as in charred remains, or when nuclear DNA may be present in only very small quantities (such as in a hair shaft). Interestingly, when authorities cannot obtain a reference sample from an individual who may be long deceased or missing, an mtDNA reference sample can be obtained from any maternally related relative. However, all individuals of the same maternal lineage will be indistinguishable by mtDNA analysis.

Although mtDNA analysis is significantly more sensitive than nuclear DNA profiling, forensic analysis of mtDNA is more rigorous, time consuming, and

FIGURE 9-19
Illustration of a human cell containing a nucleus and cell structures involved in cell functions within the cell's cytoplasm. Mitochondria units in the shape of a loop make the energy for the cell. *Courtesy Dorling Kindersley Media Library*

costly than nuclear DNA profiling. For this reason, only a handful of public and private forensic laboratories receive evidence for mtDNA determination. The FBI Laboratory strictly limits the types of cases in which it will apply mtDNA technology.

As was previously discussed, nuclear DNA is composed of a continuous linear strand of nucleotides (*A, C, G,* and *T*). By contrast, mtDNA is constructed in a circular or loop configuration. Each loop contains enough *A, C, G,* and *T* (approximately 16,569 total nucleotides) to make up 37 genes involved in mitochondrial energy generation.

Two regions of mtDNA have been found to be highly variable in the human population. These two regions have been designated hypervariable region I (HV1) and hypervariable region II (HV2), as shown in Figure 9–20. As indicated previously, the process for analyzing HV1 and HV2 is tedious. It involves generating many copies of these DNA hypervariable regions by PCR and then determining the order of the *A–T–C–G* bases constituting the hypervariable regions. This process is known as **sequencing**. The FBI Laboratory, the Armed Forces DNA Identification Laboratory, and other laboratories have collaborated to compile an mtDNA population database containing the base sequences from HV1 and HV2.

Once the sequences of the hypervariable regions from a case sample are obtained, most laboratories simply report the number of times these sequences appear in the mtDNA database maintained by the FBI. The mtDNA database contains about five thousand sequences. This approach permits an assessment of how common or rare an observed mtDNA sequence is in the database.

Interestingly, many of the sequences that have been determined in casework are unique to the existing database, and many types are present at frequencies of no greater than 1 percent in the database. Thus it is often possible to demonstrate

sequencing
A procedure used to determine the order of the base pairs that constitute DNA

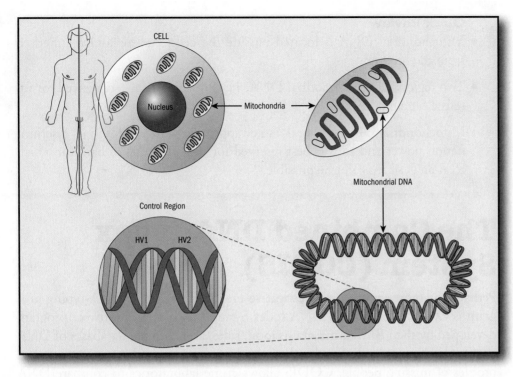

FIGURE 9–20 Every cell in the body contains hundreds of mitochondria, which provide energy to the cell. Each mitochondrion contains numerous copies of DNA shaped in the form of a loop. Distinctive differences between individuals in their mitochondrial DNA makeup are found in two specific seqments of the control region on the DNA loop known as HV1 and HV2.

how uncommon a particular mtDNA sequence is. However, even under the best circumstances, mtDNA typing does not approach STR analysis in its discrimination power. Thus, mtDNA analysis is best reserved for samples for which nuclear DNA typing is simply not possible.

The first time mtDNA was admitted as evidence in a U.S. court was in 1996 in the case of *State of Tennessee v. Paul Ware*. Here, mtDNA was used to link two hairs recovered from the crime scene to the defendant. Interestingly, in this case, blood and semen evidence was absent. Mitochondrial DNA analysis also plays a key role in the identification of human remains. An abundant amount of mtDNA is generally found in skeletal remains. Importantly, mtDNA reference samples are available from family members sharing the same mother, grandmother, great-grandmother, and so on.

One of the most publicized cases performed on human remains was the identification of the individual buried in the tomb of the Vietnam War's unknown soldier. The remains lying in the tomb were believed to belong to First Lt. Michael J. Blassie, whose A-37 warplane was shot down near An Loc, South Vietnam, in 1972. In 1984, the U.S. Army Central Identification Laboratory failed to identify the remains by physical characteristics, personal artifacts, or blood-typing results from hairs. The remains were subsequently placed in the tomb. In 1998, at the insistence of the Blassie family, the remains were disinterred for mtDNA analysis, and the results were compared to references from seven families thought to be associated with the case. The remains in the tomb were subsequently analyzed and confirmed to be consistent with DNA from Lt. Blassie's family.

MyCrimeKit:
WebExtra 9.9
See How We Inherit Our Mitochondrial DNA
www.mycrimekit.com

MyCrimeKit:
WebExtra 9.10
Look into the Structure of Mitochondrial DNA and See How It's Used for DNA Typing
www.mycrimekit.com

Quick Review

- Mitochondrial DNA is located outside the cell's nucleus and is inherited from the mother.

- Two regions of mitochondrial DNA, HV1 and HV2, are sequenced for forensic typing purposes.

- Mitochondrial DNA typing does not approach STR analysis in its discrimination power and thus is best reserved for samples, such as hair, for which STR analysis may not be possible.

The Combined DNA Index System (CODIS)

Perhaps the most significant investigative tool to arise from a DNA-typing program is CODIS (Combined DNA Index System), a computer software program developed by the FBI that maintains local, state, and national databases of DNA profiles from convicted offenders, unsolved crime-scene evidence, arrestees, and profiles of missing people. CODIS allows crime laboratories to compare DNA types recovered from crime-scene evidence to those of convicted sex offenders and other convicted criminals. This capability is of tremendous value to investigators in cases in which the police have not been able to identify a suspect. All 50 states have legislatively mandated collection of DNA samples from convicted offenders of particular crimes and establishment of DNA databases for law enforcement purposes. Thousands of CODIS matches have linked serial crimes to each other and have solved crimes by allowing investigators to match crime-scene evidence to known convicted offenders. The CODIS concept has already had a significant impact on police investigations in various states, as shown by the following case.

Currently, more than 170 public law enforcement laboratories across the United States participate in CODIS. In addition, CODIS is used by more than 40 law enforcement laboratories in more than 25 countries for their own DNA database inquiries. As previously mentioned, state laws now require the acquisition of DNA profiles from all convicted offenders. These profiles are continually added to state and national DNA data banks and have proven to be invaluable investigative resources for law enforcement. CODIS has produced more than 95,000 hits.

Quick Review

- CODIS is a computer software program developed by the FBI that maintains local, state, and national databases of DNA profiles from convicted offenders, unsolved crime-scene evidence, and profiles of missing people.

Collection and Preservation of Biological Evidence for DNA Analysis

Since the early 1990s, the advent of DNA profiling has vaulted biological crime-scene evidence to a stature of importance that is eclipsed only by the fingerprint. In fact, the high sensitivity of DNA determinations has even changed the way police investigators define biological evidence.

Just how sensitive is STR profiling? Forensic analysts using currently accepted protocols can reach sensitivity levels as low as 125 **picograms**. Interestingly, a human cell has an estimated 7 picograms of DNA, which means that only 18 DNA-bearing cells are needed to obtain an STR profile. However, modifications in the technology can readily extend the level of detection down to 9 cells. A quantity of DNA that is below the normal level of detection is defined as a **low copy number**. With this technology in hand, the horizon of the criminal investigator extends beyond the traditional dried blood or semen stain to include stamps and envelopes licked with saliva, a cup or can that has touched a person's lips, chewing gum, the sweat band of a hat, or a bedsheet containing dead skin cells. Likewise, skin or **epithelial cells** transferred onto the surface of a weapon, the interior of a glove, or a pen have yielded DNA results.[3]

The phenomenon of transferring DNA via skin cells onto the surface of an object has come to be called **touch DNA**. Again, keep in mind that, in theory, only 18 skin cells deposited on an object are required to obtain a DNA profile.

picogram
One-trillionth of a gram, or 0.000000000001 gram

low copy number
Fewer than 18 DNA-bearing cells

epithelial cells
The outer layer of skin cells

touch DNA
DNA from skin cells transferred onto the surface of an object by simple contact

Case Files

Cold-Hit Identification

In 1990, a series of attacks on elderly victims were committed in Goldsboro, North Carolina, by an unknown individual dubbed the Night Stalker. During one such attack in March, an elderly woman was brutally raped and almost murdered. Her daughter's early arrival home saved the woman's life. The suspect fled, leaving behind materials intended to burn the residence and the victim in an attempt to conceal the crime.

In July 1990, another elderly woman was raped and murdered in her home. Three months later, a third elderly woman was raped and stabbed to death. Her husband was also murdered. Although their house was set alight in an attempt to cover up the crime, fire and rescue personnel pulled the bodies from the house before it was engulfed in flames. DNA analysis of biological evidence collected from vaginal swabs from the three rape victims enabled authorities to conclude that the same perpetrator had committed all three crimes. However, there was no suspect.

More than ten years after these crimes were committed, law enforcement authorities retested the biological evidence from all three cases using newer DNA technology and entered the DNA profiles into North Carolina's DNA database. The DNA profile developed from the crime-scene evidence was compared to thousands of convicted-offender profiles already in the database.

In April 2001, a "cold hit" was made with an individual in the convicted-offender DNA database. The perpetrator had been convicted of shooting into an occupied dwelling, an offense that requires inclusion in the North Carolina DNA database. The suspect was brought into custody for questioning and was served with a search warrant to obtain a sample of his blood. That sample was analyzed and compared to the crime-scene evidence, confirming the DNA database match. When confronted with the DNA evidence, the suspect confessed to all three crimes.

Source: National Institute of Justice, "Using DNA to Solve Cold Cases," NIJ special report, 2002, http://www.ojp.usdoj. gov/nij/pubs_sum/194197.htm.

The ultimate sensitivity goal in forensic DNA analysis is profiling DNA extracted from one human cell. Such an accomplishment seems close to fruition. Researchers have reported obtaining STR profiles from one or two cells and have profiled DNA from single dermal ridge fingerprints.[4] Although it's premature to imply that this technology, or a comparable one, is eligible for admission in criminal trials, one cannot exclude its use in criminal and forensic intelligence investigations (see Figure 9–21). Table 9–2 illustrates the power of DNA as a creator of physical evidence.

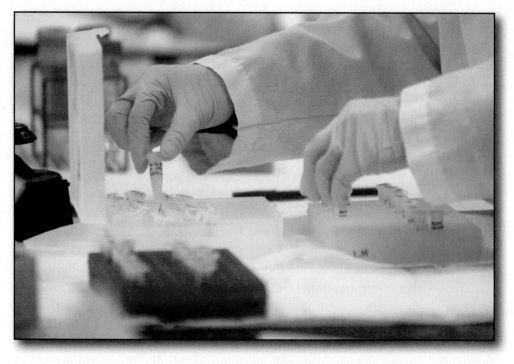

FIGURE 9–21
A criminalist inspects and extracts DNA from crime scene evidence at a DNA crime lab. *Courtesy Corbis*

Table 9–2
Location and Sources of DNA at Crime Scenes

Evidence	Possible Location of DNA on the Evidence	Source of DNA
Baseball bat or similar weapon	Handle, end	Sweat, skin, blood, tissue
Hat, bandanna, or mask	Inside	Sweat, hair, dandruff
Eyeglasses	Nose or ear pieces, lens	Sweat, skin
Facial tissue, cotton swab	Surface area	Mucus, blood, sweat, semen, ear wax
Dirty laundry	Surface area	Blood, sweat, semen
Toothpick	Tips	Saliva
Used cigarette	Cigarette butt	Saliva
Stamp or envelope	Licked area	Saliva
Tape or ligature	Inside/outside surface	Skin, sweat
Bottle, can, or glass	Sides, mouthpiece	Saliva, sweat
Used condom	Inside/outside surface	Semen, vaginal or rectal cells
Blanket, pillow, sheet	Surface area	Sweat, hair, semen, urine, saliva
"Through and through" bullet	Outside surface	Blood, tissue
Bite mark	Person's skin or clothing	Saliva
Fingernail, partial fingernail	Scrapings	Blood, sweat, tissue

Source: National Institute of Justice, U.S. Department of Justice.

Collection of Biological Evidence

Before investigators become enamored with the wonders of DNA, they should first realize that the crime scene must be treated in the traditional manner. Before the collection of evidence begins, biological evidence should be photographed close up and its location relative to the entire crime scene recorded through notes, sketches, and photographs. If the shape and position of bloodstains may provide information about the circumstances of the crime, an expert must immediately evaluate the blood evidence. The significance of the position and shape of blood-stains can best be ascertained when the expert has an on-site overview of the entire crime scene and can better reconstruct the movement of the individuals involved. The blood pattern should not be disturbed before this phase of the investigation is completed.

The evidence collector must handle all body fluids and biologically stained materials with a minimum of personal contact. All body fluids must be assumed to be infectious; hence, wearing disposable latex gloves while handling the evidence is required. Latex gloves also significantly reduce the possibility that the evidence collector will contaminate the evidence. These gloves should be changed frequently during the evidence-collection phase of the investigation. Safety considerations and avoidance of contamination also call for the wearing of face masks, shoe covers, and possibly coveralls.

Blood has great evidential value when a transfer between a victim and suspect can be demonstrated. For this reason, all clothing from both victim and suspect should be collected and sent to the laboratory for examination. This procedure must be followed even when the presence of blood on a garment does not appear obvious to the investigator. Laboratory search procedures are far more revealing and sensitive than any that can be conducted at the crime scene. In addition, blood should also be searched for in less-than-obvious places. For example, the criminal may have wiped his or her hands on materials not readily apparent to the investigator. Investigators should look for towels, handkerchiefs, or rags that may have been used and then hidden and should also examine floor cracks or other crevices that may have trapped blood.

Packaging of Biological Evidence

Biological evidence should not be packaged in plastic or airtight containers, be-cause accumulation of residual moisture could contribute to the growth of DNA-destroying bacteria and fungi. Each stained article should be packaged separately in a paper bag or a well-ventilated box. If feasible, the entire stained article should be packaged and submitted for examination. If this is not possible, dried blood is best removed from a surface with a sterile cotton-tipped swab lightly moistened with distilled water from a dropper bottle.

A portion of the unstained surface material near the recovered stain must like-wise be removed or swabbed and placed in a separate package. This is known as a **substrate control**. The forensic examiner may use the substrate swab to confirm that the results of the tests performed were brought about by the stain and not by the material on which it was deposited. However, this practice is normally not necessary when DNA determinations are carried out in the laboratory. One point

substrate control
An unstained object adjacent to an area on which biological mate-rial has been deposited

is critical: the collected swabs must not be packaged in a wet state. After collection, the swab must be air-dried for approximately five to ten minutes. Then it is best to place it in a swab box (see Figure 9–22), which has a circular hole to allow air circulation. The swab box can then be placed in a paper or manila envelope.

FIGURE 9–22
Air-dried swabs are placed in a swab box for delivery to the forensic laboratory. *Courtesy Tri-Tech, Inc., Southport, N.C., www.tritechusa.com*

All packages containing biological evidence should be refrigerated or stored in a cool location out of direct sunlight until delivery to the laboratory. However, one common exception is blood mixed with soil. Microbes present in soil rapidly degrade DNA. Therefore, blood in soil must be stored in a clean glass or plastic container and immediately frozen.

Obtaining DNA Reference Specimens

Biological evidence attains its full forensic value only when an analyst can compare each of its DNA types to known DNA samples collected from victims and suspects. For this purpose, at least 7 milliliters of whole blood should be drawn from individuals by a qualified medical person. The blood sample should be collected in a sterile vacuum tube containing the preservative EDTA (ethylenediamine tetraacetic acid). In addition to serving as a preservative, EDTA inhibits the activity of enzymes that degrade DNA. The tubes must be kept refrigerated (not frozen) while awaiting transportation to the laboratory.

In addition to blood, other options exist for obtaining standard/reference DNA specimens. The least intrusive method for obtaining a DNA standard/

buccal cells
Cells from the inner
cheek lining

reference, one that nonmedical personnel can readily use, is the *buccal swab*. A swab is placed in the subject's mouth and the inside of the cheek is vigorously swabbed, resulting in the transfer of **buccal cells** onto the swab.

With the increasing need for collection and analysis of DNA samples in forensic investigations, long-term storage of DNA has become an important consideration. FTA paper is a type of commercially available filter paper on which DNA-containing specimens are placed. The card is fixed with bacteriocidal and fungicidal materials that will protect the DNA from microbial and environmental degradation. The card allows the entrapped DNA to be stored without refrigeration for many years. Figure 9–23 illustrates the collection of a buccal swab and its transfer onto an FTA card for storage.

FIGURE 9–23
(a) A buccal swab is collected by rubbing each cheek for 15 seconds. (b) A protective film is peeled of the FTA card. (c) The swab is snapped in place against the FTA paper. (d) The FTA card is removed from the collection device and stored. *Courtesy GE Healthcare Bio-Sciences Corp. (GEHC) Piscataway, N.J., www.whatman.com*

If an individual is not available to give a DNA standard/reference sample, some interesting alternatives are available, including a toothbrush, combs and hairbrushes, a razor, soiled laundry, used cigarette butts, and earplugs. Any of these items may contain a sufficient quantity of DNA for typing. Interestingly, as investigators worked to identify the remains of victims of the World Trade Center attack on September 11, 2001, the families of the missing were asked to supply the New York City DNA Laboratory with these types of items in an effort to match recovered DNA with human remains.

Contamination of DNA Evidence

**MyCrimeKit:
WebExtra 9.11**
View DNA Forensics
www.mycrimekit.com

One key concern during the collection of a DNA-containing specimen is contamination. Contamination can occur by introducing foreign DNA through coughing or sneezing onto a stain during the collection process, or there can be a transfer of DNA when items of evidence are incorrectly placed in contact with each other during packaging. Fortunately, an examination of DNA band patterns in the laboratory readily reveals the presence of contamination. For example, with an STR, one will expect to see a two-band pattern. More than two bands suggests a mixture of DNA from more than one source.

Crime-scene investigators can take some relatively simple steps to minimize contamination of biological evidence:

1. **Change gloves before handling each new piece of evidence.**

2. **Collect a substrate control for possible subsequent laboratory examination.**

3. **Pick up small items of evidence such as cigarette butts and stamps with clean forceps. Disposable forceps are to be used so that they can be discarded after a single evidence collection.**

4. **Always package each item of evidence in its own well-ventilated container.**

A common occurrence at crime scenes is to suspect the presence of blood, but not be able to observe any with the naked eye. In these situations, the common test of choice is luminol (discussed in Chapter 8). Interestingly, luminol does not inhibit the ability to detect and characterize STRs.[5] Therefore, luminol can be used to locate traces of blood and areas that have been washed nearly free of blood without compromising the potential for DNA typing.

Case Files

Contact Lens Evidence

A woman alleged that she had been held against her will and sexually assaulted by a male friend in an apartment. During the course of the assault, a contact lens was knocked from the victim's eye. After the assault, she escaped, but because she was afraid of the threats made by her attacker, she did not report the assault to the police for three days. When the police examined the apartment, they noted that it had been thoroughly cleaned. A vacuum cleaner bag was seized for examination, and several pieces of material resembling fragments of a contact lens were discovered within the bag.

In the laboratory, approximately 20 nanograms of human DNA was recovered from the contact lens fragments. Cells from both the eyeball and the interior of the eyelids are naturally replaced every 6 to 24 hours. Therefore, both are potential sources for the DNA found. The DNA profile originating from the fragments matched the victim, thus corroborating the victim's account of the crime. The estimated population frequency of occurrence for the nine matching STRs are approximately 1 in 850 million. The suspect subsequently pleaded guilty to the offense.

STR Locus	Victim's DNA Type	Contact Lens
D3S1358	15,18	15,18
FGA	24,25	24,25
vWA	17,17	17,17
TH01	6,7	6,7
F13A1	5,6	5,6
fes/fps	11,12	11,12
D5S818	11,12	11,12
D13S317	11,12	11,12
D7S820	10,12	10,12

Source: R. A. Wickenheiser and R. M. Jobin, "Comparison of DNA Recovered from a Contact Lens Using PCR DNA Typing," Canadian Society of Forensic Science Journal 32 (1999): 67.

Quick Review

- Biological evidence should not be packaged in plastic or airtight containers because the accumulation of residual moisture could contribute to the growth of blood-destroying bacteria and fungi. Each article should be packaged separately in a paper bag or in a well-ventilated box.

- The least intrusive method for obtaining a DNA standard/reference is the buccal swab. In this procedure, cotton swabs are placed in the subject's mouth and the inside of the cheek is vigorously swabbed, resulting in the transfer of cells from the inner cheek lining onto the swab.

Chapter Review

- The gene is the fundamental unit of heredity. Each gene is composed of DNA specifically designed to control the genetic traits of our cells.

- DNA is constructed as a very large molecule made by linking a series of repeating units called nucleotides.

- Four types of bases are associated with the DNA structure: adenine (A), guanine (G), cytosine (C), and thymine (T).

- The bases on each strand of DNA are aligned in a double-helix configuration so that adenine pairs with thymine and guanine pairs with cytosine. This concept is known as complementary base pairing.

- The order in which the base pairs are arranged defines the role and function of a DNA molecule.

- DNA replication begins with the unwinding of the DNA strands in the double helix. The double helix is re-created as the nucleotides are assembled in the proper order (A with T and G with C). Two identical copies of DNA emerge from the process.

- PCR (polymerase chain reaction) is a technique for replicating or copying a portion of a DNA strand outside a living cell.

- Recombinant DNA is a process by which the DNA of an organism is altered by inserting into it fragments of DNA from another organism.

- Portions of the DNA molecule contain sequences of bases that are repeated numerous times. These tandem repeats offer a means of distinguishing one individual from another through DNA typing.

- Length differences associated with relatively long repeating DNA strands—called restriction fragment length polymorphisms (RFLPs)—formed the basis for one of the first DNA-typing procedures.

- In the laboratory, DNA molecules are cut up by a restriction enzyme and the resulting fragments are sorted out by electrophoresis.

- Materials undergoing electrophoresis are forced to move across a gel-coated plate under the influence of an electrical potential. Substances such as DNA can be separated and characterized using electrophoresis.

- A typical DNA fragment pattern shows two bands (one RFLP from each chromosome).

- Polymerase chain reaction (PCR) can amplify minute quantities of DNA. The technique evolved from an understanding of how DNA strands naturally replicate within a cell.

- PCR technology cannot be applied to RFLP DNA typing because RFLP strands are too long, often numbering in the thousands of bases. PCR is best used with DNA strands that are no longer than a couple of hundred bases.

- Long RFLP strands tend to break apart under the adverse conditions at many crime scenes. The shorter DNA strands used in PCR are more stable and less subject to degradation caused by adverse environmental conditions.

- STRs are locations on the chromosome that contain short sequences that repeat themselves within the DNA molecule. They serve as useful markers for identification because they are found in great abundance throughout the human genome.

- The entire strand of an STR is very short, less than 450 bases long. This makes STRs much less susceptible to degradation, and they are often recovered from bodies or stains that have been subjected to extreme decomposition.

- The more STRs one can characterize, the smaller the percentage of the population from which a particular combination of STRs can emanate. This gives rise to the concept of multiplexing, in which the forensic scientist can simultaneously extract and amplify a combination of different STRs.

- With STR, as little as 125 picograms of DNA is required for analysis—1/100 the amount normally required for RFLP analysis.

- Mitochondrial DNA is located outside the cell's nucleus and is inherited from the mother.

- Two regions of mitochondrial DNA, HV1 and HV2, are sequenced for forensic typing purposes.

- Mitochondrial DNA typing does not approach STR analysis in its discrimination power and thus is best reserved for samples, such as hair, for which STR analysis may not be possible.

- CODIS is a computer software program developed by the FBI that maintains local, state, and national databases of DNA profiles from convicted offenders, unsolved crime-scene evidence, and profiles of missing people.

- Biological evidence should not be packaged in plastic or airtight containers because the accumulation of residual moisture could contribute to the growth of blood-destroying bacteria and fungi. Each article should be packaged separately in a paper bag or in a well-ventilated box.

- The least intrusive method for obtaining a DNA standard/reference is the buccal swab. In this procedure, cotton swabs are placed in the subject's mouth and the inside of the cheek is vigorously swabbed, resulting in the transfer of cells from the inner cheek lining onto the swab.

Review Questions

1. New technology incorporating _____ has supplanted RFLP.
   a. PCR
   b. STR
   c. mtDNA
   d. CODIS

2. A/An _____ is composed of a sugar molecule, a phosphorus-containing group, and a base
   a. amino acid
   b. protein
   c. chromosomes
   d. nucleotide

3. DNA _____ is the synthesis of new DNA from existing DNA and begins with the unwinding of the DNA strands in the double helix.
   a. transcription
   b. translation
   c. replication
   d. cloning

4. The pairing of nucleotides *A* to *G* and *C* to *T* is known as
   a. mitochondrial DNA.
   b. complementary base pairing.
   c. polymerase chain reaction.
   d. tandem repeats.

5. The inheritable traits that are controlled by DNA arise out of its ability to direct the production of complex molecules called _____ from smaller units called _____.
   a. chromosomes; genes
   b. lipids; triglycerides
   c. proteins; nucleic acids
   d. proteins; amino acids

6. True or False: As the fundamental unit of heredity, genes instruct the body cells to make proteins that determine everything from hair color to susceptibility of disease.

7. True or False: DNA replication is accomplished using a technique known as polymerase chain reaction.

8. True or False: DNA technology is useful in identification because no two humans, except for identical twins, have the same type of tandem repeats in a strand of DNA.

9. True or False: The latest, most successful and widely used DNA profiling procedure is the short tandem repeats.

10. True or False: Mitochondrial DNA is found outside the nucleus of the cell and is inherited solely from the mother.

11. What is DNA and why is it important to forensic scientists?

12. What are genes and what is their function? Of what are genes composed and where are they located?

13. With what discovery are James Watson and Francis Crick credited?

14. Describe the basic structure of the DNA molecule. What is the name given to this type of structure?

15. Name the four bases associated with DNA. How are these bases paired on the DNA molecule?

16. How are proteins made? What determines the shape and function of a protein molecule?

17. What is the human genome? Name two medical applications of information about the human genome.

18. What is PCR? Why is it useful to forensic scientists?

19. What is recombinant DNA? How is recombinant DNA technology used to treat diabetes?

20. What are tandem repeats? How are they useful to forensic scientists?

21. What is a short tandem repeat (STR)? Why are STRs so attractive to forensic scientists?

22. Name two processes by which a forensic scientist can separate STRs for characterization. Which process is preferred and why?

23. What gene is often used to determine the sex of a DNA contributor? What characteristic of the gene allows forensic scientists to make this determination?

24. Name one advantage and three disadvantages of mtDNA analysis compared to nuclear DNA profiling.

25. What is CODIS? How is CODIS useful to forensic scientists?

26. What type of gloves should an evidence collector wear when handling biological evidence? Name two reasons for wearing this type of glove.

27. What type of packaging should not be used for biological evidence? Why? What type of packaging should be used instead for articles containing biological evidence?

28. How should packages containing biological evidence be stored until they are delivered to a laboratory? Name one common exception and describe how it should be stored.

29. List four ways to minimize contamination of biological evidence.

Quick Lab: Buccal Swab

Materials:

Swab/Q-tip
Slide
Light microscope
Methylene blue stain

Procedure:

An important part of obtaining standard/reference samples is determining the DNA profile of any individuals involved in the investigation. One way to do this is by a buccal swab. Take the swab provided by your teacher and rub the inside of your check with it. Next, rub the swab on the slide and add a drop of methylene blue stain; be careful not to get the stain on you or anything but the slide. Place a cover slip on the slide and view it under the microscope.

Follow-Up Questions:

1. How many cells were you able to see on your slide? Were you surprised by the number you saw?

2. What on the slide was stained by the methylene blue?

3. Where in the cell is the DNA located?

Application and Critical Thinking

1. The following sequence of bases is located on one strand of a DNA molecule:

   C–G–A–A–T–C–G–C–A–A–T–C–G–A–C–C–T–G

   List the sequence of bases that will form complementary pairs on the other strand of the DNA molecule.

2. Police discover a badly decomposed body buried in an area where a man disappeared some years before. The case was never solved, nor was the victim's body ever recovered. As the lead investigator, you suspect that the newly discovered body is that of the victim. What is your main challenge in using DNA typing to determine whether your suspicion is correct? How would you go about using DNA technology to test your theory?

3. You are a forensic scientist performing DNA typing on a blood sample sent to your laboratory. While performing an STR analysis on the sample, you notice a four-band pattern. What conclusion should you draw? Why?

4. A woman reports being mugged by a masked assailant, whom she scratched on the arm during a brief struggle. The victim is not sure whether the attacker was male or female. DNA analysts extract and amplify the amelogenin gene

from the epithelial cells under the victim's fingernails (allegedly belonging to the attacker) and from a buccal swab of the victim. The sample is separated by gel electrophoresis with the result shown here. The victim's amelogenin DNA is in lane 2, and the amelogenin DNA from the fingernail scraping is in lane 4. What conclusion can you draw about the attacker from this result? How did you reach this conclusion?

5. At a crime scene you encounter each of the following items. For each item, indicate the potential sources of DNA. The five possible choices are saliva, skin cells, sweat, blood, and semen.

Courtesy Evgeny Karandaev/Shutterstock

6. The 15-STR locus DNA profile of a missing person, James Dittman, is given in the following table.

STR Loci	Allele
D3S1358	15
THO1	6, 9.3
D21S11	27
D18S51	15,16
PENTA E	10
D5S818	11
D13S807	10,13
D7S820	9,10
D16S539	11,12
CSF1PO	13
PENTA D	12,13
AMELOGENIN	XY
VWA	17, 19
D8S1179	10, 13
TPOX	8, 12
FGA	21

Decomposing remains were found deep in the woods near the missing person's house. DNA from these remains was extracted, amplified, and analyzed at 15 STR loci. Compare the resulting STR readout shown on the following page to determine whether the remains could belong to James Dittman. If not, at which STR loci do the profiles differ?

**Virtual Lab:
Conduct a
DNA Analysis**

To perform a virtual DNA lab analysis, go to www.pearsoncustom. com/us/vlm/

Endnotes

1. Instructions for assembling proteins are carried from DNA to another region of the cell by ribonucleic acid (RNA). RNA is directly involved in the assembly of the protein, using the genetic code it received from DNA.

2. Applied Biosystems, 850 Lincoln Centre Drive, Foster City, CA 94404.

3. R. A. Wickenheiser, "Trace DNA: A Review, Discussion of Theory, and Application of the Transfer of Trace Quantities through Skin Contact," *Journal of Forensic Sciences* 47 (2002): 442.

4. E. K. Hanson and J. Ballantyne, "Whole Genome Amplification Strategy for Forensic Genetic Analysis Using Single or Few Cell Equivalents of Genomic DNA," *Analytical Biochemistry* 346 (2005): 246.

5. A. M. Gross et al., "The Effect of Luminol on Presumptive Tests and DNA Analysis Using the Polymerase Chain Reaction," *Journal of Forensic Sciences* 44 (1999): 837.

National Science Content Standards

Scientific Inquiry

Physical Science

Life Science

The Sam Sheppard Case: A Trail of Blood

Convicted in 1954 of bludgeoning his wife to death, Dr. Sam Sheppard achieved celebrity status when the storyline of TV's *The Fugitive* was apparently modeled on his efforts to seek vindication for the crime he professed not to have committed. Dr. Sheppard, a physician, claimed he was dozing on his living room couch when his pregnant wife, Marilyn, was attacked. Sheppard's story was that he quickly ran upstairs to stop the carnage, but was knocked unconscious briefly by the intruder. The suspicion that fell on Dr. Sheppard was fueled by the revelation that he was having an adulterous affair. At trial, the local coroner testified that a pool of blood on Marilyn's pillow contained the impression of a "surgical instrument." After Sheppard had been imprisoned for ten years, the U.S. Supreme Court set aside his conviction because of the "massive, pervasive, and prejudicial publicity" that had attended his trial.

In 1966, the second Sheppard trial commenced. This time, the same coroner was forced to back off from his insistence that the bloody outline of a surgical instrument was present on Marilyn's pillow. However, a medical technician from the coroner's office now testified that blood on Dr. Sheppard's watch was from blood spatter, indicating that Dr. Sheppard was wearing the watch in the presence of the battering of his wife. The defense countered with the expert testimony of eminent criminalist Dr. Paul Kirk. Dr. Kirk concluded that blood spatter marks in the bedroom showed the killer to be left-handed. Dr. Sheppard was right-handed.

Dr. Kirk further testified that Sheppard stained his watch while attempting to obtain a pulse reading. After less than 12 hours of deliberation, the jury failed to convict Sheppard. But the ordeal had taken its toll. Four years later Sheppard died, a victim of drug and alcohol abuse.

Crime-Scene Reconstruction: Bloodstain Pattern Analysis

10

Key Terms

angle of impact
area of convergence
area of origin
arterial spray
back spatter
cast-off
crime-scene reconstruction
drip trail pattern
expirated blood pattern
flow patterns

forward spatter
high-velocity spatter
impact spatter
low-velocity spatter
medium-velocity spatter
satellite spatter
skeletonization
transfer pattern
void

Crime-Scene Reconstruction

Previous discussions of identification and comparison have stressed laboratory work routinely performed by forensic scientists. However, there is another dimension to the role of forensic scientists in a criminal investigation: working as a team to reconstruct events before, during, and after the commission of a crime.

Reconstructing the circumstances of a crime scene entails a collaborative effort that includes experienced law enforcement personnel, medical examiners, and criminalists. All of the professionals contribute a unique perspective to develop the **crime-scene reconstruction**. Was more than one person involved? How was the victim killed? Were actions taken to cover up what actually took place? To answer these questions, everyone involved with the investigation must pay careful attention and apply logical thinking.

Crime-scene reconstruction is the method used to support a likely sequence of events at a crime scene by observing and evaluating physical evidence and statements made by individuals involved with the incident. The evidence may also include information obtained from reenactments. Therefore, reconstructions have the best chance of being accurate when investigators use proper documentation and collection methods for all types of evidence.

crime-scene reconstruction
The method used to support a likely sequence of events at a crime scene by the observation and evaluation of physical evidence and statements made by individuals involved with the incident

Principles of Crime-Scene Reconstruction

The physical evidence left behind at a crime scene plays a crucial role in reconstructing the events that took place surrounding the crime. Although the evidence alone does not describe everything that happened, it can support or contradict accounts given by witnesses and/or suspects. Information obtained from physical evidence can also generate leads and confirm the reconstruction of a crime to a jury. The collection and documentation of physical evidence is the foundation of a reconstruction. Reconstruction supports a likely sequence of events by observing and evaluating physical evidence and statements made by witnesses and those involved with the incident.

Law enforcement personnel must take proper action to enhance all aspects of the crime-scene search so as to optimize the crime-scene reconstruction. First, and most important, is securing and protecting the crime scene. Protecting the scene is a continuous endeavor from the beginning to the end of the search. Evidence that can be invaluable to reconstructing the crime can be unknowingly altered or destroyed by people trampling through the scene, rendering the evidence useless. The issue of possible contamination of evidence will certainly be attacked during the litigation process and could make the difference between a guilty and not-guilty verdict.

Before processing the crime scene for physical evidence, the investigator should make a preliminary examination of the scene as it was left by the perpetrator. Each crime scene presents its own set of circumstances. The investigator's experience and the presence or absence of physical evidence become critical factors in reconstructing a crime.

The investigator captures the nature of the scene as a whole by performing an initial walk-through of the crime scene and contemplating the events that took place. Using the physical evidence available to the naked eye, he or she can hypothesize about what occurred, where it occurred, and when it occurred. During the walk-through, the investigator must document observations and formulate how the scene should ultimately be processed.

As the collection of physical evidence begins, any and all observations should be recorded through photographs, sketches, and notes. By carefully collecting physical evidence and thoroughly documenting the crime scene, the investigator can begin to unravel the sequence of events that took place during the commission of the crime.

Personnel Involved in Reconstruction

Often reconstruction requires the involvement of a medical examiner or a criminalist. For example, a trained medical examiner may determine whether a corpse has been moved after death by evaluating the livor distribution within the body. If livor has developed in areas other than those closest to the ground, the medical examiner can reason that the victim was probably moved after death. Likewise, the examiner can determine whether the victim was clothed after death, because livor will not develop within areas of the body that are restricted by clothing. Such determinations can often reveal pertinent information that will aid the investigation.

A criminalist or trained crime-scene investigator can also bring special skills to the reconstruction of events that occurred during the commission of a crime. For example, a criminalist using a laser beam to plot the approximate bullet path in trajectory analysis can help determine the probable position of the shooter relative to that of the victim (see Figure 10–1). Other skills that a criminalist may employ during a crime-scene reconstruction analysis include blood spatter analysis (discussed in this chapter), determining the direction of impact of projectiles penetrating glass objects (Chapter 4), locating gunshot residues deposited on the victim's clothing to estimate the distance of a shooter from a target, and searching for primer residues deposited on the hands of a suspect shooter (both covered in Chapter 16).

FIGURE 10-1 A laser beam is used to determine the search area for the position of a shooter who has fired a bullet through a window and wounded a victim. The bullet path is determined by lining up the victim's bullet wound with the bullet hole in the glass pane.

Reconstruction is a team effort that involves putting together many different pieces of a puzzle (see Figure 10–2). The right connections must be made among all the parts involved so as to portray the relationship among the victim, the suspect, and the crime scene. If successful, reconstruction can play a vital role in helping a jury arrive at an appropriate verdict.

FIGURE 10-2 Crime-scene reconstruction relies on the combined efforts of medical examiners, criminalists, and law enforcement personnel to recover physical evidence and to sort out the events surrounding the occurrence of a crime.

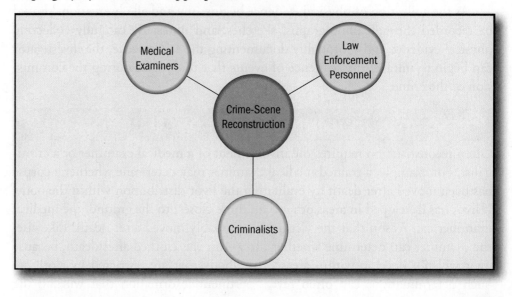

Quick Review

- Crime-scene reconstruction relies on the combined efforts of medical examiners, criminalists, and law enforcement personnel to recover physical evidence and to sort out the events surrounding the occurrence of a crime.

- Examples of crime-scene reconstruction include determining whether a body was moved after death, determining whether a victim was clothed after death, analyzing bullet trajectory, analyzing blood spatter, determining the direction from which projectiles penetrated glass objects, estimating the distance of a shooter from a target, and locating primer residue on suspects.

General Features of Bloodstain Formation

Crimes involving violent contact between individuals are frequently accompanied by bleeding and resultant bloodstain patterns. Crime-scene analysts have come to appreciate that bloodstain patterns deposited on floors, walls, ceilings, bedding, and other relevant objects can provide valuable insights into events that occurred during the commission of a violent crime. The information one is likely to uncover as a result of bloodstain pattern interpretation includes the following:

- The direction from which blood originated

- The angle at which a blood droplet struck a surface

- The location or position of a victim at the time a bloody wound was inflicted

- The movement of a bleeding individual at the crime scene

- The minimum number of blows that struck a bleeding victim
- The approximate location of an individual delivering blows that produced a bloodstain pattern

The crime-scene investigator must not overlook the fact that the location, distribution, and appearance of bloodstains and spatters may be useful for interpreting and reconstructing the events that accompanied the bleeding. A thorough analysis of the significance of the position and shape of blood patterns with respect to their origin and trajectory is exceedingly complex and requires the services of an examiner who is experienced in such determinations. Most important, the interpretation of bloodstain patterns necessitates a carefully planned control experiment using surface materials comparable to those found at the crime scene. This chapter presents the basic principles and common deductions behind bloodstain pattern analysis to give the reader general knowledge to use at the crime scene.

MyCrimeKit: WebExtra 10.1

See How Bloodstain Spatter Patterns Are Formed www.mycrimekit.com

Surface Texture

Surface texture is of paramount importance in the interpretation of bloodstain patterns; comparisons between standards and unknowns are valid only when identical surfaces are used. In general, harder and nonporous surfaces (such as glass or smooth tile) result in less spatter. Rough surfaces, such as a concrete floor or wood, usually result in irregularly shaped stains with serrated edges, possibly with **satellite spatter** (see Figure 10–3).

satellite spatter
Small drops of blood that are distributed around the perimeter of a drop or pool of blood and were produced as a result of the blood impacting the target surface

FIGURE 10-3 (a) A bloodstain from a single drop of blood that struck a glass surface after falling 24 inches. (b) A bloodstain from a single drop of blood that struck a cotton muslin sheet after falling 24 inches. *Courtesy A.Y. Wonder*

Direction and Angle of Impact

An investigator may discern the direction of travel of blood striking an object by studying the stain's shape. As the stain becomes more elliptical in shape, its direction becomes more discernible because the pointed end of a bloodstain faces its direction of travel. The distorted or disrupted edge of an elongated stain indicates the direction of travel of the blood drop. Satellite spatter coming off of parent stains will have the pointed end facing against the direction of travel. In Figure 10–4, the bloodstain pattern was produced by several droplets of blood that were traveling from left to right before striking a flat, level surface.

FIGURE 10-4   A bloodstain pattern produced by droplets of blood that were traveling from left to right. *Courtesy A.Y. Wonder*

angle of impact
The angle formed between the path of a blood drop and the surface that it contacts

It is possible to determine the impact angle of blood on a flat surface by measuring the degree of circular distortion of the stain. A drop deposited at an **angle of impact** of about 90 degrees (directly vertical to the surface) will be approximately circular in shape with no tail or buildup of blood. However, as the angle of impact deviates from 90 degrees, the stain becomes elongated in shape. Buildup of blood will show up in the larger angles, whereas longer and longer tails will appear as the angle of impact becomes smaller (see Figure 10–5).

Inside the Science

Determining the Angle of Impact of Bloodstains

The distorted or disrupted edge of an elongated stain indicates the direction of travel of the blood drop. One may establish the location or origin of bloodshed by determining the directionality of the stain and the angle at which blood came into contact with the landing surface. To determine the angle of impact, calculate the stain's length-to-width ratio and apply the formula:

$$\sin A = \frac{width\ of\ blood\ stain}{length\ of\ blood\ stain}$$

where A = the angle of impact.

For example, suppose the width of a stain is 11 mm and the length is 22 mm. Then,

$$\sin A = \frac{11mm}{22mm} = (11mm \div 22mm) = 0.50$$

A scientific calculator having the trigonometric function will calculate that the inverse sine of 0.50 is equal to a 30-degree angle.

Note: The measurements for length and width should be made with a ruler, micrometer, or photographic loupe.

FIGURE 10-5 The higher pattern is of a single drop of human blood that fell 24 inches and struck hard, smooth cardboard at 50 degrees. On this drop the collection of blood shows the direction. The lower pattern is of a single drop of human blood that fell 24 inches and struck hard, smooth cardboard at 15 degrees. On this drop the tail shows the direction. *Courtesy A.Y. Wonder*

Quick Review

- Individual bloodstains can convey to the bloodstain analyst the directionality and angle of impact of the blood when it impacted a surface. Bloodstain patterns may convey to the analyst the location of victims or suspects, the movement of bleeding individuals, and the number of blows delivered.

- Surface texture is of paramount importance in the interpretation of bloodstain patterns; rounder drops generally are produced from smooth, nonporous surfaces, whereas rough surfaces create irregular-edged drops. However, correlations between standards and unknowns are valid only if identical surfaces are used.

- The direction of travel of blood striking an object may be discerned by the stain's shape. The pointed end of a bloodstain always faces in its direction of travel.

- The angle of impact of an individual bloodstain can be approximated by the degree of distortion or lengthening of the bloodstain, or it can be more effectively estimated using the ratio of width/length of the stain.

Impact Bloodstain Spatter Patterns

The most common type of bloodstain pattern found at a crime scene is **impact spatter**. This pattern occurs when an object impacts a source of blood. The spatter projected outward and away from the source, such as an exit wound, is called **forward spatter**. **Back spatter**, sometimes called *blow-back spatter*, consists of the blood projected backward from a source, such as an entrance wound, potentially being deposited on the object or person creating the impact. Impact spatter patterns consist of many droplets radiating in direct lines from the origin of blood to the target (see <u>Figure 10–6</u>).

impact spatter
A bloodstain pattern produced when an object makes forceful contact with a source of blood, projecting drops of blood outward from the source

forward spatter
Blood that travels away from the source in the same direction as the force that caused the spatter

back spatter
Blood directed back toward the source of the force that caused the spatter

FIGURE 10-6 Impact spatter produced by an automatic weapon. The arrows show the multiple directions of travel from origin of impact as several different bullets struck the target. *Courtesy A.Y. Wonder*

Investigators have derived a common classification system of impact spatter from the velocity of a blood droplet. In general, as the force of the impact on the source of blood increases, so does the velocity of the blood drops emanating from the source. It is also generally true that as both the force and velocity of impact increase, the diameter of the resulting blood drops decreases.

Classifying Impact Spatter

Low-Velocity Spatter An impact pattern consisting of a preponderance of large separate or compounded drops with diameters of 4 millimeters or more is known as **low-velocity spatter**. This kind of spatter is normally produced by gravity alone, by a minimal force, or by an object dropping into and splashing blood from a blood pool. Low-velocity stains can result from an applied force of up to 5 feet per second.

Medium-Velocity Spatter A pattern consisting predominantly of small drops with diameters from 1 to 3 millimeters or smaller is classified as **medium-velocity spatter**. This type of impact spatter is normally associated with blunt force trauma to an individual, or other applied forces between 5 to 25 feet per second.

low-velocity spatter
An impact spatter pattern created by a force traveling at 5 feet per second or less and producing drops with diameters greater than 3 millimeters

medium-velocity spatter
An impact spatter pattern created by a force traveling at 5 to 25 feet per second and producing drops with diameters between 1 and 3 millimeters

high-velocity spatter
An impact spatter pattern created by a force traveling at 100 feet per second or faster and producing drops with diameters less than 1 millimeter

High-Velocity Spatter Very fine droplets with a preponderance of diameters of less than 1 millimeter are classified as **high-velocity spatter**. Here the spatter can result from an applied force of 100 feet per second or faster. Gunshot exit wounds or explosions commonly produce this type of spatter. However, because the droplets are very small, they may not travel far; they may fall to the floor or ground where investigative personnel could overlook them.

Using droplet size to classify impact patterns by velocity is a useful tool for giving investigators insight into the general nature of a crime. However, the classifications of low, medium, and high velocity cannot illuminate the specific events that produced the stain size pattern. For example, beatings can produce high-velocity spatter or stain size patterns that look more like low-velocity spatter. In general, one should use stain size categories very cautiously and for descriptive purposes only in evaluating impact spatter patterns. A more acceptable approach for classifying a bloodstain pattern should encompass stain size, shape, location, and distribution.

As we will learn, blood spatter patterns can arise from a number of distinctly different sources. Illustrations of patterns emanating from impact (just discussed), cast-off (on <u>pages 388–389</u>), and arterial spray (on <u>page 390</u>) are shown in <u>Figure 10–7</u>.

FIGURE 10-7 A

FIGURE 10-7 B

FIGURE 10-7
(a) The action associated with producing impact spatter.
(b) The action associated with producing cast-off spatter.
(c) The action associated with producing arterial spray spatter.
Courtesy of A.Y. Wonder

FIGURE 10-7 C

Origin-of-Impact Patterns

Impact spatter patterns can offer investigators clues that help determine the origin of the blood source and the position of the victim at the time of the impact.

Area of Convergence The **area of convergence** is the area on a two-dimensional plane from which the drops originated. This can be established by drawing straight lines through the long axis of several individual bloodstains, following the line of their tails. The intersection of these lines is the area of convergence, and the approximate area of origin will be on a line straight out from this area. Figure 10–8 illustrates how to draw lines to find an area of convergence.

An object hitting a source of blood numerous times will never produce exactly the same pattern each time. One may therefore determine the number of impacts by drawing the area of convergence for groups of stains from separate impacts.

area of convergence
The area on a two-dimensional plane where lines traced through the long axis of several individual bloodstains meet; this approximates the two-dimensional place from which the bloodstains were projected

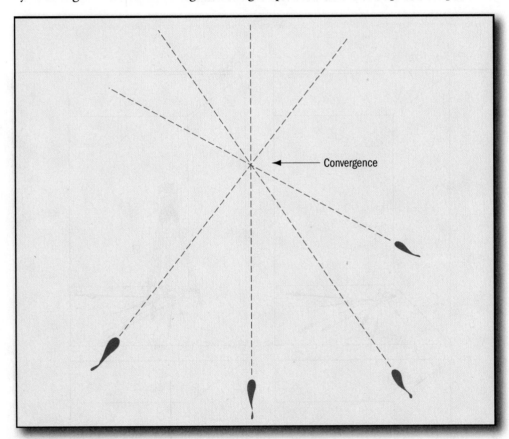

Convergence

FIGURE 10-8 An illustration of stain convergence on a two-dimensional plane. Convergence represents the area from which the stains emanated. *Courtesy Judith Bunker, J.L. Bunker & Assoc., Ocoee, FL*

Area of Origin It may also be important to determine the **area of origin** of a bloodstain pattern, the area in a three-dimensional space from which the blood was projected. This will show the position of the victim or suspect in space when the stain-producing event took place. The distribution of the drops in an impact pattern gives a general idea of the distance from the blood source to the blood-stained surface. Impact patterns produced at a distance close to the surface will appear as clustered stains. As the distance from the surface increases, so do the distribution and distance between drops.

area of origin
The location in three-dimensional space from which blood that produced a blood-stain originated. The location of the area of convergence and the angle of impact for each bloodstain is used to approximate this area

A common method for determining the area of origin at the crime scene is called the string method. Figure 10–9 illustrates the steps in the string method:

1. Find the area of convergence for the stain pattern.

2. Place a pole or stand as an axis coming from the area of convergence.

3. Attach one end of a string next to each droplet. Place a protractor next to each droplet and lift the string until it lines up with the determined angle of impact of the drop. Keeping the string in line with the angle, attach the other end of the string to the axis pole.

4. View the area of origin of the drops where the strings appear to meet. Secure the strings at this area.

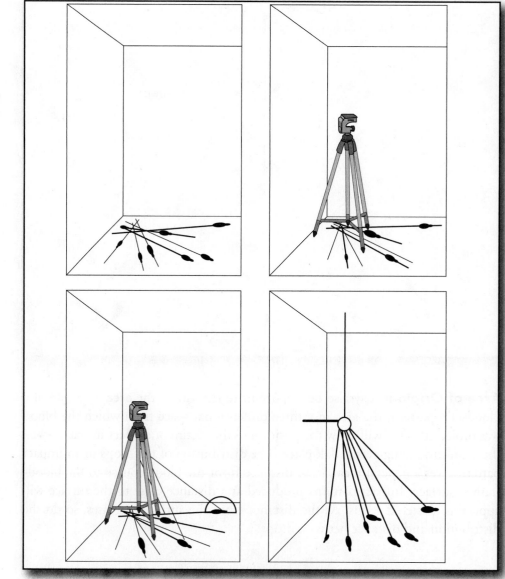

FIGURE 10-9 An illustration of the string method used at a crime scene to determine the area of origin of blood spatter. *Courtesy Bloodstain Pattern Evidence by Anita Y. Wonder, p. 47. Copyright Elsevier, 2007*

Quick Review

- An impact spatter pattern occurs when an object impacts a source of blood. This produces forward spatter projected forward from the source and back spatter projected backward from the source.

- Impact spatter patterns can be classified as low velocity (>3 mm drops), medium velocity (1–3 mm drops), or high velocity (<1 mm drops) for descriptive purposes. These categories should not be used to assume what kind of force created the pattern.

- The area of convergence is the point on a two-dimensional plane from which the drops of an impact spatter pattern originated. This area can be estimated by drawing straight lines through the long axis of several individual bloodstains, following the line of their tails.

- The area of origin of a bloodstain pattern is the area in three-dimensional space where blood was projected from, showing the position of the victim or suspect when the stain-producing event took place. The string method is commonly used at a crime scene to approximate the position of the area of origin.

More Bloodstain Spatter Patterns

Gunshot Spatter

A shooting may leave a distinct gunshot spatter pattern. This may be characterized by both forward spatter from an exit wound and back spatter from an entrance wound. Forward spatter generally leaves a pattern of very fine droplets characteristic of high-velocity spatter (see Figure 10–10). Medium and large sized drops of spatter may also be observed within the pattern.

FIGURE 10-10 The high-velocity spatter from the cone-shaped deposit of gunshot spatter. *Courtesy A.Y. Wonder*

The location of the injury, the size of the wound created, and the distance between the victim and the muzzle of the weapon all affect the amount of back spatter that occurs. Finding high-velocity spatter containing the victim's blood on a suspect can help investigators place the suspect in the vicinity when the gun was discharged. Back spatter created by a firearm discharge generally contains fewer and smaller atomized stains than does forward spatter. A muzzle blast striking an entrance wound is expected to cause the formation of atomized blood.

Depending on the distance from the victim at which the gun was discharged, some back spatter may strike the shooter and enter the gun muzzle. This is called the drawback effect. Blood within the muzzle of a gun can place the weapon in the vicinity of the gunshot wound. The presence of blow-back spatter on a weapon's muzzle is consistent with the weapon being close to the victim at the time of firing (see Figure 10–11).

FIGURE 10-11 Back spatter bloodstains entering the muzzle of a weapon discharged in close proximity to a victim. *Courtesy of Ralph R. Ristenbatt III and Robert Shaler*

Cast-Off Spatter

cast-off
A bloodstain pattern that is created when blood is flung from a blood-bearing object in motion onto a surface

A **cast-off** pattern is created when a blood-covered object flings blood in an arc onto a nearby surface. This kind of pattern commonly occurs when a person pulls a bloody fist or weapon back between delivering blows to a victim (see Figure 10–7(b)). The bloodstain tails will point in the direction in which the object was moving.

The width of the cast-off pattern created by a bloody object may help suggest the kind of object that produced the pattern. The sizes of the drops are directly related to the size of the point from which they were propelled. Drops propelled from a small or pointed surface will be smaller and the pattern more linear; drops propelled from a large or blunt surface will be larger and the pattern wider. The volume of blood deposited on an object from the source also affects the size and number of drops in the cast-off pattern. The less blood on the object, the smaller the stains produced. The pattern may also suggest whether the blow that caused the pattern was directed from right to left or left to right. The pattern will point in the direction of the backward thrust, which will be opposite the direction of the blow. This could suggest which hand the assailant used to deliver the blows.

Cast-off patterns may also show the minimum number of blows delivered to a victim. Each blow should be marked by an upward-and-downward or forward-and-backward arc pattern (see Figure 10–12). By counting and pairing the patterns, one can estimate the minimum number of blows. An investigator should

Case Files Blood Spatter Evidence

Stephen Scher banged on the door of a cabin in the woods outside Montrose, Pennsylvania. According to Scher, his friend, Marty Dillon, had just shot himself while chasing after a porcupine. The two had been skeet shooting at Scher's cabin, enjoying a friendly sporting weekend, when Dillon spotted a porcupine and took off out of sight. Scher heard a single shot and waited to hear his friend's voice. After a few moments, he chased after Dillon and found him lying on the ground near a tree stump, bleeding from a wound in his chest. Scher administered CPR after locating his dying friend, but he was unable to save Dillon, who later died from his injuries. Police found that Dillon's untied boot had been the cause of his shotgun wound. They determined that he had tripped while running with his loaded gun and shot himself. The grief-stricken Scher aroused no suspicion, so the shooting was ruled an accident.

Shortly thereafter, Scher moved from the area, divorced his wife, and married Dillon's widow. This was too suspicious to be ignored; police reopened the case and decided to reconstruct the crime scene.

The reconstruction provided investigators with several pieces of blood evidence that pointed to Scher as Dillon's murderer.

Police noticed that Scher's boots bore the unmistakable spray of high-velocity impact blood spatter, evidence that he was standing within an arm's length of Dillon when Dillon was shot. This pattern of bloodstains cannot be created while administering CPR, as Scher claimed had happened. The spatter pattern also clearly refuted Scher's claim that he did not witness the incident. In addition, the tree stump near Dillon's body bore the same type of blood spatter, in a pattern that indicated Dillon was seated on the stump and not running when he was shot. Finally, Dillon's ears were free of the high-velocity blood spatter that covered his face, but blood was on his hearing protectors found nearby. This is a clear indication that he was wearing his hearing protectors when he was shot, and they were removed before investigators arrived. This and other evidence resulted in Scher's conviction for the murder of his long-time friend Marty Dillon.

take into consideration that the first blow would only cause blood to pool to the area; it would not produce a cast-off pattern. Also, some blows may not come into contact with blood and so will not produce a pattern. The medical examiner is in the best position to estimate the number of blows a victim received.

FIGURE 10-12
The cast-off pattern created from one backward and one forward motion of an overhand swing. The larger drops are away from the victim because they're made when the weapon holds the greatest amount of blood. The smaller spatters are directed toward the victim. Source: Bloodstain Pattern Evidence by Anita Y. Wonder, p. 295. *Copyright Elsevier, 2007*

Arterial Spray Spatter

arterial spray
A characteristic bloodstain pattern containing spurts that resulted from blood exiting under pressure from an arterial injury

Arterial spray spatter is created when a victim suffers an injury to a main artery or the heart. The pressure of the continuing pumping of blood causes blood to spurt out of the injured area (see Figure 10–7(c)). Commonly, the pattern shows large spurted stains for each time the heart pumps. Some radial spikes, satellite spatter, or flow patterns may be evident because of the large volume of blood being expelled with each spurt. Drops may also be seen on the surface in fairly uniform size and shape and in parallel arrangement (see Figure 10–13).

FIGURE 10-13 Arterial spray spatter found at a crime scene where a victim suffered injury to an artery. *Courtesy Norman H. Reeves, Bloodstain Pattern Analysis, Tucson, AZ, www.bloody1.com*

The lineup of the stains shows the victim's movement. Any vertical arcs or waves in the line show fluctuations in blood pressure. The larger arterial stains are at the end of the overall pattern. The site of the initial injury to the artery can be found where the pattern begins with the biggest spurt. Arterial patterns can also be differentiated because the oxygenated blood spurting from the artery tends to be a brighter red color than blood expelled from impact wounds.

Expirated Blood Patterns

A pattern created by blood that is expelled from the mouth or nose from an internal injury is called an **expirated blood pattern**. If the blood that creates such a pattern is under great pressure, it produces very fine high-velocity spatter. Expirated blood at very low velocities produces a stain cluster with irregular edges (see Figure 10–14). The presence of bubbles of air in the drying drops can differentiate a pattern created by expirated blood from other types of bloodstains. Expirated blood also may be lighter in color when compared to impact spatter as a result of dilution by saliva. The presence of expirated blood gives an important clue as to the injuries suffered and the events that took place at a crime scene.

expirated blood pattern
A pattern created by blood that is expelled out of the nose, mouth, or respiratory system as a result of air pressure and/or airflow

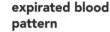

FIGURE 10-14 An example of expirated blood expelled with two wheezes from the mouth. *Courtesy A.Y. Wonder*

Void Patterns

A **void** is created when an object blocks the deposition of blood spatter onto a target surface or object (see Figure 10–15). The spatter is deposited onto the object or person instead. The blank space on the surface or object may give a clue as to the size and shape of the missing object or person. Once the object or person is found, the missing piece of the pattern should fit in, much like a puzzle piece, with the rest of the pattern. Voids may be applicable for establishing the body position of the victim or assailant at the time of the incident.

void
An area within a deposited spatter pattern that is clear of spatter, caused by an object or person blocking the area at the time of the spatter's deposition

FIGURE 10-15 A void pattern is found behind the door where the surface of the door blocked the deposition of spatter on that area. This void, and the presence of spatter on the door, shows that the door was open when the spatter was deposited. *Courtesy Norman H. Reeves*, Bloodstain Pattern Analysis, *Tucson, AZ, www.bloody1.com*

Quick Review

- Gunshot spatter can consist of both forward spatter from an exit wound and back spatter from an entrance wound; however, only back spatter will be produced if the bullet does not exit the body.

- A cast-off pattern is created when a blood-covered object flings blood in an arc onto a nearby surface. This kind of pattern commonly occurs when a person pulls a bloody fist or weapon back between delivering blows to a victim.

- The characteristic arterial spray spatter is created when a victim suffers an injury to a main artery or the heart and the pressure of the continuing pumping of blood projects blood out of the injured area in spurts, which are apparent in the pattern.

- Expired blood is expelled from the mouth or nose and may appear as very fine high-velocity spatter or large low-velocity bloodstain clusters. This kind of pattern may contain bubbles of oxygen or be mixed with saliva.

- A void pattern features an area free of spatter where an object (or person) blocks the deposition of blood spatter onto a target surface or object. Because the spatter is deposited onto the object or person instead, the shape of the void may give a clue as to the size and shape of the missing object or person.

Other Bloodstain Patterns

Not all bloodstains at a crime scene appear as spatter patterns. The circumstances of the crime often create other types of stains that can be useful to investigators.

Contact/Transfer Patterns

transfer pattern
A bloodstain pattern created when a surface that carries wet blood comes in contact with a second surface; recognizable imprints of all or a portion of the original surface or the direction of movement may be observed

When an object with blood on it touches one that does not have blood on it, this produces a contact or **transfer pattern**. Examples of transfers with features include fingerprints (see Figure 10–16), handprints, footprints, footwear prints, tool prints, and fabric prints in blood. These may provide further leads by offering individual characteristics.

The size and general shape of a tool may be seen in a simple transfer. This can lead to narrowing the possible tools by class characteristics. A transfer that shows a very individualistic feature may help point to the tool that made the pattern. Simple transfer patterns are produced when the object makes contact with the surface and the object is removed without any movement. Other transfers known as *swipe patterns* may be caused by movement of the bloody object across a surface. Generally, the pattern will lighten and "feather" as the pattern moves away from the initial contact point (Figure 10–17). However, since "feathering" is also a function of the amount of pressure being applied to the surface, the analyst must interpret directionality with care. The direction of separate bloody transfers, such as footwear prints in blood, may show the movement of the suspect, victim, or others through the crime scene after the blood was present. The first transfer pattern will be dark and heavy with blood, whereas subsequent transfers will be increasingly lighter in color. As the transfers get lighter, less and

FIGURE 10-16 A transfer pattern consisting of bloody fingerprints with apparent ridge detail. *Courtesy Lawrence A. Presley, Arcadia University*

less of the transferring object's surface will deposit visible traces of blood. Bloody shoe imprints may also suggest whether the wearer was running or walking. Running typically produces imprints with more space between them and more satellite or drop patterns between each imprint.

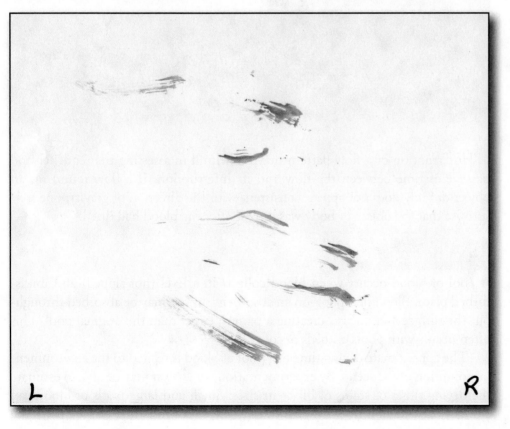

FIGURE 10-17 A series of swipe patterns moving from right to left. *Courtesy A.Y. Wonder*

flow pattern
A bloodstain pattern formed by the movement of small or large amounts of blood as a result of gravity's pull

Flows

Patterns made by drops or large amounts of blood flowing by the pull of gravity are called **flow patterns**, or flows. Flows may be formed by single drops or large volumes of blood coming from an actively bleeding wound or blood deposited on a surface from an arterial spurt. Clotting of the blood's solid parts may occur when a flow extends onto an absorbent surface.

The flow direction may show movements of objects or bodies while the flow was still in progress or after the blood had dried. Figure 10–18 illustrates a situation in which movement of the surface while the flow was still in progress led to a specific pattern.

FIGURE 10-18
The flow pattern suggests that the victim was upright and then fell while blood flowed. The assailant claimed the victim was stabbed while sleeping. *Source: Bloodstain Pattern Evidence by Anita Y. Wonder, p. 98. Copyright Elsevier, 2007*

Interruption of a flow pattern may be helpful in assessing the sequence and passage of time between the flow and its interruption. If a flow found on an object or body does not appear consistent with the direction of gravity, one may surmise that the object or body was moved after the blood had dried.

Pools

A pool of blood occurs when blood collects in a level (not sloped) and undisturbed place. Blood that pools on an absorbent surface may be absorbed throughout the surface and diffuse, creating a pattern larger than the original pool. This often occurs with pools on beds or sofas.

The approximate drying time of a pool of blood is related to the environmental condition of the scene. By experimentation, an analyst may be able to estimate the drying times of stains of different sizes. Small and large pools of blood can aid in reconstruction by providing an estimate of the time that elapsed since the blood was deposited. Considering the drying time of a blood pool can yield information about the timing of events that accompanied the incident.

The edges of a stain will dry to the surface, producing a phenomenon called **skeletonization** (see Figure 10–19). This usually occurs within 50 seconds of deposition of drops, and longer for larger volumes of blood. If the central area of the pooled bloodstain is altered by wiping, the skeletonized perimeter will be left intact. This can be used to interpret whether movement or activity occurred shortly after the pool was deposited, or whether the perimeter had time to skeletonize before the movement occurred. This may be important for classifying the source of the original stain.

skeletonization
The process by which the edges of a stain dry to the surface in a specific period of time (dependent on environmental and surface conditions). Skeletonization will remain apparent even after the rest of the bloodstain has been disturbed from its original position

FIGURE 10-19
Skeletonization is shown in a bloodstain that was disturbed after the edges had time to skeletonize. *Courtesy Norman H. Reeves*, Bloodstain Pattern Analysis, *Tucson, AZ, www. bloody1.com*

Drip Trail Patterns

A **drip trail pattern** is a series of drops that are separate from other patterns, formed by blood dripping off an object or injury. The stains form a kind of line or path usually made by the suspect after injuring or killing the victim, or they can show the movement of a wounded victim. It may simply show movement, lead to a discarded weapon, or provide identification of the suspect by his or her own blood. Investigators often see this type of pattern in stabbings during which

drip trail pattern
A pattern of bloodstains formed by the dripping of blood off a moving surface or person in a recognizable pathway separate from other patterns

the suspect cuts himself or herself as a result of the force necessary to stab the victim. Figure 10–20 shows a drip trail pattern away from the center of action at a crime scene.

FIGURE 10-20
A drip trail pattern leads away from the center of the mixed bloodstain pattern. *Courtesy Norman H. Reeves*, Bloodstain Pattern Analysis, *Tucson, AZ, www.bloody1.com*

The shape of the stains in a drip trail pattern can help investigators determine the direction and speed at which a person was moving. The tails of the drops in a drip trail pattern point in the direction the person was moving. More circular stains are found where the person was moving slowly enough to not form tails. This information may be helpful in reconstruction.

Documenting Bloodstain Pattern Evidence

Blood spatter patterns of any kind can provide a great deal of information about the events that took place at a crime scene. For this reason, investigators should note, study, and photograph each pattern and drop. This must be done to accurately record the location of specific patterns and to distinguish the stains from which laboratory samples were taken. The photographs and sketches can also point out specific stains used in determining the direction of force, angle of impact, and area of origin.

Just as in general crime-scene photography, the investigator should create photographs and sketches of the overall pattern to show the orientation of the pattern to the scene. The medium-range documentation should include pictures and sketches of the whole pattern and the relationships between individual stains

Case Files Bloodstain Reconstruction

An elderly male was found lying dead on his living room floor. He had been beaten about the face and head, then stabbed in the chest and robbed. The reconstruction of bloodstains found on the interior front door and the adjacent wall documented that the victim was beaten about the face with a fist and struck on the back of the head with his cane. A three-dimensional diagram and photograph illustrating the evidential bloodstain patterns is shown in Figures 1(a) and (b).

FIGURE 1 (a) A three-dimensional diagram illustrating bloodstain patterns that were located, documented, and reconstructed. (b) A crime-scene photograph of bloodstained areas. (a) *Courtesy Judith Bunker, J.L. Bunker & Assoc., Ocoee, Fla.* (b) *Courtesy Sarasota County (Fla.) Sheriff's Department*

(A)

(B)

(continued)

Case Files

(continued)

A detail photograph of bloodstains next to the interior door is shown in <u>Figure 2</u>. Arrow 1 in Figure 2 points to the cast-off pattern directed left to right as blood was flung from the perpetrator's fist while inflicting blows. Arrow 2 in Figure 2 points to three transfer impression patterns directed left to right as the perpetrator's bloodstained hand contacted the wall as the fist blows were being inflicted on the victim. Arrow 3 in Figure 2 points to blood flow from the victim's wounds as he slumped against the wall.

FIGURE 2 Positions of impact spatter from blows that were inflicted on the victim's face. *Courtesy Judith Bunker, J.L. Bunker & Assoc., Ocoee, Fla.*

FIGURE 3

(a) A laboratory test pattern showing an impact spatter. The size and shape of the stains demonstrate a forceful impact 90 degrees to the target. (b)A laboratory test pattern illustrating a cast-off pattern directed left to right from an overhead swing. (c) A laboratory test pattern showing a repetitive transfer impression pattern produced by a bloodstained hand moving left to right across the target. (d) A laboratory test pattern illustrating vertical flow patterns. The left pattern represents a stationary source; the right pattern was produced by left-to-right motion. *Courtesy Judith Bunker, J.L. Bunker & Assoc., Ocoee, Fla.*

Case Files

(continued)

(A)   **(B)**   **(C)**

FIGURE 4
(a) A convergence of impact spatter patterns associated with beating with a fist. (b) The convergence of impact spatter associated with the victim falling to the floor while bleeding from the nose. (c) The convergence of impact spatter associated with the victim while face down at the door, being struck with a cane. *Courtesy Judith Bunker, J.L. Bunker & Assoc., Ocoee, Fla.*

Figure 3 contains a series of laboratory test patterns created to evaluate the patterns contained within Figure 2. Figure 4 shows how the origin of individual impact spatter patterns located on the wall and door and emanating from the bleeding victim can be documented by the determination of separate areas of convergence.

A suspect was apprehended three days later, and he was found to have an acute fracture of the right hand. When he was confronted with the bloodstain evidence, the suspect admitted striking the victim, first with his fist, then with a cane, and finally stabbing him with a kitchen knife.

The suspect pleaded guilty to three first-degree felonies.

within the pattern. The close-up photographs and sketches should show the dimensions of each individual stain. Close-up photographs should be taken with a scale of some kind apparent in the photograph.

Two common methods of documenting bloodstain patterns place attention on the scale of the patterns. The *grid method* involves setting up a grid of squares of known dimensions over the entire pattern using string and stakes (see <u>Figure 10–21</u>). All overall, medium-range, and close-up photographs are taken with and without the grid. The second method, called the *perimeter ruler method*, involves setting up a rectangular border of rulers around the pattern and then placing a small ruler next to each stain. In this method, the large rulers show scale in the overall and medium-range photos, whereas the small rulers show scale in the close-up photographs (see <u>Figure 10–22</u>). Some investigation teams use tags in close-up photographs to show evidence numbers or other details.

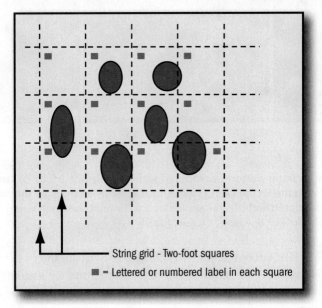

String grid - Two-foot squares

■ = Lettered or numbered label in each square

FIGURE 10-21
The grid method may be used for photographing bloodstain pattern evidence. *Source: R.R. Ogle, Jr., Crime Scene Investigation & Reconstruction, 2nd ed., Prentice Hall, Upper Saddle River, NJ, 2007*

Measurement rulers

Small metric rulers

Areas with bloodstain patterns

FIGURE 10-22
The perimeter ruler method may be used for photographing bloodstain pattern evidence. *Source: R.R. Ogle, Jr., Crime Scene Investigation & Resconstruction, 2nd ed., Prentice Hall, Upper Saddle River, NJ, 2007*

An area-of-origin determination may be calculated at the discretion of the bloodstain analyst when the circumstances of the case warrant such a determination. All measurements of stains and calculations of angle of impact and point of origin should be recorded in crime-scene notes. Especially important stains can be roughly sketched within the notes.

Only some jurisdictions have a specialist on staff to decipher patterns either at the scene or from photographs at the lab. Therefore, it is important that all personnel be familiar with patterns to properly record and document them for use in reconstruction.

Quick Review

- Transfer patterns are created when an object with blood on it makes simple contact with a surface or moves along a surface. The direction of movement may be shown by feathering of the pattern.

- Flows may originate from a single drop or a large amount of blood. The direction of the flow is caused by gravity, so the direction of a pattern may suggest the original position of the surface when the flow was formed.

- A pool is formed where large amounts of blood collect. The pool may be absorbed into the surface of deposition over time.

- The presence of skeletonization of the perimeter of a bloodstain suggests that the stain was disturbed after the edges had sufficient time to skeletonize.

- A drip trail pattern is separate from other patterns, and it is formed by single blood drops dripping off an object or injury.

- Photographs and sketches should first be created of the overall pattern to show orientation of the pattern to the scene.

- Medium-range and close-up photographs may use the grid method or perimeter ruler method to show the orientation and relative size of the pattern and individual stains.

Chapter Review

- Crime-scene reconstruction relies on the combined efforts of medical examiners, criminalists, and law enforcement personnel to recover physical evidence and to sort out the events surrounding the occurrence of a crime.

- Examples of crime-scene reconstruction include determining whether a body was moved after death, determining whether a victim was clothed after death, analyzing bullet trajectory, analyzing blood spatter, determining the direction from which projectiles penetrated glass objects, estimating the distance of a shooter from a target, and locating primer residue on suspects.

- Individual bloodstains can convey to the bloodstain analyst the directionality and angle of impact of the blood when it impacted a surface. Bloodstain patterns may convey to the analyst the location of victims or suspects, the movement of bleeding individuals, and the number of blows delivered.

- Surface texture is of paramount importance in the interpretation of bloodstain patterns; rounder drops generally are produced from smooth, nonporous surfaces, whereas rough surfaces create irregular-edged drops. However, correlations between standards and unknowns are valid only if identical surfaces are used.

- The direction of travel of blood striking an object may be discerned by the stain's shape. The pointed end of a bloodstain always faces in its direction of travel.

- The angle of impact of an individual bloodstain can be approximated by the degree of distortion or lengthening of the bloodstain, or it can be more effectively estimated using the ratio of width/length of the stain.

- An impact spatter pattern occurs when an object impacts a source of blood. This produces forward spatter projected forward from the source and back spatter projected backward from the source.

- Impact spatter patterns can be classified as low velocity (>3 mm drops), medium velocity (1–3 mm drops), or high velocity (<1 mm drops) for descriptive purposes. These categories should not be used to assume what kind of force created the pattern.

- The area of convergence is the point on a two-dimensional plane from which the drops of an impact spatter pattern originated. This area can be estimated by drawing straight lines through the long axis of several individual bloodstains, following the line of their tails.

- The area of origin of a bloodstain pattern is the area in three-dimensional space where blood was projected from, showing the position of the victim or suspect when the stain-producing event took place. The string method is commonly used at a crime scene to approximate the position of the area of origin.

- Gunshot spatter can consist of both forward spatter from an exit wound and back spatter from an entrance wound; however, only back spatter will be produced if the bullet does not exit the body.

- A cast-off pattern is created when a blood-covered object flings blood in an arc onto a nearby surface. This kind of pattern commonly occurs when a person pulls a bloody fist or weapon back between delivering blows to a victim.

- The characteristic arterial spray spatter is created when a victim suffers an injury to a main artery or the heart and the pressure of the continuing pumping of blood projects blood out of the injured area in spurts, which are apparent in the pattern.

- Expirated blood is expelled from the mouth or nose and may appear as very fine high-velocity spatter or large low-velocity bloodstain clusters. This kind of pattern may contain bubbles of oxygen or be mixed with saliva.

- A void pattern features an area free of spatter where an object (or person) blocks the deposition of blood spatter onto a target surface or object. Because the spatter is deposited onto the object or person instead, the shape of the void may give a clue as to the size and shape of the missing object or person.

- Transfer patterns are created when an object with blood on it makes simple contact with a surface or moves along a surface. The direction of movement may be shown by feathering of the pattern.

- Flows may originate from a single drop or a large amount of blood. The direction of the flow is caused by gravity, so the direction of a pattern may suggest the original position of the surface when the flow was formed.

- A pool is formed where large amounts of blood collect. The pool may be absorbed into the surface of deposition over time.

- The presence of skeletonization of the perimeter of a bloodstain suggests that the stain was disturbed after the edges had sufficient time to skeletonize.

- A drip trail pattern is separate from other patterns, and it is formed by single blood drops dripping off an object or injury.

- Photographs and sketches should first be created of the overall pattern to show orientation of the pattern to the scene.

- Medium-range and close-up photographs may use the grid method or perimeter ruler method to show the orientation and relative size of the pattern and individual stains.

Quick Lab: Blood Drop Analysis

Materials:

Simulated blood*
Dropper
Construction paper
Ruler
Scientific calculator

Procedure:

By examining a single blood drop at a crime scene, we can determine some important information that may help to reconstruct what occurred. One piece of data we can gather is the angle of impact for a blood drop. For this activity, start by creating some blood drops on the construction paper. Use the dropper to place drops of blood on the paper and be sure to squirt the blood at different angles onto the paper. Remember, you want drops, not a puddle. Once you have created about ten drops at different angles, let the blood dry. Once dry, use the ruler to measure the width and length of each drop in millimeters. Record your data. To determine the angle at which each blood drop impacted, use the calculator to solve the equation width/length = sin of the angle of impact. The sin of the angle of impact can be converted to the angle of impact by hitting the arcsin button ($\sin^{-1}$) on the calculator. This is the angle at which the blood drop fell onto the surface.

Follow-Up Questions:

1. How would knowing the angle of impact of a blood drop be helpful in an investigation?

2. Did any of your drops fall at a 90-degree angle? If so, what shape were they?

3. Create a graph of showing angle of impact vs. blood drop length using the data from your ten blood drops. Explain whether there is a correlation between these two pieces of data.

*Available from Forensics Source, www.forensicssource.com

Quick Lab:
Blood Spatter Analysis

Materials:

Sheet of blank paper
Water-soluble red paint
Paintbrush and pointed stirring stick

Procedure:

Cast-off blood spatter is often of great help to investigators in reconstructing events at the scene of a violent crime. In particular, the shape and appearance of cast-off bloodstains can indicate the relative positions of the victim and assailant during the crime and the type of weapon used. For this exercise, students should be matched up in teams of two. Each member of the pair, working separately, will make a series of spatters on the blank paper with the red paint. Using the paintbrush, make three stains by flicking a small amount of red paint onto the paper. Hold the brush at differing angles to the paper when making each stain. One should be made at a shallow angle, the second at a steeper angle, and the third at an even steeper angle. Now make similar marks using the stirring stick instead of the paintbrush. Let the paint dry, then mark the stains A, B,C, D, E, and F. Be sure to record which instrument made each mark and the angle (shallow, steep, very steep) at which it was made. (It is best to alternate making marks with one instrument, then the other, rather than making all 3 marks with the paintbrush, then all with the stirring stick.) Now pair up with your partner and exchange sheets. Answer the following questions:

Follow Up Questions:

1. Which marks were made by the paintbrush and which were made by the stick? How do you know this?

2. For each instrument, list the stains from shallowest to steepest. How did you determine the relative angles of each stain?

3. What would the presence of shallow-angle bloodstains suggest about the relative position of victim and assailant? What would a steeper angle suggest?

Review Questions

1. Violent contact between individuals at a crime scene frequently produces bleeding and results in the formation of
   a. footwear impressions.
   b. bloodstain patterns.
   c. blood typing.
   d. rigor mortis.

2. A drop of blood that strikes a surface at an angle of impact of approximately 90° will be close to _____ in shape.
   a. elongated
   b. elliptical
   c. teardropped
   d. circular

3. The classification system of impact spatter is based on the size of drops resulting from the velocity of the blood drops produced, and patterns can be classified as _____, _____, or _____ impact spatter.
   a. low-blow; medium-blow; high-blow
   b. low-velocity; medium-velocity; high-velocity
   c. small; medium; large
   d. circular; elliptical; elongated

4. The _____ method is used at the crime scene to determine the area of origin.
   a. perimeter ruler
   b. grid
   c. string
   d. cast-off

5. The edges of a bloodstain will generally skeletonize within _____ of deposition and be left intact even if the central area of a bloodstain is altered by a wiping motion.
   a. 50 seconds
   b. 10 seconds
   c. 50 minutes
   d. 3 hours

6. True or False: Harder and less porous surfaces result in less spatter, whereas rough surfaces produce stains with more spatter and serrated edges.

7. True or False: Movement of a bloody object across a surface causes the pattern to darken as the object moves away from point of contact.

8. True or False: Footwear transfer patterns created by an individual who was running typically show imprints with more space between them as compared to those of an individual who was walking.

9. True or False: The direction of a flow pattern may show movements of objects or bodies while the flow was still in progress or after the blood has dried.

10. True or False: Each bloodstain pattern found at a crime scene does not have to be noted, studied, and photographed.

11. What is crime-scene reconstruction?

12. In which of the following ways can physical evidence aid in crime-scene reconstruction? (You may choose more than one response.)
    a. by supporting or contradicting statements given by witnesses and/or suspects
    b. by describing exactly what happened at the crime scene
    c. by confirming the accuracy of a crime-scene reconstruction to a jury
    d. by distinguishing between individual and class characteristics
    e. by generating leads that may help investigators solve the case

13. Give at least three examples of a specialized task a criminalist might perform in crime-scene reconstruction.

14. Which of the following is of paramount importance in the interpretation of bloodstain patterns?
    a. the direction of impact
    b. the surface texture
    c. the angle of impact
    d. the amount of blood

15. How can an investigator tell the direction of travel of blood from the shape of a bloodstain?

16. What is the difference between the shape of a bloodstain that impacts a surface at a low angle and one that impacts at a higher angle?

17. What is the difference between forward spatter and back spatter? Which is more likely to be deposited on the object or person creating the impact?

18. In general, as both the force and velocity of impact increase, what happens to the diameter of the resulting blood drops?

19. Why might investigators overlook some high-velocity spatter?

20. Define the terms *area of convergence* and *area of origin* and explain what each reveals to an investigator.

21. Name three factors that affect the amount of backward spatter produced by a gunshot wound.

22. What is the drawback effect? How is it helpful to an investigator?

23. What determines the size of blood drops in a cast-off pattern? Explain.

24. What is expirated blood? Name two ways to distinguish expirated blood from other types of bloodstains.

Virtual Lab: Blood Spatter Evidence

To perform a virtual lab analysis of blood spatter, go to www.pearsoncustom.com/us/vlm

25. What is a void pattern? How might a void pattern be useful to investigators?

26. What is a transfer pattern? How is a simple transfer pattern created?

27. How does the first transfer pattern in a series differ from subsequent ones?

28. What is a flow pattern? What should one surmise if a flow found on an object or body does not appear consistent with the direction of gravity?

29. How can pools of blood aid in reconstructing a crime scene?

30. Explain how the shape of stains in a drip trail pattern can help investigators determine the direction and speed at which a person was moving.

31. Name and describe two methods for documenting bloodstain patterns.

Application and Critical Thinking

1. After looking at the bloodstains in the figure, answer the following questions:
   a. Which three drops struck the surface closest to a 90-degree angle? Explain your answer.
   b. Which three drops struck the surface farthest from a 90-degree angle? Explain your answer.
   c. In what direction were drops 2 and 7 traveling when they struck the surface? Explain your answer

2. Investigator Priscilla Wright arrives at a murder scene and finds the body of a victim who suffered a gunshot wound but sees no blood spatter on the wall or floor behind it. What should she conclude from this observation?

3. Investigator Terry Martin arrives at an assault scene and finds a cast-off pattern consisting of tiny drops of blood in a very linear arc pattern on a wall near the victim. What does this tell him about the weapon used in the crime?

Learning Objectives

After studying this chapter you should be able to:

- Recognize and understand the cuticle, cortex, and medulla areas of hair

- List the three phases of hair growth

- Appreciate the distinction between animal and human hairs

- List hair features that are useful for microscopic comparison of human hairs

- Explain proper collection of forensic hair evidence

- Describe and understand the role of DNA typing in hair comparisons

- Understand the differences between natural and manufactured fibers

- List the properties of fibers that are most useful for forensic comparisons

- Describe proper collection of fiber evidence

- Recognize the major contributors to the development of forensic science

National Science Content Standards

Scientific Inquiry

Physical Science

Jeffrey MacDonald: Fatal Vision

The grisly murder scene that confronted police on February 17, 1970, is one that cannot be wiped from memory. Summoned to the Fort Bragg residence of Captain Jeffrey MacDonald, a physician, police found the bludgeoned body of MacDonald's wife. She had been repeatedly knifed, and her face was smashed to a pulp. MacDonald's two children, ages 2 and 5, had been brutally and repeatedly knifed and battered to death.

Suspicion quickly fell on MacDonald. To the eyes of investigators, the murder scene had a staged appearance. MacDonald described a frantic effort to subdue four intruders who had slashed at him with an ice pick. However, the confrontation left MacDonald with minor wounds and no apparent defensive wounds on his arms. MacDonald then described how he had covered his slashed wife with his blue pajama top. Interestingly, when the body was removed, blue threads were observed under the body. In fact, blue threads matching the pajama top turned up throughout the house—19 in one child's bedroom, including one beneath her fingernail, and two in the other child's bedroom. Eighty-one blue fibers were recovered from the master bedroom, and two were located on a bloodstained piece of wood outside the house.

Later forensic examination showed that the 48 ice pick holes in the pajama top were smooth and cylindrical, a sign that the top was stationary when it was slashed. Also, folding the pajama top demonstrated that the 48 holes actually could have been made by 21 thrusts of an ice pick. This coincided with the number of wounds that MacDonald's wife sustained. As described in the book *Fatal Vision*, which chronicled the murder investigation, when MacDonald was confronted with adulterous conduct, he replied, "You guys are more thorough than I thought." MacDonald is currently serving three consecutive life sentences.

Trace Evidence I: Hairs and Fibers

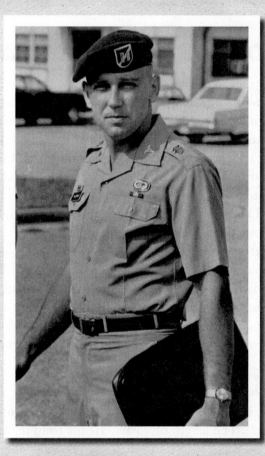

Key Terms

anagen phase

catagen phase

cortex

cuticle

follicular tag

macromolecule

manufactured fibers

medulla

mitochondrial DNA

molecule

monomer

natural fibers

nuclear DNA

polymer

telogen phase

The trace evidence transferred between individuals and objects during the commission of a crime, if recovered, often corroborates other evidence developed during the course of an investigation. Although in most cases physical evidence cannot by itself positively identify a suspect, laboratory examination may narrow the origin of such evidence to a group that includes the suspect. Using many of the instruments and techniques we have already examined, the crime laboratory has developed a variety of procedures for comparing and tracing the origins of physical evidence. This chapter and those that follow discuss how to apply these techniques to the analysis of the types of physical evidence most often encountered at crime scenes. We begin with a discussion of hairs and fibers.

Forensic Examination of Hair

Hair is encountered as physical evidence in a wide variety of crimes. However, any review of the forensic aspects of hair examination must start with the observation that it is not yet possible to individualize a human hair to any single head or body through its morphology, or structural characteristics. Over the years, criminalists have tried to isolate the physical and chemical properties of hair that could serve as individual characteristics of identity. Partial success has finally been achieved by isolating and characterizing the DNA present in hair.

The importance of hair as physical evidence cannot be overemphasized. Its removal from the body often denotes physical contact between a victim and perpetrator and hence a crime of a serious or violent nature. When hair is properly collected at the crime scene and submitted to the laboratory along with enough standard/reference samples, it can provide strong corroborative evidence for placing an individual at a crime site. The first step in the forensic examination of hair logically starts with its color and structure, or morphology, and, if warranted, progresses to the more detailed DNA extraction, isolation, and characterization.

Morphology of Hair

Hair is an appendage of the skin that grows out of an organ known as the hair follicle. The length of a hair extends from its root or bulb embedded in the follicle, continues into the shaft, and terminates at the tip end. The shaft, which is composed of three layers—the **cuticle**, **cortex**, and **medulla**—is most intensely examined by the forensic scientist (see Figure 11–1).

The Cuticle Two features that make hair a good subject for establishing individual identity are its resistance to chemical decomposition and its ability to retain structural features over a long period of time. Much of this resistance and stability is attributed to the cuticle, a scale structure covering the exterior of the hair. The cuticle is formed by overlapping scales that always point toward the tip end of each hair. The scales form from specialized cells that have hardened (keratinized) and flattened in progressing from the follicle. There are three basic patterns that describe the appearance of the cuticle: cornal, spinous, and imbricate (see Figure 11–2).

cuticle
The scale structure covering the exterior of the hair

cortex
The main body of the hair shaft

medulla
A cellular column running through the center of the hair

FIGURE 11–1 Cross section of skin showing hair growing out of a tubelike structure called the follicles.

Cortex
Cuticle

Follicle
Root

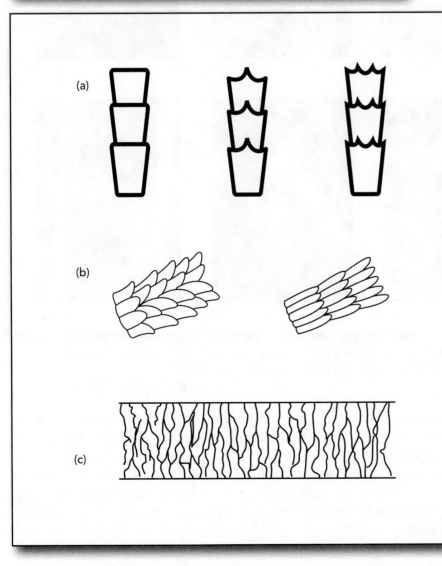

FIGURE 11–2
(a) The coronal, or crownlike scale pattern resembles a stack of paper cups.
(b) Spinous or petal-like scales are triangular in shape and protrude from the hair shaft.
(c) The imbricate or flattened-scale type consists of overlapping scales with narrow margins.

(a)

(b)

(c)

Although the scale pattern is not a useful characteristic for individualizing human hair, the variety of patterns formed by animal hair makes it an important feature for species identification. Figure 11–3 shows the scale patterns of some animal hairs and of a human hair as viewed by the scanning electron microscope. Another method of studying the scale pattern of hair is to make a cast of its surface. This is done by embedding the hair in a soft medium, such as clear nail polish or softened vinyl. When the medium has hardened, the hair is removed, leaving a clear, distinct impression of the hair's cuticle, ideal for examination with a compound microscope.

FIGURE 11–3 Scale patterns of various types of hair. (a) Human head hair (600x), (b) dog (1250x), (c) deer (120x), (d) rabbit (300x), (e) cat (2000x), and (f) horse (450x).

The Cortex Contained within the protective layer of the cuticle is the cortex, the main body of the hair shaft. The cortex is made up of spindle-shaped cortical cells aligned in a regular array, parallel to the length of the hair. The cortex derives its major forensic importance from the fact that it is embedded with the pigment granules that give hair its color. The color, shape, and distribution of these granules provide important points of comparison among the hairs of different individuals.

The structural features of the cortex are examined microscopically after the hair has been mounted in a liquid medium with a refractive index close to that of the hair. Under these conditions, the amount of light reflected off the hair's surface is minimized, and the amount of light penetrating the hair is optimized.

The Medulla The medulla is a collection of cells that looks like a central canal running through a hair. In many animals, this canal is a predominant feature, occupying more than half of the hair's diameter. The *medullary index* measures the diameter of the medulla relative to the diameter of the hair shaft and is normally expressed as a fraction. For humans, the index is generally less than one-third; for most other animals, the index is one-half or greater.

The presence and appearance of the medulla vary from individual to individual and even among the hairs of a given individual. Not all hairs have medullae, and when they do exist, the degree of medullation can vary. In this respect, medullae may be classified as being either continuous, interrupted, fragmented, or absent (see Figure 11–4). Human head hairs generally exhibit no medullae or have fragmented ones; they rarely show continuous medullation. One noted exception is the Mongoloid race, whose members usually have head hairs with continuous medullae. Also, most animals have medullae that are either continuous or interrupted.

Continuous   Interrupted   Fragmented

FIGURE 11–4
Medulla patterns.

Another interesting feature of the medulla is its shape. Humans, as well as many animals, have medullae that give a nearly cylindrical appearance. Other animals exhibit medullae that have a patterned shape. For example, the medulla of a cat can best be described as resembling a string of pearls, whereas members of the deer family show a medullary structure consisting of spherical cells occupying the entire hair shaft. Figure 11–5 illustrates medullary sizes and forms for a number of common animal hairs and a human head hair.

A searchable database on CD-ROM of the 35 most common animal hairs encountered in forensic casework is commercially available.[1] This database allows an examiner to rapidly search for animal hairs based on scale patterns and/or medulla type using a computer. A typical screen presentation arising from such a data search is shown in Figure 11–6.

The Root The root and other surrounding cells within the hair follicle provide the tools necessary to produce hair and continue its growth. Human head hair grows in three developmental stages, and the shape and size of the hair root is determined by the hair's current growth phase. The three phases of hair growth are the **anagen, catagen,** and **telogen phases.**

In the anagen phase (the initial growth phase), which may last up to six years, the root is attached to the follicle for continued growth, giving the root bulb a flame-shaped appearance (Figure 11–7[a]). When pulled from the root, some hairs in the anagen phase have a **follicular tag**. With the advent of DNA analysis, this follicular tag is important for individualizing hair.

anagen phase
The initial growth phase during which the hair follicle actively produces hair

catagen phase
A transition stage between the anagen and telogen phases of hair growth

telogen phase
The final growth phase in which hair naturally falls out of the skin

(a)   (b)   (c)

(d)   (e)   (f)

FIGURE 11–5 Medulla patterns for various types of hair. (a) Human head hair (400x), (b) dog (400x), (c) deer (500x), (d) rabbit (450x), (e) cat (400x), and (f) mouse (500x).

follicular tag
A translucent piece of tissue surrounding the hair's shaft near the root that contains the richest source of DNA associated with hair

Hair continues to grow, but at a decreasing rate, during the catagen phase, which can last anywhere from two to three weeks. In the catagen phase, roots typically take on an elongated appearance (Figure 11–7[b]) as the root bulb shrinks and is pushed out of the hair follicle. Once hair growth ends, the telogen phase begins and the root takes on a club-shaped appearance (Figure 11–7[c]). Over two to six months, the hair is pushed out of the follicle, causing the hair to be naturally shed.

Identification and Comparison of Hair

Most often the prime purpose for examining hair evidence in a crime laboratory is to establish whether the hair is human or animal in origin, or to determine whether human hair retrieved at a crime scene compares with hair from a particular individual.

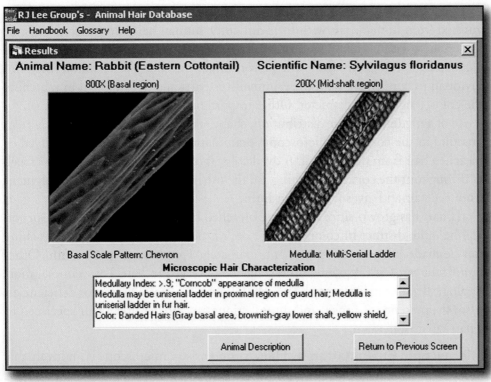

FIGURE 11–6
Information on rabbit
hair contained within
the *Forensic Animal
Hair Atlas.*
*Courtesy RJ Lee Group,
Inc. Monroeville, Pa.*

A careful microscopic examination of hair reveals morphological features that can distinguish human hair from animal hair. The hair of various animals also differs enough in structure that the examiner can often identify the species. Before reaching such a conclusion, however, the examiner must have access to a comprehensive collection of reference standards and the accumulated experience of hundreds of prior hair examinations. Scale structure, medullary index, and medullary shape are particularly important in hair identification.

FIGURE 11–7
Hair roots in the:
(a) anagen phase,
(b) catagen phase, and
(c) telogen phase (100x)
*Courtesy Charles A.
Linch*

The most common request when hair is used as forensic evidence is to determine whether hair recovered at the crime scene compares to hair removed from a suspect. In most cases, such a comparison relates to hair obtained from the scalp or pubic area. Ultimately, the evidential value of the comparison depends on the degree of probability with which the examiner can associate the hair in question with a particular individual.

Factors in Comparison of Hair Although animal hair normally can be distinguished from human hair with little difficulty, human hair comparisons must be undertaken with extreme caution. Hair tends to exhibit variable morphological characteristics, not only from one person to another but also within a single individual. In comparing hair, the criminalist is particularly interested in matching the color, length, and diameter. Other important features are the presence or absence of a medulla and the distribution, shape, and color intensity of the pigment granules in the cortex. A microscopic examination may also distinguish dyed or bleached hair from natural hair. A dyed color is often present in the cuticle as well as throughout the cortex. Bleaching, on the other hand, tends to remove pigment from the hair and gives it a yellowish tint.

If hair has grown since it was last bleached or dyed, the natural-end portion will be quite distinct in color. An estimate of the time since dyeing or bleaching can be made because hair grows approximately 1 centimeter per month. Other significant but less frequent features may be observed in hair. For example, morphological abnormalities may be present because of certain diseases or deficiencies. Also, the presence of fungal and nit infections can further link a hair specimen to a particular individual.

Microscopic Examination of Hair A comparison microscope is an invaluable tool that allows the examiner to view the questioned and known hair together, side by side. Any variations in the microscopic characteristics will thus be readily observed. Because hair from any part of the body exhibits a range of characteristics, it is necessary to have an adequate number of known hairs that are representative of all of its features when making a comparison.

Although microscopic comparison of hairs has long been accepted as an appropriate approach for including and excluding questioned hairs against standard/reference hairs, many forensic scientists have long recognized that this approach is subjective and is highly dependent on the skills and integrity of the analyst, as well as the hair morphology being examined. However, until the advent of DNA analysis, the forensic science community had no choice but to rely on the microscope to carry out hair comparisons.

Any lingering doubts about the necessity of augmenting microscopic hair examinations with DNA analysis evaporated with the publication of an FBI study describing significant error rates associated with microscopic comparison of hairs.[2] Hair evidence submitted to the FBI for DNA analysis between 1996 and 2000 was examined both microscopically and by DNA analysis. Approximately 11 percent of the hairs (9 out of 80) in which FBI hair examiners found a positive microscopic match between questioned and standard/reference hairs were found to be nonmatches when they were later subjected to DNA analysis. The course of events is clear; microscopic hair comparisons must be regarded by police and courts as presumptive in nature, and all positive microscopic hair comparisons must be confirmed by DNA determinations.

Questions about Hair Examination A number of questions may be asked to further ascertain the present status of forensic hair examinations. The answers to these questions can be of great significance to the investigator working with hair evidence.

Can the Body Area from Which a Hair Originated Be Determined? Normally it is easy to determine the body area from which a hair came. For example, scalp hairs generally show little diameter variation and have a more uniform distribution of pigment when compared to other body hairs. Pubic hairs are short and curly, with wide variations in shaft diameter, and usually have continuous medullae. Beard hairs are coarse, are normally triangular in cross-section, and have blunt tips acquired from cutting or shaving.

Can the Racial Origin of Hair Be Determined? In many instances, the examiner can distinguish hair originating from members of different races; this is especially true of Caucasian and Negroid head hair. Negroid hairs are normally kinky, containing dense, unevenly distributed pigments. Caucasian hairs are usually straight or wavy, with very fine to coarse pigments that are more evenly distributed when compared to Negroid hair. Sometimes a cross-sectional examination of hair may help identify race. Cross-sections of hair from Caucasians are oval to round in shape, whereas cross-sections of Negroid hair are flat to oval in shape. However, all of these observations are general, with many possible exceptions. The criminalist must approach the determination of race from hair with caution and a good deal of experience.

Can the Age and Sex of an Individual Be Determined from a Hair Sample? The age of an individual cannot be learned from a hair examination with any degree of certainty except with infant hair. Infant hairs are fine and short and have fine pigmentation. Although the presence of dye or bleach on the hair may offer some clue to sex, present hairstyles make these characteristics less valuable than they were in the past. The recovery of nuclear DNA either from tissue adhering to hair or from the root structure of the hair will allow a determination of whether the hair originated from a male or female.

Is It Possible to Determine Whether Hair Was Forcibly Removed from the Body? A microscopic examination of the hair root may establish whether the hair fell out or was pulled out of the skin. A hair root with follicular tissue (root sheath cells) adhering to it, as shown in Figure 11–8, indicates a hair that has been pulled out either by a person or by brushing or combing. Hair naturally falling off the body has a bulbous-shaped root free of any adhering tissue.

The absence of sheath cells cannot always be relied on for correctly judging whether hair has been forcibly pulled from the body. In some cases the root of a hair is devoid of any adhering tissue even when it has been pulled from the body. Apparently, an important consideration is how quickly the hair is pulled out of the head. Hairs pulled quickly from the head are much more likely to have sheath cells compared to hairs that have been removed slowly from the scalp.[3]

FIGURE 11–8
Forcibly removed head hair, with follicular tissue attached.

Case Files

The Central Park Jogger Case Revisited

On April 19, 1989, a young woman left her apartment around nine p.m. to jog in New York's Central Park. Nearly five hours later, she was found comatose lying in a puddle of mud in the park. She had been raped, her skull was fractured, and she had lost 75 percent of her blood. When the woman recovered, she had no memory of what happened to her. The brutality of the crime sent shock waves through the city and seemed to fuel a national perception that crime was running rampant and unchecked through the streets of New York.

Already in custody at the station house of the Central Park Precinct was a group of 14- and 15-year-old boys who had been rounded up leaving the park earlier in the night by police who suspected that they had been involved in a series of random attacks. Over the next two days, four of the teenagers gave videotaped statements, which they later recanted, admitting to participating in the attack. Ultimately, five of the teenagers were charged with the crime.

Interestingly, none of the semen collected from the victim could be linked to any of the defendants. However, according to the testimony of a forensic analyst, two head hairs collected from the clothing of one of the defendants microscopically compared to those of the victim, and a third hair collected from the same defendant's T-shirt microscopically compared to the victim's pubic hair. Besides these three hairs, a fourth hair was found microscopically similar to the victim's. This hair was recovered from the clothing of Steven Lopez, who was originally charged with rape but not prosecuted for the crime.

Hairs were the only pieces of physical evidence offered by the district attorney to directly link any of the teenagers to the crime. The five defendants were convicted and ultimately served from 9 to 13 years.

In August 1989, more than three months after the jogger attack, New York Police arrested a man named Matias Reyes, who pleaded guilty to murdering a pregnant woman, raping three others, and committing a robbery. In January 2002, Reyes also confessed to the Central Park attack. Follow-up tests revealed that Reyes's DNA compared to semen recovered from the jogger's body and her sock. Other DNA tests showed that the hairs offered into evidence at the original trial did not come from the victim, and so could not be used to link the teenagers to the crime as the district attorney had argued. After an 11-month reinvestigation of the original charges, a New York State Supreme Court judge dismissed all the convictions against the five teenage suspects in the Central Park jogger case.

A courtroom sketch of the trial proceeding in Central Park Jogger case. *Courtesy AP World Wide Photos*

Are Efforts Being Made to Individualize Human Hair? As we saw in <u>Chapter 9</u>, forensic scientists routinely isolate and characterize individual variations in DNA. Forensic hair examiners can link human hair to a particular individual by characterizing the **nuclear DNA** in the hair root or in follicular tissue adhering to the root (see <u>Figure 11–8</u>). Recall that the follicular tag is the richest source of DNA associated with hair. In the absence of follicular tissue, an examiner must extract DNA from the hair root.

The growth phase of hair is a useful predictor of the likelihood of successfully typing DNA in human hair.[4] Examiners have a higher success rate in extracting DNA from hair roots in the anagen phase or from anagen-phase hairs entering the catagen phase of growth. Telogen-phase hairs have an inadequate amount of DNA for typing. Because most hairs are naturally shed and are expected to be in the telogen stage, these observations do not portend well for hairs collected at crime scenes. However, some crime scenes are populated with forcibly removed hairs that are expected to be rich sources for nuclear DNA.

When a questioned hair does not have adhering tissue or a root structure amenable to isolation of nuclear DNA, there is an alternative—**mitochondrial DNA**. Unlike the nuclear DNA described earlier, which is located in the nuclei of practically every cell in our bodies, mitochondrial DNA is found in cellular material outside the nucleus. Interestingly, unlike nuclear DNA, which is passed down to us from both parents, mitochondrial DNA is transmitted only from mother to child. Importantly, many more copies of mitochondrial DNA are located in our cells as compared to nuclear DNA. For this reason, the success rate of finding and typing mitochondrial DNA is much greater from samples, such as hair, that have limited quantities of nuclear DNA. Hairs 1–2 centimeters long can be subjected to mitochondrial analysis with extremely high odds of success. This subject is discussed in greater detail in <u>Chapter 9</u>.

Can DNA Individualize a Human Hair? In some cases, the answer is yes. As we learned in <u>Chapter 9</u>, nuclear DNA produces frequencies of occurrence as low as one in billions or trillions. On the other hand, mitochondrial DNA cannot individualize human hair, but its diversity within the human population often permits exclusion of a significant portion of a population as potential contributors of a hair sample. Ideally, the combination of a positive microscopic comparison and an association through nuclear or mitochondrial DNA analysis strongly links a questioned hair and standard/reference hairs. However, a word of caution: mitochondrial DNA cannot distinguish microscopically similar hairs from different individuals who are maternally related.

Collection and Preservation of Hair Evidence

When questioned hairs are submitted to a forensic laboratory for examination, they must always be accompanied by an adequate number of standard/reference samples from the victim of the crime and from individuals suspected of having deposited hair at the crime scene. We have learned that hair from different parts of the body varies significantly in its physical characteristics. Likewise, hair from any one area of the body can also have a wide range of characteristics. For this

nuclear DNA
DNA that is present in the nucleus of a cell and that is inherited from both parents

mitochondrial DNA
DNA present in small structures (mitochondria) outside the nucleus of a cell; mitochondria supply energy to the cell; this form of DNA is inherited maternally (from the mother)

MyCrimeKit: WebExtra 11.1
Step into the Role of the First Officer Responding to a Violent Crime Scene
www.mycrimekit.com

Case Files Hair Evidence

Figure Bill Cosby and his son Ennis Cosby.
Courtesy Redux Pictures

The murder of Ennis Cosby, son of entertainer Bill Cosby, at first appeared unsolvable. It was a random act. When his car tire went flat, Ennis pulled off the road and called a friend on his cellular phone to ask for assistance. Shortly thereafter, an assailant demanded money and, when Cosby didn't respond quickly enough, shot him once in the temple. Acting on a tip from a friend of the assailant, police investigators later found a .38-caliber revolver wrapped in a blue cap miles from the crime scene. Mikail Markhasev was arrested and charged with murder.

At trial, the district attorney introduced firearms evidence to show that the recovered gun had fired the bullet aimed at Cosby. However, a single hair also recovered from the cap dramatically linked Markhasev to the crime. Los Angeles Police Department forensic analyst Harry Klann identified six DNA markers from the follicular tissue adhering to the hair root that matched Markhasev's DNA. This particular DNA profile is found in one out of 15,500 members of the general population. Upon hearing all of the evidence, the jury deliberated and convicted Markhasev of murder.

reason, the questioned and standard/reference hairs must come from the same area of the body; one cannot, for instance, compare head hair to pubic hair. It is also important that the collection of standard/reference hair be carried out in a way to ensure a representative sampling of hair from any one area of the body.

Forensic hair comparisons generally involve either head hair or pubic hair. Collecting 50 full-length hairs from all areas of the scalp normally ensures a representative sampling of head hair. Likewise, a minimum collection of 24 full-length pubic hairs should cover the range of characteristics present in this type of hair. In rape cases, care must first be taken to comb the pubic area with a clean comb to remove all loose foreign hair present before the victim is sampled for standard/reference hair. The comb should then be packaged in a separate envelope.

Because a hair may vary in color and other morphological features over its entire length, the entire hair is collected. This requirement is best accomplished by either pulling the hair out of the skin or clipping it at the skin line. During an autopsy, hair samples are routinely collected from a victim of suspicious death. Because the autopsy may occur early in an investigation, the need for hair standard/reference samples may not always be apparent. However, one should never rule out the possible involvement of hair evidence in subsequent investigative findings. Failure to make this simple collection may result in complicated legal problems later.

Quick Review

- The hair shaft is composed of three layers called the cuticle, cortex, and medulla and is most intensely examined by the forensic scientist.

- When comparing strands of hair, the criminalist is particularly interested in matching the color, length, and diameter. Other important features for comparing hair are the presence or absence of a medulla and the distribution, shape, and color intensity of pigment granules in the cortex.

- The probability of detecting DNA in hair roots is more likely for hair being examined in its anagen or early growth phase as opposed to its catagen or telogen phases.

- The follicular tag, a translucent piece of tissue surrounding the hair's shaft near the root, is a rich source of DNA associated with hair. Mitochondrial DNA can also be extracted from the hair shaft.

- All positive microscopic hair comparisons must be confirmed by DNA analysis.

Forensic Examination of Fibers

Just as hair left at a crime scene can serve as identification, the same logic can reasonably be extended to the fibers that compose our fabrics and garments. Fibers may become important evidence in incidents that involve personal contact—such as homicide, assault, and sexual offenses—in which cross-transfers may occur between the clothing of suspect and victim. Similarly, the force of impact between a hit-and-run victim and a vehicle often leaves fibers, threads, or even whole pieces of clothing adhering to parts of the vehicle. Fibers may also become fixed in screens or glass broken in the course of a breaking-and-entering attempt.

Regardless of where and under what conditions fibers are recovered, their ultimate value as forensic evidence depends on the criminalist's ability to narrow their origin to a limited number of sources or even to a single source. Unfortunately, mass production of garments and fabrics has limited the value of fiber evidence in this respect, and only rarely do fibers recovered at a crime scene provide individual identification with a high degree of certainty.

Types of Fibers

For centuries, humans depended on fibers derived from natural sources such as plants and animals. However, early in the 20th century, the first manufactured fiber—rayon—became a practical reality, followed in the 1920s by the introduction of cellulose acetate. Since the late 1930s, scientists have produced dozens of new fibers. In fact, the development of fibers, fabrics, finishes, and other textile-processing techniques has made greater advances since 1900 than in the preceding five thousand years of recorded history. Today, such varied items as clothing, carpeting, drapes, wigs, and even artificial turf attest to the predominant role that manufactured fibers have come to play in our culture and environment. When discussing forensic examination of fibers, it is convenient to classify them into two broad groups: *natural* and *manufactured*.

Natural Fibers **Natural fibers** are wholly derived from animal or plant sources. Animal fibers constitute most natural fibers encountered in crime laboratory examinations. These include hair coverings from such animals as sheep (wool), goats (mohair, cashmere), camels, llamas, alpacas, and vicuñas. Fur fibers include those obtained from animals such as mink, rabbit, beaver, and muskrat.

Forensic examination of animal fibers uses the same procedures discussed in the previous section for the forensic examination of animal hairs. Identification and comparison of such fibers relies solely on a microscopic examination of color and morphological characteristics. Again, a sufficient number of standard/reference specimens must be examined to establish the range of fiber characteristics of the suspect fabric.

By far the most prevalent plant fiber is cotton. The wide use of undyed white cotton fibers in clothing and other fabrics has made its evidential value almost meaningless, although the presence of dyed cotton in a combination of colors has, in some cases, enhanced its evidential significance. The microscopic view of cotton fiber shown in Figure 11–9 reveals its most distinguishing feature—a ribbonlike shape with twists at irregular intervals.

natural fibers
Fibers derived entirely from animal or plant sources

Manufactured Fibers Beginning with the introduction of rayon in 1911 and the development of nylon in 1939, **manufactured fibers** have increasingly replaced natural fibers in garments and fabrics. Such fibers are marketed under hundreds of different trade names. To reduce consumer confusion, the U.S. Federal Trade Commission has approved "generic" or family names for the grouping of all manufactured fibers. Many of these generic classes are produced by several manufacturers and are sold under a confusing variety of trade names. For example, in the United States, polyesters are marketed under names that include Dacron, Fortrel, and Kodel. In England, polyesters are called Terylene. Table 11–1 lists major generic fibers, along with common trade names and their characteristics and applications.

The first machine-made fibers were manufactured from raw materials derived from cotton or wood pulp. These materials are processed, and pure cellulose is extracted from

FIGURE 11–9 Photomicrograph of cotton fiber (450x).

manufactured fibers
Fibers derived from either natural or synthetic polymers

them. Depending on the type of fiber desired, the cellulose may be chemically treated and dissolved in an appropriate solvent before it is forced through the small holes of a spinning jet, or spinneret, to produce the fiber. Fibers manufactured from natural raw materials in this manner are classified as *regenerated fibers* and commonly include rayon, acetate, and triacetate, all of which are produced from regenerated cellulose.

Table 11–1
Major Generic Fibers

Major Generic Fiber	Characteristics	Major Domestic and Industrial Uses
Acetate	• Luxurious feel and appearance • Wide range of colors and lusters • Excellent drapability and softness • Relatively fast-drying • Shrink-, moth-, and mildew-resistant	*Apparel*: Blouses, dresses, foundation garments, lingerie, linings, shirts, slacks, sportswear *Fabrics*: Brocade, crepe, double knits, faille, knitted jerseys, lace, satin, taffeta, tricot *Home Furnishings*: Draperies, upholstery *Other*: Cigarette filters, fiberfill for pillows, quilted products
Acrylic	• Soft and warm • Wool-like • Retains shape • Resilient • Quick-drying • Resistant to moths, sunlight, oil, and chemicals	*Apparel*: Dresses, infant wear, knitted garments, skiwear, socks, sportswear, sweaters *Fabrics*: Fleece and pile fabrics, facing fabrics in bonded fabrics, simulated furs, jerseys *Home Furnishings*: Blankets, carpets, draperies, upholstery *Other*: Auto tops, awnings, hand-knitting and craft yarns, industrial and geotextile fabrics Resistant to moths, sunlight, oil, and chemicals
Aramid	• Does not melt • Highly flame-resistant • Great strength • Great resistance to stretch • Maintains shape and form at high temperatures	Hot-gas filtration fabrics, protective clothing, military helmets, protective vests, structural composites for aircraft and boats, sailcloth, tires, ropes and cables, mechanical rubber goods, marine and sporting goods

Bicomponent	• Thermal bonding • Self bulking • Very fine fibers • Unique cross-sections • The functionality of special polymers or additives at reduced cost	Uniform distribution of adhesive; fiber remains a part of structure and adds integrity; customized sheath materials to bond various materials; wide range of bonding temperatures; cleaner, environmentally friendly (no effluent); recyclable; lamination/molding/densification of composites
Lyocell	• Soft, strong, absorbent • Good dyeability • Fibrillates during wet processing to produce special textures	*Apparel:* Dresses, slacks, coats
Melamine	• White and dyeable • Flame resistance and low thermal conductivity • High-heat dimensional stability • Processable on standard textile equipment	*Fire-Blocking Fabrics*: Aircraft seating, fire blockers for upholstered furniture in high-risk occupancies (e.g., to meet California TB 133 requirements) *Protective Clothing*: Firefighters' turnout gear, insulating thermal liners, knit hoods, molten metal splash apparel, heat-resistant gloves *Filter Media*: High-capacity, high-efficiency, high-temperature baghouse air filters
Modacrylic	• Soft • Resilient • Abrasion and flame resistant • Quick-drying • Resists acids and alkalies • Retains shape	*Apparel*: Deep-pile coats, trims, linings, simulated fur, wigs and hairpieces *Fabrics*: Fleece fabrics, industrial fabrics, knit-pile fabric backings, nonwoven fabrics *Home Furnishings*: Awnings, blankets, carpets, flame-resistant draperies and curtains, scatter rugs *Other*: Filters, paint rollers, stuffed toys

Nylon	• Exceptionally strong	*Apparel*: Blouses, dresses, foundation garments, hosiery, lingerie and underwear, raincoats, ski and snow apparel, suits, windbreakers
	• Supple	
	• Abrasion resistant	
	• Lustrous	*Home Furnishings*: Bedspreads, carpets, draperies, curtains, upholstery
	• Easy to wash	
	• Resists damage from oil and many chemicals	*Other*: Air hoses, conveyor and seat belts, parachutes, racket strings, ropes and nets, sleeping bags, tarpaulins, tents, thread, tire cord, geotextiles
	• Resilient	
	• Low in moisture absorbency	
Olefin	• Unique wicking properties that make it very comfortable	*Apparel*: Pantyhose, underwear, knitted sports shirts, men's half-hose, men's knitted sportswear, sweaters
	• Abrasion resistant	
	• Quick-drying	*Home Furnishings*: Carpet and carpet backing, slipcovers, upholstery
	• Resistant to deterioration from chemicals, mildew, perspiration, rot, and weather	
	• Sensitive to heat	*Other*: Dye nets, filter fabrics, laundry and sandbags, geotextiles, automotive interiors, cordage, doll hair, industrial sewing thread
	• Soil resistant	
	• Strong; very lightweight	
	• Excellent colorfastness	
Polyester	• Strong	*Apparel*: Blouses, shirts, career apparel, children's wear, dresses, half-hose, insulated garments, ties, lingerie and underwear, permanent-press garments, slacks, suits
	• Resistant to stretching and shrinking	
	• Resistant to most chemicals	
	• Quick-drying	*Home Furnishings*: Carpets, curtains, draperies, sheets, pillowcases
	• Crisp and resilient when wet or dry	
	• Wrinkle and abrasion resistant	*Other*: Fiberfill for various products, fire hose, power belting, ropes and nets, tire cord, sail, V-belts
	• Retains heat-set pleats and creases	
	• Easy to wash	

PBI	• Extremely flame resistant	Suitable for high-performance protective apparel such as firefighters' turnout coats, astronaut space suits, and applications in which fire resistance is important
	• Outstanding comfort factor combined with thermal and chemical stability properties	
	• Will not burn or melt	
	• Low shrinkage when exposed to flame	
Rayon	• Highly absorbent	*Apparel*: Blouses, coats, dresses, jackets, lingerie, linings, millinery, rainwear, slacks, sports shirts, sportswear, suits, ties, work clothes
	• Soft and comfortable	
	• Easy to dye	*Home Furnishings*: Bedspreads, blankets, carpets, curtains, draperies, sheets, slipcovers, tablecloths, upholstery
	• Versatile	
	• Good drapability	*Other*: Industrial products, medical-surgical products, nonwoven products, tire cord
Spandex	• Can be stretched 500 percent without breaking	*Articles (in which stretch is desired):* Athletic apparel, bathing suits, delicate laces, foundation garments, golf jackets, ski pants, slacks, support and surgical hose
	• Can be stretched repeatedly and recover original length	
	• Lightweight	
	• Stronger and more durable than rubber	
	• Resistant to body oils	

Source: American Fiber Manufacturers Assoc. Inc., Washington, D.C., http://www.fibersource.com/f-tutor/q-guide.htm.

Most of the fibers currently manufactured are produced solely from synthetic chemicals and are therefore classified as synthetic fibers. These include nylons, polyesters, and acrylics. The creation of synthetic fibers became a reality only when scientists developed a method of synthesizing long-chained molecules called **polymers**.

In 1930, chemists discovered an unusual characteristic of one of the polymers under investigation. When a glass rod in contact with viscous material in a beaker was slowly pulled away, the substance adhered to the rod and formed a fine

polymer
A substance composed of a large number of atoms that are usually arranged in repeating units

filament that hardened as soon as it entered the cool air. Furthermore, the cold filaments could be stretched several times their extended length to produce a flexible, strong, and attractive fiber. This first synthetic fiber was improved and then marketed as nylon. Since then, fiber chemists have successfully synthesized new polymers and have developed more efficient methods for manufacturing them. These efforts have produced a multitude of synthetic fibers.

Polymers The polymer is the basic chemical substance of all synthetic fibers. Indeed, an almost unbelievable array of household, industrial, and recreational products is manufactured from polymers; these include plastics, paints, adhesives, and synthetic rubber. Polymers exist in countless forms and varieties and with the proper treatment can be made to assume different chemical and physical properties.

As we have already observed, chemical substances are composed of basic structural units called **molecules**. The molecules of most materials are composed of just a few atoms; for example, water, H_2O, has 2 atoms of hydrogen and 1 atom of oxygen. The heroin molecule, $C_{21}H_{23}O_5N$, contains 21 atoms of carbon, 23 atoms of hydrogen, 5 atoms of oxygen, and 1 atom of nitrogen. Polymers, on the other hand, are formed by linking a large number of molecules, so that a polymer often contains thousands or even millions of atoms. This is why polymers are often referred to as **macromolecules**, or "big" molecules.

Simply, a polymer can be pictured as resembling a long, repeating chain, with each link representing the basic structure of the polymer (see Figure 11–10). The repeating molecular units in the polymer, called **monomers**, are joined end to end, so that thousands link to form a long chain. What makes polymer chemistry so fascinating is the countless possibilities for linking different molecules. By simply varying the chemical structure of the monomers, and by devising numerous ways to weave them together, chemists have created polymers that exhibit different properties. This versatility enables polymer chemists to synthesize glues, plastics, paints, and fibers.

molecule
Two or more atoms held together by chemical bonds

macromolecule
A molecule with a high molecular mass

monomer
The basic unit of structure from which a polymer is constructed

Monomer

FIGURE 11–10 The chain-link model of a segment of a polymer molecule. The molecule may contain as many as several million monomer units or links.

Not all polymers are synthesized in the chemical laboratory; nature has produced polymers that humans have not yet been able to copy. For example, the proteins that form the basic structure of animal hairs, as well as of all living matter, are polymers, composed of thousands of amino acids linked in a highly organized arrangement and sequence. Similarly, cellulose (the basic ingredient of wood and cotton) and starch are both natural polymers built by the combination of several thousand carbohydrate monomers, as shown in Figure 11–11. Hence, the synthesis of manufactured fibers merely represents an extension of chemical principles that nature has used to produce hair and vegetable fibers.

FIGURE 11–11
Starch and cellulose are natural carbohydrate polymers consisting of a large number of repeating units or monomers.

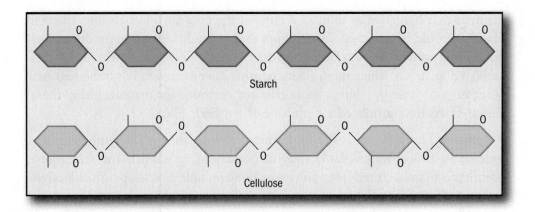

Starch

Cellulose

Identification and Comparison of Manufactured Fibers

The evidential value of fibers lies in the criminalist's ability to trace their origin. Obviously, if the examiner is presented with fabrics that can be exactly fitted together at their torn edges, the fabrics must be of common origin.

More often, however, the criminalist obtains a limited number of fibers for identification and comparison. Generally, in these situations obtaining a physical match is unlikely, and the examiner must resort to a side-by-side comparison of the standard/reference and crime-scene fibers.

Microscopic Examination of Fibers The first and most important step in the examination is a microscopic comparison for color and diameter using a comparison microscope. Unless these two characteristics agree, there is little reason to suspect a match. Other morphological features that may aid in the comparison are lengthwise striations (lined markings) on the surface of some fibers and the pitting of the fiber's surface with delustering particles (usually titanium dioxide) added in the manufacturing process to reduce shine (see Figure 11–12).

FIGURE 11–12
Photomicrographs of synthetic fibers:
(a) cellulose triacetate (450x) and
(b) olefin fiber embedded with titanium dioxide particles (450x).

(a)

(b)

The cross-sectional shape of a fiber may also help characterize the fiber (see Figure 11–13).[5] In the early 1980s, Wayne Williams was charged and tried for the murder of two individuals in the Atlanta, Georgia region. During the eight week trail, evidence linking Williams to those murders and to the murder of ten other individuals was introduced. An essential part of the government's case was the numerous fibers linking Williams to these murders. For example, unusually shaped yellow-green fibers discovered on a number of the murder victims were linked to a carpet in the Williams home. This fiber was a key element in proving Williams's guilt. A photomicrograph of this unusually shaped fiber is shown in Figure 11–14.

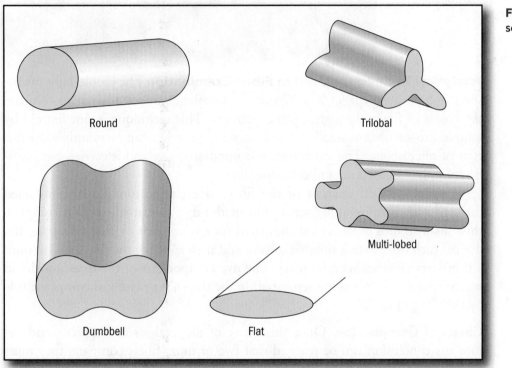

FIGURE 11–13 Cross-sectional shapes of fibers.

Although two fibers may seem to have the same color when viewed under the microscope, compositional differences may exist in the dyes that were applied to them during their manufacture. In fact, most textile fibers are impregnated with a mixture of dyes selected to obtain a desired shade or color. The significance of a fiber comparison is enhanced when the forensic examiner can show that the questioned and standard/reference fibers have the same dye composition.

FIGURE 11–14
A scanning electron photomicrograph of the cross-section of a nylon fiber removed from a sheet used to transport the body of a murder victim. The fiber, associated with a carpet in Wayne Williams's home, was manufactured in 1971 in relatively small quantities. *Courtesy Federal Bureau of Investigation, Washington, D.C.*

Analytical Techniques Used in Fiber Examination The visible-light microspectrophotometer (pages 274-275) is a convenient way for analysts to compare the colors of fibers through spectral patterns. This technique is not limited by sample size—a fiber as small as 1 millimeter long or less can be examined by this type of microscope. The examination is nondestructive and is carried out on fibers simply mounted on a microscope slide.

A more detailed analysis of the fiber's dye composition can be obtained through a chromatographic separation of the dye constituents. To accomplish this, small strands of fibers are compared for dye content by first extracting the dye off each fiber with a suitable solvent and then spotting the dye solution onto a thin-layer chromatography plate. The dye components of the questioned and standard/reference fibers are separated on the thin-layer plate and compared side by side for similarity.[6]

Chemical Composition. Once this phase of the analysis is complete, and before any conclusion can be reached that two or more fibers compare, they must be shown to have the same chemical composition. In this respect, tests are performed to confirm that all of the fibers involved belong to the same broad generic class. Additionally, the comparison will be substantially enhanced if it can be demonstrated that all of the fibers belong to the same subclassification within their generic class. For example, at least four different types of nylon are available in commercial and consumer markets, including nylon 6, nylon 6–10, nylon 11, and nylon 6–6. Although all types of nylon have many properties in common, each may differ in physical shape, appearance, and dyeability because of modifications in basic chemical structure. Similarly, a study of more than two hundred different samples of acrylic fibers revealed that they could be divided into 24 distinguishable groups on the basis of their polymeric structure and microscopic characteristics.[7]

Textile chemists have devised numerous tests for determining the class of a fiber. However, unlike the textile chemist, the criminalist frequently does not have the luxury of having a substantial quantity of fabric to work with and must therefore select tests that will yield the most information with the least amount of material. Only a single fiber may be available for analysis, and often this may amount to no more than a minute strand recovered from a fingernail scraping of a homicide or rape victim.

Birefringence. A useful physical property of fibers is that many manufactured fibers exhibit double refraction or birefringence (discussed in Chapter 4). Synthetic fibers are manufactured by melting a polymeric substance or dissolving it in a solvent and then forcing it through the fine holes of a spinneret. The polymer emerges as a fine filament, with its molecules aligned parallel to the length of the filament (see Figure 11–15). Just as the regular arrangement of atoms produces a crystal, so will the regular arrangement of the fiber's polymers cause crystallinity in the finished fiber. This crystallinity makes a fiber stiff and strong and gives it the optical property of double refraction.

FIGURE 11–15
In the production of manufactured fibers, the bulk polymer is forced through small holes to form a filament in which all the polymers are aligned in the same direction.

Polarized white light passing through a synthetic fiber is split into two rays that are perpendicular to each other, causing the fiber to display polarization or interference colors when viewed under a polarizing microscope (see Figure 11–16). Depending on the class of fiber, each polarized plane of light has a characteristic index of refraction. This value can be determined by immersing the fiber in a fluid with a comparable refractive index and observing the disappearance of the Becke line under a polarizing microscope. Table 11–2 lists the two refractive indices of some common classes of fibers, along with their birefringence. The virtue of this technique is that a single microscopic fiber can be analyzed in a nondestructive manner.

FIGURE 11–16
A photomicrograph of nylon fibers displaying interference colors when observed between the crossed polars of a polarizing microscope (50x). *Courtesy Williams Randle, Missouri State Highway Patrol crime laboratory, Jefferson City, Mo.*

Infrared Absorption. The polymers that compose a manufactured fiber, just as in any other organic substance, selectively absorb infrared light in a characteristic pattern. Infrared spectrophotometry thus provides a rapid and reliable method for identifying the generic class, and in some cases the subclasses, of fibers. The infrared microspectrophotometer combines a microscope with an infrared spectrophotometer (see page 277). Such a combination makes possible the infrared analysis of a small single-strand fiber while it is being viewed under a microscope.[8]

Table 11–2
Refractive Indices of Common Textile Fibers

| Fiber | Refractive Index | | |
	Parallel	Perpendicular	Birefringence
Acetate	1.478	1.477	0.001
Triacetate	1.472	1.471	0.001
Acrylic	1.524	1.520	0.004
Nylon			
Nylon 6	1.568	1.515	0.053
Nylon 6–6	1.582	1.519	0.063
Polyester			
Dacron	1.710	1.535	0.175
Kodel	1.642	1.540	0.102
Modacrylic	1.536	1.531	0.005
Rayon			
Cuprammonium rayon	1.552	1.520	0.032
Viscose rayon	1.544	1.520	0.024

Note: The listed values are for specific fibers, which explains the precise values given. In identification work, such precision is not practical; values within 0.02 or 0.03 of those listed will suffice.

Significance of Fiber Evidence

Once a fiber match has been determined, the question of the significance of such a finding is bound to be raised. No analytical technique permits the criminalist to associate a fiber strand definitively to any single garment. Furthermore, except in the most unusual circumstances, no statistical databases are available for determining the probability of a fiber's origin. Considering the mass distribution of synthetic fibers and the constantly changing fashion tastes of our society, it is highly unlikely that such data will be available in the foreseeable future.

Despite these limitations, one should not discount or minimize the significance of a fiber association. An enormous variety of fibers exists in our society. By simply looking at the random individuals we meet every day, we can see how unlikely it is to find two different people wearing identically colored fabrics (with the exception of blue denims or white cottons). There are thousands of different-colored fibers in our environment. Combine this with the fact that forensic scientists compare not only the color of fibers but also their size, shape, microscopic appearance, chemical composition, and dye content, and one can now begin to appreciate how unlikely it is to find two indistinguishable colored fibers emanating from randomly selected sources.

Furthermore, the significance of a fiber association increases dramatically if the analyst can link two or more distinctly different fibers to the same object. Likewise, the associative value of fiber evidence is dramatically enhanced if it is accompanied by other types of physical evidence linking a person or object to a crime. As with most class evidence, the significance of a fiber comparison is dictated by the circumstances of the case; by the location, number, and nature of the fibers examined; and, most important, by the judgment of an experienced examiner.

Collection and Preservation of Fiber Evidence

MyCrimeKit: WebExtra 11.2
Assume the Duties of an Evidence-Collection Technician at a Violent Crime Scene
www.mycrimekit.com

As criminal investigators have become more aware of the potential contribution of trace physical evidence to the success of their investigations, they have placed greater emphasis on conducting thorough crime-scene searches for evidence of forensic value. Their skill and determination at carrying out these tasks is tested in the collection of fiber-related evidence. Fiber evidence can be associated with virtually any type of crime. It usually cannot be seen with the naked eye and thus easily can be overlooked by someone not specifically searching for it.

An investigator committed to optimizing the laboratory's chances for locating minute strands of fibers identifies and preserves potential "carriers" of fiber evidence. Relevant articles of clothing should be packaged carefully in paper bags. Each article must be placed in a separate bag to avoid cross-contamination of evidence. Scrupulous care must be taken to prevent articles of clothing from different people or from different locations from coming into contact. Such articles must not even be placed on the same surface before packaging. Likewise, carpets, rugs, and bedding are to be folded carefully to protect areas suspected of containing fibers. Car seats should be carefully covered with polyethylene sheets to protect fiber evidence, and knife blades should be covered to protect adhering fibers. If a body is thought to have been wrapped at one time in a blanket or carpet, adhesive tape lifts of exposed body areas may reveal fiber strands.

Occasionally the field investigator may need to remove a fiber from an object, particularly if loosely adhering fibrous material may be lost in transit to the laboratory. These fibers must be removed with a clean forceps and placed in a small sheet of paper, which, after folding and labeling, can be placed inside another container. Again, scrupulous care must be taken to prevent contact between fibers collected from different objects or from different locations.

In the laboratory, the search for fiber evidence on clothing and other relevant objects, as well as in debris, is time consuming and tedious and will test the skill and patience of the examiner. The crime-scene investigator can manage this task by collecting only relevant items for examination. The crime-scene investigator must pinpoint areas where a likely transfer of fiber evidence occurred and then ensure proper collection and preservation of these materials.

Case Files Fatal Vision Revisited

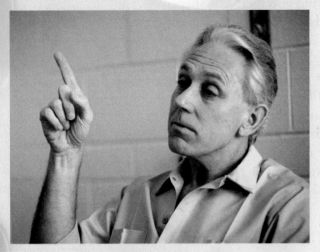

Jeffrey MacDonald in 1995 at Sheridan, Oregon, Federal Correctional Institution. *Courtesy AP Wide World Photos*

Dr. Jeffrey MacDonald was convicted in 1979 of murdering his wife and two young daughters. The events surrounding the crime and the subsequent trial were recounted in Joe McGinniss's best-selling book *Fatal Vision*. The focus of MacDonald's defense was that intruders entered his home and committed these violent acts. Eleven years after this conviction, MacDonald's attorneys filed a petition for a new trial, claiming the existence of "critical new" evidence.

The defense asserted that wig fibers found on a hairbrush in the MacDonald residence were evidence that an intruder dressed in a wig entered the MacDonald home on the day of the murder. Subsequent examination of this claim by the FBI Laboratory focused on a blond fall (a type of artificial hair extension) frequently worn by MacDonald's wife. Fibers removed from the fall were shown to clearly match fibers on the hairbrush. The examination included the use of infrared microspectrophotometry to demonstrate that the suspect wig fibers were chemically identical to fibers found in the composition of the MacDonald fall (see Figure 1). Hence, although wig fibers were found at the crime scene, the source of these fibers could be accounted for—they came from Mrs. MacDonald's fall.

Another piece of evidence cited by MacDonald's lawyers was a bluish-black woolen fiber found on the body of Mrs. MacDonald. They claimed that this fiber compared to a bluish-black woolen fiber recovered from the club used to assault her. These wool fibers were central to MacDonald's defense that the "intruders" wore dark-colored clothing. Initial examination showed that the fibers were microscopically indistin-

guishable. However, the FBI also compared the two wool fibers by visible-light microspectrophotometry. Comparison of their spectra clearly showed that their dye compositions differed, providing no evidence of outside intruders (see Figure 2). Ultimately, the U.S. Supreme Court denied the merits of MacDonald's petition for a new trial.

FIGURE 1

A fiber comparison made with an infrared spectrophotometer. The infrared spectrum of a fiber from Mrs. MacDonald's fall compares to a fiber recovered from a hairbrush in the MacDonald home. These fibers were identified as modacrylics, the most common type of synthetic fiber used in the manufacture of human hair goods. *Courtesy SA Michael Malone, FBI Laboratory, Washington, D.C.*

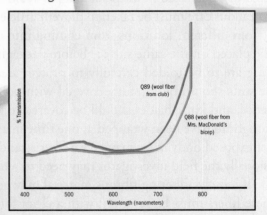

FIGURE 2

The visible-light spectrum for the woolen fiber recovered from Mrs. MacDonald's body is clearly different from that of the fiber recovered from the club used to assault her. *Courtesy SA Michael Malone, FBI Laboratory, Washington, D.C.*

Source: B. M. Murtagh and M. P. Malone, "Fatal Vision Revisited," Police Chief (June 1993): 15.

Quick Review

- Fibers may be classified into two broad groups: *natural* and *manufactured*.

- Most fibers currently manufactured are produced solely from synthetic chemicals and are therefore classified as *synthetic fibers*. They include nylons, polyesters, and acrylics.

- Microscopic comparisons between questioned and standard/reference fibers are initially undertaken for color and diameter characteristics. Other features that could be important in comparing fibers are striations on the surface of the fiber, the presence of delustering particles, and the cross-sectional shape of the fiber.

- The visible-light microspectrophotometer is a convenient way for analysts to compare the colors of fibers through spectral patterns.

- Infrared spectrophotometry and the polarizing microscope are reliable methods for identifying the chemical composition of fibers.

- Fiber evidence collected at each location should be placed in separate containers to avoid cross-contamination. Care must be taken to prevent articles of clothing from different people or from different locations from coming into contact.

Chapter Review

- The hair shaft is composed of three layers called the cuticle, cortex, and medulla and is most intensely examined by the forensic scientist.

- When comparing strands of hair, the criminalist is particularly interested in matching the color, length, and diameter. Other important features for comparing hair are the presence or absence of a medulla and the distribution, shape, and color intensity of pigment granules in the cortex.

- The probability of detecting DNA in hair roots is more likely for hair being examined in its anagen or early growth phase as opposed to its catagen or telogen phases.

- The follicular tag, a translucent piece of tissue surrounding the hair's shaft near the root, is a rich source of DNA associated with hair. Mitochondrial DNA can also be extracted from the hair shaft.

- All positive microscopic hair comparisons must be confirmed by DNA analysis.

- Fibers may be classified into two broad groups: natural and manufactured.

- Most fibers currently manufactured are produced solely from *synthetic chemicals* and are therefore classified as synthetic fibers. They include nylons, polyesters, and acrylics.

- Microscopic comparisons between questioned and standard/reference fibers are initially undertaken for color and diameter characteristics. Other features that could be important in comparing fibers are striations on the surface of the fiber, the presence of delustering particles, and the cross-sectional shape of the fiber.

- The visible-light microspectrophotometer is a convenient way for analysts to compare the colors of fibers through spectral patterns.

- Infrared spectrophotometry and the polarizing microscope are reliable methods for identifying the chemical composition of fibers.

- Fiber evidence collected at each location should be placed in separate containers to avoid cross-contamination. Care must be taken to prevent articles of clothing from different people or from different locations from coming into contact.

Review Questions

1. The _____ is important for the individualization of hair.
   a. cuticle
   b. cortex
   c. follicular tag
   d. medulla

2. The final growth phase in which hair naturally falls out of the skin is called the
   a. telogen phase.
   b. anagen phase.
   c. catagen phase.
   d. follicular phase.

3. The most prevalent plant fiber is
   a. hemp.
   b. cotton.
   c. wool.
   d. mohair.

4. Which of the following is not a manufactured fiber grouping?
   a. polyester
   b. rayon
   c. mohair
   d. spandex

5. In the examination of fibers, the first and most important step in the examination will be
   a. a microscopic comparison for color and diameter using a comparison microscope.
   b. a determination of whether the fiber is natural or manufactured.
   c. synthesizing long-chained molecules into a polymer.
   d. analyzing the individual characteristics of the material.

6. True or False: Because of advances in forensic technology and the equipment available, it is now possible to individualize human hair through its morphology.

7. True or False: Two of the features that make hair a good subject for establishing individual identity are its resistance to chemical decomposition and its ability to retain structural features over a long period of time.

8. True or False: Most often, when hair evidence is present in a criminal case, the primary purpose is to establish the identity of the individual when no other means is available.

9. True or False: The ultimate value of fibers as forensic evidence will depend on the criminalist's ability to narrow their origin to a limited number of sources or even to a single source.

10. True or False: Properties frequently used to identify fibers are refractive index and an IR spectrum.

11. What is hair and what organ produces it?

12. Name and briefly define the three layers of the hair shaft.

13. What two features make hair a good subject for establishing individual identity? To which layer of the hair shaft are much of these features attributed?

14. The scale pattern of the cuticle is an important feature for characterizing _____ hair.

15. What is the main forensic importance of the cortex?

16. What is the difference between the medullae of human and animal hairs? Name one exception to this among humans.

17. Name the three phases of hair growth. A criminalist is more likely to collect DNA from hairs in which stage of growth? Why?

18. Why must microscopic human hair comparisons be undertaken with extreme caution?

19. In comparing hairs, what aspects of the hair is the criminalist particularly interested in matching? Name at least one other important feature that the criminalist may compare.

20. Which of the following questions cannot be answered with a microscopic examination of hair?
    a. whether a hair came from a 25-year-old or an infant
    b. whether a hair is from a man or a woman
    c. whether a hair is from a scalp or a beard
    d. whether the hair is consistent with Caucasian or Negroid hair

21. What types of hairs found at a crime scene are most likely to provide useful DNA evidence? Why?

22. What part of a hair is most likely to yield useful DNA evidence?

23. Why must questioned hairs and standard/reference hairs being compared come from the same area of the body?

24. Hairs from which parts of the body are most often used for hair comparisons?

25. Why should the entire hair be collected when performing a hair comparison?

26. Define polymer and monomer. Why are polymers sometimes known as macromolecules?

27. Which of the following is not an example of a natural polymer?
    a. starch
    b. cellulose
    c. sugar
    d. protein

28. What two morphological characteristics does a criminalist first compare when examining fibers with a microscope? What other features may be important in such a comparison?

29. What analytical technique does a criminalist use to analyze the composition of the dye in a fiber?

30. Describe three analytical techniques for comparing the color of two fibers.

Application and Critical Thinking

1. Indicate the phase of growth of each of the following hairs:
   a. the root is club-shaped
   b. the hair has a follicular tag
   c. the root bulb is flame-shaped
   d. the root is elongated

2. A criminalist studying a dyed sample hair notices that the dyed color ends about 1.5 centimeters from the tip of the hair. Approximately how many weeks before the examination was the hair dyed? Explain your answer.

3. Following are descriptions of several hairs; based on these descriptions, indicate the likely race of the person from whom the hair originated.
   a. evenly distributed, fine pigmentation
   b. continuous medullation
   c. dense, uneven pigmentation
   d. wavy with a round cross-section

4. Criminalist Pete Evett is collecting fiber evidence from a murder scene. He notices fibers on the victim's shirt and trousers, so he places both of these items of clothing in a plastic bag. He also sees fibers on a sheet near the victim, so he balls up the sheet and places it in separate plastic bag. Noticing fibers adhering to the windowsill from which the attacker gained entrance, Pete carefully removes them with his fingers and places them in a regular envelope. What mistakes, if any, did Pete make while collecting this evidence?

5. For each of the following human hair samples, indicate the medulla pattern present.

A. _____   D. _____   G. _____

B. _____   E. _____   H. _____

C. _____   F. _____   I. _____

6. The most common scale patterns found on hairs are generally classified as coronal, spinous, and imbricate. Examine the scale casts of animal hairs shown here and indicate the scale pattern of each.

A. _____   B. _____

_____   _____

C. _____   D. _____

_____   _____

E. _____   F. _____

_____   _____

G. _____   H. _____

_____   _____

7. A young child is kidnapped from her school playground. Shown on the left is a reference sample of the kidnapped child's hair. The only cars that left the parking lot before the child was discovered to be missing were those of four cafeteria workers. The car of each worker was searched and hairs collected. These recovered hairs are shown on the right. Which recovered hair, if any, is consistent with that of the victim and warrants further investigation?

Hair from car of Worker A

Hair from car of Worker B

Reference Hair from Victim

Hair from car of Worker C

Hair from car of Worker D

Virtual Lab: Forensic Hair Analysis

To perform a virtual hair analysis, go to www.pearsoncustom.com/us/vlm/

Virtual Lab: Examination of Textile Fibers by Microscopy

To perform a virtual fiber examination lab, go to www.pearsoncustom.com/us/vlm/

Endnotes

1. J. D. Baker and D. L. Exline, Forensic Animal Hair Atlas: A Searchable Database on CD-ROM. RJ Lee Group, Inc., 350 Hochberg Rd., Monroeville, PA 15146.

2. M. M. Houk and B. Budowle, "Correlation of Microscopic and Mitochondrial DNA Hair Comparisons," *Journal of Forensic Sciences* 47 (2002): 964.

3. L. A. King, R. Wigmore, and J. M. Twibell, "The Morphology and Occurrence of Human Hair Sheath Cells," *Journal of the Forensic Science Society* 22 (1982): 267.

4. C. A. Linch et al., "Evaluation of the Human Hair Root for DNA Typing Subsequent to Microscopic Comparison," Journal of Forensic Sciences 43 (1998): 305.

5. S. Palenik and C. Fitzsimons, "Fiber Cross-Sections: Part I," *Microscope* 38 (1990): 187.

6. D. K. Laing et al., "The Standardisation of Thin-Layer Chromatographic Systems for Comparisons of Fibre Dyes," *Journal of the Forensic Science Society* 30 (1990): 299.

7. M. C. Grieve, "Another Look at the Classification of Acrylic Fibres, Using FTIR Microscopy," *Science & Justice* 35 (1995): 179.

8. M. W. Tungol et al., "Analysis of Single Polymer Fibers by Fourier Transform Infrared Microscopy: The Results of Case Studies," *Journal of Forensic Sciences* 36 (1992): 1027.

National Science Content Standards

  Scientific Inquiry

 Science and Technology

 Physical Science

 Science in Personal and Social Perspective

 Life Science

What Killed Napoleon?

Napoleon I, emperor of France, was sent into exile on the remote island of St. Helena by the British after his defeat at the Battle of Waterloo in 1815. St. Helena was hot, unsanitary, and rampant with disease. There, Napoleon was confined to a large reconstructed agricultural building known as Longwood House. Boredom and unhealthy living conditions gradually took their toll on Napoleon's mental and physical state. He began suffering from severe abdominal pains and experienced swelling of the ankles and general weakness of his limbs. From the fall of 1820, Napoleon's health began to deteriorate rapidly until death arrived on May 5, 1821. An autopsy concluded the cause of death to be stomach cancer.

It was inevitable that dying under British control, as Napoleon did, would bring with it numerous conspiratorial theories to account for his death. One of the more fascinating inquiries was conducted by a Swedish dentist, Sven Forshufvud, who systematically correlated the clinical symptoms of Napoleon's last days to those of arsenic poisoning. For Forshufvud, the key to unlocking the cause of Napoleon's death rested with Napoleon's hair. Forshufvud arranged to have Napoleon's hair measured for arsenic content by neutron activation analysis and found it consistent with arsenic poisoning over a lengthy period of time. Nevertheless, the cause of Napoleon's demise is still a matter for debate and speculation. Other Napoleon hairs collected in 1805 and 1814 have also shown high concentrations of arsenic, giving rise to the speculation that Napoleon was innocently exposed to arsenic. Even hair collected from Napoleon's three sisters, son, and first wife show significant levels of arsenic. Some question whether Napoleon even had clinical symptoms associated with arsenic poisoning. In truth, forensic science may never be able to answer the question "What killed Napoleon?"

Trace Evidence II: Metals, Paint, and Soil

Key Terms

alpha particle	gamma ray
atomic mass	isotope
atomic number	line spectrum
beta particle	mineral
continuous spectrum	neutron
electron	nucleus
electron orbital	proton
emission spectrum	pyrolysis
excited state	radioactivity

Considering that most materials originate from the earth's crust, it is not surprising that they are rarely obtained in pure form; instead, they include numerous elemental impurities that usually must be eliminated through industrial processing. However, it is usually not economically feasible to completely exclude all such minor impurities, especially if their presence has no effect on the appearance or performance of the final product. For this reason, many manufactured products, and even most natural materials, contain small quantities of elements present in concentrations of less than 1 percent, which are known as trace elements.

Forensic Analysis of Metals

For the criminalist, the presence of trace elements is particularly useful because they provide "invisible" markers that may establish the source of a material or at least provide additional points for comparison. For example, comparison of trace elements present in two metallic specimens may provide data on their source or origin. Table 12–1 illustrates how two types of brass alloys can readily be distinguished by their elemental composition.

Forensic investigators have examined the evidential value of trace elements present in metallic objects as well as paint, soil, glass, and fibers. One example is the examination of the bullet and bullet fragments recovered after the assassination of President John F. Kennedy.

Evidence in the Assassination of President Kennedy

Ever since President Kennedy was killed in 1963, questions have lingered about whether Lee Harvey Oswald was part of a conspiracy to assassinate the president, or a lone assassin. The Warren Commission, the official government body appointed to investigate the shooting, concluded that Oswald acted alone. This conclusion was criticized widely at the time it was reported and has been a source of controversy since that day.

Reconstructing the Assassination In arriving at its conclusions, the Warren Commission reconstructed the crime as follows: from a hidden position on the sixth floor of the Texas School Book Depository building, Oswald fired three shots from behind the president. The president was struck by two bullets, with one bullet totally missing the president's limousine. One bullet hit the president in the back, exited his throat, and went on to strike Texas Governor John Connally, who was sitting in a jump seat in front of the president. The bullet hit Connally in his back, exited his chest, struck his right wrist, and temporarily lodged in his left thigh. This bullet was later found on the governor's stretcher at the hospital. A second bullet in the skull fatally wounded the president.

FIGURE 12–1
President John F. Kennedy, Governor John Connally of Texas, and Mrs. Jacqueline Kennedy ride through Dallas moments before the assassination. *Courtesy Corbis/Bettmann*

Table 12–1
Elemental Analysis of Brass Alloys

	High-Tensile Brass (percentage)	Manganese Brass Element (percentage)
Copper	57.0	58.6
Aluminum	2.8	1.7
Zinc	35.0	33.8
Manganese	2.13	1.06
Iron	1.32	0.90
Nickel	0.48	1.02
Tin	0.64	1.70
Lead	0.17	0.72
Silicon	0.08	Nil

Source: R. L. Williams, "An Evaluation of the SEM with X-Ray Microanalyzer Accessory for Forensic Work," in Scanning Electron Microscopy/1971, O. Johari and I. Corvin, eds. (Chicago: IIT Research Institute, 1971), p. 541.

In a room at the Texas School Book Depository, a 6.5-millimeter Mannlicher-Carcano military rifle was found with Oswald's palm print on it. Also found were three spent 6.5-millimeter Western Cartridge Co./Mannlicher-Carcano (WCC/MC) cartridge cases. Oswald, an employee of the depository, had been seen there that morning and also a few minutes after the assassination, disappearing soon thereafter. He was apprehended a few miles from the depository nearly two hours after the shooting.

Questions and Criticisms Critics of the Warren Commission have long argued that evidence proves that Oswald did not act alone. Eyewitness accounts and acoustical data interpreted by some experts have been used to contend that a second shooter fired at the president from a region in front of the limousine (the so-called grassy knoll). Furthermore, critics argue that the Warren Commission's reconstruction of the crime assumed that only one bullet caused both the president's throat wound and Governor Connally's back wound. Critics contend that such damage would have deformed and mutilated a bullet. Instead, the recovered bullet showed some flattening, no deformity, and only about 1 percent weight loss.

In 1977 the U.S. House of Representatives Select Committee on Assassinations requested that the bullet taken from Connally's stretcher—along with bullet fragments recovered from the car and various wound areas—be examined for trace element levels. Because lead alloys used to manufacture bullets contain an assortment of trace elements, analysis of those trace elements provides a possible means for characterizing lead bullets. For example, antimony is often added to lead as a hardening agent; copper, bismuth, and silver are other trace elements commonly found in bullet lead.

Investigators compared the antimony and silver content of the bullet and bullet fragments recovered after the assassination. Previous studies had amply demonstrated that the levels of these two elements are particularly important for characterizing WCC/MC bullets. Bullet lead from this type of ammunition ranges in antimony concentration from 20 to 1,200 parts per million (ppm) and 5 to 15 ppm in silver content.

As can be seen in Table 12–2, the samples designated Q1 (the Connally stretcher bullet) and Q9 (bullet fragments from Connally's wrist) are indistinguishable from one another in antimony and silver content. The samples designated Q4 and Q5 (fragments from Kennedy's brain) are indistinguishable in antimony and silver content from samples Q2 and Q14 (fragments recovered from two different areas in the car). However, all four of those samples are different from Q1 and Q9.

Table 12–2
Antimony and Silver Concentrations in the Kennedy Assassination Bullets

Sample	Silver (parts per million)[a]	Antimony (parts per million)	Sample Description
Q1	8.8 ± 0.5	833 ± 9	Connally stretcher bullet
Q9	9.8 ± 0.5	797 ± 7	Fragments from Connally's wrist
Q2	8.1 ± 0.6	602 ± 4	Large fragment from car
Q4, 5	7.9 ± 0.3	621 ± 4	Fragments from Kennedy's brain
Q14	8.2 ± 0.4	642 ± 6	Small fragments found in car

[a]One part per million equals 0.0001 percent.

Source: Reprinted with permission from V. P. Guinn, "JFK Assassination: Bullet Analyses," Analytical Chemistry 51 (1979): 484 A. Copyright 1979, American Chemical Society.

Conclusions From studying these results, we can derive the following conclusions:

1. There is evidence of only two bullets—one composed of 815 ppm antimony and 9.3 ppm silver, the other composed of 622 ppm antimony and 8.1 ppm silver.

2. Both bullets have a composition highly consistent with WCC/ MC bullet lead, although other sources cannot be ruled out entirely.

3. The bullet found on the Connally stretcher also damaged Connally's wrist. The absence of bullet fragments from the back wounds of Kennedy and Connally prevented any effort at linking these wounds to the stretcher bullet.

None of these conclusions can verify absolutely the Warren Commission's reconstruction of the assassination, but the results are at least consistent with the commission's findings. Further, in 2003, an ABC TV television broadcast showed the results of a ten-year 3-D computer animation study of the events of November 22, 1963. The animation graphically showed that the bullet wounds were completely consistent with Kennedy's and Connally's positions at the time of the shooting, and that by following the bullet's trajectory backward they could be found to have originated from a narrow cone including only a few windows of the sixth floor of the School Book Depository. The analyses on the Kennedy assassination bullets used a method known as *neutron activation analysis*, one of several forensic techniques we will examine in this chapter.

Atomic Structure

To understand the principle behind neutron activation analysis, one must first understand the fundamental structure of the atom. Each atom is composed of elementary particles that are collectively known as subatomic particles. The most important subatomic particles are the **proton**, **electron**, and **neutron**.

The properties of the proton, neutron, and electron are summarized in the following table:

Particle	Symbol	Relative Mass	Electrical Charge
Proton	P	1	+
Neutron	n	1	0
Electron	e	1/1837	−

As you can see, the masses of the proton and neutron are each about 1,837 times the mass of an electron. The proton has a positive electrical charge; the electron has a negative charge equal in magnitude to that of the proton; and the neutron is a neutral particle with neither a positive nor a negative charge.

A popular descriptive model of the atom, and the one that will be adopted for the purpose of this discussion, pictures an atom as consisting of electrons orbiting

proton
A positively-charged particle that is one of the basic structures in the nucleus of an atom

electron
A negatively-charged particle that is one of the fundamental structural units of the atom

neutron
A particle with no electrical charge that is one of the basic structures in the nucleus of an atom

nucleus
The core of an atom, consisting of protons and neutrons

a central **nucleus** composed of protons and neutrons—an image that is analogous to our solar system, in which the planets revolve around the sun (see Figure 12–2).[1] To maintain a zero net electrical charge, the number of protons in the nucleus must always equal the number of electrons in orbit around the nucleus.

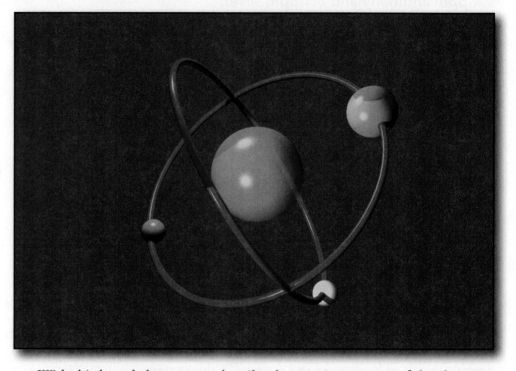

FIGURE 12–2
A popular model of the atom likens the electrons to planets orbiting the "sun" of the nucleus.
Courtesy Getty Images - Stone Allstock

With this knowledge, we can describe the atomic structure of the elements. For example, hydrogen has a nucleus consisting of one proton and no neutrons, and it has one orbiting electron. Helium has a nucleus comprising two protons and two neutrons, with two electrons in orbit around the nucleus (see Figure 12–3).

FIGURE 12–3
The atomic structures of hydrogen and helium.

atomic number
The number of protons in the nucleus of an atom

The behavior and properties that distinguish one element from another must be related to the differences in the atomic structure of each element. One such distinction is that each element possesses a different number of protons. This number is called the **atomic number** of the element. As we look back at the periodic table on page. 114, we see that the elements are numbered consecutively. Those numbers represent the atomic number or number of protons associated with each element. An element is therefore a collection of atoms that all have the same number of protons. Thus, each atom of hydrogen has one and only one proton, each atom of helium has 2 protons, each atom of silver has 47 protons, and each atom of lead has 82 protons in its nucleus.

Isotopes and Radioactivity

Although the atoms of a single element must have the same number of protons, nothing prevents them from having different numbers of neutrons. The total number of protons and neutrons in a nucleus is known as the **atomic mass** number. Atoms with the same number of protons but differing solely in the number of neutrons are called **isotopes**.

For example, hydrogen consists of three isotopes: ordinary hydrogen, which has one proton and no neutrons in its nucleus, and two other isotopes called deuterium and tritium. Deuterium (or heavy hydrogen) also has one proton, but contains one neutron as well. Tritium has one proton and two neutrons in its nucleus.

Therefore, all the isotopes of hydrogen have an atomic number of 1 but differ in their atomic mass numbers. Hydrogen has an atomic mass of 1, deuterium a mass of 2, and tritium a mass of 3. The atomic structures of these isotopes are shown in Figure 12–4.

atomic mass
The sum of the number of protons and neutrons in the nucleus of an atom

isotope
An atom differing from another atom of the same element in the number of neutrons it has in its nucleus

Hydrogen   Deuterium   Tritium

FIGURE 12–4
Isotopes of hydrogen

Like hydrogen, most elements have two or more isotopes. Tin, for example, has ten isotopes. Many of these isotopes are quite stable, and the isotopes of any one element have indistinguishable properties. Others, however, are not as stable and decompose over time by a process known as radioactive decay. **Radioactivity** is the emission of high-energy subatomic particles that accompanies the spontaneous disintegration of unstable nuclei.

Radioactivity is composed of three types of radiation: **alpha particle**, **beta particle** and **gamma rays**. Alpha are helium atoms stripped of their orbiting electrons; thus, they are positively charged particles. Each alpha ray particle has a mass approximately four times that of a hydrogen atom. Beta are electrons, and gamma rays are a form of electromagnetic radiation similar to X-rays (discussed in Chapter 4), but of a higher frequency and energy. Fortunately, most naturally occurring isotopes are not radioactive, and those that are—radium, uranium, and thorium—are found in such small quantities in the earth's crust that their radioactivity presents no hazard to human survival.

When an atom is bombarded with neutrons, some neutrons are captured to form new isotopes. This is what happens in a nuclear reactor. A nuclear reactor is simply a source of neutrons that bombard the atoms of a specimen, thereby creating radioactive isotopes. The nucleus of an atom that has captured one or more neutrons is said to be activated, and it often begins to decompose immediately, emitting radioactivity.

radioactivity
The emission of high-energy subatomic particles that accompanies the spontaneous disintegration of unstable nuclei

alpha particle
Radiation composed of helium atoms minus their orbiting electrons

beta particle
Radiation composed of electrons

gamma ray
A high-energy form of electromagnetic radiation

Case Files Death by Radiation Poisoning

In November, 2006, Alexander V. Litvinenko lay at death's door step in a London hospital. He was in excruciating pain and had symptoms which included hair loss, the inability to make blood cells, and gastrointestinal distress. His organs slowly failed as he lingered for three weeks before dying. British investigators soon confirmed that Litvinenko died from the intake of polonium-210, a radioactive element, in what appeared to be its first use as a murder weapon (see the figure).

Pine Bar of the Millennium Hotel in London. At the meeting, Mr. Litvinenko drank tea out of a teapot later found to be highly radioactive. British officials have accused Lugovoi of poisoning Litvinenko. The precise nature of the evidence against him has not been made clear. However, investigators have linked him and Mr. Kovtun to a trail of polonium-210 radioactivity stretching from hotel rooms, restaurants, bars, and offices in London to Hamburg, Germany, and to British Airways planes that had flown to Moscow. Each man has denied killing Mr. Litvinenko.

Alexander Litvinenko, former KGB agent, before and after he became sick. *Courtesy AP Wide World Photos (left) and Getty Images, Inc.-Getty News (right)*

Litvinenko's death almost immediately set off an international uproar. Litvinenko, a former KGB operative, had become a vocal critic of the Russian spy agency FSB, the domestic successor to the KGB. In 2000, he fled to London, where he was granted asylum. Litvinenko continued to voice his criticisms of the Russian spy agency and also became highly critical of Russia's president, Vladimir Putin. Just before his death, he was believed to have compiled an incriminating report regarding the activities of senior Kremlin officials on behalf of a British company looking to invest millions in a project in Russia.

Suspicions immediately fell onto Andrei Lugovoi and Dmitri Kovtun, business associates of Mr. Litvinenko. Lugovoi was himself a former KGB officer. On the day he fell ill, Litvinenko met Lugovoi and Kovtun at the

Polonium-210 is highly radioactive and very toxic. By weight, it is about 250 million times as toxic as cyanide, so a particle the size of a dust particle could be fatal. It emits a radioactive ray known as an alpha particle. This form of radiation cannot penetrate the skin, so polonium-210 is effective as a poison can only be effective if it is swallowed, breathed in, or injected. The particles disperse through the body and first destroy fast-growing cells, like those in bone marrow, blood, hair, and the digestive tract. That would be consistent with Mr. Litvinenko's symptoms. There is no antidote for polonium poisoning.

Polonium does have industrial uses and is produced by commercial or institutional nuclear reactors. Polonium-210 has been found to be ideal for making antistatic devices that remove dust from film and lenses, as well as paper and textile plants. Its non-body-penetrating rays produce an electric charge on nearby air. Bits of dust with static attract the charged air, which neutralizes them. Once free of static, the dust is easy to blow or brush away. Manufacturers of such antistatic devices take great pains to make the polonium hard to remove from their products.

Neutron Activation Analysis

Forensic chemists can characterize the trace elements in a specimen by bombarding it with neutrons and measuring the energy of the gamma rays emitted by the activated isotopes. The gamma rays of each element are associated with characteristic energy values, and thus exhibit unique levels of energy. This technique, known as neutron activation analysis, is depicted in Figure 12–5. Once an element has been identified, its concentration can be measured by the intensity of its gamma-ray radiation; the intensity of the radiation is directly proportional to the concentration of the element in a specimen.

FIGURE 12–5
The neutron activation process requires the capture of a neutron by the nucleus of an atom. The new atom is now radioactive and emits gamma rays. A director permits identification of the radioactive atoms present by measuring the energies and intensities of the gamma rays emitted.

The major advantage of neutron activation analysis is that it provides a nondestructive method for identifying and quantitating trace elements. A median detection sensitivity of one-billionth of a gram (1 nanogram) makes neutron activation analysis one of the most sensitive methods available for quantitative detection of many elements. Further, neutron activation can simultaneously analyze 20 to 30 elements. A major drawback to the technique is its expense. Only a handful of crime laboratories have access to a nuclear reactor; in addition, sophisticated analyzers are needed to detect and discriminate gamma-ray emissions.

Table 12–3
Concentration of Trace Elements in Copper Wire

	Selenium	Gold	Antimony	Silver
Control Wire				
A1	2.4	0.047	0.16	12.7
A2	3.5	0.064	0.27	17.2
A3	2.6	0.050	0.20	13.3
A4	1.9	0.034	0.21	12.6
Suspect Wire				
B	2.3	0.042	0.15	13.0

Note: Average concentration measured in parts per million.

Source: Reprinted by permission of ASTM International from R. K. H. Chan, "Identification of Single-Stranded Copper Wires by Nondestructive Neutron Activation Analysis," Journal of Forensic Sciences 17 (1972): 93.

Neutron activation has been used to characterize trace elements in metals, drugs, paint, soil, gunpowder residues, and hair. A typical illustration of its application occurred during the investigation of a theft of copper telegraphic wires in Canada. Four lengths of copper wire (A_1, A_2, A_3, A_4) found at the scene of the theft were compared by neutron activation with a length of copper wire (B) seized at a scrap yard and suspected of being stolen. All were bare, single-strand wire with the same general physical appearance and a diameter of 0.28 centimeter.

Prior experiments had revealed that significant variations could be expected in the concentration levels of the trace elements selenium, gold, antimony, and silver for wires originating from different sources. Analysts compared these elements present in the wire involved in the theft. After exposing the wires to neutrons in a nuclear reactor, neutron activation analysis revealed a match between A_1 and B that was well within experimental error (see Table 12–3). The findings suggested a common origin of the control and suspect wires.

Quick Review

- Trace elements are small quantities of elements present in concentrations of less than 1 percent. They provide "invisible" markers that may establish the source of a material or provide additional points for comparison.

- The three most important subatomic particles are the proton, neutron, and electron. The proton has a positive electrical charge, the neutron has no electrical charge, and the electron has a negative electrical charge.

- Atomic number indicates the number of protons in the nucleus of an atom. Atomic mass refers to the total number of protons and neutrons in a nucleus.

- An isotope is an atom differing from other atoms of the same element in the number of neutrons in its nucleus.

- Radioactivity is the emission of high-energy subatomic particles that accompanies the spontaneous disintegration of the nuclei of unstable isotopes. The three types of radiation are alpha particles, beta particles, and gamma rays.

- In neutron activation analysis, a sample is bombarded with neutrons and the energy of the gamma rays emitted by the activated isotopes is measured. The gamma rays of each element are associated with characteristic energy values that helps identify the specific element that produces them.

Forensic Examination of Paint

Our environment contains millions of objects whose surfaces are painted. Thus paint, in one form or another, is one of the most prevalent types of physical evidence received by the crime laboratory.

Paint as physical evidence is perhaps most frequently encountered in hit-and-run and burglary cases. For example, a chip of dried paint or a paint smear may be transferred to the clothing of a hit-and-run victim on impact with an automobile, or paint smears could be transferred onto a tool during a burglary. Obviously, in many situations a transfer of paint from one surface to another could impart an object with an identifiable forensic characteristic.

In most circumstances, the criminalist must compare two or more paints to establish their common origin. For example, such a comparison may associate an individual or a vehicle with the crime site. However, the criminalist need not be confined to comparisons alone. Crime laboratories often help identify the color, make, and model of an automobile by examining small quantities of paint recovered at an accident scene. Such requests, normally made in hit-and-run cases, can lead to the apprehension of the responsible vehicle.

Composition of Paint

Paint is composed of a binder and pigments, as well as other additives, all dissolved or dispersed in a suitable solvent. Pigments impart color and hiding (or opacity) to paint and are usually mixtures of different inorganic and organic compounds added to the paint by the manufacturer to produce specific colors and properties. The binder is a polymeric substance that provides the support medium for the pigments and additives. After paint has been applied to a surface, the solvent evaporates, leaving behind a hard polymeric binder and any pigments that are suspended in it.

One of the most common types of paint examined in the crime laboratory is finishes from automobiles. Manufacturers apply a variety of coatings to the body of an automobile; this adds significant diversity to automobile paint and contributes to the forensic significance of automobile paint comparisons. The automotive finishing system for steel usually consists of at least four organic coatings:

Electrocoat Primer. The first layer applied to the steel body of a car is the electrocoat primer. The primer, consisting of epoxy-based resins, is electroplated onto the steel body of the automobile to provide corrosion resistance. The resulting coating is uniform in appearance and thickness. The color of these primers ranges from black to gray.

Primer Surfacer. Originally responsible for corrosion control, the surfacer usually follows the electrocoat layer and is applied before the basecoat. Primer surfacers are epoxy-modified polyesters or urethanes. The function of this layer is to completely smooth out and hide any seams or imperfections, because the basecoat will be applied on this surface. This layer is highly pigmented. Color pigments are used to minimize color contrast between primer and topcoats. For example, a light-gray primer may be used under pastel shades of a colored topcoat; a red oxide may be used under a dark-colored topcoat.

Basecoat. The next layer of paint on a car is the basecoat or colorcoat. This layer provides the color and aesthetics of the finish and represents the "eye appeal" of the finished automobile. The integrity of this layer depends on its ability to resist weather, UV radiation, and acid rain. Most commonly, an acrylic-based polymer comprises the binder system of basecoats. Interestingly, the choice of automotive pigments is dictated by toxic and environmental concerns. Thus, the use of lead, chrome, and other heavy-metal pigments has been abandoned in favor of organic-based pigments. There is also a growing trend toward pearl luster or mica pigments. Mica pigments are coated with layers of metal oxide to generate interference colors. Also, the addition of aluminum flakes to automotive paint imparts a metallic look to the paint's finish.

Clearcoat. An unpigmented clearcoat is applied to improve gloss, durability, and appearance. Most clearcoats are acrylic based, but polyurethane clearcoats are increasing in popularity. These topcoats provide outstanding etch resistance and appearance.

Microscopic Examination of Paint

The microscope has traditionally been and remains the most important instrument for locating and comparing paint specimens. Considering the thousands of paint colors and shades, it is quite understandable why color, more than any other property, imparts paint with its most distinctive forensic characteristics. Questioned and known specimens are best compared side by side under a stereoscopic microscope for color, surface texture, and color layer sequence (see Figure 12–6).

The importance of layer structure for evaluating the evidential significance of paint evidence cannot be overemphasized. When paint specimens possess colored layers that match in number and sequence of colors, the examiner can begin to relate the paints to a common origin. How many layers must be matched before the criminalist can conclude that the paints come from the same source? There is no one accepted criterion. Much depends on the uniqueness of each layer's color

FIGURE 12–6
A stereoscopic micro-
scope comparison of
two automotive paints
The questioned paint on
the left has a layer structure consistent with the
control paint on the right
*Courtesy Leica Microsys-
tems, Inc., Buffalo, N.Y.,
www.leica-microsystems.
com*

and texture, as well as the frequency with which the particular combination of colors under investigation is observed. Because no books or journals have compiled this type of information, the criminalist is left to his or her own experience and knowledge when making this decision.

Unfortunately, most paint specimens do not have a layer structure of sufficient complexity to allow them to be individualized to a single source (see Figure 12–7). However, the diverse chemical composition of modern paints provides additional points of comparison between specimens. Specifically, a thorough comparison of paint must include a chemical analysis of the paint's pigments, its binder composition, or both.

FIGURE 12–7
Red paint chips pealing
off a wall revealing
underlying layers.
*Courtesy Getty Images -
Photodisc*

Analytical Techniques Used in Paint Comparison

The wide variation in binder formulations in automobile finishes provides significant information. More important, paint manufacturers make automobile finishes in hundreds of varieties; this knowledge is most helpful to the criminalist who is trying to associate a paint chip with one car as distinguished from the thousands of similar models that have been produced in any one year. For instance, there are more than a hundred automobile production plants in the United States and Canada. Each can use one paint supplier for a particular color or vary suppliers during a model year. Although a paint supplier must maintain strict quality control over a paint's color, the batch formulation of any paint binder can vary, depending on the availability and cost of basic ingredients.

Characterization of Paint Binders An important extension of the application of gas chromatography to forensic science is the technique of **pyrolysis** *gas chromatography*. Many solid materials commonly encountered as physical evidence—for example, paint chips, fibers, and plastics—cannot be readily dissolved in a solvent for injection into the gas chromatograph. Thus, under normal conditions these substances cannot be subjected to gas chromatographic analysis. However, materials such as these can be heated, or pyrolyzed, to high temperatures (500–1,000°C) so that they will decompose into numerous gaseous products. Pyrolyzers permit these gaseous products to enter the carrier gas stream, where they flow into and through the GC column. The pyrolyzed material can then be characterized by the pattern produced by its chromatogram, or pyrogram.

Pyrolysis gas chromatography is particularly invaluable for distinguishing most paint formulations. In this process, paint chips as small as 20 micrograms are decomposed by heat into numerous gaseous products and are sent through a gas chromatograph.

As shown in Figure 12–8, the polymer chain is decomposed by a heated filament, and the resultant products are swept into and through a gas chromatograph column. The separated decomposition products of the polymer emerge and are recorded. The pattern of this chromatogram or "pyrogram" distinguishes one polymer from another. The result is a pyrogram that is sufficiently detailed to reflect the chemical makeup of the binder. Figure 12–9 illustrates how the patterns produced by paint pyrograms can differentiate acrylic enamel paints removed from two different automobiles.

Infrared spectrophotometry is still another analytical technique that provides information about the binder composition of paint.[2] Binders selectively absorb infrared radiation to yield a spectrum that is highly characteristic of a paint specimen.

Characterization of Paint Pigments The elements that constitute the inorganic pigments of paints can be identified by a variety of techniques: emission spectroscopy, neutron activation analysis, and X-ray spectroscopy. The emission spectrograph for example, can simultaneously detect 15 to 20 elements in most automobile paints. Some of these elements are relatively common to all paints

pyrolysis
The decomposition of organic matter by heat

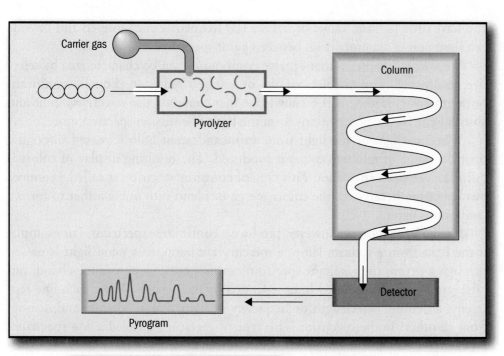

FIGURE 12–8
Schematic diagram of pyrolysis gas chromatography.

FIGURE 12–9
Paint pyrograms of acrylic enamel paints.
(a) Paint from a Ford model and
(b) paint from a Chrysler model.
Courtesy Varian Inc., Palo Alto, Calif.

and have little forensic value; others are less frequently encountered and provide excellent points of comparison between paint specimens.

We saw in Chapter 5 that organic compounds can be characterized by selective absorption of ultraviolet, visible, or infrared radiation. Equally significant to the forensic chemist is the knowledge that elements also selectively emit and absorb light. These observations form the basis of emission spectroscopy.

When sunlight or the light from an incandescent bulb is passed through a prism, a range of rainbow colors is produced. The resulting display of colors is called an **emission spectrum**. This type of emission spectrum is called a **continuous spectrum** because all the colors merge or blend into one another to form a continuous band.

Not all light sources, however, produce a continuous spectrum. For example, if the light from a sodium lamp, a mercury arc lamp, or a neon light is passed through a prism, the resultant spectrum consists not of a continuous band, but of several individual colored lines separated by dark spaces. Here, each line represents a definite wavelength or frequency of light that is separate and distinct from all others in the spectrum. This type of spectrum is called a **line spectrum**. Figure 12–10 shows the line spectra of three elements. If a solid or liquid is vaporized and "excited" by exposure to high temperature, each element that is present emits light composed of select frequencies that are characteristic of the element. This spectrum is in essence a "fingerprint" of an element and offers a practical method of identification for liquid media such as paint. Sodium vapor, for example, always shows the same line spectrum, which differs from the spectrum of all other elements.

emission spectrum
Light emitted from a source and separated into its component colors or frequencies

continuous spectrum
A type of emission spectrum showing a continuous band of colors all blending into one another

line spectrum
A type of emission spectrum showing a series of lines separated by black areas, each line represents a definite wavelength or frequency

FIGURE 12–10
Some characteristic emission spectra.

Inside the Science
The Carbon Arc Emission Spectrograph

An emission spectrograph is an instrument used to obtain and record the line spectra of elements. This instrument requires a means for vaporizing and exciting the atoms of elements so that they emit light, a means for separating this light into its component frequencies, and a means of recording the resultant spectrum. A simple emission spectrograph is depicted in Figure 1.

FIGURE 1 Parts of a simple emission spectrograph.

The specimen under investigation is inserted between two carbon electrodes through which a direct current arc is passed. The arc produces enough heat to vaporize and excite the specimen's atoms. A lens collects the light emitted by the excited atoms and focuses it onto a prism that disperses it into component frequencies. The separated frequencies of light are then directed toward a photographic plate, where they are recorded as line images. Normally, a specimen consists of numerous elements; hence, the typical emission spectrum contains many lines.

Each element in the spectrum can be identified when it is compared to a standard chart that shows the position of the principal spectral lines of all the elements. However, forensic analysis usually requires a rapid comparison of the elemental composition of two or more specimens. This is easily accomplished by comparing the emission spectra line for line, as illustrated in Figure 2, in which the emission spectra of two paint chips are shown to be comparable.

FIGURE 2 A comparison of paint chips 1 and 2 by emission spectrographic analysis. A line-for-line comparison shows that the paints have the same elemental composition.

Inside the Science

The Origin of Emission Spectra

To explain the origin of atomic spectra, we must focus on the **electron orbitals** of the atom. As electrons move around the nucleus, they are confined to a path from which they cannot stray. This orbital path is associated with a definite amount of energy and is therefore called an *energy level*. Each element has its own set of characteristic energy levels at varying distances from the nucleus. Some levels are occupied by electrons; others are empty.

An atom is in its most stable state when all of its electrons are positioned in their lowest possible energy orbitals. When an atom absorbs energy, such as heat or light, its electrons are pushed into higher-energy orbitals. In this condition, the atom is in an **excited state**. However, because energy levels have fixed values, only a definite amount of energy can be absorbed in moving an electron from one level to another. This is an important observation; atoms absorb only a definite value of energy, and all other energy values are excluded, as shown in the figure.

A specific frequency of light is required to cause this transition, and its energy must correspond to the exact energy difference between the two orbitals involved. This energy difference is expressed by the relationship $E = hf$, where E represents the energy difference between the two orbitals, f is the frequency of absorbed light, and h is a universal constant called Planck's constant. Any energy value that is more or less than this difference will not produce the transition. Hence, an element is selective in the frequency of light it will absorb, and this selectivity is determined by the electron energy levels each element possesses.

In the same manner, if atoms are exposed to intense heat, enough energy will be generated to push electrons into unoccupied higher-energy orbitals. Normally the electron does not remain in this excited state for long, and it quickly falls back to its original energy level. As the electron falls back, it releases energy. An emission spectrum shows that this energy loss comes about in the form of light emission (see the figure). The frequency of light emitted is again determined by the relationship $E = hf$, where E is the energy difference between the upper and lower energy levels and f is the frequency of emitted light. Because each element has its own characteristic set of energy levels, each emits a unique set of frequency values. The emission spectrum thus provides a "picture" of the energy levels that surround the nucleus of each element.

(a) The absorption of light by an atom, causing an electron to jump into a higher orbital, (b) The emission of light by an atom, caused by an electron falling back to a lower orbital.

Thus, we see that as far as atoms are concerned, energy is a two-way street. Energy can be put into the atom at the same time that energy is given off; what goes in must come out. The chemist can study the atom using either approach.

Inductively Coupled Plasma Emission Spectrometry (ICP) Recently, inductively coupled plasma (ICP) emission spectrometry has supplanted carbon arc emission spectroscopy for most applications. Like emission spectroscopy, ICP identifies and measures elements through light energy emitted by excited atoms. However, instead of using an electrical arc, the atoms are excited by placing the sample in a hot plasma torch. The torch is designed as three concentric quartz tubes through which argon gas flows (see Figure 12–11). A radio-frequency (RF) coil that carries a current is wrapped around the tubes. The RF current creates an intense magnetic field.

electron orbital
The path of electrons as they move around the nuclei of atoms, each orbital is associated with a particular electronic energy level

excited state
The state in which an atom absorbs energy and an electron moves from a lower to a higher energy level

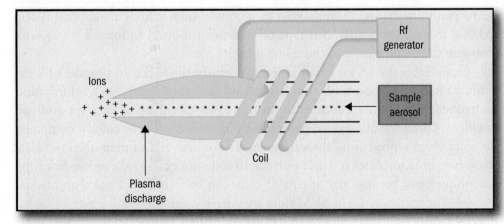

FIGURE 12–11 The creation of charged particles in the touch of an ICP discharge.

The process begins when a high-voltage spark is applied to the argon gas flowing through the torch. This strips some electrons from their argon atoms. These electrons are then caught and accelerated in the magnetic field such that they collide with other argon atoms, stripping off still more electrons. The collision of electrons and argon atoms continues in a chain reaction, breaking down the gas into argon atoms, argon ions, and electrons, forming an *inductively coupled plasma discharge*. The discharge is sustained by RF energy that is continuously transferred to it from the coil.

The plasma discharge acts like a very intense continuous flame generating temperatures in the range of 7,000–10,000°C. The sample, in aerosol form, is then introduced into the hot plasma, where it collides with the energetic argon electrons and generates charged particles (ions). The ions emit light of characteristic wavelengths that correspond to the identity of the elements in the sample.

The Significance of Paint Evidence

Once a paint comparison is completed, the task of assessing the significance of the finding begins. How certain can one be that two similar paints came from the same surface? For instance, a casual observer sees countless identically colored automobiles on our roads and streets. If this is the case, what value is a comparison of a paint chip from a hit-and-run scene to paint removed from a suspect car?

From previous discussions it should be apparent that far more is involved in paint comparison than matching surface paint colors. Paint layers beneath a surface layer offer valuable points of comparison. Furthermore, forensic analysts can detect subtle differences in paint binder formulations, as well as major or minor differences in the elemental composition of paint. Obviously, these properties cannot be discerned by the naked eye.

The significance of a paint comparison was convincingly demonstrated from data gathered at the Centre of Forensic Sciences, Toronto, Canada.[3] Paint chips randomly taken from 260 vehicles located in a local wreck yard were compared by color, layer structure, and, when required, by infrared spectroscopy. All were distinguishable except for one pair. In statistical terms, these results signify that if a crime-scene paint sample and a paint standard/reference sample removed from a suspect car compare by the previously discussed tests, the odds against the crime-scene paint originating from another randomly chosen vehicle are approximately 33,000 to one. Obviously, this type of evidence is bound to forge a strong link between the suspect car and the crime scene.

Crime laboratories are often asked to identify the make and model of a car from a very small amount of paint left behind at a crime scene. Such information is frequently of use in a search for an unknown car involved in a hit-and-run incident. Often the questioned paint can be identified when its color is compared to color chips representing the various makes and models of manufactured cars. However, in many cases it is not possible to state the exact make or model of the car in question, because any one paint color can be found on more than one car model. For instance, General Motors may have used the same paint color for several production years on cars in its Cadillac, Buick, and Chevrolet lines.

Color charts for automobile finishes are available from various paint manufacturers and refinishers (see Figure 12–12). Since 1975, the Royal Canadian Mounted Police Forensic Laboratories have been systematically gathering color and chemical information on automotive paints. This computerized database, known as PDQ (Paint Data Query), allows an analyst to obtain information on paints related to automobile make, model, and year. The database contains such parameters as automotive paint layer colors, primer colors, and binder

Inside the Science

ICP Analysis of Bullets

Mutilated bullets often are not suitable for traditional microscopic comparisons against an exemplar test-fired bullet. In such situations, ICP has been used to obtain an elemental profile of the questioned bullet fragment for comparison against an unfired bullet generally found in the possession of the suspect.

For a number of years forensic scientists have been aware of significant compositional differences among lead sources for the manufacture of lead-based bullets. Knowledge of these differences can be valuable when comparing bullets that are too mutilated to analyze with a microscope. Compositional differences in trace elements are typically reflected in the copper, arsenic, silver, antimony, bismuth, cadmium, and tin profiles of lead bullets.

When two or more bullets have comparable elemental compositions, evidence of their similarity may be offered in a court of law. In this respect, the comparison of lead bullets faces the same quandary as most common types of class physical evidence. The forensic analyst must convince a jury that the test results are meaningful to a criminal inquiry in the absence of any supporting statistical or probability data. Furthermore, creating meaningful databases to define the statistical significance of bullets compared by elemental profiles is currently an unrealistic undertaking.

Nevertheless, the significant diversity of bullet lead compositions in our population, like other class evidence such as fibers, hairs, paint, plastics, and glass, makes their chance occurrence at a crime scene and subsequent link to a defendant highly unlikely. However, care must be taken to avoid giving the impression that elemental profiles constitute a definitive match. Given the millions of bullets produced each year, one cannot conclusively rule out the possibility of a coincidental match with a non-case-related bullet.

composition (see Figure 12–13). A number of U.S. laboratories have access to PDQ.[4] Also, some crime laboratories maintain an in-house collection of automotive paints associated with various makes and models, as shown in Figure 12–14.

FIGURE 12–12
Automotive color chart of various car models. *Courtesy Damian Dovanganes, AP Wide World Photos*

FIGURE 12–13
(a) Home screen for PDQ database.
(b) Partial list of autopaints contained in the PDQ database. *Courtesy Royal Canadian Mounted Police*

Collection and Preservation of Paint Evidence

As has already been noted, paint chips are most likely to be found on or near people or objects involved in hit-and-run incidents. The recovery of loose paint chips from a garment or from the road surface must be done with the utmost care to keep the paint chip intact. Paint chips may be picked up with a tweezers or scooped up with a piece of paper. Paper druggist folds and glass or plastic vials make excellent containers for paint. If the paint is smeared on or embedded in garments or objects, the investigator should not attempt to remove it; instead, it is best to package the whole item carefully and send it to the laboratory for examination.

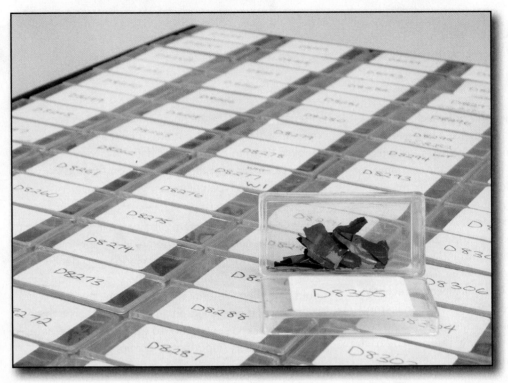

FIGURE 12–14
A crime laboratory's automotive paint library. Paints were collected at an automobile impound yard and then cataloged for rapid retrieval and examination.
Courtesy Royal Canadian Mounted Police

When a transfer of paint occurs in hit-and-run situations (such as to the clothing of a pedestrian victim), uncontaminated standard/reference paint must always be collected from an undamaged area of the vehicle for comparison in the laboratory. The collected paint must be close to the area of the car that is suspected of being in contact with the victim. This is necessary because other portions of the car may have faded or been repainted.

Standard/reference samples are always removed so as to include all the paint layers down to the bare metal. This is best accomplished by removing a painted section with a clean scalpel or knife blade. Samples ¼ inch square are sufficient for laboratory examination. Each paint sample should be separately packaged and marked with the exact location of its recovery.

When a cross-transfer of paint occurs between two vehicles, again all of the layers, including the foreign as well as the underlying original paints, must be removed from each vehicle. A standard/reference sample from an adjacent undamaged area of each vehicle must also be taken in such cases. Carefully wipe the blade of any knife or scraping tool used before collecting each sample, to avoid cross-contamination of paints.

Tools used to enter buildings or safes often contain traces of paints as well as other substances such as wood and safe insulation. Care must be taken not to lose this type of trace evidence. The scene investigator should not try to remove the paint; instead, he or she should package the tool for laboratory examination. Standard/reference paint should be collected from all surfaces suspected of having been in contact with the tool. Again, all layers of paint must be included in the sample.

When the tool has left its impression on a surface, standard/reference paint is collected from an uncontaminated area adjacent to the impression. No attempt should be made to collect the paint from the impression itself. If this is done, the impression may be permanently altered and its evidential value lost.

Case Files

The Predator

September in Arizona is hot and dry, much like the rest of the year—but September 1984 was a little different. Unusually heavy rains fell for two days, which must have seemed fitting for the friends and family of 8-year-old Vicki Lynn Hoskinson. Vicki went missing on September 17 of that year, and her disappearance was investigated as a kidnapping. A schoolteacher who knew Vicki remembered a suspicious vehicle loitering near the school that day, and he happened to jot down the license plate number. This crucial tip led police to 28-year-old Frank Atwood, recently paroled from a California prison. Police soon learned that Atwood had been convicted for committing sex offenses and for kidnapping a boy. This galvanized the investigators, who realized Vicki could be at the mercy of a dangerous and perverse man.

The only evidence the police had to work with was Vicki's bike, which was found abandoned in the middle of the street a few blocks from her home. Police found scrapes from her bike pedal on the underside of the gravel pan on Atwood's car, as well as pink paint apparently transferred from Vicki's bike to Atwood's front bumper. The police believed that Atwood deliberately struck Vicki while she was riding her bicycle, knocking her to the ground.

The pink paint on Atwood's bumper was first looked at microscopically and then examined by pyrolysis gas chromatography. This technique provides investigators with a "fingerprint" pattern of the paint sample, enabling them to compare this paint to any other paint evidence. In this case, the pink paint on Atwood's bumper matched the paint from Vicki's bicycle.

Vicki's skeletal remains were discovered in the desert, several miles away from her home, in the spring of 1985. Positive identification was made using dental records, but investigators wanted to see if the remains could help them determine how long she had been dead. Atwood was jailed on an unrelated charge three days after Vicki disappeared, so the approximate date of death was very important to proving his guilt.

Investigators found adipocere, a white, fatty residue produced during decomposition, inside Vicki's skull. This provided evidence that moisture was present around Vicki's body after her death, which did not make sense considering she was found in the Arizona desert! A check of the weather revealed that there had been an unusual amount of rainfall at only one time since Vicki was last seen alive: a mere 48 hours after her disappearance. This put Vicki's death squarely within Frank Atwood's three-day window of opportunity between her disappearance and his arrest. Frank Atwood was sentenced to death in 1987 for the murder of Vicki Lynn Hoskinson. He remains on death row awaiting execution.

Quick Review

- Paint spread onto a surface dries into a hard film that is best described as consisting of pigments and additives suspended in the binder.

- Questioned and known paint specimens are best compared side by side under a stereoscopic microscope for color, surface texture, and color layer sequence.

- Pyrolysis gas chromatography and infrared spectrophotometry are used to distinguish most paint binder formulations.

- Emission spectroscopy and inductively coupled plasma are techniques available for determining the elemental composition of paint pigments.

- PDQ (Paint Data Query) is a computerized database that allows an analyst to obtain information on paints related to automobile make, model, and year.

Forensic Analysis of Soil

The term soil has many definitions; however, for forensic purposes, soil may be thought of as any disintegrated surface material, natural or artificial, that lies on or near the earth's surface. Therefore, forensic examination of soil not only is concerned with analysis of naturally occurring rocks, minerals, vegetation, and animal matter; it also encompasses detection of such manufactured objects as glass, paint chips, asphalt, brick fragments, and cinders, whose presence may impart soil with characteristics that make it unique to a particular location. When this material is collected accidentally or deliberately in a manner that associates it with a crime under investigation, it becomes valuable physical evidence.[5]

The Significance of Soil Evidence

The value of soil as evidence rests with its prevalence at crime scenes and its transferability between the scene and the criminal. Thus, soil or dried mud found adhering to a suspect's clothing or shoes or to an automobile, when compared to soil samples collected at the crime site, may link a suspect or object to the crime scene. As with most types of physical evidence, forensic soil analysis is comparative in nature; soil found in the possession of the suspect must be carefully collected to be compared to soil samplings from the crime scene and its vicinity.

However, one should not rule out the value of soil even if the site of the crime has not been ascertained. For instance, small amounts of soil may be found on a person or object far from the actual site of a crime. A geologist who knows the local geology may be able to use geological maps to direct police to the general vicinity where the soil was originally picked up and the crime committed.

Forensic Examination of Soil

Most soils can be differentiated by their gross appearance. A side-by-side visual comparison of the color and texture of soil specimens is easy to perform and provides a sensitive property for distinguishing soils that originate from different locations. Soil is darker when it is wet; therefore, color comparisons must always be made when all the samples are dried under identical laboratory conditions. It is estimated that there are nearly 1,100 distinguishable soil colors; hence, color offers a logical first step in a forensic soil comparison (see Figure 12-15).

FIGURE 12–15
A color chart is displayed behind three soil samples.

Microscopic Examination of Soil Low-power microscopic examination of soil reveals the presence of plant and animal materials as well as of artificial debris. Further high-power microscopic examination helps characterize minerals and rocks in earth materials. Although this approach to forensic soil identification requires the expertise of an investigator trained in geology, it can provide the most varied and significant points of comparison between soil samples. Only by carefully examining and comparing the minerals and rocks naturally present in soil can one take advantage of the large number of variations between soils and thus add to the evidential value of a positive comparison.[6]

A **mineral** is a naturally occurring crystal, and like any other crystal, its physical properties—for example, color, geometric shape, density, and refractive index or birefringence—are useful for identification. More than 2,200 minerals exist; however, most are so rare that forensic geologists usually encounter only about 20 of the more common ones. Rocks are composed of a combination of minerals and therefore exist in thousands of varieties on the earth's surface. They are usually identified by characterizing their mineral content and grain size (see Figure 12–16).

Considering the vast variety of minerals and rocks and the possible presence of artificial debris in soil, the forensic geologist is presented with many points of comparison between two or more specimens. The number of comparative points and their frequency of occurrence must be considered before concluding similarity between specimens and judging the probability of common origin.

Rocks and minerals not only are present in earth materials but also are also used to manufacture a wide variety of industrial and commercial products. For example, the tools and garments of an individual suspected of breaking into a safe often contain traces of safe insulation. Safe insulation may be made from a wide

mineral
A naturally occurring crystalline solid

FIGURE 12– 16
A mineral viewed under a microscope. *Courtesy Chris Palenik, Ph. D., Microtrace, Elgin, IL., www.microtracescientific. com*

combination of mineral mixtures that provide significant points of identification. Similarly, building materials such as brick, plaster, and concrete blocks are combinations of minerals and rocks that can easily be recognized and compared microscopically to similar minerals found on the breaking-and-entering suspect.

Variations in Soil

The ultimate forensic value of soil evidence depends on its variation at the crime scene. If, for example, soil is indistinguishable for miles surrounding the location of a crime, it will have limited value in associating soil found on the suspect with that particular site. Significant conclusions relating a suspect to a particular location through a soil comparison may be made when variations in soil composition occur every 10–100 yards from the crime site. However, even when such variations do exist, the forensic geologist usually cannot individualize soil to any one location unless an unusual combination of rare minerals, rocks, or artificial debris can be located.

No statistically valid forensic studies have examined the variability of soil evidence. A study conducted in southern Ontario, Canada, seems to indicate that soil in that part of Canada shows extensive diversity. It estimated a probability of less than 1 in 50 of finding two soils that are indistinguishable in both color and mineral properties but originate in two different locations separated by a distance of 1,000 feet. Based on these preliminary results, similar diversity may be expected in the northern United States, Canada, northern Europe, and eastern Europe. However, such probability values can only generally indicate the variation of soil within these geographical areas. Each crime scene must be evaluated separately to establish its own soil variation probabilities.

Collection and Preservation of Soil Evidence

When gathering soil specimens, the evidence collector must give primary consideration to establishing the variation of soil at the crime-scene area. For this reason, standard/reference soils should be collected at various intervals within a 100-yard radius of the crime scene, as well as at the site of the crime, for comparison to the questioned soil. Soil specimens also should be collected at all possible alibi locations that the suspect may claim.

All specimens gathered should be representative of the soil that was removed by the suspect. In most cases, only the top layer of soil is picked up during the commission of a crime. Thus, standard/reference specimens must be removed from the surface without digging too deeply into the unrepresentative subsurface layers. Approximately a tablespoon or two of soil is all the laboratory needs for a thorough comparative analysis. All specimens collected should be packaged in individual containers, such as plastic vials. Each vial should be marked to indicate the location at which the sampling was made.

Soil found on a suspect must be carefully preserved for analysis. If it is found adhering to an object, as in the case of soil on a shoe, the investigator must not remove it. Instead, each object should be individually wrapped in paper, with the soil intact, and transmitted to the laboratory. Similarly, loose soil adhering to garments should not be removed; these items should be carefully and individually wrapped in paper bags and sent to the laboratory for analysis. Care must be taken that particles that may accidentally fall off the garment during transportation will remain in the paper bag.

When a lump of soil is found, it should be collected and preserved intact. For example, an automobile tends to collect and build up layers of soil under the fenders, body, and so on. The impact of an automobile with another object may jar some of this soil loose. Once the suspect car has been apprehended, a comparison of the soil left at the scene with soil remaining on the automobile may help establish that the car was present at the accident scene. In these situations, separate samples are collected from under all the fender and frame areas of the vehicle; care is taken to remove the soil in lump form in order to preserve the order in which the soil adhered to the car. Undoubtedly, during the normal use of an automobile, soil will be picked up from numerous locations over a period of months and years. This layering effect may impart soil with greater variation, and hence greater evidential value, than that normally associated with loose soil.

The prevalence of soil in our environment makes it a common type of physical evidence at crime scenes. Proper collection and preservation by the criminal investigator will help ensure that a proper scientific examination can support investigative conclusions placing a suspect or object at the crime scene. Equally important is that soil, like other types of physical evidence, when properly collected and examined may exonerate the innocent from involvement in a crime.

Quick Review

- A side-by-side visual comparison of the color and texture of soil specimens provides a way to distinguish soils that originate from different locations.

- Minerals are naturally occurring crystalline solids found in soil. Their physical properties—for example, color, geometric shape, density, and refractive index or birefringence—are useful for characterizing soils.

Case Files Soil: The Silent Witness

Alice Redmond was reported missing by her husband on a Monday night in 1983. Police learned that she had been seen with a co-worker, Mark Miller, after work that evening. When police questioned Miller, he stated that the two just "drove around" after work and then she dropped him off at home. Despite his statement, Miller was the prime suspect because he had a criminal record for burglary and theft.

Alice's car was recovered in town the following morning. The wheel wells were thickly coated in mud, which investigators hoped might provide a good lead. These hopes were dampened when police learned that Alice and her husband had attended a motorcycle race on Sunday, where her car was driven through deep mud.

After careful scrutiny, analysts found two colors of soil on the undercarriage of Alice's car. The thickest soil was brown; on top of the brown layer was a reddish soil that looked unlike anything in the county. Investigators hoped the reddish soil, which had to have been deposited sometime after the Sunday night motorcycle event and before the vehicle was discovered on Tuesday morning, could link the vehicle to the location of Alice Redmond.

An interview with Mark Miller's sister provided a break in the case. She told police that Mark had visited her on Monday evening. During that visit, he confessed that he had driven Alice in her car across the Alabama state line into Georgia, killed her, and buried her in a remote location. Now that investigators had a better idea where to look for Alice, forensic analysts took soil samples that would prove or disprove Miller's sister's story.

Each field sample was dried and compared for color and texture by eye and stereomicroscopy to the reddish-colored soil gathered from the car. Next, soils that compared to the car were passed through a series of mesh filters, each of a finer gauge than the last. In this way, the components of the soil samples were physically separated by size. Finally, each fraction was analyzed and compared for mineral composition with the aid of a polarizing light microscope.

Only samples collected from areas across the Alabama state line near the suspected dump site were consistent with the topmost reddish soil recovered from Alice's car. This finding supported Miller's sister's story and was instrumental in Mark Miller's being charged with murder and kidnapping. After pleading guilty, the defendant led the authorities to where he had buried the body. The burial site was within a half mile of the location where forensic analysts had collected a soil sample consistent with the soil removed from Alice's vehicle.

Source: T. J. Hopen, "The Value of Soil Evidence," in M. M. Houck, ed., Trace Evidence Analysis: More Cases in Mute Witnesses, M. M. Houck, ed. (Elsevier Academic Press, Burlington, Mass.: Elsevier Academic Press, 2004), pp. 105–122.

Inside the Science

Nuclear Forensics

Nuclear forensics has emerged as a critical profession on the forefront in the war on terrorism. Nuclear forensic scientists are responsible for developing the means to analyze nuclear materials recovered from either the capture of intercepted intact nuclear materials or from post-explosion debris created as a result of a nuclear explosion. Nuclear forensics is becoming an increasingly important tool in the fight against illegal smuggling and trafficking of radiological and nuclear materials. In the United States, Lawrence Livermore National Laboratory and with seven other Department of Energy (DOE) national laboratories have been tasked by the Federal Bureau of Investigation and the Department of Homeland Security with developing the nation's technical forensics capability for nuclear and radiological materials. Organizations such as the European Commission's Institute for Transuranium Elements, located in Karlsruhe, Germany, have extended nuclear forensic capabilities onto an international scale.

View of a nuclear power plant. *Courtesy Corbis*

A major focus of nuclear forensics is identifying signatures, which are the physical, chemical, and isotopic characteristics that distinguish one nuclear or radiological material from another. An example is stolen containers of uranium diverted during one of the mining, milling, conversion, enrichment, or fuel fabrication steps used to convert uranium ore to enriched fuel for nuclear power plants.

Inside the Science (CONTINUED)

Researchers analyze the material's chemical and isotopic composition, which includes measuring the amounts of trace elements as well as the ratio of parent isotopes to daughter isotopes. These measurements help to determine the source location and sample's age. They also examine the material's morphological characteristics such as shape, size, and texture. Analytical methods include electron microscopy, X-ray diffraction, and mass spectrometry. In addition, as a sample is moved from place to place, it picks up trace evidence such as pollen, hairs, fibers, and plant DNA, and fingerprints. These so-called route materials may provide information about who has handled a sample and the path it has traveled.

Contracts with major U.S. uranium fuel suppliers have provided researchers with samples and manufacturing data. Forensic scientists are also seeking to obtain samples of uranium products worldwide to analyze the products' isotopic and trace-element content, grain size, and microstructure. Nations with nuclear capabilities are beginning to share information about their nuclear fuel processes and materials. The development of databases is essential to the nuclear forensic scientist's mission of identifying the origin of nuclear materials intercepted in the black market or associated with a terrorist event.

Chapter Review

- Trace elements are small quantities of elements present in concentrations of less than 1 percent. They provide "invisible" markers that may establish the source of a material or provide additional points for comparison.

- The three most important subatomic particles are the proton, neutron, and electron. The proton has a positive electrical charge, the neutron has no electrical charge, and the electron has a negative electrical charge.

- Atomic number indicates the number of protons in the nucleus of an atom. Atomic mass refers to the total number of protons and neutrons in a nucleus.

- An isotope is an atom differing from other atoms of the same element in the number of neutrons in its nucleus.

- Radioactivity is the emission of high-energy subatomic particles that accompanies the spontaneous disintegration of the nuclei of unstable isotopes. The three types of radiation are alpha particle rays, beta particle rays, and gamma rays.

- In neutron activation analysis, a sample is bombarded with neutrons and the energy of the gamma rays emitted by the activated isotopes is measured. The gamma rays of each element are associated with characteristic energy values that helps identify the specific element that produces them.

- Paint spread onto a surface dries into a hard film that is best described as consisting of pigments and additives suspended in the binder.

- Questioned and known paint specimens are best compared side by side under a stereoscopic microscope for color, surface texture, and color layer sequence.

- Pyrolysis gas chromatography and infrared spectrophotometry are used to distinguish most paint binder formulations.

- Emission spectroscopy and inductively coupled plasma are techniques available for determining the elemental composition of paint pigments.

- PDQ (Paint Data Query) is a computerized database that allows an analyst to obtain information on paints related to automobile make, model, and year.

- A side-by-side visual comparison of the color and texture of soil specimens provides a way to distinguish soils that originate from different locations.

- Minerals are naturally occurring crystalline solids found in soil. Their physical properties—for example, color, geometric shape, density, and refractive index or birefringence—are useful for characterizing soils.

Review Questions

1. The nucleus of an atom contains:
    a. neutrons.
    b. neutrons and electrons.
    c. protons and electrons.
    d. protons and neutrons.

2. Atoms having the same atomic number but different atomic masses are called:
    a. isobars.
    b. isotopes.
    c. isotherms.
    d. isomers.

3. One of the most common types of paint examined in the crime laboratory involves
    a. finishes from fingernail polish on a victim's hands.
    b. finishes emanating from automobiles.
    c. finishes from the "bluing" of a firearm.
    d. finishes from furniture varnish at a crime scene.

4. _____ is a computerized database that allows an analyst to obtain information relating to an automobile's make, model, and year. is:
    a. CODIS
    b. AFIS
    c. PCR
    d. PDQ

5. Forensic soil comparison includes the comparison of color because
    a. color is an individual characteristic.
    b. soil color allows the examiner to determine the location of its origin.
    c. there are nearly 1,100 distinguishable soil colors so it offers a logical first step in soil comparison.
    d. color in soil is unique to a location.

6. True or False: "Trace elements" are important for the criminalist because they provide "invisible" markers that may establish the source of a material or at least provide additional points for comparison.

7. True or False: The major advantage of neutron activation analysis is that it provides a nondestructive method for identifying and quantifying trace elements.

8. True or False: Pyrolysis gas chromatography has proven to be an invaluable technique for distinguishing most paint pigments.

9. True or False: At the crime laboratory, a criminalist can determine the exact make and model of a car in question based on paint chips left behind at a crime scene.

10. True or False: When soil is found on a suspect's garments or shoes, the investigator should remove the soil by gently scraping the soil into an airtight container for later analysis.

11. What are trace elements?

12. Forensic analysis of the bullets recovered after the assassination of President John F. Kennedy focused on the concentration of what two trace elements?

13. Which of the following conclusions can be drawn from the forensic analysis of the bullets recovered after the assassination of President John F. Kennedy?
   a. The analysis absolutely verified the findings of the Warren Commission.
   b. The analysis cast doubt on the findings of the Warren Commission.
   c. The analysis generally supported the findings of the Warren Commission.
   d. The analysis absolutely disproved the findings of the Warren Commission.

14. Name the three most important subatomic particles and their electrical charges, and indicate where each is located in the atom.

15. How does atomic number differ from atomic mass?

16. What is radioactivity? What are the three types of radiation?

17. Briefly describe the process of neutron activation analysis.

18. In what types of criminal cases is paint evidence most frequently encountered?

19. Describe the basic composition of paint. What component of paint evaporates after paint is applied to a surface?

20. What characteristics does a criminalist look for when comparing paint chips under a microscope? Which of these characteristics is most important in evaluating the significance of paint evidence?

21. What technique has largely supplanted carbon arc emission spectroscopy for most applications? What is the main difference between the two techniques?

22. Why must paint collected from a vehicle involved in a hit-and-run accident be taken from the area of the car suspected of being in contact with the victim?

23. How should the investigator handle the collection of trace paint evidence left on a tool?

24. What is the first step in a forensic soil comparison?

25. What is a mineral? How are minerals useful in forensic soil analysis?

26. From what areas should standard/reference soils be collected when gathering soil evidence?

Application and Critical Thinking

1. Using the periodic table shown in Chapter 4, determine the atomic numbers for antimony, tin, barium, and lead. Which do you think has the largest atomic mass? Which do you think has the smallest atomic mass? Explain your answers.

2. You are investigating a hit-and-run accident and have identified a suspect vehicle. Describe how you would collect paint to determine whether the suspect vehicle was involved in the accident. Be sure to indicate the tools you would use and the steps you would take to prevent cross-contamination.

3. Criminalist Jared Heath responds to the scene of an assault on an unpaved lane in a rural neighborhood. Rain had fallen steadily the night before, making the area quite muddy. A suspect with very muddy shoes was apprehended nearby, but claimed to have picked up the mud either from his garden or from the unpaved parking lot of a local restaurant. Jared uses a spade to remove several samples of soil, each about 2 inches deep, from the immediate crime scene, and places each in a separate plastic vial. He collects the muddy shoes and wraps them in plastic as well. At the laboratory, he unpackages the soil samples and examines them carefully, one at a time. He then analyzes the soil on the shoes to see if it matches the soil from the crime scene. What mistakes, if any, did Jared make in his investigation?

Endnotes

1. Actually, the electrons are moving so rapidly around the nucleus that they are best visualized as an electron cloud spread out over the surface of the atom.

2. P. G. Rodgers et al., "The Classification of Automobile Paint by Diamond Window Infrared Spectrophotometry, Part I: Binders and Pigments," *Canadian Society of Forensic Science Journal* 9 (1976): 1; T. J. Allen, "Paint Sample Presentation for Fourier Transform Infrared Microscopy," *Vibration Spectroscopy* 3 (1992): 217.

3. G. Edmondstone, J. Hellman, K. Legate, G. L. Vardy, and E. Lindsay, "An Assessment of the Evidential Value of Automotive Paint Comparisons," *Canadian Society of Forensic Science Journal* 37 (2004): 147.

4. J. L. Buckle et al., "PDQ—Paint Data Queries: The History and Technology behind the Development of the Royal Canadian Mounted Police Laboratory Services Automotive Paint Database," *Canadian Society of Forensic Science Journal* 30 (1997): 199. An excellent discussion of the PDQ database is also available in A. Beveridge, T. Fung, and D. MacDougall, "Use of Infrared Spectroscopy for the Characterisation of Paint Fragments," in B. Caddy, ed., *Forensic Examination of Glass and Paint* (New York: Taylor & Francis, 2001), pp. 222–233.

5. E. P. Junger, "Assessing the Unique Characteristics of Close-Proximity Soil Samples: Just How Useful Is Soil Evidence?" *Journal of Forensic Sciences* 41 (1996), 27.

6. W. J. Graves, "A Mineralogical Soil Classification Technique for the Forensic Scientist," *Journal of Forensic Sciences* 24 (1979): 323; M. J. McVicar and W. J. Graves, "The Forensic Comparison of Soil by Automated Scanning Electron Microscopy," *Canadian Society of Forensic Science Journal* 30 (1997): 241.

Learning Objectives

After studying this chapter, you should be able to:

- List the conditions necessary to initiate and sustain combustion
- Understand the three mechanisms of heat transfer
- Recognize the telltale signs of an accelerant-initiated fire
- Describe how to collect physical evidence at the scene of a suspected arson
- Describe laboratory procedures used to detect and identify hydrocarbon residues

National Science Content Standards

 Scientific Inquiry

 Physical Science

 Science in Personal and Social Perspective

Debora Green— Poisoning the American Dream

On the face of it, the Farrar family had it all. Dr. Debora Green, a nonpracticing oncologist, and her husband, Dr. Michael Farrar, had an opulent home in an exclusive Kansas City suburb. Michael, a cardiologist, had a successful practice that enabled Debora to stay home to raise their three loving children, Tim, Kate, and Kelly.

In late 1995, Michael Farrar was hospitalized for a mysterious illness. Michael entered a revolving door of excruciating stomach pain and recovery, framed in the context of his failing marriage. Unknown to outsiders, Michael had initially asked Debora for a divorce in 1994.

Michael's suspicion of foul play was aroused when he found a large number of castor bean packets in Debora's purse. She had used the castor beans to poison Michael's food; they contain ricin, a deadly poison.

On the night of October 24, 1995, the Green house became engulfed in flames and was destroyed. Michael Farrar was sleeping elsewhere while the couple were beginning a legal separation preceding their divorce. Their daughter Kate, then 10 years old, escaped the fire by exiting her bedroom window, scaling the garage roof, and jumping to safety into the arms of her mother, who was standing outside the house. Their son Tim, 13, and daughter Kelly, 6, were killed in the blaze that consumed their home.

Fire investigators quickly realized that they were confronting a criminal case of arson. Unconnected fires had occurred in various rooms of the house. Throughout the first floor of the house, pour patterns were obvious where someone had spread accelerants—flammable substances used to spread the fire more quickly—on the floors. Heavy soaking of the carpet on the stairways leading to the children's rooms would have created a wall of fire effectively blocking the children's escape route. This arsonist was also a murderer.

Police arrested Debora and charged her with two counts of first-degree murder and aggravated arson. Psychological evaluation of the defendant concluded that she had a schizoid personality that was masked by a high degree of intelligence. Debora Green is currently serving a life sentence in a Missouri prison. Her psychotic behavior became the subject of Ann Rule's novel *Bitter Harvest*.

Forensic Aspects of Fire Investigation

Key Terms

accelerant
combustion
endothermic reaction
energy
exothermic reaction
flammable range
flash point
glowing combustion

heat of combustion
hydrocarbon
ignition temperature
modus operandi
oxidation
pyrolysis
spontaneous combustion

Forensic Investigation of Arson

Arson often presents complex and difficult circumstances to investigate. Normally these incidents are committed at the convenience of a perpetrator who has thoroughly planned the criminal act and has left the crime scene long before any official investigation is launched. Furthermore, proving commission of the offense is more difficult because of the extensive destruction that frequently dominates the crime scene. The contribution of the criminalist is only one aspect of a comprehensive and difficult investigative process that must establish a motive, the **modus operandi**, and a suspect.

modus operandi
An offender's pattern of operation

The criminalist's function is limited; usually he or she is expected only to detect and identify relevant chemical materials collected at the scene and to reconstruct and identify igniters. Although a chemist can identify trace amounts of gasoline or kerosene in debris, no scientific test can determine whether an arsonist has used a pile of rubbish or paper to start a fire. Furthermore, a fire can have many accidental causes, including faulty wiring, overheated electric motors, improperly cleaned and regulated heating systems, and cigarette smoking—which usually leave no chemical traces. Thus, the final determination of the cause of a fire must consider numerous factors and requires an extensive on-site investigation. The ultimate determination must be made by an investigator whose training and knowledge have been augmented by the practical experiences of fire investigation.

The Chemistry of Fire

Humankind's early search to explain the physical concepts underlying the behavior of matter always bestowed a central and fundamental role on fire. To ancient Greek philosophers, fire was one of the four basic elements from which all matter was derived. The medieval alchemist thought of fire as an instrument of transformation, capable of changing one element into another. One ancient recipe expresses its mystical power as follows: "Now the substance of cinnabar is such that the more it is heated, the more exquisite are its sublimations. Cinnabar will become mercury, and passing through a series of other sublimations, it is again turned into cinnabar, and thus it enables man to enjoy eternal life."

Today, we know of fire not as an element of matter but as a transformation process during which oxygen is united with some other substance to produce noticeable quantities of heat and light (a flame). Therefore, any insight into why and how a fire is initiated and sustained must begin with the knowledge of the fundamental chemical reaction of fire—**oxidation**.

oxidation
The combination of oxygen with other substances to produce new substances

Oxidation

In a simple description of oxidation, oxygen combines with other substances to produce new products. Thus, we may write the chemical equation for the burning of methane gas, a major component of natural gas, as follows:

$$CH_4 + 2O_2 \longrightarrow CO_2 + 2H_2O$$

methane   oxygen   yields   carbon dioxide   water

However, not all oxidation proceeds in the manner that one associates with fire. For example, oxygen combines with many metals to form oxides. Thus, iron forms a red-brown iron oxide, or rust, as follows (see <u>Figure 13–1</u>):

$$4Fe + 3O_2 \longrightarrow 2Fe_2O_3$$
iron   oxygen   yields   iron oxide

FIGURE 13–1
Rust forming on iron is an example of oxidation. *Courtesy Nichola Gissing-Debut Art, Getty Images-Digital Vision*

Yet chemical equations do not give us a complete insight into the oxidation process. We must consider other factors to understand all of the implications of oxidation or, for that matter, any other chemical reaction. Methane burns when it unites with oxygen, but merely mixing methane and oxygen does not produce a fire. Nor, for example, does gasoline burn when it is simply exposed to air. However, lighting a match in the presence of any one of these fuel–air mixtures (assuming proper proportions) produces an instant fire.

What are the reasons behind these differences? Why do some oxidations proceed with the outward appearances that we associate with a fire, while others do not? Why do we need a match to initiate some oxidations, but others proceed at room temperature? The explanation lies in a fundamental but abstract concept—energy.

Energy

Energy can be defined as the ability or potential of a system or material to do work. Energy takes many forms, such as heat energy, electrical energy, mechanical energy, nuclear energy, light energy, and chemical energy. For example, when methane is burned, the stored chemical energy in methane is converted to energy in the form of heat and light. This heat may be used to boil water or to provide high-pressure steam to turn a turbine. This is an example of converting chemical energy to heat energy to mechanical energy. The turbine can then be used to generate electricity, transforming mechanical energy to electrical energy. Electrical energy may then be used to turn a motor. In other words, energy can enable work to be done; heat is energy.

The quantity of heat from a chemical reaction comes from the breaking and formation of chemical bonds. Methane is a molecule composed of one carbon atom bonded with four hydrogen atoms:

An oxygen molecule forms when two atoms of the element oxygen bond:

$$O = O$$

In chemical changes, atoms are not lost but merely redistributed during the chemical reaction; thus, the products of methane's oxidation will be carbon dioxide:

$$O = C = O$$

and water:

$$H - O - H$$

This rearrangement, however, means that the chemical bonds holding the atoms together must be broken and new bonds formed. We now have arrived at a fundamental observation in our dissection of a chemical reaction—that molecules must absorb energy to break apart their chemical bonds, and that they liberate energy when their bonds are re-formed.

The amount of energy needed to break a bond and the amount of energy liberated when a bond is formed are characteristic of the type of chemical bond involved. Hence, a chemical reaction involves a change in energy content; energy is going in and energy is given off. The quantities of energies involved are different for each reaction and are determined by the participants in the chemical reaction.

Combustion

All oxidation reactions, including the **combustion** of methane, are examples of reactions in which more energy is liberated than is required to break the chemical bonds between atoms. Such reactions are said to be **exothermic**. The excess energy is liberated as heat, and often as light, and is known as the **heat of combustion**. Table 13–1 summarizes the heats of combustion of some important fuels in fire investigation.

Although we will not be concerned with them, some reactions require more energy than they eventually liberate. These reactions are known as **endothermic reactions**.

endothermic reaction
A chemical transformation in which heat energy is absorbed from the surroundings

Table 13–1
Heats of Combustion of Fuels

Fuel	Heat of Combustion[a]
Crude oil	19,650 Btu/gal
Diesel fuel	19,550 Btu/lb
Gasoline	19,250 Btu/lb
Methane	995 Btu/cu ft
Natural gas	128–1,868 Btu/cu ft
Octane	121,300 Btu/gal
Wood	7,500 Btu/lb
Coal, bituminous	11,000–14,000 Btu/lb
Anthracite	13,351 Btu/lb

[a]A Btu (British thermal unit) is defined as the quantity of heat required to raise the temperature of 1 pound of water 1°F at or near its point of maximum density.

Source: John D. DeHaan, Kirk's Fire Investigation, 2nd ed. Upper Saddle River, N.J.: Prentice Hall, 1983.

Thus, all reactions require an energy input to start them. We can think of this requirement as an invisible energy barrier between the reactants and the products of a reaction (see Figure 13–2). The higher this barrier, the more energy required to initiate the reaction. Where does this initial energy come from? There are many sources of energy; however, for the purpose of this discussion we need to look at only one—heat.

FIGURE 13–2
An energy barrier must be hurdled before reactants such as methane and oxygen can combine with one another to form the products of carbon dioxide and water.

Heat The energy barrier in the conversion of iron to rust is relatively small, and it can be surmounted with the help of heat energy in the surrounding environment at normal outdoor temperatures. Not so for methane or gasoline; these energy barriers are quite high, and a high temperature must be applied to start the oxidation of these fuels. Hence, before any fire can result, the temperature of these fuels must be raised enough to exceed the energy barrier. Table 13–2 shows that this temperature, known as the **ignition temperature**, is quite high for common fuels.

Once combustion starts, enough heat is liberated to keep the reaction going by itself. In essence, the fire becomes a chain reaction, absorbing a portion of its own liberated heat to generate even more heat. The fire burns until either the oxygen or the fuel is exhausted.

ignition temperature
The minimum temperature at which a fuel spontaneously ignites

Normally, a lighted match provides a convenient igniter of fuels. However, the fire investigator must also consider other potential sources of ignition—for example, electrical discharges, sparks, and chemicals—while reconstructing the initiation of a fire. All of these sources have temperatures higher than the ignition temperature of most fuels.

Table 13–2
Ignition Temperatures of Some Common Fuels

Fuel	Ignition Temperature, °F
Acetone	869
Benzene	928
Fuel oil #2	495
Gasoline (low octane)	536
Kerosene (fuel oil #1)	410
n-Octane	428
Petroleum ether	550
Turpentine	488

Source: John D. DeHaan, Kirk's Fire Investigation, 4th ed. Upper Saddle River, N.J.: Prentice Hall, 1997.

Speed of Reaction Although the liberation of energy explains many important features of oxidation, it does not explain all characteristics of the reaction. Obviously, although all oxidations liberate energy, not all are accompanied by a flame; witness the oxidation of iron to rust. Therefore, one other important consideration will make our understanding of oxidation and fire complete: the rate or speed at which the reaction takes place.

A chemical reaction, such as oxidation, takes place when molecules combine or collide with one another. The faster the molecules move, the greater the number of collisions between them and the faster the rate of reaction. Many factors influence the rate of these collisions. In our description of fire and oxidation, we consider only two: the physical state of the fuel and the temperature.

Physical State of Fuel. A fuel achieves a reaction rate with oxygen sufficient to produce a flame only when it is in the gaseous state, because only in this state can molecules collide frequently enough to support a flaming fire. This remains true whether the fuel is a solid such as wood, paper, cloth, or plastic, or a liquid such as gasoline or kerosene.

For example, the conversion of iron to rust proceeds slowly because the iron atoms cannot achieve a gaseous state. The combination of oxygen with iron is thus restricted to the surface area of the metal exposed to air, a limitation that severely reduces the rate of reaction. On the other hand, the reaction of methane and oxygen proceeds rapidly because all the reactants are in the gaseous state. The speed of the reaction is reflected by the production of noticeable quantities of heat and light (a flame).

Fuel Temperature. How, then, does a liquid or solid maintain a gaseous reaction? In the case of a liquid fuel, the temperature must be high enough to vaporize the fuel. The vapor that forms burns when it mixes with oxygen and combusts as a flame. The **flash point** is the lowest temperature at which a liquid gives off sufficient vapor to form a mixture with air that will support combustion. Once the flash point is reached, the fuel can be ignited by some outside source of temperature to start a fire. The ignition temperature of a fuel is always considerably higher than the flash point. For example, gasoline has a flash point of –50°F; however, an ignition temperature of 495°F is needed to start a gasoline fire.

With a solid fuel such as wood, the process of generating vapor is more complex. A solid fuel burns only when exposed to heat intense enough to decompose the solid into gaseous products. This chemical breakdown of solid material is known as **pyrolysis**. The gaseous products of pyrolysis combine with oxygen to produce a fire (see Figure 13–3). Here again, fire can be described as a chain reaction. A match or other source of heat initiates the pyrolysis of the solid fuel, the gaseous products react with oxygen in the air to produce heat and light, and this heat in turn pyrolyzes more solid fuel into volatile gases.

flash point
The minimum temperature at which a liquid fuel produces enough vapor to burn

FIGURE 13–3
Intense heat causes solid fuels such as wood to decompose into gaseous products, a process called *pyrolysis. Courtesy David Trood/Image Bank/ Getty Images*

Typically, the rate of a chemical reaction increases when the temperature is raised. The magnitude of the increase varies from one reaction to another and also from one temperature range to another. For most reactions, a 10°C (18°F) rise in temperature doubles or triples the reaction rate. This observation explains in part why burning is so rapid. As the fire spreads, it raises the temperature of the fuel–air mixture, thus increasing the rate of reaction; this in turn generates more heat, again increasing the rate of reaction. Only when the fuel or oxygen is depleted does this vicious cycle come to a halt.

The Fuel–Air Mix As we have seen from our discussion about gaseous fuel, air (oxygen) and sufficient heat are the basic ingredients of a flaming fire. There is

flammable range
The entire range of possible gas or vapor fuel concentrations in air that are capable of burning

glowing combustion
Combustion on the surface of a solid fuel in the absence of heat high enough to pyrolyze the fuel

also one other consideration—the gas fuel–air mix. A mixture of gaseous fuel and air burns only if its composition lies within certain limits. If the fuel concentration is too low (lean) or too great (rich), combustion does not occur. The concentration range between the upper and lower limits is called the **flammable range**. For example, the flammable range for gasoline is 1.3–6.0 percent. Thus, in order for a gasoline–air mix to burn, gasoline must make up at least 1.3 percent, and no more than 6 percent, of the mixture.

Glowing Combustion Although a flaming fire can be supported only by a gaseous fuel, in some instances a fuel can burn without a flame. Witness a burning cigarette or the red glow of hot charcoals (see Figure 13–4). These are examples of **glowing combustion** or smoldering. Here combustion occurs on the surface of a solid fuel in the absence of heat high enough to pyrolyze the fuel. Interestingly, this phenomenon generally ensues long after the flames have gone out. Wood, for example, tends to burn with a flame until all of its pyrolyzable components have been expended; however, wood's carbonaceous residue continues to smolder long after the flame has extinguished itself.

FIGURE 13–4 Red-hot charcoals are an example of glowing combustion. *Courtesy Paul Sisul/ Stone/Getty Images*

spontaneous combustion
A fire caused by a natural heat-producing process in the presence of sufficient air and fuel

Spontaneous Combustion One interesting phenomenon often invoked by arson suspects as the cause of a fire is **spontaneous combustion**. Actually, the conditions under which spontaneous combustion can develop are rather limited and rarely account for the cause of a fire. Spontaneous combustion is the result of a natural heat-producing process in poorly ventilated containers or areas. For example, hay stored in barns provides an excellent growing medium for bacteria whose activities generate heat. If the hay is not properly ventilated, the heat builds to a level that supports other types of heat-producing chemical reactions in the hay. Eventually, as the heat rises, the ignition temperature of hay is reached, spontaneously setting off a fire.

Another example of spontaneous combustion involves the ignition of improperly ventilated containers containing rags soaked with certain types of highly unsaturated oils, such as linseed oil. Heat can build up to the point of ignition as a result of a slow heat-producing chemical oxidation between the air and the oil. Of course, storage conditions must encourage the accumulation of the heat over a prolonged period of time. However, spontaneous combustion does not occur with hydrocarbon lubricating oils, and it is not expected to occur with most household fats and oils.

In summary, three requirements must be satisfied to initiate and sustain combustion:

1. A fuel must be present.

2. Oxygen must be available in sufficient quantity to combine with the fuel.

3. Heat must be applied to initiate the combustion, and sufficient heat must be generated to sustain the reaction.

Heat Transfer

Consider how a structural fire begins. The typical scenario starts with heat ignition at a single location. It may be an arsonist lighting a gasoline-soaked rag, a malfunctioning electric appliance sparking, or an individual falling asleep while smoking a cigarette in bed. How does a flame initially confined to a single location spread to engulf an entire structure? Understanding the anatomy of a fire begins with comprehending how heat travels through a burning structure.

The previous section stressed the importance of the role of heat in generating sufficient fuel vapors to support combustion, as well as the requirement that the heat source be hot enough to ignite the fuel's vapor. Once the fire begins, the heat generated by the fuel's reaction with air is fed back into the fuel–air mix to keep the chemical reaction going.

As a fire progresses, the heat created by the combustion process tends to move from a high-temperature region to one at a lower temperature. Understanding heat transfer from one location to another is important for reconstructing the origin of a fire, as well as for understanding why and how fire spreads through a structure. The three mechanisms of heat transfer are conduction, radiation, and convection.

Conduction Movement of heat through a solid object is caused by a process called conduction, in which electrons and atoms within the heated object collide with one another. Heat always travels from hot areas of a solid to cold ones by conduction. Solids whose atoms or molecules have loosely held electrons are good conductors of heat. Metals have the most loosely held electrons and are therefore excellent conductors of heat. Thus, when you insert one end of a metal object into an open flame, the entire object quickly becomes hot to the touch.

Materials that have electrons firmly attached to their molecules are poor conductors of heat. Poor conductors are called insulators. Wood is a good insulator; for that reason, metal objects that are subject to intense heat (such as skillets and saucepans) often have wooden handles (see Figure 13–5).

FIGURE 13–5
The wooden handle
on this saucepan is a
poor conductor of heat.
*Courtesy Topham,
The Image Works*

In reconstructing a fire scene, it's important to keep in mind that heat may be transported through metals such as beams, nails, fasteners, bolts, and other good conductors to a location far from the initial heat source. Any fuel in contact with the conductor may be ignited, creating a new fire location. On the other hand, the conductivity of wood, plastic, and paper is very low, meaning that heat emanating from these surfaces does not spread well and does not cause ignitions far from the initial heat source.

Radiation *Radiation* is the transfer of heat energy from a heated surface to a cooler surface by electromagnetic radiation. A hot surface emits electromagnetic radiation of various wavelengths, and in a fire scene the electromagnetic radiation moves in a straight line from one surface to another. Radiant heat plays a key role in understanding how fire spreads throughout a structure. For example, all surfaces that face the fire are exposed to radiant heat and burst into flames when the surface reaches their ignition temperature. In very large fires, nearby structures and vehicles are often ignited at a distance by radiant heat.

Convection *Convection* is the transfer of heat energy by movement of molecules within a liquid or gas. Water being heated on a stove illustrates the concept of convection. As the water molecules on the bottom of the pot move faster, they spread apart and become less dense, causing them to move upward. Denser, cooler water molecules then migrate to the bottom of the pot. In this way, convection currents keep the fluid stirred up as warmer fluid moves away from the heat source and cooler fluid moves toward the heat source. Likewise, warm air expands, becoming less dense and causing it to rise and move toward the cooler surrounding air.

In a structural fire, the gaseous hot products of combustion expand, and convection moves the hot gases to the upper portions of the structure (see Figure 13–6). The convected hot gases become a source of heat, radiating heat energy downward onto all the surfaces below them. The hot surfaces of the exposed objects often pyrolyze or break down, releasing gaseous molecules. The phenomenon known as *flashover* occurs when all the combustible fuels simultaneously ignite, engulfing the entire structure in flame.

FIGURE 13–6
Convection causes flames to rise to the upper floor of a burning structure. *Courtesy Dave Frazier, Danita Delimont Photography*

Quick Review

- Oxidation is the combination of oxygen with other substances to produce new substances.

- Combustion is rapid combination of oxygen with another substance, accompanied by production of noticeable heat and light.

- In an exothermic reaction, heat energy is liberated. In an endothermic reaction, heat energy is absorbed from the surroundings.

- Pyrolysis is the chemical breakdown of solid organic matter by heat. The gaseous products of pyrolysis combine with oxygen to produce a fire.

- Spontaneous combustion is fire caused by a natural heat-producing process in the presence of sufficient air and fuel.

- To initiate and sustain combustion, (1) a fuel must be present, (2) oxygen must be available in sufficient quantity to combine with the fuel, and (3) heat must be applied to initiate the combustion, and sufficient heat must be generated to sustain the reaction.

- The three mechanisms of heat transfer are conduction, radiation, and convection. Conduction is the movement of heat through a solid object. Radiation is the transfer of heat energy from a heated surface to a cooler surface by electromagnetic radiation. Convection is the transfer of heat energy by the movement of molecules within a liquid or gas.

Searching the Fire Scene

accelerant
Any material used to start or sustain a fire

The arson investigator should begin examining a fire scene for signs of arson as soon as the fire has been extinguished. Most arsons are started with petroleum-based **accelerants** such as gasoline or kerosene. Thus, the presence of containers capable of holding an accelerant arouse suspicions of arson. Discovery of an ignition device ranging in sophistication from a candle to a time-delay device is another indication of possible arson. A common telltale sign of arson is an irregularly shaped pattern on a floor or on the ground (see Figure 13–7) resulting from pouring an accelerant onto the surface. In addition to these visual indicators, investigators should look for signs of breaking and entering and theft, and they should begin interviewing any eyewitnesses to the fire.

FIGURE 13–7
Irregularly shaped pattern on the ground resulting from a poured ignitable liquid.
Courtesy Franklin County Crime Scene Unit, North Carolina

Timelines of Investigation

Time constantly works against the arson investigator. Any accelerant residues that remain after a fire is extinguished may evaporate within a few days or even hours. Furthermore, safety and health conditions may necessitate that cleanup and salvage operations begin as quickly as possible. Once this occurs, a meaningful investigation of the fire scene is impossible. Accelerants in soil and vegetation can be rapidly degraded by bacterial action. Freezing samples containing soil or vegetation is an effective way to prevent this degradation.

The need to begin an *immediate* investigation of the circumstances surrounding a fire even takes precedence over the requirement to obtain a search warrant to enter and search the premises. The Supreme Court, explaining its position on this issue, stated in part:

. . . Fire officials are charged not only with extinguishing fires, but with finding their causes. Prompt determination of the fire's origin may be necessary to prevent its recurrence, as through the detection of continuing dangers such as faulty wiring or a defective furnace. Immediate investigation may also be necessary to preserve evidence from intentional or accidental destruction. And, of course, the sooner the officials complete their duties, the less will be their subsequent interference with the privacy and the recovery efforts of the victims. For these reasons, officials need no warrant to remain in a building for a reasonable time to investigate the cause of a blaze after it has been extinguished. And if the warrantless entry to put out the fire and determine its cause is constitutional, the warrantless seizure of evidence while inspecting the premises for these purposes also is constitutional. . . .

In determining what constitutes a reasonable time to investigate, appropriate recognition must be given to the exigencies that confront officials serving under these conditions, as well as to individuals' reasonable expectations of privacy.[1]

Locating the Fire's Origin

A search of the fire scene must focus on finding the fire's origin, which will prove most productive in any search for an accelerant or ignition device. In searching for a fire's specific point of origin, the investigator may uncover telltale signs of arson such as evidence of separate and unconnected fires or the use of "streamers" to spread the fire from one area to another. For example, the arsonist may have spread a trail of gasoline or paper to cause the fire to move rapidly from one room to another.

There are no fast and simple rules for identifying a fire's origin. Normally a fire tends to move upward, and thus the probable origin is most likely closest to the lowest point that shows the most intense characteristics of burning. Sometimes as the fire burns upward, a V-shaped pattern forms against a vertical wall, as shown in Figure 13–8. Because flammable liquids always flow to the lowest point, more severe burning found on the floor than on the ceiling may indicate the presence of an accelerant. If a flammable liquid was used, charring is expected to be more intense on the bottom of furniture, shelves, and other items rather than the top.

However, many factors can contribute to the deviation of a fire from normal behavior. Prevailing drafts and winds; secondary fires due to collapsing floors and roofs; the physical arrangement of the burning structure; stairways and elevator shafts; holes in the floor, wall, or roof; and the effects of the firefighter in suppressing the fire are all factors that the fire investigator must consider before determining conclusive findings.

Once located, the point of origin should be protected to permit careful investigation. As at any crime scene, nothing should be touched or moved before notes, sketches, and photographs are taken. An examination must also be made

Virtual Lab: Arson Detection— The Recovery of Flammable Liquids

To perform a virtual arson detection lab, go to: www.pearsoncustom. com/us/vlm/

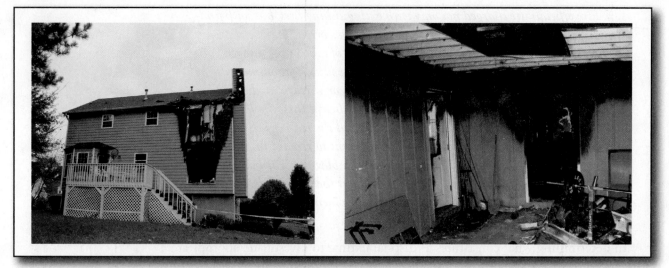

FIGURE 13–8 Typical V patterns illustrating upward movement of the fire.
Courtesy John Lentini

for possible accidental causes, as well as for evidence of arson. The most common materials used by an arsonist to ensure the rapid spread and intensity of a fire are gasoline and kerosene or, for that matter, any volatile flammable liquid.

Searching for Accerlerants

Fortunately, only under the most ideal conditions will combustible liquids be entirely consumed during a fire. When the liquid is poured over a large area, a portion of it will likely seep into a porous surface, such as cracks in the floor, upholstery, rags, plaster, wallboards, or carpet. Enough of the liquid may remain unchanged to permit its detection in the crime laboratory. In addition, when a fire is extinguished with water, the evaporation rate of volatile fluids may be slowed, because water cools and covers materials through which the combustible liquid may have soaked. Fortunately, water does not interfere with laboratory methods used to detect and characterize flammable liquid residues.

The search for traces of flammable liquid residues may be aided by the use of a sensitive portable vapor detector or "sniffer" (see Figure 13–9). This device can rapidly screen suspect materials for volatile residues by sucking in the air surrounding the questioned sample. The air is passed over a heated filament; if a combustible vapor is present, it oxidizes and immediately increases the temperature of the filament. The rise in filament temperature is then registered as a deflection on the detector's meter.

FIGURE 13–9
Portable hydrocarbon detector. *Courtesy Sirchie Finger Print Laboratories, Inc., Youngsville, N.C., www.sirchie.com*

Of course, such a device is not a conclusive test for a flammable vapor, but it is an excellent screening device for checking suspect samples at the fire scene. Another approach is to use dogs that have been trained to recognize the odor of hydrocarbon accelerants.

Collection and Preservation of Arson Evidence

Two to three quarts of ash and soot debris must be collected at the point of origin of a fire when arson is suspected. The collection should include all porous materials and all other substances thought likely to contain flammable residues. These include such things as wood flooring, rugs, upholstery, and rags.

Packaging and Preservation of Evidence

Specimens should be packaged immediately in airtight containers so possible residues are not lost through evaporation. New, clean paint cans with friction lids are good containers because they are low cost, airtight, unbreakable, and available in a variety of sizes (see Figure 13–10). Wide-mouthed glass jars are also useful for packaging suspect specimens, provided that they have airtight lids. Cans and jars should be filled one-half to two-thirds full, leaving an air space in the container above the debris.

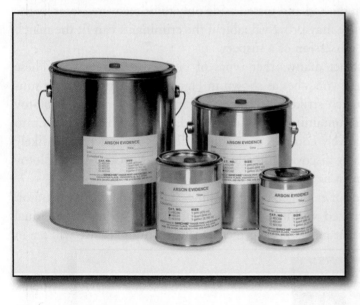

FIGURE 13–10
Various sizes of paint cans suitable for collecting debris at fire scenes. *Courtesy Sirchie Finger Print Laboratories, Inc., Youngsville, N.C., www.sirchie.com*

Large bulky samples should be cut to size at the scene as needed so that they will fit into available containers. Plastic polyethylene bags are not suitable for packaging specimens because they react with hydrocarbons and permit volatile hydrocarbon vapors to be depleted. Fluids found in open bottles or cans must be collected and sealed. Even when such containers appear empty, the investigator is wise to seal and preserve them in case they contain trace amounts of liquids or vapors.

Substrate Control

The collection of all materials suspected of containing volatile liquids must be accompanied by a thorough sampling of similar but uncontaminated control specimens from another area of the fire scene. This is known as *substrate control*. For example, if an investigator collects carpeting at the point of origin, he or she must sample the same carpet from another part of the room, where it can be reasonably assumed that no flammable substance was placed.

In the laboratory, the criminalist checks the substrate control to be sure that it is free of any flammables. This procedure reduces the possibility (and subsequent argument) that the carpet was exposed to a flammable liquid such as a cleaning solution during normal maintenance. In addition, laboratory tests on the unburned control material may help analyze the breakdown products from the material's exposure to intense heat during the fire. Common materials such as plastic floor tiles, carpet, linoleum, and adhesives can produce volatile hydrocarbons when they are burned. These breakdown products can sometimes be mistaken for an accelerant.

Igniters and Other Evidence

The scene should also be thoroughly searched for igniters. The most common igniter is a match. Normally the match is completely consumed during a fire and is impossible to locate. However, there have been cases in which, by force of habit, matches have been extinguished and tossed aside only to be recovered later by the investigator. This evidence may prove valuable if the criminalist can fit the match to a book found in the possession of a suspect.

Arsonists can construct many other types of devices to start a fire. These include burning cigarettes, matches as shown in Figure 13–11, firearms, ammunition, a mechanical match striker, electrical sparking devices, and a "Molotov cocktail"—a glass bottle containing flammable liquid with a cloth rag stuffed into it and lit as a fuse. Relatively complex mechanical devices are much more likely to survive the fire for later discovery. The broken glass and wick of the Molotov cocktail, if recovered, must be preserved as well.

One important piece of evidence is the clothing of the suspected perpetrator. If this individual is arrested within a few hours of initiating the fire, residual quantities of the accelerant may still be present in the clothing. As we will see in

FIGURE 13–11
Three matches (Spec. 3, 4, 5) discarded at the scene of an arson are each shown to fit into a matchbook (Spec. 1) found in the suspect's possession. Such evidence strongly links the crime scene and the suspect.

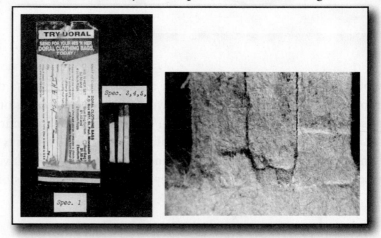

the next section, the forensic laboratory can detect extremely small quantities of accelerants, making the examination of a suspect's clothing a feasible investigative approach. Each item of clothing should be placed in a separate airtight container, preferably a new, clean paint can.

Quick Review

- Telltale signs of arson include evidence of separate and unconnected fires, the use of "streamers" to spread the fire from one area to another, and evidence of severe burning found on the floor as opposed to the ceiling of a structure.

- Other common signs of arson at a fire scene are the presence of accelerants and the discovery of an ignition device.

- Porous materials at the suspected point of origin of a fire should be collected and stored in airtight containers.

Analysis of Flammable Residues

Criminalists are nearly unanimous in judging the gas chromatograph to be the most sensitive and reliable instrument for detecting and characterizing flammable residues. Most arsons are initiated by petroleum distillates, such as gasoline and kerosene, that are composed of a complex mixture of **hydrocarbons**. The gas chromatograph separates the hydrocarbon components of these liquids and produces a chromatographic pattern characteristic of a particular petroleum product.

hydrocarbon
Any compound consisting of only carbon and hydrogen

The Headspace Technique

Before accelerant residues can be analyzed, they first must be recovered from the debris collected at the scene. The easiest way to recover accelerant residues from fire-scene debris is to heat the airtight container in which the sample is sent to the laboratory. When the container is heated, any volatile residue in the debris is driven off and trapped in the container's enclosed airspace. The vapor or headspace is then removed with a syringe, as shown in Figure 13–12.

FIGURE 13–12
Removal of vapor from an enclosed container for gas chromatographic analysis.

When the vapor is injected into the gas chromatograph, it is separated into its components, and each peak is recorded on the chromatogram. One way of classifying ignitable liquids is by their boiling point range, which is related to the number of carbon molecules that are present in the mixture of hydrocarbons comprising an ignitable fuel. A common classification system characterizes ignitable liquids based on their boiling-point range, which is related to the number of carbon molecules, as light, medium, and heavy petroleum distillates. Figure 13–13 illustrates examples of chromatograms for light, medium, and heavy petroleum distillates.

FIGURE 13–13
Chromatograms of ignitable liquids.
(a) light petroleum distillate
(b) medium petroleum distillate
(c) heavy petroleum distillate.

The identity of the volatile residue is determined when the pattern of the resultant chromatogram is compared to patterns produced by known petroleum products. For example, in Figure 13–14, a gas chromatographic analysis of debris recovered from a fire site shows a chromatogram similar to a known gasoline standard, thus proving the presence of gasoline.

FIGURE 13–14
Gas chromatograph of vapor from a genuine gasoline sample. (bottom) Gas chromatograph of vapor from debris recovered at a fire site. Note the similarity of the known gasoline to vapor removed from the debris.

Vapor Concentration

One major disadvantage of the headspace technique is that the size of the syringe limits the volume of vapor that can be removed from the container and injected into the gas chromatograph. To overcome this deficiency, many crime laboratories augment the headspace technique with a method called *vapor concentration*. One setup for this analysis is shown in Figure 13–15.

FIGURE 13–15
Apparatus for accelerant recovery by vapor concentration. The vapor in the enclosed container is exposed to charcoal, a chemical absorbent, where it is trapped for later analysis.

A charcoal-coated strip, similar to that used in environmental monitoring badges, is placed within the container holding the debris that has been collected from the fire scene.[2] The container is then heated to about 60°C for about one hour. At this temperature, a significant quantity of accelerant vaporizes into the container airspace. The charcoal absorbs the accelerant vapor with which it comes into contact. In this manner, over a short period of time, a significant quantity of the accelerant will be trapped and concentrated onto the charcoal strip.

Once the heating procedure is complete, the analyst removes the charcoal strip from the container and recovers the accelerant from the strip by washing it with a small volume of solvent (carbon disulfide). The solvent is then injected into the gas chromatograph for analysis. The major advantage of using vapor concentration with gas chromatography is its sensitivity. By absorbing the accelerant into a charcoal strip, the forensic analyst can increase the sensitivity of accelerant detection at least a hundredfold over that of the conventional headspace technique.

An examination of Figure 13–14 shows that identifying an accelerant such as gasoline by gas chromatography is an exercise in pattern recognition. Typically a forensic analyst compares the pattern generated by the sample to chromatograms from accelerant standards obtained under the same conditions. The pattern of gasoline, as with many other accelerants, can easily be placed in a searchable library. An invaluable reference known as "The Ignitable Liquids Reference Collection" or (ILRC) is found on the Internet at http://ilrc.ucf.edu. The ILRC is a useful collection showing chromatographic patterns for approximately 500 ignitable liquids.

FIGURE 13–16 Chromatogram of a residue sample collected at a fire scene (a) shows a pattern somewhat like that of gasoline (b). However, a definitive conclusion that the unknown contained gasoline could be obtained only after extraneous peaks were eliminated from the unknown by the use of GC/MS (c).

Gas Chromatography/Mass Spectrometry

On occasion, discernible patterns are not obtainable by gas chromatography. This may be due to a combination of accelerants, or to the mixing of accelerant residue with heat-generated breakdown products of materials burning at the fire scene. Under such conditions, a gas chromatographic pattern can be difficult, if not impossible, to interpret. In these cases, gas chromatography combined with mass spectrometry (discussed in Chapter 5) has proven valuable for solving difficult problems in the detection of accelerant residues.

Complex chromatographic patterns can be simplified by passing the separated components emerging from the gas chromatographic column through a mass spectrometer. As each component enters the mass spectrometer, it is fragmented into a collection of ions. The analyst can then control which ions will be detected and which will go unnoticed. In essence, the mass spectrometer acts as a filter allowing the analyst to see only the peaks associated with the ions selected for a particular accelerant. In this manner, the chromatographic pattern can be simplified by eliminating extraneous peaks that may obliterate the pattern.[3] The process is illustrated in Figure 13–16.

Quick Review

- Most arsons are initiated by petroleum distillates such as gasoline and kerosene.

- The gas chromatograph is the most sensitive and reliable instrument for detecting and characterizing flammable residues. A gas chromatograph separates the hydrocarbon components and produces a chromatographic pattern characteristic of a particular petroleum product.

- By comparing select gas chromatographic peaks recovered from fire-scene debris to known flammable liquids, a forensic analyst may be able to identify the accelerant used to initiate the fire.

- Complex chromatographic patterns can be simplified by passing the separated components emerging from the gas chromatographic column through a mass spectrometer.

Chapter Review

- Oxidation is the combination of oxygen with other substances to produce new substances.

- Combustion is rapid combination of oxygen with another substance, accompanied by production of noticeable heat and light.

- In an exothermic reaction, heat energy is liberated. In an endothermic reaction, heat energy is absorbed from the surroundings.

- Pyrolysis is the chemical breakdown of solid organic matter by heat. The gaseous products of pyrolysis combine with oxygen to produce a fire.

- Spontaneous combustion is fire caused by a natural heat-producing process in the presence of sufficient air and fuel.

- To initiate and sustain combustion, (1) a fuel must be present, (2) oxygen must be available in sufficient quantity to combine with the fuel, and (3) heat must be applied to initiate the combustion, and sufficient heat must be generated to sustain the reaction.

- The three mechanisms of heat transfer are conduction, radiation, and convection. Conduction is the movement of heat through a solid object. Radiation is the transfer of heat energy from a heated surface to a cooler surface by electromagnetic radiation. Convection is the transfer of heat energy by the movement of molecules within a liquid or gas.

- Telltale signs of arson include evidence of separate and unconnected fires, the use of "streamers" to spread the fire from one area to another, and evidence of severe burning found on the floor as opposed to the ceiling of a structure.

- Other common signs of arson at a fire scene are the presence of accelerants and the discovery of an ignition device.

- Porous materials at the suspected point of origin of a fire should be collected and stored in airtight containers.

- Most arsons are initiated by petroleum distillates such as gasoline and kerosene.

- The gas chromatograph is the most sensitive and reliable instrument for detecting and characterizing flammable residues. A gas chromatograph separates the hydrocarbon components and produces a chromatographic pattern characteristic of a particular petroleum product.

- By comparing select gas chromatographic peaks recovered from fire-scene debris to known flammable liquids, a forensic analyst may be able to identify the accelerant used to initiate the fire.

- Complex chromatographic patterns can be simplified by passing the separated components emerging from the gas chromatographic column through a mass spectrometer.

Review Questions

1. If combustion is to be initiated and sustained, all of the following elements must be present except
   a. the presence of a fuel.
   b. the availability of oxygen.
   c. the application of heat.
   d. the elimination of carbon monoxide.

2. Most arson fires are started with
   a. lead-based paints.
   b. an oxidizing agent.
   c. petroleum-based accelerants.
   d. highly unsaturated oils.

3. The quantity of heat from a chemical reaction comes from
   a. the breaking and formation of chemical bonds.
   b. the presence of oxygen in the reaction.
   c. the emission of radiation.
   d. the composition of the fuel–air mix.

4. A search of the fire scene must focus on
   a. collecting trace evidence for later chemical analysis.
   b. estimating the value of monetary loss.
   c. ascertaining whether or not a crime has been committed.
   d. finding the fire's origin.

5. A gas chromatograph identifies an accelerant by a chromatogram's
   a. length.
   b. size.
   c. pattern.
   d. peak shape.

6. True or False: The criminalist plays a central role in the detection of arson and the subsequent apprehension of the suspected arsonist based on a determination as to the cause of a fire.

7. True or False: The flash point of a liquid fuel is the highest temperature at which a liquid gives off sufficient vapor to form a mixture with air that will support combustion.

8. True or False: Radiation is the transfer of heat energy by electromagnetic radiation.

9. True or False: Fire evidence can be contained in manila envelopes or plastic bags.

10. True or False: The most important instrument for identifying accelerants in the laboratory is the mass spectrometer.

11. What is oxidation?

12. Molecules must absorb energy to _____, and they liberate energy when _____.

13. What is combustion? Why is rusting not accompanied by combustion?

14. How does an exothermic reaction differ from an endothermic reaction?

15. A fire will burn until either of which two components is exhausted?

16. Name two factors that influence the speed of reaction of a fire.

17. In what physical state must a fuel exist in order to produce combustion when it reacts with oxygen? Why must it be in this state?

18. How high must the temperature of a liquid fuel be before the fuel will burn? What is the term for the lowest temperature at which this occurs?

19. What is pyrolysis? How does pyrolysis produce fire?

20. How does the fuel–air mix affect combustion?

21. Define and give two examples of glowing combustion.

22. Define *spontaneous combustion* and give two examples of conditions under which it may occur.

23. What three requirements must be satisfied to initiate and sustain combustion?

24. List and define the three mechanisms of heat transfer.

25. What is an insulator? Give an example of a good insulator.

26. List three common signs of arson at a fire scene.

27. Name three reasons why arson investigators must work quickly to collect evidence at a fire scene.

28. What are streamers? What does evidence of their presence at a fire scene suggest?

29. Why should fire evidence be packaged in airtight containers?

30. What instrument do most criminalists consider the most sensitive and reliable for detecting and characterizing flammable residues?

31. What is headspace? How is it recovered?

32. What is the main advantage of vapor concentration over the headspace technique?

Application and Critical Thinking

1. Indicate which method of heat transfer is most likely to be responsible for each of the following:
   a. ignition of papers in the room where a fire starts
   b. ignition of electrical wiring in a room adjoining the fire's point or origin
   c. ignition of roof timbers
   d. ignition of a neighboring house

2. It is late August in Houston, Texas, and you are investigating a fire that occurred at a facility that stores motor oils and other lubricating oils. A witness points out a man who allegedly ran from the structure about the same time that the fire started. You question the man, who turns out to be the owner of the facility. He tells you that he was checking his inventory when barrels of waste motor oil stored in an unventilated back room spontaneously burst into flames. The owner claims that the fire spread so rapidly that he had to flee the building before he could call 911. After speaking with several employees, you learn that the building has no air conditioning and that the oil had been stored for almost a year in the cramped back room. You also learn from a detective assisting on the case that the owner increased his insurance coverage on the facility within the past three months. Should you believe the owner's story, or should you suspect arson? Upon what do you base your conclusion?

3. Criminalist Mick Mickelson is collecting evidence from a fire scene. He gathers about a quart of ash and soot debris collected from several rooms surrounding the point of origin. He stored the debris in a new, clean paint can, filled about three-quarters full. Seeing several pieces of timber that he believes may contain accelerant residues, he cuts them and places them in airtight plastic bags. A short time later, a suspect is arrested and Mick searches him for any signs of an igniter or accelerants. He finds a cigarette lighter on the suspect and seizes it for evidence before turning the suspect over to the police. What mistakes, if any, did Mick make in collecting evidence?

4. Classify the following chromatograms of ignitable liquids below as low, medium, or high petroleum distillates. Refer to Figure 13-13.

A. _____

B. _____

C. _____

D. _____

E. _____

F. _____

G. _____

Virtual Lab: Arson Detection— The Recovery of Flammable Liquids

To perform a virtual flammable liquid recovery and identification lab, go to www.pearsoncustom.com/us/vlm/

Endnotes

1. Michigan v. Tyler, 436 U.S. 499 (1978).

2. R. T. Newman et al., "The Use of Activated Charcoal Strips for Fire Debris Extractions by Passive Diffusion. Part 1: The Effects of Time, Temperature, Strip Size, and Sample Concentration," *Journal of Forensic Sciences* 41 (1996): 361.

3. M. W. Gilbert, "The Use of Individual Extracted Ion Profiles versus Summed Extracted Ion Profiles in Fire Debris Analysis," *Journal of Forensic Sciences* 43 (1998): 871.

Learning Objectives

After studying this chapter you should be able to:

- **Understand how explosives are classified**

- **List some common commercial, homemade, and military explosives**

- **Describe how to collect physical evidence at the scene of an explosion**

- **Describe laboratory procedures used to detect and identify explosive residues**

National Science Content Standards

 Scientific Inquiry

 Physical Science

 Science and Technology

 Science in Personal and Social Perspective

 History and Nature of Science

The Oklahoma City Bombing

It was the biggest act of mass murder in U.S. history. On a sunny spring morning in April 1995, a Ryder rental truck pulled into the parking area of the Alfred P. Murrah federal building in Oklahoma City. The driver stepped down from the truck's cab and casually walked away. Minutes later, the truck exploded into a fireball, unleashing enough energy to destroy the building and kill 168 people, including 19 children and infants in the building's day care center.

Later that morning, an Oklahoma Highway Patrol officer pulled over a beat-up 1977 Mercury Marquis being driven without a license plate. On further investigation, the driver, Timothy McVeigh, was found to be in possession of a loaded firearm and charged with transporting a firearm. At the explosion site, remnants of the Ryder truck were located, and the truck was quickly traced to a renter—Robert Kling, an alias for Timothy McVeigh. Coincidentally, the rental agreement and McVeigh's driver's license both used the address of McVeigh's friend, Terry Nichols.

Investigators later recovered McVeigh's fingerprint on a receipt for 2,000 pounds of ammonium nitrate, a basic explosive ingredient. Forensic analysts also located PETN residues on the clothing McVeigh wore on the day of his arrest. PETN is a component of detonating cord. After three days of deliberation, a jury declared McVeigh guilty of the bombing and sentenced him to die by lethal injection.

Forensic Investigation of Explosions

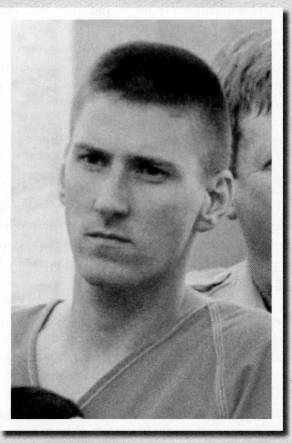

Key Terms

black powder

deflagration

detonating cord

detonation

explosion

high explosive

low explosive

oxidizing agent

primary explosive

safety fuse

secondary explosive

smokeless powder (double-base)

smokeless powder (single-base)

X-ray diffraction

Explosions and Explosives

The ready accessibility of potentially explosive laboratory chemicals, dynamite, and, in some countries, an assortment of military explosives has provided the criminal element of society with a lethal weapon. Unfortunately for society, explosives have become an attractive weapon to criminals bent on revenge, destruction of commercial operations, or just plain mischief.

Although politically motivated bombings have received considerable publicity worldwide, in the United States most bombing incidents are perpetrated by isolated individuals rather than by organized terrorists. These incidents typically involve homemade explosives and incendiary devices. The design of such weapons is limited only by the imagination and ingenuity of the bomber.

Like arson investigation, bomb investigation requires close cooperation of a group of highly specialized individuals trained and experienced in bomb disposal, bomb-site investigation, forensic analysis, and criminal investigation. The criminalist must detect and identify explosive chemicals recovered from the crime scene as well as identify the detonating mechanisms. This special responsibility concerns us for the remainder of this chapter.

The Chemistry of Explosions

explosion
A chemical or mechanical action caused by combustion, accompanied by creation of heat and rapid expansion of gases

Like fire, an **explosion** is the product of combustion accompanied by the creation of gases and heat. However, the distinguishing characteristic of an explosion is the rapid rate of the reaction. The sudden buildup of expanding gas pressure at the origin of the explosion produces the violent physical disruption of the surrounding environment.

Our previous discussion of the chemistry of fire referred only to oxidation reactions that rely on air as the sole source of oxygen. However, we need not restrict ourselves to this type of situation. For example, explosives are substances that undergo a rapid exothermic oxidation reaction, producing large quantities of gases. This sudden buildup of gas pressure constitutes an explosion. Detonation occurs so rapidly that oxygen in the air cannot participate in the reaction; thus, many explosives must have their own source of oxygen.

oxidizing agent
A substance that supplies oxygen to a chemical reaction

Chemicals that supply oxygen are known as **oxidizing agents**. One such agent is found in black powder, a *low explosive*, which is composed of a mixture of the following chemical ingredients:

75 percent potassium nitrate (KNO_3)

15 percent charcoal (C)

10 percent sulfur (S)

In this combination, oxygen-containing potassium nitrate acts as an oxidizing agent for the charcoal and sulfur fuels. As heat is applied to black powder, oxygen is liberated from potassium nitrate and simultaneously combines with charcoal and sulfur to produce heat and gases (symbolized by ↑), as represented in the following chemical equation:

$$3C \quad + \quad S \quad + \quad 2KNO_3 \quad \longrightarrow$$
carbon   sulfur   potassium nitrate   yields

$$3CO_2\uparrow \quad + \quad N_2\uparrow \quad + \quad K_2S$$

carbon dioxide   nitrogen   potassium sulfide

Some explosives have their oxygen and fuel components combined within one molecule. For example, the chemical structure of nitroglycerin, the major constituent of dynamite, combines carbon, hydrogen, nitrogen, and oxygen:

$$\begin{array}{ccccccc}
 & H & & H & & H & \\
 & | & & | & & | & \\
H - & C & - & C & - & C & - H \\
 & | & & | & & | & \\
 & NO_2 & & NO_2 & & NO_2 &
\end{array}$$

When nitroglycerin detonates, large quantities of energy are released as the molecule decomposes, and the oxygen recombines to produce large volumes of carbon dioxide, nitrogen, and water.

Consider, for example, the effect of confining an explosive charge to a relatively small, closed container. On detonation, the explosive almost instantaneously produces large volumes of gases that exert enormously high pressures on the interior walls of the container. In addition, the heat energy released by the explosion expands the gases, causing them to push on the walls with an even greater force. If we could observe the effects of an exploding lead pipe in slow motion, we would first see the pipe's walls stretch and balloon under pressures as high as several hundred tons per square inch. Finally, the walls would fragment and fly outward in all directions. This flying debris or shrapnel constitutes a great danger to life and limb in the immediate vicinity.

On release from confinement, the gaseous products of the explosion suddenly expand and compress layers of surrounding air as they move outward from the origin of the explosion. This blast effect, or outward rush of gases, at a rate that may be as high as 7,000 miles per hour creates an artificial gale that can overthrow walls, collapse roofs, and disturb any object in its path. If a bomb is sufficiently powerful, more serious damage will be inflicted by the blast effect than by fragmentation debris (see Figure 14–1).

FIGURE 14–1   A violent explosion.
© Stefan Zaklin/Corbis. All Rights
Reserved

Types of Explosives

The speed at which explosives decompose varies greatly from one to another and permits their classification as *high* and *low* explosives. In a low explosive, this speed is called the speed of **deflagration** (burning). It is characterized by very rapid oxidation that produces heat, light, and a subsonic pressure wave. In a high explosive, it is called the speed of detonation. **Detonation** refers to the creation of a supersonic shock wave within the explosive charge. This shock wave breaks the chemical bonds of the explosive charge, leading to the near instantaneous buildup of heat and gases.

Low Explosives Low explosives, such as black and smokeless powders, decompose relatively slowly at rates up to 1,000 meters per second. Because of their slow burning rates, they produce a propelling or throwing action that makes them suitable as propellants for ammunition or skyrockets. However, the danger of this group of explosives must not be underestimated, because when any one of them is confined to a relatively small container, it can explode with a force as lethal as that of any known explosive.

Black Powder and Smokeless Powder. The most widely used explosives in the low-explosive group are black powder and smokeless powder. The popularity of these two explosives is enhanced by their accessibility to the public. Both are available in any gun store, and black powder can easily be made from ingredients purchased at any chemical supply house as well.

Black powder is a relatively stable mixture of potassium nitrate or sodium nitrate, charcoal, and sulfur. Unconfined, it merely burns; thus it commonly is used in safety fuses that carry a flame to an explosive charge. A **safety fuse** usually consists of black powder wrapped in a fabric or plastic casing. When ignited, a sufficient length of fuse will burn at a rate slow enough to allow a person adequate time to leave the site of the pending explosion. Black powder, like any other low explosive, becomes explosive and lethal only when it is confined.

The safest and most powerful low explosive is **smokeless powder**. This explosive usually consists of nitrated cotton or nitrocellulose (**single-base powder**) or nitroglycerin mixed with nitrocellulose (**double-base powder**). The powder is manufactured in a variety of grain sizes and shapes, depending on the desired application (see Figure 14–2).

deflagration
A very rapid oxidation reaction accompanied by the generation of a low-intensity pressure wave that can disrupt the surroundings

detonation
An extremely rapid oxidation reaction accompanied by a violent disruptive effect and an intense, high-speed shock wave

low explosive
An explosive with a velocity of detonation less than 1,000 meters per second

black powder
Normally, a mixture of potassium nitrate, carbon, and sulfur in the ratio 75/15/10

safety fuse
A cord containing a core of black powder, used to carry a flame at a uniform rate to an explosive charge

smokeless powder (single-base)
An explosive consisting of nitrocellulose

smokeless powder (double-base)
An explosive consisting of a mixture of nitrocellulose and nitroglycerin

FIGURE 14–2
Samples of smokeless powders.

Chlorate Mixtures. The only ingredients required for a low explosive are fuel and a good oxidizing agent. The oxidizing agent potassium chlorate, for example, when mixed with sugar, produces a popular and accessible explosive mix. When confined to a small container—for example, a pipe—and ignited, this mixture can explode with a force equivalent to a stick of 40 percent dynamite.

Some other commonly encountered ingredients that may be combined with chlorate to produce an explosive are carbon, sulfur, starch, phosphorus, and magnesium filings. Chlorate mixtures may also be ignited by the heat generated from a chemical reaction. For instance, sufficient heat can be generated to initiate combustion when concentrated sulfuric acid comes in contact with a sugar–chlorate mix.

Gas–Air Mixtures. Another form of low explosive is created when a considerable quantity of natural gas escapes into a confined area and mixes with a sufficient amount of air. If ignited, this mixture results in simultaneous combustion and sudden production of large volumes of gases and heat. In a building, walls are forced outward by the expanding gases, causing the roof to fall into the interior, and objects are thrown outward and scattered in erratic directions with no semblance of pattern.

Mixtures of air and a gaseous fuel explode or burn only within a limited concentration range. For example, the concentration limits for methane in air range from 5.3 to 13.9 percent. In the presence of too much air, the fuel becomes too diluted and does not ignite. On the other hand, if the fuel becomes too concentrated, ignition is prevented because there is not enough oxygen to support the combustion.

Mixtures at or near the upper concentration limit ("rich" mixtures) explode; however, some gas remains unconsumed because there is not enough oxygen to complete the combustion. As air rushes back into the origin of the explosion, it combines with the residual hot gas, producing a fire that is characterized by a whoosh sound. This fire is often more destructive than the explosion that preceded it. Mixtures near the lower end of the limit ("lean" mixtures) generally cause an explosion without accompanying damage due to fire.

High Explosives High explosives include dynamite, TNT, PETN, and RDX. They detonate almost instantaneously at rates of 1,000–8,500 meters per second, producing a smashing or shattering effect on their target. Unlike a low explosive, high explosives do not have to be containerized in order to amplify the damaging effect of their shock waves. High explosives are classified into two groups—primary and secondary explosives—based on their sensitivity to heat, shock, or friction.

Primary explosives are ultrasensitive to heat, shock, or friction, and under normal conditions they detonate violently instead of burning. For this reason, they are used to detonate other explosives through a chain reaction and are often referred to as primers. Primary explosives provide the major ingredients of blasting caps and include lead azide, lead styphnate, and diazodinitrophenol (see Figure 14–3). Because of their extreme sensitivity, these explosives are rarely used as the main charge of a homemade bomb.

high explosive
An explosive with a velocity of detonation greater than 1,000 meters per second

primary explosive
A high explosive that is easily detonated by heat, shock, or friction

FIGURE 14–3
Blasting caps. The left and
center caps are initiated by
an electrical current; the
right cap is initiated by a
safety fuse.

secondary explosive
A high explosive that is
relatively insensitive to
heat, shock, or friction

Secondary explosives are relatively insensitive to heat, shock, or friction, and
they normally burn rather than detonate when ignited in small quantities in open
air. This group comprises most high explosives used for commercial and military
blasting. Some common examples of secondary explosives are dynamite, TNT
(trinitrotoluene), PETN (pentaerythritol tetranitrate), RDX (cyclotrimethyl-
enetrinitramine), and tetryl (2,4,6-trinitrophenylmethylnitramine).

Dynamite. It is an irony of history that the prize most symbolic of humanity's
search for peace—the Nobel Peace Prize—should bear the name of the developer
of one of our most lethal discoveries—dynamite. In 1867, the Swedish chemist
Alfred Nobel, searching for a method to desensitize nitroglycerin, found that
when kieselguhr, a variety of diatomaceous earth, absorbed a large portion of
nitroglycerin, it became far less sensitive but still retained its explosive force.
Nobel later decided to use pulp as an absorbent because kieselguhr was a heat-
absorbing material.

This so-called pulp dynamite was the beginning of what is now known as the
straight dynamite series. These dynamites are used when a quick shattering action
is desired. In addition to nitroglycerine and pulp, present-day straight dynamites
also include sodium nitrate (which furnishes oxygen for complete combustion)
and a small percentage of a stabilizer, such as calcium carbonate.

All straight dynamite is rated by strength; the strength rating is determined by
the weight percentage of nitroglycerin in the formula. Thus, a 40 percent straight

dynamite contains 40 percent nitroglycerin, a 60 percent grade contains 60 percent nitroglycerin, and so forth. However, the relative blasting power of different strengths of dynamite is not directly proportional to their strength ratings. A 60 percent straight dynamite, rather than being three times as strong as a 20 percent, is only one and one-half times as strong (see Figure 14–4).

FIGURE 14–4
Sticks of dynamite.
Courtesy AP Wide World Photos

Ammonium Nitrate Explosives. In recent years, nitroglycerin-based dynamite has all but disappeared from the industrial explosives market. Commercially, these explosives have been replaced mainly by ammonium nitrate–based explosives, that is, water gels, emulsions, and ANFO explosives. These explosives mix oxygen-rich ammonium nitrate with a fuel to form a low-cost, stable explosive.

Typically, water gels have a consistency resembling that of set gelatin or gel-type toothpaste. They are characterized by their water-resistant nature and are employed for all types of blasting under wet conditions. These explosives are based on formulations of ammonium nitrate and sodium nitrate gelled with a natural polysaccharide such as guar gum. Commonly, a combustible material such as aluminum is mixed into the gel to serve as the explosive's fuel.

Emulsion explosives differ from gels in that they consist of two distinct phases, an oil phase and a water phase. In these emulsions, a droplet of a supersaturated solution of ammonium nitrate is surrounded by a hydrocarbon serving as a fuel. A typical emulsion consists of water, one or more inorganic nitrate oxidizers, oil, and emulsifying agents. Commonly, emulsions contain micron-sized glass, resin, or ceramic spheres known as microspheres or microballoons. The size of these spheres controls the explosive's sensitivity and detonation velocity.

Ammonium nitrate soaked in fuel oil is an explosive known as ANFO. Such commercial explosives are inexpensive and safe to handle and have found wide applications in blasting operations in the mining industry. Ammonium nitrate in the form of fertilizer makes a readily obtainable ingredient for homemade explosives. Indeed, in an incident related to the 1993 bombing of New York City's

World Trade Center, the FBI arrested five men during a raid on their hideout in New York City, where they were mixing a "witches' brew" of fuel oil and an ammonium nitrate–based fertilizer.

TATP. Triacetone triperoxide (TATP) is a homemade explosive that has been used as an improvised explosive by terrorist organizations in Israel and other Middle Eastern countries. It is prepared by reacting the common ingredients of acetone and hydrogen peroxide in the presence of an acid catalyst such as hydrochloric acid.

TATP is a friction- and impact-sensitive explosive that is extremely potent when confined in a container such as a pipe. The 2005 London transit bombings were caused by TATP-based explosives and provide ample evidence that terrorist cells have moved TATP outside the Middle East. A London bus destroyed by one of the TATP bombs is shown in Figure 14–5.

A plot to blow up ten international plane flights leaving Britain for the United States with a "liquid explosive" apparently involved plans to smuggle the peroxide-based TATP explosive onto the planes. This plot has prompted authorities to prohibit airline passengers from carrying liquids and gels onto planes.

FIGURE 14–5
A London bus destroyed by a TATP-based bomb. *Courtesy AP Wide World Photos*

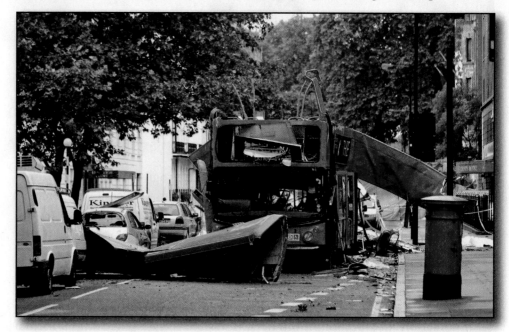

Military High Explosives. No discussion of high explosives would be complete without a mention of military high explosives. In many countries outside the United States, the accessibility of high explosives to terrorist organizations makes them common constituents of homemade bombs. RDX, the most popular and powerful military explosive, is often encountered in the form of a pliable plastic of doughlike consistency known as composition C–4 (a U.S. military designation).

TNT was produced and used on an enormous scale during World War II and may be considered the most important military bursting charge explosive. Alone or in combination with other explosives, it has found wide application in shells, bombs, grenades, demolition explosives, and propellant compositions (see Figure 14–6). Interestingly, military "dynamite" contains no nitroglycerin but is composed of a mixture of RDX and TNT. Like other military explosives, TNT is rarely encountered in bombings in the United States.

Case Files Liquid Explosives

In 2006, security agencies in the United States and Great Britain uncovered a terrorist plot to use liquid explosives to destroy commercial airlines operating between the two countries. Of the hundreds of types of explosives, most are solid. Only about a dozen are liquid. But some of those liquid explosives can be readily purchased, and others can be made from hundreds of different kinds of chemicals that are not difficult to obtain. After the September 11 attacks, worries about solid explosives became the main concern. In 2001, Richard Reid was arrested for attempting to destroy an American Airlines flight flying out of Paris. Authorities later found a high explosive with a TATP (triacetone triperoxide), detonator hidden in the lining of his shoe. It is therefore not surprising that terrorists turned to liquids in this latest plot. A memo issued by federal security officials about the plot to blow up ten international planes highlighted a type of liquid explosive based on peroxide. The most common peroxide-based explosive is TATP, which can be used as a detonator or a primary explosive and has been used in terrorist-related bombings and by Palestinian suicide bombers.

In theory, scientists know how to detect peroxide-based explosives. The challenge is to design ma-chines that can perform scans quickly and efficiently on thousands of passengers passing through airport security checks. Current scanning machines at airports are designed to detect nitrogen-containing chemicals and are not designed to detect peroxide-containing explosive ingredients. Since 9/11, security experts have worried about the possibility of liquid explosives in the form of liquids and gels getting onto airliners.

Not having the luxury of waiting for newly designed scanning devices capable of ferreting out dangerous liquids to be in place at airports, authorities decided to use a commonsense approach: to restrict the types and quantities of liquids that a passenger can carry onto a plane.

Liquids and gels discarded by airline passengers before boarding. *Stefano Paltera, AP Wide World Photos*

FIGURE 14–6 Military explosives in combat use. *Courtesy US Army/Getty Images/Time Life Pictures*

detonating cord
A cordlike explosive containing a core of high-explosive material, usually PETN; also called primacord

PETN is used by the military in TNT mixtures for small-caliber projectiles and grenades. Commercially, the chemical is used as the explosive core in a **detonating cord** or primacord. Instead of the slower-burning safety fuse, a detonating cord is often used to connect a series of explosive charges so that they will detonate simultaneously.

Detonators. Unlike low explosives, bombs made of high explosives must be detonated by an initiating explosion. In most cases, detonators are blasting caps composed of copper or aluminum cases filled with lead azide as an initiating charge and PETN or RDX as a detonating charge. Blasting caps can be initiated by means of a burning safety fuse or by an electrical current.

Homemade bombs camouflaged in packages, suitcases, and the like are usually initiated with an electrical blasting cap wired to a battery. An unlimited number of switching-mechanism designs have been devised for setting off these devices; clocks and mercury switches are favored. Bombers sometimes prefer to employ outside electrical sources. For instance, most automobile bombs are detonated when the ignition switch of a car is turned on.

> **Quick Review**
> - Explosives are substances that undergo a rapid oxidation reaction with the production of large quantities of gases. The sudden buildup of gas pressure leads to the explosion.
>
> - The speed at which an explosive decomposes determines whether it is classified as a high or low explosive.
>
> - The most widely used low explosives are black powder and smokeless powder. Common high explosives include ammonium nitrate–based explosives (water gels, emulsions, and ANFO explosives).
>
> - Among the high explosives, primary explosives are ultrasensitive to heat, shock, and friction and provide the major ingredients found in blasting caps. Secondary explosives normally constitute the main charge of a high explosive.

Collection and Analysis of Evidence of Explosives

The most important step in the detection and analysis of explosive residues is the collection of appropriate samples from the explosion scene. Invariably, undetonated residues of the explosive remain at the site of the explosion. The detection and identification of these explosives in the laboratory depend on the bomb-scene investigator's skill and ability to recognize and sample the areas most likely to contain such materials.

Detecting and Recovering Evidence of Explosives

The most obvious characteristic of a high or contained low explosive is the presence of a crater at the origin of the blast. Once the crater has been located, all loose soil and other debris must immediately be removed from the interior of the hole and preserved for laboratory analysis. Other good sources of explosive residues are objects located near the origin of detonation. Wood, insulation, rubber, and other soft materials that are readily penetrated often collect traces of the explosive. However, nonporous objects near the blast must not be overlooked. For instance, residues can be found on the surfaces of metal objects near the site of an explosion. Material blown away from the blast's origin should also be recovered because it, too, may retain explosive residues.

The entire area must be systematically searched, with great care given to recovering any trace of a detonating mechanism or any other item foreign to the explosion site. Wire-mesh screens are best used for sifting through debris. All personnel involved in searching the bomb scene must take appropriate measures to avoid contaminating the scene, including dressing in disposable gloves, shoe covers, and overalls.

Ion Mobility Spectrometer In pipe-bomb explosions, particles of the explosive are frequently found adhering to the pipe cap or to the pipe threads, as a result of either being impacted into the metal by the force of the explosion or being deposited in the threads during the construction of the bomb. One approach for screening objects for the presence of explosive residues in the field or the laboratory is the ion mobility spectrometer (IMS).[1] A portable IMS is shown in Figure 14–7.

FIGURE 14–7
A portable ion mobility spectrometer used to rapidly detect and tentatively identify trace quantities of explosives. *Courtesy GE Ion Track, Wilmington, Mass.*

FIGURE 14–8
Schematic diagram of an ion mobility spectrometer. A sample is introduced into an ionization chamber, where bombardment with radioactive particles emitted by an isotope of nickel converts the sample to ions. The ions move into a drift region where ion separation occurs based on the speed of the ions as they move through an electric field.

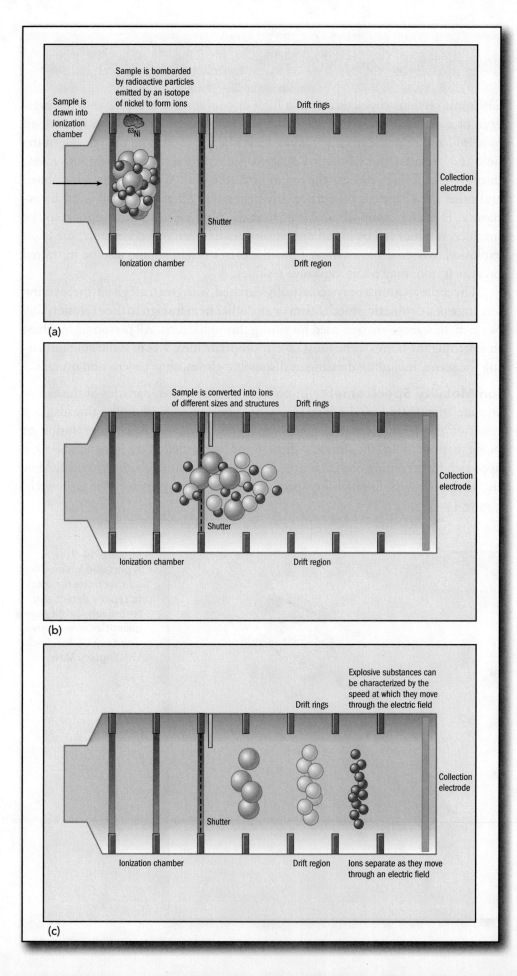

This handheld detector uses a vacuum to collect explosive residues from suspect surfaces. Alternatively, the surface suspected of containing explosive residues is wiped down with a Teflon-coated fiberglass disc and the collected residues are then drawn into the spectrometer off the disc. Once in the IMS, the explosive residues are vaporized by the application of heat. These vaporized substances are exposed to a beam of electrons or beta rays emitted by radioactive nickel and converted into electrically charged molecules or ions. The ions are then allowed to move through a tube (drift region) under the influence of an electric field. A schematic diagram of an IMS is shown in Figure 14–8.

The preliminary identification of an explosive residue can be made by noting the time it takes the explosive to move through the tube. Because ions move at different speeds depending on their size and structure, they can be characterized by the speed at which they pass through the tube. Used as a screening tool, this method rapidly detects a full range of explosives, even at low detection levels. However, all results need to be verified through confirmatory tests.

The IMS can detect plastic explosives as well as commercial and military explosives. More than 10,000 portable and full-size IMS units are currently used at airport security checkpoints, and more than 50,000 handheld IMS analyzers have been deployed for chemical-weapons monitoring in various armed forces.

Collection and Packaging All materials collected for examination by the laboratory must be placed in airtight sealed containers and labeled with all pertinent information. Soil and other soft, loose materials are best stored in metal airtight containers such as clean paint cans. Debris and articles collected from different areas are to be packaged in separate airtight containers. Plastic bags should not be used to store evidence suspected of containing explosive residues. Some explosives can escape through the plastic. Sharp-edged objects should not be allowed to pierce the sides of a plastic bag. It is best to place these types of items in metal containers.

Quick Review

- The entire bomb site must be systematically searched to recover any trace of a detonating mechanism or any other item foreign to the explosion site. Objects located at or near the origin of the explosion must be collected for laboratory examination.

- The most obvious characteristic of a high or contained low explosive is the presence of a crater at the origin of the blast.

- A device widely used to screen objects for the presence of explosive residues is the ion mobility spectrometer.

- All materials collected at bombing scenes must be placed in airtight containers such as clean paint cans.

Analysis of Evidence Explosives

When the bomb-scene debris and other materials arrive at the laboratory, everything is first examined microscopically to detect particles of unconsumed explosive. Portions of the recovered debris and detonating mechanism, if found, are carefully viewed under a low-power stereoscopic microscope in a painstaking effort to locate particles of the explosive. Black powder and smokeless powder are relatively easy to locate in debris because of their characteristic shapes and colors (see Figure 14–2). However, dynamite and other high explosives present the microscopist with a much more difficult task and often must be detected by other means.

Following microscopic examination, the recovered debris is thoroughly rinsed with acetone. The high solubility of most explosives in acetone ensures their quick removal from the debris. When a water-gel explosive containing ammonium nitrate or a low explosive is suspected, the debris should be rinsed with water so that water-soluble substances (such as nitrates and chlorates) will be extracted. Table 14–1 lists a number of simple color tests the examiner can perform on the acetone and water extracts to screen for the presence of organic and inorganic explosives, respectively.

Table 14–1
Color Spot Tests for Common Explosives

Substance	Reagent Greiss[a]	Diphenylamine[b]	Alcoholic KOH[c]
Chlorate	No color	Blue	No color
Nitrate	Pink to red	Blue	No color
Nitrocellulose	Pink	Blue-black	No color
Nitroglycerin	Pink to red	Blue	No color
PETN	Pink to red	Blue	No color
RDX	Pink to red	Blue	No color
TNT	No color	No color	Red
Tetryl	Pink to red	Blue	Red-violet

[a]*Greiss reagent: Solution 1—Dissolve 1 g sulfanilic acid in 100 mL 30% acetic acid. Solution 2—Dissolve 0.5 g N-(1-napthyl) ethylenediamine in 100 mL methyl alcohol. Add solutions 1 and 2 and a few milligrams of zinc dust to the suspect extract.*

[b]*Diphenylamine reagent: Dissolve 1 g diphenylamine in 100 mL concentrated sulfuric acid*

[c]*Alcoholic KOH reagent: Dissolve 10 g of potassium hydroxide in 100 mL absolute alcohol*

Screening and Confirmation Tests Once collected, the acetone extract is concentrated and analyzed using color spot tests, thin-layer chromatography (TLC), high-performance liquid chromatography (HPLC), and gas chromatography/mass spectrometry. The presence of an explosive is indicated by a well-defined spot on a TLC plate with an *Rf* value corresponding to that of a known explosive—for example, nitroglycerin, RDX, or PETN.

The high sensitivity of HPLC also makes it useful for analyzing trace evidence of explosives. HPLC operates at room temperature and hence does not cause explosives, many of which are temperature sensitive, to decompose during their analysis. When a water-gel explosive containing ammonium nitrate or a low explosive is suspected, the debris should be rinsed with water so that water-soluble substances (such as nitrates and chlorates) will be extracted.

When sufficient quantities of explosives are recoverable, confirmatory tests may be performed by either infrared spectrophotometry or **X-ray diffraction**. The former produces a unique "fingerprint" pattern for an organic explosive, as shown by the IR spectrum of RDX in Figure 14–9. The latter provides a unique diffraction pattern for inorganic substances such as potassium nitrate and potassium chlorate.

X-ray diffraction
An analytical technique for identifying crystalline materials

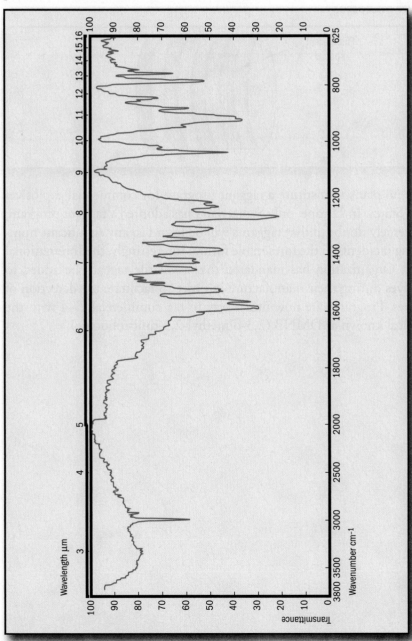

FIGURE 14–9   Infrared spectrum of RDX.

Taggants An explosive "taggant" program has been proposed to further enhance a bomb-scene investigator's chances of recovering useful evidence at a postexplosion scene. Under this proposal, tiny color-coded chips the size of sand grains would be added to commercial explosives during their manufacture. Some of these chips would be expected to survive an explosion and be capable of recovery at explosion scenes. To aid in their recovery, the chips are made both fluorescent and magnetic sensitive. Hence, investigators can search for taggants at the explosion site with magnetic tools and ultraviolet light.

The taggant chip is arranged in a color sequence that indicates where the explosive was made and when it was produced (see Figure 14–10). With this knowledge, the explosive can be traced through its distribution chain to its final legal possessor. The taggant colors are readily observed and are read with the aid of a low-power microscope.

FIGURE 14–10
Cross-section of a taggant. The color sequence of the recovered taggant is observed with the aid of a low-power microscope. The colors are then matched to a color code to yield information about the plant of manufacture, production lot, and purchasers of the explosive material.

There are no plans to institute a taggant program for commercial explosives in the United States. In Europe, only Switzerland has adopted a taggant program; thus, it is extremely doubtful that taggants will be found in any significant number of bombing incidents in the foreseeable future. Interestingly, the International Civil Aviation Organization has mandated that a volatile taggant be added to plastic explosives during their manufacture in order to facilitate the detection of these explosives. Programs are now under way to tag commercial C–4 with the volatile chemical known as DMNB (2,3-dimethyl-2,3-dinitrobutane).

Inside the Science

X-Ray Diffraction

One way to elicit information about how elements have combined into a particular substance is to aim a beam of X-rays at the material and study how the X-rays interact with the atoms that compose the substance under investigation. This technique is known as X-ray diffraction.

X-ray diffraction can be applied only to the study of solid, crystalline materials—that is, solids with a definite and orderly arrangement of atoms. For example, sodium chloride (common table salt) is crystalline. Fortunately, many substances, including 95 percent of all inorganic compounds, are crystalline and are thus identifiable by X-ray diffraction analysis. The atoms in a crystal may be thought of as being composed of a series of parallel planes. As the X-rays penetrate the crystal, a portion of the beam is reflected by each of the atomic planes. As the reflected beams leave the crystal's planes, they combine with one another to form a series of light and dark bands known as a diffraction pattern. Every compound produces a unique diffraction pattern, thus giving analysts a means for "fingerprinting" compounds.

Figure 1 illustrates the X-ray diffraction process. Diffraction patterns for potassium nitrate and potassium chlorate, two common constituents of homemade explosives, are shown in Figure 2. Comparing a questioned specimen with a known X-ray pattern is a rapid and specific way to prove chemical identity.

Photographic plate

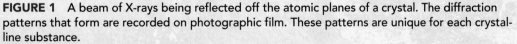

FIGURE 1 A beam of X-rays being reflected off the atomic planes of a crystal. The diffraction patterns that form are recorded on photographic film. These patterns are unique for each crystalline substance.

Inside the Science (CONTINUED)

FIGURE 2 X-ray patterns for (a) potassium nitrate and (b) potassium chlorate.

Quick Review

- Debris collected at explosion scenes is examined microscopically for unconsumed explosive particles.

- Recovered debris may be thoroughly rinsed with organic solvents and analyzed by testing procedures that include color spot tests, thin-layer chromatography, and gas chromatography/mass spectrometry.

- Unconsumed explosives are identified by either infrared spectrophotometry or X-ray diffraction.

Chapter Review

- Explosives are substances that undergo a rapid oxidation reaction with the production of large quantities of gases. The sudden buildup of gas pressure leads to the explosion.

- The speed at which an explosive decomposes determines whether it is classified as a high or low explosive.

- The most widely used low explosives are black powder and smokeless powder. Common high explosives include ammonium nitrate–based explosives (water gels, emulsions, and ANFO explosives).

- Among the high explosives, primary explosives are ultrasensitive to heat, shock, and friction and provide the major ingredients found in blasting caps. Secondary explosives normally constitute the main charge of a high explosive.

- The entire bomb site must be systematically searched to recover any trace of a detonating mechanism or any other item foreign to the explosion site. Objects located at or near the origin of the explosion must be collected for laboratory examination.

- The most obvious characteristic of a high or contained low explosive is the presence of a crater at the origin of the blast.

- A device widely used to screen objects for the presence of explosive residues is the ion mobility spectrometer.

- All materials collected at bombing scenes must be placed in airtight containers such as clean paint cans.

- Debris collected at explosion scenes is examined microscopically for unconsumed explosive particles.

- Recovered debris may be thoroughly rinsed with organic solvents and analyzed by testing procedures that include color spot tests, thin-layer chromatography, and gas chromatography/mass spectrometry.

- Unconsumed explosives are identified by either infrared spectrophotometry or X-ray diffraction.

Review Questions

1. Which type of explosive is classified into two groups, primary and secondary?
   a. low explosives
   b. medium explosives
   c. high explosives
   d. all explosives

2. Low explosives decompose at rates that vary up to
   a. 1,000 miles per hour.
   b. 1,000 meters per second.
   c. 1,000 meters per hour.
   d. 7,000 miles per hour.

3. In recent years, dynamite has been replaced commercially by
   a. PETN.
   b. nitroglycerin.
   c. TATP.
   d. ammonium nitrate–based explosives.

4. The single most important step in the detection and analysis of explosive residues is
   a. the collection of appropriate samples from the explosion scene.
   b. the determination of whether it is a low or a high explosive.
   c. the creation of a chain-of-custody form.
   d. locating the ignition source.

5. After bomb-scene debris has been examined microscopically, the next step is to
   a. examine the explosive using spectrophotometry.
   b. use X-ray diffraction to "fingerprint" the organic explosive.
   c. rinse the recovered debris with acetone to separate the debris from explosive material.
   d. view the detonating mechanism with a low-power stereoscopic microscope.

6. True or False: The speed at which explosives decompose varies greatly from one to another and permits their classification as high and low explosives.

7. True or False: The most widely used explosives in the low-explosive group are black powder and smokeless powder.

8. True or False: Military high explosives include RDX, TNT, and PETN.

9. True or False: Debris and particles collected from different areas at an explosion site are to be packaged in separate plastic containers.

10. True or False: The ion mobility spectrometer has become a widely used instrument for detecting the presence of explosive residues on objects.

11. What produces the violent physical disruption associated with an explosion?

12. What is the difference between deflagration and detonation?

13. What is the difference between low explosives and high explosives?

14. What is a safety fuse and what is it used for?

15. What ingredients are required to create a low explosive?

16. What are the two classes of high explosives? What is the difference between the two classes?

17. What are the main ingredients in straight dynamite? What other substances also are included in modern straight dynamites and what purpose do they serve?

18. What types of explosives largely have replaced dynamite for industrial uses? What are the advantages of these types of explosives?

19. What is ANFO?

20. Which is the most powerful and popular military explosive?

21. What is a detonator? What is the composition of most detonators?

22. What is the most obvious postexplosion characteristic of a high or contained low explosive?

23. How are soil and other soft loose materials collected at the scene of an explosion best stored?

24. What is the first procedure typically used to analyze bomb-scene debris that arrives in the laboratory?

25. List three procedures commonly used as screening tests for explosive residues.

26. Name two confirmatory tests for the presence of intact explosives located in debris.

27. What is a taggant? What purpose do taggants serve?

Application and Critical Thinking

1. The following pieces of evidence were found at separate explosion sites. For each item, indicate whether the explosion was more likely caused by low or high explosives, and explain your answer.
   a. lead azide residues
   b. nitrocellulose residues
   c. ammonium nitrate residues
   d. scraps of primacord
   e. potassium chlorate residues

2. Which color test or tests would you run first on a suspect sample to test for evidence of each of the following explosives? Explain your answers.
   a. tetryl
   b. TNT
   c. chlorate
   d. nitrocellulose

3. Criminalist Matt Weir is collecting evidence from the site of an explosion. Arriving on the scene, he immediately proceeds to look for the crater caused by the blast. After finding the crater, he picks through the debris at the site by hand, looking for evidence of detonators or foreign materials. Matt collects loose soil and debris from the immediate area, placing the smaller bits in paper folded into a druggist fold. Larger items he stores in plastic bags for transportation to the laboratory. What mistakes, if any, did Matt make in collecting and storing this evidence?

Endnotes

1. T. Keller et al., "Application of Ion Mobility Spectrometry in Cases of Forensic Interest," *Forensic Science International* 161 (2006): 130.

National Science Content Standards

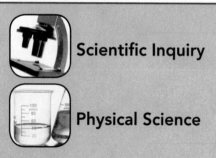

Scientific Inquiry

Physical Science

James Earl Ray: Conspirator or Lone Gunman?

Since his arrest in 1968 for the assassination of Dr. Martin Luther King, Jr., endless speculation has swirled around the motives and connections of James Earl Ray. Ray was a career criminal who was serving time for armed robbery when he escaped from the Missouri State Prison almost one year before the assassination. On April 3, 1968, Ray arrived in Memphis, Tennessee. The next day he rented a room at Bessie Brewer's Rooming House, across the street from the Lorraine Motel where Dr. King was staying.

At 6:00 p.m., Dr. King left his second-story motel room and stepped onto the balcony. As King turned toward his room, a shot rang out, striking the civil rights activist. Nothing could be done to revive him, and Dr. King was pronounced dead at 7:05 p.m. As the assailant ran on foot from Bessie Brewer's, he left a blanket-covered package in front of a nearby building and then drove off in a white Mustang. The package contained a high-powered rifle equipped with a scope, a radio, some clothes, a pair of binoculars, a couple of beer cans, and a receipt for the binoculars. Almost a week after the shooting, the white Mustang was found abandoned in Atlanta, Georgia.

Fingerprints later identified as James Earl Ray's were found in the Mustang, on the rifle, on the binoculars, and on a beer can. In 1969, Ray entered a guilty plea in return for a sentence of 99 years. Although a variety of conspiracy theories surround this crime, the indisputable fact is that a fingerprint put the rifle that killed Martin Luther King, Jr., in the hands of James Earl Ray.

Fingerprints

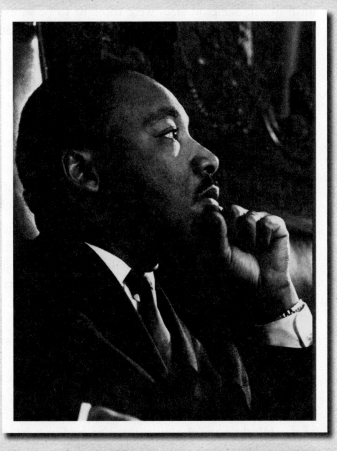

Key Terms

anthropometry
arch
digital imaging
fluoresce
iodine fuming
latent fingerprint
livescan
loop
ninhydrin

Physical Developer
pixel
plastic print
portrait parlé
ridge characteristics (minutiae)
sublimation
superglue fuming
visible print
whorl

History of Fingerprinting

Since the beginnings of criminal investigation, police have sought an infallible means of human identification. The first systematic attempt at personal identification was devised and introduced by a French police expert, Alphonse Bertillon, in 1883. The Bertillon system relied on a detailed description (**portrait parlé**) of the subject, combined with full-length and profile photographs and a system of precise body measurements known as **anthropometry**.

The use of anthropometry as a method of identification rested on the premise that the dimensions of the human bone system remained fixed from age 20 until death. Skeleton sizes were thought to be so extremely diverse that no two individuals could have exactly the same measurements. Bertillon recommended routine taking of 11 measurements of the human anatomy, including height, reach, width of head, and length of the left foot (see Figure 1–3).

For two decades, this system was considered the most accurate method of identification. But in the early years of the 20th century, police began to appreciate and accept a system of identification based on the classification of finger ridge patterns known as fingerprints. Today, the fingerprint is the pillar of modern criminal identification.

Early Use of Fingerprints

The Chinese used fingerprints to sign legal documents as far back as three thousand years ago. Whether this practice was performed for ceremonial custom or as a means of personal identity remains a point of conjecture lost to history. In any case, the examples of fingerprinting in ancient history are ambiguous, and the few that exist did not contribute to the development of fingerprinting techniques as we know them today.

Several years before Bertillon began work on his system, William Herschel, an English civil servant stationed in India, started requiring natives to sign contracts with the imprint of their right hand, which was pressed against a stamp pad for the purpose. The motives for Herschel's requirement remain unclear; he may have envisioned fingerprinting as a means of personal identification or just as a form of the Hindu custom that a trace of bodily contact was more binding than a signature on a contract. In any case, he did not publish anything about his activities until after a Scottish physician, Henry Fauld, working in a hospital in Japan, published his views on the potential application of fingerprinting to personal identification.

In 1880, Fauld suggested that skin ridge patterns could be important for the identification of criminals. He told about a thief who left his fingerprint on a whitewashed wall, and how in comparing these prints with those of a suspect, he found that they were quite different. A few days later, another suspect was found whose fingerprints compared with those on the wall. When confronted with this evidence, the individual confessed to the crime.

Fauld was convinced that fingerprints furnished infallible proof of identification. He even offered to set up at his own expense a fingerprint bureau at Scotland Yard to test the practicality of the method. But his offer was rejected in favor of the Bertillon system. This decision was reversed less than two decades later.

portrait parlé
A verbal description of a perpetrator's physical characteristics and dress provided by an eyewitness

anthropometry
A system of identification of individuals by measurement of parts of the body, developed by Alphonse Bertillon

Early Classification of Fingerprints

The extensive research into fingerprinting conducted by another Englishman, Francis Galton, provided the needed impetus that made police agencies aware of its potential application. In 1892, Galton published his classic textbook *Finger Prints*, the first book of its kind on the subject (see Figure 15–1). In his book, Galton discussed the anatomy of fingerprints and suggested methods for recording them. He also proposed assigning fingerprints to three pattern types—loops, arches, and whorls. Most important, the book demonstrated that no two prints are identical and that an individual's prints remain unchanged from year to year. At Galton's insistence, the British government adopted fingerprinting as a supplement to the Bertillon system.

FIGURE 15–1
The cover of Sir Francis Galton's book *Finger Prints* which discusses the anatomy of fingerprints, how to record them, and classification by the three pattern types—loops, arches, and whorls.

The next step in the development of fingerprint technology was the creation of classification systems capable of filing thousands of prints in a logical and searchable sequence. Dr. Juan Vucetich, an Argentinian police officer fascinated by Galton's work, devised a workable concept in 1891. His classification system has been refined over the years and is still widely used today in most Spanish-speaking countries. In 1897, another classification system was proposed by an Englishman, Sir Edward Richard Henry (see Figure 15–2). Four years later, Henry's system was adopted by Scotland Yard. Today, most English-speaking countries, including the United States, use some version of Henry's classification system to file fingerprints.

FIGURE 15–2
Sir Edward Richard Henry, British pioneer of fingerprinting for identification purposes.

Adoption of Fingerprinting

Early in the 20th century, Bertillon's measurement system began to fall into disfavor. Its results were highly susceptible to error, particularly when the measurements were taken by people who were not thoroughly trained. The method was dealt its most severe and notable setback in 1903 when a convict, Will West, arrived at Fort Leavenworth prison. A routine check of the prison files startlingly revealed that a William West, already in the prison, could not be distinguished from the new prisoner by body measurements or even by photographs. In fact, the two men looked just like twins, and their measurements were practically the same. Subsequently, fingerprints of the prisoners clearly distinguished them.

In the United States, the first systematic and official use of fingerprints for personal identification was adopted by the New York City Civil Service Commission in 1901. The method was used for certifying all civil service applications. Several American police officials received instruction in fingerprint identification at the 1904 World's Fair in St. Louis from representatives of Scotland Yard. After the fair and the Will West incident, fingerprinting began to be used in earnest in all major cities of the United States. In 1924, the fingerprint records of the Bureau of Investigation and Leavenworth were merged to form the nucleus of the identification records of the new Federal Bureau of Investigation. The FBI has the largest collection of fingerprints in the world. By the beginning of World War I, England and practically all of Europe had adopted fingerprinting as their primary method of identifying criminals.

In 1999, the admissibility of fingerprint evidence was challenged in the case of *United States* v. *Byron C. Mitchell* in the Eastern District of Pennsylvania. The defendant's attorneys argued that fingerprints could not be proven unique under the guidelines cited in *Daubert* (see page 25). Government experts vigorously disputed this claim. After a four-and-a-half-day Daubert hearing, the judge upheld the admissibility of fingerprints as scientific evidence and ruled that (1) human friction ridges are unique and permanent and (2) human friction ridge skin arrangements are unique and permanent.

Fundamental Principles of Fingerprints

Since Galton's time, and as a result of his efforts, fingerprints have become an integral part of policing and forensic science. The principal reason for this is that fingerprints constitute a unique and unchanging means of personal identification. In fact, fingerprint analysts have formulated three basic principles of fingerprints that encompass these notions of the uniqueness and stability of fingerprint identification.

First Principle: Fingerprint Is an Individual Characteristic; No Two Fingers Have Yet Been Found to Possess Identical Ridge Chacteristics

The acceptance of fingerprint evidence by the courts has always been predicated on the assumption that no two individuals have identical fingerprints. Early fingerprint experts consistently referred to Galton's calculation, showing the possible existence of 64 billion different fingerprints, to support this contention. Later, researchers questioned the validity of Galton's figures and attempted to devise mathematical models to better approximate this value. However, no matter what mathematical model one refers to, the conclusions are always the same: the probability for the existence of two identical fingerprint patterns in the world's population is extremely small.

Not only is this principle supported by theoretical calculations, but just as important, it is verified by the millions of individuals who have had their prints classified during the past 110 years—no two have ever been found to be identical. The FBI has nearly 50 million fingerprint records in its computer database and has yet to find an identical image belonging to two different people.

The individuality of a fingerprint is not determined by its general shape or pattern but by a careful study of its **ridge characteristics** (also known as **minutiae**). The identity, number, and relative location of characteristics such as those illustrated in Figure 15–3 impart individuality to a fingerprint. If two prints are to match, they must reveal characteristics that not only are identical but have the same relative location to one another in a print. In a judicial proceeding, a point-by-point comparison must be demonstrated by the expert, using charts similar to the one shown in Figure 15–4, in order to prove the identity of an individual.

ridge characteristics (minutiae)
Ridge endings, bifurcations, enclosures, and other ridge details, which must match in two fingerprints in order for their common origin to be established

FIGURE 15–3
Fingerprint ridge
characteristics.
*Courtesy Sirchie Finger
Print Laboratories, Inc.,
Youngsville, N.C.,
www.sirchie.com*

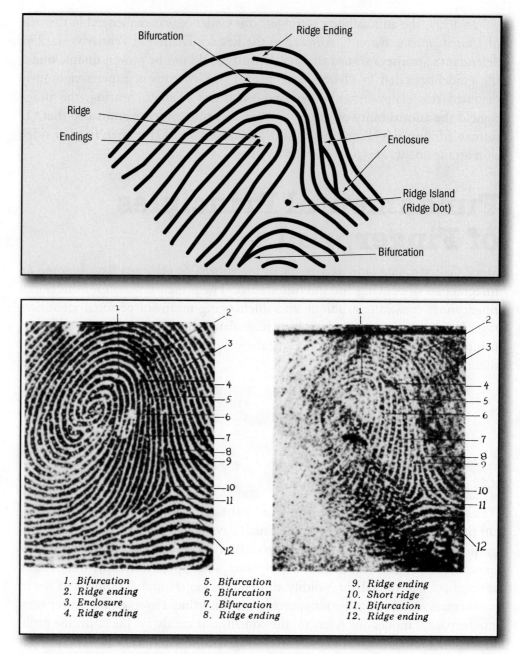

FIGURE 15–4
A fingerprint exhibit
illustrating the match-
ing ridge characteristics
between the crime-
scene print and an inked
impression of one of the
suspect's fingers.

1. Bifurcation   5. Bifurcation   9. Ridge ending
2. Ridge ending   6. Bifurcation   10. Short ridge
3. Enclosure   7. Bifurcation   11. Bifurcation
4. Ridge ending   8. Ridge ending   12. Ridge ending

An expert can easily compare the characteristics of the complete fingerprint; the average fingerprint has as many as 150 individual ridge characteristics. However, most prints recovered at crime scenes are partial impressions, showing only a segment of the entire print. Under these circumstances, the expert can compare only a small number of ridge characteristics from the recovered print to a known recorded print.

For years, experts have debated how many ridge comparisons are necessary to identify two fingerprints as the same. Numbers that range from 8 to 16 have been suggested as being sufficient to meet the criteria of individuality. However, the difficulty in establishing such a minimum is that no comprehensive statistical study has ever determined the frequency of occurrence of different ridge characteristics and their relative locations. Until such a study is undertaken and completed, no meaningful guidelines can be established for defining the uniqueness of a fingerprint.

In 1973, the International Association for Identification, after a three-year study of this question, concluded that "no valid basis exists for requiring a predetermined minimum number of friction ridge characteristics which must be present in two impressions in order to establish positive identification." Hence, the final determination must be based on the experience and knowledge of the expert, with the understanding that others may profess honest differences of opinion on the uniqueness of a fingerprint if the question of minimal number of ridge characteristics exists. In 1995, members of the international fingerprint community at a conference in Israel issued the Ne'urim Declaration, which supported the 1973 International Association for Identification resolution.

Second Principle: A Fingerprint Remains Unchanged During an Individual's Lifetime

Fingerprints are a reproduction of friction skin ridges found on the palm side of the fingers and thumbs. Similar friction skin can also be found on the surface of the palms and soles of the feet. Apparently, these skin surfaces have been designed by nature to provide our bodies with a firmer grasp and a resistance to slippage. A visual inspection of friction skin reveals a series of lines corresponding to hills (ridges) and valleys (grooves). The shape and form of the skin ridges are what one sees as the black lines of an inked fingerprint impression.

Skin is composed of layers of cells. Those nearest the surface make up the outer portion of the skin known as the epidermis, and the inner skin is known as the *dermis*. A cross-section of skin (see Figure 15–5) reveals a boundary of cells separating the epidermis and dermis. The shape of this boundary, made up of *dermal papillae*, determines the form and pattern of the ridges on the surface of the skin. Once the dermal papillae develop in the human fetus, the ridge patterns remain unchanged throughout life except to enlarge during growth.

Ridge island
Sweat pores
Epidermis
Papillae
Dermis
Duct of sweat gland
Sweat gland
Nerves of touch

FIGURE 15–5
Cross-section of human skin.

Each skin ridge is populated by a single row of pores that are the openings for ducts leading from the sweat glands. Through these pores, perspiration is discharged and deposited on the surface of the skin. Once the finger touches a surface, perspiration, along with oils that may have been picked up by touching the hairy portions of the body, is transferred onto that surface, thereby leaving an impression of the finger's ridge pattern (a fingerprint). Prints deposited in this manner are invisible to the eye and are commonly referred to as **latent fingerprints.**

Although it is impossible to change one's fingerprints, some criminals have tried to obscure them. If an injury reaches deeply enough into the skin and damages the dermal papillae, a permanent scar forms. However, for this to happen, such a wound would have to penetrate 1 to 2 millimeters beneath the skin's surface. Indeed, efforts at intentionally scarring the skin can only be self-defeating, for it is totally impossible to obliterate all of the ridge characteristics on the hand, and the presence of permanent scars merely provides new characteristics for identification.

Perhaps the most publicized attempt at obliteration was that of the notorious gangster John Dillinger, who tried to destroy his own fingerprints by applying a corrosive acid to them. Prints taken at the morgue after he was shot to death, compared with fingerprints recorded at the time of a previous arrest, proved that his efforts had been fruitless (see Figure 15–6).

latent fingerprint
A fingerprint made by the deposit of oils and/or perspiration; it is invisible to the naked eye

FIGURE 15–6
The right index finger impression of John Dillinger, before scarification on the left and afterward on the right. Comparison is proved by the 14 matching ridge characteristics. *Courtesy Institute of Applied Science, Youngsville, N.C.*

Third Principle: Fingerprints Have General Ridge Patterns That Permit Them to Be Systematically Classified

All fingerprints are divided into three classes on the basis of their general pattern: **loops, whorls,** and **arches.** Sixty to 65 percent of the population have loops, 30 to 35 percent have whorls, and about 5 percent have arches. These three classes form the basis for all ten-finger classification systems presently in use.

A loop must have one or more ridges entering from one side of the print, recurring, and exiting from the same side. If the loop opens toward the little finger, it is called an *ulnar loop*; if it opens toward the thumb, it is a *radial loop*. The pattern area of the loop is surrounded by two diverging ridges known as *type lines*. The ridge point at or nearest the type-line divergence and located at or directly in front of the point of divergence is known as the delta. To many, a fingerprint delta resembles the silt formation that builds up as a river flows into the entrance of a lake—hence, the analogy to the geological formation known as a *delta*. All loops must have one delta. The core, as the name suggests, is the approximate center of the pattern. A typical loop pattern is illustrated in Figure 15–7.

loop
A class of fingerprints characterized by ridge lines that enter from one side of the pattern and curve around to exit from the same side of the pattern

whorl
A class of fingerprints that includes ridge patterns that are generally rounded or circular in shape and have two deltas

arch
A class of fingerprints characterized by ridge lines that enter the print from one side and flow out the other side

FIGURE 15–7   Loop pattern.

Whorls are divided into four distinct groups, as shown in Figure 15–8: plain, central pocket loop, double loop, and accidental. All whorl patterns must have type lines and at least two deltas. A plain whorl and a central pocket loop have at least one ridge that makes a complete circuit. This ridge may be in the form of a spiral, oval, or any variant of a circle. If an imaginary line drawn between the two deltas contained within these two patterns touches any one of the spiral ridges, the pattern is a plain whorl. If no such ridge is touched, the pattern is a central pocket loop.

FIGURE 15–8   Whorl patterns.

As the name implies, the double loop is made up of two loops combined into one fingerprint. Any whorl classified as an accidental either contains two or more patterns (not including the plain arch) or is a pattern not covered by other categories. Hence, an accidental may consist of a combination loop and plain whorl or loop and tented arch.

Arches, the least common of the three general patterns, are subdivided into two distinct groups: plain arches and tented arches, as shown in Figure 15–9. The plain arch is the simplest of all fingerprint patterns; it is formed by ridges entering from one side of the print and exiting on the opposite side. Generally, these ridges tend to rise in the center of the pattern, forming a wavelike pattern. The tented arch is similar to the plain arch except that instead of rising smoothly at the center, there is a sharp upthrust or spike, or the ridges meet at an angle that is less than 90 degrees.[1] Arches do not have type lines, deltas, or cores.

FIGURE 15–9
Arch patterns.

Plain   Tented

With a knowledge of basic fingerprint pattern classes, we can now begin to develop an appreciation for fingerprint classification systems. However, the subject is far more complex than can be described in a textbook of this nature. The student seeking a more detailed treatment of the subject would do well to consult the references cited at the end of the chapter.

Quick Review

- Fingerprints are a reproduction of friction skin ridges found on the palm side of the fingers and thumbs.

- The basic principles underlying the use of fingerprints in criminal investigations are as follows: (1) A fingerprint is an individual characteristic because no two fingers have yet been found to possess identical ridge characteristics; (2) a fingerprint remains unchanged during an individual's lifetime; and (3) fingerprints have general ridge patterns that permit them to be systematically classified.

- All fingerprints are divided into three classes on the basis of their general pattern: loops, whorls, and arches.

- The individuality of a fingerprint is determined not by its general shape or pattern, but by a careful study of its ridge characteristics. The expert must demonstrate a point-by-point comparison in order to prove the identity of an individual.

- When the finger touches a surface, perspiration and oils are transferred onto that surface, leaving a fingerprint. Prints deposited in this manner are invisible to the eye and are commonly referred to as latent or invisible fingerprints.

Classification of Fingerprints

The original Henry system, as adopted by Scotland Yard in 1901, converted ridge patterns on all ten fingers into a series of letters and numbers arranged in the form of a fraction. However, the system as it was originally designed could accommodate files of up to only 100,000 sets of prints. Thus, as collections grew in size, it became necessary to expand the capacity of the classification system. In the United States, the FBI, faced with the problem of filing ever-increasing numbers of prints, expanded its classification capacity by modifying and extending the original Henry system. These modifications are collectively known as the FBI system and are used by most agencies in the United States today. Although we will not discuss all of the different divisions of the FBI system, a description of just one part, the primary classification, will provide an interesting insight into the process of fingerprint classification.

The primary classification is part of the original Henry system and provides the first classification step in the FBI system. Using this classification alone, all of the fingerprint cards in the world could be divided into 1,024 groups. The first step in obtaining the primary classification is to pair up fingers, placing one finger in the numerator of a fraction, the other in the denominator. The fingers are paired in the following sequence:

R. Index	R. Ring	L. Thumb	L. Middle	L. Little
R. Thumb	R. Middle	R. Little	L. Index	L. Ring

The presence or absence of the whorl pattern is the basis for determination of the primary classification. If a whorl pattern is found on any finger of the first pair, it is assigned a value of 16; on the second pair, a value of 8; on the third pair, a value of 4; on the fourth pair, a value of 2; and on the last pair, a value of 1. Any finger with an arch or loop pattern is assigned a value of 0. Approximately 25 percent of the population falls into the 1/1 category; that is, all their fingers have either loops or arches.

After values for all ten fingers are obtained in this manner, they are totaled, and 1 is added to both the numerator and denominator. The fraction thus obtained is the primary classification. For example, if the right index and right middle fingers are whorls and all the others are loops, the primary classification is

$$\frac{16 + 0 + 0 + 0 + 0 + 1}{0 + 8 + 0 + 0 + 0 + 1} = \frac{17}{9}$$

A fingerprint classification system cannot in itself unequivocally identify an individual; it merely provides the fingerprint examiner with a number of candidates, all of whom have an indistinguishable set of prints in the system's file. The identification must always be made by a final visual comparison of the suspect print's and file print's ridge characteristics; only these features can impart individuality to a fingerprint. Although ridge patterns impart class characteristics to the print, the type and position of ridge characteristics give it its individual character.

Quick Review
- The primary classification is the first step in classifying fingerprints under the FBI system. The presence or absence of the whorl pattern is the basis for determination of the primary classification.

Automated Fingerprint Identification Systems

The Henry system and its subclassifications have proven to be a cumbersome system for storing, retrieving, and searching for fingerprints, particularly as fingerprint collections grow in size. Nevertheless, until the emergence of fingerprint computer technology, this manual approach was the only viable method for maintaining fingerprint collections. Since 1970, technological advances have made possible the classification and retrieval of fingerprints by computers. Automated Fingerprint Identification Systems (AFISs) have proliferated throughout the law enforcement community.

In 1999, the FBI initiated full operation of the Integrated Automated Fingerprint Identification System (IAFIS), the largest AFIS in the United States, which links state AFIS computers with the FBI database. This database contains nearly 50 million fingerprint records. However, an AFIS can come in all sizes ranging from the FBI's to independent systems operated by cities, counties, and other agencies of local government (see Figure 15–10). Unfortunately, these local systems often cannot be linked to the state's AFIS system because of differences in software configurations.

How AFIS Works

The heart of AFIS technology is the ability of a computer to scan and digitally encode fingerprints so that they can be subject to high-speed computer processing. The AFIS uses automatic scanning devices that convert the image of a fingerprint into digital minutiae that contain data showing ridges at their points of termination (ridge endings) and the branching of ridges into two ridges (bifurcations). The relative position and orientation of the minutiae are also determined, allowing the computer to store each fingerprint in the form of a digitally recorded geometric pattern.

FIGURE 15–10
An AFIS system designed for use by local law enforcement agencies. *Courtesy AFIX Technologies Inc., Pittsburg, KS 66762, www.afix.net*

The computer's search algorithm determines the degree of correlation between the location and relationship of the minutiae for both the search and file prints. In this manner, a computer can make thousands of fingerprint comparisons in a second. For example, a set of ten fingerprints can be searched against a file of 500,000 ten-finger prints (ten-prints) in about eight-tenths of a second. During the search for a match, the computer uses a scoring system that assigns prints to each of the criteria set by an operator. When the search is complete, the computer produces a list of file prints that have the closest correlation to the search prints. All of the selected prints are then examined by a fingerprint expert, who makes the final verification of the print's identity. Thus, the AFIS makes no final decisions on the identity of a fingerprint, leaving this function to the eyes of a trained examiner.

The speed and accuracy of ten-print processing by AFIS have made possible the search of single latent crime-scene fingerprints against an entire file's print collection. Before AFIS, police were usually restricted to comparing crime-scene fingerprints against those of known suspects. The impact of the AFIS on no-suspect cases has been dramatic. In its first year of operation, San Francisco's AFIS computer conducted 5,514 latent fingerprint searches and achieved 1,001 identifications—a hit rate of 18 percent. This compares to the previous year's average of 8 percent for manual latent-print searches.

As an example of how an AFIS computer operates, one system has been designed to automatically filter out imperfections in a latent print, enhance its image, and create a graphic representation of the fingerprint's ridge endings and bifurcations and their direction. The print is then computer searched against file prints. The image of the latent print and a matching file print are then displayed side by side on a high-resolution video monitor, as shown in <u>Figure 15–11</u>. The matching latent and file prints are then verified and charted by a fingerprint examiner at a video workstation.

FIGURE 15–11
A side-by-side comparison of a latent print against a file fingerprint is conducted in seconds, and their similarity rating (SIM) is displayed on the upper-left portion of the screen.
Courtesy Sirchie Finger Print Laboratories, Inc., Youngsville, N.C., www.sirchie.com

livescan
An inkless device that captures the digital images of fingerprints and palm prints and electronically transmits the images to an AFIS

The stereotypical image of a booking officer rolling inked fingers onto a standard ten-print card for ultimate transmission to a database has, for the most part, been replaced with digital-capture devices (**livescan**) that eliminate ink and paper (see Figure 15–12). The livescan captures the image on each finger and the palms as they are lightly pressed against a glass platen. These livescan images can then be sent to the AFIS database electronically, so that within minutes the booking agency can enter the fingerprint record into the AFIS database and search the database for previous entries of the same individual.

FIGURE 15–12
Livescan technology enables law enforcement personnel to print and compare a subject's fingerprints rapidly, without inking the fingerprints.
Courtesy of Motorola, Inc., Motorola Printrak LiveScan

Case Files

The Night Stalker

Richard Ramirez committed his first murder in June 1984. His victim was a 79-year-old woman who was stabbed repeatedly and sexually assaulted and then had her throat slashed. It would be eight months before Ramirez murdered again. In the spring, Ramirez began a murderous rampage that resulted in 13 additional killings and 5 rapes.

Richard Ramirez, the Night Stalker. *Courtesy Bettmann/ CORBIS. All Rights Reserved.*

His modus operandi was to enter a home through an open window, shoot the male residents, and savagely rape his female victims. He scribed a pentagram and the words *Jack the Knife* on the wall of one of his victims, and another victim reported that he forced her to "swear to Satan" during the assault. His identity still unknown, the news media dubbed him the "Night Stalker." As the body count continued to rise, public hysteria and a media frenzy prevailed.

The break in the case came when the license plate of what seemed to be a suspicious car related to a sighting of the Night Stalker was reported to the police. The police determined that the car had been stolen and eventually located it, abandoned in a parking lot. After processing the car for prints, police found one usable partial fingerprint. This fingerprint was entered into the Los Angeles Police Department's brand-new AFIS computerized fingerprint system.

Without AFIS, it would have taken a single technician, manually searching Los Angeles's 1.7 million print cards, 67 years to come up with the perpetrator's prints. Thanks to AFIS, it took only a few seconds to locate and identify them. The Night Stalker was identified as Richard Ramirez, who had been fingerprinted following a traffic violation some years before. Police searching the home of one of his friends found the gun used to commit the murders, and jewelry belonging to his victims was found in the possession of Ramirez's sister. Ramirez was convicted of murder and sentenced to death in 1989. He remains on death row.

Considerations with AFIS

AFIS has fundamentally changed the way criminal investigators operate, allowing them to spend less time developing suspect lists and more time investigating the suspects generated by the computer. However, investigators must be cautioned against overreliance on a computer. Sometimes a latent print does not make a hit because of the poor quality of the file print. To avoid these potential problems, investigators must still print all known suspects in a case and manually search these prints against the crime-scene prints.

AFIS computers are available from several different suppliers. Each system scans fingerprint images and detects and records information about minutiae (ridge endings and bifurcations); however, they do not all incorporate exactly the same features, coordinate systems, or units of measure to record fingerprint information. These software incompatibilities often mean that although state systems can communicate with the FBI's IAFIS, they do not communicate with each other directly. Likewise, local and state systems frequently cannot share information with each other. Many of these technical problems will be resolved as more agencies follow transmission standards developed by the National Institute of Standards and Technology and the FBI.

> **Quick Review**
> - The FBI fingerprint database known as AFIS converts the image of a fingerprint into digital minutiae that contain data showing ridges at their points of termination (ridge endings) and their branching into two ridges (bifurcations).
>
> - Livescan is an inkless device that captures digital images of fingerprints and palm prints and electronically transmits them to an AFIS.

Methods of Detecting Fingerprints

Through common usage, the term *latent fingerprint* has come to be associated with any fingerprint discovered at a crime scene. Sometimes, however, prints found at the scene of a crime are quite visible to the eye, and the word latent is a misnomer.

Actually, there are three kinds of crime-scene prints. **Visible prints** are made by fingers touching a surface after the ridges have been in contact with a colored material such as blood, paint, grease, or ink; **plastic prints** are ridge impressions left on a soft material such as putty, wax, soap, or dust; and latent or invisible prints are impressions caused by the transfer of body perspiration or oils present on finger ridges to the surface of an object.

Locating Fingerprints

Locating visible or plastic prints at the crime scene normally presents little problem to the investigator, because these prints are usually distinct and visible to the eye. Locating latent or invisible prints is obviously much more difficult and requires the use of techniques to make the print visible. Although the investigator can choose from several methods for visualizing a latent print, the choice depends on the type of surface being examined.

Hard and nonabsorbent surfaces (such as glass, mirror, tile, and painted wood) require different development procedures from surfaces that are soft and porous (such as papers, cardboard, and cloth). Prints on the former are preferably developed by the application of a powder or treatment with superglue, whereas prints on the latter generally require treatment with one or more chemicals.

Sometimes the most difficult aspect of fingerprint examination is the location of prints. Recent advances in fingerprint technology have led to the development of an ultraviolet image converter for the purpose of detecting latent fingerprints.

visible print
A fingerprint made when the finger deposits a visible material such as ink, dirt, or blood onto a surface

plastic print
A fingerprint impressed in a soft surface

Case Files

The Mayfield Affair

On March 11, 2004, a series of ten explosions at four sites occurred on commuter trains traveling to or near the Atocha train station in Madrid, Spain. The death toll from these explosions was nearly 200, with more than 1,500 injured. On the day of the attack, a plastic bag was found in a van previously reported as stolen. The bag contained copper detonators like those used on the train bombs.

On March 17, the FBI received electronic images of latent fingerprints that were recovered from the plastic bag, and a search was initiated on the FBI's IAFIS. A senior fingerprint examiner encoded seven minutiae points from the high-resolution image of one suspect latent fingerprint and initiated an IAFIS search matching the print to Brandon Mayfield. Mayfield's prints were in the FBI's central database because they had been taken when he joined the military, where he served for eight years before being honorably discharged as a second lieutenant.

After a visual comparison of the suspect and file prints, the examiner concluded a "100 percent match." The identification was verified by a retired FBI fingerprint examiner with more than 30 years of experience who was working under contract with the bureau, as well as by a court-appointed independent fingerprint examiner (see the figure).

Mayfield, age 37, a Muslim convert, was arrested on May 6 on a material witness warrant. The U.S. Attorney's Office came up with a list of Mayfield's potential ties to Muslim terrorists, which they included in the affidavit they presented to the federal judge who ordered his arrest and detention. The document also said that although no travel records were found for Mayfield, "It is believed that Mayfield may have traveled under a false or fictitious name." On May 24, after the Spaniards had linked the print from the plastic bag to an Algerian national, Mayfield's case was thrown out. The FBI issued him a highly unusual official apology, and his ordeal became a stunning embarrassment to the U.S. government.

The impact of the Mayfield affair on fingerprint technology as currently practiced and the weight courts will assign to fingerprint matches remain open questions.

(a) Questioned print recovered in connection with the Madrid bombing Investigation (b) File print of Brandon Mayfield
(a) *Source U.S. Department of Justice, Washington, D.C.*

This device, called the Reflected Ultraviolet Imaging System (RUVIS), can locate prints on most nonabsorbent surfaces without the aid of chemical or powder treatments (see Figure 15–13).

(see Figure 15–13)

FIGURE 15–13
A Reflected Ultraviolet Imaging System allows an investigator to directly view surfaces for the presence of untreated latent fingerprints. *Courtesy Sirchie Finger Print Laboratories, Inc., Youngsville, N.C., www.sirchie.com*

RUVIS detects the print in its natural state by aiming UV light at the surface suspected of containing prints. When the UV light strikes the fingerprint, the light is reflected back to the viewer, differentiating the print from its background surface. The transmitted UV light is then converted into visible light by an image intensifier. Once the print is located in this manner, the crime-scene investigator can develop it in the most appropriate fashion (see Figure 15–14).

FIGURE 15–14
Using a Reflected Ultraviolet Imaging System with the aid of a UV lamp to search for latent fingerprints. *Courtesy Sirchie Finger Print Laboratories, Inc., Youngsville, N.C., www.sirchie.com*

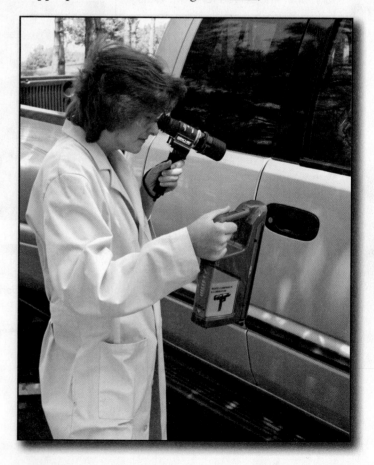

Developing Latent Prints

Several techniques are available to the criminalist to develop latent prints on a variety of surfaces. These include chemical methods such as powders and iodine fuming and the use of laser light.

Fingerprint Powders Fingerprint powders are commercially available in a variety of compositions and colors. These powders, when applied lightly to a non-absorbent surface with a camel's-hair or fiberglass brush, readily adhere to perspiration residues and/or deposits of body oils left on the surface (see Figure 15–15).

FIGURE 15–15
Developing a latent fingerprint on a surface by applying a fingerprint powder with a fiberglass brush. *Courtesy Sirchie Finger Print Laboratories, Inc., Youngsville, N.C., www.sirchie.com*

Experienced examiners find that gray and black powders are adequate for most latent-print work; the examiner selects the powder that affords the best color contrast with the surface being dusted. Hence, the gray powder, composed of an aluminum dust, is used on dark-colored surfaces. It is also applied to mirrors and metal surfaces that are polished to a mirrorlike finish, because these surfaces photograph as black. The black powder, composed basically of black carbon or charcoal, is applied to white or light-colored surfaces.

Other types of powders are available for developing latent prints. A magnetic-sensitive powder can be spread over a surface with a magnet in the form of a Magna Brush. A Magna Brush does not have any bristles to come in contact with the surface, so there is less chance that the print will be destroyed or damaged. The magnetic-sensitive powder comes in black and gray and is especially useful on such items as finished leather and rough plastics, on which the minute texture of the surface tends to hold particles of ordinary powder. Fluorescent powders are also used to develop latent fingerprints. These powders fluoresce under ultraviolet light. By photographing the fluorescence pattern of the developing print under UV light, it is possible to avoid having the color of the surface obscure the print.

Iodine Fuming Of the several chemical methods used for visualizing latent prints, **iodine fuming** is the oldest. Iodine is a solid crystal that, when heated, is transformed into a vapor without passing through a liquid phase; such a trans-

iodine fuming
A technique for visualizing latent fingerprints by exposing them to iodine vapors

sublimation
A physical change from the solid directly into the gaseous state

formation is called **sublimation**. Most often, the suspect material is placed in an enclosed cabinet along with iodine crystals (see Figure 15–16). As the crystals are heated, the resultant vapors fill the chamber and combine with constituents of the latent print to make it visible.

Unfortunately, iodine prints are not permanent and begin to fade once the fuming process is stopped. Therefore, the examiner must photograph the prints immediately on development in order to retain a permanent record. Also, iodine-developed prints can be fixed with a 1 percent solution of starch in water, applied by spraying. The print turns blue and lasts for several weeks to several months.

The reasons why latent prints are visualized by iodine vapors are not yet fully understood. Many believe that the iodine fumes combine with fatty oils; however, there is also convincing evidence that the iodine may actually interact with residual water left on a print from perspiration.[2]

FIGURE 15–16 A heated fuming cabinet. *Courtesy Sirchie Finger Print Laboratories, Inc., Youngsville, N.C., www.sirchie.com*

ninhydrin
A chemical reagent used to develop latent fingerprints on porous materials by reacting with amino acids in perspiration

Ninhydrin Another chemical used for visualizing latent prints is **ninhydrin**. The development of latent prints with ninhydrin depends on its chemical reaction to form a purple-blue color with amino acids present in trace amounts in perspiration. Ninhydrin (triketohydrindene hydrate) is commonly sprayed onto the porous surface from an aerosol can. A solution is prepared by mixing the ninhydrin powder with a suitable solvent, such as acetone or ethyl alcohol; a 0.6 percent solution appears to be effective for most applications.

Generally, prints begin to appear within an hour or two after ninhydrin application; however, weaker prints may be visualized after 24 to 48 hours. The development can be hastened if the treated specimen is heated in an oven or on a hot plate at a temperature of 80–100°C. The ninhydrin method has developed latent prints on paper as old as 15 years.

Physical Developer
A silver nitrate–based reagent formulated to develop latent fingerprints on porous surfaces

Physical Developer Physical Developer is a third chemical mixture used for visualizing latent prints. Physical Developer is a silver nitrate–based liquid reagent. This method has gained wide acceptance by fingerprint examiners, who have found it effective for visualizing latent prints that remain undetected by the previously described methods. Also, this technique is effective for developing latent fingerprints on porous articles that may have been wet at one time.

For most fingerprint examiners, the chemical method of choice is ninhydrin. Its extreme sensitivity and ease of application have all but eliminated the use of iodine for latent-print visualization. However, when ninhydrin fails, development with Physical Developer may provide identifiable results. Application of Physical Developer washes away any traces of proteins from an object's surface; hence, if one wishes to use all of the previously mentioned chemical development methods on the same surface, it is necessary to first fume with iodine, follow this treatment with ninhydrin, and then apply Physical Developer to the object.

Superglue Fuming In the past, chemical treatment for fingerprint development was reserved for porous surfaces such as paper and cardboard. However, since 1982, a chemical technique known as **superglue fuming** has gained wide popularity for developing latent prints on nonporous surfaces such as metals, electrical tape, leather, and plastic bags.[3] See Figure 15–17.

FIGURE 15–17
Superglue fuming a nonporous metallic surface in the search for latent fingerprints. *Courtesy Sirchie Finger Print Laboratories, Inc., Youngsville, N.C., www.sirchie.com*

superglue fuming
A technique for visualizing latent fingerprints on nonporous surfaces by exposing them to cyanoacrylate vapors; named for the commercial product Super Glue

Superglue is approximately 98–99 percent cyanoacrylate ester, a chemical that interacts with and visualizes a latent fingerprint. Cyanoacrylate ester fumes can be created when superglue is placed on absorbent cotton treated with sodium hydroxide. The fumes can also be created by heating the glue. The fumes and the evidential object are contained within an enclosed chamber for up to six hours. Development occurs when fumes from the glue adhere to the latent print, usually producing a white-appearing latent print. Interestingly, small enclosed areas, such as the interior of an automobile, have been successfully processed for latent prints with fumes from superglue.

Through the use of a small handheld wand, cyanoacrylate fuming is now easily done at a crime scene or in a laboratory setting. The wand heats a small cartridge containing cyanoacrylate. Once heated, the cyanoacrylate vaporizes, allowing the operator to direct the fumes onto the suspect area (see Figure 15–18).

(a) (b)

FIGURE 15–18 (a) A handheld fuming wand uses disposable cartridges containing cyanoacrylate. The wand is used to develop prints at the crime scene and (b) in the laboratory. *Courtesy Sirchie Finger Print Laboratories, Inc., Youngsville, N.C., www.sirchie.com*

Other Techniques for Visualization In recent years, researchers have explored a variety of new processes applicable to the visualization of latent fingerprints. However, for many years progress in this field was minimal. Fingerprint specialists traditionally relied on three chemical techniques—iodine, ninhydrin, and silver nitrate—to reveal a hidden fingerprint. Then, superglue fuming extended chemical development to prints deposited on nonporous surfaces.

Another hint of things to come emerged with the discovery that latent fingerprints could be visualized by exposure to laser light. This laser method took advantage of the fact that perspiration contains a variety of components that **fluoresce** when illuminated by laser light.

The next advancement in latent-fingerprint development occurred with the discovery that fingerprints could be treated with chemicals that would induce fluorescence when exposed to laser illumination. For example, application of zinc chloride after ninhydrin treatment or application of the dye rhodamine 6G after superglue fuming caused fluorescence and increased the sensitivity of detection on exposure to laser illumination. The discovery of numerous chemical developers for visualizing fingerprints through fluorescence quickly followed. This knowledge set the stage for the next advance in latent-fingerprint development—the *alternate light source*.

With the advent of chemically induced fluorescence, lasers were no longer needed to induce fingerprints to fluoresce through perspiration residues. High-intensity light sources or alternate light sources have proliferated and all but replaced laser lights (see Figure 15–19). High-intensity quartz halogen or xenon-arc light sources can be focused on a suspect area through a fiber-optic cable. This light can be passed through several filters, giving the user more flexibility in selecting the wavelength of light to be aimed at the latent print. Alternatively, lightweight, portable alternate light sources that use light-emitting diodes (LEDs) are also commercially available (see Figure 15–20).

fluoresce
To emit visible light when exposed to light of a shorter wavelength

FIGURE 15–19
An alternate light source system incorporating a high-intensity light source.
Courtesy Foster & Freeman Limited, Worcestershire, U.K., www.fosterfreeman.co.uk

FIGURE 15–20
Lightweight handheld alternate light source that uses an LED light source.
Courtesy Foster & Freeman Limited, Worcestershire, U.K., www.fosterfreeman.co.uk

In most cases, these light sources have proven to be as effective as laser light in developing latent prints, and they are commercially available at costs significantly less than those of laser illuminators. Furthermore, these light sources are portable and can be readily taken to any crime scene.

A large number of chemical treatment processes are available to the fingerprint examiner (see Figure 15–21), and the field is in a constant state of flux. Selection of an appropriate procedure is best left to technicians who have developed their skills through casework experience.

Newer chemical processes include a substitute for ninhydrin called DFO (1,8-diazafluoren-9-one). This chemical visualizes latent prints on porous materials when exposed to an alternate light source. DFO has been shown to develop 2.5 times more latent prints on paper than ninhydrin. A chemical called 1,2-indanedione is also emerging as a potential reagent for the development of latent fingerprints on porous surfaces. 1,2-indanedione gives both good initial color and strong fluorescence when reacted with amino acids derived from prints and thus has the potential to provide in one process what ninhydrin and DFO can do in two different steps. Dye combinations known as RAM, RAY, and MRM 10 when used in conjunction with superglue fuming have been effective in visualizing latent fingerprints by fluorescence.

FIGURE 15–21
(a) Latent fingerprint visualized by cyanoacrylate fuming
(b) Fingerprint treated with cyanoacrylate and a blue/green fluorescent dye
(c) Fingerprint treated with cyanoacrylate and rhodamine 6G fluorescent dye
(d) Fingerprint treated with cyanoacrylate and the fluorescent dye combination RAM
(e) Fingerprint visualized by the fluorescent chemical DFO
(f) Fingerprint visualized by Redwop fluorescent fingerprint powder
(g) A bloody fingerprint detected by laser light without any chemical treatment
(h) A bloody fingerprint detected by laser light after spraying with merbromin and hydrogen peroxide

(a, c–e, g–h) Courtesy North Carolina State Bureau of Investigation, Raleigh, N.C.,
(b) Courtesy 3M Corp., Austin, Texas
(f) Courtesy Melless Griot Inc., Carlsbad, Calif.

(a)

(b)

(c)

(d)

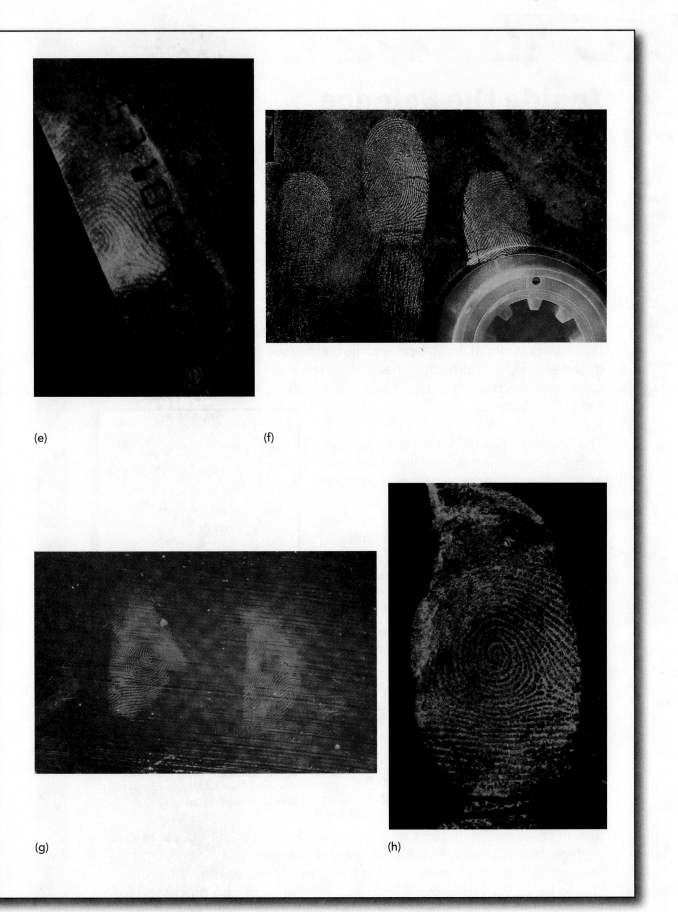

(e)

(f)

(g)

(h)

Inside the Science
Fluorescence

Fluorescence occurs when a substance absorbs light and re-emits the light in wavelengths longer than that of the illuminating source. Importantly, substances that emit light or fluoresce are more readily seen either with the naked eye or through photography than are non-light-emitting materials. The high sensitivity of fluorescence serves as the underlying principle of many of the new chemical techniques used to visualize latent fingerprints.

The earliest use of fluorescence to visualize fingerprints came with the direct illumination of a fingerprint with argon–ion lasers. This laser type was chosen because its blue-green light output induced some of the perspiration components of a fingerprint to fluoresce (see the figure). The major drawback of this approach is that the perspiration components of a fingerprint are often present in quantities too minute to observe even with the aid of fluorescence.

The fingerprint examiner, wearing safety goggles containing optical filters, visually examines the specimen being exposed to the laser light. The filters absorb the laser light and permit the wavelengths at which latent-print residues fluoresce to pass through to the eyes of the wearer. The filter also protects the operator against eye damage from scattered or reflected laser light. Likewise, latent-print residue producing sufficient fluorescence can be photographed by placing this same filter across the lens of the camera. Examination of specimens and photography of the fluorescing latent prints are carried out in a darkened room.

Schematic depicting latent-print detection with the aid of a laser. A fingerprint examiner, wearing safety goggles containing optical filters, examines the specimen being exposed to the laser light. The filter absorbs the laser light and permits the wavelengths at which latent-print residues fluoresce to pass through to the eyes of the examiner.
Courtesy Federal Bureau of Investigation, Washington, D.C.

Studies have demonstrated that common fingerprint-developing agents do not interfere with DNA-testing methods used for characterizing bloodstains.[4] Nonetheless, in cases involving items with material adhering to their surfaces and/or items that will require further laboratory examinations, fingerprint processing should not be performed at the crime scene. Rather, the items should be submitted to the laboratory, where they can be processed for fingerprints in conjunction with other necessary examinations.

Quick Review

- Visible prints are made when fingers touch a surface after the ridges have been in contact with a colored material such as blood, paint, grease, or ink.

- Plastic prints are ridge impressions left on a soft material, such as putty, wax, soap, or dust.

- Latent prints deposited on hard and nonabsorbent surfaces (such as glass, mirror, tile, and painted wood) are usually developed by the application of a powder, whereas prints on porous surfaces (such as papers and cardboard) generally require treatment with a chemical.

- Examiners use various chemical methods to visualize latent prints, such as iodine fuming, ninhydrin, and Physical Developer.

- Superglue fuming develops latent prints on nonporous surfaces.

- Latent fingerprints can also be treated with chemicals that induce fluorescence when exposed to a high-intensity light or an alternate light source.

Preservation of Developed Prints

Once the latent print has been visualized, it must be permanently preserved for future comparison and possible use in court as evidence. A photograph must be taken before any further attempts at preservation. Any camera equipped with a close-up lens will do; however, many investigators prefer to use a camera specially designed for fingerprint photography. Such a camera comes equipped with a fixed focus to take photographs on a 1:1 scale when the camera's open eye is held exactly flush against the print's surface (see Figure 15–22). In addition, photographs must be taken to provide an overall view of the print's location with respect to other evidential items at the crime scene.

FIGURE 15–22
Camera fitted with an adapter designed to give an approximate 1:1 photograph of a fingerprint. *Courtesy Sirchie Finger Print Laboratories, Inc., Youngsville, N.C., www.sirchie.com*

Once photographs have been secured, one of two procedures is to be followed. If the object is small enough to be transported without destroying the print, it should be preserved in its entirety. The print should be covered with cellophane so it will be protected from damage. On the other hand, prints on large immovable objects that have been developed with a powder can best be preserved by "lifting." The most popular type of lifter is a broad adhesive tape similar to Scotch tape. Fingerprint powder is applied to the print, and the surface containing the print is covered with the adhesive side of the tape. When the tape is pulled up, the powder is transferred to the tape. Then the tape is placed on a properly labeled card that provides a good background contrast with the powder.

A variation of this procedure is the use of an adhesive-backed clear plastic sheet attached to a colored cardboard backing. Before it is applied to the print, a celluloid separator is peeled from the plastic sheet to expose the adhesive lifting surface. The tape is then pressed evenly and firmly over the powdered print and pulled up (see Figure 15–23). The sheet containing the adhering powder is now pressed against the cardboard backing to provide a permanent record of the fingerprint.

FIGURE 15–23
"Lifting" a fingerprint.
*Courtesy Sirchie Finger
Print Laboratories, Inc.,
Youngsville, N.C.,
www.sirchie.com*

digital imaging
A process through which a picture is converted into a series of square electronic dots known as pixels; the picture is manipulated by computer software that changes the numerical value of each pixel

pixel
A square electronic dot that is used to compose a digital image

Digital Imaging for Fingerprint Enhancement

When fingerprints are lifted from a crime scene, they are not usually in perfect condition, making the analysis that much more difficult. Computers have advanced technology in most fields, and fingerprint identification has not been left behind. With the help of digital imaging software, fingerprints can now be enhanced for the most accurate and comprehensive analysis.

Digital imaging is the process by which a picture is converted into a digital file. The image produced from this digital file is composed of numerous square electronic dots called **pixels**. Images composed of only black and white elements are referred to as grayscale images. Each pixel is assigned a number according to its intensity. The grayscale image is made from the set of numbers to which a pixel may be assigned, ranging from 0 (black) to 255 (white). Once an image is digitally stored, it is manipulated by computer software that changes the numerical value of each pixel, thus altering the image as directed by the user. Resolution reveals the degree of detail that can be seen in an image. It is defined in terms of dimensions, such as 800 × 600 pixels. The larger the numbers, the more closely the digital image resembles the real-world image.

The input of pictures into a digital imaging system is usually done through the use of scanners, digital cameras, and video cameras. After the picture is changed to its digital image, several methods can be employed to enhance the image. The overall brightness of an image, as well as the contrast between the image and the background, can be adjusted through contrast-enhancement methods. One approach used to enhance an image is *spatial filtering*. Several types of filters produce various effects. A low-pass filter is used to eliminate harsh edges by reducing the intensity difference between pixels. A second filter, the high-pass filter, operates by modifying a pixel's numerical value to exaggerate its intensity difference from that of its neighbor. The resulting effect increases the contrast of the edges, thus providing a high contrast between the elements and the background.

Frequency analysis, also referred to as *frequency Fourier transform* (FFT), is used to identify periodic or repetitive patterns such as lines or dots that interfere with the interpretation of the image. These patterns are diminished or eliminated to enhance the appearance of the image. Interestingly, the spacings between fingerprint ridges are themselves periodic. Therefore, the contribution of the fingerprint can be identified in FFT mode and then enhanced. Likewise, if ridges from overlapping prints are positioned in different directions, their corresponding frequency information is at different locations in FFT mode. The ridges of one latent print can then be enhanced while the ridges of the other are suppressed.

Color interferences can pose a problem when analyzing an image. For example, a latent fingerprint found on paper currency or a check may be difficult to analyze because of the distracting colored background. With the imaging software, the colored background can simply be removed to make the image stand out (see Figure 15–24). If the image itself is a particular color, such as a ninhydrin-developed print, the color can be isolated and enhanced to distinguish it from the background.

FIGURE 15–24
A fingerprint being enhanced in Adobe Photoshop. In this example, on the left is the original scan of an inked fingerprint on a check. On the right is the same image after using Adobe Photoshop's Channel Mixer to eliminate the green security background. *Courtesy Imaging Forensics, Fountain Valley, Calif., www.imagingforensics.com*

Digital imaging software also provides functions in which portions of the image can be examined individually. With a scaling and resizing tool, the user can select a part of an image and resize it for a closer look. This function operates much like a magnifying glass, helping the examiner view fine details of an image.

An important and useful tool, especially for fingerprint identification, is the compare function. This specialized feature places two images side by side and allows the examiner to chart the common features on both images simultaneously (see Figure 15–25). The zoom function is used in conjunction with the compare tool. As the examiner zooms into a portion of one image, the software automatically zooms into the second image for comparison.

FIGURE 15–25
Current imaging software allows fingerprint analysts to prepare a fingerprint comparison chart. The fingerprint examiner can compare prints side by side and display important features that are consistent between the fingerprints. The time needed to create a display of this sort digitally is about 30 to 60 minutes. *Courtesy Imaging Forensics, Fountain View, Calif., www.imagingforensics.com*

Although digital imaging is undoubtedly an effective tool for enhancing and analyzing images, it is only as useful as the images it has to work with. If the details do not exist on the original images, the enhancement procedures are not going to work. The benefits of digital enhancement methods are apparent when weak images are made more distinguishable.

Quick Review

- Once a latent print has been visualized, it must be permanently preserved for future comparison and for possible use as court evidence. A photograph must be taken before any further attempts at preservation are made.

- A common method for preserving prints developed with a powder is lifting the print with an adhesive tape.

- Digital imaging is a process through which a picture is converted into a series of square electronic dots known as pixels. Digital imaging can be used to enhance fingerprints.

Chapter Review

- Fingerprints are a reproduction of friction skin ridges found on the palm side of the fingers and thumbs.

- The basic principles underlying the use of fingerprints in criminal investigations are as follows: (1) A fingerprint is an individual characteristic because no two fingers have yet been found to possess identical ridge characteristics; (2) a fingerprint remains unchanged during an individual's lifetime; and (3) fingerprints have general ridge patterns that permit them to be systematically classified.

- All fingerprints are divided into three classes on the basis of their general pattern: loops, whorls, and arches.

- The individuality of a fingerprint is determined not by its general shape or pattern, but by a careful study of its ridge characteristics. The expert must demonstrate a point-by-point comparison in order to prove the identity of an individual.

- When the finger touches a surface, perspiration and oils are transferred onto that surface, leaving a fingerprint. Prints deposited in this manner are invisible to the eye and are commonly referred to as latent or invisible fingerprints.

- The primary classification is the first step in classifying fingerprints under the FBI system. The presence or absence of the whorl pattern is the basis for determination of the primary classification.

- The FBI fingerprint database known as AFIS converts the image of a fingerprint into digital minutiae that contain data showing ridges at their points of termination (ridge endings) and their branching into two ridges (bifurcations).

- Livescan is an inkless device that captures digital images of fingerprints and palm prints and electronically transmits them to an AFIS.

- Visible prints are made when fingers touch a surface after the ridges have been in contact with a colored material such as blood, paint, grease, or ink.

- Plastic prints are ridge impressions left on a soft material, such as putty, wax, soap, or dust.

- Latent prints deposited on hard and nonabsorbent surfaces (such as glass, mirror, tile, and painted wood) are usually developed by the application of a powder, whereas prints on porous surfaces (such as papers and cardboard) generally require treatment with a chemical.

- Examiners use various chemical methods to visualize latent prints, such as iodine fuming, ninhydrin, and Physical Developer.

- Superglue fuming develops latent prints on nonporous surfaces.

- Latent fingerprints can also be treated with chemicals that induce fluorescence when exposed to a high-intensity light or an alternate light source.

- Once a latent print has been visualized, it must be permanently preserved for future comparison and for possible use as court evidence. A photograph must be taken before any further attempts at preservation are made.

- A common method for preserving prints developed with a powder is lifting the print with an adhesive tape.

- Digital imaging is a process through which a picture is converted into a series of square electronic dots known as pixels. Digital imaging can be used to enhance fingerprints.

Quick Lab: Fingerprinting

Materials:

Several sheets of blank paper
Fingerprinting pad (if available) or ink pad
Magnifying glass

Procedure:

Fingerprinting is perhaps the oldest method of scientific forensic identification. No two sets of same fingerprints are the same, yet they all exhibit characteristics that allow investigators to classify them for quicker identification. In this exercise, students should be matched up in teams of three. Each member of the group should roll the fingerprint of the right index finger of another group member onto a piece of paper. The paper should contain a print from every team member. Now, roll a print from each team member onto a separate blank piece of paper. Do NOT write the names of the team members on these papers. When the ink is dry, shuffle the papers and set two aside at random. Using the magnifying glass, each person on the team has 2 minutes to compare the unknown print to the named prints and determine who made it. Answer the following questions individually, then compare notes as a team and see if everyone agreed on the identity of the print.

Follow Up Questions:

1. Who do you believe made the unknown print?

2. What is the general pattern of the print – arch, loop, or whorl?

3. Did everyone in the team agree on the identity of the unknown print?

Review Questions

1. The International Association for Identification concluded that the minimum number of friction ridge characteristics which must be present in two impressions in order to establish positive identification is
   a. six.
   b. eight.
   c. ten.
   d. There is no minimum number.

2. For most fingerprint examiners, the chemical method of choice for visualizing latent prints is
   a. ninhydrin.
   b. iodine.
   c. silver nitrate.
   d. chlorate.

3. What was the original fingerprinting system adopted by Scotland Yard in 1901 which converted ridge patterns on all ten fingers into a series of letters and numbers arranged in the form of a fraction?
   a. Bertillon system
   b. Fauld system
   c. Henry system
   d. Galton system

4. Attempts at changing one's fingerprints by trying to obscure them has led to
   a. renewed efforts on the part of law enforcement to categorize the obliterated fingerprints.
   b. the creation of a new class of criminal who can avoid detection through currently available fingerprinting technology.
   c. the possibility of permanent scarring, which only provides new characteristics for identification because it is impossible to obliterate all ridge characteristics.
   d. self-injurious behavior that only results in the growth of new ridge characteristics on the fingertips.

5. A technique for visualizing latent fingerprints on nonporous surfaces by exposing them to cyanoacrylate vapors is
   a. sublimation.
   b. iodine fuming.
   c. fluorescing.
   d. superglue fuming.

6. True or False: The individuality of a fingerprint is determined by its general shape or pattern, and it has been empirically demonstrated that no two fingerprints are alike.

7. True or False: The most common type of fingerprint pattern is the arch pattern.

8. True or False: AFIS, the automated fingerprint identification system, makes it possible to search a single latent crime-scene fingerprint against an entire file's print collection.

9. True or False: Studies have recently demonstrated that common fingerprint developing agents interfere with DNA testing methods used for characterizing bloodstains, so DNA testing must precede fingerprint tests.

10. True or False: Digital imaging has become an effective tool for the enhancement and analysis of images because if the details do not exist on the original image, enhancement procedures are available to make the details clearer.

11. What are fingerprints?

12. What is the first fundamental principle of fingerprints?

13. What imparts individuality to a fingerprint?

14. What are ridge characteristics? What is another name for ridge characteristics?

15. What is the second fundamental principle of fingerprints?

16. What are dermal papillae and how are they related to fingerprints?

17. What is a latent fingerprint? Briefly describe how a latent fingerprint is formed.

18. Why is it pointless to try to obscure or obliterate one's fingerprints by scarring or otherwise damaging the skin?

19. What is the third fundamental principle of fingerprints?

20. What are the three types of fingerprint patterns? Which is most common?

21. Which class of fingerprints includes ridge patterns that are generally rounded or circular and have two deltas?

22. Which type of fingerprint pattern must have at least one delta?

23. Which is the simplest of all fingerprint patterns, formed by ridges entering from one side of the print and exiting on the opposite side?

24. What is the primary classification? What is the basis for this classification?

25. What is an AFIS? What is the heart of AFIS technology?

26. When using AFIS, who makes the final verification of a print's identity?

27. What is livescan? What procedure has livescan largely replaced?

28. Name two main drawbacks to using AFIS.

29. Name the three kinds of crime-scene fingerprints.

30. How are prints from soft and porous surfaces preferably developed?

31. What is RUVIS and how does it work?

32. Name four common chemical methods for visualizing latent prints.

33. Explain how latent prints can be visualized when illuminated by laser light.

34. Name three reasons why alternate light sources have replaced lasers for visualizing latent prints.

35. What is the first thing that the criminalist must do after visualizing a print but before making any further attempts at preserving it?

36. Briefly describe how the criminalist should handle prints on small objects.

37. Describe the basic process used to "lift" a fingerprint. When should this procedure be used?

38. What is digital imaging? How is it useful for analyzing fingerprints?

39. Under what conditions is digital imaging not effective in enhancing latent fingerprints?

Application and Critical Thinking

1. Classify each of the following prints as a loop, whorl, or arch.

(1). _____   (2). _____   (3). _____

(4). _____   (5). _____   (6). _____

2. Following is a description of the types of prints from the fingers of a criminal suspect. Using the FBI system, determine the primary classification of this individual.

Finger	Right Hand	Left Hand
Thumb	Whorl	Whorl
Index	Loop	Whorl
Middle	Whorl	Arch
Ring	Whorl	Whorl
Little	Arch	Whorl

3. While searching a murder scene, you find the following items that you believe may contain latent fingerprints. Indicate whether prints on each item should be developed using fingerprint powder or chemicals.

a. a leather sofa

b. a mirror

c. a painted wooden knife handle

d. blood-soaked newspapers

e. a revolver

---

4. Criminalist Frank Mortimer is using digital imaging to enhance latent fingerprints. Indicate which features of digital imaging he would most likely use for each of the following tasks:

a. isolating part of a print and enlarging it for closer examination

b. increasing the contrast between a print and the background surface on which it is located

c. examining two prints that overlap one another

---

5. The following are fingerprint patterns of three men and a woman with criminal records for robbery. Identify the following fingerprints according to the three groups and subgroups of fingerprints.

KJ

Tented Arch_____

Accidental Whorl_____

Double Loop Whorl_____

Plain Loop_____

Ivan

Lisa

**Virtual Lab
Fingerprinting**
To perform a virtual fingerprinting lab, go to www.pearsoncustom.com/us/vlm/

Charlie

6. Count the number of bifurcations in the following print. Choose between 9, 11, and 13.

Number of bifurcations:

7. At the Museum of Culture Studies, a diary that belonged to Martin Luther King has been stolen and replaced by a fake. The only evidence is a fingerprint impression left by the thief on the fake diary. The police suspects four individuals who have had previous criminal records in similar crimes. Their fingerprints already exist in the police database. KJ, Ivan, Lisa, and Charlie are the four suspects. Carefully read the criminal's fingerprint impression and identify the suspect fingerprint that matches the most with it.

Crime Scene Fingerprint

| KJ | Ivan | Lisa | Charlie |

Endnotes

1. A tented arch is also any pattern that resembles a loop but lacks one of the essential requirements for classification as a loop.

2. J. Almag, Y. Sasson, and A. Anati, "Chemical Reagents for the Development of Latent Fingerprints II: Controlled Addition of Water Vapor to Iodine Fumes—A Solution to the Aging Problem," *Journal of Forensic Sciences* 24 (1979): 431.

3. F. G. Kendall and B. W. Rehn, "Rapid Method of Superglue Fuming Application for the Development of Latent Fingerprints," *Journal of Forensic Sciences* 28 (1983): 777.

4. C. Roux et al., "A Further Study to Investigate the Effect of Fingerprint Enhancement Techniques on the DNA Analysis of Bloodstains," *Journal of Forensic Identification* 49 (1999): 357; C. J. Frégeau et al., "Fingerprint Enhancement Revisited and the Effects of Blood Enhancement Chemicals on Subsequent Profiler Plus™ Fluorescent Short Tandem Repeat DNA Analysis of Fresh and Aged Bloody Fingerprints," *Journal of Forensic Sciences* 45 (2000): 354; and P. Grubwieser et al., "Systematic Study on STR Profiling on Blood and Saliva Traces after Visualization of Fingerprints," *Journal of Forensic Sciences* 48 (2003): 733.

Learning Objectives

After studying this chapter you should be able to:

- Describe techniques for rifling a barrel

- Recognize the class and individual characteristics of bullets and cartridge cases

- Understand the use of the comparison microscope to compare bullets and cartridge cases

- Explain the concept of the NIBIN database

- Explain the procedure for determining how far from a target a weapon was fired

- Identify the laboratory tests for determining whether an individual has fired a weapon

- Explain the forensic significance of class and individual characteristics to the comparison of tool marks, footwear, and tire impressions

- List some common field reagents used to enhance bloody footprints

National Science Content Standards

 Scientific Inquiry

 History and Nature of Science

The Beltway Snipers

During a three-week period in October 2002, ten people were killed and three others wounded as two snipers terrorized the region in and around the Baltimore–Washington metropolitan area. The arrest of John Allen Muhammad, 41, and Lee Boyd Malvo, 17, ended the ordeal. The semiautomatic .223-caliber rifle seized from them was ultimately linked by ballistics tests to eight of the ten killings. The car that Muhammad and Malvo were driving had been specially configured with one hole in the trunk through which a rifle barrel could protrude, so that a sniper could shoot from inside a slightly ajar trunk.

The major break in the case came when a friend of Muhammad's called police suggesting that Muhammad and his friend Malvo were the likely snipers. Muhammad's automobile records revealed numerous traffic stops in the Beltway area during the time of the shootings. Another break in the case came when Malvo called a priest to boast of a killing weeks before in Montgomery, Alabama. Investigators traced the claim to a recent liquor store holdup that left one person dead. Fortunately, the perpetrator of this crime left a latent fingerprint at the murder scene. Authorities quickly tracked the print to Malvo, a Jamaican citizen, through his fingerprints on file with the Immigration and Naturalization Service. A description of Muhammad's car was released to the media, leading to tips from alert citizens who noticed the car parked in a rest area with both occupants asleep.

The motive for the shooting spree was believed to be a plot to extort $10 million from local and state governments. Muhammad was sentenced to death and Malvo is currently serving life imprisonment without parole.

Firearms, Tool Marks, and Other Impressions

Key Terms

bore

breechface

caliber

choke

distance determination

ejector

extractor

firearms identification

gauge

Greiss test

grooves

lands

rifling

Just as natural variations in skin ridge patterns and characteristics provide a key to human identification, minute random markings on surfaces can impart individuality to inanimate objects. Structural variations and irregularities caused by scratches, nicks, breaks, and wear permit the criminalist to relate a bullet to a gun; a scratch or abrasion mark to a single tool; or a tire track to a particular automobile. Individualization, so vigorously pursued in all other areas of criminalistics, is frequently attainable in firearms and tool mark examination.

Although a portion of this chapter will be devoted to the comparison of surface features for the purposes of bullet identification, a complete description of the services and capabilities of the modern forensic firearms laboratory cannot be restricted to just this one subject, important as it may be. The high frequency of shooting cases means that the science of **firearms identification** must extend beyond mere comparison of bullets to include knowledge of the operation of all types of weapons, restoration of obliterated serial numbers on weapons, detection and characterization of gunpowder residues on garments and around wounds, estimation of muzzle-to-target distances, and detection of powder residues on hands. Each of these functions will be covered in this chapter.

Bullet and Cartridge Comparisons

The inner surface of the barrel of a gun leaves its markings on a bullet passing through it. These markings are peculiar to each gun. Hence, if one bullet found at the scene of a crime and another test-fired from a suspect's gun show the same markings, the suspect is linked to the crime. Because these inner surface markings, or striations, are so important for bullet comparison, it is important to know why and how they originate.

The Gun Barrel

The gun barrel is produced from a solid bar of steel that has been hollowed out by drilling. The microscopic drill marks left on the barrel's inner surface are randomly irregular and in themselves impart a uniqueness to each barrel. However, the manufacture of a barrel requires the additional step of impressing its inner surface with spiral **grooves**, a step known as **rifling**. The surfaces of the original **bore** remaining between the grooves are called **lands** (see Figure 16–1).

firearms identification
A discipline mainly concerned with determining whether a bullet or cartridge was fired by a particular weapon

grooves
The cut or low-lying portions between the lands in a rifled bore

rifling
The spiral grooves formed in the bore of a firearm barrel that impart spin to the projectile when it is fired

bore
The interior of a firearm barrel

lands
The raised portion between the grooves in a rifled bore

FIGURE 16–1 Interior view of a gun barrel, showing the presence of lands and grooves.

As a fired bullet travels through a barrel, it engages the rifling grooves. These grooves then guide the bullet through the barrel, giving it a rapid spin. This is done because a spinning bullet does not tumble end over end on leaving the barrel, but remains instead on a true and accurate course.

The diameter of the gun barrel, sketched in <u>Figure 16–2</u>, measured between opposite lands, is known as the **caliber** of the weapon. Caliber is normally recorded in hundredths of an inch or in millimeters—for example, .22 caliber and 9 mm. Actually, the term caliber, as it is commonly applied, is not an exact measurement of the barrel's diameter; for example, a .38-caliber weapon may actually have a bore diameter that ranges from 0.345 to 0.365 inch.

caliber
The diameter of the bore of a rifled firearm, usually expressed in hundredths of an inch or millimeters—for example, .22 caliber and 9 mm

FIGURE 16–2   Cross-section of a barrel with six grooves. The diameter of the bore is the caliber.

Rifling Methods Before 1940, barrels were rifled by having one or two grooves at a time cut into the surface with steel hook cutters. The cutting tool was rotated as it passed down the barrel, so that the final results were grooves spiraling to either the right or left. However, as the need for increased speed in weapons manufacture became apparent, newer techniques were developed that were far more suitable for the mass production of weapons.

The broach cutter, shown in <u>Figure 16–3</u>, consists of a series of concentric steel rings, with each ring slightly larger than the preceding one. As the broach passes through the barrel, it simultaneously cuts all grooves into the barrel at the required depth. The broach rotates as it passes through the barrel, giving the grooves their desired direction and rate of twist.

FIGURE 16–3
A segment of a broach cutter.

In contrast to the broach, the button process involves no cuttings. A steel plug or "button" impressed with the desired number of grooves is forced under extremely high pressure through the barrel. A single pass of the button down the barrel compresses the metal to create lands and grooves on the barrel walls that are negative forms of those on the button. The button rotates to produce the desired direction and rate of twist (see Figure 16–4).

FIGURE 16–4
(top) Cross-section of a .22-caliber rifled barrel. (bottom) A button used to produce the lands and grooves in the barrel.

Like the button process, the mandrel rifling hammer forging process involves no cutting of metal. A mandrel is a rod of hardened steel machined so its form is the reverse impression of the rifling it is intended to produce. The mandrel is inserted into a slightly oversized bore, and the barrel is compressed with hammering or heavy rollers into the mandrel's form.

Every firearms manufacturer chooses a rifling process that is best suited to meet the production standards and requirements of its product. Once the choice is made, however, the class characteristics of the weapon's barrel remain consistent; each has the same number of lands and grooves, with the same approximate width and direction of twist. For example, .32 caliber Smith & Wesson revolvers have five lands and grooves twisting to the right. On the other hand, Colt .32-caliber revolvers exhibit six lands and grooves twisting to the left. Although these class characteristics permit the examiner to distinguish one type or brand name of weapon from another, they do not impart individuality to any one barrel; no class characteristic can do this.

If one could cut a barrel open lengthwise, careful examination of the interior would reveal the existence of fine lines, or *striations*, many running the length of the barrel's lands and grooves. These striations are impressed into the metal as the negatives of minute imperfections found on the rifling cutter's surface, or they are produced by minute chips of steel pushed against the barrel's inner surface by a moving broach cutter. The random distribution and irregularities of these markings are impossible to duplicate exactly in any two barrels. No two rifled barrels, even those manufactured in succession, have identical striation markings. These striations form the individual characteristics of the barrel.

Comparing Bullet Markings As the bullet passes through the barrel, its surface is impressed with the rifled markings of the barrel. The bullet emerges from the barrel carrying the impressions of the bore's interior surface (see Figure 16–5). Because there is no practical way to directly compare the markings on the fired bullet and those within a barrel, the examiner must obtain test bullets fired through the suspect barrel for comparison. To prevent damage to the test bullet's markings and to facilitate the bullet's recovery, test firings are normally made into a recovery box filled with cotton or into a water tank (see Figure 16–6).

FIGURE 16–5
A bullet is impressed with the rifling markings of the barrel when it emerges from the weapon.

FIGURE 16–6
In ballistics testing, a suspect firearm is fired into a water tank. The bullet is slowed and stopped by the water, fished out undamaged, and compared to bullets from the crime scene. *Courtesy Mikael Karlsson/Arresting Images*

The number of lands and grooves, and their direction of twist, are obvious points of comparison during the initial stages of the examination. Any differences in these class characteristics immediately eliminate the possibility that both bullets traveled through the same barrel. A bullet with five lands and grooves could not possibly have been fired from a weapon of like caliber with six lands and grooves, nor could one having a right twist have come through a barrel impressed with a left twist. If both bullets carry the same class characteristics, the analyst must begin to match the striated markings on both bullets. This can be done only with the assistance of the comparison microscope (see Chapter 7).

Modern firearms identification began with the development and use of the comparison microscope. This instrument is the firearms examiner's most important tool. The test and evidence bullets are mounted on cylindrical adjustable holders beneath the objective lenses of the microscope, each pointing in the same direction (see Figure 16–7). Both bullets are observed simultaneously within the same field of view, and the examiner rotates one bullet until a well-defined land or groove comes into view.

Once the striation markings are located, the other bullet is rotated until a matching region is found. Not only must the lands and grooves of the test and evidence bullet have

FIGURE 16–7 A bullet holder beneath the objective lens of a comparison microscope. *Courtesy Leica Microsystems, Buffalo, N.Y., www.leica-microsystems.com*

identical widths, but the longitudinal striations on each must coincide. When a matching area is located, the two bullets are simultaneously rotated to obtain additional matching areas around the periphery of the bullets. Figure 16–8 shows a typical photomicrograph of a bullet match as viewed under a comparison microscope.

FIGURE 16–8
Photomicrograph of two bullets through a comparison microcope. The test bullet is on the right; the questioned bullet is on the left. *Courtesy Philadelphia Police Department Laboratory*

Considerations in Bullet Comparison Unfortunately, the firearms examiner rarely encounters a perfect match all around the bullet's periphery. The presence of grit and rust can alter the markings on bullets fired through the same barrel. More commonly, recovered evidence bullets become so mutilated and distorted on impact that they yield only a small area with intact markings.

Furthermore, striation markings on a barrel are not permanent structures; they are subject to continuing alteration through wear as succeeding bullets traverse the length of the barrel. Fortunately these changes are usually not dramatic and do not prevent the matching of two bullets fired by the same weapon. As with fingerprint comparison, there are no hard-and-fast rules governing the minimum number of points required for a bullet comparison. The final opinion must be based on the judgment, experience, and knowledge of the expert.

Frequently the firearms examiner receives a spent bullet without an accompanying suspect weapon and is asked to determine the caliber and possible make of the weapon. If a bullet appears not to have lost its metal, its weight may be one factor in determining its caliber. In some instances, the number of lands and grooves, the direction of twist, and the widths of lands and grooves are useful class characteristics for eliminating certain makes of weapons from consideration. For example, a bullet that has five lands and grooves and twists to the right could not come from a weapon manufactured by Colt, because Colts are not manufactured with these class characteristics.

Sometimes a bullet has rifling marks that set it apart from most other manufactured weapons, as in the case of Marlin rifles. These weapons are rifled by a

MyCrimeKit: WebExtra 16.1
Practice Matching Bullets with the Aid of a 3-D Interactive Illustration
www.mycrimekit.com

technique known as *microgrooving* and may have 8 to 24 grooves impressed into their barrels; few other weapons are manufactured in this fashion. In this respect, the FBI maintains a record known as the General Rifling Characteristics File. This file contains listings of class characteristics, such as land and groove width dimensions, for known weapons. It is periodically updated and distributed to the law enforcement community to help identify rifled weapons from retrieved bullets.

Unlike rifled firearms, a shotgun has a smooth barrel, so projectiles passing through a shotgun barrel are not impressed with any characteristic markings that can later be related back to the weapon. Shotguns generally fire small lead balls or pellets contained within a shotgun shell (see Figure 16–9). A paper or plastic wad pushes the pellets through the barrel on ignition of the cartridge's powder charge. By weighing and measuring the diameter of the shot recovered at a crime scene, the examiner can usually determine the size of shot used in the shell. The size and shape of the recovered wad may also reveal the gauge of the shotgun used and, in some instances, may indicate the manufacturer of the fired shell.

MyCrimeKit: WebExtra 16.2

View 3-D Shotgun Shell Illustrations
www.mycrimekit.com

FIGURE 16–9
Cross-section of a loaded shotgun shell.

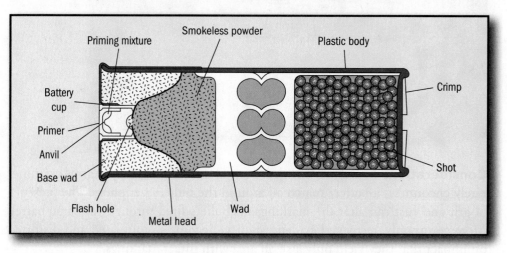

gauge
Size designation of a shotgun, originally the number of lead balls with the same diameter as the barrel that would make a pound

The diameter of the shotgun barrel is expressed by the term **gauge**.[1] The higher the gauge number, the smaller the barrel's diameter. For example, a 12-gauge shotgun has a bore diameter of 0.730 inch as contrasted to 0.670 inch for a 16-gauge shotgun. The exception to this rule is the .410-gauge shotgun, which refers to a barrel 0.41 inch in diameter.

Cartridge Cases

breechface
The rear part of a firearm barrel

The act of pulling a trigger releases the weapon's firing pin, causing it to strike the primer, which in turn ignites the powder. The expanding gases generated by the burning gunpowder propel the bullet forward through the barrel, simultaneously pushing the spent cartridge case or shell back with equal force against the **breechface**. As the bullet is marked by its passage through the barrel, the shell is also impressed with markings by its contact with the metal surfaces of the weapon's firing and loading mechanisms. As with bullets, these markings can be reproduced in test-fired cartridges to provide distinctive points of comparison for individualizing a spent shell to a rifled weapon or shotgun.

Case Files

Sacco and Vanzetti

Courtesy Corbis/Bettmann

In 1920, two security guards were viciously gunned down by unidentified assailants. The security guards were transporting shoe factory payroll, nearly $16,000 in cash, at the time of the robbery-murder. Eyewitnesses described the assailants as "Italian-looking," one with a full handlebar mustache. The robbers had used two firearms, leaving behind three different brands of shells.

Two suspects were identified and arrested—Nicola Sacco and his friend, the amply mustachioed Bartolomeo Vanzetti. After denying owning any firearms, each was found to be in possession of a loaded pistol. In fact, Sacco's pistol was .32 caliber, the same caliber as the crime-scene bullets. In Sacco's pockets were found 23 bullets matching the brands of the empty shells found at the murder scene.

This case coincided with the "Red Scare," a politically turbulent time in post–World War I America. Citizens feared socialist zealots, and the media played up these emotions. Political maneuvering and the use of the media muddied the waters surrounding the case, and the fact that both suspects belonged to anarchist political groups that advocated revolutionary violence against the government only incited public animosity toward them. Sympathetic socialist organizations attempted to turn Sacco and Vanzetti into martyrs, calling their prosecution a "witch hunt."

The outcome of the trial ultimately depended on whether the prosecution could prove that Sacco's pistol fired the bullets that killed the two security guards. At trial, the ballistics experts testified that the bullets used were no longer in production and they could not find similar ammunition to use in test firings—aside from the unused cartridges found in Sacco's pockets. A forensics expert for the prosecution concluded that a visual examination showed that the bullets matched, leading the jury to return a verdict of guilty. Sacco and Vanzetti were sentenced to death.

Because of continued public protests, a committee was appointed in 1927 to review the case. Around this time, Calvin Goddard, at the Bureau of Forensic Ballistics in New York, perfected the comparison microscope for use in forensic firearms investigations. With this instrument, two bullets are viewed side by side to compare the striations imparted to a bullet's surface as it travels through the gun's barrel. The committee asked Goddard to examine the bullets in question. A test-fired bullet from Sacco's weapon was matched conclusively by Goddard to one of the crime-scene bullets. The fates of Sacco and Vanzetti were sealed, and they were put to death in 1927.

extractor
The mechanism in a firearm by which a cartridge or fired case is withdrawn from the chamber

ejector
The mechanism in a firearm that throws the cartridge or fired case from the firearm

The shape of the firing pin is impressed into the relatively soft metal of the primer on the cartridge case, revealing the minute distortions of the firing pin. These imperfections may be sufficiently random to individualize the pin impression to a single weapon. Similarly, the cartridge case, in its rearward thrust, is impressed with the surface markings of the breechface. The breechface, like any machined surface, is populated with random striation markings that become a highly distinctive signature for individualizing its surface.

Other distinctive markings that may appear on the shell as a result of metal-to-metal contact are caused by the **extractor** and **ejector** mechanism and the magazine or clip, as well as by imperfections on the firing chamber walls. The photomicrographs in Figure 16–10 reveal a comparison of the firing pin and breechface impressions on evidence and test-fired shells.

(a)　　　　　　　　　　　　　　(b)

FIGURE 16–10 Comparison microscope photomicrograph showing a match between (a) firing pin impressions and (b) the breechface markings on two shells. *Courtesy Ronald Welsh, Bureau of Forensic Services, Central Valley Laboratory, Ripon, Calif.*

Firing pin, breechface, extractor, and ejector marks may also be impressed onto the surface of the brass portion of shells fired by a shotgun. These impressions provide points for individualizing the shell to a weapon that are just as valuable as cartridge cases discharged from a rifled firearm. Furthermore, in the absence of a suspect weapon, the size and shape of a firing pin impression and/or the position of ejector marks in relationship to extractor and other markings may provide some clue to the type or make of the weapon that fired the questioned shell, or at least eliminate a large number of possibilities.

MyCrimeKit: WebExtra 16.3
View 3-D Revolver Cartridge Illustrations
www.mycrimekit.com

Quick Review

- The manufacture of a gun barrel requires impressing its inner surface with spiral grooves, a step known as rifling. Rifling imparts spin to the projectile when it is fired, which keeps it on an accurate course.

- No two rifled barrels have identical striation markings. These striations form the individual characteristics of the barrel. The inner surface of the barrel of a gun leaves its striation markings on a bullet passing through it.

- The class characteristics of a rifled barrel include the number of lands and grooves and the width and direction of twist.

- The comparison microscope is a firearms examiner's most important tool because it allows two bullets to be observed and compared simultaneously.

- The firing pin, breechface, and ejector and extractor mechanism also offer a highly distinctive signature for individualization of cartridge cases.

- Unlike handguns, a shotgun is not rifled—it has a smooth barrel. Because of this, shotgun shells are not impressed with any characteristic markings that can be used to compare two shotgun shells to determine whether they were fired from the same weapon.

MyCrimeKit: WebExtra 16.4

3-D Pistol Cartridge Illustrations
www.mycrimekit.com

MyCrimeKit: WebExtra 16.5

3-D Rifle Cartridge Illustrations
www.mycrimekit.com

MyCrimeKit: WebExtra 16.6

View Animations that Illustrate the Firing Process and the Extraction/Ejection Process of a Semiautomatic Pistol
www.mycrimekit.com

Automated Firearms Search Systems

The use of firearms, especially semiautomatic weapons, during the commission of a crime has significantly increased throughout the United States. Because of the expense of such firearms, the likelihood that a specific weapon will be used in multiple crimes has risen. The advent of computerized imaging technology has made possible the storage of bullet and cartridge surface characteristics in a manner analogous to the storage of automated fingerprint files. Using this concept, crime laboratories can be networked, allowing them to share information on bullets and cartridges retrieved from several jurisdictions.

Early Systems

The effort to build a national computerized database for firearms evidence in the United States had a rather confusing and inefficient start in the early 1990s. Two major federal law enforcement agencies, the FBI and the Bureau of Alcohol, Tobacco, Firearms and Explosives (ATF), offered the law enforcement community competing and incompatible computerized systems.

The automated search system developed for the FBI was known as DRUG-FIRE. This system emphasized the examination of unique markings on the cartridge casings expended by the weapon. The specimen was analyzed through a microscope attached to a video camera. The magnification allowed for a close-up view to identify individual characteristics. The image was captured by a video camera, digitized, and stored in a database. Although DRUGFIRE emphasized cartridge-case imagery, the images of highly characteristic bullet striations could also be stored in a like manner for comparisons.

The *Integrated Ballistic Identification System (IBIS)*, developed for the Bureau of Alcohol, Tobacco, Firearms and Explosives, processed digital microscopic images of identifying features found on both expended bullets and cartridge casings. IBIS incorporated two software programs: Bulletproof, a bullet-analyzing module, and Brasscatcher, a cartridge-case-analyzing module. A schematic diagram of Bulletproof's operation is depicted in Figure 16–11.[2]

FIGURE 16–11   Bulletproof configuration. The sample is mounted on the specimen manipulator and illuminated by the light source from a microscope. The image is captured by a video camera and digitized. The digital image is then stored in a database, available for retrieval and com parison. The search for a match includes analyzing the width of land and groove impressions along with both rifling and individual characteristics. The Brasscatcher software uses the same system configuration but emphasizes the analysis of expended cartridge casings rather than the expended bullets. *Courtesy Forensic Technology (WAI) Inc., Côte Quebec, Canada*

NIBIN In 1999, members of the FBI and ATF joined forces to introduce the *National Integrated Ballistics Information Network (NIBIN)* program to the discipline of firearms examination. The new unified system incorporates both DRUGFIRE and IBIS technologies available in prior years. ATF has overall responsibility for the system sites, whereas the FBI is responsible for the communications network.

Agencies using the new NIBIN technology produce database files from bullets and cartridge casings retrieved from crime scenes or test fires from retrieved firearms. More than two hundred law enforcement agencies worldwide have adapted to this technology. The success of the system has been proven with more than 800,000 images compiled; nationwide, law enforcement agencies have connected more than 28,000 bullets and casings to more than one crime (see Figure 16–12).

FIGURE 16–12
Bullets A, B, C, and D were acquired in the IBIS database at different times from different crime scenes. D is a fragmented bullet that had only three land impressions available for acquisition. Upon the entry of bullet D, IBIS found a potential matching candidate in the database: B. On the far right, bullet D is compared to bullet B using IBIS imaging software. Finally, a forensic firearms examiner using the actual evidence under a conventional comparison microscope will confirm the match between B and D. *Courtesy Forensic Technology (WAI) Inc., Côte St-luc, Quebec, Canada*

For example, in a recent case, a Houston security guard was shot and killed during a botched armed robbery. A bullet and .40-caliber Smith & Wesson cartridge casing were recovered and imaged into NIBIN. Earlier that day, a robbery-turned-double-homicide left two store clerks dead. Again, two bullets and two .40-caliber Smith & Wesson cartridge casings were recovered. Once they were processed into NIBIN, a correlation was found with the murder of the security officer and a separate aggravated robbery that occurred two weeks earlier. All three crimes were linked with a firearm believed to be a .40-caliber Smith & Wesson pistol.

Further investigation into the use of a victim's credit card helped police locate two suspects. In the possession of one suspect was a .40-caliber Smith & Wesson pistol. The gun was test-fired and imaged into NIBIN. The casing from the test-fired weapon matched the evidence obtained in the robbery and the aggravated robbery-homicides. A firearms examiner verified the associations by traditional comparisons. Before this computerized technology was developed, it would have taken years, or may have been impossible, to link all of these shootings to a single firearm.

In another example, the ATF laboratory in Rockville, Maryland, received 1,466 cartridge casings from the Ovcara mass burial site in Bosnia. After processing and imaging profiles for all casings, the examiners determined that 18 different firearms were used at the site. With the help of NIBIN technology and competent examiners, jurists were able to try and convict an individual for war crimes.

NIBIN serves only as a screening tool for firearms evidence. A computerized system does not replace the skills of the firearms examiner. NIBIN can screen hundreds of unsolved firearms cases and may narrow the possibilities to several firearms. However, the final comparison will be made by a forensic examiner through traditional microscopic methods.

Ballistic Fingerprinting

Participating crime laboratories in the United States are building databases of bullet and cartridge cases found at crime scenes and those fired in tests of guns seized from criminals. As these databases come online and prove their usefulness in solving crimes, law enforcement officials and the political community are scrutinizing the feasibility of scaling this concept up to create a system of *ballistic fingerprinting*. This system would entail the capture and storage of appropriate markings on bullets and cartridges test-fired from handguns and rifles before they are sold to the public. Questions regarding who will be responsible for collecting the images and details of how will they be stored are but two of many issues to be determined. The concept of ballistic fingerprinting is an intriguing one for the law enforcement community and promises to be explored and debated intensely in the future.

Quick Review
- The advent of computerized imaging technology has made possible the storage of bullet and cartridge surface characteristics in a manner analogous to automated fingerprint files.

- Two automated firearms search systems are DRUGFIRE, developed by the FBI, and IBIS, developed by the ATF.

- NIBIN is the National Integrated Ballistics Information Network, a unified firearms search system that incorporates both DRUGFIRE and IBIS technologies.

Gunpowder Residues

Modern ammunition is propelled toward a target by the expanding gases created by the ignition of smokeless powder or nitrocellulose in a cartridge. Under ideal circumstances, all of the powder is consumed in the process and converted into the rapidly expanding gases. However, in practice the powder is never totally burned. When a firearm is discharged, unburned and partially burned particles of gunpowder in addition to smoke are propelled out of the barrel along with the bullet toward the target. If the muzzle of the weapon is sufficiently close, these products are deposited onto the target. The distribution of gunpowder particles and other discharge residues around the bullet hole permits a **distance determination**, an assessment of the distance from which a handgun or rifle was fired.

Distance Determination

In incidents involving gunshot wounds, it is often necessary to determine the distance from which the weapon was fired. For example, in incidents involving a shooting death, the suspect often pleads self-defense as the motive for the attack. Such claims are fertile grounds for distance determinations, because finding the proximity of the people involved is necessary to establish the facts of the incident. Similarly, careful examination of the wounds of suicide victims usually reveals characteristics associated with a very close-range gunshot wound. The absence of such characteristics strongly indicates that the wound was not self-inflicted and signals the possibility of foul play.

The accuracy of a distance determination varies according to the circumstances of the case. When the investigator is unable to recover a suspect weapon, the best that the examiner can do is to state whether a shot could have been fired within some distance from the target. More exact opinions are possible only when the examiner has the suspect weapon in hand and has knowledge of the type of ammunition used in the shooting.

Handguns and Rifles The precise distance from which a handgun or rifle has been fired must be determined by carefully comparing the powder residue pattern on the victim's clothing or skin to test patterns made when the suspect weapon is fired at varying distances from a target. A white cloth or a fabric comparable to the victim's clothing may be used as a test target (see Figure 16–13). Because the spread and density of the residue pattern vary widely between weapons and ammunition, such a comparison is significant only when it is made with the suspect weapon and suspect ammunition, or with ammunition of the same type and make. By comparing the test and evidence patterns, the examiner may find enough similarity in shape and density on which to judge the distance from which the shot was fired.

Without the weapon, the examiner is restricted to looking for recognizable characteristics around the bullet hole. Such findings are at best approximations made as a result of general observations and the examiner's experience. However, some noticeable characteristics should be sought. For instance, when the weapon is held in contact with or less than 1 inch from the target, a heavy concentration of smokelike vaporous lead usually surrounds the bullet entrance hole. Often

distance determination
The process of determining the distance between the firearm and a target, usually based on the distribution of powder patterns or the spread of a shot pattern

FIGURE 16–13
Test powder patterns made with a Glock 9mm luger fired at the following distances: (a) contact, (b) 6 inches, (c) 12 inches, and (d) 18 inches. *Courtesy Michelle D. Miranda, MS, D-ABC*

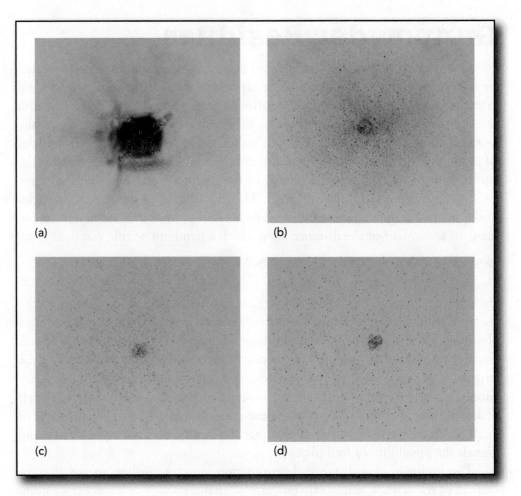

loose fibers surrounding a contact hole show scorch marks from the flame discharge of the weapon, and some synthetic fibers may show signs of being melted as a result of the heat from the discharge. Furthermore, the blowback of muzzle gases may produce a stellate (star-shaped) tear pattern around the hole. Such a hole is invariably surrounded by a rim of a smokelike deposit of vaporous lead (see Figure 16–14).

FIGURE 16–14
A contact shot.
Courtesy Michelle D.
Miranda, MS, D-ABC

A halo of vaporous lead (smoke) deposited around a bullet hole normally indicates a discharge 12–18 inches or less from the target. The presence of scattered specks of unburned and partially burned powder grains without any accompanying soot can often be observed at distances up to approximately 25 inches. Occasionally, however, scattered gunpowder particles are noted at a firing distance as far out as 36 inches. With ball powder ammunition, this distance may be extended to 6–8 feet.

Finally, a weapon that has been fired more than 3 feet from a target usually does not deposit any powder residues on the target's surface. In these cases, the only visual indication that the hole was made by a bullet is a dark ring, known as bullet wipe, around the perimeter of the entrance hole. Bullet wipe consists of a mixture of carbon, dirt, lubricant, primer residue, and lead wiped off the bullet's surface as it passes through the target. Again, in the absence of a suspect weapon, these observations are general guidelines for estimating target distances. Numerous factors—barrel length, caliber, type of ammunition, and type and condition of the weapon fired—influence the amount of gunpowder residue deposited on a target.

Shotguns The determination of firing distances involving shotguns must also be related to test firings performed with the suspect weapon, using the same type of ammunition known to be used in the crime. In the absence of a weapon, the muzzle-to-target distance can be estimated by measuring the spread of the discharged shot. With close-range shots varying in distance up to 4–5 feet, the shot charge enters the target as a concentrated mass, producing a hole somewhat larger than the bore of the barrel. As the distance increases, the pellets progressively separate and spread out. Generally speaking, the spread in the pattern made by a 12-gauge shotgun increases 1 inch for each yard of distance. Thus, a 10-inch pattern would be produced at approximately 10 yards.

Of course, this is only a rule of thumb; normally, many variables can affect the shot pattern. Other factors include the barrel length, the size and quantity of the pellets fired, the quantity of powder charge used to propel the pellets, and the choke of the gun under examination. **Choke** is the degree of constriction placed at the muzzle end of the barrel. The greater the choke, the narrower the shotgun pattern and the faster and farther the pellets will travel.

choke
An interior constriction placed at or near the muzzle end of a shotgun's barrel to control shot dispersion

Powder Residues on Garments

When garments or other evidence relevant to a shooting are received in the crime laboratory, the surfaces of all items are first examined microscopically for gunpowder residue. These particles may be identifiable by their characteristic colors, sizes, and shapes. However, the absence of visual indications does not preclude the possibility that gunpowder residue is present. Sometimes the lack of color contrast between the powder and garment or the presence of heavily encrusted deposits of blood can obscure the visual detection of gunpowder. Often, an infrared photograph of the suspect area overcomes the problem. Such a photograph may enhance the contrast, thus revealing vaporous lead and powder particles deposited around the hole (see Figure 16–15). In other situations, this may not help, and the analyst must use chemical tests to detect gunpowder residues.

FIGURE 16–15
(a) A shirt bearing a powder stain, photographed under normal light.
(b) Infrared photograph of the same shirt.

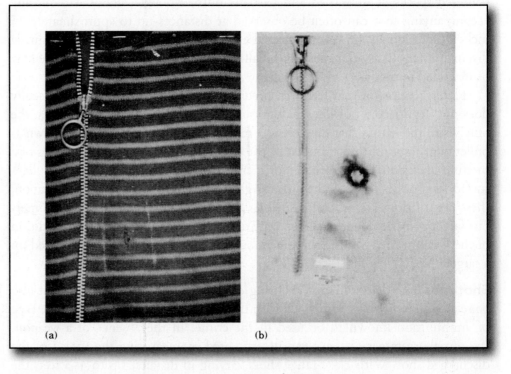

(a)   (b)

Greiss test
A chemical test used to develop patterns of gunpowder residues around bullet holes

Nitrites are one type of chemical product that results from the incomplete combustion of smokeless (nitrocellulose) powder. One test method for locating powder residues involves transferring particles embedded on the target surface to chemically treated gelatin-coated photographic paper. This procedure is known as **the Greiss test.** The examiner presses the photographic paper onto the target with a hot iron; once the nitrite particles are on the paper, they are made easily visible by chemical treatment.[3] In addition, comparing the developed nitrite pattern to nitrite patterns obtained from test firings at known distances can be useful in determining the shooting distance from the target. A second chemical test is then performed to detect any trace of lead residue around the bullet hole. The questioned surface is sprayed with a solution of sodium rhodizonate, followed by a series of oversprays with acid solutions. This treatment turns lead particles pink, followed by blue-violet.

Quick Review

- The distribution of gunpowder particles and other discharge residues around a bullet hole permits an assessment of the distance from which a handgun or rifle was fired.

- The precise distance is determined by carefully comparing the powder residue pattern on the victim's clothing to test patterns made when the suspect weapon is fired at varying distances from a target.

- The Greiss test is a chemical test used to develop patterns of gunpowder residues around bullet holes. It tests for the presence of nitrates.

Primer Residues on the Hands

The firing of a weapon not only propels residues toward the target, but also blows gunpowder and primer residues back toward the shooter (see Figure 16–16). As a result, traces of these residues are often deposited on the firing hand of the shooter, and their detection can provide valuable information as to whether an individual has recently fired a weapon.

FIGURE 16–16
When a handgun is fired, gunpowder and primer residues are normally blown back toward the hand of the shooter. *Courtesy Centre of Forensic Sciences, Toronto, Canada*

Detecting Primer Residues

Early efforts at demonstrating powder residues on the hands centered on chemical tests that could detect unburned gunpowder or nitrates. For many years, the *dermal nitrate test* was popular. It required the application of hot paraffin or wax to the suspect's hand with a paintbrush. After drying into a solid crust, the paraffin was removed and tested with diphenylamine. A blue color indicated a positive reaction for nitrates. However, the dermal nitrate test has fallen into disfavor with law enforcement agencies, owing mainly to its lack of specificity. Common materials such as fertilizers, cosmetics, urine, and tobacco all give positive reactions that are indistinguishable from that obtained for gunpowder by this test.

Efforts to identify a shooter now center on the detection of primer residues deposited on the hand of a shooter at the time of firing. With the exception of most .22-caliber ammunition, primers currently manufactured contain a blend of lead styphnate, barium nitrate, and antimony sulfide. Residues from these materials are most likely to be deposited on the thumb web and the back of the firing hand of a shooter, because these areas are closest to gases escaping along the side or back of the gun during discharge. In addition, individuals who handle a gun without firing it may have primer residues deposited on the palm of the hand coming in contact with the weapon.

However, with the handling of a used firearm, the passage of time, and the resumption of normal activities following a shooting, gunshot residues from the back of the hand are frequently redistributed to other areas, including the palms. Therefore, it is not unusual to find higher levels of barium and antimony on the palms than on the backs of the hands of known shooters. Another possibility is the deposition of significant levels of barium and antimony on the hands of an individual who is near a firearm when it is discharged.

Tests for Primer Residues

Determination of whether a person has fired or handled a weapon or has been near a discharged firearm is normally made by measuring the presence and possibly the amount of barium and antimony on the relevant portions of the suspect's hands. A variety of materials and techniques are used for removing these residues. The most popular approach, and certainly the most convenient for the field investigator, is to apply an adhesive tape or adhesive to the hand's surface in order to remove any adhering residue particles.

Swabbing Another approach is to remove any residues present by swabbing both the firing and nonfiring hands with cotton that has been moistened with 5 percent nitric acid. The front and back of each hand are separately swabbed. All four swabs, along with a moistened control, are then forwarded to the crime laboratory for analysis.

In any case, once the hands are treated for the collection of barium and antimony, the collection medium must be analyzed for the presence of these elements. High barium and antimony levels on the suspect's hand(s) strongly indicate that the person fired or handled a weapon or was near a firearm when it was discharged. Because these elements are normally present in small quantities (less than 10 micrograms) after a firing, only the most sensitive analytical techniques can be used to detect them.

Unfortunately, even though most specimens submitted for this type of analysis have been from individuals strongly suspected of having fired a gun, there has been a low rate of positive findings. The major difficulty appears to be the short time that primer residues remain on the hands. These residues are readily removed by intentional or unintentional washing, rubbing, or wiping of the hands. In fact, one study demonstrated that it is difficult to detect primer residues on cotton hand swabs taken as soon as two hours after firing a weapon.[4] Hence, some laboratories do not accept cotton hand swabs taken from living people six or more hours after a firing has occurred.

In cases that involve suicide victims, a higher rate of positives for the presence of gunshot residue is obtained when the hand swabbing is conducted before the person's body is moved or when the hands are protected by paper bags.[5] However, hand swabbing or the application of an adhesive cannot be used to detect firings with most .22-caliber rim-fire ammunition. Such ammunition may contain only barium or neither barium nor antimony in its primer composition.

SEM Testing Most laboratories that can detect gunshot residue require application of an adhesive to the shooter's hands.[6] Microscopic primer and gunpowder particles on the adhesive are then found with a scanning electron microscope (SEM). The characteristic size and shape of these particles distinguishes them from other contaminants on the hands (see Figure 16–17). When the SEM is linked to an X-ray analyzer, an elemental analysis of the particles can be conducted. A finding of a select combination of elements (lead, barium, and antimony) confirms that the particles were indeed primer residue (see Figure 16–18).

2500X   10μm

FIGURE 16–17
An SEM view of gunshot residue particles.
Courtesy Jeol USA, Inc., Peabody, Mass., www.jeolusa.com

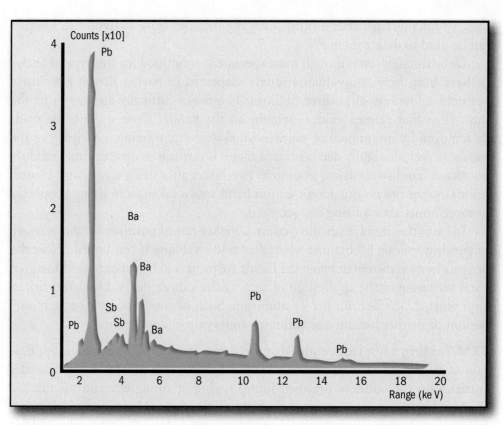

The major advantage of the SEM approach for primer residue detection is its enhanced specificity over hand swabbing. The SEM characterizes primer particles by their size and shape as well as by their chemical composition. Unfortunately, the excessive operator time required to find and characterize gunshot residue has deterred this technique's use. The availability of automated particle search and identification systems for use with scanning electron microscopes may overcome this problem. Results of work performed with automated systems show it to be significantly faster than a manual approach for finding gunshot residue particles.[7]

Other Primer Residue Tests Neutron activation analysis and flameless atomic absorption spectrophotometry are analytical methods sensitive enough to detect barium and antimony in gunshot residues in hand swabs. However, the need for access to a neutron source, expensive counting equipment, and extensive regulatory requirements limit neutron activation analysis technology to a small number of crime laboratories. On the other hand, flameless atomic absorption spectrophotometry can be purchased at a cost well within the budgets of most crime laboratories, and a number of laboratories use this instrument to detect barium and antimony on a shooter's hands.

Inside the Science

Atomic Absorption Spectrophotometry

When an atom is vaporized, it absorbs many of the same frequencies of light that it emits in an excited state. Selective absorption of light by atoms is the basis for a technique known as *atomic absorption spectrophotometry*. A simple atomic absorption spectrophotometer is illustrated in <u>the figure</u>.

Parts of a simple flame atomic absorption spectrophotometer.

In atomic absorption spectrophotometry, the specimen is heated to a temperature that is hot enough to vaporize its atoms while leaving a substantial number of atoms in an unexcited state. Normally the specimen is inserted into an air-acetylene flame to achieve this temperature. The vaporized atoms are then exposed to radiation emitted from a light source. The technique achieves great specificity by using as its radiation source a discharge tube made of the same element being analyzed in the specimen.

When the discharge lamp is turned on, it emits only the frequencies of light that are present in the emission spectrum of the element. Likewise, the sample absorbs these frequencies only when it contains the same element. Therefore, to determine the presence of antimony in a specimen, the atomic absorption spectrophotometer must be fitted with a discharge lamp that is constructed of antimony. Under these conditions, the sample absorbs light only if it contains antimony.

Once the radiation has passed through the sample, a monochromator, consisting of a prism or a diffraction grating and a slit, isolates the desired radiation frequency and transmits it to a detector. The detector converts

Inside the Science (CONTINUED)

the light into an electrical signal, the intensity of which is recorded on a strip-chart recorder.

Atomic absorption spectrophotometry measures the absorption of light by the element of interest. The concentration of the absorbing element is directly proportional to the quantity of the light absorbed. The higher the concentration of the element, the more light is absorbed. For this reason, atomic absorption spectroscopy is most useful for accurately determining an element's concentration in a sample. Furthermore, the technique is sufficiently sensitive to find wide application in detecting and quantitating elements that are present in trace levels. However, one drawback is that the analyst can determine only one element at a time, each time having to select the proper lamp to match the element under investigation.

Although atomic absorption spectrophotometry has been used for chemical analysis since 1955, it has not yet found wide application for solving forensic problems. However, a modification in the design of the instrument may change this situation. By substituting a heated graphite furnace or a heated strip of metal (tantalum) for the flame, analysts have achieved a more efficient means of atomic volatilization and as a result have substantially increased the sensitivity of the technique. Many elements can now be detected at levels that approach one-trillionth of a gram.

The high sensitivity of "flameless" atomic absorption now equals or surpasses that of most known analytical procedures. Considering the relative simplicity and low cost of the technique, atomic absorption spectrophotometry has become an attractive method for detecting and measuring the smallest levels of trace elements in physical evidence.

As far as atoms are concerned, energy is a two-way street. Energy can be put into the atom at the same time that energy is given off; what goes in must come out. The chemist can study the atom using either approach. Atomic absorption spectrophotometry carefully measures the value and amount of light energy going into the atom; emission spectroscopy collects and measures the various light energies given off. The result is the same: atoms are identified by the existence of characteristic energy levels.

Quick Review

- Firing a weapon propels residues toward the target and blows gunpowder and primer residues back toward the shooter. Traces of these residues are often deposited on the firing hand of the shooter, providing valuable information as to whether an individual has recently fired a weapon.

- Examiners measure the amount of barium and antimony on the relevant portion of the suspect's hands or characterize the morphology of particles containing these elements to determine whether a person has fired or handled a weapon or was near a discharged firearm.

Serial Number Restoration

Today, many manufactured items, including automobile engine blocks and firearms, are impressed with a serial number for identification. Increasingly the criminalist must restore such a number when it has been removed or obliterated by grinding, rifling, or punching.

Serial numbers are usually stamped on a metal body or frame, or on a plate, with hard steel dies. These dies strike the metal surface with a force that allows each digit to sink into the metal at a prescribed depth. Serial numbers can be restored because the metal crystals in the stamped zone are placed under a permanent strain that extends a short distance beneath the original numbers. When a suitable etching agent is applied, the strained area dissolves faster than the unaltered metal, thus revealing the etched pattern in the form of the original numbers (see Figure 16–19). However, if the zone of strain has been removed, or if the area has been impressed with a different strain pattern, the number usually cannot be restored.

FIGURE 16–19
Obliterated or altered serial numbers on firearms can be restored by analysts using chemical means. *Courtesy Federal Bureau of Investigation*

Before any treatment with the etching reagent, the obliterated surface must be thoroughly cleaned of dirt and oil and polished to a mirrorlike finish. The reagent is swabbed onto the surface with a cotton ball. The choice of etching reagent depends on the type of metal surface being worked on. A solution of hydrochloric acid (120 milliliters), copper chloride (90 grams), and water (100 milliliters) generally works well for steel surfaces.

Collection and Preservation of Firearms Evidence

Firearms

The Hollywood image of an investigator picking up a weapon by its barrel with a pencil or stick in order to protect fingerprints must be avoided. This practice only disturbs powder deposits, rust, or dirt lodged in the barrel, and consequently may alter the striation markings on test-fired bullets. If recovery of latent fingerprints is a primary concern, hold the weapon by the edge of the trigger guard or by the checkered portion of the grip, which usually does not retain identifiable fingerprints.

The most important consideration in handling a weapon is safety. Before any weapon is sent to the laboratory, all precautions must be taken to prevent an accidental discharge of a loaded weapon in transit. In most cases, it will be necessary to unload the weapon. If this is done, a record should first be made of the weapon's hammer and safety position; likewise, the location of all fired and unfired ammunition in the weapon must be recorded.

When a revolver is recovered, the chamber position in line with the barrel should be indicated by a scratch mark on the cylinder. Each chamber is designated with a number on a diagram, and as each cartridge or casing is removed, it should be marked to correspond to the numbered chambers in the diagram. Knowledge of the cylinder position of a cartridge casing may be useful for later determination of the sequence of events, particularly in shooting cases, when more than one shot was fired. Place each round in a separate box or envelope. If the weapon is an automatic, the magazine must be removed and checked for prints and the chamber then emptied.

As with any other type of physical evidence recovered at a crime scene, firearms evidence must be marked for identification and a chain of custody must be established. Therefore, when a firearm is recovered, an identification tag should be attached to the trigger guard. The tag should be marked to show appropriate identifying data, including the weapon's serial number, make, and model and the investigator's initials. The firearm itself may be further identified by being marked directly with a sharp-pointed scriber in an inconspicuous area of the weapon—for example, the inside of the trigger guard. This practice will avoid any permanent defacement of the weapon.

When a weapon is recovered from an underwater location, no effort must be made to dry or clean it. Instead, the firearm should be transported to the laboratory in a receptacle containing enough of the same water necessary to keep it submerged. This procedure prevents rust from developing during transport.

Ammunition

Protection of class and individual markings on bullets and cartridge cases must be the primary concern of the field investigator. Thus, extreme caution is needed when removing a lodged bullet from a wall or other object. If the bullet's surface is accidentally scratched during this operation, valuable striation markings could be obliterated. It is best to free bullets from their target by carefully breaking away the surrounding support material while avoiding direct contact with the projectile.

Bullets recovered at the crime scene should be scribed with the investigator's initials, on either the base or the nose of the bullet (see Figure 16–20). Again, obliteration of any striation markings on the bullet must be scrupulously avoided. If the bullet is badly deformed and there is no apparent place for identification, it should just be placed in a container that is appropriately marked for identification. In any case, the investigator must protect the bullet by wrapping it in tissue paper before placing it in a pillbox or an envelope for shipment to the crime laboratory.

FIGURE 16–20
Discharged evidence bullets should be marked on the base or nose. When there is more than one bullet, a number should accompany the initials. *Never* mark bullets on the side.

Minute traces of evidence such as paint and fibers may be adhering to the bullet; the investigator must take care to leave these trace materials intact. Similarly, a fired casing must be identified so as to avoid destroying marks impressed on it from the weapon. The investigator's initials should be placed near the outside or inside mouth of the shell (see Figure 16–21). Discharged shells from shotguns are initialed with ink or indelible pencil on the paper or plastic tube remaining on the shell or on the metal nearest the mouth of the shell. In incidents involving shotguns, any wads recovered should also be packaged and sent to the laboratory. An examination of the size and composition of the wad may reveal information about the type of ammunition used and the gauge of the shotgun.

FIGURE 16–21
Discharged evidence shells should be marked on the outside or inside, as close as possible to the mouth of the shell. Discharged shotgun shells should be marked on the brass, close to the paper or plastic. *Never* mark the shells where the firing pin strikes the primer.

When semiautomatic or automatic weapons have been fired, the ejection pattern of the casings can help establish the relationship of the suspect to his or her victim. For this reason, the investigator must note the exact location where a shell casing was recovered.

Gunpowder Deposits

The clothing of a firearms victim must be carefully preserved to prevent damage or disruption to powder residues deposited around a bullet or shell hole. Cutting or tearing of clothing in the area of the holes must be avoided when removing the clothing. All wet clothing should be air-dried out of direct sunlight and then folded carefully so as not to disrupt the area around the bullet hole. Each item should be placed in a separate paper bag.

> **Quick Review**
>
> - Criminalists can restore serial numbers removed or obliterated by grinding, rifling, or punching.
>
> - Because the metal crystals in the stamped zone are placed under a permanent strain that extends a short distance beneath the original numbers, the serial number can be restored through chemical etching.
>
> - A suspect firearm should never be picked up by inserting an object into its barrel because this practice may alter the striation markings on test-fired bullets.
>
> - Before unloading a suspect weapon, the weapon's hammer and safety position should be recorded, as well as the location of all fired and unfired ammunition in the weapon.
>
> - Protection of class and individual markings on bullets and cartridge cases is the primary concern of the field investigator when recovering bullets and cartridge casings.

Tool Marks

A tool mark is any impression, cut, gouge, or abrasion caused by a tool coming into contact with another object. Most often, tool marks are encountered at burglary scenes that involve forcible entry into a building or safe. Generally, these marks occur as indented impressions into a softer surface or as abrasion marks caused by the tool cutting or sliding against another object.

Comparing Tool Marks

Typically, an indented impression is left on the frame of a door or window as a result of the prying action of a screwdriver or crowbar. Careful examination of these impressions can reveal important class characteristics—that is, the size and shape of the tool. However, they rarely reveal any significant individual characteristics that could permit the examiner to individualize the mark to a single tool. Such characteristics, when they do exist, usually take the form of discernible random nicks and breaks that the tool has acquired through wear and use (Figure 16–22).

FIGURE 16–22
A comparison of a tool mark with a suspect screwdriver. Note how the presence of nicks and breaks on the tool's edge helps individualize the tool to the mark.

Just as the machined surfaces of a firearm are impressed with random striations during its manufacture, the edges of a pry bar, chisel, screwdriver, knife, or cutting tool likewise display a series of microscopic irregularities that look like ridges and valleys. Such markings are left as a result of the machining processes used to cut and finish tools. The shape and pattern of such minute imperfections are further modified by damage and wear during the life of the tool. Considering the variety of patterns that the hills and valleys can assume, it is highly unlikely that any two tools will be identical. Hence, these minute imperfections impart individuality to each tool.

If the edge of a tool is scraped against a softer surface, it may cut a series of striated lines that reflect the pattern of the tool's edge. Markings left in this manner are compared in the laboratory through a comparison microscope with test tool marks made from the suspect tool. The result can be a positive comparison, and hence a definitive association of the tool with the evidence mark, when a sufficient quantity of striations match between the evidence and test markings.

A major problem of tool mark comparisons is the difficulty in duplicating in the laboratory the tool mark left at the crime scene. A thorough comparison requires preparing a series of test marks by applying the suspect tool at various angles and pressures to a soft metal surface (lead is commonly used). This approach gives the examiner ample opportunity to duplicate many of the details of the original evidence marking. A photomicrograph of a typical tool mark comparison is illustrated in Figure 16–23.

Collecting Tool Mark Evidence

Whenever practical, the entire object or the part of the object bearing a tool mark should be submitted to the crime laboratory for examination. When removal of the tool mark is impractical, the only recourse is to photograph the marked area to scale and make a cast of the mark. Liquid silicone casting material is best for reproducing most of the fine details of the mark (see Figure 16–24). However, even under the best conditions, the clarity of many of the tool mark's minute details will be lost or obscured in a photograph or cast. Of course, this will reduce the chance of individualizing the mark to a single tool.

The crime-scene investigator must never attempt to fit the suspect tool into the tool mark. Any contact between the tool and the marked surface may alter the mark and will, at the least, raise serious questions about the integrity of the evidence. The suspect tool and mark must be packaged in separate containers, with every precaution taken to avoid contact between the tool or mark and another hard surface. Failure to protect the tool or mark from damage could result in the destruction of its individual characteristics.

Furthermore, the tool or its impression may contain valuable trace evidence. Chips of paint adhering to the mark or tool provide perhaps the best example of how the transfer of trace physical evidence can occur as a result of using a tool to gain forcible entry into a building. Obviously, the presence of trace evidence greatly enhances the evidential value of the tool or its mark and requires special care in handling and packaging the evidence to avoid losing or destroying these items.

(a) (b)

FIGURE 16–24 (a) Casting a tool mark impression with a silicone-based putty. (b) Impression alongside suspect tool. *Courtesy Sirchie Finger Print Laboratories, Inc., Youngsville, N.C., www.sirchie.com*

Quick Review

- The presence of minute imperfections on a tool imparts individuality to that tool. The shape and pattern of such imperfections are further modified by damage and wear during the life of the tool.

- The comparison microscope is used to compare crime-scene tool marks with test impressions made with the suspect tool.

Other Impressions

From time to time, other types of impressions are left at a crime scene. This evidence may take the form of a shoe, tire, or fabric impression. It may be as varied as a shoe impression left on a piece of paper at the scene of a burglary (Figure 16–25), a hit-and-run victim's garment that has come into violent contact with an automobile (Figure 16–26), or the impression of a bloody shoe print left on a floor or carpet at a homicide scene (Figure 16–27).

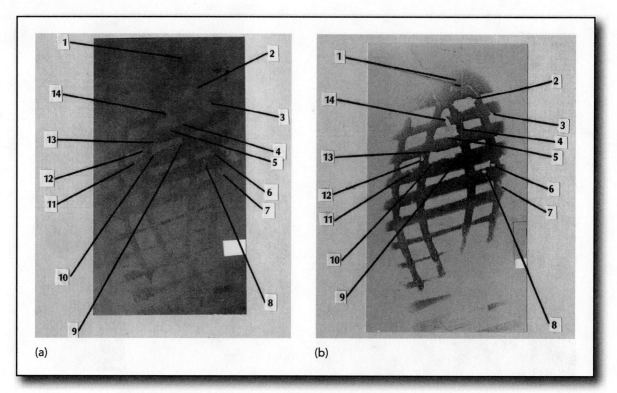

(a)

(b)

FIGURE 16–25 (a) Impression of shoe found at a crime scene. (b) Test impression made with suspect shoe. A sufficient number of points of comparison exist to support the conclusion that the suspect shoe left the impression at the crime scene.

FIGURE 16–26
A small child was found dead at the edge of a rural road near a railroad crossing, the victim of a hit-and-run driver. A local resident was suspected, but he denied any knowledge of the incident. The investigating officer noted what appeared to be a fabric imprint on the bumper of the suspect's automobile. The weave pattern of the clothing of the deceased was compared with the imprint on the bumper and was found to match. When the suspect was confronted with this information, he admitted his guilt.
Courtesy Centre of Forensic Sciences, Toronto, ON, Canada

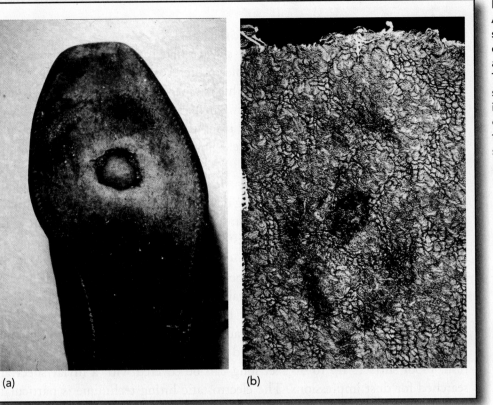

(a)   (b)

FIGURE 16–27
A bloody imprint of a shoe was found on the carpet in the home of a homicide victim. (b) The suspect's shoe, shown in (a), made the impression. Note the distinctive impression of the hole present in the shoe's sole. *Courtesy Dade County Crime Lab, Miami, Fla.*

Preserving Impressions

The primary consideration in collecting impressions at the crime scene is the preservation of the impression or its reproduction for later examination in the crime laboratory. Before any impression is moved or otherwise handled, it must be photographed (a scale should be included in the picture) to show all the observable details of the impression. Several shots should be taken directly over the impression as well as at various angles around the impression. Skillful use of side lighting for illumination will help highlight many ridge details that might otherwise remain obscured. Photographs should also be taken to show the position of the questioned impression in relation to the overall crime scene.

Although photography is an important first step in preserving an impression, it must be considered merely a backup procedure that is available to the examiner if the impression is damaged before reaching the crime laboratory. Naturally, the examiner prefers to receive the original impression for comparison to the suspect shoe, tire, garment, and so forth. In most cases when the impression is on a readily recoverable item, such as glass, paper, or floor tile, the evidence is easily transported intact to the laboratory.

Lifting Impressions

If an impression is encountered on a surface that cannot be submitted to the laboratory, the investigator may be able to preserve the print in a manner that is analogous to lifting a fingerprint. This is especially true of impressions made in light deposits of dust or dirt. A lifting material large enough to lift the entire impression should be used. Carefully place the lifting material over the entire impression. Use a fingerprint roller to eliminate any air pockets before lifting the impression off the surface.

A more exotic approach to lifting and preserving dust impressions involves the use of a portable electrostatic lifting device.[8] The principle is similar to that of creating an electrostatic charge on a comb and using the comb to lift small pieces of tissue paper. A sheet of mylar film is placed on top of the dust mark, and the film is pressed against the impression with the aid of a roller. The high-voltage electrode of the electrostatic unit is then placed in contact with the film while the unit's earth electrodes are placed against a metal plate (earth plate) (see Figure 16–28). A charge difference develops between the mylar film and the surface below the dust mark so that the dust is attached to the lifting film. In this manner, dust prints on chairs, walls, floors, and the like can be transferred to the mylar film. Floor surfaces up to 40 feet long can be covered with a mylar sheet and searched for dust impressions. The electrostatic lifting technique is particularly helpful in recovering barely visible dust prints on colored surfaces. Dust impressions can also be enhanced through chemical development (see Figure 16–29).[9]

FIGURE 16–28
Electrostatic lifting of a dust impression off a floor using an electrostatic unit. *Courtesy Sirchie Finger Print Laboratories, Inc., Youngsville, N.C., www.sirchie.com*

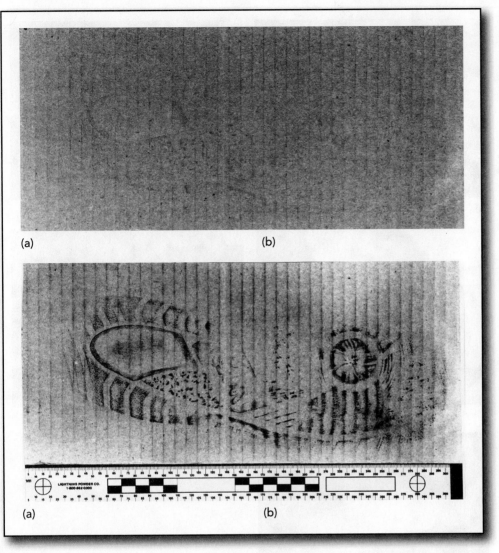

(a)   (b)

(a)   (b)

FIGURE 16–29
(a) A dust impression
     of a shoe print on
     cardboard before
     enhancement.
(b) Shoe print after
     chemical enhancement
     with Bromophenol
     Blue and exposure
     to water vapor.
*Courtesy Division of
Identification and Foren-
sic Science (DIFS), Israel
Police Headquarters,
Jerusalem, Israel*

Casting Impressions

Shoe and tire marks impressed into soft earth at a crime scene are best preserved by photography and casting.[10] Class I dental stone, a form of gypsum, is widely recommended for making casts of shoe and tire impressions. A series of photographs clearly illustrating the steps in casting an impression are found in Figure 16–30. The cast should be allowed to air-dry for 24 to 48 hours before it is shipped to the forensic science laboratory for examination. Figure 16–31 illustrates a cast made from a shoe print in mud. The cast compares to the suspect shoe.

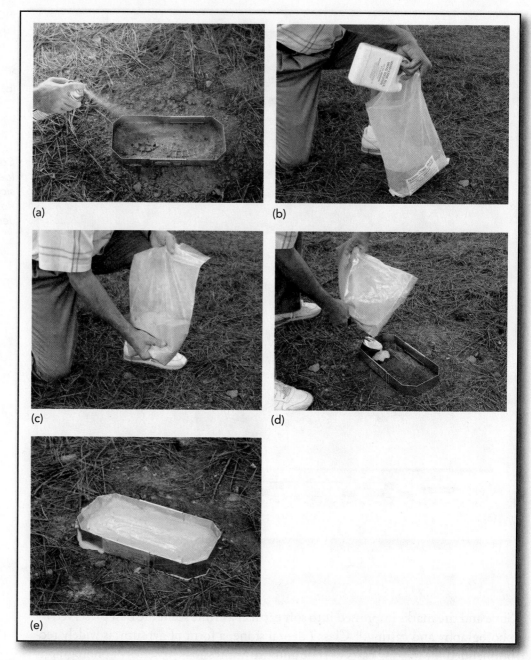

FIGURE 16–30

To cast a footwear impression at a crime scene. (a) The impression is hardened using aerosol hairspray. (b) The correct amount of water is added to a known amount of dental stone. (c) The mixture is kneaded by hand until the desired (pancake batter-like) consistency is reached. (d) The dental stone is poured into the impression using a spoon as a medium to disperse the flow. (e) The impression is filled with dental stone and allowed to dry before removal. *Courtesy Sirchie Finger Print Laboratories, Inc., Youngsville, N.C., www.sirchie.com*

(a)   (b)   (C)

FIGURE 16–31   (a) Shoe impression in mud. (b) Cast of shoe impression. (c) Shoe suspected of leaving muddy impression. *Courtesy Sirchie Finger Print Laboratories, Inc., Youngsville, N.C., www.sirchie.com*

An aerosol product known as Snow Impression Wax is available for casting snow impressions.[11] The recommended procedure is to spray three light coats of the wax at an interval of one to two minutes between layers, and then let it dry for ten minutes. A viscous mixture of Class I dental stone is then poured onto the wax-coated impression. After the casting material has hardened, the cast can be removed.

Several chemicals can be used to develop and enhance footwear impressions made with blood. In areas where a bloody footwear impression is very faint or where the subject has tracked through blood leaving a trail of bloody impressions, chemical enhancement can visualize latent or nearly invisible blood impressions (see Figure 16–32).

Several blood enhancement chemicals have been examined for their impact on STR DNA typing. None of the chemicals examined had a deleterious effect, on a short-term basis, on the ability to carry out STR DNA typing on the blood.[12]

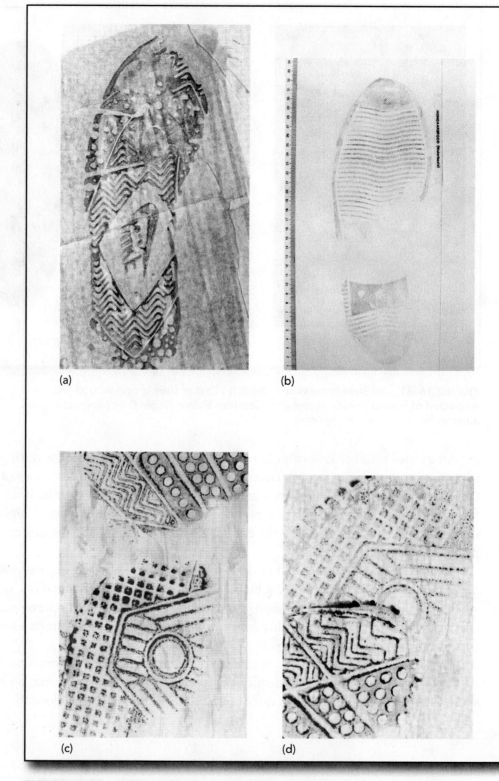

FIGURE 16–32 (a) Bloody footprint on cardboard treated with amido black. (b) Bloody footprint treated with Hungarian Red dye. (c) Bloody footprint visualized with leucocrystal violet. (d) Bloody footprint enhanced with patent blue. (e) Bloody foot impression treated with amido black. (f) Bloody footprint visualized with fushin acid dye. (g) Bloody foot impression visualized with tartrazine. (h) Bloody footprint treated with diaminobenzidine. *(a) Courtesy Dwane S. Hilderbrand and David P. Coy, Scottsdale Police Crime Laboratory, Scottsdale, Ariz. (b) Courtesy ODV Inc., South Paris, Maine. (c-h) Courtesy William Bodziak, FBI Laboratory*

(e)

(f)

(g)

(h)

Comparing Impressions

Whatever the circumstances, the laboratory procedures used to examine any type of impression remain the same. Of course, a comparison is possible only when an item suspected of having made the impression is recovered. Test impressions may be necessary to compare the characteristics of the suspect item with the evidence impression.

The evidential value of the impression is determined by the number of class and individual characteristics that the examiner finds. Agreement with respect to size, shape, or design may permit the conclusion that the impression could have been made by a particular shoe, tire, or garment; however, one cannot entirely exclude other possible sources from having the same class characteristics. More significant is the existence of individual characteristics arising out of wear, cuts, gouges, or other damage. A sufficient number or the uniqueness of such points of comparison support a finding that both the evidence and test impressions originated from one and only one source.

When tire tread impressions are left at a crime scene, the laboratory can examine the design of the impression and possibly determine the style and/or manufacturer of the tire. This may be particularly helpful to investigators when a suspect tire has not yet been located.

New computer software may help the forensic scientist compare shoe prints. For example, an automated shoe print identification system developed in England, called Shoeprint Image Capture and Retrieval (SICAR), incorporates multiple databases to search known and unknown footwear files for comparison against footwear specimens. Using the system, an impression from a crime scene can be compared to a reference database to find out what type of shoe caused the imprint. That same impression can also be searched in the suspect and crime databases to reveal whether that shoe print matches the shoes of a person who has been in custody or the shoe prints left behind at another crime scene. When matches are made during the searching process, the images are displayed side by side on the computer screen (see Figure 3–9).

Human bite mark impressions on skin and foodstuffs have proven to be important items of evidence for convicting defendants in a number of homicide and rape cases in recent years. If a sufficient number of points of similarity between test and suspect marks are present, a forensic odontologist may conclude that a bite mark was made by one particular individual (see Figure 16–33).

FIGURE 16–33
(a) Bite mark impression on the victim's forearm
(b) Upper dental model from the teeth of the suspect matches the individual teeth characteristics of the bite marks.
Courtesy Haskall Askin, D.D.S., Chief Forensic Odontologist, City of Philadelphia, Pa

(a)　　　　　　(b)

Case Files

The O. J. Simpson Trial—Who Left the Impressions at the Crime Scene?

On the night of June 12, 1994, Nicole Brown—ex-wife of football star O. J. Simpson—and her friend Ron Goldman were brutally murdered on the grounds outside her home in Brentwood, California. O. J. Simpson was arrested for their murders, but professed his innocence. At the crime scene, investigators found bloody shoe impressions along the concrete walkway leading up to the front door of Brown's condominium. These shoe impressions were of extremely high quality and of intricate detail. The news media broadcast countless images of these bloody shoe prints on television, making it obvious to the killer that those shoes would surely link him to the crime.

Famed FBI shoe print examiner William J. Bodziak investigated the footwear evidence from the scene. His first task was to identify the brand of shoe that made the marks. Because the pattern was clear and distinct, with complete toe-to-heel detail, this seemed a simple task at first. Bodziak compared this pattern to the thousands of sole patterns in the FBI's database. None matched. He then went to his reference collection of books and trade show brochures, again with no success.

Bodziak's experience told him that these were expensive, Italian-made casual dress shoes with a sole made from synthetic material. Using this knowledge, he shopped the high-end stores for a similar tread pattern, but still was unable to identify the shoes. He then drew a composite sketch of the sole and faxed the image to law enforcement agencies and shoe manufacturers and distributors worldwide. The owner of the American distributing company for Bruno Magli shoes was the only one to respond.

Further exhaustive investigation revealed that these were extremely rare shoes. There were two styles of shoe bearing this exact sole design. They were available for only two years, and from a mere 40 stores in the United States and Puerto Rico. The Lorenzo style shoe had a bootlike upper that came to the ankle. The Lyon style shoe had the lower, more typical dress shoe cut. The impressions were made by a size 12

shoe, and it was later determined that only 299 pairs of size 12 with this tread pattern were sold in the United States.

Simpson flatly denied ever owning these shoes, adding that he would never wear anything so ugly. However, he was known to wear a size 12, and photographs taken almost nine months before the murders show Simpson wearing a pair of black leather Bruno Magli Lorenzo shoes. These shoes were available in several colors, so this narrows the number of shoes matching Simpson's pair of Lorenzos (this size, color, and style) sold in the United States to 29 pairs.

Proving that Simpson owned a pair of shoes that had the exact pattern found printed in blood at the crime scene was an essential component of the case, but it was not done in time to be used during the criminal prosecution. The photographs of Simpson in his Bruno Magli shoes were released after the culmination of the criminal trial, so the jury never heard the direct evidence that Simpson owned these shoes. However, this proved to be an important link uniting Simpson with the crime scene in the civil trial. Although O. J. Simpson was acquitted of the murders of Nicole Brown and Ron Goldman in the criminal trial, he was judged responsible for their murders in the civil court case.

Quick Review

- Shoe and tire marks impressed into soft earth at a crime scene are best preserved by photography and casting.

- The electrostatic lifting technique is particularly helpful in recovering barely visible dust prints on floor surfaces.

- In areas where a bloody footwear impression is very faint or where the subject has tracked through blood, leaving a trail of bloody impressions, chemical enhancement can visualize latent or nearly invisible blood impressions.

Chapter Review

- The manufacture of a gun barrel requires impressing its inner surface with spiral grooves, a step known as rifling. Rifling imparts spin to the projectile when it is fired, which keeps it on an accurate course.

- No two rifled barrels have identical striation markings. These striations form the individual characteristics of the barrel. The inner surface of the barrel of a gun leaves its striation markings on a bullet passing through it.

- The class characteristics of a rifled barrel include the number of lands and grooves and the width and direction of twist.

- The comparison microscope is a firearms examiner's most important tool because it allows two bullets to be observed and compared simultaneously.

- The firing pin, breechblock, and ejector and extractor mechanism also offer a highly distinctive signature for individualization of cartridge cases.

- Unlike handguns, a shotgun is not rifled—it has a smooth barrel. Because of this, shotgun shells are not impressed with any characteristic markings that can be used to compare two shotgun shells to determine whether they were fired from the same weapon.

- The advent of computerized imaging technology has made possible the storage of bullet and cartridge surface characteristics in a manner analogous to automated fingerprint files.

- Two automated firearms search systems are DRUGFIRE, developed by the FBI, and IBIS, developed by the ATF.

- NIBIN is the National Integrated Ballistics Information Network, a unified firearms search system that incorporates both DRUGFIRE and IBIS technologies.

- The distribution of gunpowder particles and other discharge residues around a bullet hole permits an assessment of the distance from which a handgun or rifle was fired.

- The precise distance is determined by carefully comparing the powder residue pattern on the victim's clothing to test patterns made when the suspect weapon is fired at varying distances from a target.

- The Greiss test is a chemical test used to develop patterns of gunpowder residues around bullet holes. It tests for the presence of nitrates.

- Firing a weapon propels residues toward the target and blows gunpowder and primer residues back toward the shooter. Traces of these residues are often deposited on the firing hand of the shooter, providing valuable information as to whether an individual has recently fired a weapon.

- Examiners measure the amount of barium and antimony on the relevant portion of the suspect's hands or characterize the morphology of particles containing these elements to determine whether a person has fired or handled a weapon or was near a discharged firearm.

- Criminalists can restore serial numbers removed or obliterated by grinding, rifling, or punching.

- Because the metal crystals in the stamped zone are placed under a permanent strain that extends a short distance beneath the original numbers, the serial number can be restored through chemical etching.

- A suspect firearm should never be picked up by inserting an object into its barrel because this practice may alter the striation markings on test-fired bullets.

- Before unloading a suspect weapon, the weapon's hammer and safety position should be recorded, as well as the location of all fired and unfired ammunition in the weapon.

- Protection of class and individual markings on bullets and cartridge cases is the primary concern of the field investigator when recovering bullets and cartridge casings.

- The presence of minute imperfections on a tool imparts individuality to that tool. The shape and pattern of such imperfections are further modified by damage and wear during the life of the tool.

- The comparison microscope is used to compare crime-scene tool marks with test impressions made with the suspect tool.

- Shoe and tire marks impressed into soft earth at a crime scene are best preserved by photography and casting.

- The electrostatic lifting technique is particularly helpful in recovering barely visible dust prints on floor surfaces.

- In areas where a bloody footwear impression is very faint or where the subject has tracked through blood, leaving a trail of bloody impressions, chemical enhancement can visualize latent or nearly invisible blood impressions.

Quick Lab: Toolmarks

Materials:

6 used screwdrivers
Piece of wooden board or stiff cardboard
Jar of Play-doh or other easy-to-use modeling clay (1 for each group)

Procedure:

Toolmarks and other impressions left at a crime scene are most helpful when they exhibit individual characteristics – variations that distinguish one particular tool, tire, or shoe from all others of its type. In this exercise, students will identify tools based on their individual characteristics. Student should be matched up in teams of four or five. Place the screwdrivers on a table where they are accessible to all teams and mark each with an identifying number or letter. Each team places their modeling clay onto the board and molds it into a shape suitable to hold impressions. One team member takes the clay to the table tond makes impressions in the clay with three of the screwdrivers, noting on a separate paper which screwdrivers made each impression. When all teams have finished making impressions, teams trade their impressions with another and note which team they trade with. Each team now has 5 minutes to study the impressions and the screwdrivers and determine which ones made the impressions in the clay. The instructor should allow no more than 2 teams to study the screwdrivers at the same time.

Follow Up Questions:

1. Which screwdrivers made the impressions in your clay? Consult with the team you traded with to determine if you correctly identified all three marks.

2. Were some of the marks easier to identify than the others? What factors made identification easier?

3. Toolmarks are often found in harder substances such as wood. How would identifying toolmarks in wood be different from identifying them in clay?

Review Questions

1. The raised areas between the grooves in a rifled bore are called
   a. rifling.
   b. lands.
   c. grooves.
   d. caliber.

2. The most important tool available to the firearms examiner in the identification of firearms is
   a. the comparison microscope.
   b. the digitizing videocamera.
   c. mylar film and a high-voltage electrode.
   d. laser illumination.

3. Tool marks are most often encountered at which type of crime scene?
   a. arson
   b. homicide
   c. sexual assault
   d. burglary

4. What is the primary consideration in collecting impressions at a crime scene?
   a. the preservation of the impression or its reproduction for later use
   b. maintaining the chain of evidence
   c. the impression's admissibility in a courtroom
   d. the obliteration of the impression based on weather conditions

5. In the examination of tool mark impressions, individuality of a tool can be ascertained by
   a. patterns of grooves and lands resulting from the machining process.
   b. patterns of hills and valleys as minute imperfections.
   c. patterns of striations created by the manufacturer to trademark the tool.
   d. patterns of stains from oil and other maintenance activities.

6. True or False: Unlike other areas of criminalistics, the goal of individualization is not yet a reality in firearm and tool mark examination.

7. True or False: Rifled barrels manufactured in succession will have identical striation markings.

8. True or False: As a shotgun shell passes through a barrel, its surface is impressed with striations from the lands and grooves of the barrel.

9. True or False: Barium and antimony specimens found in primer on a suspect's hand after firing a gun remain for a period of 36 hours and confirm the suspect's involvement in a crime approximately 75 percent of the time.

10. True or False: Other forms of impressions that may constitute evidence at a crime scene include shoe, tire, and fabric impressions.

11. What is rifling and what is its purpose?

12. What are grooves and lands?

13. What is caliber?

14. List the class characteristics of a rifled barrel.

15. What are striations? How are they produced?

16. How are striations useful for comparing bullets?

17. Name three factors that can prevent a firearms examiner from obtaining a perfect match of striation markings around the periphery of two bullets.

18. How does a shotgun barrel differ from the barrel of a handgun? How does this difference affect the ability of a firearms examiner to compare shotgun shells?

19. Describe the relationship between a shotgun's gauge and the diameter of its barrel.

20. Briefly describe the sequence of events that occur from the time the trigger of a firearm is pulled to the time the bullet is fired.

21. What parts of a firearm leave impressions on a cartridge case that constitute individual characteristics of that weapon?

22. What is NIBIN?

23. What is distance determination and upon what is it based?

24. Briefly describe how a firearms examiner makes a distance determination for a handgun or rifle shot.

25. What is bullet wipe? Of what does it consist?

26. How does a firearms examiner estimate a distance determination for a shooting involving a shotgun?

27. As the distance to the target of a shotgun blast increases, what do the pellets do?

28. What is choke? How is it related to the speed, range, and spread pattern of shotgun pellets?

29. What is the Greiss test? What substance is being tested for in this procedure?

30. Name and briefly describe two popular approaches for collecting gunshot residue from a suspect's hands.

31. What device is often used to locate primer and gunpowder particles by their characteristic size and shape?

32. What is the major advantage of the SEM approach for primer residue detection? What is its major drawback?

33. Why is it possible to restore an obliterated serial number? Name two situations in which an obliterated serial number usually cannot be restored.

34. Why should a suspect firearm never be picked up by inserting an object into its barrel?

35. How should a suspect weapon discovered underwater be transported to the laboratory and why?

36. What typically imparts individual characteristics to a tool mark?

37. How does the criminalist record a tool mark for comparison when removal of the original tool mark is impractical?

38. Why must the crime-scene investigator never attempt to fit a suspect tool into a tool mark?

39. Name two procedures used to preserve impressions that cannot be submitted to the laboratory.

40. What is SICAR and how is it useful in comparing impressions?

Application and Critical Thinking

1. From each of the following descriptions of bullet holes, use general guidelines to estimate the distance from the shooter to the target.
   a. a few widely scattered gunpowder particles with no soot around the entrance hole
   b. a dark ring around the bullet hole, but no soot or gunpowder particles
   c. a halo of soot surrounding the entrance hole along with scattered specks of powder grains
   d. scorch marks and melted fibers surrounding the entrance hole

**Virtual Lab:
Tool Mark Analysis**

To perform a virtual tool mark analysis, go to www.pearsoncustom.com/us/vlm/

2. You are investigating a shooting involving a 12-gauge shotgun with a moderately high choke. The spread of the pattern made by the pellets measures 12 inches. In your opinion, which of the following is probably closest to the distance from the target to the shooter? Explain your answer and explain why the other answers are likely to be incorrect.
   a. 18 yards
   b. 12 yards
   c. 6 yards
   d. 30 yards

3. Criminalist Ben Baldanza is collecting evidence from the scene of a shooting. After locating the revolver suspected of firing the shots, Ben picks the gun up by the grip, unloads it, and places the ammunition in an envelope. He then

attaches an identification tag to the grip. Searching the scene, Ben finds a bullet lodged in the wall. He uses pliers to grab the bullet and pull it from the wall, then inscribes the bullet with his initials and places it in an envelope. What mistakes, if any, did Ben make in collecting this evidence?

4. How would you go about collecting impressions in each of the following situations?
a. You discover a shoe print in dry dirt.
b. You discover a tool mark on a windowsill.
c. You discover tire marks in soft earth.
d. You discover a shoe print on a loose piece of tile.
e. You discover a very faint shoe print in dust on a colored linoleum floor.

Endnotes

1. Originally, the number of lead balls with the same diameter as the barrel that would make a pound. For example, a 20-gauge shotgun has an inside diameter equal to the diameter of a lead ball that weighs 1/20 of a pound.

2. R. E. Tontarski, Jr., and R. M. Thompson, "Automated Firearms Evidence Comparison: A Forensic Tool for Firearms Identification—An Update," *Journal of Forensic Sciences* 43 (1998): 641.

3. P. C. Maiti, "Powder Patterns around Bullet Holes in Bloodstained Articles," *Journal of the Forensic Science Society* 13 (1973): 197.

4. J. W. Kilty, "Activity after Shooting and Its Effect on the Retention of Primer Residues," *Journal of Forensic Sciences* 20 (1975): 219.

5. G. E. Reed et al., "Analysis of Gunshot Residue Test Results in 112 Suicides," *Journal of Forensic Sciences* 35 (1990): 62.

6. G. M. Woiten et al., "Particle Analysis for the Detection of Gunshot Residue, I: Scanning Electron Microscopy/Energy Dispersive X-Ray Characterization of Hand Deposits from Firing," *Journal of Forensic Sciences* 24 (1979): 409.

7. R. S. White and A. D. Owens, "Automation of Gunshot Residue Detection and Analysis by Scanning Electron Microscopy/Energy Dispersive X-Ray Analysis (SEM/EDX)," *Journal of Forensic Sciences* 32 (1987): 1595; and W. L. Tillman, "Automated Gunshot Residue Particle Search and Characterization," *Journal of Forensic Sciences* 32 (1987): 62.

8. See R. Milne, "Electrostatic Lifting of Marks at Crime Scenes and the Development of Pathfinder," *Science & Justice* 38 (1998): 135.

9. B. Glattstein, Y. Shor, N. Levin, and A. Zeichner, "pH Indicators as Chemical Reagents for the Enhancement of Footwear Marks," *Journal of Forensic Sciences* 41 (1996): 23.

10. D. S. Hilderbrand and M. Miller, "Casting Materials—Which One to Use?" *Journal of Forensic Identification* 45 (1995): 618.

11. Available from Sirchie Finger Print Laboratories, Inc., Youngsville, N.C.

12. C. J. Frégeau et al., "Fingerprint Enhancement Revisited and the Effects of Blood Enhancement Chemicals on Subsequent Profiler Plus™ Fluorescent Short Tandem Repeat DNA Analysis of Fresh and Aged Bloody Fingerprints," *Journal of Forensic Sciences* 45 (2000): 354.

Learning Objectives

After studying this chapter you should be able to:

- Define questioned document
- Know what common individual characteristics are associated with handwriting
- List some important guidelines for collecting known writings for comparison to a questioned document
- Recognize some of the class and individual characteristics of printers and photocopiers
- List some of the techniques document examiners use to uncover alterations, erasures, obliterations, and variations in pen inks

National Science Content Standards

Scientific Inquiry

Science and Technology

Science in Personal and Social Perspective

History and Nature of Science

The Unabomber

In 1978, a parcel addressed to a Northwestern University professor exploded as it was being opened by a campus security officer. This was the start of a series of bomb-containing packages that typically were sent to universities and airlines. Considering the intended victims, the perpetrator was dubbed UN (university) A (airlines) BOM; hence, the Unabomber.

The explosives were usually housed in a pipe within a wooden box. The explosive ingredients generally were black powder, smokeless powder, or an ammonium nitrate mix. The box was filled with metal objects to create a shrapnel effect on explosion. The device typically had the initials "FC" punched into it.

The first Unabomber fatality came in 1985, when a computer store owner was killed after picking up a package left outside his business. The Unabomber emerged again in 1993 after a six-year hiatus by mailing bombs to two university professors. Their injuries were not fatal, but his next two attacks did result in fatalities.

In 1995, the case took an unexpected turn when the Unabomber promised to end his mad spree if his 35,000-word typewritten "*Manifesto*," sent to the *New York Times* and the *Washington Post*, was published. The manifesto proved to be a long, rambling rant against technology, but it offered valuable clues that broke the case. David Kaczynski realized that the manifesto's writing style and the philosophy it espoused closely resembled that of his brother, Ted. His suspicions were confirmed by linguistics experts, who carefully pored over the manifesto's content. Ted Kaczynski was arrested in Montana in 1996. Inside his ramshackle cabin were writings similar to the manifesto, three manual typewriters, and bomb-making materials. Forensic document examiners were able to match the typewritten manifesto to one of the typewriters recovered from the cabin.

Document
Examination

Key Terms

charred document

erasure

exemplar

indented writings

infrared luminescence

natural variations

obliteration

questioned document

The Document Examiner

Ordinarily, the work of the document examiner involves examining handwriting and typescript to ascertain the source or authenticity of a questioned document. However, document examination is not restricted to a mere visual comparison of words and letters. The document examiner must know how to use microscopy, photography, and even such analytical methods as chromatography to uncover all efforts, both brazen and subtle, to change the content or meaning of a document.

Alterations of documents through overwriting, erasures, or the more obvious crossing out of words must be recognized and characterized as efforts to alter or obscure the original meaning of a document. The document examiner identifies such efforts and recovers the original contents of the writing. An examiner may even reconstruct writing on charred or burned papers, or uncover the meaning of indented writings found on a paper pad after the top sheet has been removed.

questioned document
Any document about which some issue has been raised or that is the subject of an investigation

Any object that contains handwritten or typewritten markings whose source or authenticity is in doubt may be referred to as a **questioned document**. Such a broad definition covers all of the written and printed materials we normally encounter in our daily activities. Letters, checks, driver's licenses, contracts, wills, voter registrations, passports, petitions, and even lottery tickets are commonly examined in crime laboratories. However, we need not restrict our examples to paper documents. Questioned documents may include writings or other markings found on walls, windows, doors, or any other objects.

Document examiners possess no mystical powers or scientific formulas for identifying the authors of writings. They apply knowledge gathered through years of training and experience to recognize and compare the individual characteristics of questioned and known authentic writings. For this purpose, gathering documents of known authorship or origin is critical to the outcome of the examination. Collecting known writings may entail considerable time and effort and may be further hampered by uncooperative or missing witnesses. However, the uniqueness of handwriting makes this type of physical evidence, like fingerprints, one of few definitive individual characteristics available to the investigator, a fact that certainly justifies an extensive investigative effort.

Handwriting Comparisons

Document experts continually testify that no two individuals write exactly alike. This is not to say that there cannot be marked resemblances between two individuals' handwritings, because many factors make up the total character of a person's writing.

General Style

Perhaps the most obvious feature of handwriting to the layperson is its general style. As children, we all learn to write by attempting to copy letters that match a standard form or style shown to us by our teachers. The style of writing acquired by the learner is that which is fashionable for the particular time and locale. In the United States, for example, the two most widely used systems are the Palmer method, first introduced in 1880, and the Zaner-Bloser method, introduced in 1895 (see Figure 17–1). To some extent, both of these systems are taught in nearly all 50 states.

FIGURE 17–1
(top) Example of Zaner-Bloser handwriting; (bottom) Example of Palmer handwriting. *Courtesy Robert J. Phillips, Document Examiner, Audubon, New Jersey*

The early stages of learning and practicing handwriting are characterized by a conscious effort by the student to copy standard letter forms. Many pupils in a handwriting class tend at first to have writing styles that are similar to one another, with minor differences attributable to skill in copying. However, as initial writing skills improve, a child normally reaches the stage at which the nerve and motor responses associated with the act of writing become subconscious. The individual's writing now begins to take on innumerable habitual shapes and patterns that distinguish it from all others. The document examiner looks for these unique writing traits.

Variations in Handwriting

The unconscious handwriting of two different individuals can never be identical. Individual variations associated with mechanical, physical, and mental functions make it extremely unlikely that all of these factors can be exactly reproduced by any two people. Thus, variations are expected in angularity, slope, speed, pressure, letter and word spacings, relative dimensions of letters, connections, pen movement, writing skill, and finger dexterity.

Furthermore, many other factors besides pure handwriting characteristics should be considered. The arrangement of the writing on the paper may be as distinctive as the writing itself. Margins, spacings, crowding, insertions, and alignment are all results of personal habits. Spelling, punctuation, phraseology, and grammar can be personal and, if so, combine to individualize the writer.

In a problem involving the authorship of handwriting, all characteristics of both the known and questioned documents must be considered and compared. Dissimilarities between the two writings strongly indicate two writers, unless these differences can logically be accounted for by the facts surrounding the preparation of the documents. Because any single characteristic, even the most distinctive one, may be found in the handwriting of other individuals, no single handwriting characteristic can by itself be taken as the basis for a positive comparison. The final conclusion must be based on a sufficient number of common characteristics between the known and questioned writings to effectively preclude their having originated from two different sources.

What constitutes a sufficient number of personal characteristics? Here again, there are no hard-and-fast rules for making such a determination. The expert examiner can make this judgment only in the context of each particular case.

Challenges to Handwriting Comparison

When the examiner receives a reasonable amount of known handwriting for comparison, sufficient evidence to determine the source of a questioned document is usually easy to find. Frequently, however, circumstances prevent a positive conclusion or permit only the expression of a qualified opinion. Such situations usually develop when an insufficient number of known writings are available for comparison. Although nothing may be found that definitely points to the questioned and known handwriting being of different origin, not enough personal characteristics may be present in the known writings that are consistent with the questioned materials.

Difficulties may also arise when the examiner receives questioned writings containing only a few words, all deliberately written in a crude, unnatural form or all very carefully written and thought out so as to disguise the writer's natural style—a situation usually encountered with threatening or obscene letters. It is extremely difficult to compare handwriting that has been very carefully prepared to a document written with such little thought for structural details that it contains only the subconscious writing habits of the writer. However, although one's writing habits may be relatively easy to change for a few words or sentences, maintaining such an effort grows more difficult with each additional word.

When an adequate amount of writing is available, the attempt at total disguise may fail. This was illustrated by Clifford Irving's attempt to forge letters in the name of the late industrialist Howard Hughes in order to obtain lucrative publishing contracts for Hughes's life story. Figure 17–2 shows forged signatures of Howard Hughes along with Clifford Irving's known writings. By comparing these signatures, document examiner R. A. Cabbane of the U.S. Postal Inspection Service detected many examples of Irving's personal characteristics in the forged signatures.

FIGURE 17–2 Forged signatures of Howard Hughes and examples of Clifford Irving's writing. *Reprinted by permission of the American Society for Testing and Materials from the Journal of Forensic Sciences, copyright 1975*

For example, note the formation of the letter *r* in the word *Howard* on lines 1 and 3, as compared with the composite on line 6. Observe the manner in which the terminal stroke of the letter *r* tends to terminate with a little curve at the baseline of Irving's writing and the forgery. Notice the way the bridge of the *w* drops in line 1 and also in line 6. Also, observe the similarity in the formation of the letter *g* as it appears on line 1 as compared with the second signature on line 5.

The document examiner must also be aware that writing habits may be altered beyond recognition by the influence of drugs or alcohol. Under these circumstances, it may be impossible to obtain known writings of a suspect written under conditions comparable to those at the time the questioned document was prepared.

Collection of Handwriting Exemplars

exemplar
An authentic sample used for comparison purposes, such as handwriting

Collection of an adequate number of known writings (**exemplars**) is critical for determining the outcome of a comparison. Generally, known writings of the suspect furnished to the examiner should be as similar as possible to the questioned document. This is especially true with respect to the writing implement and paper. Styles and habits may be somewhat altered if a person switches from a pencil to a ballpoint pen or to a fountain pen. The way the paper is ruled, or the fact that it is unruled, may also affect the handwriting of a person who has become particularly accustomed to one type or the other. Known writings should also contain some of the words and combinations of letters present in the questioned document.

natural variations
Normal deviations found between repeated specimens of an individual's handwriting

The known writings must be adequate in number to show the examiner the range of **natural variations** in a suspect's writing characteristics. No two specimens of writing prepared by one person are ever identical in every detail. Variation is an inherent part of natural writing. In fact, a signature forged by tracing an authentic signature can often be detected even if the original and tracing coincide exactly, because no one ever signs two signatures exactly alike (see Figure 17–3).

FIGURE 17–3
No two specimens of writing from one person are ever identical.

Case Files

Hitler's Diaries

In 1981 a spectacular manuscript attributed to Adolf Hitler was disclosed by the brother of an East German general. These documents included Hitler's 27-volume diary and an unknown third volume of his autobiography, *Mein Kampf*. The existence of these works was both culturally and politically significant to the millions who were affected by World War II.

Authentication of the diaries was undertaken by two world-renowned experts, one Swiss and one American. Both declared that the handwritten manuscripts were identical to the known samples of Adolf Hitler's handwriting that they were given. Bidding wars began for publishing rights, and a major national newspaper in the United States won with a price near $4 million.

The publishing company that originally released the documents to the world market undertook its own investigation, which ultimately revealed a clever but devious plot. The paper on which the diaries were written contained a whitener that didn't exist until 1954, long after Hitler committed suicide. The manuscript binding threads contained viscose and polyester, neither of which was available until after World War II. Further, the inks used in the manuscript were all inconsistent with those in use during the year these pages were allegedly written.

Moreover, the exemplars sent to the Swiss and American experts as purportedly known examples of Hitler's handwriting were actually from the same source as the diaries. Thus, the experts were justified in proclaiming that the documents were authentic because they *were* written by the same hand—it just wasn't Hitler's. Chemical analysis of the inks later determined that the "Hitler diaries" were in fact less than one year old—spectacular, but fake!

Many sources are available to the investigator for establishing the authenticity of the writings of a suspect. An important consideration in selecting sample writings is the age of the genuine document relative to the questioned one. It is important to try to find standards that date closely in time to the questioned document. For most typical adults, basic writing changes are comparatively slow. Therefore, material written within two or three years of the disputed writing is usually satisfactory for comparison; as the age difference between the genuine and unknown specimens becomes greater, the standard tends to become less representative.

Despite the many potential sources of handwriting exemplars, obtaining an adequate set of collected standards may be difficult or impossible. In these situations, handwriting may have to be obtained voluntarily or under court order from the suspect. Ample case law supports the constitutionality of taking handwriting specimens. In *Gilbert v. California*,[1] the Supreme Court upheld the taking of handwriting exemplars before the appointment of counsel. The Court also reasoned that handwriting samples are identifying physical characteristics that lie outside the protection privileges of the Fifth Amendment. Furthermore, in *United States v. Mara*,[2] the Supreme Court ruled that taking a handwriting sample did not constitute an unreasonable search and seizure of a person and hence did not violate Fourth Amendment rights.

As opposed to nonrequested specimens (written without the thought that they may someday be used in a police investigation), requested writing samples may be consciously altered by the writer. However, the investigator can take certain steps to minimize attempts at deception. The requirement of several pages of writing normally provides enough material that is free of nervousness or attempts at deliberate disguise for a valid comparison. In addition, the writing of dictation yields exemplars that best represent the suspect's subconscious style and characteristics.

Other steps that can be taken to minimize a conscious writing effort, as well as to ensure conditions approximating those of the questioned writing, can be summarized as follows:

1. The writer should be allowed to write sitting comfortably at a desk or table and without distraction.

2. The suspect should not under any conditions be shown the questioned document or be told how to spell certain words or what punctuation to use.

3. The suspect should be furnished a pen and paper similar to those used in the questioned document.

4. The dictated text should be the same as the contents of the questioned document, or at least should contain many of the same words, phrases, and letter combinations found in the document. In handprinting cases, the suspect must not be told whether to use uppercase (capital) or lowercase (small) lettering. If, after writing several pages, the writer fails to use the desired type of lettering, he or she can then be instructed to include it. Altogether, the text must be no shorter than a page.

5. Dictation of the text should take place at least three times. If the writer is trying to disguise the writing, noticeable variations should appear among the three repetitions. Discovering this, the investigator must insist on continued repetitive dictation of the text.

6. Signature exemplars can best be obtained when the suspect is required to combine other writings with a signature. For example, instead of compiling a set of signatures alone, the writer might be asked to fill out completely 20 to 30 separate checks or receipts, each of which includes a signature.

7. Before requested exemplars are taken from the suspect, a document examiner should be consulted and shown the questioned specimens.

Quick Review

- Any object with handwriting or print whose source or authenticity is in doubt may be referred to as a questioned document.

- Document examiners gather documents of known authorship or origin and compare them to the individual characteristics of questioned writings.

- Collecting an adequate number of known writings is critical for determining the outcome of a handwriting comparison. Known writing should contain some of the words and combinations of letters in the questioned document.

- The unconscious handwriting of two different individuals can never be identical. However, the writing style of an individual may be altered beyond recognition by the influence of drugs or alcohol.

Typescript Comparisons

The document examiner analyzes not only handwritten documents, but machine-created ones as well. This includes a wide variety of devices including computer printers, photocopiers, fax machines, computer printers, and typewriters.

Photocopier, Fax, Computer Printer, and Typewriter Examination

With the emergence of digital technology, document examiners are confronted with a new array of machines capable of creating documents subject to alteration or fraudulent use. Personal computers use daisy wheel, dot-matrix, ink-jet, and laser printers. More and more, the document examiner encounters problems involving these machines, which often produce typed copies that have only inconspicuous defects.

In the cases of photocopiers, fax machines, and computer printers, an examiner may need to identify the make and model of a machine that may have been used in printing a document. Alternatively, the examiner may need to compare a questioned document with test samples printed from a suspect machine. Typically, the examiner generates approximately ten samples through each machine to obtain a sufficient representation of a machine's characteristics. A side-by-side comparison is then made between the questioned document and the printed exemplars to compare markings produced by the machine.

Photocopiers Transitory defect marks originating from random debris on the glass platen, inner cover, or mechanical portions of a copier produce images. These images are often irregularly shaped and sometimes form distinctive patterns. Thus, they become points of comparison as the document examiner attempts to link the document to suspect copiers. The gradual change, shift, or duplication of these marks may help the examiner date the document.

Fax Machines Fax machines print a header known as the *transmitting terminal identifier (TTI)* at the top of each fax page. For the document examiner, the TTI is an very important point of comparison (see Figure 17–4). The header and the document's text should have different type styles. TTIs can be fraudulently prepared and placed in the appropriate position on a fax copy. However, a microscopic examination of the TTI's print quickly reveals significant characteristics that distinguish it from a genuine TTI.

FIGURE 17–4
A fax page showing a transmitting terminal identifier (TTI).
Courtesy Melinda Alexander

In determining the fax machine's model type, the examiner usually begins by analyzing the TTI type style. The fonts of that line are determined by the sending machine. The number of characters, their style, and their position in the header are best evaluated through a collection of TTI fonts organized into a useful database. One such database is maintained by the American Society of Questioned Document Examiners.

Computer Printers Computer printer model determination requires extensive analysis of the specific printer technology and type of ink used. Visual and microscopic techniques help determine the technology and toner used. Generally printers are categorized as impact and nonimpact printers by the mechanism of their toner application. Nonimpact printers, such as ink-jet and laser printers, and impact printers, such as thermal and dot-matrix printers, all have characteristic ways of printing documents. Character shapes, toner differentiation, and toner application methods are easily determined with a low-power microscope and help the examiner narrow the possibilities of model type.

In analyzing computer printouts and faxes, examiners use the same approach for comparing the markings on a questioned document to exemplar documents generated by a suspect machine. These markings include all possible transitory patterns arising from debris and other extraneous materials. When the suspect machine is not available, the examiner may need to analyze the document's class characteristics to identify the make and model of the machine. It is important to identify the printing technology, the type of paper, the type of toner or ink used, the chemical composition of the toner, and the type of toner-to-paper fusing method used in producing the document.

Examination of the toner usually involves microscopic analysis to characterize its surface morphology, followed by identification of the inorganic and organic components of the toner. These results separate model types into categories based on their mechanical and printing characteristics. Typically, document examiners access databases to help identify the model type of machine used to prepare a questioned document. The resulting list of possibilities produced by the database hopefully reduces the number of potential machines to a manageable number. Obviously, once a suspect machine is identified, the examiner must perform a side-by-side comparison of questioned and exemplar printouts as described previously.

Typewriters Although typewriters are not used as widely as they were at one time, document examiners still analyze typescripts. Examiners are most often asked the following two questions about typewriters: (1) Can the make and model of the typewriter used to type the questioned document be identified? (2) Can a particular suspect typewriter be identified as having prepared the questioned document?

To answer the first question, the examiner must have access to a complete reference collection of past and present typefaces used by typewriter manufacturers. The two most popular typeface sizes are pica (10 letters to the inch) and elite (12 letters to the inch). Although a dozen manufacturers may use a pica or an elite typeface, many of these are distinguishable when the individual type character's style, shape, and size are compared.

As is true for any mechanical device, use of a typewriter will result in wear and damage to the machine's moving parts. These changes occur both randomly and irregularly, thereby imparting individual characteristics to the typewriter. Variations in vertical and horizontal alignment (characters are too high or low or too far left or right of their correct position) and perpendicular misalignment of characters (characters leaning to the left or to the right), as well as defects in each typeface, are valuable for proving the identity of a typewriter (see Figure 17–5).

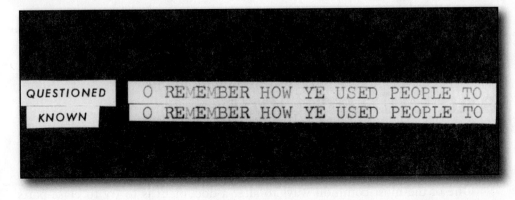

FIGURE 17–5
A portion of a typewriting comparison points to the conclusion that the same mcahine typed both specimens. Besides the smilarity in the design and size of type, note the light impression consistently made by the letter *M*. Also, the letter *E* slants to the right, almost touching *D* in the word *USED* in both specimens.

Associating a particular typewriter with a typewritten document requires comparing the questioned document to exemplars prepared from the suspect typewriter. As with handwriting, collection of proper standards is the foundation of such comparisons. In this respect, it is best if the document examiner has the questioned typewriter, allowing the examiner to prepare an adequate number of exemplars and examine the machine's typefaces. If the investigator must prepare standards from the questioned machine, a minimum of one copy in full word-for-word order of the questioned typewriting must be obtained.

Another area of investigation relates to the ribbon. An examination of the type impressions left on a ribbon may reveal the portion of the ribbon on which a particular text was typed.

When the suspect typewriter is not available for examination, the investigator must gather known writings that have been typed on the suspect machine. Ideally, material should be selected that contains many of the same combinations of letters and words found on the questioned document. The individual defects that characterize a typewriter develop and change as the machine is used; some may have changed between the preparation of the questioned and standard material. Hence, if many specimens are available, those prepared near the time of the disputed document should be collected.

Quick Review

- The examiner compares the individual type character's style, shape, and size to a complete reference collection of past and present typefaces.

- Use of a printing device results in wear and damage to the machine's moving parts in a way that is both random and irregular, thereby imparting individual characteristics to it.

- Transitory defect marks originating from random debris on the glass platen, inner cover, or mechanical portions of a copier produce irregularly shaped images that may serve as points of comparison.

- A TTI, or transmitting terminal identifier, is a header at the top of each page of a fax document. It is useful in document comparison because it serves as a way to distinguish between a real and a fraudulently prepared fax document.

- Variations in vertical and horizontal alignment and perpendicular misalignment of characters, as well as defects in each typeface, are valuable for proving the identity of a typewriter.

Alterations, Erasures, and Obliterations

Documents are often altered or changed after preparation, to hide their original intent or to perpetrate a forgery. Documents can be changed in several ways, and for each way, the application of a special discovery technique is necessary.

One of the most common ways to alter a document is to try to erase parts of it, using an India rubber eraser, sandpaper, a razor blade, or a knife to remove writing or type by abrading or scratching the paper's surface. All such attempts at erasure disturb the upper fibers of the paper. These changes are apparent when the suspect area is examined under a microscope using direct light or by allowing the light to strike the paper obliquely from one side (side lighting). Although microscopy may reveal whether an **erasure** has been made, it does not necessarily indicate the original letters or words present. Sometimes so much of the paper has been removed that identifying the original contents is impossible.

In addition to abrading the paper, the perpetrator may also obliterate words with chemicals. In this case, strong oxidizing agents are placed over the ink, producing a colorless reaction product. Although such an attempt may not be noticeable to the naked eye, examination under the microscope reveals discoloration on the treated area of the paper. Sometimes examination of the document under ultraviolet or infrared lighting reveals the chemically treated portion of the paper. Interestingly, examination of documents under ultraviolet light may also reveal fluorescent ink markings that go unnoticed in room light, as seen in Figure 17–6.

erasure
The removal of writing, typewriting, or printing from a document, normally accomplished by either chemical means or an abrasive instrument

FIGURE 17–6
(a) A twenty-dollar bill as it appears under room light.
(b) The bill illuminated with ultraviolet light reveals ink writing. *Courtesy Sirchie Finger Print Laboratories, Inc., Youngsville, N.C., www.sirchie.com*

Some inks, when exposed to blue-green light, absorb the radiation and reradiate infrared light. This phenomenon is known as **infrared luminescence**. Thus, alteration of a document with ink differing from the original can sometimes be detected by illuminating the document with blue-green light and using

infrared luminescence
A property exhibited by some dyes that emit infrared light when exposed to blue-green light

infrared-sensitive film to record the light emanating from the document's surface. In this fashion, any differences in the luminescent properties of the inks are observed (see Figure 17–7). Infrared luminescence has also revealed writing that has been erased. Such writings may be recorded by invisible residues of the original ink that remain embedded in the paper even after an erasure.

FIGURE 17–7 Part of a check stolen from a government agency as it appears to the naked eye is shown in (a). An infrared luminescence photograph was prepared of the amount figures at a magnification of 10x in (b). This clearly shows that the number 2 was added with a different ink. The accused pleaded guilty. *Courtesy Centre of Forensic Sciences, Toronto, Canada*

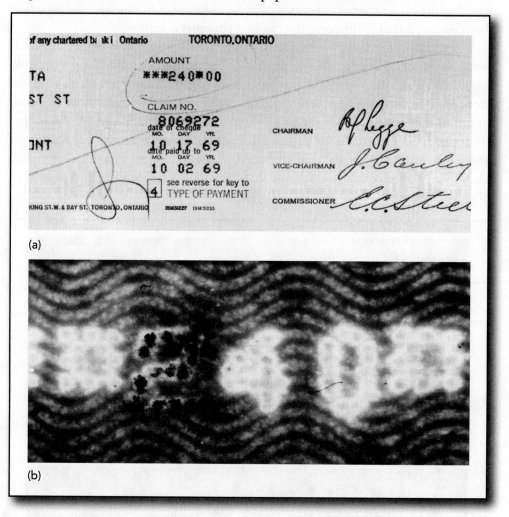

Another important application of infrared photography arises from the observation that inks differ in their ability to absorb infrared light. Thus, illuminating a document with infrared light and recording the light reflected off the document's surface with infrared-sensitive film enables the examiner to differentiate inks of a dissimilar chemical composition (see Figure 17–8).

Intentional **obliteration** of writing by overwriting or crossing out is seldom used for fraudulent purposes because of its obviousness. Nevertheless, such cases may be encountered in all types of documents. Success at permanently hiding the original writing depends on the material used to cover the writing. If it is done with the same ink as was used to write the original material, recovery will be difficult if not impossible. However, if the two inks are of a different chemical composition, photography with infrared-sensitive film may reveal the original writing. Infrared radiation may pass through the upper layer of writing while being absorbed by the underlying area (see Figure 17–9).

obliteration
Blotting out or smearing over writing or printing to make the original unreadable

FIGURE 17–8 (a) This photograph, taken under normal illumination, shows the owner of an American Express check to be "Freda C. Brightly Jones." Actually, this signature was altered. The check initially bore the signature "Fred C. Brightly Jr." (b) This photograph taken under infrared illumination, using infrared-sensitive film, clearly shows that the check was altered by adding *a* to Fred and *ones* to jr. The ink used to commit these changes is distinguishable because it absorbs infrared light, whereas the original ink does not.

FIGURE 17–9 (a) Under normal illumination it is impossible to read the obliterated text. (b) When the same document is photographed with infrared-sensitive film, the original writing is revealed. *Courtesy Centre for Forensic Sciences, Toronto, Canada*

Close examination of a questioned document sometimes reveals crossing strokes or strokes across folds of perforations in the paper that are not in a sequence that is consistent with the natural preparation of the document. Again, these differences can be shown by microscopic or photographic scrutiny.

Infrared photography sometimes reveals the contents of a document that has been accidentally or purposely charred in a fire. Another way to decipher **charred documents** involves reflecting light off the paper's surface at different angles in order to contrast the writing against the charred background (see Figure 17–10).

charred document
Any document that has become darkened and brittle through exposure to fire or excessive heat

FIGURE 17–10
Decipherment of charred papers seized in the raid of a suspected book-making establishment. The charred documents were photographed with reflected light.

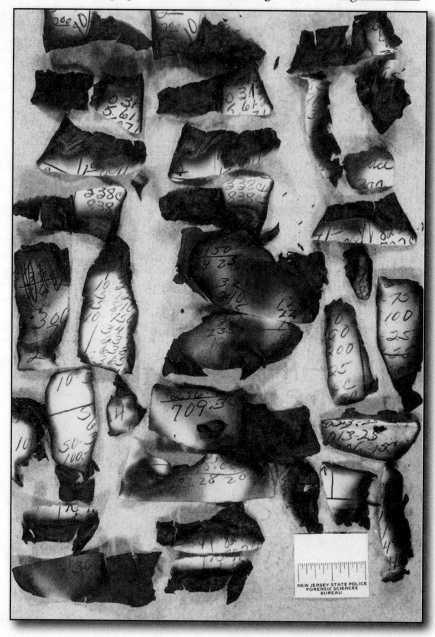

Digital image processing is the method by which the visual quality of digital pictures is improved or enhanced. *Digitizing* is the process by which the image is stored in memory. This is commonly done by scanning an image with a flatbed scanner or a digital camera and converting the image by computer into an array of digital intensity values called *pixels*, or picture elements. Once the image has been digitized, an image-editing program such as Adobe Photoshop™ is used to adjust the image. An image may be enhanced through lightening, darkening, and color and contrast controls. An example of how the technology is applied to forensic document examination is shown in Figures 17–11 and 17–12.

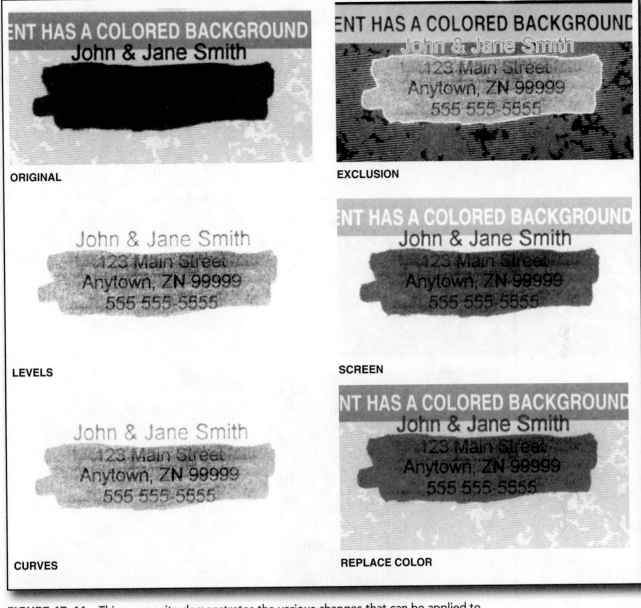

FIGURE 17–11 This composite demonstrates the various changes that can be applied to a digitized image in order to reveal information that has been obscured. Using a photo editor (Adobe Photoshop), the original was duplicated and pasted as a second layer. Colors were changed in selected areas of the image using the "screen" and "exclusion" options. "Replace color" allows the user to choose a specific color or range of colors and lighten, darken, or change the hue of the colors selected. "Level" and "curves" tools can adjust the lightest and darkest color ranges and optimize contrast, highlights, and shadow detail of the image for additional clarity. *Courtesy Lt. Robert J. Garnett, Middlesex County Prosecuter's Office, N.J.*

FIGURE 17–12

(a) Receipts have been used in investigations to establish a victim's whereabouts, provide suspects with alibis, and substantiate a host of personal conduct. Unfortunately, due to wear, age, or poor printing at the register, the receipt is often unreadable. This can be corrected using photo-editing software. In this example, the original toll receipt was scanned at the highest color resolution, which allows more than 16 million colors to be reproduced. The image was then manipulated, revealing the printed details, by adjusting the lightest and darkest levels and the color content of the image.

(b) Invoices may contain details about a transaction that are important to an investigation. The copy that ships with the merchandise may have that information blocked out. This information may be recovered using digital imaging. The left figure shows the original shipping ticket. The right figure shows the information revealed after replacing the color of the blocking pattern.

Courtesy Lt. Robert J. Garnett, Middlesex County Prosecuter's Office, N.J.

Other Document Problems

Document examiners encounter other challenges when analyzing questioned documents, including visualizing writing pressed or indented into a surface and analyzing the inks and paper used in suspect documents.

Indented Writings

Indented writings are the partially visible depressions on a sheet of paper underneath the one on which the visible writing was done. Such depressions are caused by the application of pressure on the writing instrument.

Indented writings have proved to be valuable evidence. For example, the top sheet of a bookmaker's records may have been removed and destroyed, but it still may be possible to determine the writing by the impressions left on the pad. These impressions may contain incriminating evidence supporting the charge of illegal gambling activities. When paper is studied under oblique or side lighting, its indented impressions are often readable (see Figure 17–13).

indented writings
Impressions left on paper positioned under a piece of paper that has been written on

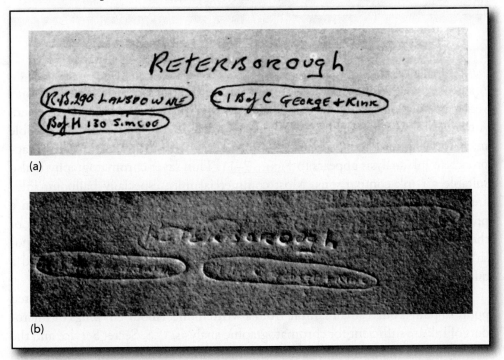

(a)

(b)

FIGURE 17–13
A suspected forger was arrested. In his car, police found written lists of the victims he intended to defraud. Some of these writings are shown in (a). A writing pad found in his house had indentations on the top page of the pad shown in (b). These indentations corresponded to the writings found in the car, further linking the suspect to the writings.
Courtesy Centre of Forensic Sciences, Toronto, Canada

An innovative approach to visualizing indented writings has been developed at the London College of Printing in close consultation with the Metropolitan Police Forensic Science Laboratory.[3] The method involves applying an electrostatic charge to the surface of a polymer film that has been placed in contact with a questioned document, as shown in Figure 17–14. Indented impressions on the document are revealed by applying a toner powder to the charged film. For many documents examined by this process, clearly readable images have been produced from impressions that could not be seen or were barely visible under normal illumination. An instrument that develops indented writings by electrostatic detection is commercially available and is routinely used by document examiners.

FIGURE 17-14
An electostatic detection apparatus (ESDA) works by applying an electrostatic charge to a document suspected of containing indented writings. The indentations are then visualized by the application of charge-sensitive toner. *Courtesy Foster & Freeman Limited, Worcestershire, U.K., www. fosterfreeman.co.uk*

FIGURE 17-14
An electostatic detection apparatus (ESDA) works by applying an electrostatic charge to a document suspected of containing indented writings. The indentations are then visualized by the application of charge-sensitive toner. *Courtesy Foster & Freeman Limited, Worcestershire, U.K., www. fosterfreeman.co.uk*

Ink and Paper Comparisons

A study of the chemical composition of writing ink present on documents may verify whether known and questioned documents were prepared by the same pen. A nondestructive approach to comparing ink lines is accomplished with a visible microspectrophotometer.[4] A case example illustrating the application of this approach to ink analysis appears in Figure 7–11. Thin-layer chromatography is also suitable for ink comparisons. Most commercial inks, especially ballpoint inks, are actually mixtures of several organic dyes. These dyes can be separated on a properly developed thin-layer chromatographic plate. The separation pattern of the component dyes is distinctly different for inks with different dye compositions and thus provides many points of comparison between a known and a questioned ink.

Ink can be removed from paper with a hypodermic needle with a blunted point to punch out a small sample from a written line. About ten plugs or microdots of ink are sufficient for chromatographic analysis. U.S. Secret Service and the Internal Revenue Service jointly maintain the U.S. International Ink Library. This collection includes more than 8,500 inks, which date back to the 1920s. Each year new pen and ink formulations are added to the reference collection. These inks have been systematically cataloged according to dye patterns developed by thin-layer chromatography (TLC; see Figure 17–15). On several occasions, this approach has been used to prove that a document has been fraudulently backdated. For example, in one instance, it was possible to establish that a document dated 1958 was backdated because a dye identified in the questioned ink had not been synthesized until 1959.

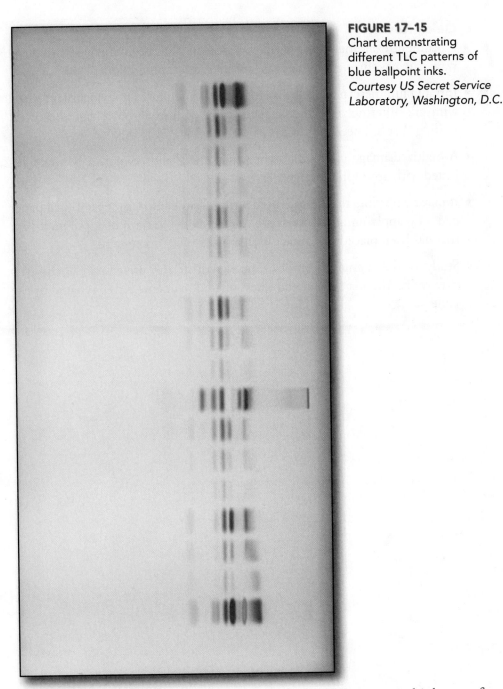

FIGURE 17–15
Chart demonstrating
different TLC patterns of
blue ballpoint inks.
*Courtesy US Secret Service
Laboratory, Washington, D.C.*

To further aid forensic chemists in ink-dating matters, several ink manufacturers, at the request of the U.S. Treasury Department, voluntarily tag their inks during the manufacturing process. The tagging program allows inks to be dated to the exact year of manufacture by changing the tags annually.

Another area of inquiry for the document examiner is the paper on which a document is written or printed. Paper is often made from cellulose fibers found in wood and fibers recovered from recycled paper products. The most common features associated with a paper examination are general appearance, color, weight, and watermarks. Other areas of examination include fiber identification and the characterization of additives, fillers, and pigments present in the paper product.

Quick Review

- Document examiners deal with evidence that has been changed in several ways, such as through alterations, erasures, and obliterations.

- Infrared luminescence can be used to detect alterations to a document made with ink differing from the original. Infrared luminescence can also reveal writing that has been erased.

- A digitized image can be lightened, darkened, and color and contrast adjusted with appropriate software.

- It may be possible to read indented writing—the impressions left on a paper pad—by applying an electrostatic charge to the surface of a polymer film that has been placed in contact with a questioned document.

- Studying the chemical composition of writing ink present on documents may verify whether known and questioned documents were prepared by the same pen.

Chapter Review

- Any object with handwriting or print whose source or authenticity is in doubt may be referred to as a questioned document.

- Document examiners gather documents of known authorship or origin and compare them to the individual characteristics of questioned writings.

- Collecting an adequate number of known writings is critical for determining the outcome of a handwriting comparison. Known writing should contain some of the words and combinations of letters in the questioned document.

- The unconscious handwriting of two different individuals can never be identical. However, the writing style of an individual may be altered beyond recognition by the influence of drugs or alcohol.

- The examiner compares the individual type character's style, shape, and size to a complete reference collection of past and present typefaces.

- Use of a printing device results in wear and damage to the machine's moving parts in a way that is both random and irregular, thereby imparting individual characteristics to it.

- Transitory defect marks originating from random debris on the glass platen, inner cover, or mechanical portions of a copier produce irregularly shaped images that may serve as points of comparison.

- A TTI, or transmitting terminal identifier, is a header at the top of each page of a fax document. It is useful in document comparison because it serves as a way to distinguish between a real and a fraudulently prepared fax document.

- Variations in vertical and horizontal alignment and perpendicular misalignment of characters, as well as defects in each typeface, are valuable for proving the identity of a typewriter.

- Document examiners deal with evidence that has been changed in several ways, such as through alterations, erasures, and obliterations.

- Infrared luminescence can be used to detect alterations to a document made with ink differing from the original. Infrared luminescence can also reveal writing that has been erased.

- A digitized image can be lightened, darkened, and color and contrast adjusted with appropriate software.

- It may be possible to read indented writing—the impressions left on a paper pad—by applying an electrostatic charge to the surface of a polymer film that has been placed in contact with a questioned document.

- Studying the chemical composition of writing ink present on documents may verify whether known and questioned documents were prepared by the same pen.

Quick Lab: Handwriting Comparison

Materials:

Piece of paper with exemplar signature (prepared by instructor)
Notebook paper
Scissors
Tape

Procedure:

Handwriting comparison is a basic tool in the arsenal of investigators looking into cases involving possible forgery. In this exercise, divined into teams of
three or four. Each team member will sign his or her name on the same piece of
paper. Your instructor will then give each student a piece of paper containing a
signature. Working alone for 2 minutes, each student will attempt to copy the
signature on a blank piece of paper. When the time has expired, use the scissors
to cut your finished "forgery" from the piece of paper and fold it so no one can
see it. One member of each team will collect the scraps of paper containing the
team's "forgeries," mix them, then unfold and tape each to the piece of paper
containing the tam members' signatures. Mark the forgeries with a letter (A,
B, C, etc.) to identify each. Each member now has 3 minutes to compare the
signatures to the "forgeries" and determine which team member created each
"forgery." Write your answers on a separate piece of paper. When all members
have finished, each team member reveals which forgery he or she created. Check
your answers to see how many you guessed correctly.

Review Questions

1. Critical to the examination of questioned documents is
   a. the preservation of the questioned document in its original form.
   b. the recognition that only handwritten or typewritten documents are suitable for examination.
   c. the gathering of documents of known authorship.
   d. the knowledge and understanding on the part of the document examiner of the current scientific formula to apply to the examination.

2. A nondestructive approach to comparing ink lines is accomplished with
   a. a comparison microscope.
   b. a visible microspectrophotometer.
   c. infrared spectroscopyluminescence.
   d. digitizing.

3. Chemical erasures of words or numbers may be revealed by examination of handwriting under
   a. visible light.
   b. X-ray fluorescence.
   c. UV light.
   d. infrared luminescence.

4. Handwriting containing inks of different chemical compositions may be distinguished by photography with
   a. UV light.
   b. visible light.
   c. IR light.
   d. all of the above

5. The age of an ink may be determined by utilizing an ink library based on analysis by
   a. gas chromatography.
   b. mass spectrometry.
   c. thin-layer chromatography.
   d. infrared spectrophotometry.

6. True or False: Because people sign their names the same way every time, if an original signature was traced over, the handwriting examiner would have to conclude that the tracing was produced by the signer of the original.

7. True or False: The age difference between genuine and unknown specimens is not an important factor in a handwriting comparison.

8. True or False: A single handwriting characteristic can by itself be taken as a basis for a positive comparison.

9. True or False: Random wear and damages to a printer impart it with class characteristics.

10. True or False: A TTI, or transmitting terminal identifier, is a header at the top of each page of a fax document.

11. What is a questioned document?

12. Name at least five characteristics of handwriting in which one might expect to encounter variations between individuals.

13. Name at least five factors besides handwriting characteristics that can impart individual variations to writing.

14. Describe two situations in which a document examiner may be prevented from coming to a positive conclusion about a questioned document.

15. What are exemplars? Why are they important for document examination?

16. What are natural variations? How can they be useful for detecting forgeries?

17. When comparing sample writing to a suspect document, the age difference between the documents should be no more than
    a. 6 to 12 months.
    b. 12 to 18 months.
    c. two to three years.
    d. five to seven years.

18. What constitutional principle did the Supreme Court address in *Gilbert v. California*, and how did the court rule?

19. What constitutional principle did the Supreme Court address in the case of *United States v. Mara*, and how did the court rule?

20. What distinguishing marks serve as points of comparison on documents produced by a photocopier?

21. What is a TTI? Name two ways in which it is useful in document comparison.

22. Name the two general categories of printers and list two examples of each type.

23. Name five important characteristics of a printer, photocopier, or fax machine that a document examiner must identify when analyzing a document in a situation in which the suspect machine is not available.

24. What two processes typically are involved in examination of toner?

25. What two questions are document examiners most often asked about typewriters?

26. What individual characteristics of a typewriter are valuable for proving its identity?

27. Name two ways in which infrared luminescence is useful in examining documents.

28. Describe two methods for visualizing indented writing.

29. Name two analytical techniques used to analyze writing inks.

30. List the most common features associated with a paper examination.

Application and Critical Thinking

1. Criminalist Julie Sandel is investigating a series of threatening notes written in pencil and sent to a local politician. A suspect is arrested, and Julie directs the suspect to prepare writing samples to compare to the writing on the notes. She has the suspect sit at a desk in an empty office and gives him a pen and a piece of paper. She begins to read one of the notes and asks the suspect to write the words she dictates. After reading about half a page, she stops, then dictates the same part of the note a second time for the suspect. At one point, the suspect indicates that he does not know how to spell one of the words, so Julie spells it for him. After completing the task, Julie takes the original notes and the dictated writing from the suspect to a document examiner. What mistakes, if any, did Julie make?

2. In each of the following situations, indicate how you would go about recovering original writing that is not visible to the naked eye.
   a. The original words have been obliterated with a different ink than was used to compose the original.
   b. The original words have been obliterated by chemical erasure.
   c. The original writing was made with fluorescent ink.
   d. The original documents have been charred or burned.

3. You have been asked to determine whether a handwritten will, supposedly prepared 30 years ago, is authentic or a modern forgery. What aspects of the document would you examine to make this determination? Explain how you would use thin-layer chromatography to help you come to your conclusion.

**Virtual Lab:
Thin-Layer Chromatography of Ink**

To perform a virtual thin-layer chromatography lab analysis of ink, go to www.pearsoncustom.com/us/vlm

Endnotes

1. 388 U.S. 263 (1967).

2. 410 U.S. 19 (1973).

3. D. M. Ellen, D. J. Foster, and D. J. Morantz, "The Use of Electrostatic Imaging in the Detection of Indented Impressions," *Forensic Science International* 15 (1980): 53.

4. P. W. Pfefferli, "Application of Microspectrophotometry in Document Examination," *Forensic Science International* 23 (1983): 129.

Learning Objectives

After studying this chapter you should be able to:

- List and describe the hardware and software components of a computer

  Understand the difference between read-only memory and random-access memory

- Describe how a hard disk drive is partitioned

- Describe the proper procedure for preserving computer evidence at a crime scene

- Understand the difference between and location of visible and latent data

- List the areas of the computer that will be examined to retrieve forensic data

National Science Content Standards

Scientific Inquiry

Science and Technology

History and Nature of Science

The BTK Killer

Dennis Rader was arrested in February 2005 and charged with committing ten murders since 1974 in the Wichita, Kansas area. The killer, whose nickname stands for "bind, torture, kill," hadn't murdered since 1991, but he resurfaced in early 2004 by sending a letter to a local newspaper taking credit for a 1986 slaying. Included with the letter were a photocopy of the victim's driver's license and three photos of her body. The BTK killer was back to his old habit of taunting the police.

Three months later, another letter surfaced. This letter detailed some of the events surrounding BTK's first murder victims. In 1974, he strangled Joseph and Julie Otero along with two of their children. Shortly after those murders, BTK sent a letter to a local newspaper in which he gave himself the name BTK. In December 2004, a package found in a park contained the driver's license of another BTK victim along with a doll covered with a plastic bag, its hands bound with pantyhose.

The major break in the case came when BTK sent a message on a computer disk to a local TV station. "Erased" information on the disk was recovered and restored by forensic computer specialists, and the disk was traced to the Christ Lutheran Church in Wichita. The disk was then quickly linked to Dennis Rader, the church council president. The long odyssey of the BTK killer was finally over.

Computer Forensics

Key Terms

bit
bookmark
byte
central processing unit (CPU)
cluster
cookies
file slack
firewall
hacking

hard disk drive (HDD)
hardware
Internet cache
Internet history
latent data
Message Digest 5 (MD5)/
  Secure Hash Algorithm (SHA)
motherboard
operating system (OS)

partition
RAM slack
random-access memory
  (RAM)
sector
software
swap file
temporary files
unallocated space
visible data

Since the 1990s, few fields have progressed as rapidly as computer technology. Computers are no longer a luxury, nor are they in the hands of just a select few. Technology and electronic data are a part of everyday life and permeate all aspects of society. Consequently, computers have become increasingly important as sources of evidence in an ever-widening spectrum of criminal activities.

Investigators frequently encounter computers and other digital devices in all types of cases. As homicide investigators sift for clues, they may inquire whether the method for a murder was researched on the Internet, whether signs of an extramarital affair can be found in e-mail or remnants of instant messages (which may provide motive for a spouse killing or murder for hire), or whether an obsessed stalker threatened the victim before a murder. Arson investigators want to know whether financial records on a computer may provide a motive in an arson-for-profit fire. A burglary investigation would certainly be aided if law enforcement determined that the proceeds from a theft were being sold online—perhaps through eBay or a similar online auction site.

Accessibility to children and the perception of anonymity has given sexual predators a way to seek out child victims online. The vulnerability of computers to hacker attacks is a constant reminder of security issues surrounding digitally stored data. Finally, the fact that computers control most of our critical infrastructure makes technology an appetizing target for would-be terrorists.

Computer forensics involves preserving, acquiring, extracting, analyzing, and interpreting computer data. Although this is a simple definition, it gets a bit more complicated. Part of this complication arises from technology itself. More and more devices are capable of storing electronic data: cell phones, personal digital assistants (PDAs), iPods, digital cameras, flash memory cards, smart cards, jump drives, and many others. Each method for extracting data from these devices presents unique challenges. However, sound forensic practices apply to all these devices. The most logical place to start to examine these practices is with the most common form of electronic data: the personal computer.

Andrew W. Donofrio is a lieutenant with the prosecutor's office in Bergen County, New Jersey, and is a leading computer forensics examiner for Bergen County, with more than 20 years' experience in law enforcement. He has conducted more than five hundred forensic examinations of computer evidence and frequently lectures on the subject throughout the state, as well as teaching multiday courses on computer forensics and investigative topics at police academies and colleges in New Jersey. Detective Sergeant Donofrio writes regularly on Internet-related and computer forensics issues for a number of law enforcement publications and has appeared as a guest expert on Internet-related stories on MSNBC.

From Input to Output: How Does the Computer Work?

Hardware versus Software

Before we get into the nuts and bolts of computers, we must establish the important distinction between hardware and software. **Hardware** comprises the physical components of the computer: the computer chassis, monitor, keyboard, mouse, hard disk drive, random-access memory (RAM), central processing unit (CPU), and so on (see Figure 18–1). The list is much more extensive but, generally speaking, if it is a computer component or peripheral that you can see, feel, and touch, it is hardware.

hardware
The physical components of a computer: case, keyboard, monitor, motherboard, RAM, HDD, mouse, and so on; generally speaking, if it is a computer component you can touch, it is hardware

FIGURE 18–1
Cutaway diagram of a personal computer.
Courtesy Tim Downs

Software, conversely, is a set of instructions compiled into a program that performs a particular task. Software consists of programs and applications that carry out a set of instructions on the hardware. Operating systems (Windows, Mac OS, Linux, Unix), word-processing programs (Microsoft Word, WordPerfect), Web-browsing applications (Internet Explorer, Safari, Firefox), and accounting applications (Quicken, QuickBooks, Microsoft Money) are all examples of software.

software
A set of instructions compiled into a program that performs a particular task

It is important not to confuse software with the physical media that it comes on. When you buy an application such as Microsoft Office, it comes on a compact disc (CD). The CD containing this suite of applications is typically referred to as software, but this is technically wrong. The CD is external computer media that contains the software; it is a container for and a medium to load the set of instructions onto the hard disk drive (the hardware).

Hardware Components

Computer Case/Chassis The case is the physical box holding the fixed internal computer components in place. Cases come in many shapes and sizes: a full upright tower chassis, a slim desktop model sitting on the desktop, or an all-in-one monitor/computer case like the iMac. For our purposes, the term *system unit* is probably most appropriate when describing a chassis seized as evidence. The term *system unit* accurately references the chassis, including the motherboard and other internal components.

Power Supply The term *power supply* is actually a misnomer, because it doesn't actually supply power—the power company does that. Rather, a computer's power supply converts power from the wall outlet to a usable format for the computer and its components. Different power supplies have different wattage ratings. The use, or more specifically the components, of the computer dictate the appropriate power supply.

motherboard
The main system board of a computer (and many other electronic devices) that delivers power, data, and instructions to the computer's components

Motherboard The main circuit board in a computer (or other electronic devices) is referred to as the **motherboard**. Motherboards contain sockets for chips (such as the CPU and ROM, discussed shortly) and slots for add-on cards. Examples of add-on cards are a video card to connect the computer to the monitor, a network card or modem to connect to an internal network or the Internet, and a sound card to connect to speakers.

Sockets on the motherboard typically accept things such as random-access memory (RAM) or the central processing unit (CPU). The keyboard, mouse, CD-ROM drives, monitor, and other peripherals or components connect to the motherboard in one way or another.

System Bus Contained on the motherboard, the system bus is a vast complex network of wires that carries data from one hardware device to another. This network is analogous to a complex highway. Data is sent along the bus in the form of ones and zeros (or, more appropriately stated, as electrical impulses representing an "on" or "off" state—this two-state computing is also known as binary computing).

central processing unit (CPU)
The part of the computer that processes information and performs computations

Central Processing Unit (CPU) The **central processing unit (CPU)**, also referred to as a processor, is the brain of the computer; it is the part of the computer that actually computes. It is the main (and typically the largest) chip that plugs into a socket on the motherboard. Basically, all operations performed by the computer are run through the CPU. The CPU carries out the program steps to perform the requested task, such as opening and working in a Microsoft™ Word document or performing advanced mathematical algorithms.

Read-Only Memory (ROM) This rather generic term describes special chips on the motherboard. ROM chips store programs called *firmware*, used to start the boot process (in which the computer starts up before the system is fully functioning) and configure a computer's components. This technology is referred to as the BIOS, for *basic input-output system*. The operation of the BIOS is relevant to several computer forensics procedures, particularly the boot sequence. As will become clear later, it is important not to boot the actual computer under investigation to the original hard disk drive. This would cause changes to the data, thus compromising the integrity of evidence. The BIOS allows investigators to control the boot process to some degree.

Random-Access Memory (RAM) Random-access memory (RAM) stores software programs and instructions while the computer is turned on; it takes the physical form of chips that plug into the motherboard. Most of the data on a computer is stored on the hard disk drive (HDD). However, if the computer had to access the HDD each time it wanted data, it would run slowly and inefficiently. Instead, the computer, aware that it may need certain data at a moment's notice, stores the data in RAM. This takes the burden off the computer's processor and hard disk drive (HDD). RAM is referred to as *volatile memory* because it is not permanent; its contents undergo constant change and are forever lost once power is taken away from the computer.

Hard Disk Drive (HDD) Generally speaking, the **hard disk drive (HDD)** is the primary component of storage in the personal computer (see Figure 18–2). It typically stores the operating system, programs, and data files created by the user, such as documents, spreadsheets, accounting information, or a company database. Unlike RAM, the HDD is permanent storage and retains its information even after the power is turned off. HDDs work off a controller that is typically part of the motherboard, but sometimes takes the form of an add-on (expansion) card plugged into the motherboard.

random-access memory (RAM)
The volatile memory of the computer; when power is turned off, its contents are lost; programs and instructions are loaded into RAM while they are in use

hard disk drive (HDD)
Typically the main storage location within the computer, consisting of magnetic platters contained in a case

FIGURE 18–2
An inside view of the platter and read/write head of a hard disk drive.
Courtesy Corbis RF

Input Devices Input devices are used to get data into the computer or to give the computer instructions. Input devices constitute part of the "user" side of the computer. Examples include the keyboard, mouse, joystick, and scanner.

Output Devices Output devices are equipment through which data is obtained from the computer. Output devices are also part of the "user" side of the computer and provide the results of the user's tasks. They include the monitor, printer, and speakers.

> **Quick Review**
>
> - Computer forensics involves preserving, acquiring, extracting, and interpreting computer data.
>
> - Software programs are applications that carry out a set of instructions.
>
> - The central processing unit (CPU) is the brain of the computer—the main chip responsible for doing the actual computing.
>
> - The motherboard is the main circuit board within a computer.
>
> - Read-only memory (ROM) chips store programs that control the boot (startup) process and configure a computer's components.
>
> - Random-access memory (RAM) is volatile memory, which is lost when power is turned off. Programs are loaded into RAM because of its faster read speed than accessing the program on the hard drive constantly.
>
> - The hard disk drive (HDD) is typically the primary location of data storage within the computer.

Putting It All Together

A person approaches the computer, sits down, and presses the power button. The power supply wakes up and delivers power to the motherboard and all of the hardware connected to the computer. At this point the flash ROM chip on the motherboard (the one that contains the BIOS) conducts a power-on self test (POST) to make sure everything is working properly.

The flash ROM also polls the motherboard to check the hardware that is attached and follows its programmed boot order, thus determining from what device it should boot. Typically the boot device is the HDD, but it can also be a CD, or USB drive. If it is the HDD, the HDD is then sent control. It locates the first sector of its disk (known as the master boot record), determines its layout (partition[s]), and boots an operating system (Windows, Mac OS, Linux, Unix). The person is then presented with a computer work environment, commonly referred to as a desktop.

Now ready to work, the user double-clicks an icon on the desktop, such as a Microsoft Word shortcut, to open the program and begin to type a document. The CPU processes this request, locates the Microsoft™ Word program on the HDD (using a predefined map of the drive called a *file system table*), carries out the programming instructions associated with the application, loads Microsoft™

Word into RAM via the system bus, and sends the output to the monitor by way of the video controller, which is either located on or attached to the motherboard.

The user then begins to type, placing the data from the keyboard into RAM. At the end, the user may print the document or simply save it to the HDD for later retrieval. If printed, the data is taken from RAM, processed by the CPU, placed in a format suitable for printing, and sent through the system bus to the external port where the printer is connected. If the document is saved, the data is taken from RAM, processed by the CPU, passed to the HDD controller (IDE, SCSI, or SATA) by way of the system bus, and written to a portion of the HDD. The HDD's file system table is updated so it knows where to retrieve that data later. In actuality, the boot process is more complex than the way it has been described here and requires the forensic examiner to possess an in-depth knowledge of its process.

The preceding example illustrates how three components perform most of the work: the CPU, RAM, and system bus. The example can get even more complicated as the user opens more applications and performs multiple tasks simultaneously (multitasking). Several tasks can be loaded into RAM at once, and the CPU is capable of juggling them all. This allows for the multitasking environment and the ability to switch back and forth between applications. All of this is orchestrated by the operating system and is written in the language of the computer—ones and zeros. The only detail missing, and one that is important from a forensic standpoint, is a better understanding of how data is stored on the hard disk drive (see Figure 18–2).

Storing and Retrieving Data

As mentioned earlier, most of the data in a computer is stored on the hard disk drive (HDD). However, before beginning to understand how data is stored on the HDD, it is first important to understand the role of the **operating system (OS)**. An OS is the bridge between the human user and the computer's electronic components. It provides the user with a working environment and facilitates interaction with the system's components. Each OS supports certain types of file systems that store data in different ways, but some support the methods of others.

operating system (OS)
Software that allows the user to interact with the hardware and manages the file system and applications

Formatting and Partitioning the HDD

Generally speaking, before an OS can store data on a HDD, the HDD must first be formatted, or prepared to accept the data in its current form. Before the HDD can be formatted, a partition must be defined. A **partition** is nothing more than a contiguous (adjacent) set of blocks (physical areas on the HDD in which data can be stored) that are defined and treated as an independent disk. Thus, a hard disk drive can hold several partitions, making a single HDD appear as several disks.

Partitioning a drive can be thought of as dividing a container that begins as nothing more than four sides with empty space on the inside. Imagine that we then cut a hole in the front of the container and place inside two drawers containing the hardware to open and close the drawers. We have just created a two-drawer filing cabinet and defined each drawer as a contiguous block of storage. A partitioning program then defines the partitions that will later hold the

partition
A contiguous set of blocks that are defined and treated as an independent disk

data on the HDD. Just as the style, size, and shape of a filing cabinet drawer can vary, so too can partitions.

After a hard drive is partitioned, it is typically formatted. The formatting process *initializes* portions of the HDD, so that they can store data, and creates the structure of the file system. There are various types of file systems—methods for storing and organizing computer files and data so they are easier to locate and access. Each has a different way of storing, retrieving, and allocating data.

At the conclusion of these steps, we say that the drive is *logically defined*. The term logically is used because no real divisions are made. If you were to crack open the HDD before or after partitioning and formatting, to the naked eye the platters would look the same.

Mapping the HDD

As shown in Figure 18–3, disks are logically divided into sectors, clusters, tracks, and cylinders. A **sector** is the smallest unit of data that a hard drive can address; sectors are typically 512 bytes in size (a **byte** is eight bits; a **bit** is a single one or zero).[1] A **cluster** usually is the minimum space allocated to a file. Clusters are groups of sectors; their size is defined by the file system, but they are always in multiples of two. A cluster, therefore, consists of two, four, six, or eight sectors, and so on. (With modern file systems, the user can exercise some control over the number of sectors per cluster.) Tracks are concentric circles that are defined around the platter. Cylinders are groups of tracks that reside directly above and below each other.

sector
The smallest unit of data addressable by a hard disk drive, generally consisting of 512 bytes

byte
A group of eight bits

bit
Short for *binary digit*; taking the form of either a one or a zero, it is the smallest unit of information on a machine

cluster
A group of sectors in multiples of two; typically the minimum space allocated to a file

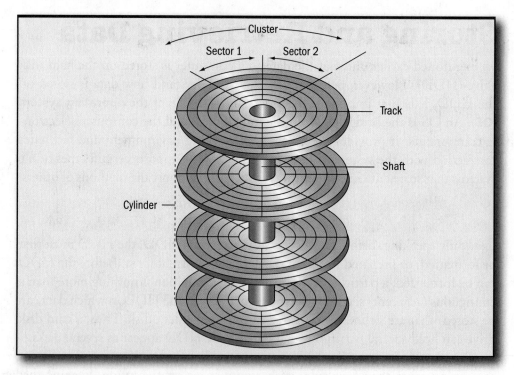

FIGURE 18–3
An inside view of the platter and read/write head of a hard disk drive.
Courtesy Corbis RF

Additionally, the HDD has a file system table (map) of the layout of the defined space in that partition. FAT file systems use a *file allocation table* (which is where the acronym *FAT* comes from) to track the location of files and folders (data) on the HDD, whereas NTFS file systems use, among other things, a *master file table (MFT)*. Each file system table tracks data in different ways, and forensic computer examiners should be versed in the technical nuances of the HDDs they examine. It is sufficient for our purposes here, however, to merely visualize the file system table as a map to where the data is located. This map numbers sectors, clusters, tracks, and cylinders to keep track of the data.

One way to envision a partition and file system is as a room full of safe-deposit boxes. The room itself symbolizes the entire partition, and the boxes with their contents represent clusters of data. In order to determine who rented which box, and subsequently where each depositor's property is, a central database is needed. This is especially true if a person rented two boxes located in opposite ends of the room. A similar situation often arises when storing data on a computer, because not all the data in a particular file or program is always stored in contiguous (adjacent) clusters on the HDD. Thus, a database tracking the locations of the safe-deposit boxes is much like a file system table tracking the location of data within the clusters.

This example is also useful to understand the concept of reformatting a HDD, which involves changing the way the disk stores data. If the database managing the locations of the safe-deposit boxes were wiped out, the property in them would still remain; we just wouldn't know what was where. So too with the hard disk drive. If a user were to wipe the file system table clean—for example, by reformatting it—the data itself would not be gone. Both the database tracking the locations of the safe-deposit boxes and the file system table tracking the location of the data in the cluster are maps—not the actual contents. (Exceptions exist with some file systems, such as an NTFS file system, which stores data for very small files right in its file system table, known as the master file table.)

Other Common Storage Devices

Although the HDD is the most common storage device for the personal computer, many others exist. Methods for storing data and the layout of that data can vary from device to device. A CD-ROM, for example, uses a different technology and format for writing data than a USB thumb drive. Fortunately, regardless of the differences among devices, the same basic forensic principles apply for acquiring the data. Common storage devices include the following:

CDs and DVDs Compact discs (CDs) and digital video discs (DVDs) are two of the most common forms of storing all sorts of external data, including music, video, and data files. Both types of media consist of plastic discs with an aluminum layer containing the data that is read by a beam of laser light in the CD/DVD reader. Different CDs are encoded in different ways, which makes forensic examination of such discs difficult at times.

Floppy Disks Although "floppies" are not as common as they once were, forensic examiners still encounter the 3.5-inch floppy disk. Floppy disks can be used to boot an operating system or to store data. They are constructed of hard plastic with a thin plastic disk on the inside. That thin plastic disk is coated with a magnetic iron oxide material. The disk stores data in a similar fashion to the hard disk drive. By today's standards, floppy disks don't hold much data.

USB Thumb Drives and Smart Media Cards These devices, which can store a large amount of data, are known as *solid-state storage devices* because they have no moving parts. Smart media cards are typically found in digital cameras and PDAs, whereas USB thumb drives come in many shapes, sizes, and storage capacities.

Tapes Tapes come in many different formats and storage capacities. Each typically comes with its own hardware reader and sometimes a proprietary application to read and write its contents. Tapes and thumb drives are typically used for backup purposes and consequently have great forensic potential.

Network Interface Card (NIC) Very rarely do we find a computer today that doesn't have a NIC. Whether they are on a local network or the Internet, when computers need to communicate with each other, they typically do so through a NIC. NICs come in many different forms: add-on cards that plug into the motherboard, hard-wired devices on the motherboard, add-on cards (PCMCIA) for laptops, and universal serial bus (USB) plug-in cards, to name a few. Some are wired cards, meaning they need a physical wired connection to participate on the network, and others are wireless, meaning they receive their data via radio waves.

> **Quick Review**
>
> - The computer's operating system (OS) is the bridge between the human user and the computer's electronic components. It provides the user with a working environment and facilitates interaction with the system's components.
>
> - Formatting is the process of preparing a hard disk drive to store and retrieve data in its current form.
>
> - A sector is the smallest unit of data that a hard drive can address. A cluster usually is the minimum space allocated to a file. Clusters are groups of sectors.
>
> - A FAT is a file allocation table. It tracks the location of files and folders on the hard disk drive.

Processing the Electronic Crime Scene

Processing the electronic crime scene has a lot in common with processing a traditional crime scene. The investigator must first ensure that the proper legal requirements (search warrant, consent, and so on) have been met so that the scene can be searched and the evidence seized. The investigator should then devise a plan of approach based on the facts of the case and the physical location.

Documenting the Scene

The scene should be documented in as much detail as possible before disturbing any evidence and before the investigator lays a finger on any computer components. Of course there are circumstances in which an investigator may have to act quickly and pull a plug before documenting the scene, such as when data is in the process of being deleted.

   Crime-scene documentation is accomplished through two actions: sketching and photographing. The electronic crime scene is no different. The scene should be sketched in a floor plan fashion (see Figure 18–4) and then overall photographs of the location taken. In a case in which several computers are connected together in a network, a technical network sketch should also be included if possible.

FIGURE 18–4
Rough sketch made at a crime scene, with necessary measurements included.

   After investigators photograph the overall layout, close-up photographs should be shot. A close-up photograph of any running computer monitor should be taken. All the connections to the main system unit, such as peripheral devices (keyboard, monitor, speakers, mouse, and so on), should be photographed. If necessary, system units should be moved delicately and carefully to facilitate the connections photograph (see Figure 18–5). Close-up photographs of equipment serial numbers should be taken if practical.

FIGURE 18–5
Back of a computer showing all connections.

At this point, investigators must decide whether to perform a live acquisition of the data, perform a system shutdown (as in the case of server equipment), pull the plug from the back of the computer,[2] or a combination thereof. Several factors influence this decision. For example, if encryption is being used and pulling the plug will encrypt the data, rendering it unreadable without a password or key, pulling the plug would not be prudent. Similarly, any data that exists in RAM and has not been saved to the HDD will be lost if power to the system is discontinued. Regardless of how investigators decide to proceed, the equipment most likely will be seized. Exceptions exist in the corporate environment, where servers are fundamental to business operations.

After the photographs and sketches are complete, but before disconnecting the peripherals from the computer, a label should be placed on the cord of each peripheral, with a corresponding label placed on the port to which it is connected. A numbering scheme should be devised to identify the system unit if several computers are at the scene (Figure 18–6). The combination of sketching, photographing, and labeling should adequately document the scene, prevent confusion of which component went with which system unit, and facilitate reconstruction if necessary for lab or courtroom purposes.

Forensic Image Acquisition

Once a computer has been seized, the data it contains must be obtained for analysis. The number of electronic items that potentially store evidentiary data are too vast to cover in this section. The hard disk drive will be used as an example, but the same "best practices" principles apply for other electronic devices as well.

The goal in obtaining data from a HDD is to do so without altering even one bit of data. Thus, throughout the entire process, the forensic computer examiner must use the least intrusive method to retrieve data. Because booting a HDD to its operating system changes many files and could potentially destroy evidentiary data, obtaining data is generally accomplished by removing the HDD from the system and placing it in a laboratory forensic computer so that a *forensic image*

FIGURE 18–6
Back of a computer with each component correlated with its port.

can be created. However, the BIOS of the seized computer sometimes interprets the geometry of the HDD differently than the forensic computer does. *Geometry* refers to the functional dimensions of a drive, including the number of heads, cylinders, and sectors per track. In these instances, the image of the HDD must be obtained using the seized computer.

Regardless of the computer in which the HDD is placed, the examiner must ensure that, when creating the forensic image, the drive to be analyzed is in a "write-blocked" read-only state in which no new data can be added to the drive. Furthermore, the examiner needs to be able to prove that the forensic image he or she obtained includes every bit of data and caused no changes (writes) to the HDD.

To this end, a sort of fingerprint of the drive is taken before and after imaging through the use of a **Message Digest 5 (MD5)/Secure Hash Algorithm (SHA)**, or similar algorithm. Before imaging the drive, the algorithm is run, and a 32-character alphanumeric string is produced based on the drive's contents. The algorithm is then run against the resulting forensic image. If nothing changed, the same alphanumeric string is produced, thus demonstrating that the image is all-inclusive of the original contents and that nothing was altered in the process.

A forensic image of the data on a hard disk drive (or any type of storage medium) is merely an exact duplicate of the entire contents of that medium. In other words, all portions of a hard disk drive—even blank portions—are copied from the first bit (one or zero) to the last. Why would investigators want to copy what appears to be blank or unused portions of the HDD? The answer is simple: to preserve *latent data*, discussed later in the chapter. Data exists in areas of the drive that are, generally speaking, unknown and inaccessible to most end users. This data can be valuable as evidence. Therefore, a forensic image—one that copies every single bit of information on the drive—is necessary.[3] A forensic image differs from a backup or standard copy in that it takes the entire contents, not only data the operating system is aware of.

Many forensic software packages come equipped with a method to obtain a forensic image. The most popular software forensic tools—EnCase, Forensic

Message Digest 5 (MD5)/Secure Hash Algorithm (SHA)
A software algorithm used to "fingerprint" a file or contents of a disk in order to verify the integrity of data; in forensic analysis it is typically used to verify that an acquired image of suspect data was not altered during the process of imaging

Toolkit (FTK), Forensic Autopsy (Linux-based freeware), and SMART (Linux-based software by ASR Data)—all include a method to obtain a forensic image. All produce self-contained image files that can then be interpreted and analyzed. They also allow image compression to conserve storage. The fact that self-contained, compressed files are the result of forensic imaging allows many images from different cases to be stored on the same forensic storage drive. This makes case management and storage much easier (see Figure 18–7).

FIGURE 18–7 Screen shot of EnCase Software. *Courtesy EnCase, www.encase.com*

Quick Review

- Aspects of a computer that should be photographed close up at an electronic crime scene include (1) the screen of any running computer monitor, (2) all the connections to the main system unit, such as peripheral devices (keyboard, monitor, speakers, mouse, and so on), and (3) equipment serial numbers.

- Two situations in which an investigator would not unplug a computer at an electronic crime scene are (1) if encryption is being used and pulling the plug will encrypt the data, rendering it unreadable without a password or key, and (2) if data exists in RAM that has not been saved to the HDD, and will thus be lost if power to the system is discontinued.

- The primary goal in obtaining data from a HDD is to do so without altering even one bit of data. To this end, a Message Digest 5 (MD5)/Secure Hash Algorithm (SHA) takes a "fingerprint" of a hard disk drive (HDD) before and after forensic imaging.

Analysis of Electronic Data

Analysis of electronic data is virtually limitless and bound only to the level of skill of the examiner. The more familiar an examiner is with computers, operating systems, application software, data storage, and a host of other disciplines, the more prepared he or she will be to look for evidentiary data.

Because computers are vast and complex, discussing each area, file, directory, log, or computer process that could potentially contain evidentiary data is beyond the scope of one chapter—and may be beyond the scope of an entire book. What follows are some of the more common areas of analysis. While reading this section, reflect on your own knowledge of computers and consider what other data might be of evidentiary value and where it might be found.

Visible Data

The category of **visible data** includes all information that the operating system is presently aware of and thus is readily accessible to the user. Here we present several common types of visible data considered in many investigations. This list is by no means exhaustive and can include any information that has value as evidence.

Data/Work Product Files One place to find evidence is in documents or files produced by the suspect. This category is extremely broad and can include data from just about any software program. Microsoft Word and WordPerfect word-processing programs typically produce text-based files such as typed documents and correspondence. These programs, and a host of other word-processing programs, have replaced the typewriter. They are common sources of evidence in criminal cases, particularly those involving white-collar crime.

Also relevant in white-collar crime and similar financial investigations are any data related to personal and business finance. Programs such as QuickBooks and Peachtree accounting packages can run the entire financial portion of a small to midsize business. Similarly, personal bank account records in the computer are often managed with personal finance software such as Microsoft Money and Quicken. Moreover, criminals sometimes use these programs as well as spreadsheet applications to track bank accounts stolen from unsuspecting victims. Forensic computer examiners should familiarize themselves with these programs, the ways in which they store data, and methods for extracting and reading the data.

Advances in printer technology have made high-quality color printing both affordable and common in many homes. Although this is a huge benefit for home office workers and those interested in graphic arts, the technology has been used for criminal gain. Counterfeiting and check and document fraud are easily perpetrated by most home computer users. All that is required is a decent ink-jet printer and a scanner. Including the computer, a criminal could set up a counterfeiting operation for less than $1500. Examiners must learn the graphics and photo-editing applications used for such nefarious purposes. Being able to recognize the data produced by these applications and knowing how to display the images is key to identifying the evidence.

visible data
All data that the operating system is presently aware of and thus is readily accessible to the user

Page File Data When an application is running, the program and the data being accessed are loaded into RAM. A computer's RAM can read data much faster than the hard disk drive, which is why the programs are loaded here. RAM, however, has its limits. Some computers have more than a gigabyte or two. Regardless of the amount, though, most operating systems (Microsoft Windows™, Linux, and so on) are programmed to conserve RAM when possible. This is where the *Page file* comes in. The operating system attempts to keep only data and applications that are presently being used in RAM. Other applications that were started, but are currently waiting for user attention, may be swapped out of RAM and written to the **Page file** on the hard disk drive.[4]

Page file
A file or defined space on the HDD to which data is written, or swapped, to free RAM for applications that are in use

For example, a manager of a retail store may want to type a quarterly report based on sales. The manager starts Microsoft Word™ and begins his report. Needing to incorporate sales figure data from a particular spreadsheet, he opens Microsoft Excel™. Depending on what is running on the computer, the original Word document may be swapped from RAM to the swap space on the HDD to free up space for Excel™. As the manager goes back and forth between the programs (and maybe checks his e-mail in between), this swapping continues. Data that is swapped back and forth is sometimes left behind in the memory space. Even as this area is constantly changed, some of the data is orphaned in unallocated space, an area of the HDD discussed later in this chapter.

Page file can be defined as a particular file or even a separate HDD partition, depending on the operating system and file system type. Data in the memory space can be read by examining the HDD through forensic software or a utility that provides a binary view, such as Norton Disk Editor™ or WinHex™ (see Figure 18–8).

FIGURE 18–8
As the user switches between applications and performs multiple tasks, data is swapped back and forth between RAM and the computer's hard drive. This area on the hard drive is referred to as *memory space*.

Swapping of data between RAM and the hard drive's swap space or page file

Swap space

RAM module (chip)

temporary files
A copy of the current file that the computer saves in memory automatically and updates periodically

Temporary Files Any user who has suffered a sudden loss of power in the middle of typing a document can attest to the value of a **temporary file**. Most programs automatically save a copy of the file being worked on in a temporary file. After typing a document, working on a spreadsheet, or working on a slide presentation, the user can save the changes, thus promoting the temporary copy to an actual file. This is done as a sort of backup on the fly. If the computer experiences a sudden loss of power or other catastrophic failure, the temporary file can be recovered, limiting the amount of data lost. The loss is limited because the temporary file is not updated in real time. Rather, it is updated periodically (typically defaulted to every ten minutes in most programs), depending on the application's settings.

Temporary files can sometimes be recovered during a forensic examination. Some of the data that may have been orphaned from a previous version may be recoverable, if not the complete file. This is true even when a document has been typed and printed, but never saved. The creation of the temporary file makes it possible for some of this "unsaved" data to be recovered during analysis.

Another type of temporary file valuable to the computer investigator is the *print spool file*. When a print job is sent to the printer, a spooling process delays the sending of the data so the application can continue to work while the printing takes place in the background. To facilitate this, a temporary print spool file is created; this file typically includes the data to be printed and information specific to the printer. There are different methods for accomplishing this, and thus the files created as a result of this process vary. It is sometimes possible to view the data in a readable format from the files created during the spooling process.

Latent Data

The term **latent data** includes data that are blocked (not necessarily intentionally) from a user's view. It includes areas of files and disks that typically are not apparent to the computer user, but contain data nonetheless. Latent data are one of the reasons a forensic image of the media is created. If a standard copy were all that was produced, only the logical data (that which the operating system is aware of) would be captured. Getting every bit of data ensures that potentially valuable evidence in latent data is not missed.

Once the all-inclusive forensic image is produced, how are the latent data viewed? Utilities that allow a user to examine a hard disk drive on a binary level (ones and zeros) are the answer. Applications such as Norton Disk Editor™ and WinHex™ provide this type of access to a hard disk drive or other computer media. Thus, these applications, sometimes also referred to as hex editors (for the hexadecimal shorthand of computer language), allow all data to be read on the binary level independent of the operating system's file system table. Utilities such as these can write to the media under examination, thus changing data. Consequently, a software or hardware write-blocker should be used.

A more common option in data forensics is to use specialized forensic examination software. EnCase™ and Forensic Toolkit for Windows™ and SMART™ and Forensic Autopsy for Linux™ are examples of forensic software. Each allows a search for evidence on the binary level and provides automated tools for performing common forensic processing techniques. Examiners should be cautious, however, about relying too heavily on automated tools. Merely using an automated tool without understanding what is happening in the background and why evidentiary data may exist in particular locations would severely impede the ability to testify to the findings.

Slack Space Slack space is empty space on a hard disk drive created because of the way the HDD stores files. Recall that although the smallest unit of data measure is one bit (either a one or a zero), a HDD cannot address or deal with such a

latent data
Areas of files and disks that are typically not apparent to the computer user (and often not to the operating system), but contain data nonetheless

small unit. In fact, not even a byte (eight bits) can be addressed. Rather, the smallest unit of addressable space by a HDD is the sector. HDDs typically group sectors in 512-byte increments, whereas CD-ROMs allocate 2,048 bytes per sector.

If the minimum addressable unit of the HDD is 512 bytes, what happens if the file is only 100 bytes? In this instance there are 412 bytes of slack space. It does not end here, however, because of the minimum cluster requirement. As you may recall, clusters are groups of sectors used to store files and folders. The cluster is the minimum storage unit defined and used by the logical partition. It is because of the minimum addressable sector of the HDD and the minimum unit of storage requirement of the volume that we have slack space.

Minimum cluster allocation must be defined in a sector multiple of two. Thus, a cluster must be a minimum of two, four, six, or eight sectors, and so on. Returning to our initial example of the 100-byte file, suppose an HDD has a two-sectors-per-cluster volume requirement. This means that the HDD will isolate a minimum of two 512-byte sectors (a total of 1,024 bytes) of storage space for that 100-byte file. The remaining 924 bytes would be slack space (see Figure 18–9).

FIGURE 18–9
Slack space illustrated in a two-sector cluster. Cluster sizes are typically greater than two sectors, but two sectors are displayed here for simplicity.

To illustrate this point, let us expand on the previous example of safe-deposit boxes. The bank offers safe-deposit boxes of a particular size. This is the equivalent of the HDD's clusters. A person wanting to place only a deed to a house in the box gets the same size box as a person who wants to stuff it full of cash. The former would have empty space should he or she desire to place additional items in the box. This empty space is the equivalent of slack space. But what if the box becomes full and the person needs more space? That person must then get a second box. Similarly, if a file grows to fill one cluster and beyond, a second cluster (and subsequent clusters as needed) is allocated. The remaining space in the second cluster is slack space. This continues as more and more clusters are allocated depending on file size and file growth.

This example is a bit of an oversimplification because there are actually two types of slack space: RAM slack and file slack. **RAM slack** occupies the space from where the actual (logical) data portion of the file ends to where the first allocated sector in the cluster terminates. **File slack**, therefore, occupies the remaining space of the cluster.

RAM slack
The area beginning at the end of the logical file and terminating at the end of that sector; in some older operating systems this area is padded with information in RAM

file slack
The area that begins at the end of the last sector that contains logical data and terminates at the end of the cluster

Let us go back to the 100-byte file with the two-sectors-per-cluster minimum requirement. Following the end of the logical data (the end of the 100 bytes), the remaining 412 bytes of that sector is RAM slack; the additional 512 bytes completing the cluster is then file slack. See Figure 18–10 for a visual depiction. The question now becomes: What can I expect to find in slack space, and why is this important? The answer: junk—valuable junk.

HDD

FIGURE 18–10   File slack.

RAM slack is a concept that was more relevant in older operating systems. Remember that the minimum amount of space the HDD can address is the 512-byte sector. Therefore, if the file size is only 100 bytes, the remaining space must be padded. Some operating systems pad this area with data contained in RAM. This could include Web pages, passwords, data files, or other data that existed in RAM when the file was written. Modern Windows operating systems pad this space with zeros, but some examinations may still yield valuable data in this area.

File slack, on the other hand, can contain a lot of old, orphaned data. To illustrate this point, let's take the 100-byte file example a bit further. Let's say that before the 100-byte file was written to the HDD, occupying one cluster (two sectors totaling 1024 bytes), a 1,000-byte file occupied this space but was deleted by the user. When a file is "deleted" the data still remains behind, so it is probably a safe bet that data from the original 1,000-byte file remains in the slack space of the new 100-byte file now occupying this cluster. This is just one example of why data exists in file slack and why it may be valuable as evidence.

In one final attempt to illustrate this point, let us again build on our safe-deposit box analogy. Suppose a person rents two safe-deposit boxes, each box representing a sector and the two combined representing a cluster. If that person places the deed to his house in the first box, the remaining space in that box would be analogous to RAM slack. The space in the second box would be the equivalent of file slack. The only difference is that unlike the empty spaces of the safe-deposit box, the slack space of the file most likely contains data that may be valuable as evidence.

The data contained in RAM and file slack is not really the concern of the operating system. As far as the OS is concerned, this space is empty and therefore ready to be used. Until that happens, however, an examination with one of the aforementioned tools will allow a look into these areas, thus revealing the orphaned data. The same is true for unallocated space.

Unallocated Space Latent evidentiary data also resides in **unallocated space**. What is unallocated space, how does data get in there, and what is done to access this space?

If we have an 80-GB hard drive and only half of the hard drive is filled with data, then the other half, or 40 GB, is unallocated space (see <u>Figure 18–11</u>). Returning to our safe-deposit box analogy, if the entire bank of safe-deposit boxes contains 100 boxes, but only 50 are currently in use, then the other 50 would be the equivalent of unallocated space. The HDD's unallocated space typically contains a lot of useful data. The constant shuffling of files on the HDD causes data to become orphaned in unallocated space as the logical portion of the file is rewritten to other places. Some examples of how data is orphaned may help.

unallocated space
The area of the HDD that the operating system (file system table) sees as empty (containing no logical files) and ready for data; simply stated, it is the unused portion of the HDD, but is not necessarily empty

FIGURE 18–11
Simplistic view of a hard drive platter demonstrating the concept of unallocated space.

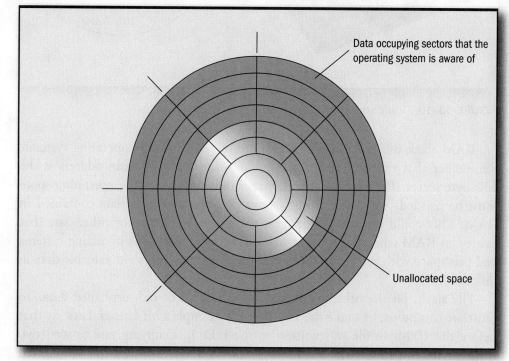

Data occupying sectors that the operating system is aware of

Unallocated space

Defragmenting. Defragmenting a HDD involves moving noncontiguous data back together. Remember that the HDD has minimum space reservation requirements. Again, if a file requires only 100 bytes of space, the operating system may allocate much more than that for use. If the file grows past what has been allocated for it, another cluster is required. If, however, a different file occupies the next cluster in line, then the operating system will have to find another place for that first file on the drive. In this scenario, the file is said to be *fragmented* because data for the same file is contained in noncontiguous clusters. In the case of the HDD, the shuffling of files causes data to be orphaned in unallocated space.

Ultimately, fragmentation of numerous files can degrade the performance of a HDD, causing the read/write heads to have to traverse the platters to locate the data. Defragmenting the HDD takes noncontiguous data and rearranges it so it is in contiguous clusters. Building yet again on our safe-deposit box analogy, if a renter eventually needs to store more property than his original box can hold, the bank will rent him a second box. If, however, all the boxes around his are occupied and the only free one is in another section of the room, then his property is "fragmented." The bank would have to "defrag" the safe-deposit boxes to get the property of users with more than one box into adjacent boxes.

Swap File/Swap Space. Recall that a computer uses the HDD to maximize the amount of RAM by constantly swapping data in and out of RAM to a predetermined location on the HDD, thus freeing valuable RAM. The constant read and write operations of RAM cause a constant change in the page file or memory space. Data can become orphaned in unallocated space from this constant swapping to and from the HDD.

Deleted Files. The deletion of files is another way that data becomes orphaned in unallocated space. Data from deleted files can manifest itself in different ways during a forensic examination. The actions that occur when a file is deleted vary among file systems. However, generally speaking, the data is not gone. For example, consider what happens when a user or program deletes a file in a Windows operating system with a FAT file system. When a file is deleted, the first character in the file's directory entry (its name) is replaced with the Greek letter sigma. When the sigma replaces the first character, the file is no longer viewable through conventional methods and the operating system views the space previously occupied by the file as available. The data, however, is still there.

This example doesn't account for the actions of the Windows Recycle Bin. When the Windows operating system is set up to merely place the deleted file in the Recycle Bin, the original directory entry is deleted and one is created in the Recycle folder for that particular user. The new Recycle folder entry is linked to another file, the *info* or *info2* file, which includes some additional data, such as the location of the file before its deletion in case the user wishes to restore it to that location. Detailed discussions of the function of the Recycle Bin are beyond the scope of this chapter, but suffice it to say that even when the Recycle Bin is emptied, the data usually remains behind until overwritten. Moreover, Windows NTFS partitions and Linux EXT partitions handle deleted files differently, but in both cases data typically remains.

What if a new file writes data to the location of the original file? Generally speaking, the data is gone. This is, of course, unless the new file only partially overwrites the original. In this instance we return to the unallocated-space orphaned-data scenario. If a file that occupied two clusters is deleted and a new file overwrites one of the clusters, then the data in the second cluster is orphaned in unallocated space. Of course, yet a third file can overwrite the second cluster entirely, but until then the data remains in unallocated space.

Let us once again look to our safe-deposit box analogy. If, for example, the owner of two safe-deposit boxes stopped renting them, the bank would list them as available. If the owner didn't clean them out, the contents would remain unchanged. If a new owner rented one of the boxes, the contents from the former owner would be replaced with the new owner's possessions. The second box would therefore still contain orphaned contents from its previous owner. The contents would remain in this "unallocated box" space until another renter occupies it.

Quick Review

- The types of computer evidence can be grouped under two major subheadings: visible and latent data.

- Visible data is data that the operating system is aware of and thus is easily accessible to the user. It includes any type of user-created data, such as word-processing documents, spreadsheets, accounting records, databases, and pictures.

- Temporary files created by programs as a sort of backup on the fly can prove valuable as evidence. Data in the swap space (used to conserve the valuable RAM within the computer system) can also yield evidentiary data.

- Latent data is data that the operating system is not aware of. The constant shuffling of data through deletion, defragmentation, swapping, and so on is one of the ways data is stored in latent areas.

- Latent data can exist in both RAM slack and file slack. RAM slack is the area from the end of the logical file to the end of the sector. File slack is the remaining area from the end of the final sector containing data to the end of the cluster.

- Latent data may be found in unallocated space—space on a HDD that the operating system sees as empty and ready for data.

- When a user deletes files the data typically remains behind, so deleted files are another source of latent data.

Forensic Analysis of Internet Data

It's important from the investigative standpoint to be familiar with the evidence left behind from a user's Internet activity. A forensic examination of a computer system reveals quite a bit of data about a user's Internet activity. The data described next would be accessed and examined using the forensic techniques outlined in the previous sections of this chapter.

Internet Cache

Evidence of Web browsing typically exists in abundance on the user's computer. Most Web browsers (Internet Explorer™, Safari™, and Firefox™) use a caching system to expedite Web browsing and make it more efficient. This was particularly true in the days of dial-up Internet access. When a user accesses a Web site, such as the *New York Times* home page, the data is fed from that server (in this example the *New York Times*), via the Internet service provider, over whatever type of connection the user has, to his or her computer. If that computer is accessing the Internet via a dial-up connection, the transfer of the *New York Times* home page may take a while, because the data transfer rate and capabilities (bandwidth) of the telephone system is limited. Even with the high-speed access of a DSL line or cable connection, conservation of bandwidth is always a consideration. Taking that into account, Web browsers store (cache) portions of the pages visited onto the local hard disk drive. This way, if the page is revisited, portions of it can be reconstructed more quickly from this saved data, rather than having to pull it yet again from the Internet and use precious bandwidth.

This **Internet cache** is a potential source of evidence for the computer investigator. Portions of, and in some cases, entire visited Web pages can be reconstructed. Even if deleted, these cached files can often be recovered (see the section on deleted data). Investigators must know how to search for this data within the particular Web browser used by a suspect.

Internet cache
Portions of visited Web pages placed on the local hard disk drive to facilitate quicker retrieval once revisited

Internet Cookies

Cookies provide another area where potential evidence can be found. To appreciate the value of cookies you must first understand how they get onto the computer and their intended purpose. **Cookies** are placed on the local hard disk drive by Web sites the user has visited, if the user's Web browser (such as Internet Explorer™) is set to allow this to happen. Microsoft Internet Explorer places cookies in a dedicated directory. The Web site uses cookies to track certain information about its visitors, such as the history of visits, purchasing habits, passwords, and personal information used to recognize the user for later visits.

Consider a user who registers for an account at the Barnes and Noble bookstore Web site, and then returns to the same site from the same computer a few days later. The site will then display "Welcome, *Your User Name.*" This data is retrieved from the cookie file placed on the user's hard disk drive by the Web site during the initial visit and registration with the site.

It is helpful to think of cookies almost like a Caller ID for Web sites. The site recognizes and retrieves information about the visitor, as when a salesperson recognizes the caller from a Caller ID display and quickly pulls the client's file. Cookie files can be a valuable source of evidence. In Internet Explorer™, they take the form of plain text files, which can typically be opened with a standard text viewer or word-processing program, revealing part of the data. The existence of the files themselves, regardless of the information contained within, can be of evidentiary value to show a history of Web visits.

A typical cookie may resemble the following: rsaferstein@forensicscience.txt. From this we can surmise that someone using the local computer login *rsaferstein* accessed the forensic science Web site. It is possible that the cookie was placed there by an annoying pop-up ad, but considered against other evidence in the computer data, the presence of this cookie may be of corroborative value.

cookies
Files placed on a computer from a visited Web site; they are used to track visits and usage of that site

Internet History

Most Web browsers track the history of Web page visits for the computer user. This is probably done merely for a matter of convenience. Like the "recent calls" list on a cell phone, the **Internet history** provides an accounting of sites most recently visited, with some storing weeks' worth of visits. Users can go back and access sites they recently visited just by going through the browser's history. Most Web browsers store this information in one particular file; Internet Explorer™ uses the *index.dat* file. On a Microsoft Windows™ system, an *index.dat* file is created for each login user name on the computer.

Internet history
An accounting of Web sites visited; different browsers store this information in different ways

The history file can be located and read with most popular computer forensic software packages. It displays the uniform resource locator (URL) of each Web site, along with the date and time the site was accessed. An investigation involving Internet use almost always includes an examination of Internet history data.

In some respects, the term "*Internet history*" is wrong because it doesn't encompass all of its functions. Several browsers—Internet Explorer™, for one—store other valuable evidence independent of Internet access. It is not uncommon to see files accessed over a network listed in the history. Similarly, files accessed on external media, such as CDs, or thumb drives, may also appear in the history. Regardless, the Internet history data is a valuable source of evidence worthy of examination (see Figure 18–12).

FIGURE 18–12
The Internet history displays more than just web browsing activity. Here we see Microsoft Word documents and a picture accessed on the current day.

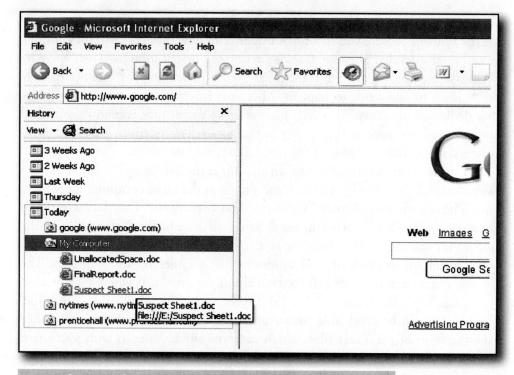

Bookmarks and Favorite Places

bookmark
A feature that enables the user to designate favorite sites for fast and easy access

Another way users can access Web sites quickly is to store them in their **bookmarks** or "Favorites." Like a preset radio station, Web browsers allow users to bookmark Web sites for future visits (see Figure 18–13). A lot can be learned from a user's bookmarked sites. You may learn what online news a person is interested in or what type of hobbies he or she has. You may also see that person's favorite child pornography or computer hacking sites bookmarked.

In Microsoft Internet Explorer™ the favorites are kept in a folder with link (shortcut) files to a particular URL. They can be organized in subfolders or grouped by type. The same is true for the Firefox™ web browser, except that Firefox™ bookmarks are stored in a document created in hypertext markup language (HTML), the same language interpreted by Web browsers themselves.

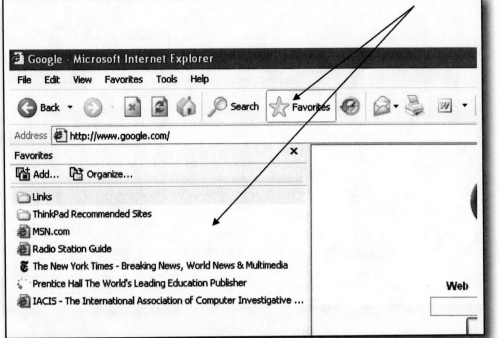

FIGURE 18–13
Bookmarks or favorite places can be saved for quick access in most web browsers.

Forensic Investigation of Internet Communications

Computer investigations often begin with or are centered on Internet communication. Whether it is a chat conversation among many people, an instant message conversation between two individuals, or the back-and-forth of an e-mail exchange, human communication has long been a source of evidentiary material. *Regardless of the type, investigators are typically interested in communication.*

Role of the IP

With all of the computer manufacturers and software developers, some rules are necessary for computers to communicate on a global network. Just as any human language needs rules for people to communicate successfully, so does the language of computers. Computers that participate on the Internet, therefore, must be provided with an address known as an Internet protocol (IP) address from the Internet service provider to which they connect.

IP addresses take the form ###.###.###.###, in which, generally speaking, ### can be any number from 0 to 255. A typical IP address might look like this: 66.94.234.13. Not only do these IP addresses provide the means by which data can be routed to the appropriate location, but they also provide the means by which most Internet investigations are conducted (see Figure 18–14). Thus, the IP address may lead to the identity of a real person. If an IP address is the link to the identity of a real person, then it is quite obviously valuable for identifying someone on the Internet.

FIGURE 18–14
Two computers communicating by sending data to each other's IP address via the Internet. An IP address is assigned to each computer by its respective Internet service provider (ISP).

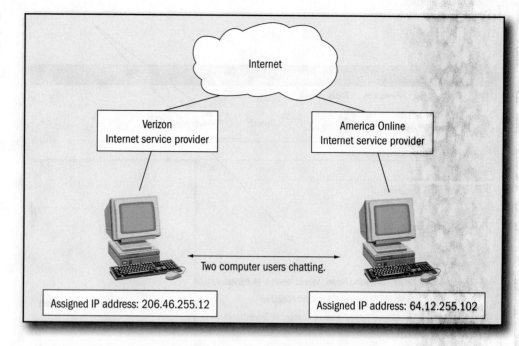

To illustrate, let's assume that a user of the Internet, fictitiously named John Smith, connects to the Internet from his home by way of a Verizon™ DSL connection. Verizon™ in this case would be responsible for providing Smith with his IP address. Verizon™ was issued a bank of IP addresses to service its customers from a regulatory body designed to track the usage of IP addresses (obviously so no two were used at the same time).

Suppose that Smith, while connected to the Internet, decides to threaten an ex-girlfriend by sending her an e-mail telling her he is going to kill her. That e-mail must first pass through Smith's Internet service provider's computers (in this case, Verizon™) on its way to its destination—Smith's ex-girlfriend. The e-mail would be stamped by the servers that it passes through, and this stamp would include the IP address given to Smith by Verizon™ for his session on the Internet.

An investigator responsible for tracking that e-mail would locate the originating IP address stamped in the e-mail header. That IP address could be researched using one of many Internet sites (http://www.samspade.org, http://www.arin.net) to determine which Internet service provider was given this IP as part of a block to service its customers (see Figure 18–15). The investigator then files a subpoena with the Internet service provider (Verizon™) asking which of its customers was using that IP address on that date and time.

IP addresses are located in different places for different methods of Internet communications. E-mail has the IP address in the header portion of the mail. This may not be readily apparent and may require a bit of configuration to reveal. Each e-mail client is different and needs to be evaluated on a case-by-case basis. For an instant message or chat session, the particular provider (the one providing the chat mechanism—AOL™, Yahoo™, and so on) would be contacted to provide the user's IP address.

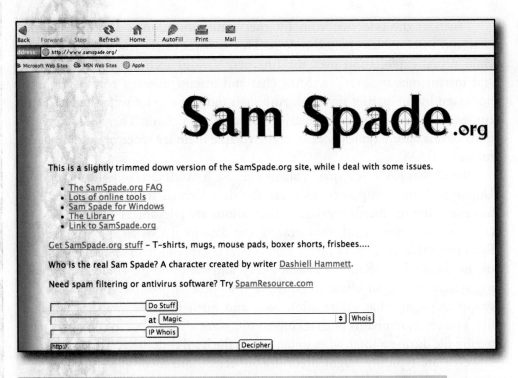

FIGURE 18–15
Sites such as
www.samspade.org
can be used to track
the origins of an IP
address. *Courtesy
Word to the Wise*

E-Mail, Chat, and Instant Messaging

E-mail can be read by a number of *clients* or software programs. Two of the most popular ways to access, read, and store e-mail in today's Internet environment, however, are Microsoft Outlook and an Internet browser. Some people even use a combination of the two.

If an e-mail account is linked through Microsoft Outlook, then the e-mail is stored in a compound file (a file with several layers). Typically, a compound file exists for received (inbox), sent, and deleted e-mail. Users can also create new categories (shown as folders in Outlook) and categorize saved e-mail there. Most computer forensic software applications can view (mount) these compound files so that the e-mail can be seen, including any file attachments. These files can also be imported into a clean copy (one not attached to an account) of Microsoft Outlook and the e-mail viewed there. Investigators must also be aware that in a computer network environment, the user's Outlook files may not reside on his or her workstation computer, but rather on a central mail or file server.

Most accounts offer the ability to access e-mail through a Web-based interface as well. This way, users can access their e-mail remotely from other computers. For e-mail accessed through a Web browser, the information presented earlier on Internet-based evidence applies. The Web interface converts the e-mail into a document suitable for reading in a Web browser. Consequently, Web-based e-mail is often found in the Internet cache. This is particularly true of free Internet e-mail providers such as Hotmail and Yahoo.

Much of the evidence from Internet communication is also derived from chat and instant message technology. This is particularly true in the world of child sexual exploitation over the Internet. Various technologies provide chat and instant message services. Most chat and instant message conversations are not saved by the parties involved. Although most of the software does allow for conversation archiving, it is typically turned off by default. Therefore, conversations of this nature typically exist in the volatile memory space of random-access memory (RAM).

Recall that RAM is termed volatile because it holds data only if it has power. Unplugging the computer will cause the data located in RAM to be lost. If, however, chat or instant message conversations are relevant as evidence and the computer was turned off, thus erasing the data in RAM, all may not be lost. Remember that there is an interaction between the computer system's RAM and the hard disk drive. RAM is a commodity, and therefore the computer's operating system makes an effort to conserve it as best as possible. This is done by swapping/paging that information back and forth into the swap space/paging file. Therefore, remnants of chat conversations are often found in the swap space/paging file during a forensic examination of the hard disk drive. These remnants, however, are typically fragmented, disconnected, and incomplete. Therefore, if the chat or instant message is still present on the screen (and thus probably still in RAM) the investigator needs a method by which to preserve and collect it.

A detailed discussion of capturing volatile data from RAM is beyond the scope of this chapter. Suffice it to say that many commercial forensic software packages can capture this data. Similarly, Linux-based tools can accomplish this as well. The examiner may even be able to export the data remotely to another device. Regardless of the method, the data needs to be acquired.

Furthermore, many programs such as America Online Instant Messenger™, Yahoo Messenger™, and mIRC™ (Internet Relay Chat) create files regarding the rooms or channels a user chatted in or the screen names with which a user sent instant messages. Each application needs to be researched and the computer forensic examination guided by an understanding of how it functions.

Unauthorized computer intrusion, more commonly referred to as **hacking**, is the concern of every computer administrator. Hackers penetrate computer systems for a number of reasons. Sometimes the motive is corporate espionage; other times it is merely for bragging rights within the hacker community. Most commonly, though, a rogue or disgruntled employee with some knowledge of the computer network is looking to cause damage. Whatever the motivation, corporate America frequently turns to law enforcement to investigate and prosecute these cases.

Generally speaking, when investigating an unauthorized computer intrusion, investigators concentrate their efforts in three locations: *log files, volatile memory*, and *network traffic*. Logs typically document the IP address of the computer that made the connection. Logs can be located in several locations on a computer network. Most servers on the Internet track connections made to them through the use of logs. Additionally the router (the device responsible for directing data) may contain log files detailing connections.

**MyCrimeKit:
WebExtra 18.1**

Follow the trail of an e-mail as it travels through the Internet
www.mycrimekit.com

hacking
Has various meanings, but is frequently used as a slang term for an unauthorized computer or network intrusion

Similarly, devices known as **firewalls** may contain log files listing computers that were allowed access to the network or an individual system. Firewalls are devices (taking the form of either hardware or software) that permit only requested traffic to enter a computer system (or, more appropriately, a network). In other words, if a user didn't send out a request for Internet traffic from a specific system, the firewall should block its entry. If the log files captured the IP address of the intruder, then revealing the user behind the IP is the same process as for e-mail. Investigating a computer intrusion, however, does get a bit more complicated than this.

Frequently, in cases of unlawful access to a computer network, the perpetrator attempts to cover the tracks of his or her IP address. In these instances, advanced investigative techniques may be necessary to discover the hacker's true identity. When an intrusion is in progress, the investigator may have to capture volatile data (data in RAM). The data in RAM at the time of an intrusion may provide valuable clues into the identity of the intruder, or at least his or her method of attack. As in the case of an instant message or chat conversation, the data in RAM needs to be acquired.

Another standard tactic for investigating intrusion cases is to document all programs installed and running on a system, in order to discover malicious software installed by the perpetrator to facilitate entry. The investigator uses specialized software to document running processes, registry entries, open ports, and any installed files.

Additionally, the investigator may want to capture live network traffic as part of the evidence collection and investigation process. Traffic that travels the network does so in the form of data packets. In addition to data, these packets also contain source and destination IP addresses. If the attack requires two-way communication, as in the case of a hacker stealing data, then data needs to be transmitted back to the hacker's computer using the destination IP address. Once this is learned, the investigation can focus on that system. Moreover, the type of data that is being transmitted on the network may be a clue as to what type of attack is being launched, whether any important data is being stolen, or what types of malicious software, if any, are involved in the attack.

firewall
Hardware or software designed to protect intrusions into an Internet network

Quick Review

- An investigator tracking the origin of an e-mail seeks out the sender's IP address in the e-mail's header. Chat and instant messages are typically located in a computer's random-access memory (RAM).

- Tracking the origin of unauthorized computer intrusions (hacking) requires investigating a computer's log file, RAM, and network traffic.

- A firewall is a device designed to protect against intrusions into a computer network.

Chapter Review

- Computer forensics involves preserving, acquiring, extracting, and interpreting computer data.

- Software programs are applications that carry out a set of instructions.

- The central processing unit (CPU) is the brain of the computer—the main chip responsible for doing the actual computing.

- The motherboard is the main circuit board within a computer.

- Read-only memory (ROM) chips store programs that control the boot (startup) process and configure a computer's components.

- Random-access memory (RAM) is volatile memory, which is lost when power is turned off. Programs are loaded into RAM because of its faster read speed.

- The hard disk drive (HDD) is typically the primary location of data storage within the computer.

- The computer's operating system (OS) is the bridge between the human user and the computer's electronic components. It provides the user with a working environment and facilitates interaction with the system's components.

- Formatting is the process of preparing a hard disk drive to store and retrieve data in its current form.

- A sector is the smallest unit of data that a hard drive can address. A cluster usually is the minimum space allocated to a file. Clusters are groups of sectors.

- A FAT is a file allocation table. It tracks the location of files and folders on the hard disk drive.

- Aspects of a computer that should be photographed close up at an electronic crime scene include (1) the screen of any running computer monitor, (2) all the connections to the main system unit, such as peripheral devices (keyboard, monitor, speakers, mouse, and so on), and (3) equipment serial numbers.

- Two situations in which an investigator would not unplug a computer at an electronic crime scene are (1) if encryption is being used and pulling the plug will encrypt the data, rendering it unreadable without a password or key, and (2) if data exists in RAM that has not been saved to the HDD, and will thus be lost if power to the system is discontinued.

- The primary goal in obtaining data from a HDD is to do so without altering even one bit of data. To this end, a Message Digest 5 (MD5)/Secure Hash Algorithm (SHA) takes a "fingerprint" of a hard disk drive (HDD) before and after forensic imaging.

- The types of computer evidence can be grouped under two major subheadings: visible and latent data.

- Visible data is data that the operating system is aware of and thus is easily accessible to the user. It includes any type of user-created data, such as word-processing documents, spreadsheets, accounting records, databases, and pictures.

- Temporary files created by programs as a sort of backup on the fly can prove valuable as evidence. Data in the swap space (used to conserve the valuable RAM within the computer system) can also yield evidentiary data.

- Latent data is data that the operating system is not aware of. The constant shuffling of data through deletion, defragmentation, swapping, and so on is one of the ways data is stored in latent areas.

- Latent data can exist in both RAM slack and file slack. RAM slack is the area from the end of the logical file to the end of the sector. File slack is the remaining area from the end of the final sector containing data to the end of the cluster.

- Latent data may be found in unallocated space—space on a HDD that the operating system sees as empty and ready for data.

- When a user deletes files the data typically remains behind, so deleted files are another source of latent data.

- An investigator tracking the origin of an e-mail seeks out the sender's IP address in the e-mail's header. Chat and instant messages are typically located in a computer's random-access memory (RAM).

- Tracking the origin of unauthorized computer intrusions (hacking) requires investigating a computer's log file, RAM, and network traffic.

- A firewall is a device designed to protect against intrusions into a computer network.

Review Questions

1. Which of the following is not a utility for quickly accessing Web pages a user has visited previously?
   a. bookmarks
   b. Internet history
   c. a search engine
   d. a favorites

2. Which of the following carries data from one hardware device to another?
   a. system bus
   b. central processing unit (CPU)
   c. random-access memory (RAM)
   d. network interface card (NIC)

3. The volatile memory of the computer is known as
   a. ROM.
   b. BIOS.
   c. RAM.
   d. the CPU.

4. Areas of files and disks that are not apparent to the user, and sometimes not even to the operating system, are called
   a. missing data.
   b. latent data.
   c. exceptional data.
   d. hidden data.

5. An investigator responsible for tracking e-mail communication would begin by locating
   a. the computer that originated the questioned e-mail.
   b. the receiving IP address.
   c. the originating IP address.
   d. the ISP customer database assigned an IP address.

6. True or False: Processing the electronic crime scene has very little in common with processing a traditional crime scene and requires that the investigator take a substantially different approach.

7. True or False: The goal in obtaining data from a HDD is to do so without altering any data.

8. True or False: If so motivated, most home computer users could easily perpetrate counterfeiting and check and document fraud using a decent ink-jet printer and a scanner.

9. True or False: The service that is most commonly used in conjunction with the Internet is e-mail.

10. True or False: Because Web browsers typically do not use a caching system, evidence of Web browsing is not typically available to the forensic examiner.

11. What is the difference between hardware and software?

12. What are CDs, DVDs, and other containers for programs that are loaded into the memory of a computer called?

13. What is a computer's motherboard?

14. What type of memory stores software programs and instructions while the computer is turned on? Because it is not permanent, and its contents are forever lost once power is taken away from the computer, what is it also called?

15. What is firmware? What is another name for firmware? Why is it important to forensic computer investigation?

16. What is the role of the computer's operating system (OS)?

17. What is formatting? Why must a hard disk drive be formatted?

18. What are sectors and clusters? How are they related to one another?

19. What is the smallest unit of information on a computer? What do eight of them constitute?

20. What is a FAT and what purpose does it serve?

21. Name two situations in which an investigator would not immediately unplug a computer at an electronic crime scene.

22. What is the purpose of a Message Digest 5 (MD5)/Secure Hash Algorithm (SHA)? Why would a forensic computer examiner run such an algorithm?

23. Why would investigators want to copy blank or unused portions of the HDD?

24. What is swap space?

25. In which of the following places would a computer forensic investigator not look for latent data?
    a. RAM slack
    b. file slack
    c. unallocated space
    d. temporary files

26. What is slack space?

27. What is fragmentation? What effect does fragmentation have on a hard disk drive (HDD)?

28. What is an IP address? What form do addresses typically take?

29. What is a human-readable name assigned to an IP address called?

30. What is a browser?

31. What is the purpose of an Internet cache?

32. List three places where a forensic computer examiner might look to determine what Web sites a computer user has visited recently.

33. Why is an IP important to forensic computer examination?

34. What is hacking? Who most commonly engages in hacking, and for what purpose?

35. What is a firewall and how does it work?

Application and Critical Thinking

1. If a file system defines a cluster as six sectors, how many bits of information can be stored on each cluster? Explain your answer.

2. Criminalist Tom Parauda is investigating the scene of a crime involving a computer. After he arrives, he photographs the overall scene and takes close-up shots of all the connections to the single computer involved, as well as photos of the serial numbers of the computer and all peripheral devices. Tom then labels the cord to each peripheral device, then disconnects them from the computer. After making sure that all data in RAM has been saved to the hard disk drive, he unplugs the computer from the wall. What mistakes, if any, did Tom make?

3. You are investigating a case in which an accountant is accused of keeping fraudulent books for a firm. Upon examining his computer, you notice that the suspect uses two different accounting programs that are capable of reading the same types of files. Given this information, where would you probably begin to search for latent data on the computer and why?

4. You are examining two computers to determine the IP address from which several threatening e-mails were sent. The first computer uses Microsoft Outlook as an e-mail client, and the second uses a Web-based e-mail client. Where would you probably look first for the IP addresses in each of these computers?

Endnotes

1. One million bytes is referred to as a megabyte (MB); 1 billion bytes is termed a gigabyte (GB).

2. Pulling the plug should always be done by removing the plug that is connected to the back of the computer. If a plug is removed from the wall, it may be unknowingly connected to a battery backup (UPS). Under these circumstances, the UPS may cause an alert to the system and keep the unit powered on.

3. In this instance, *bit* is both metaphorical and literal. Every bit of information is needed, so we must get it all. So too every bit, as in the smallest unit of data storage—a one or a zero—must be imaged.

4. Actually, the more appropriate term is probably *paging* as opposed to swapping. This is because entire programs are typically not swapped in and out of memory to the swap space; rather, *pages* of memory are placed there.

Careers in
Forensic Science

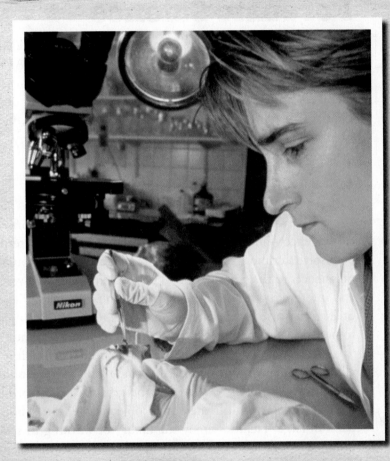

In previous chapters we have encountered some of the many disciplines within forensic science pathology, toxicology, anthropology, archaeology, and entomology, to name a few. However, the profession of forensic science encompasses an even wider range of activities, with work taking place in the field, the laboratory, and the courtroom. In this chapter, we will explore some of the various careers within forensic science and discuss the kind of training necessary to pursue each.

Disciplines in Forensic Science

The wide variety of activities comprising forensic science is reflected in the structure of the American Academy of Forensic Sciences (AAFS), the largest forensic science organization in the world. Each of the five thousand scientists who are members of the AAFS belongs to one of the academy's 11 divisions: Criminalistics, Digital & Multimedia Sciences, Engineering Sciences, General, Jurisprudence, Odontology, Pathology/Biology, Physical Anthropology, Psychiatry/Behavioral Science, Questioned Documents, and Toxicology.

Criminalistics

As we have seen throughout this text, the criminalist works primarily with physical evidence—analyzing, comparing, identifying, and interpreting items that may help solve a crime. The criminalist applies techniques from the physical and natural sciences to the examination of physical evidence. However, examining, testing, and interpreting results are only part of the responsibilities of the criminalist. He or she must also effectively communicate technical details and scientific findings to nonspecialist members of the law enforcement community.

The extent and depth of versatility expected of the forensic scientist are usually determined by the size of the crime laboratory's staff. Scientists in smaller laboratories are often expected to be generalists, performing a wide variety of tasks in order to fulfill the varied objectives of the laboratory. Their counterparts in larger facilities enjoy the luxury of working in specialized areas, relying on a teamwork approach to provide the spectrum of scientific skills needed for the comparison or identification of physical evidence. Currently there is a huge demand for forensic DNA analysts. Generally these positions require a graduate degree in biochemistry or forensic science.

In addition to his or her technical responsibilities, the newly trained criminalist must discover and master the role of the expert witness. A good courtroom demeanor and the ability to communicate thoughts and ideas in clear, concise terms are absolutely essential if the scientist's examination and conclusions are to be properly and effectively presented at a hearing or in court.

Education and Training The minimum educational requirement is a bachelor's degree in a science such as chemistry, biology, physics, or molecular biology. Coursework must include mathematics, chemistry, and/or biology. Many government criminalist positions have either local or national civil service educational and work experience requirements. Interested job applicants should inquire with appropriate civil service authorities to determine these requirements for a particular jurisdiction. The criminalist also participates in continuing education courses throughout his or her career to remain current with the ever-changing technology and procedures in the field. The American Board of Criminalistics (http://www. criminalistics.com) offers certification for trained criminalists who pass a rigorous examination.

Career Opportunities Criminalists work in a wide array of settings, including forensic laboratories in local, regional, and state police and sheriff's departments and in district attorneys' offices. They may also serve federal agencies such as the U.S. military; Drug Enforcement Administration (DEA); Alcohol, Tobacco, Firearms and Explosives (ATF); Federal Bureau of Investigation (FBI); Department of Justice (DOJ); U.S. Postal Service (USPS); Secret Service (SS); Central Intelligence Agency (CIA); and U.S. Fish and Wildlife Service. Trained criminalists also may teach at community colleges and universities.

Forensic Engineering

Forensic engineers apply principles of engineering to resolve legal issues, primarily in civil, rather than criminal cases. However, a forensic engineer may also assist in criminal matters or cases involving violation of government regulations. These areas of activity cover investigations into structural failure; reconstruction of automobile accidents; exploring the causes of fires or explosions; and evaluation of construction, manufacturing, or maintenance procedures. The forensic engineer's work applies in personal-injury suits, construction claims, contract or warranty disputes, patent or copyright infringements, and criminal and regulatory matters. Certification in the forensic engineering sciences is available from the International Institute of Forensic Engineering Sciences (http://www.iifes.org).

Education and Training The minimum educational requirement for a forensic engineer is a bachelor's degree in engineering or an allied science. However, an advanced degree is desirable, as is registration in a professional engineering society. Because of the wide range of engineering disciplines, a forensic engineer should have professional experience in the particular field(s) of engineering that are the subject of his or her investigation.

Career Opportunities Although some forensic engineers work for sizable corporations or government agencies, most are either self-employed or employed by small firms. Some forensic engineers hold a full-time job in another field (such as engineering consulting or teaching) and perform forensic services on a part-time or contract basis.

Forensic Odontology

As we saw in previous chapters, forensic odontology applies the principles of dental science to law. This includes such activities as identifying human remains through dental analysis as well as comparing bite marks, using both physical and biological dental evidence. Forensic odontologists frequently are called upon after catastrophic events involving large numbers of casualties for which identification from other physical remains is difficult or impossible. Another important area of forensic dentistry is bite mark analysis in cases of assault, rape, and/or homicide. Bite mark analysis may involve collecting saliva for DNA profiling and matching.

Education and Training The forensic odontologist must of course possess a Doctor of Dental Science (D.D.S.) degree, but this basic education by itself is not sufficient to function in this field. Courses in forensic science and medicolegal death investigation are strongly recommended. Additional courses and advanced training in approved forensic techniques and procedures are required to prepare a forensic odontologist to conduct proper crime-scene investigations. Several professional organizations, including the American Board of Forensic Odontology, the American Society of Forensic Odontology, the New York Society of Forensic Dentistry, and the New York County Dental Society, offer advanced training in this field. The American Board of Forensic Odontology (http://www.abfo.org) serves as a highly regarded credentialing body for forensic dentists.

Career Opportunities Most forensic odontologists are engaged in private dental practice. They typically have either formal appointments or consulting relationships with coroners, medical examiners' offices, state and local government agencies, and branches of the military. They also often offer private consultations for insurance companies and law firms. Qualified forensic odontologists frequently provide expert testimony in criminal and civil cases involving personal injuries, worker's compensation, malpractice suits, potential violations of the dentist–patient relationship, and identification of bite marks in criminal cases. Once a commitment is made to enter this field, the dental investigator needs to be current in the most accurate methods available, be aware of ethical values and conflicts, and possess the dedication to render assistance in a timely and professional manner.

Forensic Pathology

Forensic pathology is the application of the principles of pathology—and medicine in general—to the legal process. Forensic pathologists perform autopsies to determine the causes of an individual's death and the circumstances surrounding the death. Understanding the circumstances of a person's death allows the pathologist to determine whether the death was the result of natural causes, an accident, suicide, or homicide. Forensic pathologists also identify remains using medical information, dental records, and other peculiarities of an individual. Forensic pathologists help public health officials recognize and control epidemic diseases. Clinical forensic pathologists study patterns of injury in living people to help law investigations into crimes such as child and elder abuse. The principal professional organization for forensic pathologists is the National Association of Medical Examiners (http://www.thename.org).

Education and Training Forensic pathologists undergo the same training and education as any medical doctor: four years of college, followed by four years of medical school, and then a residency in pathology. After college, medical school, internship, and residency, an additional one- or two-year fellowship in forensic pathology must be completed. This is then followed by certification in pathology or one of its subspecialties from the American Board of Pathology.

Career Opportunities Forensic pathologists are usually employed by city, county, or state medical examiners' offices and hospitals. Some federal government agencies, such as the Centers for Disease Control (CDC) and the Armed Forces Institute of Pathology (AFIP), also employ forensic pathologists.

Forensic Anthropology

Forensic anthropologists are trained in the study of human skeletal biology, and they typically use this training to identify deceased individuals when skeletal remains are the only useful evidence. They also determine whether recovered bones are human or nonhuman and determine sex based on skeletal structure. Forensic pathologists may estimate the cause and time of death when remains are unsuitable for examination by a pathologist.

Education and Training Forensic anthropologists usually earn a Ph.D. in anthropology with an emphasis on human osteology (the study of bones) and anatomy. Practical experience in forensic anthropology typically is required before a court accepts an individual as an expert witness in the field. The American Board of Forensic Anthropology (ABFA) (http://www.theabfa.org) provides professional certification for experts in the field of forensic anthropology. To earn certification, an individual must submit case reports for review that demonstrate practical experience in the field. The applicant must also pass both a written and a practical examination.

Career Opportunities Most forensic anthropologists work out of laboratories at major research institutions or universities. In addition, various state and local medical examiner offices use forensic anthropologists as medical investigators or administrators. The federal government employs forensic anthropologists at the U.S. Army Central Identification Laboratory and the Armed Forces Institute of Pathology. State and federal law enforcement agencies also hire physical anthropologists to act as special agents and laboratory personnel. The largest group of forensic anthropologists works for the military in the U.S. Army's Central Identification Laboratory in Hawaii. A major professional organization in this field is the American Association of Physical Anthropologists (http://www.physanth.org).

Forensic Psychology and Psychiatry

The forensic psychologist or psychiatrist deals with issues of human behavior and mental illness as they relate to matters of civil and criminal law. This involves such activities as determining an individual's competence to stand trial, testify, or waive legal representation, and determining whether mental illness mitigates a suspect's responsibility for his or her actions. For example, the forensic psychiatrist often gives an opinion about whether a defendant may be innocent by reason of mental illness or defect. Other areas in which such expertise is applied includes cases of involuntary psychiatric hospitalization, a patient's right to refuse treatment, and competency to participate in do-not-resuscitate decisions. Forensic psychology includes psychological evaluation and expert testimony regarding such criminal forensic issues as trial competency and forensic behavioral analysis.

Education and Training Forensic psychiatrists are medical doctors who complete a course of study similar to that of forensic pathologists. This includes four years of college followed by medical school and residency training in psychiatry. Some forensic psychiatrists take an additional year or two of postresidency training in psychiatry and the law, and many continue independent study and on-the-job training after completing their formal education. The American Board of Psychiatry and Neurology offers certification in forensic psychiatry for those who pass special examinations. Forensic psychologists usually obtain a Ph.D. degree and are licensed by a state board, and may be board certified by the American Board of Professional Psychology (http://www.abpp.org).

Career Opportunities As with other professionals in the psychiatric profession, forensic psychiatrists and forensic psychologists may be employed in private practice, by hospitals, or by city, county, state, or federal government agencies. They often work in a prison or state hospital setting. The major professional organization for forensic psychiatrists is the American Academy of Psychiatry and the Law (http://www.aapl.org).

Document Examiners

As we saw in Chapter 17, the document examiner analyzes questioned documents and related material, such as ink, paper, toner from a copier or fax, and computer printers. Detecting forged documents and counterfeit currency is a large part of the document examiner's work.

Education and Training Document examiners should possess at least a bachelor's degree, preferably in a scientific field. Several colleges and universities offer questioned-document or related courses as part of criminal justice, forensic science, or criminalistics degree programs, although no document examination degree programs currently exist. In addition to a college education, the prospective document examiner must complete an apprenticeship program lasting approximately two years under the direct supervision of a full member or fellow of the questioned-documents section of the AAFS, a member of the American Society of Questioned Document Examiners, or a diplomate of the American Board of Forensic Document Examiners (http://www.abfde.org).

Career Opportunities Forensic document examiners are often consultants working in private practice, but many large police organizations, as well as most state and federal law enforcement agencies, also employ forensic document experts.

Forensic Toxicology

Forensic toxicology deals with the effects of drugs and chemicals on the human body and the application of that knowledge to questions of law. Forensic toxicologists perform a wide range of activities, including determining whether an individual has consumed illegal drugs and identifying the substances involved. Forensic toxicologists are often called upon to determine whether an individual was driving under the influence of alcohol or drugs. They may be involved in postmortem toxicology, which involves determining the contribution drugs or chemicals make to the circumstances of a death. The forensic toxicologist investigates cases as varied as animal poisoning, the use of drugs in sexual assault, and drug use and doping in human and animal sports. Currently, many forensic toxicologists are employed by private laboratories engaged in conducting workplace drug testing and forensic urine testing on employees of organizations and industries associated with the public's safety or engaged in performing hazardous work.

Education and Training Training for a career in forensic toxicology requires a bachelor's degree in a physical science, ideally including a solid background in chemistry and coursework in pharmacology. Several colleges and universities offer graduate coursework in forensic toxicology at the master's or Ph.D. level. Membership in the forensic toxicology section of AAFS requires at least one year of additional experience and further requirements of scholarly work or advanced study. The American Board of Forensic Toxicology and the Forensic Toxicologist Certification Board offer professional certification to scientists with work experience in forensic toxicology. A major forensic toxicology organization is the Society of Forensic Toxicologists (http://www.soft-tox.org).

Career Opportunities Many forensic toxicologists work in police laboratories, medical examiners' offices, and workplace drug-testing laboratories. Other career opportunities for forensic toxicologists exist in hospitals, universities, corporations, and agencies that monitor drug use in sports.

College Courses in Forensic Science

Degree Programs in Forensic Science

It is something of an irony that, although most of the careers discussed previously require at least a bachelor's degree, few colleges and universities in the United States offer undergraduate or graduate degrees in forensic science. Institutions offering Forensic Science Education Programs Accreditation Commission (FEPAC) accredited undergraduate and graduate programs include the following:

University of Alabama at Birmingham, Birmingham, AL: Conditional Accreditation for the Master of Science in Forensic Science

Albany State University, Albany, GA: Accreditation for the Bachelor of Science Degree in Forensic Science

University at Albany (SUNY at Albany), Albany, NY: Accreditation for the Master of Science Degree in Forensic Science

Arcadia University, Glenside, PA: Accreditation for the Master of Science Degree in Forensic Science

Cedar Crest College, Allentown, PA: Accreditation for the Bachelor of Science Degree in Chemistry, Biochemistry, Biology, and Genetic Engineering with a concentration in Forensic Science

Duquesne University, Pittsburg, PA: Conditional Accreditation for the Master of Science in Forensic Science

Eastern Kentucky University, Richmond, KY: Accreditation for the Bachelor of Science Degree Program in Forensic Science

Florida International University, Miami, FL: Accreditation for both the Certificate Programs in conjunction with the Bachelor of Science Degree in a natural science such as chemistry or biology and the Master of Science in Forensic Science

University of Illinois at Chicago, Chicago, IL: Conditional Accreditation for the Master of Science in Forensic Science

John Jay College of Criminal Justice (CUNY), New York, NY: Conditional Accreditation for the Bachelor of Science degree in Forensic Science

Marshall University, Huntington, WV: Accreditation for the Master of Science Degree in Forensic Science

Metropolitan State College of Denver, Denver, CO: Accreditation for the Bachelor of Science Degree Program in Chemistry with a concentration in Criminalistics

Michigan State University, East Lansing, MI: Accreditation for the Master of Science Degree Program (biology and chemistry tracks)

University of Mississippi, University, MS: Accreditation for the Bachelor of Science degree in Forensic Science

University of New Haven, West Haven, CT: Accreditation for the Bachelor of Science degree in Forensic Science

Ohio University, Athens, OH: Accreditation for the Bachelor of Science Degree in Forensic Chemistry Program

Oklahoma State University, Tulsa, OK: Accreditation for the Master of Science Degree in Forensic Science

The Pennsylvania State University, University Park, PA: Accreditation for the Bachelor of Science Degree in Forensic Science

Sam Houston State University, Huntsville, TX: Accreditation for the Master of Science Degree in Forensic Science

University of North Texas, Denton, TX: Accreditation for the Certificate Programs in Conjunction with the Bachelor of Science Degree in Biochemistry, Biology, and Chemistry

Virginia Commonwealth University, Richmond, VA: Accreditation for both the Bachelor of Science Degree in Forensic Science and the Master of Science Degree in Forensic Science Programs

West Chester University, West Chester, PA: Accreditation for the Bachelor of Science Degree in Forensic and Toxicological Chemistry

West Virginia University, Morgantown, WV: Accreditation for the Bachelor of Science Degree—Forensic and Investigative Science Program

This is not to suggest, however, that course and degree programs in forensic sciences are not available at other colleges and universities. In fact, more than a hundred schools offer associate's, bachelor's, and master's degrees in some area of forensic science, and others provide seminars and courses in forensic specialties such as DNA typing and profiling. Although most of these programs have not been accredited by the FEPAC, most working forensic scientists obtained their education and degrees from non-FEPAC-accredited schools. A complete list of undergraduate and graduate programs in forensic science in the United States and abroad can be found at the AAFS Web site, http://www.aafs.org.

A small number of schools have initiated programs and courses in computer forensics. Interested students should search out schools on the AAFS Web site for these programs.

Required College Courses

Certain natural science courses are required for any student in forensic science. Unlike other criminal justice professionals, a forensic scientist requires a foundation in chemistry, biology, physics, and mathematics. The minimum general core requirements recommended for undergraduate forensic science programs include the following:

- General chemistry I and II and lab for science majors (eight credit hours)

- Organic chemistry I and II and lab (eight credit hours)

- Biology I and II for science majors (four to eight credit hours; classes with laboratory components are preferable, if available)

- Physics I and II for science majors and lab (eight credit hours)

- Calculus (three credit hours)

- Statistics for science majors (three credit hours)

An undergraduate degree in forensic science is expected to be an interdisciplinary degree that includes substantial laboratory work and an emphasis on advanced coursework in chemistry or biology. Students can use these additional courses to begin to specialize along a forensic science discipline track, such as forensic biology or forensic chemistry. Specialized science courses may be selected from any of the following:

- Biochemistry

- Molecular biology

- Genetics

- Population genetics

- Inorganic chemistry

- Analytical/quantitative chemistry

- Physical chemistry
- Instrumental analysis
- Cell biology
- Pharmacology
- Calculus II
- Microbiology

As you can see, the path to becoming a forensic scientist is neither brief nor easy. It begins with rigorous college coursework, typically followed by additional training and certification in the specific area of forensic science one chooses to pursue. It involves lifelong learning and the dedication to seek out the newest and best methods to gather, analyze, and interpret data needed to solve all types of crimes.

Despite these hurdles, forensic science is a fascinating profession that challenges one's scientific knowledge, powers of observation, critical-thinking skills, deductive and inductive reasoning, and ability to think creatively and imagine various possible scenarios when presented with facts and physical evidence. Hopefully, this text will provide both a spark of interest and the basic information that will spur you to take the first steps toward pursuing a career in this challenging and ever-evolving field.

Appendix:
Guides to the Collection of Physical Evidence—FBI

	Amount Desired		
Specimen	Standard	Evidence	Send By
Abrasives	Not less than one ounce.	All	Registered mail or equivalent
Ammunition (Live Cartridges)			Live ammunition must be shipped via Federal Express. The following guidelines must be followed to comply with U.S. Department of Transportation regulations. Pack ammunition in a cardboard container. Label invoices FEDERAL EXPRESS. The shipper's certification for restricted articles must be included. The outside of the container must be labeled ORMD AIR, CARTRIDGES SMALL ARMS. The shipping papers must also include the weight in grams.
Anonymous Extortion Letters, and Bank Robbery Notes		Documentary evidence condition in which it was found. It should not be folded, torn, marked, soiled, stamped, written on, or handled unnecessarily. Protect the evidence from inadvertent indented writing. Mark documents unobtrusively by writing the collector's initials, date, and other information with a pencil. Whenever possible, submit the original evidence to the Laboratory. The lack of detail in photocopies makes examinations difficult. Copies are sufficient for reference file searches.	Registered mail or equivalent.
Bullets (projector without cartridge) (Live Cartridges)		All found.	Same as Ammunition
Cartridge Cases (shells only)		All	Same as Ammunition

Source: Courtesy of the Federal Bureau of Investigation, Washington, D.C.

Identification	Wrapping and Packing	Remarks
Outside container: type of material, date obtained, investigator's name or initials.	Submit abrasives in heat-sealed or resealable plastic bags or paint cans. Avoid using paper or glass containers.	Abrasives settle in oil and fuel. Submit the oil and fuel from the engine sump and/or filters. Abrasives embed in bearings and other parts. Submit the bearings and other parts.
Same as above.	Ammunition components such as bullets, cartridge cases and shotshell casings can be sent via registered mail through the U.S. Postal Service. Evidence should be packaged separately and identified by date, time, location, collector's name, case number, and evidence number.	Unless specific examination of the cartridge is essential, do not submit.
Initial and date each document, if advisable.	Use proper enclosure. Place in envelope and seal with "Evidence" tape or transparent cellophane tape. Flap side of envelope should show: (1) wording "Enclosure(s) to FBI from (name of submitting office)," (2) title of case, (3) brief description of contents, (4) file number, if known. Staple to original letter of transmittal.	Do not handle with bare hands. Advise if evidence should be treated for latent fingerprints. Whenever possible, submit the original evidence to the laboratory. The lack of detail in photocopies makes examination difficult. Copies are sufficient for reference file searches.
Do not mark bullets, cartridges, and cartridge cases, and shotshells and shotshell casings. The date, time, location, collector's name, case number, and evidence number should be on the container.	Pack tightly in cotton or soft paper in pill, match, or powder box. Place in box. Label outside of box as to contents.	Unnecessary handling obliterates marks.
Same as above.	Same as above.	Spent cartridge cases.

	Amount Desired		
Specimen	Standard	Evidence	Send By
Casts (Dental or Die Stone Casts of Tire Treads and Shoe Prints)	Send in suspects shoes and tired. Photographs and sample impressions are usually not suitable by comparison.	All shoe prints and entire circumference of tires.	Registered mail or equivalent
Checks (fraudulent)		See Anonymous Letter (p. 508)	Registered mail or equivalent
Check Protector, Rubber Stamp, and/or Date Stamp Known Standards (if possible, send actual device)	Obtain several copies in full word-for-word order of each questioned check-writer impression. If unable to forward rubber stamps, prepare numerous samples with different degrees of pressure.		Registered mail or equivalent
Clothing		All	Registered mail or equivalent
DNA Examinations (see pp. 520-522)			
Documents (charred or burned)		All	Registered mail or equivalent
Drugs: 1. Liquids		All	Registered mail or equivalent
2. Powders, Pills, and Solids		All to 30 g.	Registered mail or equivalent

EXPLOSIVES: Detonators, Blasting Caps, Detonating Cord, Black Powder, Smokeless Powder, Explosives, and Accessories, call FBI Laboratory, for shipping instructions.

Fibers	Entire garment or other cloth item.	All	Registered mail or equivalent
Firearms (unloaded weapons)		Firearms must be packaged and shipped separately from live ammunition. All firearms must be unloaded.	Firearms and ammunition components such as bullets, cartridge cases, and shotshell casings can be sent via registered mail through the U.S. Postal Service. Evidence must be packaged separately and identified by date, time, location, collector's name, case number, and evidence number.

Identification	Wrapping and Packing	Remarks
On back of cast before it hardens, write location and date taken, and investigator's name or initials.	Wrap in paper and cover with suitable packing material to prevent breakage. Label "Fragile." Plaster of Paris is no longer recommended.	For shoeprint and tire tread file searches, submit quality photographs of the impressions. If photographs are not available, submit cases, lifts, or the original evidence. Detailed sketches or photocopies are acceptable.
See Anonymous Letters on p. 503.	See Anonymous Letters on p. 503.	Advise what parts are questioned or known. Furnish physical description of subject.
Place name or initials, date, name of make and model, etc., on sample impressions.	See Anonymous Letters on p. 503	Do not disturb inking mechanisms on printing devices.
Mark directly on garment or use string tag indicating type of evidence, date obtained, investigator's name or initials.	Wrap each article individually. Place in strong container with identification written on outside of package.	Do not cut out stains; leave clothing whole. If wet, hang in room to dry before packing.
Outside container: Indicate if fragile, date obtained, investigator's name or initials.	Pack in rigid container between layers of cotton.	If moisture is added use atomizer, otherwise, not recommended.
Affix label to bottle in which found, including date it was found and investigator's name or initials.	Make sure container does not leak. Seal with tape to prevent any loss.	Mark "Fragile." If possible, use heat-seal plastic bags.
Outside of pillbox: affix label with date found and investigator's name or initials.	Seal with tape to prevent any loss.	If powder, pills, or solids are found in paper bags, place them in paper bags to prevent any loss. Do not submit used drug field test kits with evidence.
Outside container or on the object fibers are adhering, include date and investigator's name or initials.	Use folder paper or pillbox. Seal edges and openings with tape.	No not place loose in an envelope.
Do not mark the firearm. Firearms should be identified with a tag containing the caliber, make, model, and serial number. The date, time, owner(s)' name(s), location, collector's name, case number, and evidence number should be on the container.	Wrap in paper and identify contents of packages. Place in cardboard box or wooden box.	The firearm should be handled minimally to avoid loss or destruction of evidence. Do not allow objects to enter or contact the firearm's barrel, chamber, or other operating surface.

	Amount Desired			
Specimen	Standard		Evidence	Send By
Flash Paper	One sheet		All to 5 sheets.	Call FBI Laboratory.
Gasoline	10 ml		All to 10 ml	Call Chemistry-Toxicology Unit for instructions
General Unknown: 1. Solids (nonhazardous)	10 gm		All to 10 gm	Registered mail or equivalent
2. Liquids (nonhazardous)	10 ml		All to 10 ml	Registered mail or equivalent
Glass Fractures			All	Registered mail or equivalent
Glass Particles	Submit the victim(s) and suspect's air-dried clothing. Each item must be packaged separately in a paper bag. Search for particles in the victim(s)' and suspect(s)' hair, skin, and wounds. Submit particles in leakproof containers such as film canisters or plastic pill bottles. Do not use paper or glass containers. Search for particles in vehicles by vacuuming each section of the vehicle separately. Do not use tape for covering glass particles. Submit vacuum sweepings in leakproof containers. Do not use paper or glass containers.		All	Registered mail or equivalent

Identification	Wrapping and Packing	Remarks
Outside container: label indicating date and investigator's name and initials.	Flash paper is a hazardous material. Do not store flash paper near combustible materials. Seal flash paper in polyethylene envelopes and refrigerate.	
Outside container: label indicating type of material, date, and investigator's name or initials.	Use an all-metal container packed in a wooden box.	An all-metal container should be used for its fireproof qualities.
Outside container: label indicating date and investigators name or initials.	Same as Drugs (see p. 510)	Call Chemistry-Toxicology Unit for instructions
Same as Liquid Drugs (see p. 510)	Same as Liquid Drugs (see p. 510)	Same as above.
Label the sides of the glass in the frame INSIDE and OUTSIDE. Label the glass where it was removed in the frame such as TOP, BOTTOM, LEFT, and RIGHT.	Wrap each piece separately in cotton. Pack in sturdy container to prevent shifting and breakage. Identify contents.	Submit all glass pieces so that the pieces can be fitted together to identify the radial cracks near and at the point(s) of impact and to increase the probability of matching edges. Pack all glass separately and securely to avoid shifting and breaking during transport.
Outside container: label indicating date and investigator's name or initials.	Place in film canister or plastic vial. Seal and protect against breakage.	Submit samples of glass from each broken window or source in leakproof containers such as film canisters or plastic pill bottles. Avoid using paper or glass containers.

	Amount Desired		
Specimen	**Standard**	**Evidence**	**Send By**
Gunshot Residues The Laboratory provides gunshot residue examinations to assist FBI field office investigations only.		Usually gunshot residue examinations will only be performed when samples are collected from living person's hands. Gunshot residue evidence must be collected within five hours of exposure to the discharge of a firearm.	
On cloth only to determine weapon to target distance		All	Clothing submitted for gunshot residue examinations should be handled carefully, air dried, and wrapped separately in paper. Clothing with blood must be air dried and labeled BIOHAZARD on the inner and outer containers. The date, time, location, collector's name, case number, and evidence number should be on the container.
Hair	Twenty-five full-length hairs from different parts of head and/or pubic region.	All	Registered mail or equivalent
Handwriting and Hand Printing Known Standards			Registered mail or equivalent
Insulation 1. Glass wool	1' mass from each suspect area	All	Registered mail or equivalent
2. Safe	Sample all damaged areas.	All	Registered mail or equivalent
Matches	One to two books of paper. One full box of wood.	All	Federal Express, UPS, or equivalent
Obliterated, Eradicated, or Indented Writing		Same as Anonymous Letters (see p. 508)	Registered mail or equivalent

Identification	Wrapping and packing	Remarks
		Collecting gunshot residue samples requires five adhesive lifts suitable scanning electron microscopic analysis. Dab the adhesive side of the stub against the surface (right palm, back of right hand, left palm, back of left hand). Use one stub per sampling surface. The remaining stub will be used as a control. Label each sampling surface stub (e.g., RIGHT PALM, BACK OF RIGHT HAND). Cap and seal the stubs in separate, resealable plastic bags.
Outside container: Indicate date, obtained from whom, description, name or initials.	Dry and package individually in **unused** brown wrapping paper or brown grocery bag.	The deposition of gunshot residue on evidence such as clothing varies with the distance from the muzzle of the firearm to the target. Patterns of gunshot residue can be duplicated using a questioned firearm and ammunition combination fired into test materials and known distances. These patterns serve as a basis for estimating muzzle-to-garment distances.
Outside container: Type of material, date, and investigator's name or initials.	Folded paper or pillbox. Seal edges and opening with tape.	Do not place loose in envelope.
Indicate from whom obtained, voluntary statement included in appropriate place, date obtained, and investigator's name or initials.	Same as Anonymous Letters (see p. 508).	Same as Anonymous Letters (see p. 508).
Outside of container: type of material, date, name or initials	Use pillbox or plastic vial. Seal to prevent any loss. Safe insulation can adhere to persons, clothing, tools, bags, and loot and can transfer to vehicles. If possible, submit the evidence to the Laboratory for examiners to remove the debris. Package each item of evidence in a separate paper bag. Do not process tools for latent prints.	Submit known and questioned debris in leakproof containers such as film canisters or plastic pill bottles. Avoid using paper or glass containers. Pack to keep lumps intact.
Same as above.		
Outside container: label indicating type of material, date, and investigator's name or initials.	Pack in metal container and in larger package to prevent shifting. Pack matches in box or metal container to prevent friction between matches.	Keep and label: "Keep away from fire."
Same as Anonymous Letters (see p. 508)	Same as Anonymous Letters (see p. 508)	Advise whether bleaching or staining methods may be used. Avoid folding.

Specimen	Amount Desired		Send By
	Standard	**Evidence**	
Organs of the Body		200 g of each organ.	Call Chemistry-Toxicology Unit for instructions.
Paint: Liquid	Original unopened container up to ¼ pint, if possible.	All to ¼ pint.	Registered mail or equivalent
Solid (paint chips or scrapings)	At least ½ sq. in. of solid, with all layers represented.	Standard: Control paint chips must be collected from the suspected source of the evidentiary paint. Controls must be taken from an area close to, but not in, any damaged area. If no damage is obvious, controls should be taken from several areas of the suspect substrate. Each layer can be a point of comparison. Controls must have all of the layers of paint to the substrate.	Registered mail or equivalent
Rope, Twine, and Cordage	One yard or amount available.	Submit the entire rope or cord. If the rope or cord must be cut, specify which end was cut during evidence collection. Label the known and questioned samples. Handle the sections of rope or cord carefully to prevent loss of trace material or contamination.	Registered mail or equivalent
Saliva Samples	1.5" diameter stain in center of filter paper.	All	Registered mail or equivalent
Shoe Print Lifts (impressions on hard surfaces)	Photograph before making lift of dust impression.	For shoeprint and tire tread comparisons, submit original evidence whenever possible (shoes, tires, photographic negatives, casts, lifts).	Registered mail or equivalent

Identification	Wrapping and Packing	Remarks
Each biological specimen must be placed in a separate, labeled, sealed glass tube, plastic cup, or heat-sealed or resealable plastic bag. Affix BIOHAZARD labels to the inside and outside containers.	To avoid deterioration, biological specimens must be refrigerated or frozen during storage and shipping. Pack so that no breakage, leakage, or contamination occurs.	Submit a copy of the autopsy or incident report. Describe the symptoms of the suspect(s) or victim(s) at the time of the crime or prior to the death. List any known or questioned drugs consumed by or prescribed for the suspect(s) or victim(s). Describe any known or questioned environmental exposure to toxic substances but the suspect(s) or victim(s).
Outside Container: Type of material, origin if known, date, investigator's name or initials. Same as above.	Use friction-top paint can or large-mouth, screw-top jar. If glass, pack to prevent breakage. Use heavy corrugated paper or wooden box. Package paint specimens in leakproof containers such as vials or pillboxes. Do not stick paint particles on adhesive tape. Do not use plastic bags, cotton, or envelopes to package paint specimens.	Protect spray can nozzles to keep them from going off. Avoid contact w/adhesive materials. Wrap to protect paint smears. Do not use envelopes, paper/plastic bags, or glass vials. Avoid contact with adhesive materials. Wrap so as to protect smear. If *small amount:* seal round pillbox, film canister, or plastic vial to protect against leakage/breakage.
On tag or container: Type of material, date, investigator's name or initials.	Submit in heat-sealed or resealable plastic or paper bags.	
Outside envelope and on filter paper: Type of sample, name of donor, date of collection, and collector's initials or name.	Seal in envelope.	Stain should be circled in pencil for identification. Filter paper available from hospitals and drugstores. Allow to dry.
On lifting tape or paper attached to tape: date, investigator's name or initials.	Prints in dust are easily damaged. Fasten print or lift to bottom of box so that nothing will rub against it.	Always secure crime-scene area until show prints or tire treads are located and preserved.

Specimen	Amount Desired		Send By
	Standard	Evidence	
Soils and Minerals	Samples from areas near pertinent spot	Collect soil samples from the immediate crime scene area and from the logical access and/or escape route(s). Collect soil samples at a depth that is consistent with the depth from which the questioned soil may have originated. If possible, collect soil samples from alibi areas such as the yard or work area of the suspect(s).	Registered mail
Tape (Adhesive Tape)	Recovered roll.	All	Registered mail or equivalent
Tools/Toolmarks	Send in the tool. If impractical, make several impressions on similar materials as evidence using entire marking area of tool.	If it is not possible to submit the tool-marked evidence, submit a cast of the toolmark.	Registered mail or equivalent.
Typewriting Known standards	See Anonymous Letters (p. 508)		Registered mail or equivalent
Wire	3 ft. (Do not kink.)	All (Do not kink.)	Registered mail or equivalent
Wood	One foot or amount available.	All	Registered mail or equivalent

Identification	Wrapping and Packing	Remarks
Outside container: Type of material, date, investigator's name or initials.	Do not remove soil adhering to shoes, clothing, and tools. Do not process tools for latent prints. Air-dry the soil and the clothing and package separately in paper bags. Carefully remove soil adhering to vehicles. Air-dry the soil and package separately in paper bags.	Ship known and questioned debris separately to avoid contamination. Submit known and questioned soil in leakproof containers such as film canisters or plastic pill bottles. Do not use paper envelopes or glass containers. Pack to keep lumps intact.
Same as above.	Place on waxed paper, cellophane, or plastic.	Do not cut, wad, distort, or separate tapes that are stuck together.
On object or on tag attached to an opposite end from where toolmarks appear: date recovered and investigator's name or initials.	After marks have been protected with soft paper, wrap in strong wrapping paper, place in strong box, and pack to prevent shifting.	Photographs locate tool-marks but are of no value for identification purposes. Obtain samples of any material deposited on the tools. To avoid contamination, do not place the tool against the toolmarked evidence. Submit the tool rather than making test cuts or impressions. Mark the ends of the evidence and specify which end was cut during evidence collection.
On specimens: serial number, brand, model, etc., date recovered, and investigator's name or initials.	Wrap securely.	Do not kink wire.
On label or tab: Describe type of material, date, investigator's name or initials.	Wrap securely.	Do not kink wire.
Same as above.	Submit wood in heat-sealed or resealable plastic or paper bags.	

DNA Examinations

Deoxyribonucleic acid (DNA) is analyzed in body fluids, stains, and other biological tissues recovered from evidence. The results of DNA analysis of questioned biological samples are compared with the results of DNA analysis of known samples. This analysis can associate victim(s) and/or suspect(s) with each other or with a crime scene.

There are two sources of DNA used in forensic analyses. Nuclear DNA (nDNA) is typically analyzed in evidence containing blood, semen, saliva, body tissues, and hairs that have tissue at their root ends. Mithochondrial DNA (mtDNA) is typically analyzed in evidence containing naturally shed hairs, hair fragments, bones, and teeth.

If DNA evidence is not properly documented, collected, packaged, and preserved, it will not meet the legal and scientific requirements for admissibility in a court of law.

- If it is not properly documented, its origin can be questioned.

- If it is not properly collected, biological activity can be lost.

- If it is not properly packaged, contamination can occur.

- If it is not properly preserved, decomposition and deterioration can occur.

When DNA evidence is transferred by direct or secondary (indirect) means, it remains on surfaces by absorption or adherence. In general, liquid biological evidence is absorbed into surfaces, and solid biological evidence adheres to surfaces. Collecting, packaging, and preserving DNA evidence depends on the liquid or solid state and the condition of the evidence.

The more that evidence retains its original integrity until it reaches the laboratory, the greater the possibility of conducting useful examinations. It may be necessary to use a variety of techniques to collect suspected body fluid evidence.

Blood Examinations

Examinations can determine the presence or absence of blood in stains. Examinations can also determine whether blood is human or not. Blood examinations cannot determine the age or the race of a person. Conventional serological techniques are not adequately informative to positively identify a person as the source of a stain.

Collecting Known Samples

Blood

- Only qualified medical personnel should collect blood samples from a person.

- Collect at least two 5-ml tubes of blood in purple-top tubes with EDTA as an anticoagulant for DNA analysis. Collect drug- or alcohol-testing samples in gray-top tubes with NaF (sodium fluoride).

- Identify each tube with the date, time, subject's name, location, collector's name, case number, and evidence number.

- Refrigerate, do not freeze blood samples. Use cold packs, not dry ice, during shipping.

- Pack liquid blood tubes individually in Styrofoam or cylindrical tubes with absorbent material surrounding the tubes.

- Label the outer container KEEP IN A COOL DRY PLACE, REFRIGERATE ON ARRIVAL, and BIOHAZARD.
- Submit to the laboratory as soon as possible.

Blood on a Person

- Absorb suspected **liquid blood** onto a clean cotton cloth or swab. Leave apportion of the cloth or swab unstained as a control. Air-dry the cloth or swab and pack in clean paper or an envelope with sealed corners. Do not use plastic containers.
- Absorb suspected **dried blood** onto a clean cotton cloth or swab moistened with distilled water. Leave a portion of the cloth or swab unstained as a control. Air-dry the cloth or swab and pack in clean paper or an envelope with sealed corners. Do not use plastic containers.

Blood on Surfaces or in Snow or Water

- Absorb suspected **liquid blood** or **blood clots** onto a clean cotton cloth or swab. Leave a portion of the cloth or swab unstained as a control. Air-dry the cloth or swab and pack in clean paper or an envelope with sealed corners. Do not use plastic containers.
- Collect suspected **blood in snow or water** immediately to avoid further dilution. Eliminate as much snow as possible. Place in a clean airtight container. Freeze the evidence and submit as soon as possible to the laboratory.

Bloodstains

- Air-dry **wet bloodstained garments.** Wrap **dried bloodstained garments** in clean paper. Do not place wet or dried garments in plastic or airtight containers. Place all debris or residue from the garments in clean paper or an envelope with sealed corners.
- Air-dry small suspected **wet bloodstained objects** and submit the objects to the laboratory. Preserve bloodstain patterns. Avoid creating additional stain patterns during drying and packaging. Pack to prevent stain removal by abrasive action during shipping. Pack in clean paper. Do not use plastic containers.
- When possible, cut a large sample of suspected **bloodstains from immovable objects** with a clean, sharp instrument. Collect an unstained control sample. Pack to prevent stain removal by abrasive action during shipping. Pack in clean paper. Do not use plastic containers.
- Absorb suspected dried bloodstains on immovable objects onto a clean cotton cloth or swab moistened with distilled water. Leave a portion of the cloth or swab unstained as a control. Air-dry the cloth or swab and pack in clean paper or an envelope with sealed corners. Do not use plastic containers.

Blood Examination Request Letter

A blood examination request letter must contain the following information:

- A brief statement of facts relating to the case.
- Claims made by the suspect(s) regarding the source of the blood.
- Whether animal blood is present.

- Whether the stains were laundered or diluted with other body fluids.

- Information regarding the victim(s)' and suspect(s)' health such as AIDS, hepatitis, or tuberculosis.

Semen and Semen Stains

- Absorb suspected **liquid semen** onto a clean cotton cloth or swab. Leave a portion of the cloth or swab unstained as a control. Air-dry the cloth or swab and pack in clean paper or an envelope with sealed corners. Do not use plastic containers.

- Submit small suspected **dry semen-stained objects** to the laboratory. Pack to prevent stain removal by abrasive action during shipping. Pack in clean paper. Do not use plastic containers.

- When possible, cut a large sample of suspected **semen stains from immovable objects** with a clean, sharp instrument. Collect an unstained control sample. Pack to prevent stain removal by abrasive action during shipping. Pack in clean paper. Do not use plastic containers.

- Absorb suspected dried semen stains on immovable objects onto a clean cotton cloth or swab moistened with distilled water. Leave a portion of the cloth or swab unstained as a control. Air-dry the swab or cloth and place in clean paper or an envelope with sealed corners. Do not use plastic containers.

Seminal Evidence from Sexual Assault Victim(s)

- Sexual assault victim(s) must be medically examined in a hospital or a physician's office using a standard sexual assault evidence kit to collect vaginal, oral, and anal evidence.

- Refrigerate and submit the evidence as soon as possible to the laboratory.

Buccal (Oral) Swabs

- Use clean cotton swabs to collect buccal (oral) samples. Rub the inside surfaces of the cheeks thoroughly.

- Air-dry the swabs and place in clean paper or an envelope with sealed corners. Do not use plastic containers.

- Identify each sample with the date, time subject's name, location, collector's name, case number, and evidence number.

- Buccal samples do not need to be refrigerated.

Saliva and Urine

- Absorb suspected **liquid saliva or urine** onto a clean cotton cloth or swab. Leave a portion of the cloth unstained as a control. Air-dry the cloth or swab and pack in clean paper or an envelope with sealed corners. Do not use plastic containers.

- Submit suspected small, **dry saliva- or urine-stained objects** to the laboratory. Pack to prevent stain removal by abrasive action during shipping. Pack in clean paper or an envelope with sealed corners. Do not use plastic containers.

- When possible, cut a large sample of suspected **saliva or urine stains from immovable objects** with a clean, sharp instrument. Collect an unstained control sample. Pack to prevent stain removal by abrasive action during shipping. Pack in clean paper. Do not use plastic containers.

- Pick up **cigarette butts** with gloved hands or clean forceps. Do not submit ashes. Air-dry and place the cigarette butts from the same location (e.g., ashtray) in clean paper or an envelope with sealed corners. Do not submit the ashtray unless a latent print examination is requested. Package the ashtray separately. Do not use plastic containers.

- Pick up **chewing gum** with gloved hands or clean forceps. Air-dry and place in clean paper or an envelope with sealed corners. Do not use plastic containers.

- Pick up **envelops and stamps** with gloved hands or clean forceps and place in a clean envelope. Do not use plastic containers.

Hair

- Pick up hair carefully with clean forceps to prevent damaging the root tissue.

- Air-dry hair mixed with suspected body fluids.

- Package each group of hair separately in clean paper or an envelope with sealed corners. Do not use plastic containers.

- Refrigerate and submit as soon as possible to the Laboratory.

Tissues, Bones, and Teeth

- Pick up suspected tissues, bones, and teeth with gloved hands or clean forceps.

- Collect 1–2 cubic inches of red skeletal muscle.

- Collect 3–5 inches of long bone such as the fibula or femur.

- Collect teeth in the following order:

    1. nonrestored molar
    2. nonrestored premolar
    3. nonrestored canine
    4. nonrestored front tooth
    5. restored molar
    6. restored premolar
    7. restored canine
    8. restored front tooth

- Place tissue samples in a clean, airtight plastic container without formalin or formaldehyde.

- Place teeth and bone samples in clean paper or an envelope with sealed corners.

- Freeze the evidence, place in Styrofoam containers, and ship overnight on dry ice.

INDEX

Chapter Opener Image Credits

Cover: ©Don Farrall/Getty Images

Chapter 1: AP Wide World Photos

Chapter 2: AP Wide World Photos

Chapter 3: Modesto Police Department Handout/AP Wide World Photos

Chapter 4: John A. Rizzo, Getty Images, Inc. – Photodisc

Chapter 5: Alain Masiero/SYGMA, Corbis-NY

Chapter 6: PA/Topham, The Image Works

Chapter 7: The Granger Collection

Chapter 8: AP Wide World Photos

Chapter 9: AP Wide World Photos

Chapter 10: Corbis/Bettmann

Chapter 11: AP Wide World Photos

Chapter 12: Jacques-Louis David (French, 1748-1825) "Napoleon in His Study" 1812, oil on canvas, National Gallery of Art, Washington. Samuel H. Kress Collection. © Board of Trustees, National Gallery of Art, Washington. Photo by Lyle Peterzell.

Chapter 13: Dave Kaup, AP Wide World Photos

Chapter 14: Reuters New Media, Inc./Corbis

Chapter 15: Corbis/Bettmann

Chapter 16: AP Wide World Photos

Chapter 17: AP Wide World Photos

Chapter 18: AP Wide World Photos

Chapter 19: Dr. Jurgen Scriba, Photo Researchers, Inc.

Appendix: Tri-Tech, Inc., Southport, NC, www.tritechusa.com